Preface

This guide to Australia is one of the new generation of Baedeker guides.

These guides, illustrated throughout in colour, are designed to meet the needs of the modern traveller. They are quick and easy to consult, with the principal places of interest described in alphabetical order, and the information is presented in a format that is both attractive and easy to follow.

This guide is devoted to Australia, the continent of kangaroos and koalas, of shimmering heat in the outback and magnificent beaches on the Pacific and the Indian Ocean. It is in three parts. The first part gives a general account of the country, its topography, climate, flora and fauna, population, government and administration, education and science, economy, transport, history, famous people, art and culture. The second part begins with a number of suggested itineraries and then describes places of tourist interest within the various states and territories. The third part contains a variety of practical information. Both the sights and the practical information are listed in alphabetical order.

With natural wonders like the Olgas in the empty interior and glittering metropolises like Perth on the coast, Australia is a continent of fascinating contrasts

The new Baedeker guides are noted for their concentration on essentials and their convenience of use. They contain numerous specially drawn plans and colour illustrations; and at the end of the book is a large map making it easy to locate the various places described in the "A to Z" section of the guide with the help of the co-ordinates given at the head of each entry.

Contents

Nature, Culture, History
Pages 9–85

Sights from A to Z
Pages 87–535

Practical Information from A to Z
Pages 537–597

Baedeker Specials

Welcome D

Welcome down under! Welcome to the land of kangaroos and koalas, of red rocks and eucalyptus trees – the country to which Britain exported its criminals in the 19th century. But things are far different now: Australia is now attracting increasing numbers of visitors, drawn not only by the lure of a distant land but by the special attractions and experiences that Australia has to offer – the vast empty expanses of the outback, the shell-spangled beaches, the opal fields and gold mines, the great modern metropolises like Sydney, Melbourne and Perth. With an area of just under 3 million square miles, measuring 2000 miles from north to south and 2500 from east to west, Australia is the smallest of the continents, but it is still more than thirty times the size of the United Kingdom. It ranges from the tropical rain forests of the north by way of arid stony, sandy and salt desert and steppe country to the Mediterranean-like climate of the south. The extreme south of the continent and the offshore island of Tasmania lie in a temperate zone with a climate similar to that of Europe. Adventurous travellers and nature-lovers will find plenty to interest them in Australia: spectacular natural phenomena like Ayers

Ayers Rock

A great natural landmark and a place of Aboriginal legend

Whitsunday Islands

A tropical island paradise in Queensland

ɔwn Under

Rock gleaming red in the sunshine; the Olgas; the world's largest coral reef, over 1200 miles long; the tropical hinterland of Cairns; the Kakadu National Park near Darwin; the wild Flinders Ranges; the inhospitable salt deserts round Lake Eyre. But Australia, once the "unknown southern land" (*terra australis incognita),* also has much to offer in the way of art and culture – from the rock drawings by the country's original prehistoric inhabitants in the remote outback by way of the arts and crafts of the Aborigines to magnificent achievements of modern engineering and architecture, perhaps the most striking of which is the Sydney Opera House. The fifth continent, with a population of less than 6 inhabitants to the square mile, is called both by Australians and by visitors the "lucky country" – its immense size and wildness a source of fascination particularly to visitors from the densely populated countries of the western world. Travelling to the other side of the globe, they can experience for a while life in a different world and explore an unspoiled natural paradise – even if it is only a once-in-a-lifetime visit. It must be hoped that Australia will long remain a "lucky country".

Adelaide

A modern metropolis in South Australia

Melbourne

Australia's first capital and the world's third largest "Greek" city

ydney

ɪe of the great cities of ɜ world, magnificently uated, with breathtaking ɔdern architecture

Facts and Figures

General

Area

Although with an area of 7,687,000sq.km/2,968,000sq.miles Australia is the smallest of the continents it is still of enormous size. Its greatest extent from north to south is 3180km/1976 miles, from east to west over 4000km/2485 miles. It is comparable in size with the United States (excluding Alaska); for a comparison with Europe see the map on p. 10.

Australia in the world

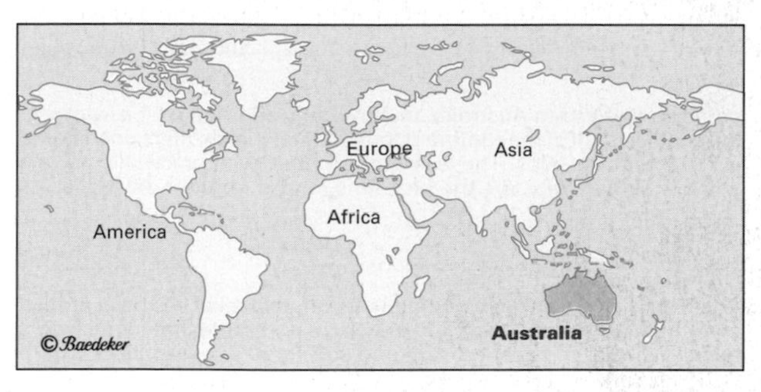

This arid continent does not lend itself to a balanced pattern of economic development. The population has risen to just under 18 million, but the average population density is only 2.3 to the sq. kilometre (just under 6 to the sq. mile). This low density is a result of the extreme topographical conditions which offer such attractions to visitors. Australia has some 200 million hectares/500 million acres of waste land, land which remains completely unused by man – the great expanses of desert and steppe country in the arid interior. In addition there are 191 million hectares/472 million acres of grazing land used for extensive stock-farming, with over 64 hectares/160 acres for every head of cattle and over 8 hectares/20 acres for every sheep. This empty interior of the country is now drawing increasing numbers of visitors.

Scenic attractions

In addition to the striking landscapes of the interior Australia has many other attractions – its endless beaches with their ideal conditions for bathing, fishing and water sports and, most spectacular of all, the Great Barrier Reef, the world's largest coral reef.

Concentrations of population

The population of Australia is concentrated in the state capitals situated round its coasts. These great conurbations are spaciously laid out, with detached houses, gardens and many public parks, and their population has ready access to unspoiled nature in the country's National Parks and nature reserves.

Reversal of the seasons

For visitors from the northern hemisphere the reversal of the seasons and the change of climate is often an additional benefit. During the northern hemisphere's winter with its frequently unattractive weather conditions they will find the southern half of Australia enjoying summer and a magnificent climate. In February, March and April, which in the northern hemisphere are often rainy, it is hot late summer in Australia. The northern autumn and early winter (October/November) are Australia's spring, with a fascinating profusion of wild flowers

◀ *Aborigines dancing*

Australia compared with Europe

This map gives some idea of the size of Australia by superimposing the outline of the European heartland on the map of Australia. It can be seen that the main European land mass, from Portugal in the west to Greece in the east, fits comfortably into the Australian continent.

particularly Western Australia. In June, July and August it is winter in the southern half of the continent, but a winter which offers good skiing in the Australian Alps. These winter months, with practically no rain and low air humidity, are the best time to visit northern Australia.

Topography

An ancient continent

Australia is a very ancient continent. Its original relief has been eroded away and levelled out, and it is only here and there that harder rocks have been able to resist erosion and still stand out prominently from the level surrounding country (Ayers Rock, Olgas, Mount Connor, MacDonnell and Musgrave Ranges).

The flattest of the continents

The surface topography of Australia consists of great expanses of territory with gradual transitions between them. It is the flattest of the continents, with uncomplicated patterns of relief extending over large areas. In profile Australia has the form of a large dish with a raised rim, formed in the east and south-east by the Great Dividing Range, in the south-west by the Darling Range and in the north-west by the Hamersley Range and the Kimberley.

The driest of the continents

Australia is also the driest of the continents. The peripheral hills keep rainfall away from the interior of the country; and the base rocks and surface topography lead to the creation of underground reserves of water, extending far into the arid interior, which can be tapped by artesian wells.

Eastern Highlands

On the east coast of the continent geological folding movements combined with volcanic activity have produced a highland belt extending from Tasmania in the south to Cape York in the north and rising at some points to over 1000m/3300ft: Cradle Mountain (TAS), Australian Alps (VIC and NSW), Southern Tablelands, Blue Mountains, New England Plateau (NSW), McPherson Range (NSW and QLD), Atherton Tableland (QLD). Volcanic activity, combined with folding processes, has left its mark on the landscape in such features as Mount Warning (NSW), a gigantic lava plug, and the conical hills in Warrumbungle National Park, which have a similar origin.

Ranges of hills

In southern Queensland the Great Dividing Range breaks up into a number of parallel ranges, giving the highland belt an east–west extent of up to 500km/300 miles. After the rise in sea level towards the end of the last Ice Age the most easterly foothills of the highlands became islands of great scenic beauty, like the Whitsunday group off Proserpine (QLD).

Coastal plain

The coastal plain below the highland belt increases in width from south to north. In the south the steep scarp of the peripheral hills frequently reaches right down to the sea. Only at the estuaries of rivers are there inlets with beautiful sandy beaches and sites for settlements. This attractive topography is found all along the east coast. On the borders of New South Wales and Queensland the plain becomes broader, with room for extensive stretches of beach. Here there have developed important holiday and tourist centres (Gold Coast, Sunshine Coast). At the northern tip of Queensland there are few sandy beaches and the coastal regions are increasingly occupied by mangrove forests.

Great Barrier Reef

Off the north-eastern coast of Australia is the Great Barrier Reef, the largest continuous area of corals in the world (20,000sq.km/ 7700sq.miles). It extends parallel to the coast for 1800km/1100 miles, with the outside of the reef only 15km/9 miles off the coast in the north but as much as 400km/250 miles in the south.

Central Lowlands

Plains

To the west the Eastern Highlands merge very gradually into the great plains of the interior. The lowlands of central Australia extend from the Gulf of Carpentaria in the north to the estuary of the Murray River in the south. In earlier geological epochs this area was covered by the sea. The lowest depression is round Lake Eyre (12m/40ft below sea level). Here end numerous rivers which rise on the western slopes of the Great Dividing Range; but it is only occasionally, after unusually heavy rain, that these rivers have any water in them. The rivers in this "Channel Country" have very flat beds, so that in the event of heavy rain there may be sudden flash floods.

Salt lakes

This can also happen with the lakes in this area, which have no outlets, on those occasions when the rivers do supply them with water. As a result the size and form of these salt lakes, which are usually dry, can alter markedly. Normally they are covered with a salt crust which glistens in the sunshine with a reddish shimmer.

Gulf of Carpentaria

In the north is the plain round the Gulf of Carpentaria, with rivers which drain into the gulf. Here too heavy rain during the Australian summer can lead to flooding, cutting off farms and settlements for weeks at a time.

Murray and Darling Rivers

At the south end of the Central Lowlands is the Murray/Darling river system. The Murray, which rises in the Australian Alps, is Australia's longest river (2557km/1589 miles), and its catchment area accounts for 15% of the country's total area. Thanks to an extensive system of artificial lakes and pipelines (the Snowy Mountains scheme) water from the Snowy River is diverted into the Murray, which as a result, along with its tributary the Murrumbidgee, carries enough water to irrigate 1.2 million hectares/3 million acres of land.

Great Dividing Range

The central Australian depression is bounded on the east by the Great Dividing Range. In the west the land also rises gradually and merges into the Great Western Plateau. This trough form provides the conditions for the formation of an artesian water reserve. The Great Artesian Basin has the largest underground reservoir of water in the world, a resource of great importance for pastoral farming. This tableland, at an average height of between 250m/820ft and 800m/2625ft above sea level, rises to its greatest height on the west coast, with the Darling Range, the western edge of the Darling Plateau, the Hamersley Range in the north-east and the uplands of the Kimberley in the north.

Darling Plateau

The Darling Plateau, with what are probably the oldest rocks in Australia, is rich in minerals (gold, nickel, bauxite, iron ore). Only the higher south-western rim of the plateau has enough rainfall to nourish a rich vegetation (forests of karri trees). The arid interior of the plateau has a sparse scrub vegetation, with many salt lakes.

Hamersley Range

The Hamersley Range has rich deposits of iron ore, and the high iron content gives large areas of the surface soil a reddish tinge. The landscape is diversified by a number of deeply indented river gorges, particularly in Hamersley Gorge National Park.

Kimberley Range

Greater geological variety and more marked relief is found in the Kimberley Range, ancient rocks with deeply indented river valleys (e.g.

Geikie Gorge National Park) and bizarre rock formations created by weathering (e.g. in Bungle Bungle National Park).

Arnhem Land

Like the Kimberley, Arnhem Land has differentiated and more varied coastal forms.

Barkly Tableland Nullarbor Plain

The Barkly Tableland and Nullarbor Plain consist of limestone, with underground caves, rivers and lakes. The Nullarbor Plain is fringed by rugged and spectacular cliffs 200m/650ft high on the Great Australian Bight.

Flinders Ranges

The plateaux of southern Australia were formed by folding movements, combined with later sinkings. The most attractive scenically are the Flinders Ranges, extending far inland.

MacDonnell and Musgrave Ranges

Geological formations also pattern the landscape in the great expanses of the interior. Particularly striking are the MacDonnell and Musgrave Ranges. In earlier geological periods rivers cut deeply into the rock, exposing the geological structure (e.g. the Simpson Gap, Emily Gap and Jessie Gap in the MacDonnell Ranges).

Ayers Rock and the Olgas

Out of the sandy plain between the MacDonnell and the Musgrave Ranges rise Australia's best known hills, Ayers Rock and the Olgas. A hard sandstone formation which had originally come into being some 600 million years ago as the bottom of a lake was so displaced by folding movements 300 million years ago that the hard stratum of sandstone now rises vertically out of the ground to a height of 350m/1150ft, with a circumference of 8km/5 miles. The other end of the stratum comes to the surface in the Olgas; but since at this point the strata are not vertical and the sandstone is of a coarser grain the rock has been much dissected by weathering.

Rivers and lakes

Only in the north and south-west of the Great Western Plateau are there rivers with a periodic and sometimes a perennial flow. In the interior there are only the remains of earlier river systems, with no regular flow of water. The occasional rainfall seeps away in the old river beds and the numerous lakes with no outlets.

Deserts

In the Australian deserts – the Great Victoria Desert, the Gibson Desert, the Great Sandy Desert and the Tanami Desert – there are great expanses marked by long parallel lines of sand dunes. These areas have a scanty vegetation cover nourished by dew. Only after the rare falls of rain is the sandy desert briefly transformed into a sea of blossom. There are also smaller areas of stony desert.

Coastal Forms · Beaches · Waves

TAS, VIC, NSW, QLD

In these states the beaches are mainly shingly and sandy, the sand becoming finer and the beaches broader towards the north. Apart from the Sydney area there are few steep stretches of coast.

North-east coast

Within the shelter of the Great Barrier Reef there are beaches of fine sand and lagoons. A tidal range of between 2 and 6 metres (6½ and 20 feet) leads to the formation of broad expanses of sandy mud-flats. To the north of Townsville limestone crust formations ("beach rock") appear more frequently and limestone pebbles become commoner.

West coast of Queensland

Here the coast varies between fine sand and mud. The beaches are mostly narrow, and in estuaries and inlets have great expanses of mangroves and salt marsh vegetation. There are no steeply scarped coasts.

Northern Territory

In this area, with greater tidal ranges, there are broad stretches of sand or mud flats and the beaches are mostly narrow, with fine sand. The flat shore regions, particularly in estuaries and inlets, have been colonised by mangroves and salt marsh vegetation. Along the Kimberley, Darwin and Arnhem Land coasts there are, thanks to the coral reefs offshore, increased quantities of shingle on the beaches.

Western Australia

At the Kimberley the coasts are fringed by cliffs, with broad reefs of limestone reaching out to sea. Farther south the coasts are mostly flat, though here too there are stretches with reefs. For the most part the beaches are sandy.

West coast

In the northern part of the west coast there are stretches of cliffs, with intervening flat sandy beaches and inlets, particularly south of Carnarvon and in Shark Bay. There are shallow lagoons and inlets with broad sandy beaches, with frequent intrusions of beach rock and sometimes a profusion of shells. To the south of Geraldton, down to the south-western tip of Australia, the beaches are mainly sandy and shingly, with some beach rock; the proportion of shingle increases towards the south.

South coast

In the western section of the south coast the beaches are mostly broad and sandy, often with lagoons and chains of tall dunes in inlets and river estuaries. Farther east, bordering the Nullarbor Plain, rugged cliffs predominate, with small, narrow and inaccessible beaches.

South Australia

Along the western part of the coast (Nullarbor Plain) there are cliffs and broad sandy beaches with dunes. To the east there are sandstone cliffs up to 200m/650ft high; they are particularly impressive to the west of Adelaide and in western Victoria (along the Great Ocean Road).

Waves

To the south of the Tropic of Capricorn, along the west coast and off Tasmania the waves mainly come in from the south-west; on the south-east and east coasts they come from the south-east; and to the north of the Tropic of Capricorn they come from differing directions. Waves over 2.50m/8ft high are particularly common at certain seasons of the year to the south of the Tropic. The highest proportion is found on the Great Australian Bight, where over a period of six months more than 30% of all waves are over 2.50m/8ft high. The frequency of high waves declines steadily towards the north, reaching a minimum figure of under 10% on the north coast.

The waves mainly take the form of a slow swell from the same direction, though their direction, height and frequency may be modified by storm conditions, particularly on the south coast and off Tasmania. In summer the swell on the south-east coast may also be affected by the trade winds and by the alternation of offshore and onshore winds near the coast in the course of the day. To the north of the Tropic of Capricorn, as a result of the protection afforded by reefs and lagoons, there is no uniformity in the height and direction of the waves. The passage of cyclones brings with it the danger of storm tides and tidal waves from different directions.

Surfing

The coasts of Australia offer ideal conditions for surfing, which is possible on almost all sandy and easily accessible beaches without underwater reefs. The finest waves for surfing are the high swells of the south-east and south coasts.

Particularly fine too is the south coast of Queensland, with magnificent waves, beautiful beaches and warm water. The north coast and parts of the west coast of Queensland are less suitable for surfing because of their protective reefs and mainly light, shifting winds.

Wind-surfing

The north coast is more suitable for wind-surfing, thanks to the frequently changing onshore winds and the absence of high waves.

Climate

Geographical factors

The climate of Australia is influenced by three geographical factors:

- the geographical situation of the main land mass between 15° and 35° S, in the tropics and subtropics with their intensive radiation;
- the compactness and size of the continent (7.7 million sq.km/3 million sq.miles), with only slight interpenetration of land and sea, the main exceptions being the Great Australian Bight in the south and the Gulf of Carpentaria in the north; and
- the mainly flat surface topography, with only a few higher ranges of hills to attract rain in the east and north-west.

Twelve typical weather stations in Australia

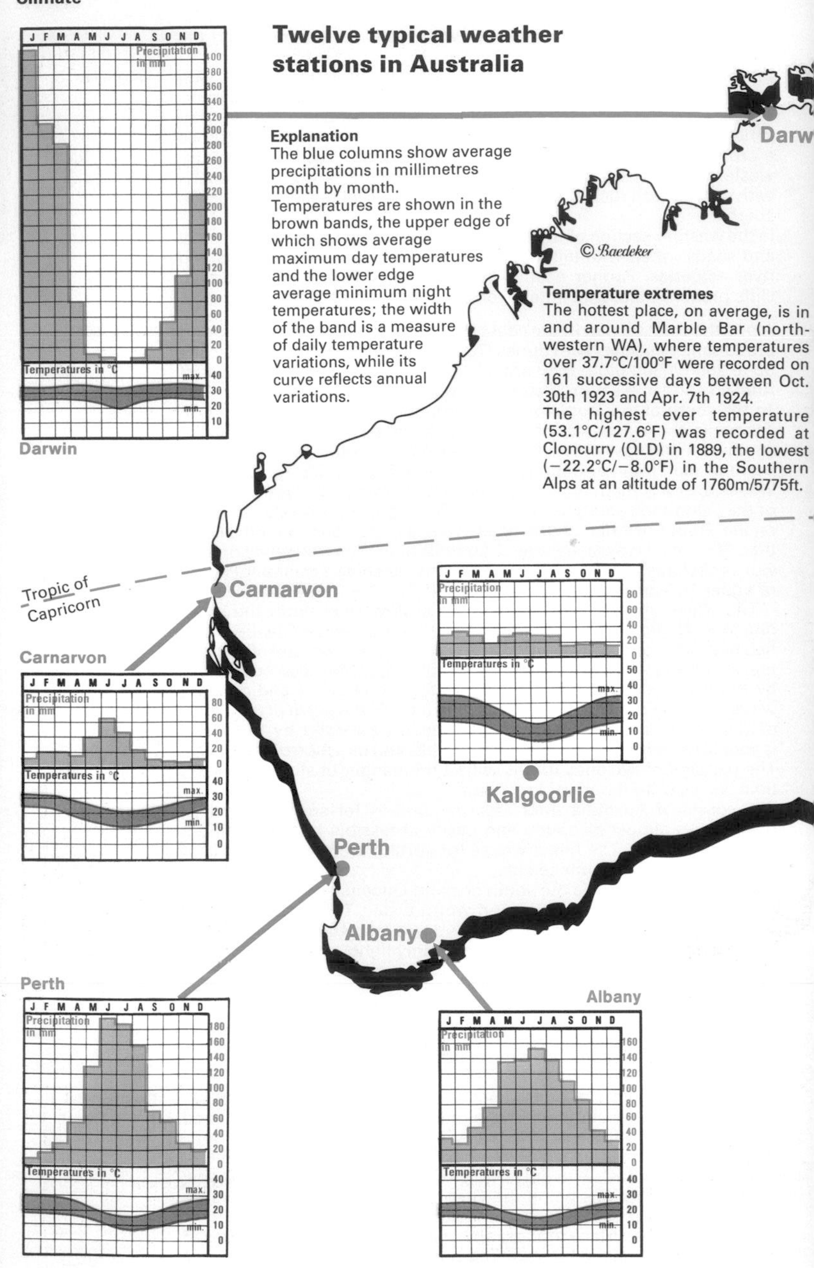

Explanation
The blue columns show average precipitations in millimetres month by month.
Temperatures are shown in the brown bands, the upper edge of which shows average maximum day temperatures and the lower edge average minimum night temperatures; the width of the band is a measure of daily temperature variations, while its curve reflects annual variations.

Temperature extremes
The hottest place, on average, is in and around Marble Bar (north-western WA), where temperatures over 37.7°C/100°F were recorded on 161 successive days between Oct. 30th 1923 and Apr. 7th 1924.
The highest ever temperature (53.1°C/127.6°F) was recorded at Cloncurry (QLD) in 1889, the lowest (−22.2°C/−8.0°F) in the Southern Alps at an altitude of 1760m/5775ft.

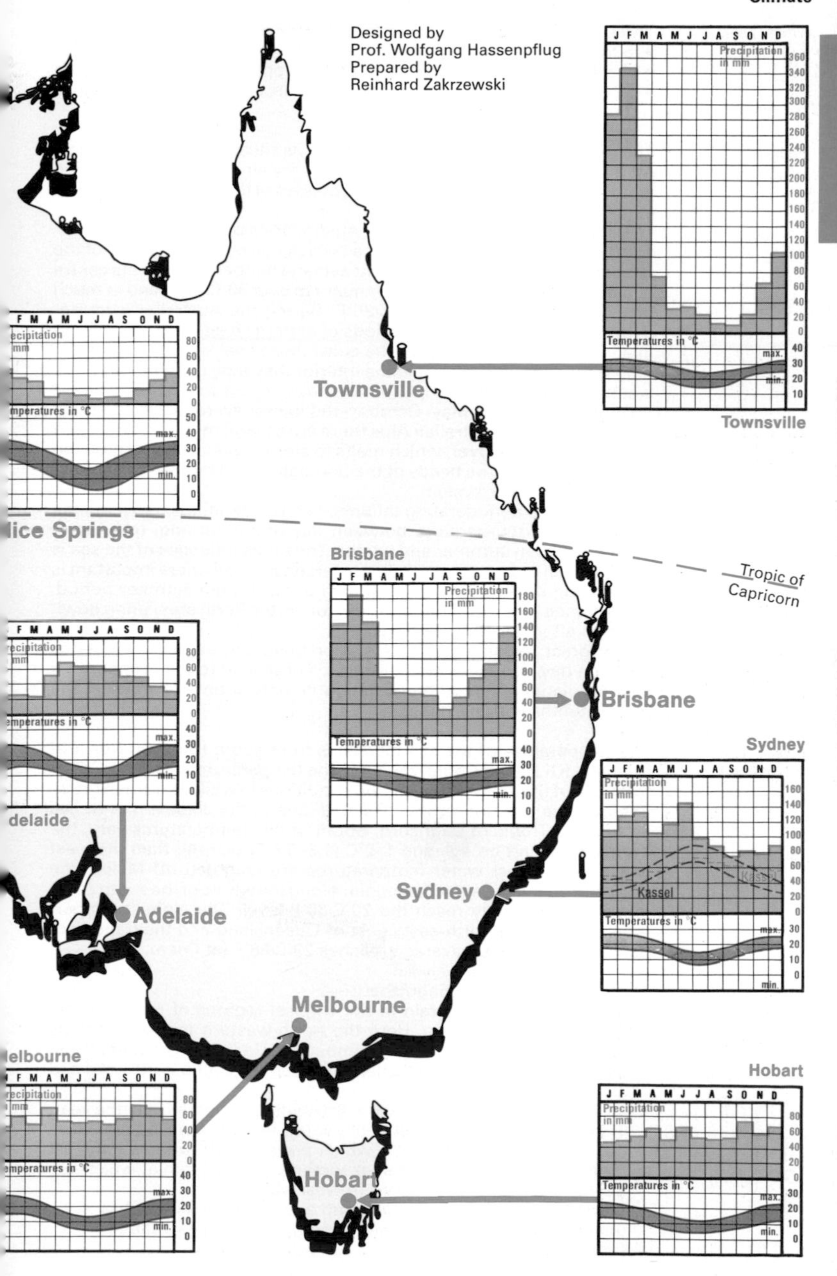
Designed by
Prof. Wolfgang Hassenpflug
Prepared by
Reinhard Zakrzewski
Townsville
Brisbane
Sydney
Adelaide
Melbourne
Hobart
lice Springs
Tropic of Capricorn
J F M A M J J A S O N D
Precipitation in mm
Temperatures in °C
max.
min.
Kassel

Climate

Climatic zones

Three broad climatic zones can be distinguished in Australia:
- a tropical zone to the north of the Tropic of Capricorn;
- a subtropical zone to the south of the Tropic;
- a cool temperate zone in the extreme south (Victoria) and in Tasmania.

Temperatures

The climate of Australia is determined by its situation in the subtropical high-pressure zone, which gives it clear, dry air and brilliant sunshine almost all year round. The great land masses of the continent act like an enormous heating area.

At its greatest east–west extent Australia lies on the Tropic of Capricorn, exposed to hot, dry air masses which make it the "hottest" of the continents. Within this great extent average temperatures in the centre and north of the country rise in January to over 30°C/86°F, and in much of the north-west to over 35°C/95°F. During the Australian summer (November–April) there are periods of extreme heat (over 40°C/104°F) in all parts of the country. On the coast these heat waves seldom last longer than three days, but in the interior they may continue for three weeks or even longer.

During the winter (May–October) the lowest average temperatures are in July. In the Australian Alps there are several months of frost and continuous snow cover, which melts to stock the reservoirs supplying water for meeting the needs of the population and regulating the flow of the Murray river system.

Moderating influence of the sea

The sea exerts a moderating influence on temperatures, reducing the differences of temperature between day and night and, to a lesser extent, between summer and winter. The direct influence of the sea is of course felt only in the narrow coastal zones. Much more important is the cooling effect of onshore winds during the hot summer period. These winds (e.g. the "Fremantle doctor" in the Perth area) bring down the high afternoon temperatures.

Day/night variations

In the great expanses of the interior there are extreme variations between day and night temperatures. These lead to the formation of dew on plants, giving the vegetation its only supply of water in the many months without rain.

Water temperatures

The temperature of the sea increases from south to north. North of Brisbane (QLD) and Carnarvon (WA) the temperature is over 20°C/68°F throughout the year, providing the conditions in which coral can grow. The average position of the 20°C/68°F line in the coldest month lies around the Tropic of Capricorn. South of this temperatures vary, the east coast being on average 1–2°C (1.8–3.6°F) warmer than the west coast. The lowest water temperatures are recorded off Melbourne (VIC) and on the coasts of Tasmania. Along the whole of the south coast temperatures barely reach the 20°C/68°F level. The highest temperatures are on the north-east coast of Queensland and the Cape York peninsula, where the average reaches 29°C/86°F (at Coen).

Rainfall

Three zones can be distinguished:
- the zone of summer rain in the tropical regions of northern and north-eastern Australia. Here the north-western monsoon brings heavy rain, particularly in December and January. The rainfall can be particularly violent in the land masses projecting northward and also as a result of cyclones.
- a transitional zone with an even distribution of rainfall over the year. This zone is at its broadest in the south-east. It takes in the coastal plains of New South Wales, which are exposed to the south-east trade winds, and the states of Victoria and Tasmania, which are almost continuously exposed to west winds.
- the zone of winter rain in the south and south-west, which is under the influence of the rain-bringing west winds, mainly from May to October.

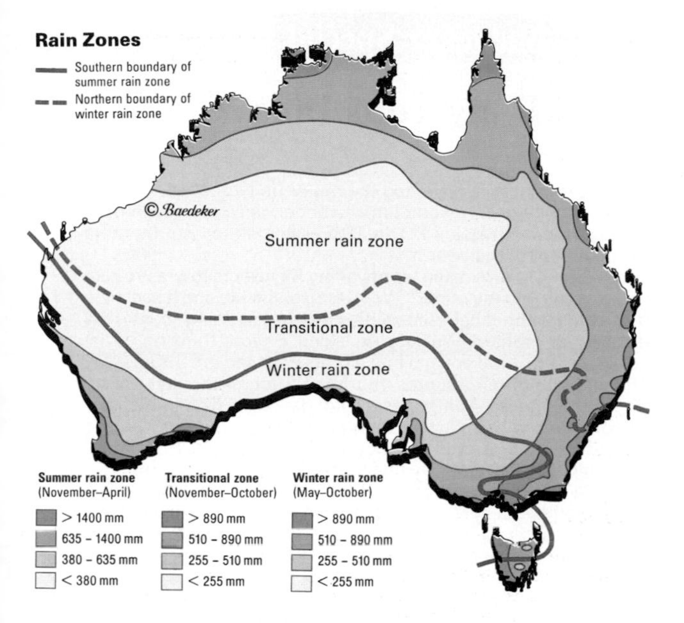

Rainfall is also influenced by the seasonal displacement of the high-pressure zone from north to south. During the Australian summer (November–April) this lies in the southern half of the continent, while the north has heavy monsoon rains, which lead to serious flooding, particularly in December and January. With the high humidity of the air the high temperatures are almost intolerable, making the summer months a bad time to visit the north. In the southern half of the continent, with the exception of the extreme south-east, there is usually no rain at all during the summer. Combined with the agreeable temperatures this provides an ideal climate for the sun-hungry visitor from more northerly latitudes.

Wet and dry seasons

In winter the subtropical high-pressure zone moves north again. This keeps the monsoon rain away from Australia and brings the northern part of the country a dry period (May–October). This is the best time of year for a visit to northern Australia. The displacement of the high-pressure zone brings the south into the sphere of influence of the west winds. South-western Australia, western Tasmania and parts of south-eastern Australia now get winter rain. Variations in the movement of the subtropical high-pressure zone are frequent, and have catastrophic consequences in areas which otherwise have little rain – the northern zone of winter rain, the transitional zone and the southern zone of summer rain – bringing heavy falls of rain, flooding and damage by erosion. On the east coast and in Tasmania the weather is influenced by the south-eastern trade winds, while on the north-east coast the monsoon rains bring heavy falls, reaching maxima for the country: thus between 1924 and 1980 the area south of Cairns had an average annual rainfall of 4203mm/165in. Elsewhere in the foreland of the peripheral hills of eastern Australia there is also heavy rainfall by orographic precipitation (average about 2500mm/98in.). In spite of these exceptional figures, however, Australia is still, after Antarctica, the world's driest continent, some 52% of its area having an annual rainfall of under 300mm/12in.

Baedeker Special

A Dangerous Hole

It is true that not many people have had the opportunity of observing our planet from space. If they had – I sometimes wonder since my seven days with the German space-lab mission D 1 in 1985 – would they not be more careful in their treatment of their earth?

The striking and thought-provoking words of my Russian fellow-astronaut Vladimir Shatalov come into my mind: "We look up to the sky and it seems to be infinite. We breathe without being conscious that we are doing so, as if it is a thing to be taken for granted. We keep speaking without thinking of the endlessness of space. And then you get into a spacecraft and are thrust away from the earth, and within ten minutes you burst through the layer of air beyond which is nothingness – emptiness, cold, darkness! The immeasurable blue ocean of the sky which allows us to breathe and protects us from the abyss of space and death has turned out to be a mere fragile skin. How fatal it is to damage in even the slightest way this protective covering of life!"

When, around 1987, weather and research satellites began to send back to their control centres the first evidence of a hole in the delicate ozone layer which protects life on earth, alarm bells sounded, and not only in scientific circles. It became clear that one of the causes of the sharp increase in skin cancer which health authorities had observed for many years was men's thoughtless treatment of their planet. And but for space travel, it may be remarked in passing, we should probably not even know of the existence of the ozone layer. To dismiss the existence and the growth of the hole in the ozone layer as a pure natural phenomenon would not only be wrong: it would be negligent and fatal for the future of our planet.

Ozone is a gas with three oxygen atoms in the molecule. It is formed under the influence of short-wave ultraviolet rays of molecular oxygen emitted by the sun. Ozone absorbs this radiation, which in high concentration is dangerous to life on earth, and then breaks down into its individual atoms. The atomic oxygen thus released is then taken up by molecular oxygen, so that there is a balance between the build-up and the disintegration of ozone.

The chlorofluorocarbons, formerly regarded as harmless and environmentally neutral, have now been identified as the "killers" of ozone. These aggressive gases, until recently used in refrigerators and air-conditioning plants and as the propellant in aerosols, have the fateful quality of rising slowly (over a period of 10–15 years) through the earth's atmosphere. During their rise they remain chemically stable, but they then meet the ozone layer in the stratosphere, which begins at a height of between 8 and 17km (5 and 11 miles), varying according to season and geographical latitude, and at a height of around 45km/28 miles merges into the stratopause. Here they filter out the sun's ultraviolet radiation, and in the process the chlorine atoms contained in the chlorofluorocarbons are released and attack the ozone molecules.

Satellite photographs show that the hole in the ozone layer over Antarctica, in which the earth's rotation produces particular weather conditions, has grown considerably in size over the few years since its discovery. The photographs opposite, taken by a satellite camera specially constructed for studying the hole in the ozone layer, show clearly how the hole has increased in size; and almost exactly in the centre of the hole can be seen the Australian continent. And when it is remembered that the chlorofluorocarbons were

Baedeker Special

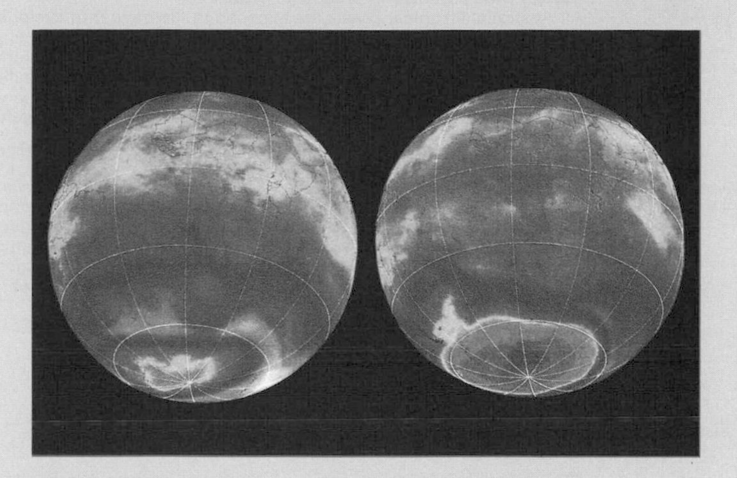

The hole in the ozone layer over the Antarctic is increasing in size
Photographs taken from space, 1977 (left) and 1987 (right)

widely used until a few years ago and take up to 15 years to reach the ozone layer it can be seen that in spite of the fall in world production of chlorofluorocarbons it will be many years before the problem can be reduced.

In the course of our D 1 mission in 1985, orbiting at an angle of 57° to the Equator, we had an excellent opportunity to estimate the possible effects of the hole in the ozone layer. That the Australian continent and its inhabitants must be particularly affected, both now and in the future, is evident from its situation on the globe. It can also be seen that a country with little cloud cover and many sunny days is particularly in need of protection from the dangerous ultraviolet radiation. It has since been shown that in the months between October and December the ozone layer here has lost all its previous concentration up to a height of 18km/11 miles and beyond this has preserved only half its previous level. Australia's near neighbour New Zealand has the highest incidence of skin cancer in the world, with up to 12,000 new cases recorded every year. It is to be feared that this life-endangering disease will show a marked increase in Australia, and thereafter perhaps in other continents as well. It is up to all of us to secure our survival by showing more care in our treatment of planet earth. My American fellow-astronaut Edgar Mitchell spoke from the heart when he said "The high point of our trip was the insight that the universe is harmonious, useful and creative. The low point was the realisation that mankind does not behave in accordance with that insight." Should not these words give us cause for thought?

Professor Ernst W. Messerschmid, the author of this note, was a member of the German space-lab mission D 1, which between October 30th and November 6th 1985 made 112 orbits of the earth at a height of 324km/200 miles in the space shuttle "Challenger". Along with five other scientists from Germany, the Netherlands and the United States and two American pilots he carried out numerous scientific experiments in space. He is now professor of space travel systems at Stuttgart University.

Bush fires

As a result of the long periods of drought bush fires are frequent in Australia. After the last period of drought (1981–83) there were great bush fires in the south-east of the country, reaching in South Australia and Victoria right down to the coast. The most recent fires in the Sydney area attracted international headlines.

Cyclones

All Australia's tropical coasts are exposed to the danger of cyclones. On average there are two cyclones every year off the north-west coast and three off the north-east coast. One in two or three of the cyclones comes close to the coast or strikes the land. The period of greatest frequency is between January and April. South of 20° S the cyclones die down and turn west. Thus the whole of Western Australia can suffer the effects of a cyclone (heavy rain).

Weather hazards for visitors

In these extreme climatic conditions travel in some parts of Australia at certain times of year is not without its hazards for visitors – for example the stresses created by extremely high temperatures and the danger of being cut off from the outside world or prevented from reaching their destination by flooding. When planning a trip to Australia, therefore, they should check up on temperatures and rainfall – information which is readily available for all parts of the country.

For journeys in the outback it is essential to take sufficient supplies of water.

Flora and Fauna

Natural vegetation

The natural vegetation of Australia is determined by the distribution of temperatures and rainfall in time and space, and the flora of the continent has adjusted to varying natural conditions in an enormous range of variations. It is predominantly an endemic flora: that is, a plant world found only in Australia. Early forms of vegetation have been preserved in Australia since the breaking of the land connection which once existed between Asia and Australia.

Eucalyptus (gums)

There are more than 500 species of eucalyptus, which in its adaptation to natural conditions has evolved very varying growth forms. The type of eucalyptus thought of as particularly characteristic of Australia is represented by the great forests on the south-western and south-eastern periphery of the continent.

Acacias (wattles)

Commoner in the interior of the continent are the acacias (wattles), which have developed an even wider range of species in their adaptation to the extreme conditions of the interior.

Rain forest

In the areas of forest and woodland in the extreme south-west of the continent and along the east coast in the foreland of the Great Dividing Range, with a growing period of over nine months in the year, trees grow to heights of up to 60m/200ft. On the north-east coast the rainfall pattern permits the growth of vegetation throughout the year. In this area are found the various types of rain forest.

Woodlands

Towards the interior of the country the pattern of tree cover varies in accordance with climatic conditions. Here the climate does not favour a dense growth of forest, and instead there are areas of more open woodland with an undergrowth of shrubs and grass in which the trees grow to heights of around 20m/65ft. These open woodlands with areas of grazing offered suitable conditions for pastoral farming (cattle and sheep). As the trees were felled the area available for grazing was steadily increased. To save the labour of rooting out the trees they were caused to decay by the process of "rind-barking". Much woodland was also cleared to provide land for growing wheat.

Changes in natural eco-systems 1770–1970

Eco-systems	Desert	Grasslands	Scrublands	Woodlands	Forest	Rain Forest
Growing period in months	<1	1–5	1–5	5–9	>9	12
Percentage of total area 1770	12.8	52.2	11.0	17.0	5.0	2.0
Percentage of total area 1970	12.8	9.7	6.5	2.0	1.5	0.3

Scrublands Mallee scrub, mulga scrub

Farther into the interior are expanses of scrubland, with a scrub of sclerophyllous (hard-leaved) species, known as "mallee scrub" when eucalypts predominate and as "mulga scrub" when acacias are dominant. Here the growing period ranges between 1 and 5 months. A third type is salt bush steppe, in which growths are generally lower and sparser.

Grasslands

The vegetation form which has changed most is the grasslands. These are areas in north-eastern Australia and the arid interior with expanses of tufted grass interrupted by bushes and shrubs, wattles and eucalypts. Not all the grasses in these extensive grass steppes were palatable to grazing stock. Thus spinifex grass, for example, was left untouched and consequently spread. Other grasses such as Mitchell grass appealed particularly to cattle. As a result the patterm of the grasslands changed by selection and over-grazing.

Deserts

The deserts have resisted development for stock-farming, and their area has remained practically unchanged.

Imported plants

With 20,000 different species of plant, Australia has an enormous range of variation. Although only 10% of these have been imported within the last two centuries they occupy considerable areas of land. They are mainly agricultural plants (various species of grain, grasses, pulses, clover and tropical plants such as sugar-cane). There are extensive plantations of spruce for building timber. Some imported plants brought with them pests which were new to the country.

National Parks

Australia's vegetation is so varied and so fascinating that the changes which have been brought about by human intervention are not always realised. The numerous National Parks and similar reserves are designed to preserve the natural vegetation and if possible to re-establish species that have disappeared.

Bottle tree

Sturt's desert pea

Banksia

A carnivorous plant

Eucalyptus

Crocodile

Kangaroo

Emu

Kookaburra

Baedeker Special

The Koala is not so Cuddly

The koala was in a fair way to become Australia's heraldic animal. "But," my old friend Ron Baxter used to say, scratching his reddish beard, "what can you do with an animal that spends two-thirds of the day having a kip in a tree and the rest of its time eating?" Then he would tip up his broad-brimmed hat, take a good pull at his Foster's beer and add, "And has a kangaroo ever scratched you or piddled on you?"

Ron had got the story about being piddled on from an Australian minister of tourism, no less, a man named John Brown who had complained vigorously about the koala. The koala was by no means the cuddly little creature it was cracked up to be, he had said. "It stinks, it scratches you and it is covered with fleas." It does not appear that these accusations gave rise to any great storm of indignation in Australia; but this button-eyed and snub-nosed little Australian bear with its soft silver-grey fur and rather ungainly appearance has its defenders. A koala will scratch you only if you take hold of it, and the emptying of its bladder is due purely to fright.

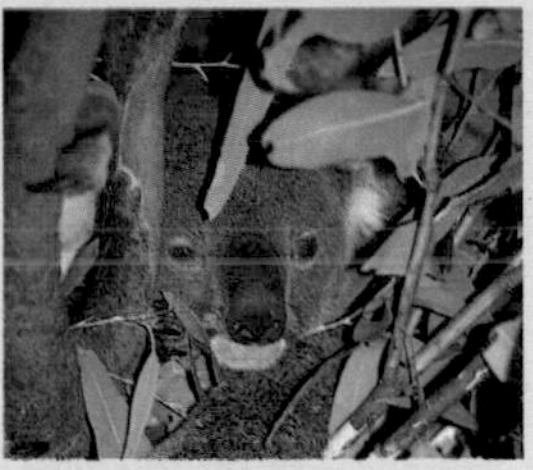

Koala in the Land of Cockaigne

But there is no dispute over the koala's disposition for sleepy lethargy. This tree-dwelling marsupial (scientific name *Phascolarctus cinereus),* which can reach a length of over 80cm/2½ft, is a nocturnal animal which comes to life only in the evening twilight but then is very active indeed. Then – unless his sleeping quarters have been in a eucalyptus tree – he sets out in quest of the eucalyptus leaves which he likes best. He is very choosy in selecting his food: if he does not like the taste he will not touch it. There are over 500 species of eucalyptus in Australia, but only a dozen or so appeal to the koala. He eats between 600 and 1250 grams (21 and 44 ounces) per day – or rather per night, for he sleeps throughout the day. This diet gives his skin the strong smell for which koalas are notorious.

The koala had a narrow escape from becoming an endangered species, to be seen only in a few zoos. The popularity of its soft grey fur, which was appreciated from the 18th century onwards for providing a warm head-covering, and the ruthless felling of the eucalyptus trees which provided its favourite food brought it to the verge of extinction. The killing or capture of the koala has been banned since 1927, but the mass felling of eucalyptus trees continues.

It is estimated that there are still something like half a million koalas in Australia. There are a few dozen in captivity in zoos round the world, and for many years people wondered why they did not survive long in these conditions. Now, however, botanists have discovered that koalas thrive on a particular mixture of eucalyptus leaves – some that have a stimulating effect and others that make them sleepy. The difficulty of finding the right combination of leaves out of the wide range of possibilities means that koalas kept in zoos slowly but surely pine and die.

Fauna

The National Parks also protect Australia's distinctive fauna. Thanks to its isolated situation it has preserved some primitive species which are found nowhere else. Alongside relatively few of the so-called higher mammals (flying foxes, bats, some rodents) there are egg-laying mammals (duck-billed platypus, echidna) and marsupials, of which there are some 130 species. The best known are the kangaroos (around 50 species), of different sizes and adapted to very varied living conditions. In the marsupials the young are born in an embryonic state and continue their development in a pouch on the mother's body, to which the tiny embryos must make their own way after being born. Even in the largest species, which reach the height of a man, the kangaroo embryo is no more than 2.5cm (1 inch) long. Marsupials which run upright (mainly the kangaroo) have the pouch on the mother's belly; climbing species (the koala and some 40 other species) have it on the back, as do marsupials which grub for their food (e.g. the wombat).

Koala

The best known of the climbing marsupials is the koala or native bear. The tiny embryo makes its way to the pouch on its mother's back and is suckled there for seven months, after which the mother carries it pickaback for another six months. Koalas are mainly nocturnal and eat only certain species of eucalyptus. They frequently suffer from chills and eye troubles and have been decimated by disease as well as by having been hunted in the past for their fur. They are still found in eastern and south-eastern Australia particularly in Victoria, where their numbers are increasing.

Gliding marsupials

The gliding or flying marsupials have adapted to their living conditions in a different way. They have membranes between their front and rear legs which enable them to glide for distances of up to 100 metres, carrying their young on their back.

Tasmanian wolf, Tasmanian devil

The Tasmanian wolf (Tasmanian tiger) and Tasmanian devil were driven to extinction in mainland Australia by the dingos which were brought in by immigrants from south-eastern Asia more than 10,000 years ago and by the increasing aridity of the climate. The Tasmanian Devil has survived only in Tasmania, which was cut off from Australia by the rise in sea level at the end of the last Ice Age, before the arrival of the dingos.

Birds

Australia is also unique in its rich and colourful bird life with 700 bird species recorded. Its insular situation was of less significance in the development of birds than of land animals, and there was some interchange of species with Asia. Species lacking in Australia include flamingoes, vultures and woodpeckers.

Emu

The emu ranks with the kangaroo as one of Australia's heraldic animals. A flightless bird, it grows to a height of 1.50m/5ft and a weight of almost 60kg/130lb. It is still frequently encountered in the outback.

Parrots

Australia has many species of parrots, cockatoos, rosellas and budgerigars being particularly common. Huge swarms of budgerigars and zebra finches gather at watering points in the interior.

Kookaburra

The kookaburra is another typically Australian species. It has a loud cackling cry which has earned it the name of laughing jackass.

Lyrebird

The lyrebird is noted for its magnificent plumage, and was formerly hunted for its long tail feathers; it is now a protected species. It has a remarkable ability to imitate the cries of other birds.

Other rare species are the jabiru, Australia's only stork, and the brolga crane.

Water birds

Australia has innumerable species of water birds, particularly in the north of the country. During the dry Australian winter flocks of ducks, geese and herons, together with spoonbills, pelicans and kingfishers can be observed at close quarters on the remaining stretches of water. The black swan is found only in Australia.

Penguins

Dwarf penguins are found on the southern Australian coasts and in Tasmania ("penguin parade" on Phillip Island, VIC).

Reptiles

Turtles

Australia also has an extraordinary variety of reptiles. Along the north coast and on beaches on the islands of the Great Barrier Reef turtles lay their eggs.

Crocodiles

Saltwater crocodiles (salties) are found in coastal regions in northern Australia. They are usually about 4m/13ft long but may be larger, and are dangerous to man. The freshwater crocodile is harmless; it is only around 2.5m/8ft long and lives on plants, fish and small river creatures.

Lizards

There are lizards all over Australia: some 500 species, ranging in length from 5cm/2in. to 2.50m/8ft, are known. An unusual species is the frilled lizard, which seeks to frighten off its enemies by expanding its frill and rearing up on its hind legs.

Snakes

Some 140 species of snake have been identified in Australia, from species only a few inches long to the python, which can be up to 7m/23ft long. Around 20 species are poisonous. There are now effective antidotes against snakebite, but it is preferable to take avoiding action. When walking through undergrowth it is advisable to stride firmly and make a noise, whereupon almost all snakes will get out of the way.

Spiders

There are poisonous species – the funnel-web spider (found particularly in and around Sydney) and the redback spider (all over Australia) – which should be avoided.

Corals

On the fantastic world of coral on the Great Barrier Reef, see the Baedeker Special on pp. 288–89.

Whale sharks

The wide-mouthed whale shark, the largest of all fish (up to 18m/60ft long), lives in tropical waters and is found on the west coast of Australia. It feeds on corals and plankton.

Imported animals

The original fauna of Australia has been much affected by the import of animals from other countries. Since the imported animals for the most part found no natural enemies they multiplied at a disproportionate rate. The native fauna was no match for the new arrivals and was reduced in numbers and sometimes exterminated. Since the arrival of Europeans in 1788 17 species of mammals, three species of lizard and one species of bird are known to have become extinct. The natural fauna of Australia was decimated not only by hunting and by the imported animals (cattle, sheep, goats, water buffalo, rabbits, foxes, cats) but also by the development of agriculture, which radically altered the natural landscape and curtailed the habitats of the native fauna. The smaller marsupials are now under threat from imported animals (particularly cats and foxes) which have run wild.

Rabbits

The rabbits which were brought into Australia in the mid 19th century proved particularly disastrous. They multiplied at such a rate that 3000km/1865 miles of rabbit-proof fences had to be erected to keep them out of grazing land. Only the deliberate spread of myxomatosis has checked the rabbit plague.

Toads

The toads which were introduced into Queensland to combat pests in the sugar-cane plantations also developed into a plague.

National Parks

Australia's fenced-in animal reserves and National Parks are designed to preserve endangered species such as the rare rock kangaroos and long-nosed bandicoots. The clearance of forest and the creation of huge areas of grazing for cattle and sheep have provided improved living conditions for emus and the larger kangaroos; and the soft paws of the kangaroos do not damage the soil, always threatened by erosion, or the grassland as do the hard hooves of imported European animals.

Wildlife viewing

Many visitors to Australia are disappointed by seeing so few animals in the wild. In farming country, however, wild animals (many of which are of nocturnal habit) are unwanted competitors for food. Unpleasantly close and dangerous encounters with kangaroos are frequent occurrences on roads in the outback. During the dry Australian winter there are opportunities for observing animals (waterfowl, crocodiles) at watering-points in northern Australia.

Typical Australian animals which are rarely met with in the wild (platypuses and echidnas, the Tasmanian devil, wombats, koalas, parrots and parakeets, etc.) can be seen in the zoos in the large cities and in the many privately run zoos.

Dangers for bathers
Jellyfish

On bathing beaches in the tropical north of Australia the main hazard for bathers during the Australian summer is the highly poisonous box jellyfish. Antidotes (usually vinegar) which neutralise the venom in the tentacles are often available from beach kiosks.

Sharks

Outside the summer season there is little risk in swimming in the sea, at any rate in shallow coastal waters. In deeper waters there may be danger from sharks.

Natural and Man-Made Landscapes

Agriculture

Unlike the Aborigines (see Population), who had adjusted to their environment, the white settlers had from the outset great difficulty in coming to terms with natural conditions in Australia. For many decades the first colonies of convicts and settlers were dependent on the arrival of supplies from the home country. It soon became clear that the living standards normal in Britain could not be achieved in Australia from local resources. In order to be able to import the goods which the country lacked it was necessary to have products which could be exported in return. The development of the colony was thus mainly a quest for export products of economic value.

Sheep-farming

It took thirty years for the wool produced on Australian sheep farms to become the country's first major export product. The number of sheep increased by leaps and bounds, reaching 60 million by 1850 and 180 million forty years later. By about 1900 70% of the wool sold on the London wool market came from Australia. The basis for the wool boom was the importation of merino sheep from Britain and Germany which

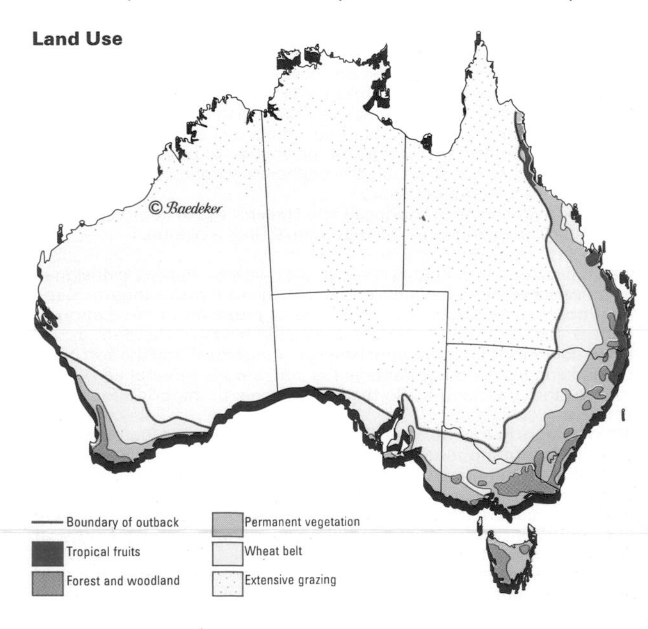

in Australia produced wool of the finest qualities. The best grazing land for sheep was in the coastal areas and also farther inland, where vast expanses of wooded grassland were available for grazing without the need for cultivation. There seemed no limit to the expansion of the sheep-farming areas. The natural grassland was exploited by sheep-farmers (squatters) who neither owned nor leased the land. Later these de-facto arrangements developed into legal tenancies.

Cattle-farming

Cattle-farming developed alongside this boom in sheep-farming, particularly in the interior of Queensland, where its extension was promoted by the availability of artesian water supplies. In the last few decades the demand for meat for hamburgers has considerably expanded the market for Australian beef. Cattle farms have now also been established in the Northern Territory and in the north of Western Australia.

Cattle farms are leased out by the State, in Western Australia up to a limit of 200,000 hectares/500,000 acres, in the Northern Territory up to 800,000 hectares/2,000,000 acres, in the other states without limit of size. The lease is for a period of from 30 to 50 years. The history of cattle-farming in Australia has not been one of uninterrupted development. There have been repeated setbacks due to the fall of prices in world markets, though the risks can be reduced by a combination of cattle and sheep farming. The industry has also suffered from periodic devastating periods of drought (1895–1903, 1911–16, 1965–67, 1981–83).

Wheat

After wool and meat Australia's third great agricultural export has been wheat. The necessary conditions for the development of the wheat-growing areas were created by the gold boom which spread over the whole country in the second half of the 19th century. The gold boom brought Australia a great increase in population, trebling it in some areas. This created a large market for agricultural produce within Australia itself, and wheat production expanded to such an extent that there was soon a surplus available for export.

Urban settlement zone

There are favourable conditions for the development of agriculture and forestry in a narrow strip along the east coast, in the south-east and south-west and in Tasmania. These areas have an annual rainfall of well over 500mm/20in. Temperature and rainfall conditions are particularly favourable in a narrow coastal strip extending south from Cairns (QLD) into northern New South Wales.

Sugar-cane

In this area tropical crops, in particular sugar-cane, are grown. The processing of sugar-cane is now mechanised and the cane is transported to the numerous sugar factories on narrow-gauge railways.

Grazing land

In terms of area grazing land is predominant in the humid coastal zone. Most of it is of first-rate quality, requiring less than a hectare (2½ acres) per head of cattle. From the early pioneering days the area of grassland was increased by the clearance of trees and the introduction of new types of grass.

Eucalyptus forest

In the humid coastal zone, which occupies 45 million hectares (110 million hectares), or 5.8% of the whole area of Australia, the natural vegetation has been preserved only in wooded and forest areas. These forests are on the higher ground, on the slopes running up to the highlands of eastern Australia and, in the south-west, to the Darling Range. The eucalyptus forests have not been much altered by forestry management, and large areas have been declared protected reserves. The finest eucalypts in these forest areas are the karri tree in the south-west and the mountain ash (giant gum) in Victoria, New South Wales and Tasmania. Australians often distinguish eucalyptus trees by their bark: gum trees are those which cast off their bark completely and have smooth trunks, while iron-bark trees have a firm and deeply furrowed bark. Half way between the two are the stringy bark trees, which cast off the bark only from the trunk and the larger branches.

Natural and Man-Made Landscapes

Tropical rain forest

Conurbations and axes of development

Tropical rain forest is found mainly in northern Queensland. Large areas are now under statutory protection (e.g. Daintree National Park). Axes of development are gradually extending from the two great conurbations of Sydney and Brisbane along the east coast of Australia and north and south of Perth on the west coast. The situation is less satisfactory in Victoria, South Australia and Tasmania.

Rural settlement zone

Inland from the urban settlement zone extends the rural settlement zone. This area between the humid coastal strip and the arid interior is Australia's core agricultural zone, within which lie the whole of the wheat belt (40.3 million hectares/99.5 million acres) and the irrigated areas with their vegetables, vineyards, orchards of citrus and other fruits and cotton plantations. As a result of alternation in the use of land in the wheat belt between wheat and grazing for stock this zone accounts for 60% of the country's stock of sheep and 40% of its head of cattle. Measures of rationalisation (e.g. the amalgamation of farms) have led to a flight from the land. Small agricultural supply centres have lost their viability and been abandoned, and the larger regional centres have often been able to survive only as a result of government measures promoting decentralisation.
Throughout the rural settlement zone the development of agriculture has displaced the natural vegetation. Only occasional patches of woodland, odd uncultivated areas and the National Parks give some idea of the variety of vegetation which once flourished here.

Outback

Some 81% of the total area of Australia is accounted for by the vast expanses of the interior, the outback, in which no more than 4% of the population live. Climatic conditions are unfavourable, and except in the extreme north there is significant rainfall for less than five months in the year. All that can be contemplated in the way of agricultural development, therefore, is extensive stock-farming. In some parts of the outback the natural vegetation has been changed, though not completely displaced; but the outback remains the one part of Australia in which visitors can get some impression of an unspoiled natural landscape.

National Parks and nature reserves

In two hundred years of white settlement more than 70% of the original plant and animal world has been changed. Arable and pastoral farming, timber felling and mining have much reduced the natural bush. It is now essential to protect the remaining "wilderness" areas, if possible to extend them and to preserve this natural world which is now threatened with exploitation and destruction. The native flora and fauna, extraordinary landscapes and scenic beauties, the endangered rain

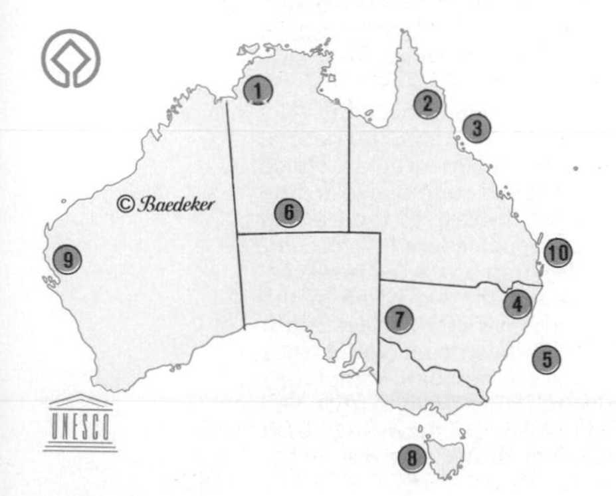

World Heritage Areas

C=Cultural heritage
N=Natural heritage

(in order of inclusion in UNESCO's World Heritage List)

1 Kakadu National Park (C, N)
2 Wet Tropics of Queensland (N)
3 Great Barrier Reef (N)
4 Australian Rainforest Parks (N)
5 Lord Howe Island Group (N)
6 Uluru National Park (Ayers Rock; N)
7 Wilandra Lakes Region (C, N)
8 Tasmanian Wilderness (N)
9 Shark Bay (N)
10 Fraser Island (N)

forests, coastal areas and wetlands, and also places of historical or cultural importance (Aboriginal cult sites, evidence of early white settlement, etc.) have been taken into state or federal guardianship and scheduled as protected areas. But National Parks – along with State Parks, Nature Reserves and State Recreation Areas – are not merely natural landscapes worthy of being preserved, they are also for people, giving them an opportunity to experience nature and the environment in a relaxed way and to learn to accept responsibility for nature.
The first Australian National Park (now known as the Royal National Park), to the south of Sydney, was established in 1879 "for public rest, recreation and pleasure". The largest of the National Parks is Kakadu National Park in the Northern Territory, which has an area of almost 2 million hectares (5 million acres). The Great Barrier Reef Marine Park is the world's largest marine reserve, taking in an area of 35 million hectares (86 million acres).
By 1994 there were over 200 National Parks and Reserves and over 2700 other protected areas totalling 22.16 million hectares (54.74 million acres). Altogether 6.4% of the land area of Australia was protected in this way. Since then a number of other protected areas have been established, and more will follow.
Thus thanks to the greatly increased public interest in the protection of nature and the environment as well as to government action Australia has been able to preserve its rain forests, unspoiled hill, coastal and island regions, wetlands and wild, untamed rivers.

Population

A young nation

The population structure of Australia has been favourably influenced by the immigration of mainly young people. In 1990 30.5% of Australians were under 20 and only 10.5% were over 65.

Growth of population in the capitals

The population of the state and national capitals increased sharply between 1971 and 1990. In Adelaide (SA) and Perth (WA) the increase was 73%, in Melbourne (VIC) 70.3%, in Sydney (NSW) 62.8%, in Darwin (NT) 46.6%, in Brisbane (QLD) 44.8%, in Hobart (TAS) 40.2% and in Canberra (ACT), the national capital, no less than 99.6%.

Aborigines

The original Australians

The Aborigines had lived in Australia for some 40,000 years before the arrival of the Europeans. Their ancestors had come from southern Asia in the remote past and taken possession of the whole continent, which in those days had more rain than it has now. The original population adapted successfully to their barren environment. Their society and culture were much more differentiated than the new arrivals from Britain were prepared to admit. In their eyes the natives were primitive and at best pitiable savages of repellent ugliness, lacking the blessings of civilisation, naturally inferior and doomed to extinction. In fact, however, the Aborigines had learned over many millennia to come to terms with changing natural conditions; they were skilled in observing nature and tracking game and unsurpassed in their ability to find water and food. It is estimated that when the first settlers arrived in 1788 there were some 300,000 Aborigines, distributed over the whole continent in between 500 and 600 tribes.

At first, when the white settlers began to take over their land the Aborigines reacted with alarm and astonishment to the light-skinned and fully clothed intruders – believing, indeed, that they were their own remote ancestors returning. Soon, however, the picture of peaceable

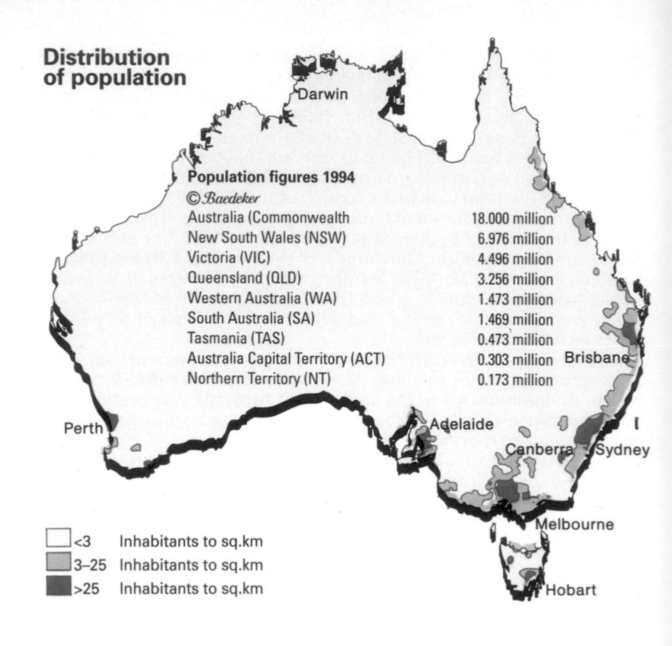

colonisation changed its aspect, as the conquerors exerted increasing pressure on the natives. The establishment of penal camps, settlements and stock farms led to the expulsion of the Aborigines from their hereditary tribal lands and hunting grounds and the destruction of their habitat and culture. Their traditional food-gathering and hunting areas were taken from them, their sacred places and ceremonial sites desecrated. Embittered by this treatment, they took up arms against the invaders, following their usual guerrilla tactics. But for every white man they killed or wounded there were ruthless reprisals, sparing neither women or children. Under the Proclamation of Native Outlawry (1816) Aborigines could be killed with impunity. The darkest chapter in the short history of white Australia deprived the people who had occupied the land from time immemorial of their roots, making them homeless and (in a literal sense) fair game for their oppressors. When they took the squatters' sheep or cattle in their hunting – having no conception of personal property – they were themselves hunted down and driven into the bush or killed.

The only areas where the Aborigines could still pursue their ancestral way of life were the desert-like centre of Australia and the rough country of the "Top End" in the north, where the inhospitable terrain formed a barrier to European expansion. On the large cattle stations they were able to find work in accordance with their traditional way of life. The worst off were – and still are – the rootless Aborigines in the slums of the cities, where they receive social assistance providing a bare minimum existence but have little prospect of integration into Australian society and accordingly fall victim to alcohol and disease or take to crime. As a result the number of Aborigines has fallen dramatically. There are none at all in Tasmania, and the total number in the whole of Australia in 1986, according to official figures, was only 227,645 (in 1994 303,261, representing 1.5% of the population), mainly in Queensland (61,268), New South Wales (59,011), Western Australia (37,789) and the Northern Territory

(34,739). Since the 1960s the Aborigines have been fighting stubbornly, and with some success, for the recovery of their ancestral land. In the Northern Territory a law passed in 1977 recognised their land rights and gave them control of some of their principal cult sites (e.g. Ayers Rock). Since then the Aboriginal Land Trusts have recovered around a third of the area of the Northern Territory, which is now administered by Aboriginal Land Councils and can be entered only with written permission. In the other states discussion of the Aborigines' claims is continuing.

In present-day Australia, which claims to be multi-cultural, racism still exists and the Aborigines are still treated as second-class citizens, in spite of the fact that they were given the vote in 1967.

Languages

The Aborigines speak more than 200 languages, sometimes very different from one another, with a remarkably rich vocabulary and with variations between everyday language and cult language. In the earliest days of European settlement Captain Arthur Phillip, commander of the First Fleet in 1788, was surprised to discover that a native at Sydney Cove could not understand the language of the neighbouring tribe on the Hawkesbury River.

Social structure

The concept of personal possessions was unknown to the Aborigines except for hunting weapons and sacred stones or wooden objects (tjuringas). The social structure was extremely complex. Individual families or clans belonged to a particular tribe which met at certain places and certain times for ceremonies and festivals. There were no tribal chiefs or leaders, but a special position was occupied by the old men of the tribe as preservers of the traditional creation myths and ceremonies and custodians of certain secret cult objects (stones, boomerangs) which were often taboo for women and children. Family relationships were complicated, centred on totems (mostly animals and plants) which to those concerned were sacred and might not be hunted, killed or eaten. The system of totems also regulated marriage relationships. Great importance was attached to the initiation rites for young men, who on entering the adult world gained access to the secret knowledge of the old.

Cosmology

The cosmology of the Aborigines was centred on a Dreamtime in the distant past when their remote forefathers had given life to the dead earth in human or animal form. All striking natural features – waterholes, hills, gorges, caves and prominent trees – were an expression of these creative forces, which were regularly celebrated in ceremonies, myths, songs and plays. As descendants of the beings of the Dreamtime and on their behalf the Aborigines revered and preserved, but never plundered, their environment. The tribal territory was their lebensraum and their home: deprived of it, they were left rootless.

On the art of the Aborigines see pp. 68–69, on their music pp. 74 and 78, on their flag p. 36.

European Settlement

Australia a place of exile for criminals

The "First Fleet" (1788) and many later convoys brought to Australia only convicts and the troops sent out to guard them. The convicts were compelled to work hard, but after serving their sentence were allowed to stay in the colony as free men ("emancipists") and work as craftsmen or on the land. The officers of the guard forces, the New South Wales Corps (popularly known as the "Rum Corps"), did well out of the allocation of land and the use of convict labour for their own purposes.

The position of the young British colony was by no means secure. France also showed interest in the South Pacific area, and voyages of exploration by the French (D'Entrecasteaux, La Pérouse, Baudin) took them along the Australian coasts. While circumnavigating the continent in 1802 Matthew Flinders encountered Baudin off the southern Australian coast, and on his voyage home experienced French hostility

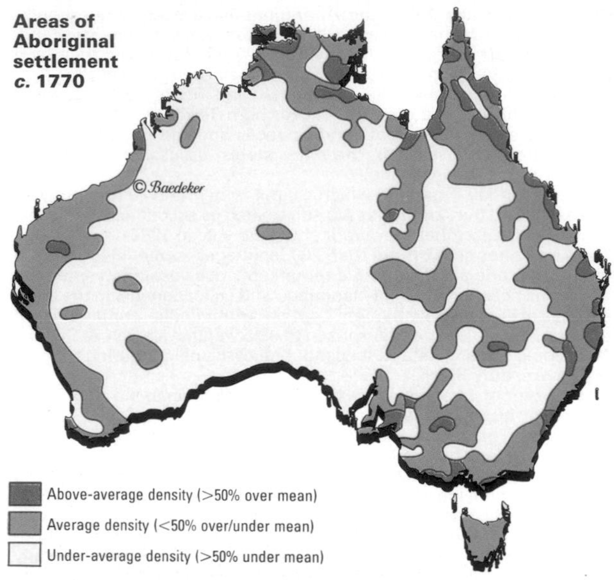

at first hand, being held prisoner for some years on the island of Mauritius. In order to forestall French claims the British government was determined to establish further settlements, which frequently failed (e.g. in Tasmania, Victoria, Western Australia and on the Cobourg peninsula in the tropical north). By 1868, when the transportation of convicts to Western Australia, the last colony to be established, came to an end, over 160,000 convicts had been sent to Australia. The numbers of free settlers had also increased steadily, and Australia had become one of the classic immigration countries, though never possessing the same fascination for immigrants as America. By around 1850 Australia had over 400,000 white inhabitants, of whom 20% were convicts.

Gold rush

In the second half of the 19th century the gold rush, starting in Victoria and New South Wales and spreading over the whole continent like a tidal wave, attracted great numbers of immigrants from all over the world. By 1870 the population of Australia was 1,647,000, having multiplied fourfold over the previous twenty years. The industrial development of Sydney, Melbourne and Adelaide suffered a setback in the economic depression of the late 19th century, and this was reflected in a fall in immigration. Only Western Australia, where the gold rush reached a final peak, escaped the effects of the depression.

First Census 1901

In 1901, the year in which the Commonwealth of Australia was established, the first Australian Census was held (subsequently to be followed by others at five-yearly intervals). It showed that Australia had a population of 3,774,000 (excluding the Aborigines).

White Australia policy

Immigration from China and the South Sea islands was banned by the Immigration Restriction Act, a reflection of the racist "White Australia" policy which arose out of the riots by Chinese workers during the gold-mining period and was also directed against the Kanakas who provided a cheap labour force on the sugar-cane plantations, working in conditions akin to slavery. Undesirable immigrants were kept out with the aid of the "dictation test" which they were required to undergo.

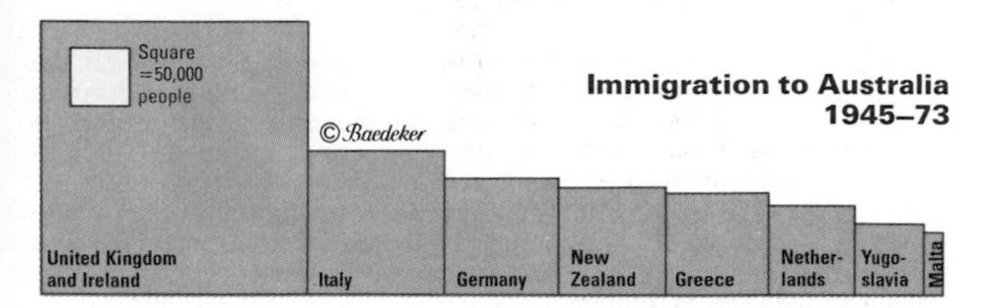

"Populate or perish"

After the turn of the century, and particularly after the First World War, the policy was to promote planned immigration from Britain. Decisive points were the world economic crisis of 1929 and the Second World War. Japanese attacks on the thinly populated north and north-east of Australia gave additional force to the slogan of this policy, "Populate or perish".

Australia, lying close to the densely populated regions of South-East Asia, needed more people, and now gladly opened its frontiers to streams of homeless and persecuted people from Europe, war-ravaged and divided by the Iron Curtain. Thanks to the influx of millions of new immigrants and to a high birth rate the population of Australia rose from 7.5 million in 1945 to 11 million in 1966. By 1976 some 2.6 million inhabitants of Australia had not been born there.

Immigration from Europe

2.3 million of the new immigrants came from Europe – 1,117,000 from Britain and Ireland, 280,000 from Italy, 153,000 from Greece, 144,000 from Yugoslavia, 108,000 from Germany, 92,000 from the Netherlands, 56,000 each from Poland and Malta. The areas of origin moved from Eastern Europe to Northern and Central Europe and then to Southern Europe. The immigrants from the Mediterranean countries developed a system of "chain migration" in which the Greeks, Yugoslavs, Italians and Maltese who were already settled in Australia brought in other members of their families – sometimes, indeed, whole villages. This gave the newcomers a feeling of security in their new country, and also led to the concentration of particular ethnic groups in particular places: thus by 1971 more than 41% of immigrants in Melbourne were from Italy, Greece or Malta and in Sydney 32% of immigrants came from these countries.

The immigrants made for the large cities, where there were jobs to be had in their developing industry. With this large-scale immigration from many different countries Australia became a multi-cultural society. It is estimated that but for these great waves of immigration the population of Australia in 1980 would have been around 9 million: in fact it was 14.78 million.

Abandonment of White Australia policy

Australia's immigration policy changed in 1966, when the discriminatory White Australia policy was abandoned. This led to a considerable increase in the number of immigrants from the countries of Asia, and Australia also took in large numbers of Vietnamese refugees. More recently the difficult economic situation has led to a stricter control of immigrants, preference being given to those with families already established in Australia and to those with skills which are in short supply.

Social services

Australia had a state social insurance scheme at an early stage, and old age pensions were introduced in 1909. The present extensive system of social assistance and insurance is highly cost-intensive. Social services are a federal responsibility, with the states as executive agents. Health services are well developed in spite of the great distances to be covered, and the remoter parts of the country are served by the Flying Doctor Service (see Baedeker Special, p. 275).

Language and Religion

Language
English and "Strine"

The language of Australia is English, with spelling generally on the British pattern; but there is also a very characteristic colloquial form of English ("Strine") with numerous slang terms and colourful turns of phrase (for examples see Practical Information, Language). The first Australianisms were taken over from the Aboriginal names of objects, animals and places. With the ending of the White Australia policy in the 1960s the pressure on immigrants to integrate into Australian life was relaxed; but applicants for Australian citizenship must still have an adequate knowledge of English.

Multi-cultural variety

In the past fifty years, over 500,000 refugees and displaced persons have made their homes in Australia, the highest humanitarian intake per capita in the world. In 1994–95, 70% of the 87,428 settler arrivals were from non-English speaking countries and in the same period, Australia's humanitarian program provided 13,000 resettlement places.

Religion

Under the Australian constitution all churches and religious communities have equal rights and are independent of the State. Although the national Censuses carried out every five years ask for information about a person's religion the answer to this question is optional, and in 1986 25% of the population did not answer it.

Most Australians (75%) claim to belong to one or other Christian denomination. 23.9% of them are Anglicans (members of the Church of England in Australia), 16.1% are Catholics, 7.6% belong to the Uniting Church, 3.6% are Presbyterian and 2.7% are Orthodox.

The non-Christian religions accounted for only 2% of the population in 1986. Around a third of them are Muslims, a quarter are Buddhists and a fifth are Jews.

Government and Administration

Colonies and states

The six states of the Commonwealth of Australia - New South Wales (NSW), Queensland (QLD), South Australia (SA), Tasmania (TAS), Victoria (VIC) and Western Australia (WA) - were originally British colonies. Then in 1850 the Australian Colonies Government Act gave them their own governments, based on a constitution, with a two-chamber parliament, a prime minister and a cabinet.

The new system was brought into effect in New South Wales, Victoria

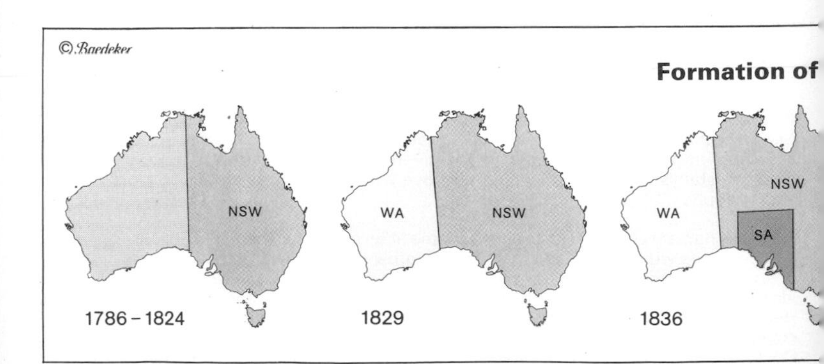

and Tasmania in 1855–56, in South Australia in 1857, in Queensland in 1859 (after its separation from New South Wales; upper house abolished in 1922) and in Western Australia in 1890. The various colonies had developed independently and in competition with each other – a situation reflected, for example, in the different gauges of their railways. There were considerable economic differences between the colonies: thus New South Wales believed in free trade while Victoria imposed protective tariffs.

Commonwealth of Australia

The British government's insistence in the 1880s on the amalgamation of the states' armed forces was followed up by a famous speech by the prime minister of New South Wales, Henry Parker, at Tenterfield on October 24th 1889 in which he called for a common Australian army and, as an eventual aim, a central Australian government. There was much resistance to the idea in the individual states, and New Zealand decided against joining in; but at last in 1900 a draft constitution for an Australian federation was put forward in London, signed by the Queen and brought into force on January 1st 1901. The Commonwealth of Australia now came into being, with Sir Edmund Barton as its first prime minister.

Canberra; ACT

The capital of the Commonwealth is Canberra, situated in the Australian Capital Territory (ACT) which was carved out of New South Wales in 1911. Until the government moved to Canberra in 1927 the main functions of the capital were performed by Melbourne (VIC). Finally the new Parliament Building in Canberra was inaugurated in 1988.

Parliamentary monarchy and federation

Australia is a parliamentary monarchy closely based on the British model, but also a federation whose constitution shows many similarities to that of the United States. In recent years British influence has been steadily reduced, although the Queen is still head of state, represented in Australia by a governor-general. Since the 1960s the governor-general has always been a native Australian, not a Briton as in the past. Since 1986 the constitutional link with Britain has practically fallen into abeyance, and Australia is expected to be declared a republic in 2001.

Legislature

The federal legislature consists of two houses, the Senate or upper house (76 senators, twelve per state and two per territory) and the House of Representatives or lower house (148 members, the number from each state varying according to population). The members of the House of Representatives are elected by majority vote for a three-year term. The senators are elected by proportional representation for a six-year term, with half the seats coming up for re-election every three years. The Crown is represented by the governor-general.

Voting is obligatory in federal elections and in state elections to the

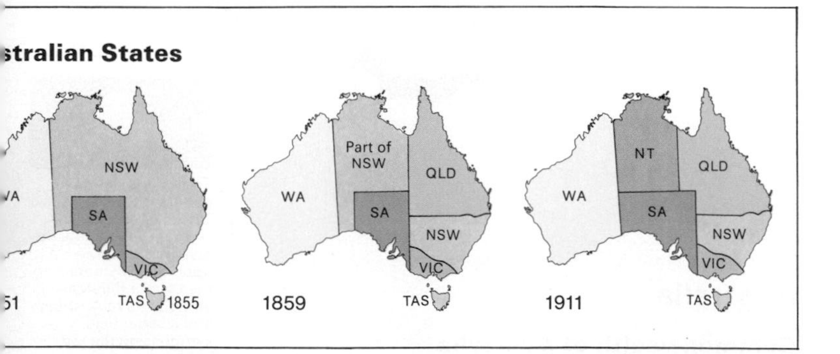

National flag

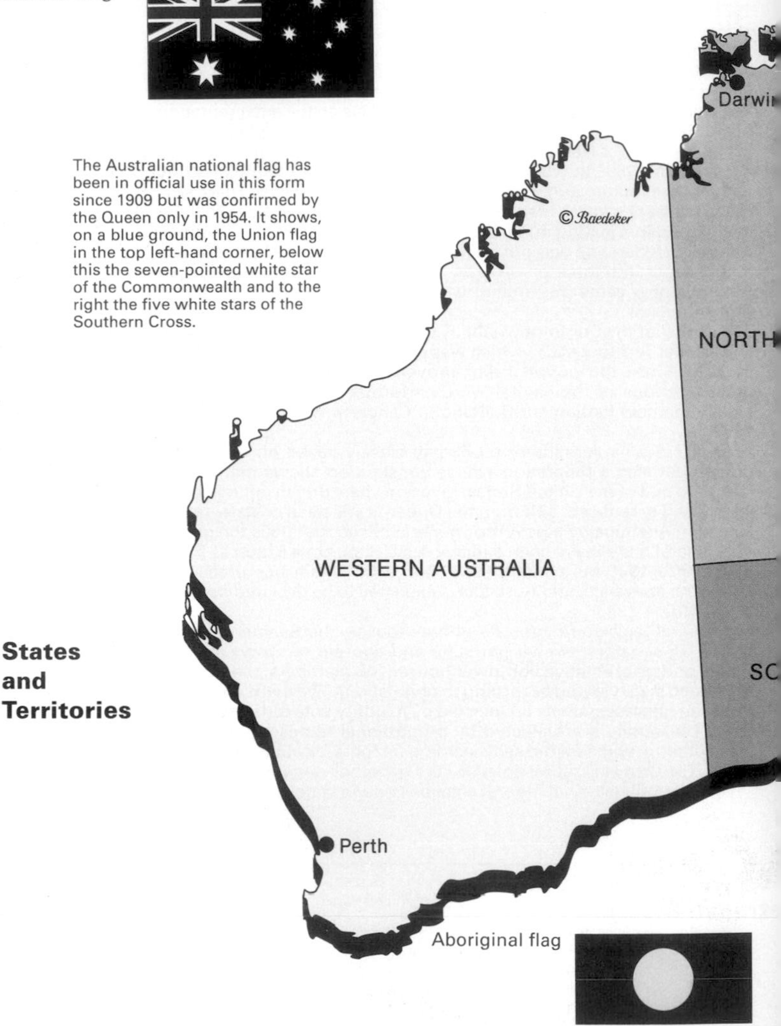

The Australian national flag has been in official use in this form since 1909 but was confirmed by the Queen only in 1954. It shows, on a blue ground, the Union flag in the top left-hand corner, below this the seven-pointed white star of the Commonwealth and to the right the five white stars of the Southern Cross.

States and Territories

Aboriginal flag

The Aborigines have had their own flag since 1972. It shows in the centre a yellow sun, the giver of life, on an upper field symbolising the black indigenous inhabitants of Australia and a lower field symbolising the red earth.

Australia

Commonwealth of Australia

Coat of arms

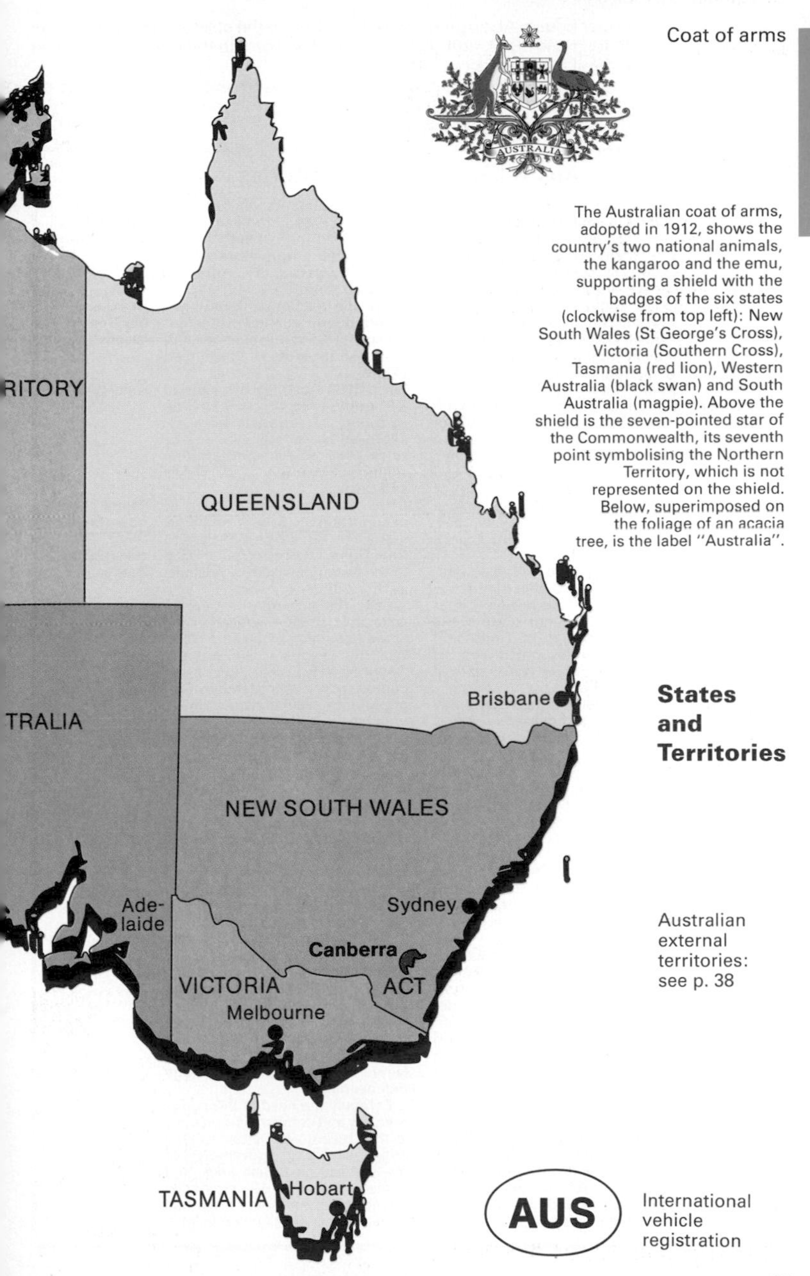

The Australian coat of arms, adopted in 1912, shows the country's two national animals, the kangaroo and the emu, supporting a shield with the badges of the six states (clockwise from top left): New South Wales (St George's Cross), Victoria (Southern Cross), Tasmania (red lion), Western Australia (black swan) and South Australia (magpie). Above the shield is the seven-pointed star of the Commonwealth, its seventh point symbolising the Northern Territory, which is not represented on the shield. Below, superimposed on the foliage of an acacia tree, is the label "Australia".

States and Territories

Australian external territories: see p. 38

AUS International vehicle registration

upper house. Aborigines were admitted to the electoral register for the first time in 1962, and they have been subject to the obligatory vote in federal elections since 1984.

Britain was the first country in the world to give women the vote (in 1886), and this example was followed by Australia in 1901 when the Commonwealth was established.

Australian External Territories

Territory of Cocos Islands
Cocos Islands or Keeling Islands: numerous small coral islands (total area 14.2sq.km/5.5sq.miles; pop. 600, mainly Malays; coconuts, export of copra) in the north-eastern Indian Ocean 1000km/620 miles south-west of Java and 2750km/1710 miles north-west of Perth (WA); under Australian administration since 1955. Can be visited only with special permission.

Christmas Island Territory
Christmas Island (135sq.km/-52sq.miles; pop. 1200; export of phosphates): in the north-eastern Indian Ocean 350km/220 miles south-west of Java and 1400km/870 miles north-west of North West Cape (WA); under Australian administration since 1958. Can be visited only with special permission.

Ashmore and Cartier Islands
Ashmore Island (1.89sq.km/-0.7sq.miles) and Cartier Island: two small islands in the western Timor Sea 200km/125 miles south of the Indonesian island of Timor and 400km/250 miles north-west of Cape Londonderry (WA); part of Northern Territory.

Coral Sea Islands Territory
Coral Sea Islands: several small uninhabited archipelagos – Willis Group (Willis Island, with weather station; South Island, Raine Island), Chilcott Island, Diamond Islets, Tregosse Islets – in the Coral Sea, north-east of the Great Barrier Reef; administered by Norfolk Island (see below); no access.

Territory of Norfolk Island
Norfolk Island (36.3sq.km/-14sq.miles; pop. 2300; chief place Kingston): in the south-western Pacific 800km/500 miles north-west of North Cape on New Zealand's North Island and 1650km/1025 miles north-east of Sydney (NSW); convict settlement from 1788; Australian territory since 1983; now inhabited by descendants of the "Bounty" mutineers (1789; "Islanders") and immigrants from Australia ("Mainlanders"); developing tourist trade; income from duty-free status and sale of stamps; Bounty Day celebrated on June 8th.

Lord Howe Island and Ball's Pyramid
Lord Howe Island and Ball's Pyramid: two small Pacific islands (together 13sq.km/5sq.miles) discovered in 1788; 700km/435 miles north-east of Sydney; belong to New South Wales.

Macquarie Island
Macquarie Island: an Antarctic island (176sq.km/68sq.miles) 1480km/920 miles south of Tasmania and administered from there; Australian Antarctic research station.

Heard and MacDonald Islands
Heard and MacDonald Islands: two uninhabited islands (together 417sq.km/161sq.miles) in the Antarctic south-west of the Indian Ocean.

Antarctica
Since 1938 Australia has claimed 4.5 million sq.km (1.7 million sq.miles) of Antarctic territory, explored by several expeditions since 1911; scientific observation stations at Mawson, Casey, Wilkes and Davis.

Papua-New Guinea (since 1975 a sovereign state
After a complicated pattern of occupation by Britain and Germany the British part of eastern New Guinea was assigned in 1906 to the Commonwealth of Australia as the Territory of Papua.

After the surrender of German colonial forces to Australian troops at the beginning of the First World War the League of Nations put "German New Guinea" (which had been directly administered by Germany since 1899) under Australian mandate in 1921.

After the Second World War (during which part of the Territory of Papua and the mandated territory were occupied by the Japanese from 1942 to 1944) the League of Nations mandate passed to the United Nations. In 1949 the UN mandated territory and the Australian colony were joined in the Territory of Papua and New Guinea under Australian sovereignty. This territory developed from 1951 (first legislative assembly) in stages into an independent state. In December 1973 it was granted self-government (except for foreign policy and defence, which remained the responsibility of Australia); and finally on September 16th 1975 the new state of Papua New Guinea became fully independent.

Formally the head of this parliamentary and democratic monarchy is the Queen, who is represented by a governor. The government of the state is on British lines, and since 1977 the 19 provincial government authorities have had certain rights of self-government.

Constitutional changes by referendum

Changes in the Australian constitution must be approved by a national referendum. Approval requires a majority of electors in a majority of states, and the proposal must also be approved by both houses of parliament or by one of the houses twice within three months.

States and territories

The six states have their own parliaments (all consisting of two chambers except in Queensland) and their own governments, the nominal head of which is a governor representing the Crown. In 1978 the Northern Territory was granted extensive powers of self-government. The Australian Capital Territory is still directly administered by the Commonwealth government.

Local government

In the three-tier structure of Australian government the third level is that of local government, with city councils and shire councils, numbering 883 in all (including ten Aboriginal councils in the Northern Territory and Queensland).

Executive

Executive power is nominally in the hands of the governor-general assisted by the executive council. In practice the prime minister and his cabinet, though formally appointed by the governor-general, are selected from the party or coalition which has a majority in parliament. The states are responsible for executing laws passed by the federal parliament; in case of conflict federal law takes precedence over state law.

Judicature

The supreme court of the Commonwealth is the High Court of Australia, which is both a court of appeal and a constitutional court. Australian law is based on the common law of England supplemented by statute law.

Ombudsmen

There are ombudsmen on the Scandinavian model at both federal and state level. Standing above party, they investigate complaints by citizens and associations against the government, ministries, government agencies and the police.

Parties

The oldest Australian party is the Australian Labor Party (ALP), which grew out of the Labour Electoral League (founded in Sydney in 1891).

The Liberal Party of Australia (LP) was founded in 1944 on the initiative of Sir Robert Menzies as a reaction to the disunity of the 18 different anti-Labor organisations. Menzies was prime minister from 1949 to 1966.

The National Party (NP) was founded in 1920 as the Australian Country Party, which had its roots in the associations of farmers established after the economic depression of the late 19th century. In 1975 the Australian Country Party changed its name to the National Country Party of Australia, and finally in 1982 it became the National Party. It has usually partnered the Liberal Party in a coalition.

The Australian Democrats (AD) split off from the Liberal Party in 1977. Their few seats in the Senate have frequently enabled them to hold the balance of power.

During the 1980s a number of new political parties were formed, mostly concerned with environmental problems and the plight of the Aborigines. The best known is the Nuclear Disarmament Party (NDP), a leading part in which is played by the rock star Peter Garnett. The "green" parties managed to send representatives to Parliament from Tasmania.

Trade unions

Australia has some 300 trade unions on the British model, grouped in four umbrella organisations, the largest of which is the Australian Council of Trade Unions (ACTU), bringing together around 150 trade unions with a total of 2.6 million members. Strikes are frequent and often unpredictable. They can paralyse whole branches of the economy (e.g. the 1989 strike by pilots of Australian domestic airlines).

Baedeker Special

School of the Air

Patrick, youngest of the four sons of a sheep-farmer in the Australian outback, is nine and has been going to school for almost three years. But his teacher sees him only at very irregular intervals, for she is exactly 485 kilometres (300 miles) away in a modest building in Head Street, Alice Springs. And yet pupil and teacher know each other very well; Patrick is familiar with the voice of his teacher, which he hears for an hour and a half every weekday from the crackling loudspeaker of his little radio.

So when Patrick goes to school he sits down at the table in the kitchen-livingroom of his parents' farm, takes out his schoolbooks and notebooks and switches on the radio. "Good morning!" comes the familiar voice from the ether, and teacher and pupil get down at once to business. "Take your English book and open it at page 36!" Patrick takes up his book, opens it at the right page, and the lesson begins.

This method of teaching is unique in the world: a demonstration of the inventiveness of the Australians in coping with the problems of life in the outback.

The first school of the air was established in 1951 to give children living far away from any school at least a rudimentary education. There are now 26 of these schools scattered over the whole of the continent and providing education for some 2000 children between the ages of six and eleven. The teachers are specially trained in the technique of teaching in front of a microphone rather than a class. Since there is no blackboard on which they can illustrate some particularly difficult point they must know how to adapt their teaching to a different medium as imaginatively as possible.

There is no other way to provide education in the remote outback, for the journey to and from the nearest school would take Patrick almost the whole day. Once a week Patrick's father drives almost 100 kilometres (62 miles) to the nearest little town to take in the week's food supply and pick up Patrick's school work at the post office. The packet includes a video cassette and Patrick's last composition. At the foot of the little story Kathleen, his teacher in Alice Springs, has written "Well done!", and Patrick is naturally proud of this praise from the distant town which he knows only from his parents' accounts.

When Patrick wants to ask his teacher a question he presses the "Speak" key on the microphone. Discipline in the use of the radio is important, for Patrick is only one out of eleven pupils scattered over an area of almost 1500 sq. kilometres (580 sq. miles). Sometimes the teacher is besieged by several pupils all trying to speak at once and she has to admonish them, "One after the other, please!" But that is seldom necessary, for the pupils realise that teaching can only be done properly if they take it in turn to speak; and of course each of them can learn from the other children's questions.

Once a year the children meet for a few days of intensive teaching in a school camp. This also gives them personal contact with the teachers and fellow-pupils whom during the rest of the year they only hear on the radio.

It is evident to both parents and teachers that however good the teaching the School of the Air can give only a basic education. Older children have to go to a boarding school or stay with friends or relatives in the nearest town.

At the end of the teaching period Kathleen says goodbye to her pupils and switches off the radio. But her day's work is by no means done. Piled up on her desk is their written work, brought by the postman that morning, waiting to be corrected . . .

Education and Science

Schools
School of the Air

An Australian institution which has been much admired is the School of the Air, which provides education by radio for children on remote farms and in tiny settlements in the empty interior of Australia. Based, like the famous Flying Doctor Service (see Baedeker Special, p. 275), on the use of two-way radio, it was founded in Alice Springs in 1951. There are now thirteen School of the Air bases in the Northern Territory, six in Queensland, five in Western Australia and one each in New South Wales and South Australia, serving a total area of around 2.5 million sq.km (970,000 sq.miles). Most of them can be visited on school days.

Compulsory school attendance

School attendance has been compulsory for all children since 1869. It applies to children between the ages of 6 and 15 (in Tasmania 16). Under the constitution education is a responsibility of the states and territories, though the financing of the school system has increasingly been taken over by the federal government. Most schools are state-run and provide education free (about 7500), but there are also some 2500 private schools charging fees, mostly run by the churches (mainly Roman Catholic). The first school in Australia was the Catholic Marist High School in Parramatta, founded in 1821.

Integration of Aborigines

The National Aboriginal and Torres Strait Islander Education Policy (AEP), introduced in 1988, is designed to foster the education of Aboriginal children, previously disadvantaged. They now attend the ordinary primary and secondary schools, and there are also special school programmes laying emphasis on the cultural heritage of the Aborigines.

The wearing of school uniform is fairly general, and groups of children in uniform on a school trip are a common feature of the street scene.

Primary education – often preceded by a period of pre-school education – lasts six or seven years, secondary education from the seventh or eighth to the twelfth year of schooling. In addition to schools providing general education there are vocational schools. The school certificate obtained at the end of the secondary course is a prerequisite for admission to higher education.

Special schools

There are also special schools for ill and handicapped children, as well as radio educational programmes and lectures broadcast on the national radio system.

Teacher training

Teachers in nursery and primary schools take a three-year training course at a college of advanced education. Teachers at secondary schools usually have an academic qualification followed by a teacher training course which includes practical experiemce.

Adult education

There are further education courses for adults in evening schools, technical colleges and some universities.

Multi-cultural education

The number of non-English-speaking immigrants has increased considerably, particularly since the Second World War. The Australian educational system seeks to support the different ethnic groups in preserving their own language and culture; but at the same time immigrants are encouraged to develop their command of English in order to improve their prospects of training and employment and to promote their social integration.

Higher education

The first Australian university was established in Sydney in 1850. Higher education is now provided by numbers of universities and colleges. There are two types of college, either private or state-run – colleges of advanced education (CAE) and colleges of technical and further education (TAFE). In 1989 there were 68 higher educational establishments, but under a policy of amalgamation the number is due to be reduced to 35 or 30. The first private university in Australia, Bond University in Gold Coast (QLD), was opened in 1989; 30% of the students are from other countries. Since 1989 students have had to make a substantial contribution to the cost of their studies; and the fees, particularly for foreign students without bursaries, are high. The total number of students is around 500,000, over half of them women.

Science and research

Higher education leading to academic degrees is offered by the universities and by colleges of advanced education (CAE), more strongly oriented towards vocational and practical training, which were formally granted equal status with universities in 1989. Vocational training is provided by a number of private colleges and by over 200 colleges of technical and further education (TAFE) run by individual states, which grant industrial, commercial, technical and artistic qualifications.

Research

In addition to university institutes there are special state-run research institutes and private research establishments run by industrial firms. The states support mainly research and development in agriculture and mining. The most important research organisation on the federal level is the Commonwealth Scientific and Industrial Research Organisation (CSIRO), founded in 1949, with around 100 laboratories and a staff of 7000.

Research and observation stations

Given Australia's geographical situation, institutes for space monitoring, weather observation and research in the fields of astronomy and astrophysics play a major role. The data reception station in Alice Springs (NT) records signals from international satellites carrying out terrestrial and marine reconnaissance which are processed and interpreted in Canberra (ACT). Tracking stations at Tidbinbilla (ACT) and Yarragadee (WA) run by the Australian Department of Science in association with the US National Aeronautics and Space Administration (NASA) monitor the orbits of satellites in space and play an important part in communications with space shuttles and satellites. In Melbourne is one of the three international weather stations (the others being in Washington DC and Moscow), and there is a regional weather station in Darwin (NT). Also of great importance in astronomical, astrophysical and radiophysical research are powerful telescopes at Siding Springs Mountain (NSW), Parkes (NSW), Culgoora (NSW) and Mount Stromlo (ACT). The Australian Nuclear Science and Technology Organisation (ANSTO) is based at Lucas Heights, 30km/19 miles south-west of Sydney, with the only two nuclear reactors in Australia (which is a producer of uranium), used exclusively for research. A research station in Alice Springs (NT), run jointly by Australia and the United States, helps to monitor the international agreement on the cessation of atomic tests.

Antarctic research

Australia has a number of observation stations in Antarctica and, in association with other countries, organises expeditions and research in accordance with the Antarctic Treaty of 1959.

Economy

Concentration of industry in cities

From the beginning of the colonial era industry was concentrated in the principal towns, where there were facilities for the industrial processing of both imported raw materials and materials for export. The concentration of industrial employment in the conurbations reached its peak in 1971–72, when 87.7% of all industrial jobs in Western Australia were in Perth, 85.4% of jobs in Victoria were in Melbourne, 82.9% of jobs in South Australia were in Adelaide and 76.4% of jobs in New South Wales were in Sydney (excluding the industrial towns of Newcastle and Wollongong). The main contributors to this development were European immigrants, who had a disproportionate share of employment in craft production and industry. The expansion of heavy industry during the Second World War and its development after the war brought the proportion of the working population employed in the industrial sector to around 29% in 1960.

Boom in raw materials

In the 1970s investment moved to the mining sector. Only large multinational concerns could bear the risks of development in remote and climatically unfavourable areas and of heavy dependence on prices in world markets. There was now a boom in raw materials, and by 1980 Australia was the world leader in the export of iron ore, lead and bauxite, taking second place in the export of coal and wolfram and third place in zinc. Australia is also the world's fourth largest producer of gold.

Job cuts

Some branches of industry, e.g. textiles and shoe manufacture, could be preserved only by high protective tariffs. Jobs in craft production and industry were cut, reducing their share of the total working population to 21% in 1980. Mining, too, failed to provide enough new jobs, since the use of high technology in both the working and the export of minerals reduced the amount of manpower required. In order to compete in world markets firms were forced to amalgamate, and expensive human labour was replaced by machinery. The proportion of the working population employed in agriculture fell from 13% in 1960 to 6% in 1980, but in spite of this Australia in 1980 was the world's largest exporter of beef and wool and took second place in the export of mutton and lamb and third place in the export of wheat and sugar.

Exports

Australia's principal export is coal, which accounts for 12% of total exports; most of it comes from the large new opencast workings in central Queensland. The mining areas in New South Wales (Hunter Valley) supply coal for iron-smelting and energy production in Australia and also contribute to exports. The second largest export is gold (7% of total exports), followed by wool (6%), iron ore from the large mining areas in the Pilbara region (5%) and aluminium oxide (4%).

Imports

A dominant position among Australian imports is occupied by machinery and plant, which account for 33% of total imports. After this come transport equipment (16%), chemicals and oil derivates (12%), unfinished metal products (steel, etc.; 5%) and paper and associated materials (5%).

Balance of trade

Prices of Australian exports in world markets come repeatedly under pressure and show a long-term falling trend. Part of the trouble, in the case of agricultural produce, results from subsidies for producers in the European Union and the United States. The situation is very different with imports, the prices of which show a long-term rising trend. As a result the terms of trade for Australia are unfavourable. In order to maintain a reasonable balance of trade it is necessary to export ever greater quantities of mining and agricultural products.

Trading partners

Australia's most important trading partners are Japan, which accounts for 27% of the total volume of foreign trade, followed by the United States (10%), South Korea (6%), Singapore (6%), New Zealand (5%) and Germany (2%).

Growth of services sector

The only part of the economy to show a rising trend is the services sector. The proportion of the working population employed in this sector rose from 58% in 1960 to 73% in 1980 and is now over 75%.

Domestic tourism

The coastal regions have an excellent infrastructure for recreational activities and the holiday trade, and as a result the existing tourist and holiday resorts are growing in size and new ones are being established. These facilities for leisure and recreation have given a boost to domestic tourism.

International tourism

The overloading of tourist and holiday facilities is minimised by the fact that Australians and foreign visitors tend to go on holiday at different times. The main Australian holiday seasons are October, April and above all January, during the Australian summer. Foreign visitors (except in December) show a different trend.

Objectives of the tourist industry

The government seeks to promote investment in the tourist industry by offering tax incentives. In current development programmes great importance is attached to international tourism, both as an earner of foreign currency and a creator of employment. Official projections set the target for the year 2000 (Olympic year) at 6.5 million (compared with 1 million in 1984 and 3.5 million in 1994–95. In order to achieve this target new ideas are to be developed and new tourist attractions offered. Particular attention is to be given to "eco-tourism", for which Australia is well equipped, with its numerous National Parks, some of them of enormous size, and its other nature reserves. It is also planned to involve the Aborigines more closely in the development of the tourist trade. Experience in the Northern Territory has shown that guided tours of Aboriginal territory by the Aborigines themselves are a good introduction to their mental world and way of life.
Until now Australia has attracted visitors mainly from Japan, New Zealand, Great Britain, the USA and Germany. In the future, however, it is seen as a key tourist market for those from places such as China, Vietnam, South Africa, the Near East and countries of Central and South America.

Transport

Roads

Australia's first road was built in 1789–91 between Sydney and the settlement of Parramatta, 22km/13½ miles inland. Under Governor Macquarie, from 1810 onwards, new roads were built and existing ones improved to a total of more than 400km/250 miles, including a road through the Blue Mountains to Bathurst which was of great importance for the development of the young colony. In 1835 the construction of a road between Sydney and Melbourne was begun. At this period the roads were no more than rough tracks on which travel was uncomfortable and difficult. With the discovery of gold new roads became necessary and could be afforded. And finally the coming of the motor car brought new dimensions to road construction. During the Second World War almost 6000km/3730 miles of new roads were built and 8000km/5000 miles of existing roads upgraded to facilitate the movement of troops and supplies, among them the legendary Stuart Highway between Adelaide and Darwin. By the end of the 1980s Australia had a network of over 800,000km/500,000 miles of roads, of which around a third were surfaced (asphalt or concrete). Since 1995, national road charges have been introduced to many states, once fully implemented, this system will allow vehicles to travel interstate at less expense and without permits.

Buses

Buses play an important part in both long-distance and local traffic all over Australia, often in co-operation with the state railways. Regular overland buses link the cities and the states. For long-distance journeys Interstate and Intercity buses are the cheapest form of transport. On bus services in Australia see Practical Information, Buses.

Road trains

The "road trains" – heavy articulated trucks with two, and sometimes three or more, trailers – which operate in the outback are mainly used in the transport of cattle: the modern "beef roads" have taken the place of the old cattle tracks to the railway loading points. The road trains now carry over four times as much freight as the railways.

Railways

The first steam train in Australia ran in 1854 between Melbourne and its port, and this was soon followed by the construction of numerous railway lines in the eastern colonies by private companies. By 1901, when the Commonwealth of Australia came into being, all the states except Tasmania and Western Australia were linked by rail. Great problems were caused by the use of three different gauges, and it was only around 1930 that it became possible to travel from Sydney to Perth without changing trains. Except on one or two lines on which steam trains still operate as a tourist attraction all locomotives are electric or diesel. The national railway network has a total length of just under 40,000km/25,000 miles (for map of services, see Practical Information, Railways). There are some 5500km/3400 miles of private railways – iron ore trains, particularly in the Pilbara region (WA) and sugar-cane and coal trains in Queensland. As a means of conveying passengers and freight the railways have long been outstripped by road transport, but it is planned to increase their competitiveness by the development of high-speed trains (VFT, very fast trains) travelling at speeds of up to 350km/220 miles an hour.

Trams

Trams as a form of urban transport have survived only in Melbourne and Adelaide (to Glenelg). There are plans to bring a section of the old tramway system in Sydney back into operation as a tourist attraction.

Monorail

In Sydney a monorail system has operated since 1988 between the business centre and Darling Harbour.

Air services

The first solo flights to Australia from Britain (Bert Hinkler) and America (Charles Kingsford Smith) in 1928 were hailed worldwide as a major advance. The Australian national airline QANTAS is the world's second oldest airline, having been established in 1920 as the Queensland and Northern Territory Aerial Services Ltd (from whose initials it took its name); at first confined to domestic routes, it began flying international services in 1934.

Australia has one of the densest networks of air services in the world, with more than 400 airports and airfields either publicly or privately run. Most of the domestic services are flown by the Ansett group, followed in second place by Qantas. For maps showing the routes flown by both airlines, see Practical Information, Air Services.

For covering long distances in Australia the domestic air services are an excellent and time-saving alternative to the long and time-consuming journeys by bus or rail. Since 1980 domestic air services have been deregulated, leaving airlines free to compete with one another in fares and services offered.

Shipping

As early as 1789 the "Rose Hill Packet", the first ship built in Australia, was transporting passengers and freight on the Parramatta River, whose estuary forms Sydney's harbour (Port Jackson). After the dissolution of the East India Company in 1813 sea-going ships were also built in Australia.

River shipping

In the past shipping on the Murray, Darling and Murrumbidgee was an important form of transport. Later, when road and rail transport had superseded the old paddle-steamers, some of the old boats, like the "Murray Queen", took on a new lease of life in providing pleasure trips and cruises.

Ferries

Ferries also played an important part, as they still do, in cities with a complex pattern of coastal waters. The sailing ferries gave place to steamboats, and these in turn were succeeded by motor ships. For travellers to Tasmania the car ferry "Spirit of Tasmania" (Melbourne to Davenport) offers an alternative to flying, though heavy seas frequently make the ferries a less attractive proposition.

Seaports

Before aircraft displaced ships as the regular form of passenger transport the ports of the principal cities were the usual gateway of Australia for new immigrants. Nowadays the passenger terminals have been decommissioned and only a few cruise liners make the long passage to Australia.

Transport

The most important ports for coastal shipping, container ships and freighters carrying ore and coal are Sydney and Newcastle in New South Wales, Melbourne and Geelong in Victoria, Brisbane in Queensland, Hyalla in South Australia and Fremantle and Port Hedland in Western Australia.

History

Prehistory

Australia has been called a window through which we can glimpse the remote history of the earth; for over large areas of the continent, particularly on the western Australian plateau, very ancient rocks lie directly on the surface without any overlay of later sediments. In the light of the theory of plate tectonics and the comparative study of flora and fauna the old widely held theory that the Australian continent split off from the mainland of Asia at a very remote period can no longer be maintained. It is now generally believed that until the Mesozoic era Australia was part of the great southern continent of Gondwana, which itself stemmed from the primeval continent known as Pangaea. Perhaps 100 million years ago Gondwanaland broke up and Africa, India and New Zealand became detached from it. At this period Australia was still attached to South America and Antarctica, breaking free only some 50 or 60 million years ago. It then drifted north until it crashed into the Eurasian and Pacific plates of the earth's crust, leading to mountain folding movements and volcanic activity. And finally the rise in sea level at the end of the last Ice Age, some 10,000 years ago, cut off New Guinea, Tasmania and other islands (e.g. Kangaroo Island) from the mainland of Australia.

The earliest inhabitants of Australia are believed to have moved in from southern Asia, at least 40,000 years ago and possibly much earlier, either over land bridges which then still existed or by sea. The first inhabitants are now known as Aboriginals: the older names of "Australian negroes" or "black Australians" were incorrect, since they were not of African but of Asian origin. At the time they moved into Australia the climate was wetter and the whole continent was suitable for human occupation. As the climate grew increasingly arid the Aborigines adapted to their barren environment. When white settlement began at the end of the 18th century Australia had an estimated population of some 300,000 people, who ranged over their tribal territories in small groups, living as hunters and gatherers.

Discovery of Australia

Map, pp. 48–49

Medieval ideas

Long before the discovery of Australia medieval European scholars believed in the existence of a southern continent. The ancient Greeks had held that there must be a southern half of the earth as a counterpart to the northern half which they knew; and around A.D. 150 Ptolemy had developed this theory of symmetry and postulated the existence of an unknown southern world (*terra australis incognita*) separated from the known world by a girdle of fire and a sea full of dangers. Thereafter this mysterious "Southland" was frequently mentioned and represented in imaginative drawings.

It is possible that Chinese seafarers, who from the 9th century A.D. onwards were sailing to the east coast of Africa and parts of Indonesia, may also have reached the northern coasts of Australia. From the 11th century fishermen from Macassar on Celebes (Sulawesi) regularly visited the north coast of Australia in quest of the trepang or sea slug (bêche-de-mer), regarded as a great delicacy. When Marco Polo sailed back from China to Venice in 1292 he did not pass through Australian

Exploration of Australia 1770–1876

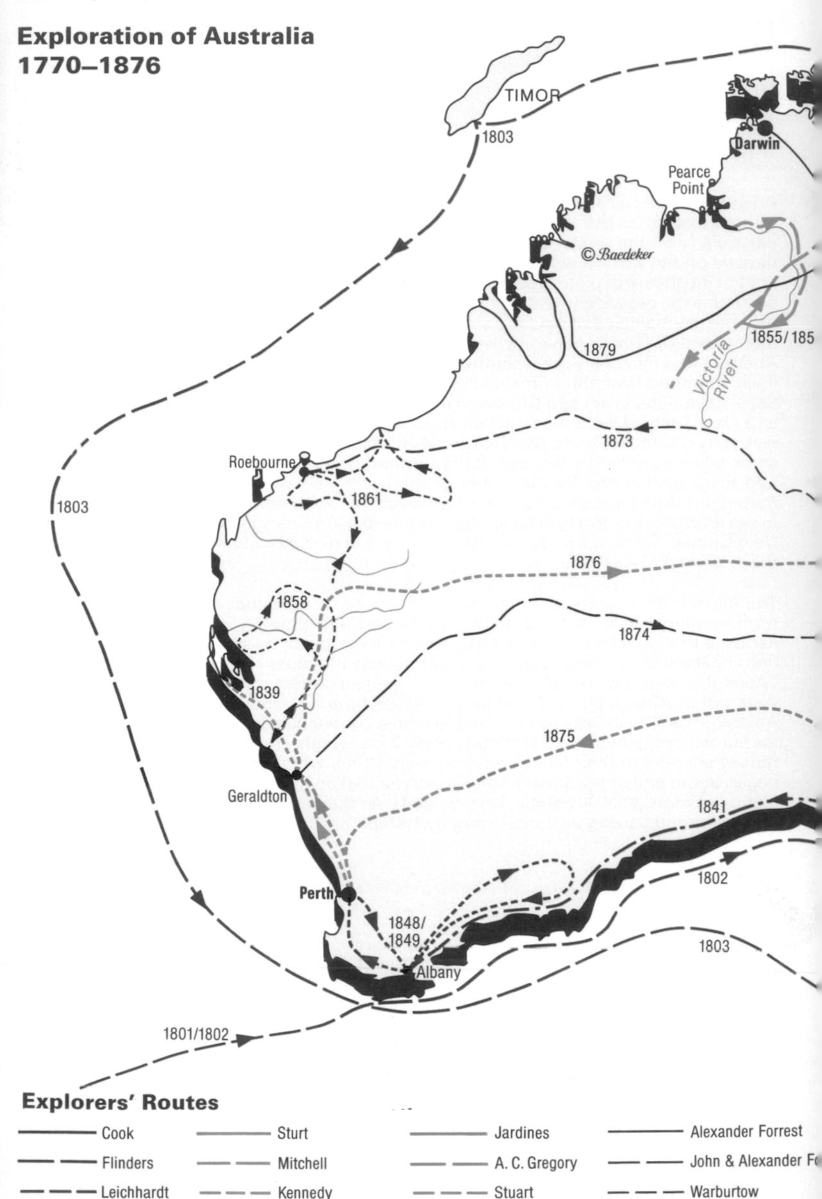

Explorers' Routes

Cook	Sturt	Jardines	Alexander Forrest
Flinders	Mitchell	A. C. Gregory	John & Alexander Fo
Leichhardt	Kennedy	Stuart	Warburtow
Eyre	Bass & Flinders	McKinlay	Burke & Wills
Rower	Grey	Giles	T. F. Gregory

Exploration of Australia 1770–1876

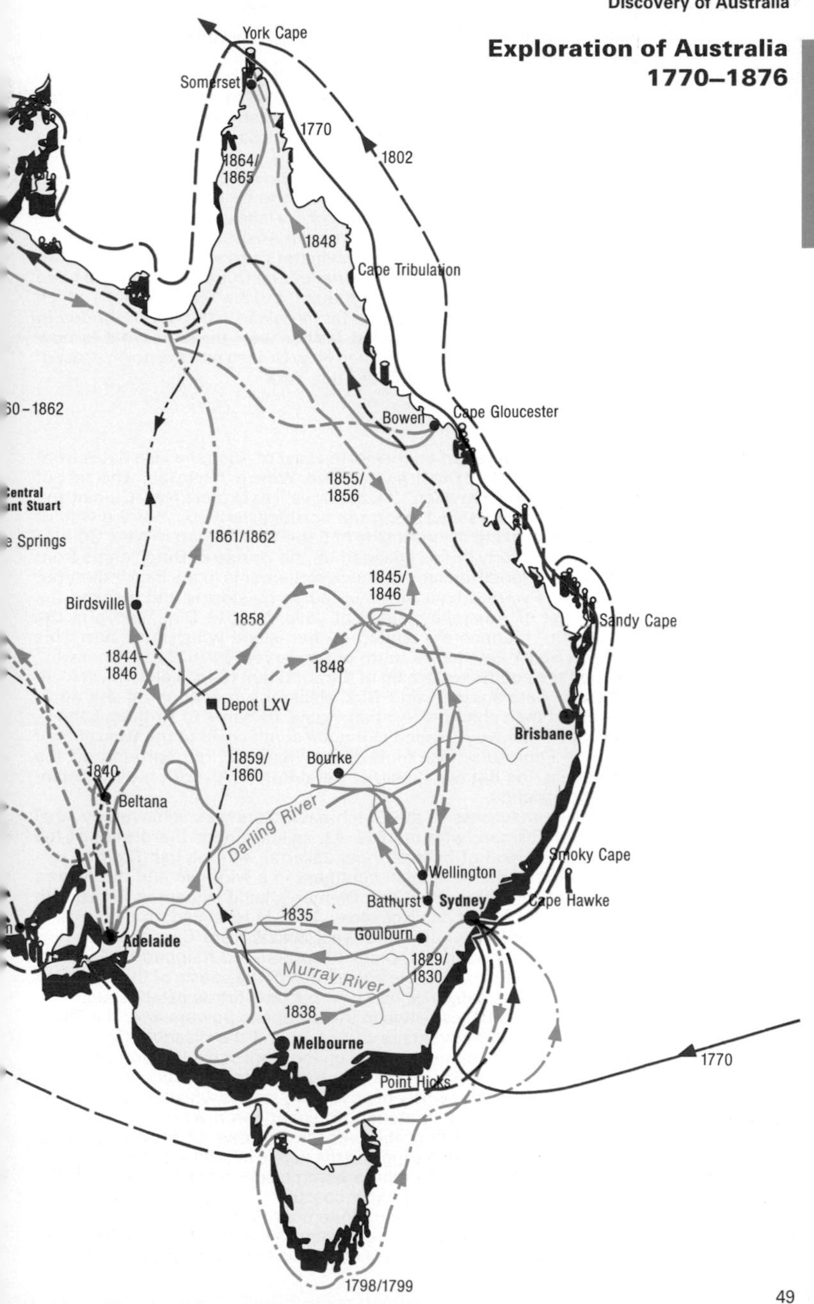

waters, but in his account of his travels he referred to a land south of Java which was rich in gold and shells.

A Portuguese landing?

From the 15th century, when Spain and Portugal were vying for predominance at sea, the unknown "Southland" moved nearer. It seems likely that the Portuguese landed on the Australian coast, for in 1516 they established a settlement on Timor, less than 500km/310 miles from Australia.

A French map of Australia?

There is still controversy over the "Dieppe Maps", drawn between 1536 and 1550 for the Dauphin and said to be based on Portuguese sources, which show to the south of Java a land called Java la Grande – perhaps, or perhaps not, the first map of Australia.

Spanish navigators

In the early 17th century Spanish navigators also sailed close to Australia. An expedition led by Pedro Fernandez de Quiros set out from Lima (Peru) to explore the southern continent; but the Terra Australis which they claimed to have found was in fact an island in the New Hebrides. In 1606 Luis Vaez de Torres sailed farther west through what is now known as the Torres Strait between New Guinea and the north coast of Australia, almost within sight of Cape York.

Dutch discovery of Australia

The first reliable report on the north coast of Australia also dates from 1606. We owe it to a Dutch sea-captain, Willem Janszoon, who set out from Java in the "Duyfken" ("Little Dove") to explore New Guinea and other islands and sailed along the north-eastern coast of the Gulf of Carpentaria, taking the west side of Cape York for part of New Guinea. The north-easterly winds speeded up the course of Dutch ships from the Cape of Good Hope to the Dutch settlements in the East Indies, but some ships were driven off their course by storms and reached the west coast of Australia instead of Java. In 1616 Dirk Hartog in the "Endracht" ("Concord") landed on the island which now bears his name in Shark Bay, to the south of Carnarvon. In 1622 the "Leeuwin" reached the south-western tip of the continent (Cape Leeuwin, WA). In 1623 Jan Carstenszoon and Dirk Meliszoon reconnoitred the north coast, and their ship the "Arnhem" gave its name to Arnhem Land.

In 1627 Peter Nuyts sailed along the south coast to the west side of the Eyre Peninsula (SA). In 1629 the "Batavia" ran aground off the west coast, the Batavia Coast, at Geraldton (WA), with the Houtman-Abrolhos Islands.

Abel Tasman

The greatest success of the Dutch navigators was achieved by Abel Janszoon Tasman, who in 1642–43, sailing under the orders of the governor-general of Batavia (now Jakarta), Antonij van Diemen, circumnavigated the Australian continent in a wide arc and discovered Tasmania, which he called Van Diemen's Land (renamed in the 19th century in honour of its discoverer). In 1644 he sailed on a voyage of discovery along the north and west coasts from Cape York to Port Hedland. These reconnaissances, recorded and mapped by Tasman, gave Dutch seamen accurate knowledge of the coasts of this southern continent whose existence had now become firmly established.

William Dampier

Changed relationships between the European powers after the Thirty Years' War, to the advantage of Britain and the disadvantage of the Dutch, led British seamen to carry on the work of exploration begun by the Dutch. The first British seafarer to come to Australia was William Dampier, a pirate and writer of adventure stories who sailed round the world in quest of new material. He spent some weeks studying the north-west coast (north of the present-day town of Broome on King Sound), finding the landscape and the native inhabitants equally repellent. In 1699 he returned with a commission from the Admiralty to explore the north and north-west coasts.

Willem de Vlamingh

In 1696–97 another Dutchman, Willem de Vlamingh, explored south-western Australia. He discovered Rottnest Island, off Perth, and named it after the quokkas (a species of marsupial) which he took for rats, and the Swan River, which he named after the numerous black swans he saw there. From Mandurah he followed the coast north to the West Cape.

By the end of the 17th century European seamen had established the course of the north and west coasts, the south coast as far as the middle of the Great Australian Bight and the south coast of Tasmania, which until the early 19th century was believed to be part of the Australian mainland.

Captain Cook

In the second half of the 18th century French ships appeared in the South Pacific. Louis-Antoine de Bougainville set out on a circumnavigation of the globe which took him, in his passage from Tahiti and Samoa, close to the Queensland coast. The obstacle presented by the Great Barrier Reef led him to change his course. Then some years later Captain James Cook was sent by the Royal Navy to Tahiti to observe the transit of Venus on June 3rd 1769, which would make it possible to establish the exact distance between the earth and the sun. He set sail from Plymouth in the "Endeavour" on August 26th 1768, accompanied by Charles Green, an astronomer, Sir Joseph Banks, a botanist, and a Swedish botanist, David Solander, and the transit of Venus was duly observed.

The second part of Cook's expedition was devoted to a secret reconnaissance of the southern continent with a view to taking possession of it. For this purpose the "Endeavour" was to sail south as far as the 40th degree of latitude. In the course of this voyage Cook discovered the Society Islands, naming them after the Royal Society. He then continued to New Zealand (which had been discovered by Tasman in 1642) and established that it consisted of two islands. Then, driven by storms, he sailed west.

On Friday April 19th 1770, at 6 o'clock in the morning, Lieutenant Hicks sighted an unknown land (Point Hicks, VIC). Cook believed that it was Van Diemen's Land and set his course northward along the east coast of Australia. On April 28th he tried to land at the site of what is now Port Kembla, but the surf was too strong. On the following day he anchored in the sheltered bay which was named Botany Bay by Banks because of its abundant vegetation. Each day he hoisted the British flag, tried to establish contact with the natives and assisted the scientists in the collection of plants and seeds. Then on May 6th the "Endeavour" weighed anchor and continued north, passing Port Jackson Bay, later to become Sydney's harbour. Cook gave names to many of the natural features, particularly inlets, islands and hills, which he saw from the ship, and they are still known by these names.

The northward voyage continued without incident until on the moonlit night of June 11th 1770, at high water, the "Endeavour" struck a hidden reef off the coast of the Cape York peninsula, to the north of Cairns, and ran aground. To release the ship Cook jettisoned much of its ballast, and after temporary measures to stem the leak in Weary Bay the "Endeavour" was beached for repair at Cooktown.

The expedition was unable to continue until the beginning of August 1770. On the 17th of the month the "Endeavour" nearly came to grief again while passing through the Great Barrier Reef, which Cook did not recognise for what it was; but, with Hicks going ahead of the ship in a boat to find a safe channel, the "Endeavour" was able to thread its way through these uncharted waters.

On August 21st Cook reached the tip of Cape York and, landing on Possession Island, took possession of the whole of the east of the new land in the name of King George III, naming it New South Wales.

After Cook's return to Britain in 1771 the Admiralty took great care to keep his discoveries secret. A complete report was not published until 1893 (though an unauthorised version soon appeared), and Cook's secret orders to take possession of the new land were not made public until 1923.

Cook did not discover Australia, for the existence of this *terra australis* had long been known. His merit was to explore the east coast of the continent with its advantages for human settlement – its sheltered inlets, natural harbours and promising vegetation. He laid the foundations which eighteen years later enabled Captain (later Governor) Arthur Phillip, in command of the "First Fleet", with 778 convicts and some 500 seamen and guards on board, to establish a penal colony at Port Jackson. The First Fleet reached Botany Bay on a long voyage from London via Teneriffe, Rio de Janeiro and Cape Town.

Cook undertook two further voyages, in 1772–75 and 1776–79, looking for a northern passage between the Atlantic and the Pacific. On his third voyage he discovered the Hawaiian Islands, where he was killed on February 14th 1779 in a fight with the natives. He himself was thus not available to advise the commander of the First Fleet, but Joseph Banks, his companion on his first voyage, was a powerful advocate for the colonisation of Australia.

In 1798–99 Matthew Flinders and George Bass sailed round Tasmania, demonstrating that it was an island and not part of mainland Australia. Then between December 1801 and May 1802 they sailed along the whole of the south coast of Australia, from Cape Leeuwin to Sydney; and finally concluded their voyage in June 1803 by sailing round the whole continent and returning to Sydney.

Exploration of the Interior

Map, pp. 48–49

After the survey of the Australian coastline was complete a succession of daring explorers began to advamce step by step into the interior. It was not merely scientific interest that drove scientists and adventurers to risk – and sometimes to lose – their lives in these expeditions. The expectation of profit and the acquisition of land provided a powerful motive: those who financed the expeditions were hoping to gain access to great areas of grazing land and rich mineral resources. The young penal colony at Sydney had an ideal natural harbour in Port Jackson, but the surrounding country was unproductive and the settlement had to live through years when food was scarce.

Exploration round Sydney

Soon after landing Governor Phillip ordered a series of expeditions into the immediate surroundings of Sydney. As early as May 1788 Broken Bay and Pittwater, north of the town, had been explored, and further journeys reached the foot of the Blue Mountains and the Hawkesbury River; it was not realised until 1791 that the Hawkesbury and the Nepean River belonged to the same river system.

Expeditions to west, north and south

After 1813, when Gregory Blaxland, William Wentworth and Willian Lawson found a route through the barrier of the Blue Mountains, the colony, hitherto confined to its narrow stretch of territory, was able to expand westward, and Bathurst became the first settlement in the interior. This westward extension of the colony provided a base for the exploration of south-eastern Australia by John Oxley, Allan Cunningham, Hamilton Hume and William Hovell, Angus McMillan and Paul Strzelecki. From Bathurst Oxley explored the Lachlan River in 1817, and in the following year followed the Macquarie River in an attempt to find a large lake which was believed to lie in the interior. He then crossed the Liverpool Plains and at Port Macquarie, at the mouth of the Hastings River, returned to the coast, which he followed south to Port Stephens. On a third expedition in 1823 he sailed north from Sydney to Moreton Bay (Brisbane) and Port Curtis (Gladstone). Cunningham travelled north from Bathurst to the Liverpool Plains (1823) and from the Hunter River to Brisbane (1827–28). This inland route gave access to the good grazing land on the New England plateau and the fertile soils of the Darling Downs. In 1824 Hume and Hovell travelled through south-eastern Australia, roughly on the line of the present-day Hume

Highway, to Corio Bay (south-west of Melbourne), but miscalculated their position and thought they had reached Western Port (south-east of Melbourne). They opened up the interior of Victoria and explored the rivers flowing down from the Snowy Mountains. Many settlers followed in the explorers' footsteps.

Thomas Mitchell

In 1831–32 Thomas Livingston Mitchell, who had been appointed surveyor-general of New South Wales in 1828, explored the north-west of the colony in an attempt to find a legendary river north of the Gwydir which was believed to flow into the Gulf of Carpentaria. In 1835 he followed the course of the Darling River to Menindee, and in 1836, starting out from Orange, he explored the Lachlan River, the Murrumbidgee and the Murray as far as its junction with the Darling at Mildura. To the south and south-west he found the rich grazing lands of Victoria's Western District, which he celebrated as "Australia Felix".

McMillan and Strzelecki

The exploration of the "Australian Alps" (the Snowy Mountains) was the work of McMillan and Strzelecki. In 1839–41, starting from Currawong Station, McMillan explored the south-eastern Snowy Mountains as far as South Gippsland. In 1840 Count Paul Edmund de Strzelecki set out from Goulburn, climbed the highest peak in the range, naming it Mount Kościusko after the Polish freedom fighter Tadeusz Kościuszko (1746–1817), and continues through southern Gippsland to near Western Port.

Edward Eyre

Between 1837 and 1839 Edward Eyre explored the Eyre Peninsula and tried, unsuccessfully, to find an inland route from Canberra through Victoria to Adelaide. In 1840 he penetrated far into the desertic north of what is now Victoria, reaching the shores of the salt lake which now bears his name. In 1841 he undertook an arduous journey with his native companion Wylie through the Nullarbor desert from Port Lincoln (SA) to Albany (WA).

Ludwig Leichhardt

In 1844–45 Ludwig Leichhardt, an immigrant of German origin, achieved the first crossing of the continent from the east coast (Moreton Bay, Brisbane) to the north coast (Port Essington, on the Cobourg Peninsula), a distance of over 5000km/3100 miles through northern Queensland and along the Gulf of Carpentaria. On a second expedition in which he planned to cross the continent from east to west, he and his companions disappeared without trace (1848).

Charles Sturt

In 1844 Charles Sturt, who had previously, in 1838, followed the Murray River to its outfall into Lake Alexandrina (SA), set out northward from Adelaide in search of the huge lake which was believed to exist in the centre of the continent. He and his companions braved the intense heat of the Simpson Desert, the south-eastern part of which is named after him (Sturt's Stony Desert), and on September 8th 1845 reached its most northerly point, north-west of Birdsville.

Edmund Kennedy; Frank and Alexander Jardine

An ill-prepared expedition led by Edward Kennedy which set out to travel from the coast of northern Queensland (Rockingham Bay) to the tip of Cape York ended tragically. The ten members of the expedition, including Kennedy, died as a result of the rigours of the journey through swamp and jungle or were killed by Aborigines. The Cape York peninsula was finally reached in 1864–65 by two brothers, Frank and Alexander Jardine, who drove a herd of cattle along its west coast to Somerset, at its northern tip.

Augustus and Francis Gregory

In 1855–56 Augustus Gregory travelled through the tropical north of Australia, starting from the Victoria River and following the Gulf of Carpentaria through northern Queensland to Brisbane. In 1858 he and his brother Francis crossed Queensland to Innamincka, looking for the missing Ludwig Leichhardt, and then found a way through the salt lakes southward to Adelaide. Between 1858 and 1861 Francis Gregory opened up the unknown north-west of Western Australia as a cattle-grazing region.

Burke and Wills

Two further expeditions set out to achieve a crossing of the continent from south to north, one starting from Melbourne, the other from Adelaide. On August 20th 1860 a well-equipped expedition sponsored by the government and led by Robert O'Hara Burke and William John Wills set out from Melbourne. In December 1860 Burke decided to establish a base camp, Depot LXV, at Cooper's Creek so that a party of four (Burke, Wills, Gray, King) could push on rapidly with the best camels to the Gulf of Carpentaria. At the end of January 1861 the party reached the Gulf of Carpentaria but could make no progress through the mangrove swamps and turned back, returning to Depot LXV on the evening of April 21st, only to discover that the other members of the expedition had left that morning to cross the desert to their main camp at Menindee. In spite of the food that had been left for them and of help from the local Aborigines Burke and Wills died. Gray had already died on the return journey, and only King survived in the care of the Aborigines. Another member of the expedition, Wilhelm Brahe, who had been in charge of the base camp, returned to Cooper's Creek but did not realise that the advance party were there, since they had left no traces. In 1863 Burke and Wills were given a state funeral in Melbourne.

John McDouall Stuart

Burke and Wills' rival John McDouall Stuart finally succeeded, after two unsuccessful attempts, in completing the south–north crossing of the continent from Adelaide. In March 1860 he set out with two companions from Chambers Creek in the north of South Australia and travelled through the "Red Centre" of Australia, becoming the first white man to see many of the present-day tourist sights and naming them, usually after his sponsors – Chambers Pillar, the Finke River the MacDonnell Ranges (after the governor of South Australia). He gave the mountain in the centre of Australia the name of Central Mount Sturt, later changed to Central Mount Stuart. At Attack Creek, north of Tennant Creek, illness and hostile Aborigines compelled him to turn back. After his return a larger party was formed, and by May 1861 this second expedition had got beyond Attack Creek, but on July 12th, when it had reached Burke Creek, it had once again to give up. Then Stuart set out for the third time with ten companions. He discovered Daly Waters Creek, which he named after the new governor of South Australia, and then continued by way of the Roper, Chambers and Katherine Rivers to reach Van Diemen Gulf, at the mouth of the Mary River, some 100km/60 miles north-east of the site of present-day Darwin. The return journey ended tragically: Stuart survived, but he was almost completely blind, totally exhaused and too weak to ride.

As a result of Stuart's exploration of central and northern Australia the administration of the Northern Territory was transferred in 1863 from New South Wales to South Australia. The overland telegraph line from Adelaide to Darwin largely followed his route. His expedition was in effect the climax in the exploration of the Australian interior. He established that there was no large lake – nothing but arid and lifeless desert.

Exploration in the 1870s

The desert regions of Western Australia were explored in the 1870s. In 1873 Peter E. Warburton travelled through the Great Desert from Alice Springs to Roebourne. In 1875 Ernest Giles explored the Great Victorian Desert and in 1876 the Gibson Desert, a journey on which his companion Gibson died. In the early seventies John Forrest, later a prominent politician and in 1890 first prime minister of Western Australia, explored the southern part of the Gibson Desert, travelling from Geraldton to Adelaide. His brother Alexander Forrest travelled through the Kimberley region from Derby (Beagle Bay) to the overland telegraph line north of the Tanami Desert, preparing the way for the extensive pastoral farming of the Kimberley region.

By around 1880 the exploration of the interior had been largely completed; but there were still some blank spots on the map of Australia until the 1930s – remote areas which could only be surveyed from the air.

Chronology

Australoid tribes from South-East Asia move south over still existing land bridges, "island-hopping" by way of the Indonesian islands to New Guinea. Before the end of the last Ice Age, some 12,000 years ago, the sea level was much lower and New Guinea and Tasmania were still attached to the Australian continent. Stone implements and human bones between 20,000 and more than 40,000 years old have been found at Penrith, near Sydney (NSW), Lake Mungo (NSW), Oenpelli in Arnhem Land (NT), Kutikina (TAS) and Devil's Lair (WA).	40,000 years ago (or still earlier)
Marco Polo, returning from China to Venice, reports seeing a large southern land.	1292–95
Pedro Fernandez de Quiros lands in the New Hebrides and names them Tierra Australia. Luís Vaez de Torres sails through the Torres Strait between Cape York and New Guinea. Willem Janszoon becomes the first European to land on Australia, at Duyfken Point, near Weipa on the west coast of Cape York.	1606
Frederik de Houtman reconnoitres the Houtman-Abrolhos Islands.	1616
The Dutch ship "Leeuwin" reaches the south-western tip of Australia (Cape Leeuwin).	1622
Pieter Nuyts sails along the south coast of Australia for some 1500km/930 miles to the Great Australian Bight.	1627
The "Batavia", commanded by François Pelsaert, is wrecked on a reef off the west coast: mutiny and murder by the crew, followed by severe punishment of the ringleaders.	1629
Abel Tasman discovers the southern tip of Tasmania (known until 1856 as Van Diemen's Land) and the South Island of New Zealand.	1642–43
Tasman sails along the north and north-west coasts of Australia.	1644
William Dampier, pirate and writer of adventure stories, lands on the north-west coast, the first Englishman to reach Australia, and gives a detailed amd uncomplimentary account of the unknown and inhospitable land.	1688
Willem de Vlamingh, the last of the Dutch navigators who played an important part in the discovery of Australia, explores Rottnest Island (off Perth, WA) and the Swan River to the south-west.	1696–97
William Dampier surveys the north-west coast and discovers the islands of the Dampier Archipelago.	1699
Antoine de Bougainville is prevented by the Great Barrier Reef from claiming the east coast of Australia for France.	1768
On his first voyage round the world Captain James Cook discovers the North Island of New Zealand and sails round both islands.	1769
Cook surveys the east coast of "New Holland" and anchors in Botany Bay. In the Great Barrier Reef, to the north of Cairns, the "Endeavour" strikes a reef and has to be repaired (at Cooktown). Landing on Possession Island, Cook takes possession of the eastern part of the continent in the name of King George III. He then returns to London by way of the Torres Strait and Batavia (Jakarta).	1770
On his second voyage Cook sails into Antarctic waters and proves that there is no other unknown southern land. In 1774 he discovers Norfolk Island.	1772–74
Landing of the First Fleet in Botany Bay. Captain Phillip, first governor of the colony, selects Port Jackson as the site for the settlement of Sydney. The French navigator La Pérouse arrives in Botany Bay six days after the First Fleet; on the voyage home his ship and its crew are lost. Discovery of Lord Howe Island.	1788
Antoine Bruny d'Entrecasteaux reconnoitres the south coast of Tasmania, the Derwent River and the channel between Bruny Island and the main island.	1792–93

Chronology

1798–99	Bass and Flinders sail round Tasmania (previously thought to be attached to mainland Australia), discover the Tamar River and reconnoitre the Bass Strait between Tasmania and Victoria.
1802–03	Flinders sails round the whole of Australia and off Adelaide encounters his French rival Thomas-Nicolas Baudin, who had explored the south-east coast to the west of Wilsons Promontory. On his voyage home Flinders is taken prisoner on Mauritius and kept in a French prison for seven years.
1804	David Collins founds Hobart in Sullivan Cove on the Derwent River (Tasmania).
1813	Blaxland, Wentworth and Lawson find a route through the Blue Mountains, and the colony rapidly extends westward.
1817	Oxley follows the Lachlan and Macquarie Rivers inland, hoping to find the rumoured large lake in the interior. He discovers the Liverpool Plains (New England) and Port Macquarie.
1823	Oxley discovers the Brisbane River.
1824	Hume and Hovell pioneer the overland route from the east to the south coast by way of the Snowy Mountains and the Murray River.
1825	Van Diemen's Land is separated from New South Wales. (In 1856 it becomes self-governing and is renamed Tasmania.)
1826	Penal colony founded by Lockyer at Albany (WA).
1826–27	Penal colony founded by Logan in Moreton Bay.
1827	Stirling surveys the Swan River (WA). Cunningham discovers the fertile Darling Downs in southern Queensland. Stirling founds a settlement (soon abandoned) in Raffles Bay (Cobourg Peninsula) on the north coast.
1829	Fremantle takes possession of western Australia for Britain. Foundation of Perth.
1829–30	Sturt explores the Murrumbidgee, names the Murray River and discovers its junction with the Darling River.
1831	Proclamation of the colony of Western Australia (which gets its own government only in 1890).
1831–36	Mitchell surveys the Darling and Murray river system, the most important in New South Wales. His work promotes the settlement of Victoria.
1835	The Henty family, disappointed by Western Australia, settle in Portland Bay, on the western border of Victoria. John Batman, from Tasmania, selects the site of the settlement which becomes Melbourne.
1836	Establishment of the colony of South Australia (which gets its own government in 1856).
1839–40	Exploration of the Australian Alps (Snowy Mountains) by McMillan and Strzelecki.
1840	Transportation of convicts to New South Wales ceases.
1841	Eyre crosses the Nullarbor Plain.
1844–45	Leichhardt crosses the continent from Brisbane in the east to Port Essington in the north; on his second expedition westward he disappears.
1850–51	Proclamation of the colony of Victoria (own government 1855). Beginning of gold rush in New South Wales and Victoria; thereafter gold fever spreads over the whole continent, reaching its peak in 1892–93 at Kalgoorlie/Coolgardie (WA).
1855–56	Independent governments established in New South Wales and South Australia.
1859	Queensland becomes the last colony, with its own government.
1860	Stuart reaches the MacDonnell Ranges and the geographical centre of the Australian continent.
1860–61	Burke and Wills cross the continent from Melbourne to the Gulf of Carpentaria, but die on the return journey.
1862	At his third attempt Stuart succeeds in crossing the continent from Adelaide to the north coast.
1868	Transportation of convicts to Western Australia ceases.

Completion of the overland telegraph line from Adelaide to Darwin, following Stuart's route. The laying of a cable from Java speeds up communications between Britain and eastern Australia.	1872
The Commonwealth of Australia comes into being on January 1st. Melbourne has important functions as temporary capital. Beginning of the "White Australia" policy directed against non-European immigrants.	1901
The Northern Territory and Australian Capital Territory come under the authority of the federal government.	1911
During the First World War Australian and New Zealand forces suffer heavy losses at Gallipoli. Since then April 25th has been Australia's National Day - Anzac Day (Anzac: from the initials of Australian and New Zealand Army Corps).	1915
Parliament and the government move to the new capital, Canberra.	1927
Proclamation of the Australian Antarctic Territory.	1936
Australian troops fight in the Second World War, suffering heavy losses in Europe.	1939-45
Bombing of Darwin by Japanese aircraft; Japanese submarines in Sydney harbour. Concept of the Brisbane Line, the core area south of a line from Adelaide to Brisbane. Australia lies in the South West Pacific Area and is under American command (General MacArthur).	1942
Huge influx (over 3 million) of immigrants, mostly young: "Populate or perish" policy.	from 1945
ANZUS Pact (Australia, New Zealand, United States).	1951
Australia joins SEATO (South-East Asia Treaty Organisation).	1954
15th Summer Olympics in Melbourne	1956
End of the "White Australia" immigration policy with its "dictation test"; no discrimination against immigrants of any nationality. Increased immigration from Asia; many refugees from Indochina.	1958
On Christmas Day Cyclone Tracy devastates Darwin.	1974
Sensational dismissal of Prime Minister Gough Whitlam by Governor-General Sir John Kerr.	1975
The land rights of the Aborigines in the Northern Territory are recognised.	1977
Bush fires and flooding after a long period of drought, particularly in Victoria, South Australia, the Northern Territory, Queensland and Western Australia.	1983
Bicentennial (200th anniversary) of the arrival of the First Fleet. Demonstrations by Aborigines.	1988
Areas of land in the Northern Territory are assigned to the Aborigines (September 10th). Earthquake in Newcastle, NSW (December 28th).	1989
Australia announces that it is sending two warships to join the international fleet in the Gulf War.	1990
Agreement is reached on the proposal to work out a new constitution by January 1st 2001. (The date when it is planned that Australia will relinquish any constitutional ties with Great Britain)	1991
In elections to the House of Representatives the Labor Party wins for the fifth time in succession (March 13th).	1993
A much-publicised solar energy motor car race is held on the stretch between Darwin and Adelaide; Japanese manufacturers "win by a nose".	1993
At the turn of the year there are devastating bush fires, particularly round Sydney. The Royal National Park, 36km/22 miles south of the city, is completely destroyed. Nature demonstrates, however, that it has adapted itself to frequent fires, and within a few months the vegetation is in process of regeneration.	1993-94
As a result of the extreme aridity violent sandstorms sweep across the whole continent from west to east (May).	1994
During his visit to Australia and Sydney (19th Jan.), Pope John Paul II beatifies Mary MacKillop, the first Australian woman to be so blessed.	1995
After thirteen years of Labour rule the Liberal Pary/National Party coalition wins an overwhelming victory (2nd March). John W. Howard, the Liberal leader, becomes the 25th prime minister.	1996
In the Northern Territory the law authorising voluntary euthanasia is passed (1st July)	1996
Summer Olympics due to be held in Sydney.	2000

Famous People

This section contains brief biographies, in alphabetical order, of notable, and sometimes internationally famous, people who were born, lived or died in Australia.

Sir Reginald Myles Ansett (1909–81)

Reginald Ansett was born at Inglewood in the gold-mining district of Victoria. His father ran a bicycle repair workshop before going to Europe to serve in the First World War. The children and their mother lived in Melbourne, where they ran a knitwear factory and Reginald was trained as a knitting machine operator. In 1929 he learned to fly as a member of the Australian Aero Club. He spent some time as a surveyor in the Northern Territory but, finding it too lonely, resolved to try his luck in the haulage business. Then in 1933, in an attempt to reduce the deficit on running the railways, the government introduced the Transport Regulation Act, which prohibited road transport from competing with the railways. Ansett then took to the air, and in 1936 began to fly daily air services between Hamilton and Melbourne. This was the birth of Ansett Airways. Ansett was knighted for his services to transport in 1969.

Sir Joseph Banks (1743–1820)

A man of wide culture and a keen botanist, Joseph Banks was the son of a country squire and member of parliament. In 1766 he was a member of an expedition to Labrador and Newfoundland, and in 1768–71, along with the Swedish botanist David Carl Solander, accompanied Cook on his first voyage round the world, with Banks paying all expenses. When in Botany Bay he devoted himself to identifying and collecting plants, but was also enthusiastic about the prospects of future settlement in Australia, earning him the style of "father of Australia". His likeness appears on the Australian five dollar note.

Bushrangers

Bushrangers appeared in Australia almost at the beginning of white settlement, when convicts who succeeded in escaping sought refuge in the impenetrable bush and lived by robbery. An early example was "Black Caesar", a negro convict from the West Indies who took to the bush but was finally cornered and shot in 1796. Particularly vicious were the escaped convicts of Van Diemen's Land (Tasmania), the notorious "Vandemonians", who formed organised bands. The goldfields produced unheard-of wealth, and it was easy for the bushrangers to ambush and plunder gold transports and mailcoaches. Notorious loners, before the time of the Kelly Gang (see Baedeker Special, "Ned Kelly's Brief Career", p. 61), were Dan Morgan, who was shot in April 1865 at Wangaratta (VIC), and Ben Hall, killed at Forbes (NSW) in May 1865. Captain Thunderbolt (Frederick Ward) died in 1870 at Uralla in New England (NSW). Frank Gardiner, who was condemned in 1864 to 32 years in prison, was released in 1874 and expelled from the country. Andrew George Scott, a lay preacher from Bacchus Marsh, later became famous as "Captain Moonlite" and was executed for the murder of a policeman. After the development of telegraph and railway services throughout the country the life of the bushrangers became more difficult.

James Cook (1728–79)

James Cook joined the Royal Navy in 1755, and from 1758 to 1767 was employed on cartographic surveys on the St Lawrence River and in Newfoundland. In 1768 he was appointed commander of an expedition sent to Tahiti to observe the transit of Venus on June 3rd 1760. Thereafter he discovered, named and surveyed the neighbouring island groups. He had secret orders, which only became known much later,

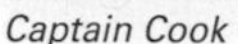

Captain Cook

Erroll Flynn

Ludwig Leichhardt

requiring him to look for the fabled southern continent. On April 19th 1770, having been driven past Tasmania in a storm, he reached the south-eastern tip of Australia and soon afterwards arrived in Botany Bay. He then continued up the coast through the Great Barrier Reef, where he was shipwrecked, to the northern tip of the Cape York peninsula and Possession Island, where, in accordance with his secret orders, he took possession in the name of the Crown of the whole of the eastern part of the continent. Then, passing through the Torres Strait, he returned to London, where he arrived on July 12th 1771. Joseph Banks, who had accompanied Cook, advised the British government before the despatch of the First Fleet in 1788, recommending Botany Bay as a landing-place.

Cook undertook two other voyages round the world, in 1772–75 and 1776–80. On his third voyage he sailed by way of Easter Island and the New Hebrides and penetrated into the Antarctic Ocean, establishing that there was no continent farther south. His aim was to find a northern passage between the Atlantic and the Pacific. In 1778 he discovered Hawaii and sailed as far north as the Bering Strait. After a further landing in Hawaii he was killed in a fight with natives on February 14th 1779.

Errol Flynn (1909–59)

Errol Flynn, born in Hobart (TAS) of Irish descent, featured in many Hollywood films as a dashing, daredevil hero and an irresistible lover. He died in Hollywood.

John Flynn (1880–1951)

John Flynn was born in Moliagul in the Wimmera district of Victoria, the son of a teacher. He gave up his training as a teacher in Melbourne at the age of 18, and at the age of 25 joined a Presbyterian home mission group. In 1912 he was invited to assess the prospects for the Australian Inland Mission. He began his task in the outback riding on camels and was concerned about the need to provide rapid aid, transport and communications for an area of some 2 million sq. miles. This gave rise to the idea of the Flying Doctor Service (see Baedeker Special, p. 275).

Mrs Aeneas Gunn (Jeannie Gunn, née Taylor, 1870–1961)

Born in the Carlton district of Melbourne. After studying at Melbourne University she opened a private school along with her sisters. When involved in a coach accident she met her future husband, Aeneas Gunn, who had worked for many years as manager of huge cattle stations in the Northern Territory, and after their marriage went with him in 1901 to the Elsey Station on the Roper River, 300 miles south of Darwin. She was so fascinated with her experiences on the journey by rail from Darwin to Pine Creek and from there to Elsey Station, near

Mataranka, through rivers in flood and expanses of grass taller than a man, with the comradeship of the rough characters of the Never Never and with the year she spent as the only white woman in an immense surrounding area that after her husband's early death from malaria and her return to Melbourne she wrote two books – a children's book, "The Little Black Princess", based on her memories of the Aboriginal children she had known at Elsey Station, and an autobiographical work, "We of the Never Never", which sold a million copies and had even greater success as a film.

Sir Hans Heysen (1877–1968)

Born in Hamburg; along with his mother and the rest of the family joined his father in South Australia in 1883. While still at school he had shown a talent for drawing, and in Hahndorf (SA) he depicted village life in idyllic terms. After beginning work as an assistant in an ironmonger's shop he continued drawing as a hobby, attending the East Adelaide Model School after work. Exhibited in and around Adelaide from 1895 onwards; study in Europe 1899–1903; then in 1908 exhibition in Melbourne which brought him country-wide recognition. Then moved with family to Hahndorf. From 1926 mainly scenes from the bush and the Flinders Ranges with their play of colour and forms. OBE 1945; knighted 1959.

Bernhard Otto Holtermann (1838–85)

Born in Germany; emigrated to Australia (Melbourne, then Sydney) in 1858. Worked as a waiter and came in contact with gold-miners; then went to the gold-mining settlement of Hill End, where he struck it rich with his Star of Hope Mine. Now wealthy, he devoted himself to his hobby, photography, and built up a collection of over 3000 photographs of life in the goldfields and panoramic views of Australian towns, taken by himself and his colleagues Merlin and Bayliss, which were shown at many exhibitions in America and Europe in the 1870s. He was also a successful businessman, selling his wonder medicine, Holtermann's Australian Life-Preserving Drops, as well as German beer, sewing machines and telegraph apparatus. In 1883 he was elected a member of the New South Wales parliament for his home constituency of St Leonards (North Sydney).

Ned Kelly (1855–80)

On the celebrated bushranger Ned Kelly see the Baedeker Special on p. 61.

Ludwig Leichhardt (1813–48?)

Born in Brandenburg (Germany), the sixth child of a peat-cutter, Ludwig Leichhardt was able to study in Berlin and Göttingen thanks to the support of the village pastor. His future career was determined by his friendship with two English brothers Nicholson. Turned from the study of philosophy to medicine and science; moved to England; travel plans, interfered with by military service; study in Mediterranean area. In 1841, sailed from London to Australia, a voyage which took 4½ months. Then, after working on sheep stations in Moreton Bay (Brisbane), bushwalking in the hinterland. Planned great overland expedition through Queensland to the north coast (Port Essington, Cobourg Peninsula); set out in 1844. Attacked by Aborigines on June 28th 1845; his companion Gilbert killed, two others badly injured. December 17th 1845, reached Port Essington, a British military post which was soon afterwards abandoned. Returned by ship through the Torres Strait to Sydney, where he was enthusiastically received. Honoured by geographical societies in London and Paris. As a result of Leichhardt's explorations squatters now moved north with their herds of cattle. Further plans for a crossing of the continent from east to west; expedition set out in December 1846, but turned back after epidemic of fever and loss of cattle. Fresh attempt in December 1847 by a group of seven, of whom all trace was lost after April 1848.

John Macarthur (1767–1834)

Born in Plymouth (England); became a soldier in 1782. In 1789 sent to Australia, with his young family, as an ensign in the New South Wales

Baedeker Special

Ned Kelly's Brief Career

Edward Kelly, it has been said, might have turned out well. *Might:* but circumstances were against him. He was born in Beveridge, to the north of Melbourne (VIC). His father was a thick-skulled Irish convict who was forced to work for his betters; his mother smoked, drank and was ready to join in when her two sons had to stand up for themselves with their fists against the youths of the neighbourhood. Ned, as the slight boy with reddish hair and freckles came to be called, was a quick learner. When his parents found it difficult to feed him and his brother Dan he was sent to work for various farmers round the little town of Benalla. There he soon found means of relieving the hardships of life. At the tender age of ten he had learned the art of horse-stealing, and he soon came into conflict with the law and its guardians. There were plenty of models for him to follow, like the notorious bushrangers Dan Morgan, Captain Thunderbolt (Frederick Ward), Ben Hall and Frank Gardiner. Ned had just turned fourteen when he found himself in prison for the first time. He was caught stealing horses and sent down for three years. His sentence did little to improve him. He took a job in a sawmill, but this was merely a cover for other activities, and he was soon widely feared as a stealer of cattle and horses. But since his raids were almost exclusively directed against wealthy cattle-farmers he became (and remains) something of a folk hero, a Robin Hood of the outback; and when he was again caught and due to be hanged no fewer than 32,000 signatures were collected for a petition against his execution.

Ned Kelly's last fight

The good citizens who signed the petition might have spared their trouble. Ned Kelly had become "public enemy No. 1", particularly after three policemen were killed in a shoot-out with the Kelly gang. The authorities were on his track as he grew ever bolder, not only stealing cattle but raiding banks, mailcoaches and gold transports. Between his crimes he found refuge with small farmers, who respected him because he took money only from the well-to-do.

Ned Kelly died at the age of only 25. A member of his gang betrayed him to the authorities, and a manhunt began. Finally he and his gang entrenched themselves in a hotel in Glenrowan, not far from his birthplace, and there was another bloody shoot-out with the police. The police set fire to the building and the gang tried to escape. But not even Ned Kelly's home-made armour (still to be seen in the Old Gaol in Melbourne) could save him. He was shot in the leg, and his brief career came to an end. He was condemned to death and was hanged in Melbourne's Old Gaol on November 11th 1880.

Ned Kelly was not only a folk hero but also a model for many other bushrangers, most of them escaped convicts – none of whom, however, attained the fame of the boy from the slums of Greta.

Nellie Melba

Paul Strzelecki

Patrick White

Corps. In 1793 he became controller of public buildings and received his first allotment of land (100 acres at Parramatta). In 1795 he took up sheep-farming, and in the following year imported merino sheep from the Cape of Good Hope and from a flock owned by George III. After fighting a duel he was arrested and sent back to Britain for court-martial. He was acquitted, and, now in favour with the Colonial Office, showed off his samples of wool, got promises of future support and in effect laid the foundations of the Australian sheep stocks.

Sir Douglas Mawson (1882–1958)

Born in Yorkshire; as a child emigrated with his parents to Australia. A pupil of William E. David, he accompanied him on the British Antarctic expedition led by Shackleton (1907–09). Along with David and Mackay he reached the south magnetic pole after a 1260 mile trek taking 120 days. In 1911–14 he led the first Australian Antarctic expedition. Along with Ninnis and Mertz he set out with dog-sledges to explore the endless snowy wastes of King George V Land; but, 300 miles from the base camp, Ninnis fell into a crevasse with the best dogs and most of their supplies, and Mertz died of hunger and exhaustion. After the departure of the "Aurora" Mawson and his team lived through the Antarctic winter and explored great expanses of the coastal regions. In 1929 he led a further Antarctic expedition in the "Discovery", the result of which was the proclamation of the Australian Antarctic Territory in 1936. Mawson was professor of geology and mineralogy at Adelaide University from 1920 to 1952.

Nellie Melba (Dame Helen Porter Mitchell, 1861–1931)

Born in Richmond, near Melbourne, daughter of a well known builder, landowner and wine-maker; both parents were musical. After training as a singer she married Charles Armstrong in Brisbane in 1882. In 1886, with her father, husband and son, she moved to London. Training in Paris with Matilda Marchesi. Successful appearances in Brussels, London, Paris, Milan, St Petersburg and New York, particularly in Verdi, Puccini and Wagner operas. Her voice had an extraordinarily wide range, from an octave below middle B to two octaves above middle F. Her stage name of Melba was a tribute to her home town of Melbourne. She was made a Dame of the British Empire in 1918. A well known international dessert, peach Melba, bears her name.

Thomas Livingstone Mitchell (1792–1855)

Born in Scotland; enlisted in the army at the age of 16; promoted major in 1826. Sent out to New South Wales in 1827 as assistant to Surveyor-General John Oxley, whom he later succeeded. Expeditions to the upper course of the Darling River in 1831 and 1835. In 1836 a major expedition to the Murrumbidgee River and its junction with the Murray River and to the estuary of the Darling. Mitchell then turned south-west into the unknown interior of Victoria, whose unaccustomedly fresh and green landscape so delighted him that he compared it with the Garden of Eden and declared that this was "Australia Felix". In England 1837–40; publication of his "Three Expeditions into the Interior of Eastern Australia". 1844, member of the Legislative Council. 1845, large expedition to find a route across Australia to the Gulf of Carpentaria; discovery of huge expanses of grazing land ("Mitchell grass"). 1848, home leave; publication of his "Journal of an Expedition into the Interior of Tropical Australia". Mitchell also developed a steamship propeller on the basis of the boomerang and translated 16th century Portuguese poetry into English.

Albert Namatjira
(1902–59)

Albert Namatjira, a member of the Aranda tribe who was brought up as a Christian, is one of Australia's leading landscape painters. He grew up in the Lutheran mission station of Hermannsburg (NT), founded in 1879, where he learned the technique of watercolour painting at the age of 20. His work, which originally reflected aspects of Aboriginal culture but later increasingly freed itself from mythic and spiritual elements, appealed to the white society of Australia. He was unequalled in his ability to depict the scenic beauties of the "Red Centre" of Australia. The success of his pictures led to the formation of a kind of "Namatjira school" of his friends and followers. He himself stood half way between the ancient culture of the Aranda tribe and white civilisation. After years of being treated as a member of an inferior and disadvantaged race he was received by the Queen in Canberra in 1954 and was granted Australian citizenship in 1957. Nevertheless he remained close to his fellow-members of the Aranda tribe and supported them with the money gained from selling his paintings. His personal tragedy was his trial for giving liquor to an Aboriginal friend of his, for which he was sentenced in 1958 to three months in prison. He died in August 1959 and was buried in Alice Springs (NT).

Georg Balthasar von Neumayer
(1826–1909)

Born in Germany and studied in Munich; a student of the American oceanographer M. F. Maury. Involved in research into terrestrial magnetism. Went to Australia in 1852; lived in Melbourne, the goldfields of Victoria and Tasmania, where the John Ross Observatory gave him the idea of establishing an observatory in Melbourne, a plan which was supported by King Maximilian of Bavaria, Justus von Liebig, Michael Faraday and Alexander von Humboldt. 1857, foundation of the Flagstaff Observatory in Melbourne; beginning of meteorological, magnetic and astronomical observations, particularly of meteorites and polar lights. As Director of the Magnetic Survey of Victoria he established a total of 230 magnetic observatories between 1858 and 1864, and his tide gauges along the coast provided the basis for tidal forecasts. In 1863 the Observatory was moved to the south bank of the Yarra. Neumayer then left Australia and from 1875 to 1903 was Director of the Marine Observatory in Hamburg. There he promoted polar research, and was one of the organisers of the first international Polar Year in 1882–83. The German research station in the Antarctic, established in 1981, bears his name.

Helmut Newton
(b. 1920)

The Berlin-born photographer Helmut Newton emigrated to Australia as a young man, returning to Europe (Paris) in 1958. Since the early eighties he has lived in Monte Carlo. He works in the fashion and advertising fields, and has gained an international reputation for his portraits, particularly his nudes. Some of his provocative female nudes in unusual poses and settings have aroused feminist opposition.

Sidney Robert Nolan
(1917–92)

Sidney Nolan's ancestors emigrated from Ireland to Victoria. He himself was born in Carlton (Melbourne), where his father worked for many years as a tram conductor. From an early age he was interested in colours, but the teaching of painting at Prahan Technical College and the art school of the National Gallery of Victoria did not appeal to him and he preferred his own technique. At the age of 21 he decided to devote himself to painting, and lived for some time in the Australian bush. Military service took him to the thinly populated country round Nhill and Dimboola in the Wimmera (VIC), and the impression made on him by this desolate landscape is still reflected in his later work. As a boy he had been thrilled by the exploits of Ned Kelly: his grandfather had taken part, as a young policeman, in the hunt for the bushranger and was full of stories about him; and Nolan painted a series of pictures centred on Kelly after visiting the "Kelly country" of northern Victoria. Travel became a basic element in his life, and foreign countries inspired him as settings for his pictures. After a visit to Greece he painted his Gallipoli pictures, which he presented to the Australian War Memorial in Canberra in memory of his brother, who had been killed in the Second World War. In 1982 he presented his "Paradise Garden" series to the Victorian Arts Centre. This arose from his memories of a visit to central Australia as an imaginative conception of the flowers which after rain briefly transform the arid semi-desert into a paradise. Other works by Nolan can be seen in the Reserve Bank in Melbourne (the "Eureka Mural"), the Festival Arts Centre in Adelaide and the Federal Law Building in Sydney. There are pictures by Nolan, who is often seen as a forerunner of Pop Art, in many of the great museums of the world. He was knighted in 1981.

Andrew Barton Paterson ("Banjo") (1864–1941)

Born in the Australian bush north-west of Bathurst (NSW); moved to near the Lambing Flat goldfields, Young (NSW); studied law in Sydney. His first publication, a pamphlet entitled "Australia for the Australians", appeared under his own name, but he published his later poems and ballads under the pseudonym "The Banjo". His collection of ballads "The Man from Snowy River and Other Verses" (1895) was an immediate huge success. He depicted life in the bush and its great free natural expanses in powerfully expressive language, as in "Clancy of the Overflow". Around 1900 Paterson gave up his practice of law to devote himself wholly to writing. As a correspondent of the "Sydney Morning Herald" he reported from South Africa on the Boer War. Then, after spending some time in London, he went to China to report on the Boxer rising. His second volume of poems, "Rio Grande's Last Ride" (1902), was also a great success. In 1904, when he was editor of the "Sydney Evening News", he published a collection of bush songs, mostly anonymous, "The Old Bush Songs, Composed and Sung in the Bushranging, Digging and Overlanding Days". At this period he also contributed articles on Australia to the London "Times". In 1906 he published his first prose work, "An Outback Marriage", but this did not have the expressive power of his verse. He volunteered for service in the First World War, serving first as an ambulance driver in France and later in Egypt. In 1917 appeared "Saltbush Bill", a collection which included his most famous ballad, "Waltzing Matilda", Australia's unofficial national anthem. In 1988 the National Book Council Award was renamed the Banjo Award for Australian Literature in his honour.

Charles Rasp (1846?–1907)

Rasp is said to have been born near Stuttgart in south-western Germany, but there is a mystery about his early years before his arrival in Melbourne in February 1871 as a nutritional chemist with an excellent command of languages. It seems likely that he was a Prussian officer who deserted during the battle for Paris in the winter of 1870. In Australia he worked on wine-growing estates and also for a brief period in the goldfields of Victoria, before moving to the arid country north of the Barrier Ranges, where he was employed as a boundary rider on the Mount Gipps stock farm. On his rides his attention was attracted by Broken Hill, which the Aborigines called the "hill of mullock" (rubbish-heap). In 1883 he staked out his claim there and took samples for assay in Adelaide, 600km/370 miles away to the south-west. The working of the silver, lead and zinc deposits which he had discovered proved highly profitable. Rasp thereupon established the Broken Hill Proprietary Company, in which he held most of the shares.

Sir Arthur Streeton (1867–1943)

Born near Geelong (VIC), the son of a schoolmaster. His future career was determined by a chance meeting with the painters Tom Roberts and Fred McCubbin at Mentone (on Port Phillip Bay) in 1886. Roberts and McCubbin had established their painting camp at Box Hill, in wild open country, and invited the young Streeton to join them. Here he painted his first large landscapes, which brought in good money, so that he was able to give up his trade as a lithographer. His landscape "Golden Summer" (1888–89) was exhibited in London and Paris and won an award – the first for an Australian artist. Streeton founded the famous Heidelberg School (showing affinities with Impressionism) in Eaglemont, north-west of Melbourne, from which there were magnificent views of the Yarra valley. After spending some time in Egypt and London he returned briefly to Australia in 1906 as an artist of established reputation. He was knighted in 1937.

Theodor Strehlow (1908–78)

The son of Carl Strehlow, a German missionary who came to the mission station of Hermannsburg (NT) in 1894. Carl Strehlow learned the language of the Aranda tribe, translated the New Testament and recorded the myths and songs of the Aborigines. His son Theodor (Ted) grew up in Hermannsburg, familiar with both white and Aboriginal culture. After his father's death (1922) Theodor went to Adelaide to complete his education but returned to Hermannsburg in 1933 to devote himself to collecting and recording material (films, slides, recordings, card-indexed information, books) on the culture of the Aborigines. His publications "Aranda Phonetics and Grammar", "Aranda Traditions" and "Songs of Central Australia" brought him fame, but he incurred criticism for selling pictures of traditional Aboriginal ceremonies to the German illustrated magazine "Stern", reproductions of which in an Australian magazine upset the Aborigines because they broke the taboo on their secret rites.

Count Paul Edmund de Strzelecki (1797–1873)

Scion of a poor Polish noble family in Silesia; served as a volunteer in the Prussian army while still at school. Thereafter travelled and worked on an estate in Russian-occupied Poland. 1830 onwards, stays in England, study of geology and mineralogy, travels in Scottish highlands. 1834, went to America and travelled widely in Canada, the United States and South America. Then via Hawaii to New Zealand and in 1839 to Sydney, where he established close relationships with the governor, Sir George Gipps, and the explorer Philip Parker King. In 1840 he began his travels through south-eastern Australia. He explored the Australian Alps, discovered and climbed the highest peak in the Snowy Mountains and named it Mount Kosciusko in memory of the Polish freedom fighter Tadeusz Kościuszko because the form of the summit resembled Kościuszko's tomb in Cracow. He also travelled from Melbourne to Tasmania, where he explored the islands in the Bass Strait. He is commemorated by Mount Strzelecki National Park on Flinders Island. In 1843 Strzelecki returned to settle in England, where he published his "Physical Description of New South Wales, Victoria and Van Diemen's Land" (1845), a geological study which laid the foundations for later research.

John McDouall Stuart (1815–66)

Born in Scotland. Accompanied Charles Sturt on his expedition to central Australia in 1844–45. Employed as land surveyor. 1858–59, shorter expeditions to the west of Lake Eyre (SA). In 1859 a prize of £2000 was offered for the first crossing of South Australia from south to north. Stuart's first attempt at making the crossing in 1860 ended after he had reached the central point of the continent (Central Mount Stuart) at Attack Creek (near Tennant Creek); a second attempt in

1860–61, following the same route, took him as far as Burke Creek; but at his third attempt he reached the Van Diemen Gulf, at the mouth of the Mary River, on July 24th 1862, though he barely survived the return journey, ill, emaciated and blind. The overland telegraph line from Adelaide to Darwin and later the Stuart Highway and the Ghan railway line followed Stuart's route for much of the way.

Charles Sturt (1795–1869)

Born in India, the son of a lawyer in the East India Company, and brought up in England. 1813, enlisted in the army. 1826, as captain, accompanied a shipment of convicts to New South Wales. In 1828, with Hamilton Hume as assistant, he explored and mapped the Macquarie, Bogan and Castlereagh Rivers and discovered the Darling River. Then in 1829–30 he sailed on a whaler up the Murrumbidgee into the unknown – one of the most daring expeditions in the history of Australian discovery. The greatest hazards were the stumps of trees in the river and the ever-present Aborigines, but Sturt managed to establish friendly relations with the natives. After a month's travelling he reached the outflow of the Murray River into Lake Alexandrina (SA). Later, in 1838, he travelled along the Murray River with a herd of cattle to South Australia. In 1839 he became surveyor-general of New South Wales. In 1844, along with Stuart and, for part of the time, Eyre, he led a well-equipped expedition up the Murray and Darling Rivers to Lake Blanche, and on to Sturt's Stony Desert in central Australia.

Dame Joan Sutherland (b. 1926)

Joan Sutherland was born in Sydney. After her father's early death her mother encouraged her to sing, but before she began her training as a singer at the age of 19 she trained as a secretary. Naturally a mezzo-soprano, her voice was developed into a coloratura soprano, so that she was equally at home in lyrical and dramatic roles. In 1952 she joined the Royal Opera and appeared at Covent Garden; she also had great success as a concert singer. In 1959 she made her debut as Lucia in "Lucia di Lammermoor", and later enjoyed great successes in Paris, Milan and New York, where she won particular applause as an interpreter of Rossini, Bellini and Donizetti. In 1965 she returned to Australia, and in 1974 appeared for the first time in Sydney's new Opera House. She received many distinctions and honours, and in 1979 was appointed DBE. She gave her final performance in Sydney Opera House in 1990.

Patrick White (1912–90)

Born in London when his parents were on a visit to Europe. His paternal relatives had emigrated to New South Wales in 1828; his mother, a distant relative of the family, was English. Troubled by asthma as a child, he grew up in Rushcutters Bay and in the Blue Mountains. He spent four years at school (Cheltenham College) in England, with theatre visits to London and holidays in France as his only diversions. Soon he was writing his first poems. Returning to Australia, he spent some years, in accordance with family tradition, working on the land, at Adaminaby in the Snowy Mountains and Walgett in northern New South Wales. He then returned to England to read modern languages in King's College, Cambridge, spending vacations in France and Germany, and took his B.A. in 1935. Thereafter he remained in England, seeking to live by writing, mainly for the theatre. Military service in North Africa, Palestine and Greece. In 1948 he returned to Australia, but it did not live up to his memories and expectations; he complained of the "great Australian emptiness" and of the materialism and concentration on profit of urbanised post-war Australian society. He acquired the property of Dogwood, with some land, at Castle Hill, 20 miles from Sydney, in an area still spared by the expansion of the city, where he grew flowers and vegetables, bred dogs and goats and kept dairy cows. In 1955 his novel "The Tree of Man", which had previously been rejected by three British publishers, was published in America and was a huge success. His next novel, "Voss", caused some controversy in Australia, though it was well received abroad. The figure of the German explorer Voss was not, as some thought, modelled on Ludwig Leichhardt: according to White himself the stimulus for the book came from his feelings about Hitler's megalomania while serving in the North African desert. Among White's later works were "Riders in the Chariot", "The Solid Mandala", "The Vivisector", "The Eye of the Storm", "A Fringe of Leaves" and "The Twyborn Affair". He also published collections of short stories. In 1961 there was controversy over his play "The Ham Funeral", written for the Adelaide Festival of Arts, which was rejected by the Festival management but was successfully produced in Adelaide outside the Festival. Other plays had great influence on contemporary experimental theatre in Australia.

White was a committed opponent of discrimination and exploitation. He protested against the Vietnam War and against the spread of the Australian cities and supported the cause of the Aborigines and the opponents of uranium. In 1973 he was awarded the Nobel Prize for literature, which was accepted on his behalf by Sidney Nolan, but gave the money to a foundation for supporting unknown Australian writers. In 1963 he was compelled to give up his rural retreat of Dogwood, for Castle Hill had now been swallowed up by the expanding suburbs of Sydney, and returned to near the city centre (Martin Street, on Centennial Park). He collected the works of young Australian painters, some of which he bequeathed to the Art Gallery of New South Wales. His "Flaws in the Glass" (1981) is believed to be a self-portrait.

Art and Culture

Art of the Aborigines

The culture of Australia's original inhabitants goes back many thousands of years, against the mere two centuries of white occupation. The steady penetration of Australia by British stock-farmers and squatters, freed convicts, gold-seekers from many countries and mining companies meant the irrevocable end of the Aborigines' tribal territories and hunting grounds, their way of life and their conceptions of the world. From the late 19th century onwards there was intensive research into the culture and language of the Aborigines, particularly in central Australia – for example the expeditions of B. Spencer and F. J. Gillen and Carl and Theodor Strehlow's commitment to the Aranda tribe.

A special place in the art of the Aborigines is occupied by Albert Namatjira, an Aranda who was inspired by white painters living in Hermannsburg (NT) in the 1930s to paint water-colours of Australian landscape in European techniques but from the perspective of the Aborigines.

Visitors to Australia have a unique opportunity to observe a Stone Age culture close-up, even if from outside. The remains of the country's early inhabitants which are scattered all over Australia are strictly protected by law, with severe penalties for damaging them. Conducted tours led by Aborigines and presentations of their way of life and their ceremonies give at least a general impression of the way of life and the abilities of the first Australians.

Ritual significance of Aboriginal art

Rock drawings, cave paintings, bark paintings, sand pictures, totem poles, woodcarvings and basketwork – all these examples of Aboriginal art have a ritual function and are not to be seen as the work of an individual artist. They are symbols representing the relationship between men and their natural environment. The remote ancestors of the Dreamtime, supra-terrestrial beings in human or animal form, had endowed all natural phenomena – rain, water-holes, caves, rocks, trees – with a spiritual significance. The symbols on cult objects embody the forces of the Dreamtime and act as a reminder of them, and they also determine the ritual activities of the tribal communities over which they preside. The designs (geometric patterns, figures of animals) correspond to the myths and songs peculiar to the tribal group. The very production of the work of art, as the visible expression of these myths, was accompanied by magical formulae and songs. The range of designs is endless, as is the number of magical verses.

Tjurungas (central Australia)

Tjurungas were flat stones, pieces of wood on which patterns were incised with animals' teeth. Like ritual shields, sand pictures and totem poles, they were generally taboo to women and children. The colours used by the Aborigines in painting cult objects and their own bodies were provided by natural deposits of ochre in tones of red and yellow, often conveyed over long distances, and by charcoal and chalk; birds' feathers, particularly soft down feathers, were also used for decoration. The corroboree dancers representing the ancestors of the Dreamtime concealed their own identity by decorating themselves with paint or clay and feathers. Non-sacred objects, in particular hunting equipment (boomerangs, spears, throwing sticks) were also decorated with Dreamtime symbols. In central Australia the tjurungas were the central cult features: compared with them caves and painted rock overhangs were of secondary importance.

Cave paintings (northern Australia)

In northern Australia, on the other hand – in Arnhem Land (NT) and on the Cape York peninsula (QLD) – there are innumerable painted caves and rock overhangs in which the hunting tribes took refuge during the rainy season. The paintings represent legendary figures, creator ancestors of the Dreamtime, personifications of the forces of nature. The rainbow serpent symbolises the beginning of life, life-preserving water and fertility. In the "X-ray style" the internal organs of the body are shown as well as the exterior. In the "silhouette style" there are frequent outlines of hands as well as animals, human figures and hunting scenes. The cult rituals involved repeatedly touching the figures and following their outlines. The most recent paintings, curiously, also include representations of the ships and weapons of the white men.

Tiwi art

The art of the Tiwi people, who live an isolated life on Bathurst and Melville Islands (NT), show very different themes and techniques. They created impressive woodcarvings, often depicting birds and spirits. Large and brightly painted burial poles played a part in their funerary ritual. They were also skilled in basketwork.

The advance of white civilisation ended the cultic association of art with myth and ritual, and the cosmic unity of the Aboriginal world was destroyed. The magical spells and secret rites have now been almost completely demythologised. The bark and acrylic paintings, woodcarving and basketwork produced by the Aborigines still show their innate feeling for colour and form, but they are now merely craft products without their former spiritual content. There are Aboriginal shops and art galleries everywhere, but most of the profit is now made by white dealers. Even the ceremonial dances are now mainly a tourist attraction, in which the magical rituals and songs are often deliberately falsified by the actors in order to escape the wrath of their ancestors of the Dreamtime.

Art of White Australia

In the early colonial period Australian art was indistinguishable from British art. It was not until the 1880s that the "Heidelberg school" which came into being in the Melbourne suburb of Heidelberg in the Yarra valley turned deliberately away from the academic painting of Europe. Tom Roberts, Frederick McCubbin, Arthur Streeton and other members of the group painted in an Impressionist style scenes of life in the Australian bush. The Hamburg-born painter Hans Heysen (1877–1968), who lived in Hahndorf, near Adelaide, painted scenes in the south Australian bush and landscapes in the Flinders Ranges. But Australian painters and sculptors still continued to look to Europe, and liked to stay in London. Among notable 20th century figures are George Russell Drysdale (1912–89), Sidney Nolan (1917–92), Arthur Boyd (b. 1920) and Albert Tucker (b. 1914).

Around the middle of the century, when Australia, conscious of its nationhood, was increasingly moving away from its attachment to the home country, Australian art rapidly developed towards independence. Private galleries and art dealers proliferated, particularly from the late sixties onwards. It became worthwhile to collect Australian art. Among well-known contemporary artists are the painters Brett Whiteley, Fred Williams and Jeffrey Smart and the sculptors Tom Bass, Inge King and Stephen Walker. The painter and sculptor Otto Herbert Hajek (b. 1927), of Czech origin, attracted much attention with his decoration (1973–77) of the Plaza of Adelaide's Festival Centre.

Galleries

The national art galleries have been prominent in supporting Australian art. A leading place is taken by the Australian National Gallery in Canberra, but the individual states also have excellent galleries housed in imposing 19th century buildings and financed both by public and by private funds (e.g. the Art Gallery of New South Wales in Sydney and

Baedeker Special

Convicts

The lookout high up in the crow's nest was the first to sight land. He, and many others on board, had been looking forward to this moment since leaving Plymouth more than three months ago. This was the beginning of European settlement in Australia: the arrival of the "First Fleet" in Botany Bay on January 18th 1788, bringing convicts sentenced to transportation from Britain and their guards.

The British government, alarmed by the increase of crime, had decided on this means of disposing of criminals who could not be accommodated in the country's overcrowded prisons and prison hulks. Transportation would rid Britain of its undesirables and at the same time would establish a British presence in a recently discovered continent which was thought to be ripe for settlement.

Many of the prisoners were petty offenders, but even petty offences frequently earned a sentence of death; but there was increasing reluctance to hang offenders for such offences, and more often than not the sentence was commuted to transportation for a term of seven or fourteen years.

Conditions on the convict transports were harsh and squalid in the extreme. The prisoners were herded below decks in crowded and bug-ridden quarters; disease was rife, and many died during the long voyage. And conditions in the penal colonies were no better: hard labour, brutal treatment, severe punishments for the least offence against discipline.

Some of the prisoners contrived, both during the voyage and in Australia, to get better treatment by submission to authority, and those with skills which were needed in the new colony could better themselves. Thus the talents of Francis Greenway, an architect sentenced to fourteen years' transportation in 1814 for forgery, were recognised by Governor Macquarie within a few months and in 1816 he was put in charge of designing and building all government works. The name of convict architecture is still applied to these buildings. For men like Greenway who used their skills and worked hard there was a future in Australia.

But only a minority of the 160,000 convicts transported to Australia did so well for themselves as Greenway. For most of them their journey ended in the penal colonies, condemned to hard and exhausting work, punished with heavy chains and the cat-o'-nine-tails for any real or imagined offence; those who tried to escape were usually rounded up, shot by the guards or sometimes killed by the Aborigines. Relatively few – the "emancipists" – lived out their sentence to become free citizens, running a farm or working in a trade.

In 1848 the government of New South Wales ceased to take in any more convicts, and other colonies followed. Only in Western Australia were convicts regarded for another two decades as a useful source of cheap labour.

For many years Australians were ashamed to admit to being descended from a convict. Nowadays, however, most of them, in the fifth or sixth generation, take pride in the convict ancestors to whom they owe their presence in Australia.

the Art Gallery of South Australia in Adelaide). In some cities the galleries are in modern cultural centres: e.g. the National Gallery of Victoria in the Melbourne Arts Centre, the Queensland Art Gallery in Brisbane's Cultural Centre. The Cultural Centre in Perth (WA) combines both old and modern buildings. There is also the New South Wales Museum of Contemporary Art in Sydney, opened in 1991, in an Art Deco building.

Art festivals

See Practical Information, Events

Architecture

Early building in Sydney

At the beginning of the colonial period the only accommodation was in tents, which were soon replaced by miserable wooden huts. In 1799 a two-storey residence was built for Governor John Hunter in Parramatta, at the west end of Port Jackson. This first Government House was enlarged and altered in 1815 by Governor Macquarie and remained the Governor's residence until the building of Government House in Sydney in 1847.

Convict architecture
(see Baedeker Special, p. 70)

During Macquarie's governorship (1809–21) broad new streets were planned and many public buildings in Georgian style were erected in Sydney. Among them were the "Rum Hospital" and other buildings by the convict architect Francis Howard Greenway, who was transported to Australia for forgery in 1814 but by 1816 had been appointed civil architect. He was responsible for designing, among other buildings, the Macquarie Lighthouse on South Head, the Hyde Park convict barracks, St James's Church, the portico of Old Government House in Parramatta, the present Conservatorium of Music (originally built as stables for New Government House), St Matthew's Church and the Courthouse in Windsor. In their perfect proportions and the harmony of their clear and simple forms these buildings reflect the optimistic attitudes of the early colonial period. On his journeys of inspection Macquarie gave orders for the erection of decent buildings in other settlements, particularly inns, churches and official buildings. But the cost of all this building was so high that the parsimonious and suspicious government in London sent out a commissioner, John Thomas Bigge, to enquire into and report on the situation (1819–21).

Early buildings in Tasmania

Many buildings both public and private have survived from pioneering days in Tasmania, the oldest settlement after Sydney, particularly in and around Hobart and Launceston and in the Midlands. What Greenway did for Sydney John Lee Archer, a free architect sent out from London, did for Tasmania. Between 1827 and 1838 he built barracks, bridges, churches and courthouses in and around Hobart and Launceston.

From imitation to independence

Australia's earliest architecture looked to British models, and builders at the other end of the world sought to build in as British a style as possible. The neo-Gothic, classical and Renaissance styles popular at home were reproduced in Australia, particularly in churches and public buildings. The ornate urban architecture of Victorian times was well suited to demonstrate the wealth won in the goldfields.

But Australia also went its own way, for example in the architecture of the tropical and subtropical north (Queensland). In these areas houses were built on stilts, with overhanging roofs to give shade and openings to allow the circulation of air, and fronted by verandahs and colonnades – a style well adapted to the hot, moist climate of summer. Characteristic of the period, in addition to the imposing mansions, elegant country houses and homesteads (farmhouses), are the terraced houses, with their richly decorated cast-iron railings and balustrades, found in many of the older suburbs of the cities, which in recent years have been lovingly restored.

A specifically Australian architecture in the 20th century

In the 20th century Australia has developed its own distinctive architecture, no longer based on British models. An early example of genuinely Australian architecture is Sydney Harbour Bridge, with the massive single arch which has earned it the name of the "Coathanger" and the piers at each end, higher than is structurally necessary. Completed in 1932, the bridge became the city's first great landmark, now rivalled by the world-famous Opera House, designed by the Danish architect Jørn Utzon, which took 14 years to build and cost ten times as much as the original estimate. Canberra has a number of impressive public buildings dating from the second half of the 20th century – the High Court, the National Library, the National Gallery, the Academy of Science and above all New Parliament House.

In recent decades the capitals of the other states have built impressive cultural centres such as Melbourne's Art Centre, Adelaide's Festival Hall and Brisbane's Cultural Centre.

In the central areas of the state capitals the skyline is now dominated by the high-rise buildings occupied by banks and business houses, for example the circular 48-storey Australia Square Tower in Sydney. The historic old buildings of the 19th century are now surrounded by functional buildings in concrete, aluminium amd reflective glass.

In recent years the great cities have been steadily expanding, covering the surrounding countryside with featureless and space-consuming detached houses and an elaborate infrastructure, interspersed with parks and gardens – for Australians like to have plenty of space. The streets are lined with uniform functional buildings, enlivened by the ever-present advertisements.

Literature

The beginnings (18th-19th c.)

The first literary work concerned with Australia, which at the beginning of the 19th century was still known as New Holland, was a short and not very good German novel, "Adventures on a Journey to New Holland" (1801), by Therese Huber. She was familiar with the story of the discovery of Australia through her first husband, Georg Forster, who along with his father Johann Reinhold Forster accompanied Cook on his second voyage in 1772–75 and in 1789 wrote an account of "New Holland and the British Colony in Botany Bay".

In addition to various accounts of travels and descriptions of the young colonies on Port Jackson and Norfolk Island the diaries of the various expeditions into the interior (Flinders, Sturt, Mitchell, Leichhardt, Eyre) are informative about conditions in Australia in the pioneering period.

Second half of 19th century

Genuinely Australian literary works, owing nothing to British models, began to appear only in the second half of the 19th century. Novels and short stories focused on local themes – convict life, the gold-diggers, the bushrangers, life on the great cattle and sheep farms. Among writers of this period were Henry Kingsley (1830–76), William Howitt (1792–1879), Marcus A. Clarke (1846–81), Rolf Boldrewood (real name Thomas Alexander Browne, 1826–1915), Catherine H. Spence (1825–1910) and Catherine E. Macauley Martin (1848–1937). The organ and mouthpiece of Australian novelists and poets was the Sydney weekly "Bulletin", founded in 1880 by J. F. Archibald and A. G. Stephens.

The availability of this means of publication led to a great upsurge of Australian literature from around 1890 to the outbreak of the First World War, in a mood of confidence and national feeling. Leading representatives of this "national" trend were Henry A. Lawson (1867–1922), Joseph Furphy (alias Tom Collins, 1843–1912; "Such is Life", 1903), William Astley (1855–1911), Arthur H. Davis (alias Steele Rudd, 1868–1935), Dowell O'Reilly (1865–1923), Randolf Bedford (1868–1941) and Barbara Baynton (1882–1929).

Poetry

Early Australian lyric poets were Charles Harpur (1813–68), Henry Kendall (1839–82) and Adam Lindsay Gordon (1833–70).

"The Banjo" (A. B . Paterson)

The publication of a collection of anonymous bush ballads by Andrew B. Paterson ("The Banjo") in 1905 brought wide popularity to this characteristically Australian type of popular song, celebrating the heroes and hardships of the pioneering period, natural events, bushrangers and outlaws. Paterson was the author of Australia's alternative national anthem, "Waltzing Matilda". His "Man of the Snowy River" also achieved great success.

Also popular were the poems of the politically active Dame Mary Jane Gilmore (1865–1962).

Henry Handel Richardson

Very different in subject matter were the historical and psychological novels of Henry Handel Richardson (real name Ethel Richardson, 1870–1946), who was born and brought up in Australia, studied music in Leipzig and then settled in London (trilogy "The Fortunes of Richard Mahoney").

Literature between the wars

Australian literature between the wars was concerned with nature, the Australian landscape and the myths of the Aborigines (the Jindyworobak movement). Originally the main concern was with rural life; later came descriptions of the cities and their slums. The national perspective merged into an international one. After the First World War there was a sharp quantitative increase in Australian literature, and Australian prose was enriched by new narrative techniques and a concern with existential problems. In her realistic novels of social criticism Katherine S. Prichard (1883–1970) made herself the advocate of the under-privileged working classes and the Aborigines. Vance Palmer (1885–1959) also depicted the class war. In "Capricornia" (1938), in which sequential narrative gives place to a multi-layered simultaneity, A. F. Xavier Herbert (1901–84) portrayed the wretched living conditions of the Aborigines.

Patrick White

On the Nobel Prize winner Patrick White, acclaimed as the "voice of Australia", see Famous People.

Contemporary literature

A well-known name among contemporary Australian writers is the best-selling author Colleen McCullough (b. 1937; "The Thorn Birds", 1977). In his novel "The Songlines" Bruce Chatwin introduces his readers to the bizarre world of the Aboriginal myths and the rootless life of the Aborigines.

It should also be mentioned that short stories and detective novels enjoy great popularity in Australia and that excellent children's books are produced.

Theatre

Drama

During the gold fever of the second half of the 19th century theatres provided entertainment in the newly prosperous towns. European (mainly British) actors and companies made frequent tours in Australia, but these were interrupted by the Second World War. In 1954 the Australian Elizabethan Theatre Trust was founded to promote the performing arts (theatre, opera, ballet, puppet theatre), and with the support of the Trust there came into being the Australian Opera, the Australian Ballet and the National Institute of Dramatic Art (NIDA), which was established in 1958 to train actors, directors and set-designers in association with the Theatre Trust, the national broadcasting corporation (ABC) and the University of New South Wales.

Opera

The Australian Opera was established by the Theatre Trust in 1956 through the amalgamation of the National Theatre Movement and the National Opera with the object of running annual tours to the Australian cities. It became independent in 1970 and is now based in the new Opera House in Sydney.

Ballet

The Australian Ballet was established in 1962 with Dame Peggy van Praagh as director, a role in which she was succeeded by Sir Robert

Helpmann (1909–86) in 1974. The Sydney Dance Company, founded in 1965 for the training of ballet dancers as the Dance Company of New South Wales, became in 1971 the first professional ballet company in New South Wales, which under its director Graeme Murphy performs in the Sydney Opera House and has also carried out some very successful tours abroad,

The Aboriginal Islander Dance Theatre was founded in 1975 to train dancers. It concentrates particularly on the dances and cultural traditions of the Aborigines and the Torres Strait Islanders.

Festivals

See Practical Information, Events

Film

The first short films shown in Australia were part of a variety show in the Melbourne Opera House in 1896. In the same year Australia's first cinema was opened in Sydney (in Pitt Street), making it the fourth country in the world with a cinema (after France, the United States and Germany).

The first short film scenes were also shot round Sydney in 1896. In 1897 Joseph Perry, an officer of the Salvation Army in Melbourne, began to produce films with a plot, among them "Soldiers of the Cross". The first full-length film, "The Story of the Kelly Gang", was shot in Melbourne in 1906, and by 1914 almost 100 films had been produced in Australia. After the First World War Australian films were largely displaced by British and American films, and after the Second World War the federal government subsidised the production of documentary films, though these were always subject to state control. Then in 1968 an independent body, the Australian Film Institute, was established to promote Australian films.

Among successful Australian films, many of them popular abroad as well as in Australia, have been "Gallipoli", "The Last Wave", "Picnic at Hanging Rock", "My Brilliant Career", "The Man from Snowy River", "Mad Max", "The Road Warrior", "Careful, He Might Hear You" and above all "Crocodile Dundee".

The Australian Film, Television and Radio School was founded in 1973, the independent Australian Film Commission in 1975.

Film festivals

See Practical Information, Events

Music

Music of the Aborigines

The music of the Aborigines, harking back to prehistoric times, gives some impression of what the music of early human society must have been like. Music and dance are closely bound up with myth and worship, and the deliberate incomprehensibility of the singing is in keeping with its ritual content. The singing is accompanied by simple instruments – boomerangs, wooden batons and above all the didgeridoo, a wind instrument consisting of a wooden tube over 3 feet long.

Symphony orchestras

The Australian Broadcasting Corporation (ABC), established in 1983 as successor to the Australian Broadcasting Commission founded in 1932, maintains six symphony orchestras created in the six states between 1946 (Sydney Symphony Orchestra, enlarged from the Sydney Orchestra) and 1950 (Western Australia Symphony Orchestra).

Chamber music

Musica Viva, a chamber music group, gave its first concert in the Sydney Conservatorium of Music in 1945. It was the forerunner of a chamber music movement which spread over the whole of Australia and now has over 9000 members and an annual programme of more than 2000 concerts.

Music festivals

See Practical Information, Events

Aussie Rock and Pop

Thunder from Down Under

As in the rest of the western world, Australian interest in music is concentrated mainly on American light music. The government regulation requiring all radio stations to include at least 20% of Australian music in their programmes has made little difference, since the best-known Australian artistes now sound very American or British.

Quiet beginnings

The triumph of rock'n'roll in the fifties and early sixties produced a host of Elvis Presley imitators, who with the exception of Johnny O'Keefe have now fallen into well-deserved oblivion. Among his successes was "Real Wild Child" (1958), recently revived by Iggy Pop. The stars of the early beat boom were Billy Thorpe and the Aztecs. Although thirty years later Billy Thorpe still has a large and faithful public, he is practically unknown outside Australia.

The Bee Gees and Easyfever

Then in 1967, with a shot from both barrels, Australia conquered the hit parades of the world with two worldwide hits, the Easybeats' "Friday On My Mind" and the Bee Gees' "Massachusetts". By then both groups were teenagers' idols in Australia, and Easyfever was the Australian equivalent of Beatlemania elsewhere.

The Bee Gees are still among the best-known groups in the business. Kings of schmaltz in the late sixties and ten years later pioneers of the disco wave with their soundtrack for "Saturday Night Fever", the Gibb brothers are still producing new and appealing trivialities. It is all too easy to forget how brilliant their first three long-play records were and how timeless such songs as "New York Mining Disaster" and "To Love Somebody" are. Who now remembers that they once wrote Uwe Ochsenknecht's hit "Only One Woman" for The Marbles?

Easybeats

The Easybeats were not so lucky. In spite of nine excellent long-play records they were never able to repeat their international hit. But the

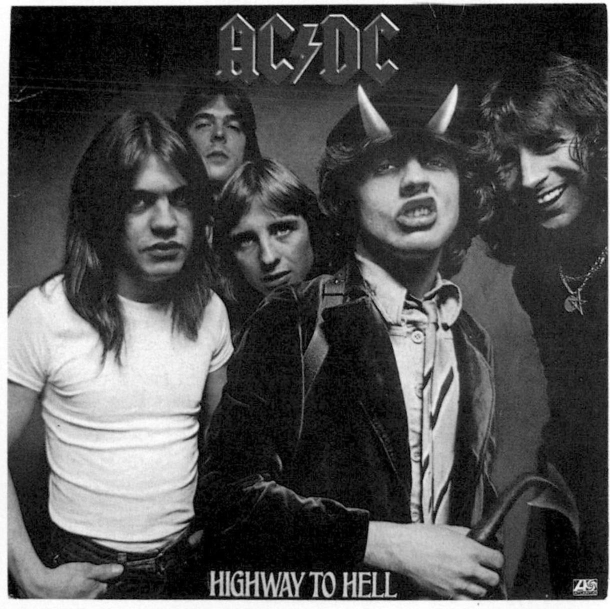

An AC/DC record sleeve of 1979

two song-writers for the Easybeats, Harry Vanda and George Young, are still the Australian counterparts to Lennon and McCartney. Of the numerous pseudonyms under which they have published the best known is Flash and the Pan. Among the groups they have started off on their careers are AC/DC and the still harder-sounding Rose Tattoo.

Oz sound

Innumerable groups influenced by the hard sound of the Rolling Stones and Pretty Things alarmed the suburbs in the mid sixties. The Master's Apprentices, the Missing Links and the Purple Hearts laid the foundations of the uncompromisingly hard "Oz sound". Bands such as Buffalo, Skyhooks, The Saints, Radio Birdman and the early AC/DC continued this tradition, so that by 1977 punk rock did not sound particularly revolutionary to Australian ears. There was always a minority market for rasping sound and crude attitudes.

During the seventies mainstream jazz returned to Anglo-American models – lightweight melody from the Little River Band and later from Air Supply, harder sounds from Cold Chisel, Roxy music borrowings from Icehouse, white reggae from Jo Jo Zep and the Falcons, and of course Sherbet, the Australian ABBA. The television programme in which the nation was introduced to the latest hits was "Countdown".

New trends in the eighties

Apart from the Little River Band no new artistes of international fame came to the fore until the eighties. In 1982 Men at Work achieved a hit with "I Come from the Land . . . Down Under", which ranks along with "Friday On My Mind" as the most widely known Australian song – alway excepting "Waltzing Matilda". INXS ("In Excess") established themselves as international top sellers, though dismissed by the envious as a poor imitation of U 2. Midnight Oil, the group centred on the bald-headed giant Peter Garret, has, musically, little new to offer, but the elements of social criticism in their lyrics have brought them a reputation as the conscience of Australian rock. They are neither the first nor the only people to speak out publicly for the rights of the Aborigines, but they are undoubtedly the loudest critics of the Australian perception of history.

AC/DC

AC/DC celebrated twenty years on the stage in 1993, This band, with "Easybeat" George Young's younger brothers, is the most reliable in Australia. At first labelled as punks because of their lack of style and later, no less inappropriately, assigned to the heavy metal camp, they are now the grey eminences of rock-hard sound, though after 1980 they had to come to terms with the loss of their trademark, the gravelly voice of Bon Scott, who was brought down by alcohol and inadequately replaced by the English singer Brian Johnson.

The independent scene

In a country of sixteen million inhabitants a hit does not mean immediate big money; but it is possible by constant appearances on the club scene to build up a regional reputation which guarantees a band's financial survival even if the sale of records does not come up to expectations. Although punk and New Wave caused less of a shock in Australia than in the rest of the world, new groups also proliferated here, among them the Sports, the Divinyls, Mental as Anything and the Finn brothers' Split Enz from New Zealand. The Finns' real breakthrough, however, came when they broke up Split Enz, with its relatively complex sound, and launched Crowded House. The forefathers of hard Australian guitar rock are Radio Birdman, whose declared models were Iggy Pop's Stooges and MC 5, and the Saints. Both of these bands toured Britain in 1977, and with their complete command of their instruments stole the show from all the local punk bands. The Saints scored a great commercial success with their hit "I'm Stranded" and, with a different team, are still active – though their music has now distinctly lost its bite.

Radio Birdman

Radio Birdman shared the fate of the Easybeats and broke up in 1979, but they are still one of the few bands with a cult following. Their original records are now beyond price, and their name is regularly mentioned when American grunge bands are asked who their models are. Over the years the founding members of the group – Deniz Tek, Rob Younger, Chris Masuak and Warwick Gilbert – kept turning up with new bands that were among the best in Australia: the Hitmen, New Race and the Screaming Tribesmen, to name only the most important. This sound, which combines hard instrumental tone in moderate tempo with polished vocal harmonies – and yet has nothing at all to do with heavy metal stereotypes – is also characteristic of the Lime Spiders, the Trilobites, the Celibate Rifles, the Hoodoo Gurus, the Exploding White Mice, the Stems and the Scientists, who were always ready to experiment and cannot therefore be precisely classified. Even musical louts like the Hard-Ons and the Cosmic Psychos have something that puts them ahead of the international competition. Gentler in sound, partly inspired by folk music and partly by psychedelic models are such groups as The Church, Died Pretty, the Triffids, the Go-Betweens, the Tymaround and the Chills, though this last group vehemently insists on its New Zealand origins. In spite of unmistakable reminiscences of the Beatles, Byrds, Doors or the Velvet Underground the music of these groups is not nostalgic. It sounds more like an up-to-date development of trends which elsewhere had fallen into oblivion. In the Beasts of Bourbon – the very name is a programme – Australia produced an outstanding rhythm and blues band which took up where the Rolling Stones after "Exile on Main Street" had left off. Their singer, Tex Perkins, has recently formed the Cruel Sea group, which is Australia's great hope for the future. Less catchy and distinctly gloomy are the musical experiments of the Hunters and Collectors and the Birthday Party, whose singer Nick Cave moved to Europe and had a great success with his group Bad Seeds. The variety and the high standard of quality of the Australian independent scene are so astonishing that it is possible here to mention only those groups which have been sold worldwide by international firms. Unfortunately none of them have achieved the great breakthrough. This is partly because Australian musicians are known to be uncompromising and stubborn; but it is evident also that they have become resigned to their fate. For thirty years Australian artistes have been trying to break into the international market; but so few have managed this that most of them nowadays would rather remain stars in their own continent than fail in America or Europe.

Today's bands

At the moment Jimmy Barnes has set out on this hazardous game. He has left his group, Cold Chisel, at the height of its success after himself becoming the superstar of the nineties in Australia with his native mainstream rock. Although he can fill stadiums in Australia he is now working his way round Europe, happy if he can get a paying audience of 500. In the very recent past the Black Sorrows, Diesel, the Screaming Jets and Daryl Braith Waite have achieved international success; but, significantly, they have done this with music which is as good as their Anglo-American models but is practically indistinguishable from them. A special position is occupied by the Clouds, for whom the international specialist press has prophesied a great future. They mingle catchy popular tunes with multi-rhythmed music to create a sound which is not only interesting and exciting but is also independent and distinctive.

Aboriginal rock

For far too long the musical heritage of the Aborigines was ignored, and it was only in 1985 that an Aboriginal band, Coloured Stone, had a chance to denounce the Australian way of life from their point of view with such titles as "No More Boomerang" or "Island of Greed". The main influence on them, apart from their native music, was reggae. A small sensation was created by the Yothu Yindi ("Mother and Child") group, whose band-leader, Manadawuy Yunupingu, is the first Aborigine with academic qualifications. They have conquered the dance floors of the western world with their mixture of traditional Aboriginal music, funk and rock and have given unprecedented popularity to archaic instruments such as the didgeridoo.

It is very much to be hoped that some of Australia's promising newcomers will win international recognition. Australian music has much more to offer than INXS, Midnight Oil or Kylie Minogue. We need only take the trouble to listen.

Media

Almost all Australians listen to the radio, watch television and read the newspapers. The freedom of the press and freedom of speech are guaranteed by law; and publishing of both newspapers and books is in private hands and free from state regulation. The extensive network of radio and television services is partly publicly run, partly private and partly non-profit-making. In the large cities the difficulty is to choose between the many channels on offer, while in the outback and in extensive farming areas the services available are much more limited.

Radio

Radio services began in 1923, when they were provided by private agencies. Public service broadcasting began in 1932 with the establishment of the Australian Broadcasting Commission, which later became the Australian Broadcasting Corporation (ABC). Commercial stations are now steadily increasing in number (in 1990 there were 170), as is the competition between them and with the public service stations. The ABC is financed by the state and is not allowed to transmit advertisements; the licence fee was abolished in 1974. A second public service system was established in 1975, the Special Broadcasting Service (SBS), which transmits programmes from Sydney and Melbourne for the non-English-speaking minorities in a total of 54 languages. A third group of public broadcasting stations (79 in 1990) provides services on regional and local level. These depend largely on volunteer staff and transmit programmes of adult and further education, music and ethnic programmes for Aborigines and particular immigrant groups. These stations are financed by voluntary contributions, membership fees and state subsidies; they are not allowed to accept advertisements.

Television

The first television transmissions in Australia were in 1956. There are now over 50 commercial stations as well as a public service, ABN Channel 2, which co-operates with commercial suppliers. The first television station run by Aborigines for Aborigines, Imparja TV, began transmitting from Alice Springs in 1988. The introduction of satellite technology (Australia's own AUSSAT, membership of Intelsat) has further commercialised the telecommunications business.

The press

Australia's first newspaper, the "Sydney Gazette and New South Wales Advertiser", appeared on March 5th 1803, published by the government and edited by George Howe. This was followed in October 1824 by the first privately-owned weekly, the "Australian", and in 1831 by the "Sydney Herald". The privately run Australian press has never been subject to any form of state control. Since the First World War there has been a steady concentration of ownership combined with a fall in standards. The many formerly independent newspapers, periodicals and magazines now belong to a small number of media groups, which have also bought up radio and television companies.

The Australian media mogul Rupert Murdoch (b. 1931 in Melbourne) became an American citizen so that he could extend his empire to the United States. Starting with the Adelaide "News" which he had inherited, he built up his News Corporation into a gigantic international business (newspapers and periodicals, publishing, television, film studios, property and financial firms all over the world). In recent years there have been violent and sometimes surprising shifts and changes in the Australian media market, and there will undoubtedly be further changes.

Traditions and Festivals

Aboriginal customs: now tourist attractions

The traditional customs of the Aborigines have long become tourist attractions. Their ceremonial dances (corroborees) and songs, formerly taboo for non-initiates, are now, like the arts and crafts of the Aborigines, the highlights of package tours, particularly in the Northern Territory, as examples of Stone Age traditions. Body painting and decoration with feathers were originally part of the sacred ritual. The dances are performed to the accompaniment of the didgeridoo and a recital, deliberately incomprehensible, of traditional myths and songs. When the cosmic conceptions of the Aborigines were still intact these dances renewed the creative activities of the Dreamtime ancestors or formed part of rites of initiation into the community. The Australian government is concerned to assimilate the now rootless Aborigines, but also recognises that they are also an important constituent in Australia's multi-cultural society. Their traditions and their art, therefore, must be preserved, and not solely in museums.

British traditions

Founded as British colonies, the Australian states have preserved some features of British life, even in the very different climate and natural conditions of Australia. In the heat of the Australian summer the streets and shopping arcades are still gay with Christmas decorations, and conservative families still celebrate the festival with turkey and plum pudding. Even in the matter of dress the Australians are still conventional: however common the leisure look on the beach and in suburban gardens, formal wear is prescribed in city offices and at dinner parties. A jacket and tie are essential for evening outings, in restaurants, clubs and casinos.

Immigrant traditions

Groups of non-British immigrants soon began to add colour to the Australian scene. German communiities in South Australia have preserved many of the customs of their homeland: thus in Hahndorf there is an annual "Schuetzenfest" (Marksmen's Festival) in January, with folk dancing, brass bands and much consumption of beer. The Cornish miners who came to the Yorke Peninsula (SA) in 1868, too, have preserved their own customs, and in May in alternate (odd-numbered) years celebrate their traditional Kernewek Lowender festival, with Cornish dancing, Cornish pasties and a wheelbarrow race.

Large numbers of Chinese immigrants came to Australia during the gold rush, living quietly and working hard, thereby falling into disfavour with their white competitors and leading to the adoption of the "White Australia" policy. The Chinese Australians, however, still retain their feeling of community: almost every city has its Chinatown, and the Chinese New Year is celebrated with colourful processions and fireworks.

The cultural pattern of Australia has been enriched by the immigration of many different races. The open immigration policy of the postwar years have made Australia a multi-cultural society, a melting-pot of nations. The racist "White Australia" policy and the obligatory assimilation of immigrants are things of the past. Many immigrants, particularly from the Mediterranean countries, came to Australia in a process of "chain migration" in which the first immigrants invited other members of their family and friends to join them, thus preserving the connection with their homeland and its way of life. Whole districts of the cities were taken over by different nationalities with their own customs, their own dances and costumes and their own gastronomic preferences.

Baedeker Special

Boomerangs

We usually think of boomerangs as instruments which when thrown return to the hand of the thrower. In fact, however, there are two types of boomerang: one which returns to the thrower and the other which after hitting its target falls to the ground. The original function of the boomerang was its use as a weapon in hunting or fighting; but it was also used as a multi-purpose implement, for throwing, digging, boring, scraping and many other uses.

Pieces of wood bent in a greater or lesser curve were in use at a very early period. Remains of aerodynamically shaped pieces of wood which are believed to date back 10,000 years or more have been found in Australia. The value attached to boomerangs is shown by the fact that they were used in cultic and ceremonial activities and were among the grave goods deposited with the dead. They also served as musical instruments, for the Aborigines still strike two boomerangs together to set the rhythm for their dances.

It is not known who gave the boomerang its name. It seems fairly certain that it was not the Aborigines, for the word does not occur in any of their 200 dialects. It has been suggested that it was derived from the term *burramanga* or *woomera* used in the Hunter Valley. It is certain at any rate that the invention of the boomerang came about by chance. There is no mystery about the physics of the boomerang: if a piece of wood is given a particular curved form and hollowed out on the underside it will follow an elliptical course and return to somewhere near its starting-point.

The combination of throwing speed and turning speed makes the boomerang a dangerous weapon. The Aborigines were able to throw a non-returning boomerang for distances of 200 yards or more without any difficulty. A skilled operator could hit an animal – preferably on the head – with such force that it was stunned and could then be finished off on the ground.

The Aborigines used a great variety of woods to make boomerangs, either returning or non-returning. Nowadays, when they are mostly used for sport, they are also made of laminated wood; and in sporting contests they may also be made of materials totally unknown to the Aborigines in the past – aluminium, plastic or even glass fibre. Often, too, they are weighted with lead to make them fly better over long distances.

The Aborigines devoted much attention to the decoration of boomerangs. After carefully finishing the surface they ornamented it with geometric patterns and sacred symbols from their mythology; for they believed that boomerangs, like so much else, stemmed from the world of Dreamtime, the origin of all existence.

Annual events

Each state has a full programme of annual events and festivals, like the day of the Melbourne Cup in the district of Flemington, Australia's most important horse race (a public holiday in Victoria). At the beginning of the Australian spring the football season ends with the Grand Final in Melbourne. In March there is the Moomba Festival in Melbourne, a carnival with a huge parade, amusement booths and fireworks. The most important sporting event in Sydney is the yacht race to Hobart on Boxing Day (December 26th); with the start of the race in Sydney a lively festival begins in Hobart. The Adelaide Arts Festival, regarded by many as *the* cultural event of the continent, has been held since 1960 in alternate (even-numbered) years. Another major sporting event is the Grand Prix for Formula 1 cars, hitherto held in Adelaide and in future to be held in Melbourne. Among Australian folk festivals are the German Schuetzenfest in Hahndorf (SA) and various wine festivals, particularly in the Barossa Valley (WA). Smaller towns too have local festivals which attract many visitors, for example the Begonia Festival in the old gold-digging town of Ballarat (VIC). Country music fans make the pilgrimage to Tamworth (NSW) for the Country Music Awards Festival. Townsville (QLD) has the Pacific Festival, a mixture of entertainment, sport and art.

The most unusual and craziest events are celebrated in the Northern Territory. Among the best-known sporting events are the Camel Cup race (Alice Springs), the Henley-on-Todd Regatta, with bottomless boats propelled by foot power, and the Beer Can Regatta in Darwin, with boats cobbled together from beer cans.

This is merely the briefest selection out of the innumerable events and festivals celebrated all over the continent. For a fuller listing, see Practical Information, Events.

Public holidays

Among officially recognised public holidays are the traditional Christian festivals, with the exception of Christmas Eve and Whitsun.

Australia Day

Australia's national day is Australia Day on January 26th, the anniversary of the arrival of the First Fleet in 1788. For the Aborigines this is a day of mourning on which they remember the beginning of the destruction of their culture and the loss of their land.

In addition to this national holiday the individual states celebrate the anniversary of their foundation: thus Western Australia has its Foundation Day in June, South Australia its Proclamation Day at the end of December. Labour Day is celebrated on different dates in the various states, in Western Australia and Victoria in March, in Queensland in May, in New South Wales, South Australia and the Australian Capital Territory in October. The Queen's birthday is celebrated in June, as in Britain, except in Western Australia, where it falls in September or October.

Anzac Day

An important day throughout Australia is Anzac Day on April 25th, a big occasion for ex-servicemen. There are numerous parades at war memorials commemorating the many members of the Australia and New Zealand Army Corps (Anzac) who fell in the Gallipoli landings on April 25th 1915 and the dead of the Second World War, the Korean War and the Vietnam War.

A feature of the Australian festival calendar is that holidays falling in the middle of the week are moved to Monday or Friday so as to make possible the long holiday weekends so popular in this leisure-oriented society.

Sport and Adventure

Games, sport and competitive activities are part of the Australian way of life. The typical Australian is a keen sportsman – whether he keeps

Baedeker Special

Adventure in the Outback

There is no signpost anywhere in Australia pointing to the outback. There is no need for one, because anyone who wants to go to this region of desolation, drought, dust and pitiless sun in the heart of Australia knows where it is. And what about the others? "They should stay where they are!" grates John MacIntire. Then the 48-year-old Irishman from Ulster screws up the sharp little eyes under his bushy eyebrows and goes on: "What is there for them here? Its too hot for them." What he really means is that the fewer of these fellows come here the more there is for those already there. He means the "bloody greenhorns" who kit themselves out in a department store and set out to look for gold.

Gold: that was the magic word that worked like a magnet in the second half of the 19th century and attracted thousands of men to this desolate country with its salt-pans, knee-high scrub and long-dried-up rivers. A man must surely be crazy to come voluntarily to this dreary waste. Many who have come here have been driven by despair, perhaps after some failure in life, but often, too, they have been drawn by the hope of a find which would allow them to live in comfort and ease for the rest of their days.

It is sometimes said that the outback is the real Australia. Extending in a broad swathe across the continent from Perth to Brisbane, it is one of the richest sources of raw materials in the world. Sitting of an evening at his small camp fire in front of his even smaller tent, John MacIntire talks of a minister from Arizona who abandoned his parish one day, leaving a note for his flock on the kitchen table. "He turned up here with a shovel and a riddle under his arm, waving a digging permit he'd got in Coolgardie for a few bloody dollars, and then he began to dig like he was a mole . . ."

The minister didn't last long, and soon returned to the bosom of the Church. That is why John likes to tell the story. "He found too much dirt," he says with a wide grin, referring to the overburden, which is always many times heavier than any gold that is found.

There are many ghost towns in the outback with the remains of fallen-in mine shafts. They grew up overnight, and were as quickly abandoned when the gold-bearing seams were worked out. The desert sand gradually covers the ruins of the buildings and the wooden crosses in the little cemeteries. All that remains is a faint memory of a time when a mere rumour was enough to bring a pack of gold-hungry prospectors within 48 hours. Most of them were after a quick lucky strike: patience was not one of their virtues.

"You can smell gold!" asserts John, pulling with two fingers at his ear lobe and at the same time rubbing his outsize nose. "You must have a nose for it, otherwise all you find in this bloody country is dirt." Not long ago, apparently, John's nose stood him in good stead when he found a few nuggets in his claim which together weighed a good eight ounces on the government purchasing agent's scales and brought John something like 2300 dollars of hard-earned money. He invested a good deal of the money in the liquid so necessary in this hot and arid country; but unfortunately the alcohol content turned out to be a few degrees too high and John collected three days in the county jail. They said I was drunk and disorderly. Me!" he says, crossing himself with an air of injured innocence. Then he admits that he he had been beaten in a drinking match with a "bloody nobody", though only after seventeen ponies, as the quarter-litre beer mugs are called here.

Pioneering days: diggers in the outback

There are thousands of adventurers like John in the outback, always on the lookout for a fast buck. "You can get bloody rich here," says John. But sometimes you don't. Some spend their lives looking for gold, finding only enough to keep them digging. Adventurers all, with gaunt faces marked by privation and dusty, sun-tanned skin. And when they go back where they came from others arrive to take their place.

But it is not only gold and precious stones that you find in the outback; there are other precious metals as well – lead, nickel and high-grade iron ore, which is worked in the Hamersley Range. Fully 30 million tons are exported annually to Japan, the United States and Europe. To transport the ore a 426km/265 mile long railway line was built from Newman, in the heart of the outback, to Port Hedland. It is estimated that the reserves of ore will last at least another half-century.

But the outback is not only a land of gold-diggers and iron-miners: it is a land of huge flocks of sheep and herds of cattle. And the land, too, of the dingoes, the small desert dogs which break into the sheep-pens at night out of sheer blood-lust and kill dozens of sheep. To keep them under control there are regularly employed dingo-hunters paid by the government; and some years ago a fence thousands of kilometres long was driven across the continent to keep them out. Much more effective, however, was the work of the dingo-hunters, using traps, poison and guns. Attempts to domesticate the dingoes and use them as police dogs were unsuccessful.

When night drops down over the outback the few bars fill up, and the drinkers at the rough-hewn bar counters fantasise about what they will do when they make the big find. "Then," says John, "just wait to see how quickly I get out of this bloody country!"

himself in training and is an active member of one of the country's innumerable sports clubs, or merely cheers on his club from the stand or the terraces, or contents himself with watching horse and dog racing and other sporting events on television.

There are over 130 national sports organisations and thousands of regional and local clubs, which are particularly active in the suburbs of the cities. All over the country elderly men and women in their white "uniforms" can be seen engaged in lawn bowling. Other favourite sports are rugby and association football, baseball, hockey, cricket, golf and tennis. The most popular team sport in summer, and the one attracting most spectators, is cricket.

Football

Four types of football are played in Australia: rugby union, rugby league, Australian rules football (similar to Gaelic football; first played in Melbourne in 1856 and originally known as Victoria rules) and association football, which has become more popular since the Second World War as a result of the influx of immigrants from Europe.

Tennis

Australia's top tennis players have made great international names for themselves. The world-famed Australian Open tournament was first held in Melbourne in 1905 as the Australian Singles Championship.

Horse-racing

Horse-racing has a long tradition in Australia. The first official race was run in Sydney in 1810. The race for the Melbourne Cup, Australia's best-known sporting event, has been run annually since 1861; the prize money is now at least a million Australian dollars. The first Tuesday in November, the day on which it is run, is a public holiday in Victoria, and at 2 o'clock on that day all eyes in Australia are on Melbourne. Horse-racing also satisfies the Australian passion for betting, and book-makers and totalisators (an Australian invention) have an annual turn-over of more than 4 billion Australian dollars.

Gambling and betting

Gambling and betting have now become respectable in Australia. Every small town has a betting office, and gaming machines are found all over the place. The first legal casino in Australia was opened in Hobart (Wrest Point Casino) and has since had many imitators (Adelaide, Melbourne, Perth, Darwin, Alice Springs, Surfers Paradise).

Two-up

The favourite Australian gambling game is two-up. Two coins (usually old copper pennies) are thrown up in the air and the punters bet on heads or tails. If the first throw does not produce two of the same, the throw is repeated until it does. This very simple game was played in the goldfields of the 19th century and on the battlefields of the 20th, and fortunes have been lost at it. Two-up is also played in the casinos, but it is mostly played illegally in clandestine two-up "schools" in which the State does not get its cut.

Betting on animals

Although most money is betted on horses and greyhounds Australians will also bet on almost any kind of animal race (cows, goats, pigs, lizards, frogs and toads).

Outdoor recreations

Most Australians live fairly close to the sea, and the beaches along the coast (as well as on lakes and rivers) are popular holiday and leisure destinations. Swimming, surfing, sailing and diving are all popular recreations.

Important figures on the long Australian beaches, which often have a dangerous undertow or heavy surf, are the lifeguards who patrol the most popular beaches, warning swimmers of possible dangers from jellyfish, sharks, dangerous currents or storm tides and rescuing those who get into trouble. The races, regattas and dry-land exercises in which the lifeguards take part are a great entertainment for both spectators and participants.

Other popular outdoor activities are angling, fishing and barbecue picnics, either round a camp-fire or in one of the many picnic areas equipped with gas-fired barbecues. During periods of drought with a high risk of fire there is usually a ban on open fires, with heavy penalties for offenders.

Australians National Hymn

Waltzing Matilda

Once a jolly swagman camped by a billabong,
Under the shade of a coolibah tree,
And he sang as he watched and waited till his billy boiled
Who'll come a-waltzing Matilda with me?

Down came a jumbuck to drink at the billabong;
Up jumped the swagman and grabbed him with glee.
And he sang as he shoved that jumbuck in his tucker-bag,
You'll come a-waltzing Matilda with me.

Up rode a squatter, mounted on his thoroughbred;
Down came the troopers, one, two, three;
Whose' that jolly jumbuck you've got in your tucker-bag?
You'll come a-waltzing Matilda with me!

Up jumped the swagman and sprang into the billabong;
"You'll never catch me alive!" said he;
And his ghost may be heard as you pass by that billabong.
You'll come a-waltzing Matilda with me!

Published by Andrew Barton "The Banjo" Paterson in "Saltbush Bill", 1917

Going bush

Many Australians, particularly the young, are enthusiasts for the "back to nature" movement. Out of a desire for adventure, or merely to escape from the monotony of life in the suburbs, many of them "go bush" for the weekend, their holidays or a longer period. This desire to get out into the arid wide open spaces of the interior is catered for by special bush shops, which supply the equipment required for bush camping, bush walking and survival training in the outback. The quest for freedom in the wilderness has revived interest in the old bush ballads of Andrew Paterson ("The Banjo": see Famous People), in particular the ever-popular "Waltzing Matilda". It is the tale of a swagman, an itinerant labourer or sheep-shearer, who is sitting by a billabong (water-hole) waiting for his billy to boil when a jumbuck (lamb) comes down to drink. He grabs it and puts it in his tucker-bag, and just then along comes the sheep-farmer, supported by three troopers. The swagman jumps into the billabong to escape arrest; and now his ghost can be heard as you pass the billabong singing "You'll come a-waltzing, Matilda, with me!" In the course of a nation-wide debate on a national anthem for Australia a referendum was held in 1977 in which "Waltzing Matilda" got roughly the same number of votes as "God save the Queen". The winner, with 44% of the votes, was "Advance, Australia Fair", a song written in 1878 which was proposed as the national anthem in 1974 by Prime Minister Gough Whitlam and after being withdrawn by Malcolm Fraser was finally adopted as Australia's anthem by Robert Hawke.

Australia from A to Z

In view of the immense extent of the Australian continent the descriptive part of this guide is divided into eight sections (see below), arranged in alphabetical order, covering the six states and two territories of the Commonwealth of Australia, shown on the following map.

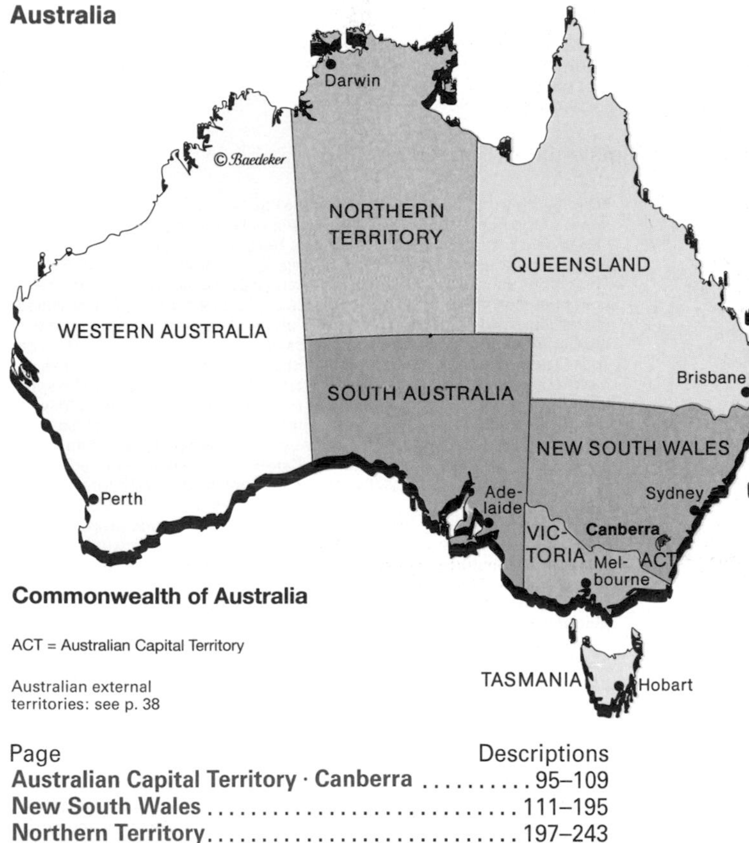

Australian external territories: see p. 38

◄ *Devil's Marbles (Northern Territory)*

Suggested Routes

It is perfectly easy to tour Australia with a sturdy car or motorcycle. All the major scenic beauties can be reached on roads or gravel tracks. Tourist offices in towns and country townships and visitor centres in the National Parks can supply good maps and detailed descriptions of the various districts; and with the help of the large map at the end of this guide individual routes or round trips can easily be worked out.

Warning

Between November and March travellers in northern Queensland and the Northern Territory may find their plans upset by heavy rain and the resultant flooding.

Australian Highlights (about 12,000km/7450 miles)

Sydney – Pacific coast – Brisbane – Great Barrier Reef – Cairns (about 3100km/ 1925 miles)

From **Sydney** the route runs north on the Pacific Highway, with magnificent views of the Pacific coast, to **Newcastle** and **Port Macquarie** on the Pacific Ocean. Then along the coast via **Coffs Harbour** to **Cape Byron**, the most easterly point in Australia. Beyond this is the **Gold Coast**, with Surfers Paradise. A short distance north is the city of **Brisbane**. From here the route continues north along the coast. A side trip can be made to **Fraser Island**, the largest sand island in the world. The road then runs along the coast of the Coral Sea, sheltered by the **Great Barrier Reef**. Places of interest on the coast are **Bundaberg**, **Gladstone** and **Rockhampton**, from which there are fascinating boat trips to the Great Barrier Reef Marine Park and **Keppel Island**. From Rockhampton the Bruce Highway continues north to **Mackay and Airlie Beach**, from which the numerous islands in the Whitsunday Archipelago can be visited. Then by way of **Townsville** and **Mission Beach** (rewarding side trip to Dunk Island) to **Cairns**, an excellent base from which to explore the world's largest coral reef and the tropical rain forest.

Cairns – Mount Isa – Darwin – Kakadu National Park (about 3000km/ 1865 miles)

From Cairns the route runs up to the **Atherton Tablelands**, from which a side trip should be made to the **Millaa Millaa Falls**. Then by way of **Mount Garnet** and **Mount Surprise** to the imposing **Undurra Lava Tubes**. Next, to the west, come **Georgetown**, **Croydon** and **Normantown**, the centre of the Gulf Country. From here the route runs south to **Cloncurry** and then west to **Mount Isa**, one of the largest mining settlements in Australia. From Mount Isa the Barkley Highway continues west into the Northern Territory; then at Barkley Roadhouse the route turns north on to the **Barkley Tableland** and at Balbirini turns west again and comes to **Daly Waters**, famed for its pub and a nearby gold-mine. From here the Stuart Highway runs north to **Mataranka** and **Katherine**, from which side trips can be made to the **Katherine Gorge** and **Kakadu National Park**. Then on to **Darwin**, Australia's most northerly city.

Darwin – Alice Springs – Ayers Rock – Adelaide (about 3600km/ 2235 miles)

From Darwin we follow the Stuart Highway south, crossing the **Sturt Plain**, passing **Lake Woods** and coming finally to **Tennant Creek**, on the north-western slopes of the **Murchison Range**. To the south of the hills are the **Devil's Marbles**. Some hours' drive farther south is **Alice Springs**, the "oasis in the heart of Australia". From here there are attractive excursions to **Simpsons Gap National Park** and the **MacDonnell Ranges** to the west, with **Ormiston Gorge**, **Finke Gorge** and **Kings Canyon National Park**. From Alice Springs the route continues through the "Red Heart" of Australia to **Ayers Rock** and the **Olgas**. We then return to the Stuart Highway and follow it south through the **Musgrave Ranges** to **Coober Pedy**, famed for its opals, in the **Stuart Ranges**. From here the route runs south through the desert and past the **Woomera** rocket range (closed military area) to **Port Augusta**, at the northern tip of Spencer Gulf. From here it is worth making a side trip north-east into the **Flinders Ranges**. To the south of Port Augusta is the imposing **Mount Remarkable**, and beyond this the little towns of **Clare** and **Gawler**. Then on to **Adelaide**, capital of South Australia, from which excursions can be made to the **Barossa Valley** and **McLaren Vale**, famed for their wine, and to **Kangaroo Island**.

Adelaide – Melbourne – Canberra – Sydney (about 2000km/ 1240 miles)

From Adelaide the Princes Highway runs south-east along Encounter Bay and **Coorong National Park** to **Kingston** and **Mount Gambier** with its crater lake. From here a side trip can be made to **Robe**, on the coast. Beyond Mount Gambier the road enters the state of Victoria. The Great Ocean Road runs via **Portland**, **Port Fairy** and **Warrnambool** to **Port Campbell** and **Apollo Bay**. On this scenic stretch of road are imposing rock formations such as the **Twelve Apostles** and the **Sentinel Rock**. Then via **Geelong** to the city of **Melbourne** on Port Phillip Bay. From here the route continues north-east along the south-eastern slopes of the **Great Dividing Range** and the coast of the Tasman Sea, passing **Port Albert**, **Sale** and **Bega**. On the way there are possible excursions to **Wilsons Promontory National Park**, **Seaspray** and **Mallacoota**. At Bega the route turns north-west, runs through the Great Dividing Range and enters the **Australian Capital Territory**, with the federal capital **Canberra**. Then north-east via **Berrima** and back to **Sydney**.

Best of the West (about 4200km/2610 miles)

Perth – Carnarvon (about 1100km/ 685 miles)

From the modern metropolis of Western Australia, **Perth**, the Brand Highway runs north through the imposing **Pinnacles**, a glistening yellow sandy desert with bizarre rock and sand formations created by wind erosion and wide variations in temperature. Rewarding excursions to **Lancelin** and **Namburg National Park**. Also worth seeing are **Green Head National Park** and the two settlements of **Greenough** and **Geraldton**. From here a side trip (340km/210 miles north-east) can be made to **Mount Magnet**. North of Geraldton Highway 1 skirts the scenically magnificent **Kalbarri National Park**, with its very impressive gorge on the Murchison River and the elegant Kalbarri Beach Resort. Some 300km/185 miles farther north, on a long peninsula in **Shark Bay**, is **Monkey Mia**, which is famed for the tame dolphins to be seen on the beach every morning. Before reaching **Carnarvon** the road runs past huge irrigated plantations of various tropical fruits.

Carnarvon – Port Hedland (about 1800km/ 1120 miles)

From Carnarvon the route continues north-east to the Minilya valley, where a road goes off on the left and runs north to **Coral Bay**, with beautiful white sand-dunes fringing the Indian Ocean and fine opportunities for snorkellers. Farther north is Ningaloo Resort, from which a boat can be taken to Ningaloo Reef, a paradise for divers. Just under an hour's drive farther north are **Cape Range National Park** and the little town of **Exmouth**, on Exmouth Gulf. After this excursion we return to Highway 1 and follow it north-east to Nanutarra. From here an excursion can be made eastwards (270km/170 miles) to **Hamersley Range National Park**. Highway 1 continues to **Dampier**, from which **Millstream Chichester National Park** can be explored. Beyond this, on the shores of the Indian Ocean, is **Port Hedland**.

Port Hedland – Derby (about 820km/ 510 miles)

The road from Port Hedland to Derby runs along the north-western edge of the Great Sandy Desert, a short distance inland from the immensely long **Eighty Mile Beach**. At the north-east end of this shell-spangled beach is the former pearl-fishing port of **Broome** with its beautifully maintained Cable Beach. From Broome the Great Northern Highway (Highway 1) runs north-east across the southern part of the Dampier Land peninsula to **Derby**, on King Sound.

Derby – Wyndham (about 930km/ 580 miles)

From Derby the route continues south-east, coming in some 260km/ 160 miles to **Fitzroy Crossing**, from which an excursion can be made to the **Geikie Gorge**. The Great Northern Highway now runs via Christmas Creek to **Halls Creek**. A few kilometres before this town a side trip can be made to **Wolfe Creek Meteorite Crater**, to the south. From Halls Creek Highway 1 runs north through the Kimberley hills, passing Mount Parker, to **Wyndham**.

Wyndham – Darwin (about 870km/ 540 miles)

From Wyndham the route runs south-east to **Kununurra**, an oasis in a desolate landscape. From here it is a short distance to **Hidden Valley National Park**. To the east of Kununurra we cross the boundary into the Northern Territory. From here a rewarding excursion can be made (1 hour's drive south) to **Lake Argyle** and the **Argyle Diamond Mine** and (another hour's drive south) to **Bungle Bungle National Park**. Some distance farther east the road skirts **Gregory National Park** and then comes to **Katherine**, the starting-point for excursions to **Katherine Gorge** and **Kakadu National Park**. Then north-west to **Darwin**.

South-Western Tip of Australia (about 1500km/930 miles)

Perth – Wave Rock (about 380km/ 235 miles)

From **Perth** the route runs east via **Mundaring** to **York** and then turns south to Brookton, from which a road runs east to Hyden, with the **Wave Rock** just to the north.

Wave Rock – Albany (about 470km/ 290 miles)

From Hyden the route runs east, passing the Dragon Rocks, and then south through a district of many lakes to **Lake King** and **Ravensthorpe**, where the road joins Highway 1, here running parallel to the south coast. From here a rewarding side trip (200km/125 miles east) can be made to **Esperance** and **Cape Le Grand National Park**. The main route continues south-west past **Fitzgerald River National Park** and through **Hassel National Park** to **Albany**, on beautiful King George Sound. From here an excursion can be made to **Stirling Range National Park**, 70km/45 miles north.

Albany – Perth (about 650km/ 405 miles)

From Albany Highway 1 runs north-west via Denmark and Walpole to **Sir James Mitchell National Park**. Beyond this, shortly before **Manjimup**, a road goes off on the left and runs west to **Pemberton National Park** and Flinders Bay, continuing via Nannup to the pretty coastal town of **Augusta** and **Leeuwin Naturaliste National Park**, at the north end of which is Geographe Bay. From Bunbury the best way back to Perth is through **Yalgorup National Park** and then via **Mandurah** and **Fremantle**.

Round Tasmania (about 1500km/930 miles)

Devonport – Launceston (about 140km/ 85 miles)

From **Devonport** (arrival point of ferry from Melbourne), on the north coast, the route runs south to **Mole Creek**, from which a rewarding excursion can be made to the Great Western Tiers, with the Marakoopa and King Solomon Caves, and the **Walls of Jerusalem National Park**. From Mole Creek the route continues westward by way of **Deloraine** to **Launceston**. From Launceston there are worthwhile excursions to the north-east, on the west side of the River Tamar to **Beaconsfield** and Asbestos Range National Park and on the east side to Georgetown or Lilydale, and to the south-east to Ben Lomond National Park.

Launceston – St Helens (about 170km/ 105 miles)

From Launceston the Tasman Highway runs north-east to **Scottsdale**. To the east is a mining region with the old settlements of Branxholm and Derby. North-east of Derby a road branches off to **Mount William National Park**. The Tasman Highway then runs down to the rising holiday resort of **St Helens** on the Tasman Sea.

St Helens – Swansea – Triabunna (about 180km/ 110 miles)

From St Helens the route runs south along the coast, passing the attractive holiday resort of Scamander, and comes to **St Marys**. It then goes over the Elephant Pass and returns to the east coast. From Chain of Lagoon a detour can be made through Douglas Apsley National Park. The main road continues along the coast to **Bicheno**, where the Tasman Highway bears southwest to **Swansea**, on Great Oyster Bay. From here there are rewarding side trips eastward to the magnificent Nine Mile Beach and the **Freycinet Peninsula**. The route continues from Swansea over the Spiky Bridge and past Little Swanport to **Triabunna**. From the southern suburb of Louisville a boat can be taken to **Maria Island**, once a convict settlement.

Triabunna – Hobart (about 90km/ 55 miles)

Beyond Triabunna the Tasman Highway runs along Prosser Bay to Orford and continues via Buckland (interesting church) to Sorell, on the Pittwater. From Sorell there are two interesting excursions – to the little town of **Richmond** (protected as a national monument), with the oldest bridge in Australia, and on the Arthur Highway to the Forestier Peninsula and beyond this to the **Tasman Peninsula**, with the former convict colony of **Port Arthur**. The main route continues from Sorell by way of Cambridge and Bellerive and over the River Derwent (Tasman Bridge) to **Hobart**, at the foot of Mount Wellington. From Hobart it is worth while taking a 100km/60 miles trip south-west to Huonville and the fertile Huon valley, continuing to Franklin and **Geeveston**, a good base from which to explore Hartz Mountains National Park, to the south-west. From Geeveston the road continues south to Dover and **Southport**, from which the Hastings Caves can be visited. An alternative excursion from Hobart is via Kingston to **Bruny Island**, the two parts of which are connected only by a narrow isthmus.

Hobart – Queenstown (about 260km/ 160 miles)

From Hobart the Lyell Highway runs up the Derwent valley to **New Norfolk**. From here an excursion (150km/95 miles) can be made on the Gordon River Road to **Mount Field National Park** and the centre of the **Tasman World Heritage Area**, with the **South West National Park** and **Franklin Gordon Wild Rivers National Park**, with Lake Pedder and Lake Gordon. From New Norfolk the Lyell Highway runs through central Tasmania and climbs to **Cradle Mountain Lake St Clair National Park**, which is also part of the Tasman World Heritage Area. It then runs down into the mining district of **Queenstown** and continues to the old port of Strahan on sheltered **Macquarie Harbour**. From here a boat trip can be taken to the primeval forest on the lower course of the Gordon River.

Queenstown – Burnie – Devonport (about 230km/ 145 miles)

From Queenstown the route runs north past the old mining settlement of **Zeehan** to the mining town of **Rosebery**, in a beautiful mountain setting (artificial lakes). 40km/25 miles north of Rosebery a road branches off to the east towards the beautiful northern part of **Cradle Mountain National Park**, with the Cradle valley and Waldheim Lodge. The main route reaches the north coast of Tasmania at Somerset, a short distance west of **Burnie**. From here a side trip should be made on the Bass Highway along the coast to the west. This leads via Wynyard to **Rocky Cape National Park**, **Smithton** and the finely situated old port of Stanley. Then back, via Burnie, to **Devonport**.

City Route (about 2700km/1680 miles)

Visitors who have only limited time at their disposal and want to see as much of Australia as possible shoulld follow the City Route from Sydney to Adelaide. This will introduce them to the densely populated south of the country and will also take in spectacular natural features, lonely mountain country and beaches and the retreats of rare animals (kangaroos, penguins).

From **Sydney** the route runs south-west by way of the Great Dividing Range to **Canberra**, the Australian capital. It then continues south to the coast, with Cape Conran, Ninety Mile Beach and Wilsons Promontory National Park. Highway 1 runs west to **Melbourne**. Then along the coast via **Geelong** to **Apollo Bay**, **Otway National Park**, **Port Campbell National Park** and Port Campbell, passing on the way the rock formations known as the **Twelve Apostles**. At **Warrnambool** the route turns north, passes **Grampians National Park** and skirts **Little Desert National Park**. Then on to **Adelaide**, capital of South Australia.

Bruce Highway (about 1800km/1120 miles)

The road from Brisbane to Cairns (described in the Australian Highlights route), the Bruce Highway, leads to some of the finest holiday destinations and bathing beaches on the east coast of Australia and also offers the possibility of excursions into the attractive hinterland and to the offshore islands and banks of coral (Flinders Island, Great Barrier Reef, etc.). At least two weeks should be allowed for the route described here.

From **Brisbane** the Bruce Highway runs along the **Sunshine Coast**, with Golden Beach and Mooloolaba, known as the "Australian Venice". It then continues along the Cooloola Coast, with the Coloured Sands; from here a boat can be taken to **Fraser Island**, a huge sandy island. At **Gladstone** it comes to the south end of the **Great Barrier Reef**, here marked by two offshore islands, Curtis Island and Heron Island. Farther north, on the Tropic of Capricorn, is **Rockhampton**, Australia's main cattle-farming centre. From here an excursion (about 40km/25 miles) can be made inland to Mount Hay Gemstone Tourist Park, where agates can be found. Then on to **Mackay**, a sugar-cane-growing centre. The next place of interest is **Airlie Beach**, from which a boat trip can be taken to the Whitsunday Islands. Then on to the Billabong Sanctuary, Queens Beach and **Townsville**, a good base for excursions to the Great Barrier Reef. Farther north are **Mount Spec National Park**, **Tully** (white-water rafting) and the beautiful **Mission Beach**, from which there are boat trips to **Dunk Island**. The Bruce Highway ends at **Cairns**, with a hinterland of dense tropical vegetation.

Stuart Highway (about 3000km/1865 miles)

Two or three weeks should be allowed for this trip through the Red Centre of Australia. It follows the route pioneered by John MacDouall Stuart (see Famous People) in 1861–62. It is best to start from Adelaide, in South Australia, and travel north via Alice Springs to Darwin. (The Stuart Highway is also briefly described in the Australian Highlights route, travelling from north to south.)

From **Adelaide** the route runs north via **Port Pirie** to **Port Augusta**, from which a rewarding side trip can be made into the **Flinders Ranges**. It then continues through the arid outback of South Australia, with its salt lakes, to the **Woomera** rocket range and **Coober Pedy**, famed for the rich finds of opals made in the surrounding area. From Coober Pedy it is a strenuous day's drive to **Ayers Rock** and the **Olgas**, off the Stuart Highway to the west. From Ayers Rock it is possible (without returning to the Stuart Highway) to make direct for the imposing **Kings Canyon**. From there a road runs south-west, passing the huge **Henbury Meteorite Crater**, to rejoin the Stuart Highway, which then continues to **Alice Springs**. From here there are interesting excursions into the surrounding area (e.g. to the MacDonnell Ranges). The main route continues north through Aboriginal territory, passing the **Devil's Marbles**, huge round boulders regarded by the Aborigines as sacred. Farther north are the old gold-mining settlement of **Tennant Creek** and **Mataranka**, at Outback town celebrated for its thermal springs. The route then runs north-west to **Darwin**, with opportunities for visiting **Katherine Gorge National Park** and **Kakadu National Park** on the way.

Australian Capital Territory Canberra

General

Australian Capital Territory

Area: 25,000sq.km/9650sq.miles
Population: 310,100

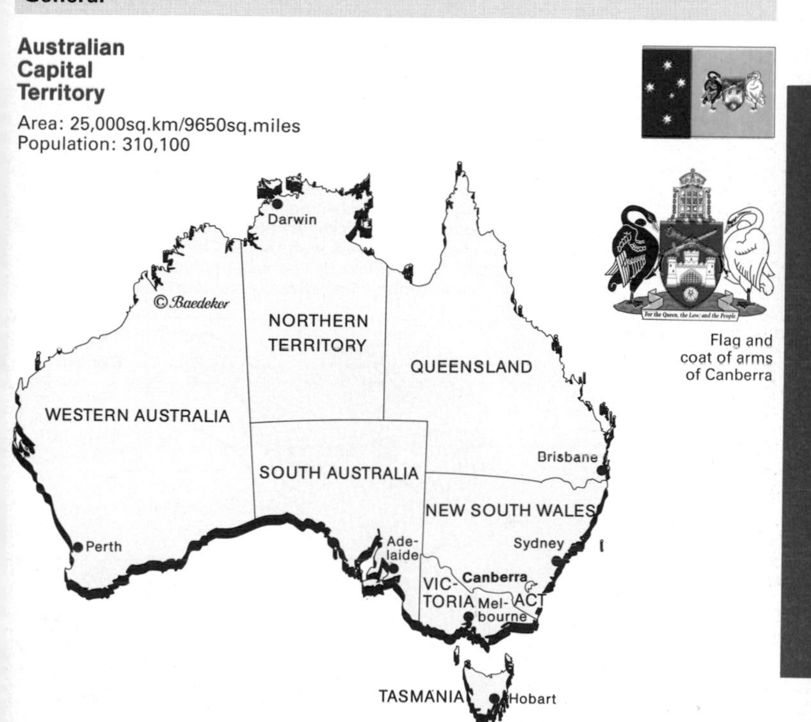

Flag and coat of arms of Canberra

Late development of Australian national consciousness

The inauguration of the Commonwealth of Australia on January 1st 1901, when Lord Hopetoun was sworn in as first governor-general in Sydney's Centennial Park, had been preceded by many years of discussion and negotiation. The independence of the various colonies, reflected particularly in their customs legislation, and the self-centred suspicion of one another which hampered their economic and other relationships stood in the way of the development of any national consciousness. The British government's call for an all-Australian defence strategy was responded to by Henry Parkes, prime minister of New South Wales, in a speech at the little town of Tenterden, close to the border with Queensland, in October 1889. In this speech, which attracted much attention at the time, he advocated a national government for the whole of Australia. In the following year a conference was held in Melbourne at which it was resolved to work out a constitution on the model of the United States and Canada. The main problem was to secure acceptance of the constitution in the individual

◀ *Canberra's central axis – Anzac Parade, Lake Burley Griffin and the Parliamentary Triangle*

colonies, particularly in New South Wales and Western Australia. It was finally agreed that the seat of government of the Commonwealth of Australia should be in New South Wales, that it should have an area of at least 100 sq. miles and – on the insistence of the other colonies – that it should be not less than 100 miles from Sydney. It was also decided that Melbourne, capital of Victoria, should be the temporary seat of government. It was not until 1909, after much competition for the privilege of housing the capital, that the location of the Australian Capital Territory and the new capital was finally decided, enabling the federal government to acquire the land in 1911. The Jervis Bay Territory to the south of Nowra was also acquired as a base for the Australian navy; and this area, now the seat of the Royal Australian Naval College, is still administered from Canberra.

Finally in 1913 the new capital was officially founded and given its name. It had taken some time to secure agreement on the name, but after the rejection of such unlikely suggestions as "Sydmeladperbrisho" (formed from the first syllables of the names of the six state capitals) the new town was named **Canberra**, after the first settlement in this area in 1824, Canberry (from an Aboriginal term meaning "place of assembly").

Canberra is a regularly planned city. An international competition for the plan of the new town in 1912 was won by the Chicago architect Walter Burley Griffin (1876–1937), whose design was modelled on the layout of Washington DC. Burley Griffin, who had never previously been in Australia,

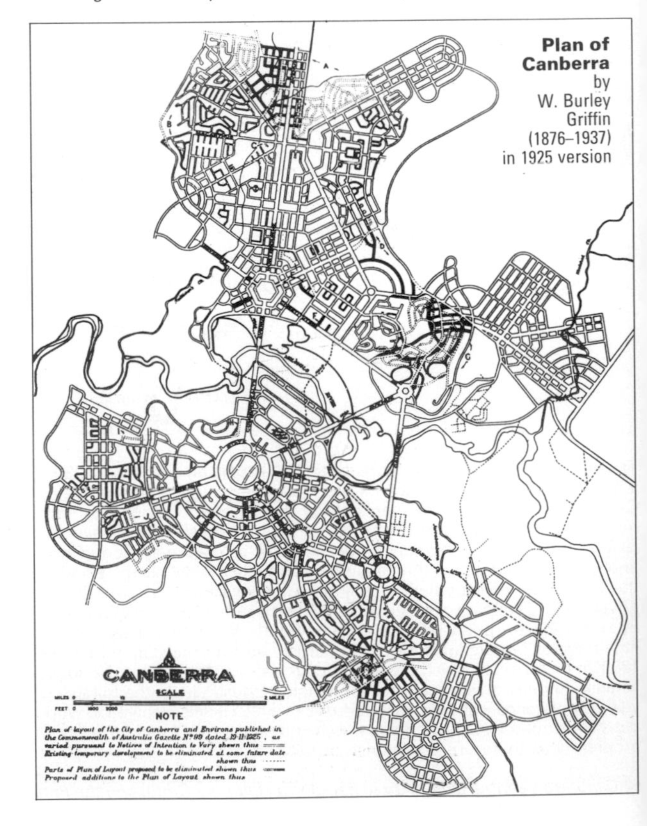

Plan of Canberra by W. Burley Griffin (1876–1937) in 1925 version

centred his layout on a triangular area with Parliament House at its apex. Today the inhabitants of the conurbation of Canberra total more than 325,000, and this number continues to grow.
The young capital is unusual in having no international airport. Its comparatively small airport lies 7km/4½ miles from the city centre and is used only for domestic flights. Nevertheless, some 2 million visitors come to Canberra every year.

Situation and ★townscape

Canberra (alt. 550m/1805ft), situated half way between Sydney and Melbourne, is surrounded by a semicircle of hills (Mount Ainslie, Red Hill, Mount Pleasant, Black Mountain). A central feature of the city is Lake Burley Griffin, a long artificial lake formed in 1964 by a dam on the Molongolo River. The lake separates the northern half of the city, with its central area (City Hill) on Vernon Circle surrounded by the London Circuit, from the southern half, with the government quarter on Capital Hill (and the embassy quarters). The two parts of the city are linked by Commonwealth Avenue and Kings Avenue, which span the lake. These two avenues, meeting at an acute angle on Capital Hill, are the two sides of a triangle which has Lake Burley Griffin and Parkes Way as its curving base.
Canberra's streets are laid out on a generous scale, with many of them flanked by gardens. Millions of trees have been planted, producing glorious autumn colours.

Sights in Canberra J 7

It is a good idea, to begin your visit by getting a general impression of the city from a viewpoint such as Black Mountain (812m/2664ft; telecommunications tower with viewing platform and revolving restaurant, open: daily 9am–10pm), to the east of the city centre, Mount Ainslie (843m/2766ft) to the north-east or Red Hill (720m/2362ft) to the south.

Parliamentary Triangle

Canberra's principal buildings lie within the Parliamentary Triangle formed by Kings Avenue, Commonwealth Avenue and Lake Burley Griffin, with

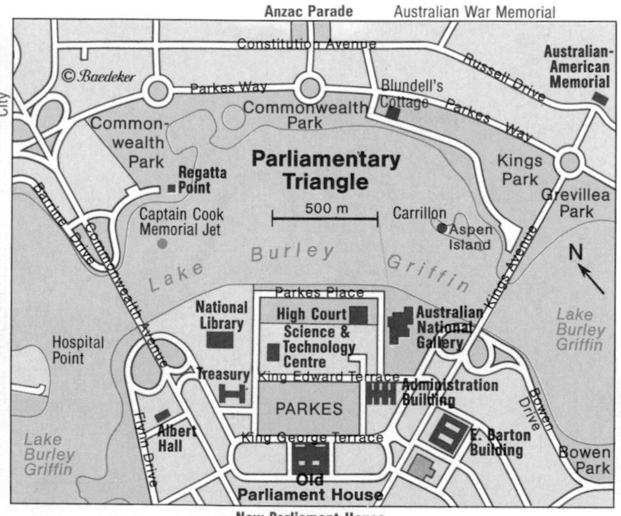

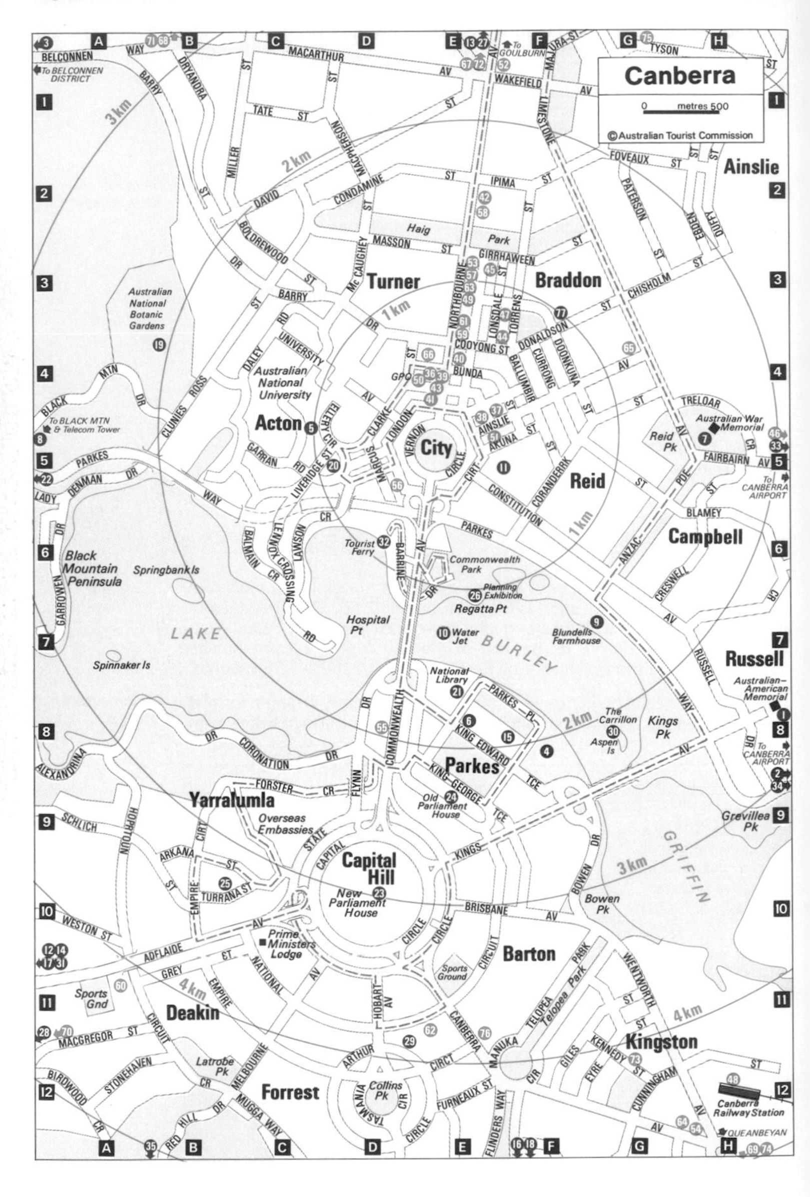
Canberra
0 metres 500
©Australian Tourist Commission
To BELCONNEN DISTRICT
To GOULBURN
To BLACK MTN & Telecom Tower
To CANBERRA AIRPORT
To QUEANBEYAN
Ainslie
Turner
Braddon
City
Acton
Reid
Campbell
Russell
Parkes
Yarralumla
Capital Hill
Barton
Deakin
Forrest
Kingston
Australian National Botanic Gardens
Australian National University
Australian War Memorial
Australian–American Memorial
Haig Park
Reid Pk
Black Mountain Peninsula
Springbank Is
Spinnaker Is
LAKE BURLEY GRIFFIN
Tourist Ferry
Commonwealth Park
Planning Exhibition
Regatta Pt
Hospital Pt
Water Jet
Blundells Farmhouse
National Library
The Carrillon
Aspen Is
Kings Pk
Grevillea Pk
Overseas Embassies
Old Parliament House
New Parliament House
Prime Ministers Lodge
Bowen Pk
Sports Ground
Sports Gnd
Latrobe Pk
Collins Pk
Telopea Park
Canberra Railway Station
GPO
1 km
2 km
3 km
4 km

Places of Interest

- Australian-American Mem'l ❶ H8
- Australian Defence Force Academy ❷ H9
- Australian Institute of Sport ❸ A1
- Australian National Gallery ❹ F8
- Aust. Nat. Botanic Gardens ⓳ B4
- Australian National Uni. ❺ C5
- Australian Science and Technology Centre (1988) ❻ E8
- Australian War Memorial ❼ H5
- Black Mountain Tower ❽ A5
- Blundell's Farmhouse ❾ G7
- Captain Cook Memorial Water Jet ❿ E7
- Canberra National Convention Centre (1988) ⓫ F5
- Canberra Space Centre ⓬ A11
- Cockington Green ⓭ E1
- Government House ⓮ A11
- High Court of Australia ⓯ F8
- Lanyon Homestead ⓰ F12
- Mt. Stromlo Observatory ⓱ A10
- Mugga Lane Zoo ⓲ E12
- National Film and Sound Archive ⓴ D5
- National Library 21 E8
- National Museum Visitor Centre 22 A5
- New Parliament House 23 D10
- Old Parliament House 24 E9
- Overseas Embassies 25 B10
- Questacon Science Centre 77 F3
- Regatta Point Planning Exhibition 26 E7
- Rehwinkel's Animal Park 27 E1
- Royal Australian Mint 28 A11
- Serbian Church 29 D11
- The Carillon 30 G8
- Tidbinbilla Nature Reserve 31 A11
- Tourist Ferry 32 D6

Lookouts

- Black Mountain ❽ A5
- Mt. Ainslie 33 H5
- Mt. Pleasant 34 H8
- Red Hill 35 A12

Tourist Information Centres

- Canberra Tourist Bureau 36 E4
- N.T. Tourist Bureau 37 E4
- Qld. Govt. Travel Centre 37 E4
- Tas. Govt. Tourist Bureau 38 E5
- Victour Travel Centre 39 E4

Airlines— City Departure Terminals

- Ansett Airlines 40 E4
- Australian Airlines 41 E4

Coach Terminals

- Ansett Pioneer 42 E2
- Greyhound 43 E4

Rent-a-Car Offices

- Avis 44 F4
- Budget 45 E3
- Hertz (Airport) 46 H5
- Thrifty 47 F3

Railway Station 48 H12

Motoring Association

- National Roads & Motorists Association (N.R.M.A.) 49 E3

Post Office

- Canberra City 50 E4

International Airline

- Qantas Airways 51 E5

Accommodation

Facilities for the handicapped

Premier

- Canberra International 52 F1
- Capital Motor Inn 53 E3
- Diplomat International 54 H12
- Hyatt Hotel Canberra 55 D8
- Noah's Lakeside Internat. 56 D5
- Parkroyal 57 E3
- The Rex Motel 58 E2
- Travelodge Canberra City 59 E4

Moderate

- Embassy 60 A11
- Downtown Speros 61 E3
- Forest Lodge Motor Inn 62 E11
- Kythera 63 E3
- Manuka Motor Inn 64 G12
- Olims Ainslie 65 G4
- Townhouse Motel 66 E4

Budget

- Canberra City Gate 67 E1
- Canberra Motor Village 68 B1
- Capt. James Cook Hotel 69 H12
- Deakin Inn 70 A11
- International Youth Hostel 71 B1
- Lyneham Motor Inn 72 E1
- Monaro Motel 73 G12
- Regency Motel 74 H12
- Tall Trees 75 G1
- Telopea Park Motel 76 E11

Canberra Explorer Bus — — — —

Shopping

Plan of Parliamentary Triangle: see p. 97

Map of surroundings: see p. 108

Australian War Memorial

1860	New Zealand
1885	Sudan
1899–1902	South Africa
1900–1901	China
1914–1918	First World War
1939–1945	Second World War
1950–1953	Korea
1950–1960	Malaya
1963–1966	Malaysia
1962–1972	Vietnam
1991	Gulf

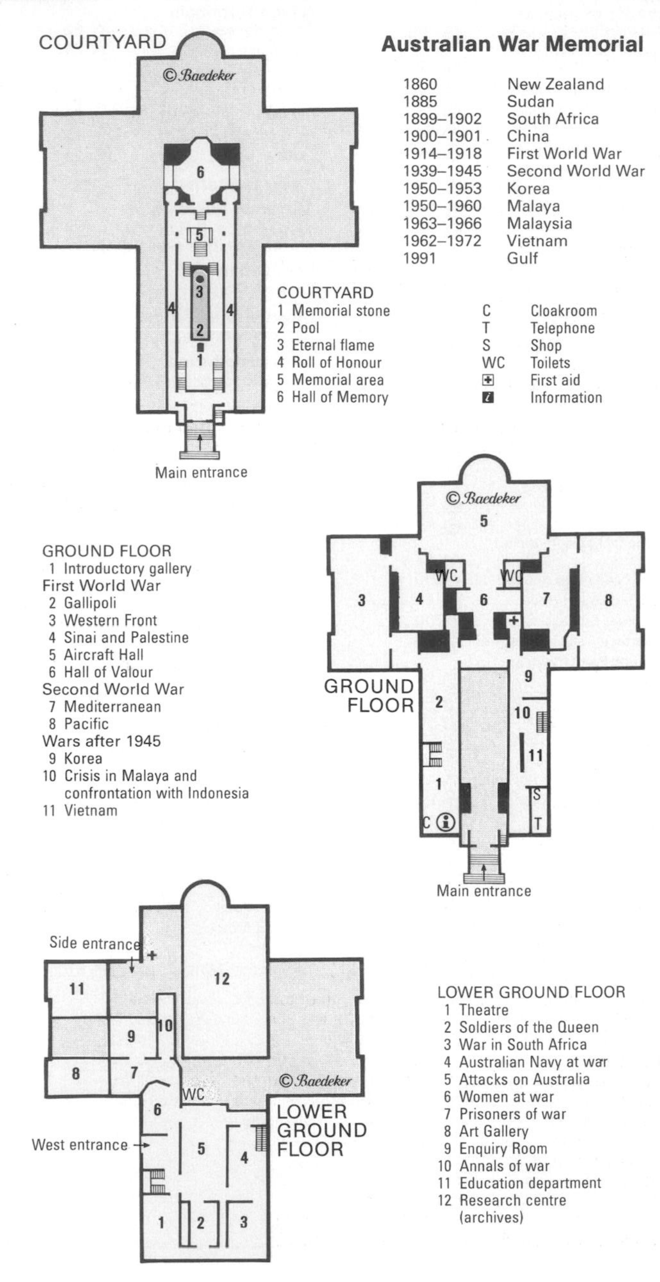

COURTYARD
1 Memorial stone
2 Pool
3 Eternal flame
4 Roll of Honour
5 Memorial area
6 Hall of Memory

C Cloakroom
T Telephone
S Shop
WC Toilets
+ First aid
i Information

GROUND FLOOR
1 Introductory gallery
First World War
2 Gallipoli
3 Western Front
4 Sinai and Palestine
5 Aircraft Hall
6 Hall of Valour
Second World War
7 Mediterranean
8 Pacific
Wars after 1945
9 Korea
10 Crisis in Malaya and confrontation with Indonesia
11 Vietnam

LOWER GROUND FLOOR
1 Theatre
2 Soldiers of the Queen
3 War in South Africa
4 Australian Navy at war
5 Attacks on Australia
6 Women at war
7 Prisoners of war
8 Art Gallery
9 Enquiry Room
10 Annals of war
11 Education department
12 Research centre (archives)

Capital Hill, the government quarter, at its southern tip and City Hill, the business centre, at its north end.

Sightseeing Canberra Explorer Bus

It is better not to try do do your sightseeing by car, since the complicated layout of the city makes finding your way difficult. A good solution is to take the Canberra Explorer Bus, which does a 25km/15 mile tour of the city taking about an hour. Buses leave from the Visitors Information Centre in the Jolimont Centre (Northbourne Avenue) at hourly intervals from 9.45am to 3.45pm. There are 24 stops at which passengers can leave the bus and rejoin it later.

★Lake Burley Griffin

The centrepiece of the city is Lake Burley Griffin, with an area of 7sq.km/2.7sq.miles, an average depth of 4.50m/15ft and a shoreline of 36km/22 miles fringed by gardens with picnic areas. A central lake was included in Burley Griffin's original plan of 1912, but it was created in its present form only in 1958. It is spanned by two bridges, Commonwealth Bridge and Kings Bridge. There is an attractive path round the lake, used by walkers, cyclists and joggers. There are cruises on the lake, starting from Acton Ferry Terminal, at the north end of Barrine Drive (where bicycles, rowing boats, sailing dinghies and pedalos can be hired). In Commonwealth Park on Regatta Point (near the landing-stages below Commonwealth Bridge) is the National Capital Planning Exhibition which illustrates the planning and development of Canberra.

Captain Cook Memorial Jet

In the lake is the Captain Cook Memorial Jet, a 137m/450ft high fountain inaugurated in 1970 on the 200th anniversary of Cook's discovery of Australia. The fountain plays (winds permitting) 10am–noon and 2–4pm and during the evenings in summer.

Globe

On the shores of the lake is an enormous globe showing Cook's voyages of discovery.

Aspen Island Carillon

On the little Aspen Island further to the south-east is a carillon which is rung twice a week (53 peals; Wed. 12.45pm, Sun. 2.45pm). It was installed in 1963 to mark the city's 50th jubilee.

Commonwealth Park

Commonwealth Park extends between Commonwealth Avenue and Anzac Parade on the north side of the lake. Developed since the sixties, it contains play areas, paddling pools, waterfalls, an amphitheatre and a path round the park. In summer there are weekly performances in the "Sunday in the Park" programme, and annually in March the park is one of the venues of the Canberra Festival.

★Anzac Parade (ill., p. 95)

Anzac Parade, lined with monuments, leads to Canberra's best known landmark, the Australian War Memorial at the foot of Mount Ainslie (Explorer Bus stop 22).

★★Australian War Memorial

The massive Byzantine-style monument commemorating Australia's war dead was designed in 1925 as something more than the ordinary war memorial, with a museum, archives, an art gallery and a library. It was inaugurated in 1941, in the middle of the Second World War. The dome and the courtyard at the entrance to the Memorial commemorate the fallen, whose names are inscribed on the walls of the colonnades. The Hall of Memories has stained glass windows, a mosaic made of millions of parts and three statues of Australian soldiers. The Memorial's collection includes over 4 million items, including 20,000 maps and several hundreds of thousands of photographs, and concentrates mainly on the two World Wars, the Korean War and the Vietnam War. At the entrance to the ground floor, on the right, are portraits of the initiators of the Memorial, the historian C. E. W. Bean and General Sir William Birdwood. Of particular interest are the collection of old aircraft and a Japanese mini-submarine from Sydney Harbour, reconstructed from its remains. The Memorial is open daily, except at Christmas, from 9am to 4.45pm. To the east and west of Anzac Parade are the oldest buildings in Canberra, dating from the time of the first white settlers in the Limestone Plains.

St John's Church

St John's Church was built in 1841 at the expense of Robert Campbell. It has fine stained glass. In the churchyard are the graves of early settlers. The schoolhouse belonging to the church (built in the 1840s and rebuilt in 1864 after a fire) now houses a museum.

Blundell's Cottage

In Kings Park, to the east of Anzac Parade, is Blundell's Cottage, the last of the modest stone houses of the early settlers, built by the Campbell family about 1860 for their farm workers (Explorer Bus stop 20). The last occupant of the house, George Blundell, lived in it for 50 years until 1933. To the south-east, near Aspen Island, is a monument to the cruiser "Canberra", sunk by the Japanese, along with three other cruisers, in 1942.

★Carillon, Aspen Island

On Aspen Island is the white Carillon Tower (Explorer Bus stop 19). The carillon of 53 bells ranging from 7kg/15lb to 6 tons in weight was a gift from the British government on Canberra's 50th birthday in 1963. The carillon plays on Sundays at 2.45pm and Wednesdays at 12.45pm.

★Australian-American Memorial

To the east of Kings Bridge and Lake Burley Griffin is the Australian-American Memorial, an aluminium column 73m/240ft high erected in 1954. It commemorates US help in the defence of Australia during the Second World War.

Duntroon

Farther east, along Russell Drive and Moreshead Drive, is Duntroon, where Australian military traditions and memories of the Campbell family who lived here meet. The mansion of Duntroon (named after Duntrune Castle in Scotland), built in the 1840s, has been occupied since 1911 by the Royal Military College for the training of officers. The mansion itself is now the officers' mess and is only occasionally open to the public. In the grounds are two First World War cannon, one captured from the Turks in Mesopotamia, the other from the Germans in France.

★★National Gallery of Australia

The National Gallery of Australia, an imposing concrete structure of cubic form with many corners and edges, was begun in 1974 and opened by Queen Elizabeth II in October 1982. It consists of eleven main galleries on three levels and a 2 hectare/5 acre sculpture garden (laid out according to the four seasons). The purchase of the collection, the largest in Australia,

The National Gallery of Australia on Lake Burley Griffin

Australian National Gallery Canberra

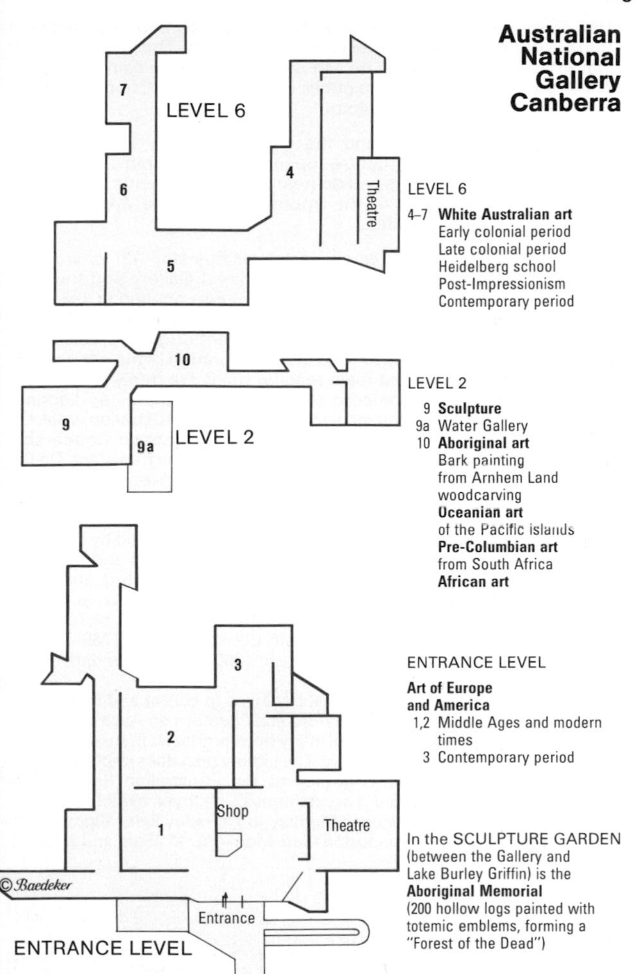

LEVEL 6

4–7 **White Australian art**
Early colonial period
Late colonial period
Heidelberg school
Post-Impressionism
Contemporary period

LEVEL 2

9 **Sculpture**
9a Water Gallery
10 **Aboriginal art**
Bark painting
from Arnhem Land
woodcarving
Oceanian art
of the Pacific islands
Pre-Columbian art
from South Africa
African art

ENTRANCE LEVEL

Art of Europe and America
1,2 Middle Ages and modern times
3 Contemporary period

In the SCULPTURE GARDEN (between the Gallery and Lake Burley Griffin) is the **Aboriginal Memorial** (200 hollow logs painted with totemic emblems, forming a "Forest of the Dead")

began in 1968 (Australian art; international art from 1971). Its particular strengths are "white" art in Australia since 1788, South-East Asian art and the art of the Aborigines, together with African, Oceanian and pre-Columbian art, European art before 1850 and modern art since 1950. The exhibits range from oil paintings and water-colours, sculpture, votive objects, decorative art, printed works, drawings, book illustrations, sketchbooks, photographs and films to ceramics, costumes and textiles. The National Gallery is open daily 10am–5pm and there are guided tours at 11.15am, 1.15 and 2.15pm.

High Court of Australia

Adjoining the National Gallery and similar in style is the imposing High Court of Australia, opened by Queen Elizabeth II in 1980. The main entrance, in front of which are fountains, leads into the 24m/80ft high Great

Hall, from which ramps lead up to the courts. The floor is paved with Carrara marble; the walls are of bullet-proof glass. The north and west walls have mural paintings by Jan Senberg (six panels on each wall). The High Court is open to the public daily (except on Good Friday and at Christmas) from 10am to 4pm.

Australian Science and Technology Centre

Between the High Court and the National Library the Australian Science and Technology Centre (open: daily 9am–5pm), which has hands-on science displays and do-it-yourself experiments designed to promote understanding of the importance and the application of technology in everyday life.

★National Library of Australia

The National Library of Australia (Explorer Bus stop 12) is, architecturally, at the opposite pole from the National Gallery and the High Court. Built in the style of a Greek temple, it was opened in 1968. The classical effect is underlined by the use of marble and travertine on the columns and the walls, and marble of different origins (Greece, Italy, Australia) and colour are also used in the decoration of the interior. The foyer, exhibition areas and main reading room are freely open to the public. In the foyer are superb stained glass windows by Leonard French and three Aubusson tapestries woven from Australian wool. On the mezzanine floor are a 1:24 scale model of Captain Cook's ship "Endeavour" and photographs of all Australian prime ministers. On the lower floor are displayed treasures from the library's collection.

The National Library was originally part of the Commonwealth Parliamentary Library but was hived off from that library and given independent status in 1960. It now has a collection, formed by purchase or donation, of over 3 million books, rare printed books and medieval manuscripts, newspapers (many of them on microfilm) and autographs and papers left by scientists, politicians and artists, as well as historic and contemporary photographs and over 6000 pictures. Its most valuable possessions are Captain Cook's journal (1768–71) and Wills' diary of his expedition with Burke in 1860–61 which ended in their deaths.

The main function of the National Library is to collect and make available for public use Australian literature and literature on Australia. Under the 1968 Copyright Act one copy of every book produced in Australia must be deposited in the National Library. The Library also does important work in the field of bibliography, producing the "Australian Bibliography Network", an integrated record of catalogues. The foyer, exhibition rooms and main reading room are open Monday to Thursday 9am–10pm, Friday to Sunday 9am–4.45pm (conducted tours Mon.– Fri. 11.45am and 2.45pm).

Old Parliament House

Old Parliament House (Explorer Bus stop 14) looks down from King George Terrace along the spacious gardens of Canberra's main axis towards the Australian War Memorial on the other side of Lake Burley Griffin. Opened by the Duke of York (later King George VI) in 1927, it was occupied by the Australian Parliament until 1988. A permanent home for Parliament was to be built only after agreement had been reached on its site and architectural style.

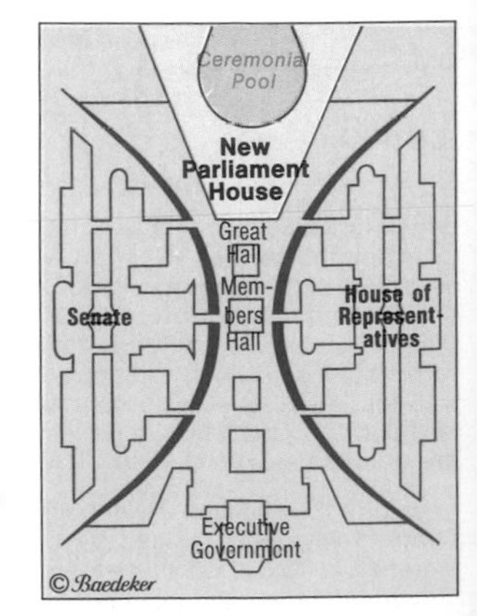

In King's Hall, the entrance lobby, are busts and portraits of Australian prime ministers and an exhibition of important documents such as Queen Victoria's agreement on July 9th 1900 to the creation of the Commonwealth of Australia on January 1st 1901.

The chambers of the House of Representatives and the Senate are modelled on the British House of Commons and House of Lords. The panelling and furnishings are of Australian woods and the carpets are patterned with Australian flora. On the left-hand side of the building, above King Edward Terrace (near the Lobby Restaurant), are the beautiful National Rose Gardens.

National Rose Gardens

New Parliament House (reached by way of Kings Avenue or Commonwealth Avenue) nestles into Capital Hill rather than dominate it. It was designed as the final fulfilment of Burley Griffin's vision of 1912. In order to fit it into its site the top of Capital Hill was levelled off. An international competition for the design of the new building was won by a New York architect, the foundation stone was laid in 1979 and Parliament House was formally opened by the Queen on May 9th 1988, the 200th anniversary of the landing of the "First Fleet" (see p. 52). (The first Parliament of the Commonwealth of Australia had met in Melbourne on May 9th 1901, and Parliament had first met in Old Parliament House on May 9th 1927.)

★★**New Parliament House**
(see plan, p. 104)

Parliament House is impressive both in size and in general effect. From the grassed walkway which forms the roof there are fine views of Canberra. The circular form of the hill is reflected in two huge circular walls and the building is topped by an elegant four-legged steel structure (weight 220 tons) supporting a flagpole 81m/266ft high; the flag measures 12m/40ft by 6m/20ft. Parliament House is open to the public daily from 9am to 5pm.

Steps lead up to the Ceremonial Pool, in the centre of which is a large mosaic (196sq.m/2110sq.ft) in the style of traditional Aboriginal sand-painting representing a gathering of Aboriginal tribes. The curving walls are of granite from Eugowra (NSW). The Great Verandah is used for the reception of guests on official occasions. In the centre of its façade is a coat

Ceremonial Pool

Australia's Parliament Building on Capital Hill

of arms in the "X-ray" style of the rock paintings of Arnhem Land. In the foyer are 48 columns of greenish-grey marble illuminated in such a way as to create the impression of a eucalyptus forest. In the foyer are cases displaying important documents, and to the left of the entrance is a bookshop. From the foyer two staircases lead up to the public terrace (view of forecourt), lounges and a large public cafeteria. The Great Hall, used for major functions, is not open to the public, but visitors can look into it from balconies on the first floor and a gallery. Adjoining the Great Hall is the Members' Hall, which can be entered only by members of Parliament. From the gallery running round the first floor visitors can gain admission to the public galleries of the two houses. The chamber of the House of Representatives (240 members), to the east, has galleries on the first and second floors. The predominant colour in the chamber is the broken green of a eucalyptus forest. The Senate chamber to the west, in the traditional red, has seating for 120 senators, but can be enlarged by means of movable walls to seat 360 for joint sittings of both houses.

Members' rooms and ministers' offices are not open to the public. A lift below the flagstaff gives access to the grassed walkway on the roof, from which it can be seen how Parliament is the focal point of the capital's street layout – the hub of a wheel whose spokes are the avenues named after the Australian state capitals.

Prime Minister's Lodge

Prime Minister's Lodge, the official residence of the prime minieter, is hidden behind a whitewashed brick wall and gardens on the south-west side of Capital Hill.

Government House

Government House, the residence of the Governor-General, is a mansion in the Yarralumla district originally built in 1891 for Frederick Campbell, grandson of Robert Campbell.

Royal Australian Mint (Deakin)

The (Royal Australian) Mint is in Denison Street (Deakin district, reached by way of Adelaide Avenue). Here all Australian coins have been minted since 1965 (previously in Melbourne). Coin making can be observed from public galleries and visitors can make their own $A1 coin on the public gallery coinery presses. Banknotes are still printed in the various states, mainly in Melbourne (VIC).

In the foyer of the Mint is a small museum, with a souvenir shop. The Mint is open Monday to Friday 9am–4pm; 9am–3pm Sat. and Sun.

Serbian Orthodox Church (Forrest)

The Serbian Orthodox Church in the Forrest district (32 National Circuit; Explorer Bus stop 16) is famed for its wall paintings (by Karl Matzek) and its gold-leaf-covered ceiling (open: daily 9am–1pm and 2–5pm).

★National Museum of Australia

At the north-west end of Lake Burley Griffin, near the Scrivener Dam (Lady Denman Drive), is the richly-stocked National Museum of Australia. The main emphasis of the exhibition is on the cultural history of the Aborigines: open Tue.–Sat. 10am–4pm, Sun. 1–4pm.

★National Aquarium and Wildlife Park

The new National Aquarium, south-west of the Scrivener Dam (12km/7½ miles from Canberra), displays in more than 60 tanks a wide range of marine life, from the tiny denizens of the reefs to huge sharks (open: daily 9am-5.30pm).

★National Botanic Gardens

National Botanic Gardens on the slopes of the Black Mountain 1km/⅔ mile west of the university and covering an area of 50ha/125 acres (open: daily 9.30am–4.30pm).

Australian National University (Acton)

The Australian National University (ANU) lies in 145 hectares/360 acres of parkland on the north side of Lake Burley Griffin (in Acton district, east of Black Mountain). The University was provided for in Burley Griffin's original plan but was not built until 1946. It now consists of two separate but closely associated parts, the Institute of Advanced Studies (research) and the School of General Studies (teaching). The University is worth a visit for the sake of its beautiful grounds, laid out by landscape artists and botanists (admission free; exhibitions).

★National Film and Sound Archive (Acton)

On McCoy Circuit in Acton is the handsome Art Deco sandstone building (1929–30) occupied by the National Film and Sound Archive

The Archive, much used by the media and by researchers, contains hundreds of thousands of film and television productions and innumerable recordings, radio programmes, scripts and printed documents. It is equipped with recorders, radio and television apparatus (open: daily 9am–5pm: charge for admission).

Australian Academy of Science

Facing the National Film and Sound Archive, in Gordon Street, can be seen the futuristic dome of the Australian Academy of Science. The shallow copper-covered dome, 45m/150ft in diameter, is borne on 16 arches. The building contains a lecture hall and various academic offices (not open to the public). The Academy was founded in 1954 on the model of the British Royal Society to promote the advance of science and honour distinguished scientists.

Business District

From the Academy of Science it is a short distance to the Business District, the focal point of the northern half of Canberra.

London Circuit

Here, round London Circuit, on City Hill at the end of Commonwealth Avenue, are concentrated the great business firms and banks. The Sydney and Melbourne Buildings with their colonnades were erected in 1926–27, on a site then surrounded by wide treeless plains. The sober glass and concrete structures which have since been built serve purely business purposes: the city's social life is mostly in the outer districts.

Civic Square

In Civic Square is a copper statue, "Ethos", originally cast in 1962 as "The Spirit of the Community". Opposite it is a three-dimensional representation of Canberra's coat of arms in cast copper-zinc.

St Kilda Merry-go-round

Outside the Theatre Centre is a sculpture of "Thespis". and nearby, in Petrie Plaza, is the old St Kilda merry-go-round, a favourite with children.

General Post Office
★Stamp collection

The General Post Office in Alinga Street has Australia's largest and most valuable collection of postage stamps.

Australian Institute of Sport (Bruce)

In the north-western district of Bruce (Leverrier Crescent), on the edge of the Black Mountain reserve, is the Australian Institute of Sport, with sports halls seating 4000 (conducted tours by athletes daily at 2pm). Open: 8.15am–5pm Mon.–Fri.; 9.45am–4.15pm Sat. and Sun.

Diplomatic missions

During the slow development of the new capital most diplomatic missions remained in Sydney (NSW) or Melbourne (VIC). First to come to Canberra, in 1936, was the British High Commission, followed in 1940 by the US Embassy.

Most of the diplomatic missions are west of Capital Hill in the Yarralumla district. For the most part they are featureless functional buildings: more interesting architecturally are the High Commission of Papua New Guinea (built in the form of a cult house, with a high patterned gable), the Greek Embassy (with marble-clad columns) and the Indonesian Embassy (with sculptures of Balinese deities).

Surroundings of Canberra

Suburbs

With the great increase in the city's population in recent years new districts and satellite towns have been developed. Among them are Woden and Tuggeranong to the south and Belconnen to the north-west. After the government offices and shops close Canberra is an empty city; thereafter life continues in the suburbs and outer districts.

Round the city are many picnic and barbecue areas, nature reserves, old settlements and other features of interest (e.g. space observatories).

Cockington Green
Ginnederra

9km/5½ miles north of the city on Barton Highway is Cockington Green, a pretty English village in miniature, adjoining the township of Ginnederra, which is older than Canberra, with craft shops and workshops.

Rehwinkel's Animal Park

24km/15 miles north of Canberra, on the Federal Highway, is Rehwinkel's Animal Park, where over 100 species of Australian animals live in a natural bush setting.

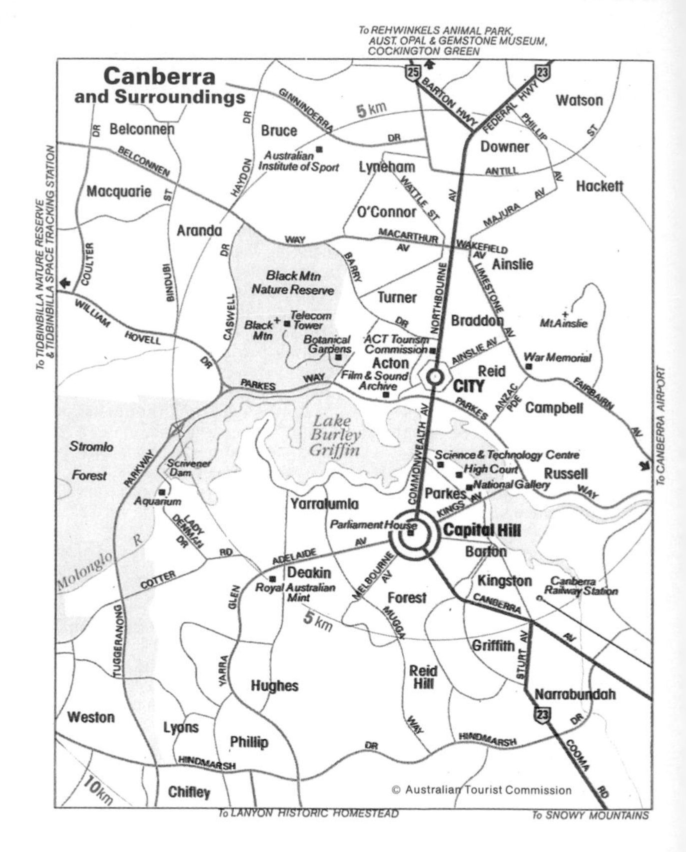

Tidbinbilla Nature Reserve

40km/25 miles south-west of Canberra is the Tidbinbilla Nature Reserve, with unspoiled natural flora and fauna.

Corin Forest Recreation Area

The nearby Corin Forest Recreation Area offers ample scope for walking and, when snow falls, for winter sports.

Lake Cotter

Lake Cotter, an artificial lake 22km/13½ miles west of Canberra, has excellent picnic sites, play areas and camping grounds.

★Mount Stromlo Observatory

Nearby is the Mount Stromlo Observatory with its large silver domes, housing the huge telescope of the Australian National University.

★Tidbinbilla Deep Space Tracking Station, Canberra Space Centre

A special attraction is the Tidbinbilla Space Station, from where the flight paths of manned space missions, satellites, etc. can be observed. In the Visitor Centre (open daily 9am–5pm) can be seen models and very interesting films and documentation relating to various expeditions.

Lanyon Homestead

The historic homestead of Lanyon (protected as a national monument), set in parkland on the Murrumbidgee River (40km/25 miles south of Canberra), recalls 19th century rural life. Here too there is a gallery of Sydney Nolan's paintings. (open: Tue–Sun. 10am–4pm.)

Cuppacumbalong

Farther south, also on the Murrumbidgee, is the old homestead of Cuppacumbalong with its cottages and outbuildings and facilities for visitors (picnic areas, craft shops, swimming in river).

Namadgi National Park

Namadgi National Park to the south of Canberra, established in 1985, covers an area of 94,000 hectares/232,000 acres, about two-fifths of the Australian Capital Territory. It includes expanses of alpine and sub-alpine wilderness as well as areas in which the original bush vegetation is being allowed to recover. There are walking tracks, camping sites and picnic areas. Here too can be seen some remains of Aboriginal culture, particularly at Yankee Hat and Rendezvous Creek (stone-settings, rock paintings, hunting grounds), and evidence of European settlement from 1830 onwards.

Namadgi National Park joins up with Alpine National Park in Victoria and Kosciusko National Park in New South Wales.

Excursions into the bush and Snowy Mountains

There is plenty of scope for excursions from Canberra into the surrounding bush, and the Snowy Mountains are not too far away. Some 230km/145 miles south, reached on the Monarco Highway and Snowy Mountains Highway, are Thredbo (see p. 156), the Snowy Mountains winter sports area and Lake Eucumbene (water sports, fishing).

Pacific beaches

It is 150km/95 miles from Canberra to the beaches on the Pacific, Batemans Bay, a favourite holiday resort at the mouth of the Clyde River (bird reserves) and the nearby old gold-mining towns of Mogo and Araluen.

New South Wales

General

Founding State
Area: 802,000sq.km/310,000sq. miles
Population: 5,974 million
Capital: Sydney

Flag

Coat of arms

Symbolic animals: platypus, kookaburra

Symbolic plant: waratah

Topography

The topography of New South Wales reflects that of Australia as a whole – the beautiful beaches on the Pacific coast, the Snowy Mountains, their peaks snow-capped in winter, the gorges of the Blue Mountains, the fertile farming and pastoral country, the inhospitable outback. The Great Dividing Range, which extends for 3200km/2000 miles from the extreme north of Queensland to the south coast of Victoria, cuts through the whole of New South Wales, dividing the state, as its name indicates, into four natural regions:

- a narrow coastal strip, only 30–80km (20–50 miles) wide, in the east;
- the high tablelands and peaks of the Great Dividing Range itself;
- the fertile farming and pastoral country which slopes gently down towards the interior of the state; and
- the arid and sparsely populated outback to the west.

◀ *Wentworth Falls in the Blue Mountains*

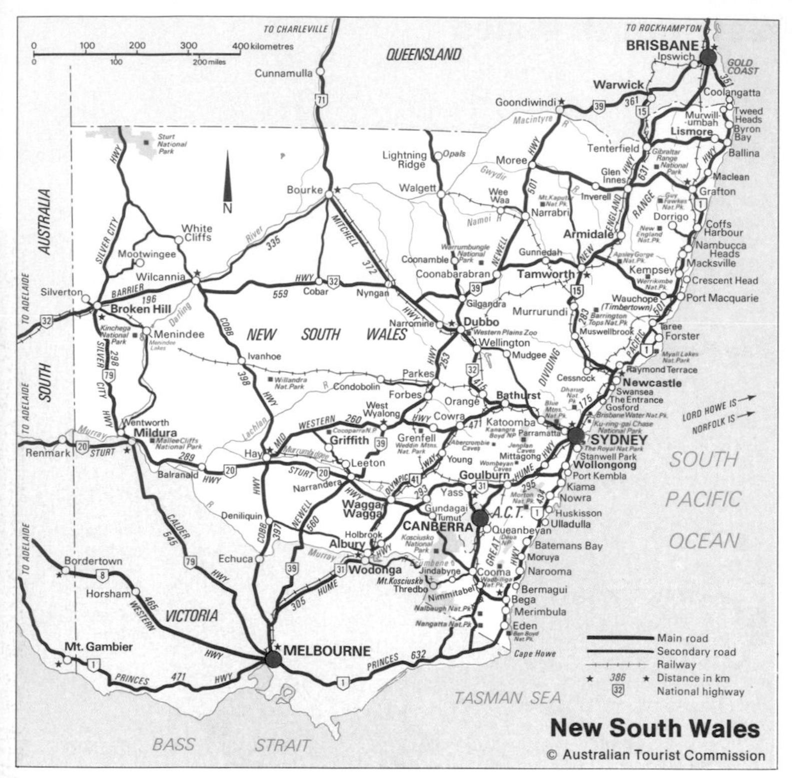

Tourist attractions

The great highlight of New South Wales, and indeed of the whole of Australia, is the state capital, Sydney, with its big-city attractions, its National Parks, its fine beaches and its facilities for water sports in the bays and inlets surrounding the city.

In the city's hinterland, beyond the Blue Mountains, are the "Golden West", with its rich grazing land, huge fields of wheat and, in the past, its gold, and the irrigated Riverina region along the rivers Murrumbidgee and Murray (fruit, rice).

To the south extend great stretches of beautiful beaches – the Illawarra or Leisure Coast, the South Coast, the Alpine Coast.

In the Snowy Mountains (Australian Alps) is the marvellous natural landscape of Kosciusko National Park, with Australia's highest mountain and a number of other peaks over 2000m/6560ft. Here there are excellent (though expensive) facilities for winter sports and endless scope for walking in summer.

From Sydney the Pacific Highway runs north through the wine-growing country in the Hunter Valley and along the Holiday Coast, with a string of beaches and holiday resorts extending along the coast into Queensland.

From the coast of northern New South Wales excursions can be made into the mountainous hinterland of New England (rain forests), where the summer is pleasantly cool.

In the far west is the outback – arid, hot, inhospitable, with salt lakes and rivers which only rarely have any flow of water.

Places of Interest from A to Z in New South Wales

Adelong J 7

Situation and characteristics

Adelong (pop. 890) is a little town in the southern highlands on the Snowy Mountains Highway which dates from gold rush times. In the mid 19th century there were some 29,000 gold-miners here, producing around 200 tons of gold (Golden Gully).

Accommodation

Hotel, motel, caravan park.

Features

Visitors can still fossick for gold here. The old buildings in the main street (Bank of New South Wales, Old Pharmacy) are protected as national monuments.

Surroundings

At Adelong Falls, 2km/1¼ miles north on the road to Gundagai, are attractive picnic areas and ruins of buildings of the gold rush period.

★Albury J 7

Situation and characteristics

Albury (pop. 43,770), the twin town of Wodonga on the borders of Victoria, lies on the north bank of the Murray River. It is a popular stopover on the Hume Highway between Sydney and Melbourne. It was here that Hume and Murray on their journey of exploration in 1824 reached the Murray, and this later became the most important crossing over the river, which here forms the boundary between New South Wales and Victoria.

Accommodation

Many motels; caravan/camping park.

Features

There is a good view of the town from Western Hill, on which there is a 30m/100ft high war memorial. In the main street (Dean Street) are a number of interesting 19th century buildings: the railway station, the courthouse, the post office and the Regional Art Centre, housed in the former town hall. The old Turk's Head Inn (Wodonga Place) is now the Regional Museum.

Surroundings

Lake Hume, a large artificial lake created by the Hume Weir in 1936, is a paradise for water sports enthusiasts and anglers. To the south can be seen the Bogong Mountains in Victoria, which are covered with snow in winter. There are day trips to the wine-growing areas round Rutherglen (VIC).

Arakoon K 6

Situation and characteristics

Arakoon, 510km/317 miles north of Sydney and 37km/23 miles east of Kempsey, is a popular leisure park on the north coast, with beautiful picnic areas. There is an attractive stretch of coast at South West Rocks.

Accommodation

Camping grounds.

★Trial Bay Gaol

A local sight is Trial Bay Gaol, which was built in 1886 but was used only for a short time. During the First World War it became an internment camp for Germans; it is now a museum. (Access: from the Pacific Highway on the road to the South West Rocks, a little to the north of Kempsey.)

★Armidale K 6

Situation

Armidale (alt 1000m/3280ft; pop. 21,500), situated in the highlands half way between Brisbane and Sydney on the New England Highway, attracts many visitors with its agreeable summer climate. A sheep station was established here in 1835, and the town was founded soon afterwards.

St Mary's Cathedral, Armidale

Accommodation	Many hotels and motels, 2 caravan/camping parks.
Features	Armidale is an attractive recreation area and tourist centre. 5km/3 miles north-west of the town is the University of New England, a spacious campus with a kangaroo and deer park. In the New England Regional Art Museum (Kentucky Street) is the valuable Hinton Collection. The Armidale Folk Museum, housed in a Victorian building (Rusden and Faulkner Streets), displays pioneer relics. Other features of interest are two cathedrals (R.C. and Anglican), Courthouse (1860) and Imperial Hotel (1889).
Surroundings	30km/19 miles east is Hillgrove, an old gold-mining settlement, with a museum. From Yarrowyck, 30km/19 miles west, there is a trail to Aboriginal cave paintings.

Oxley Wild Rivers National Park

Location; area	39km/24 miles east of Armidale; 90,000 hectares/225,000 acres.
Access	Via Armidale or from the Oxley Highway.
Facilities	Camping sites and picnic areas at the waterfalls; bush walking, rock-climbing, canoeing, fishing; viewpoints.
Features	This National Park was formed by the amalgamation of the Apsley Gorge and Yarrowitch Gorge National Parks. Wild winding rivers, waterfalls (including the 457m/1500ft high Wollomombi Falls, the Chandler Falls and the Apsley Falls) and deep gorges.

★Ballina K 5

Situation and characteristics	Ballina (pop. 29,240), a fishing port and favourite family resort, lies 35km/22 miles east of Lismore on the Pacific Highway and the estuary of the Richmond River. In the mid 19th century gold was found in the sand of the

estuary and on the beach. A predecessor of Ballina on the site was a settlement established on Shaws Bay around 1840 where timber was loaded on to ships.

Accommodation

Many motels and caravan/camping parks.

Features

The Shaws Bay Hotel in East Ballina is in the style of a well-to-do citizen's house in Sydney. There is an interesting Maritime Museum (steam riverboat exhibit; balsa-wood raft which crossed the Pacific from South America to here). Visitors can see round the Tropical Fruit Research Station and the Broadwater Sugar Mill (10km/6 miles south on the Pacific Highway).

Batemans Bay K 7

Situation and characteristics

The holiday resort of Batemans Bay (pop. 8310) lies 294km/183 miles south of Sydney on the estuary of the Clyde River. It is the nearest bathing resort to Canberra (152km/94 miles), and is famed for its crayfish and oysters and its excellent facilities for surfing, bathing and fishing in the bay.

Accommodation

Many motels and caravan/camping parks.

Surroundings

In Batehaven (1km/¾ mile east) are the Shell Museum and Birdland Animal Park (native and exotic birds; hiking trails, picnic areas).

★Bathurst J 6

Situation and characteristics

Bathurst (pop. 27,5000) lies 209km/130 miles west of Sydney on the Macquarie River and on the Great Western Highway. It is the oldest Australian settlement in the interior, laid out with streets broad enough for an ox-cart to turn. It has handsome Victorian buildings and trees brought in from Britain.

After the discovery of the route through the Blue Mountains and the construction of the first road Governor Macquarie visited the new territory in 1815, selected the site for a settlement and named it after the colonial secretary of the day, Lord Bathurst. In 1851 the first large finds of gold were made at Ophir, 35km/22 miles from the town, and by 1871 Bathurst had a population of 17,000 and was the headquarters of Cobb's mailcoach company. The gold brought Bathurst an influx of settlers and prosperity; and when the goldfields were worked out the town became the commercial centre of a large farming area.

Accommodation

Many hotels, motels and caravan/camping parks.

Features

Bathurst's fine old buildings bear witness to its 19th century prosperity. Among them are the Courthouse (1877–80), now housing the Historical Society Museum and the tourist office; the Cathedrals of St Michael and St John; a wing of Government House (so called because Macquarie stayed there in 1821) dating from about 1817; and Miss Traill's Cottage (1845).

Surroundings

8km/5 miles from the town centre on the road to Ophir is Abercrombie House, a huge baronial-style Gothic mansion of around 1870. Near the town is the most famous hill racing circuit in Australia (races in October and at Easter). In Karingal Village are the Bathurst Gold Diggings, a reconstruction of a goldfield demonstrating the different methods of winning gold, with 19th century machinery.

70km/43 miles south of the town on the road to Goulburn are the Abercrombie Caves. 80km/50 miles north-west is the old gold-mining town of Hill End (see Hill End Historic Site).

★Bega J 7

Situation and characteristics

Bega (pop. 4500) lies 450km/280 miles south of Sydney at the junction of the Princes and Snowy Mountain Highways, between the south coast with its good surfing beaches and the finest winter sports areas in the Snowy

Mountains. An earlier settlement of around 1830 was later moved to the higher bank of the river for safety from flooding. It is an important dairy farming centre with a well-known cheese factory (guided visits).

Accommodation — Several hotels, motels and caravan/camping parks.

Features — The Bega Family Museum, in a former hotel, illustrates the early period of settlement on the south coast. Several viewpoints.

Bournda National Park

Location; area — 20km/12½ miles south-east of Bega, between Tathra and Merimbula on the south coast; 2305 hectares/5693 acres.

Access — From Princes Highway via Merimbula or Bega.

Facilities — Camping sites; water sports of all kinds; walking trails, picnic areas.

Features — Bournda National Park is a coastal park on Lake Wallagoot, offering a combination of Pacific coastal scenery, Lake Wallagoot and the river valley.

Mimosa Rocks National Park

Location; area — 413km/257 miles south of Sydney; 5200 hectares/12,845 acres.

Access — From Bermagui, Bega or Tathra via Aragunnu, Haigs, Cowdroys and Nelsons Lake.

Accommodation — In Bermagui and Tathra.

Facilities — Picnic areas; walking, fishing, swimming. No drinking water.

Features — This beautiful coastal park, opened in 1973, has a 12km/7½ mile long coastline with a complex pattern of beaches, cliffs, promontories and inlets and a variety of scenery. Bunga Head and Mimosa Rocks are massive volcanic crags, partly separated from the mainland.

Bermagui K 7

Situation and characteristics — The fishing village and angling resort of Bermagui (pop. 1500) lies 362km/225 miles south of Sydney, just off the Princes Highway. Scenically impressive are its backdrop of hills (Mount Dromedary) and its rugged coast. It was much publicised for its fishing by the American sportsman and novelist Zane Grey around 1930.

Accommodation — Several motels and caravan/camping parks.

Wallaga Lake National Park

Location; area — 8km/5 miles north of Bermagui; 1200 hectares/3000 acres.

Access — Best reached by water; boats can be hired at Regatta Point, 5km/3 miles north of Bermagui. From the Princes Highway there are tracks (better for walkers than for cars) to Digmans Creek, Narira Creek and Wallaga Lake. By car the best route is via Bermagui.

Accommodation — No camping sites or facilities for visitors in the park. Motels and caravan/camping parks at Regatta Point, Beauty Point and Bermagui.

Facilities — Bush walking, picnic areas, boat hire, swimming, fishing.

Features — Wallaga Lake National Park, established in 1972, consists of a wooded area on the southern and western shores of Wallaga Lake, a coastal lagoon with many sheltered inlets.

★Berrima K 6

Situation, characteristics and history — The little settlement of Berrima (pop. 360), 150km/95 miles south-west of Sydney, was founded around 1830 and has changed very little since then; it is now protected as a national monument. The site of the settlement was selected in 1829 by Thomas Mitchell, surveyor-general of the colony. The importance of the place as a commercial and transport centre declined sharply when the railway bypassed it. The population dwindled and the houses fell into disrepair. In the last few decades, however, the beauty of the Georgian buildings has been rediscovered, artists and potters have settled in the little town and there are interesting art galleries, restaurants and shops.

Accommodation

Motels.

Features

In addition to a number of old inns there are the Gaol (built by convicts), the Courthouse and Australia's oldest hotel, the Surveyor General (1835).

Bingara K 5

Situation and characteristics

65km/40 miles west of Inverell is the little town of Bingara (pop. 1300), situated on the Gwydir River amid wooded hills. Many precious stones have been (and still are) found in the rivers and streams in this area. The All Nations Gold Mine was closed down in 1948.

Accommodation

Hotels, motel, caravan/camping park.

Features

Historical Society Museum in the town's oldest hotel (*c.* 1860). Upper Bingara Goldfields, with remains dating from gold rush days and a Chinese cemetery (25km/15½ miles south); gold panning in stream.

Surroundings

60km/37 miles east is Copeton Lake (ideal conditions for water sports).

★★Blue Mountains K 6

Situation and characteristics

For more than a hundred years the Blue Mountains have been a favourite holiday resort for the people of Sydney. Some 65km/40 miles west of the city the mountains rise steeply out of the coastal plain, combining magnificent mountain scenery (steep-sided gorges, waterfalls and rock formations) with high-quality facilities for tourists and holidaymakers.

The "City of Blue Mountains" comprises more than 20 settlements: best equipped to cater for tourists are Katoomba (see entry), Blackheath, Wentworth Falls (see Katoomba), Springwood and Glenbrook.

History

The high rock walls of the Blue Mountains were an almost impassable barrier in the early days of the colony, until in 1813 Gregory Blaxland, Henry Lawson and William Charles Wentworth discovered the passage through the mountains and thus opened up the route to the grazing land beyond, of which the settlers were in such urgent need. After 1875 well-to-do citizens of Sydney discovered the charms of the scenery and built holiday homes in the mountains which offered a refuge from the heat of summer on the coast.

Once the Blue Mountains – "blue" because of the intensification of the bluish tones of the solar spectrum by particles of eucalyptus oil suspended in the air – could be reached only by coach or by rail: nowadays they are less than 2 hours by car from the centre of Sydney. Large numbers of visitors come to Katoomba every day on coach tours or by train.

In spite of intensive tourist development along the Great Western Highway only a small part of the Blue Mountains is directly accessible for day trippers. The sheer rock faces of the mountains, which rise up to 1100m/3600ft, and the deep wooded gorges close much of the area to all but thoroughly experienced bush walkers and rock climbers. (There are rock-climbing schools running courses for beginners or more advanced climbers.)

Access

From Sydney on the Great Western Highway to Glenbrook, on the eastern edge of the Blue Mountains National Park (see below).

Accommodation

Accommodation in all categories, from mountain huts to luxury hotels.

Features

In the Australian spring (October) there are many private gardens with magnificent displays of blossom. In Leura (2km/1¼ miles east of

Vegetation in the Blue Mountains

Katoomba) there is a Gardens Festival in mid October in the National Trust garden on Devision Street, Everglades.

Zig Zag Railway

Another attraction in the Blue Mountains is the Zig Zag Railway between Bell and Lithgow, an incredibly steep line completed in 1869 and replaced in 1910 by an alternative route. In the 1960s it was partially brought back into operation by railway enthusiasts and now runs excursions drawn by steam engines.

Jenolan Caves

See Lithgow

Blue Mountains National Park

Location; area

Some 100–120km (60–75 miles) west of Sydney; 247,000 hectares/610,000 acres.

Access

There are only a few side roads giving access to the park, which lies on both sides of the Great Western Highway.

Facilities

Picnic area (in southern part of park); well-equipped visitor centre.

Features

The Blue Mountains National Park, established in 1959, is a region of impressive mountain scenery. There are three sections:

1. Northern section: Grose Valley.
   Situated on the north side of the Great Western Highway, this section extends from Springwood to Mount Victoria, with magnificent panoramic views and attractive picnic areas. The entrance is in Blackheath, opposite the railway station. Bush walking.
2. Southern section: Glenbrook.
   Extending on the south side of the Great Western Highway from Glenbrook to the Wentworth Falls (see Katoomba), it takes in the low hills which rise out of the Cumberland Plains to the west of Sydney. Entrance at Glenbrook. Walking.
3. Extension to southern section: Warragamba Reservoir.
   This section extends from south of Katoomba (see entry) to the Wom-

beyan Caves (see Mittagong) and from Lake Burragorang (Warragamba Reservoir) to the Great Dividing Range. It merges into Kanangra Boyd National Park (see entry) and has not been over-developed for tourism. Bush walking.

Walking trails

In the Blue Mountains there are numerous walking trails of varying degrees of difficulty leading to the main features of interest and viewpoints, as well as cycle tracks and bridle-paths.

Border Ranges National Park K 5

Location; area

Some 900km/560 miles north of Sydney, on the north-eastern border between New South Wales and Queensland; 31,200 hectares/77,100 acres.

Access

By way of the Tweed Range Scenic Drive, 38km/24 miles west of Murwillumbah.

Accommodation

In Murwillumbah and Kyogle.

Facilities

Scenic roads and walking trails; picnic areas and camping sites; viewpoints.

Features

Border Ranges National Park takes in part of the McPherson Ranges, adjoins Lamington National Park (QLD) and along with Nightcap National Park (see entry) lies within the caldera of Mount Warning. Originally only 583 hectares/1440 acres in extent, the park was enlarged in 1982 to an area of over 30,000 hectares/75,000 acres. It protects an expanse of the unique and very complex environment of the rain forest. From Blackbutts Lookout, on the edge of the precipitous escarpment, there are fine views of the Tweed Valley and the whole caldera.

Bourke J 6

Situation and characteristics

The far west of New South Wales is a fascinating and typically Australian region, depicted in poetry and folk tales as an endless red plain spangled with wild flowers and patterned by rocky hills and dried-up rivers. Much of the year is very pleasant, but it can be very hot in summer. Anything "back o' Bourke", it is said, is the real outback.

The town (pop. 3380) is the supply centre for a vast area of sheep country which produces over 50,000 bales of wool a year (formerly shipped downstream on the Darling River). The construction of the Bourke Weir in 1892 made it possible to grow citrus fruits and cotton in irrigated fields, amid arid plains covered with salt bush and Mitchell grass. During his 1835 expedition Thomas Mitchell built Fort Bourke. The town itself, founded around 1860, developed into an important coaching station.

Accommodation

Several hotels, motels and caravan/camping parks.

Features

The Bourke Historical Museum (45 Mitchell Street) offers an excellent survey of the history of the outback.

Surroundings

On Mount Gunderbooka, 74km/46 miles south, are caves with Aboriginal rock paintings.

Braidwood J 7

Situation and characteristics

84km/52 miles south of Goulburn is Braidwood (pop. 1100), an early settlement of around 1830 surrounded by the large grazing farms of the southern highlands. After the finding of gold in 1853 the town became the centre of the goldfields in the surrounding area.

Accommodation

Hotels, motels.

Features

Many old buildings survive from the period of the gold rush, including handsome churches, old hotels, restaurants, galleries, art and antique shops.

In the Old Royal Hotel is an interesting museum.

Brewarrina J 5

Situation and characteristics
Brewarrina (pop. 1500) is a little country town on the Darling River, 95km/59 miles east of Bourke, in the wheat and grazing country of the north-west.

Accommodation
Hotels, motels, caravan/camping park.

Features
In the bed of the Darling River is a complex of low-walled stone channels, an Aboriginal fish trap. Hence the name of the town, from an Aboriginal word meaning "good fishing".

Surroundings
Some 40km/25 miles east, on Narran Lake, is a bird sanctuary.

★Broken Hill H 6

Situation and characteristics
Broken Hill (pop. 24,460) is an artificial oasis in the arid desert landscape in the far west of New South Wales, 1170km/725 miles west of Sydney. This mining town was founded to serve the miners working the rich reserves of silver, lead and zinc discovered by Charles Rasp in 1883. In spite of its isolation and the hard living conditions the town, known as "Silver City", grew rapidly, and by the turn of the century it had a population of 20,000.

Accommodation
Hotels, motels, caravan/camping parks.

Features
The Post Office with its clock-tower dates from 1891, the Town Hall from the same period. There are a Roman Catholic cathedral and a simple iron mosque built in 1891 for the camel-men. The turn-of-the-century Trades Hall was the first trade union building in Australia: the trade unions played a dominant role in Broken Hill from the beginning. The Mining Museum occupies a former hotel of 1891.

Thanks to irrigation with water from local reservoirs and the Menindee Lakes there are attractive gardens along the Darling River. The streets are named after various chemical compounds.

Visitors can see round Delprat's Mine and the Daydream Mine, and also the premises of the School of the Air and the Flying Doctor Service.

Surroundings
To the west of Broken Hill is the ghost town of Silverton, where silver chloride was worked from 1883–89; it is now much used as a film set. Excursions: to the Menindee Lakes (110km/68 miles) and Kinchega National Park (water sports, fishing, camping) and to Mootwingee Historical Site (Aboriginal remains in Bynguano Ranges; 130km/80 miles north-east on an unsurfaced track; no petrol, water scarce). 30km/19 miles farther north is Mootwingee National Park (see entry).

Brunswick Heads K 5

Situation and characteristics
Brunswick Heads (pop. 1670) is a fishing village at the mouth of the Brunswick River, situated on the Pacific Highway 60km/37 miles south of the border with Queensland. It is now the base of a commercial fishing fleet.

Accommodation
Hotel, motels, caravan/camping park

Features
Minyon Falls; lighthouse on Cape Byron; several viewpoints. Brunswick Heads is an angler's paradise; boat hire; good beaches.

Bulahdelah K 6

Situation and characteristics
Bulahdelah (pop. 1100) lies on the Myall River and on the Pacific Highway, 95km/59 miles north-east of Newcastle. Above the little town rears Alum Mountain, on which alunite (alumstone), an important raw material for the papermaking and dyestuff industries, has been mined for more than 80 years.

Accommodation
Hotel, motels.

★Myall Lakes National Park

Location; area
12km/7½ miles east of Bulahdelah; 34,500 hectares/85,200 acres (including 10,000 hectares/25,000 acres of lakes).

Access
16km/10 miles east of Bulahdelah, from the Pacific Highway via Tea Gardens to the south along the coast.

Accommodation
Camping sites on the shores of the Broadwater Lake, bush camping; hotel and motels in Bulahdelah and Foster.

Facilities
Water sports, fishing, bush walking. Visitors must take their own drinking water.

Features
In Myall Lakes National Park is one of the largest expanses of freshwater and brackish lakes in New South Wales, with very varied scenery: dune-fringed beaches, heaths with spring flowers and a rich fauna (great numbers of waterfowl). Fine views of beautiful beaches and areas of rain forest.

Bungonia State Recreation Area J 6

Location; area
36km/22 miles east of Goulburn and 200km/125 miles south-west of Sydney; 3836 hectares/9475 acres.

Access
From Marulan on the Hume Highway south to Bungonia.

Accommodation
Motels, caravan/camping sites with excellent facilities.

Features
The park is the gateway to the wild country of the Shoalhaven valley and farther east to Morton National Park (see Moss Vale). The main features are the Bungonia cave system and views of the limestone gorge through which the Bungonia Creek flows before its junction with the Shoalhaven.

Magnificent walking country. The caves, unlit and hazardous, are for expert cavers only.

★Byron Bay K 5

Situation and characteristics
Cape Byron, named by Captain Cook after the poet's grandfather, is the most easterly point on the Australian continent. Here, 40km/25 miles north of Ballina, is the beautifully situated holiday resort of Byron Bay (pop. 3730). On Cape Byron itself is an imposing lighthouse.

Accommodation
Motels, caravan/camping sites.

Camden K 6

Situation and characteristics
Camden (pop. 18,700) lies 60km/37 miles south-west of Sydney, near Campbelltown (see entry), and like that town has grown considerably in size as a result of its proximity to the Sydney conurbation. John Macarthur acquired great areas of grazing land here in 1805 and, with his wife Elizabeth, experimented with new breeds of sheep. Also associated with Macarthur is the Elizabeth Farm House at Parramatta (see Sydney, Surroundings).

Accommodation
Motels, caravan park.

Features
The town was founded around 1840, and many old building have survived from that period (Belgenny, Camden Park House, St John's Church, Macaria, Gledswood Winery).

Campbelltown K 6

Situation and characteristics
Campbelltown (pop. 141,800), 50km/30 miles south-west of Sydney, has been since the 1970s a rapidly growing satellite town of the state capital.

Accommodation
Motels, caravan park.

Lighthouse on Cape Byron (see page 121)

Features — There are only scanty remains of the town founded by Governor Macquarie around 1820 and given his wife's maiden name.

St Peter's Church (1823), a fine example of Georgian architecture; old houses of the colonial period in Queen Street (Nos. 284–298).

Cathedral Rock National Park K 6

Location; area — 565km/351 miles north of Sydney and 69km/43 miles east of Armidale in the New England highlands; 6500 hectares/16,000 acres.

Access — By way of the road from Armidale to Ebor or from the north to Native Dog Creek on the Ebor–Guyra road, 11km/7 miles west of Ebor.

Facilities — Camping site on Native Dog Creek; good facilities for visitors on Native Dog Creek (picnic area), with footpath to Woolpack Rocks; bush walking, rock-climbing.

Features — Rock formations and buttresses such as Cathedral Rock and the Woolpack Rocks, massive granite crags which are frequently snow-capped in winter; the highest peaks after those of the Snowy Mountains (Round Mountain, 1584m/5197ft); beautiful forests, marshland and a rich fauna. From the tops of the granite crags there are fine panoramic views.

Cessnock K 6

Situation and characteristics — Cessnock (pop. 15,450), founded about 1850, lies 45km/28 miles west of Newcastle in the fertile Hunter Valley (see entry). After the opening of the first coal-mine the town grew rapidly. The gentle hills round Cessnock, particularly in the Pokolbin area, are famed for their excellent wines. Tourism is an important element in the town's economy.

Accommodation — Many hotels, motels and caravan/camping parks.

Surroundings

Nearby is the pretty little township of Wollombi, with many old buildings (church, courthouse, post office), in which many veterans of the Napoleonic wars settled in the early 19th century.

Cobar J 6

Situation and characteristics

Cobar (pop. 5600) lies 720km/450 miles north-west of Sydney on the Barrier Highway. Formerly a farming town with a cattle market and wool as the primary industry, it is now an important mining centre with a huge copper-mine opened about 1960 and a silver, lead and zinc mine opened in 1983 in which the most modern technology is used. At one time it had a population of 10,000, but the numbers declined in the 1920s after the closing of a mine which had been operating since 1870.

Accommodation

Hotels, motels, caravan/camping park.

Features

Many old buildings have survived from the town's heyday (courthouse, police office, Roman Catholic church and the Great Western Hotel, now a museum, with a verandah over 100m/330ft long). The museum illustrates very vividly the history of mining and also has sections devoted to sheep-farming, the pioneering period and the Aborigines (open: daily 10am–5pm).

A pipeline 135km/85km long brings water from Nyngan, to the east of the town, and crops now flourish in what was formerly an arid region.

Surroundings

On Mount Grenfell, 70km/45 miles north-west, are caves with Aboriginal rock paintings.

★Coffs Harbour K 6

Situation and characteristics

Coffs Harbour (originally called Korff's Harbour after the founder of the first settlement), lies 580km/360 miles north of Sydney on the Pacific Highway. The chief place on the "Holiday Coast", it is also a modern timber-shipping port. The main sources of income in the surrounding area are growing bananas and vegetables, dairy farming and fishing.

Coffs Harbour is really two towns, one on the highway and the other near the artificial harbour and railway station. The two together have a population of 19,800.

Accommodation

Many hotels, motels and caravan/camping parks.

Features

There are a number of old houses round the harbour. On Mutton Bird Island are large numbers of nesting-places. Along the coast there are beautiful beaches and excellent tourist facilities.

Surroundings

50km/30 miles west is Dorrigo National Park (see Dorrigo). 3km/2 miles north on the Pacific Highway is the concrete monstrosity called the Big Banana, housing an exhibition on the banana industry.

Condobolin J 6

Situation and characteristics

The little country town of Condobolin (pop. 3500), established about 1840, lies 475km/295 miles west of Sydney on the Lachlan River, in the centre of a red-soil plain (wool, lamb meat, wheat). Mount Tilga, to the north of the town, is the geographical centre of New South Wales.

Accommodation

Hotels, motels, caravan/camping park.

Surroundings

40km/25 miles west is the burial-place of an Aboriginal chieftain.

★Cooma J 7

Situation and characteristics

The first settlers came to the Monaro area (from the Aboriginal word *maneroo,* meaning a treeless plain) in 1827, and the settlement of Cooma

(416km/258 miles south-west of Sydney; pop. 8000) was founded in 1849. The finding of gold in 1859 at Kiandra, 90km/56 miles west, gave a boost to the development of the town. Cooma is now a favourite tourist centre at the junction of the Monaro and Snowy Mountains Highways, the jumping-off point for the Snowy Mountains.

Accommodation — Numerous hotels, motels and caravan/camping parks.

Features — In Lambie Street are twenty-one 19th century buildings, including the Raglan Gallery (the town's first inn), the Courthouse, the Old Gaol and the Post Office.

When the Snowy Mountains hydro-electric scheme was under construction (building of dams, boring of tunnels) in the fifties and sixties of this century the population of the town was multiplied by an influx of workers. The Avenue of Flags in Centennial Park displays the flags of the 27 countries from which they came. A monument commemorates the "Southern Cloud", an aircraft which crashed in the mountains in 1931 on a flight from Sydney to Melbourne and was discovered only in 1958.

Accommodation — Hotels, motel, caravan/camping park.

Surroundings — 18km/11 miles south of Cooma on the Monaro Highway is Bombala, a small settlement in the valley of that name (good trout fishing). Nearby is an old gold-mine where visitors can look for gold.

Coonabarabran J 6

Situation and characteristics — Coonabarabran (pop. 2960) lies 465km/290 miles north-west of Sydney on the Newell Highway and the Castlereagh River.

Accommodation — Several hotels, motels and caravan/camping parks.

Features — This is a good base from which to explore Warrumbungle National Park, to the west of the town. The volcanic hills offer plenty of scope for bush walking, rock-climbing and camping.

Surroundings — 8km/5 miles west of the town is Miniland, with life-size models of prehistoric animals and a museum. 24km/15 miles west, high up in the hills, is the Siding Spring Observatory, with the largest optical telescope in the southern hemisphere.

★Warrumbungle National Park

Location; area — 37km/23 miles west of Coonabarabran, in the zone of transition between the arid areas to the west and the rainy east; 21,000 hectares/52,000 acres.

Access — From Coonabarabran to the west; from Coonamble, Gulargambone and Gilgandra, on the Castlereagh Highway to the east.

Facilities — Camping grounds, picnic areas, walking trails, visitor centre.

Features — John Oxley discovered the Warrumbungles in 1818 on his second journey of exploration. In 1853 an area of 3759 hectares/9285 acres was declared a nature reserve, and in 1967 the present National Park was established. The spectacular rock buttresses and domes in the park are the result of volcanic activity. On the summits of the hills are snow gums, and in the valleys are deep gorges with springs. Along the walking trails are a number of viewpoints, with particularly impressive views at sunrise and sunset. Rich fauna; beautiful spring blossom.

Deniliquin H 7

Situation and characteristics — Deniliquin (pop. 8200) lies 771km/479 miles south-west of Sydney on the Cobb Highway and 76km/47 miles north of Echuca in an extensive irrigated area in which the main crop is rice (largest rice mill in Australia). Other products are wheat and wool. Between the Edward River and a series of lagoons is an island scheduled as a nature reserve (kangaroos, emus, etc.).

Accommodation — Several hotels, motels and caravan/camping parks.

In Warrumbungle National Park, near Coonabarabran

Features

The town has a number of interesting old buildings (Courthouse, Town Hall, Taylor's Cottage). There was formerly a well-known cattle market for dealers from Victoria. Sheep-farming is now of economic importance in the north part of the area.

Dorrigo K 6

Situation and characteristics

Dorrigo (pop. 1130), an important timber town, lies some 50km/30 miles inland from the Holiday Coast between Nambucca Heads and Coffs Harbour.

Accommodation

Hotels, motels, caravan/camping park.

Surroundings

4km/2½ miles from the town is Dorrigo National Park (see below). 40km/25 miles east, on the slopes of the New England plateau, is New England National Park (see New England).

There is good trout-fishing round the town.

Dorrigo National Park

Location; area

4km/2½ miles east of Dorrigo; 7900 hectares/19,500 acres.

Access

From the Pacific Highway via Bellingen.

Accommodation

In Dorrigo. No camping site in park.

Facilities

There is a visitor centre at the entrance to the park.

Features

The National Park was established in 1972 to protect the dense wet forests on the Dorrigo plateau. It is a fascinating wilderness of subtropical rain forest and wet eucalyptus forests with orchids, ferns, mosses and many birds and nocturnal mammals. There is heavy rain in summer, when the waterfalls are at their most impressive.

Walking trails

There are good walking trails, starting from the Glade picnic area in the north-west of the park and the Never Never picnic area in the centre, through rain forest and to the Dangar Falls.

Dubbo J 6

Situation and characteristics
Dubbo (pop. 28,100) lies 420km/260 miles north-west of Sydney on the Macquarie River and on the Newell Highway. Formerly it was an important staging-point for herds of cattle on their way to Victoria; it is now noted for its cattle market. There are also large cattle and sheep farms round the town; visitors can see round some of them by appointment.

Accommodation
Many hotels, motels and caravan/camping parks.

Features
Museum; Old Dubbo Gaol; handsome 19th century houses.

Surroundings
5km/3 miles south of the town is Western Plains Zoo, Australia's largest open-range zoo (area 300 hectares/750 acres), with animals from all parts of the world roaming in natural surroundings.

Dungog K 6

Situation and characteristics
Dungog (pop. 2110) lies 80km/50 miles north of Newcastle (see entry) on the upper course of the Williams River. The town grew out of a farming settlement established about 1820 and a military post established in 1838 to combat bushranging. It is a good base for walking in the surrounding area and visiting Barrington Tops National Park (see below).

Accommodation
Hotels, motels, caravan/camping park.

★Barrington Tops National Park

Location; area
37km/23 miles north-west of Dungog on the northern slopes of the hills running down to the Hunter Valley; 39,000 hectares/96,000 acres.

Access
Via Gloucester or via Dungog and Salisbury or, from the north, via Scone to Gloucester. The tracks for four-wheeled vehicles within the park are closed in winter.

Accommodation
Camping sites in the eastern part of the park on the Gloucester River. Hotels, motels and caravan/camping parks in Gloucester, Scone and Dungog.

Facilities
Picnic areas, walking trails, trout-fishing.

Features
The landscape of Barrington Tops National Park is dominated by the precipitous Barrington and Gloucester Tops (over 1500m/5000ft). A striking feature is the wide range of vegetation – sub-alpine plants on the plateau, subtropical rain forest in the valleys. Beautiful views; picturesque waterfalls; great numbers of birds. The 143km/89 mile drive along the Barrington Top Forest Drive is a memorable experience.

★Eden J 7

Situation and characteristics
Eden (pop. 3270), founded in whaling days, is now the most important fishing port on the south coast. The excellent natural harbour on Twofold Bay is 512km/318 miles south of Sydney. The beauty of the scenery attracts many holiday visitors.

Accommodation
Hotel, many motels and caravan/camping park.

Features
Eden Killer Whale Museum (Imlay Street; open: February to December daily 11am–4pm, January 10am–5pm). Good, safe beach; excellent fishing. To north and south of the town extends the Ben Boyd National Park (see below). Also worth visiting is Mount Imlay National Park.

Near Eden are the ruins of the former rival settlement of Boydtown, founded by Benjamin Boyd in 1842; the old Sea Horse Inn is still open.

Ben Boyd National Park

Location; area
490km/305 miles south of Sydney on both sides of Twofold Bay; 9438 hectares/23,311 acres.

Access
For the northern part of the park, 8km/5 miles north of Eden, side road off Princes Highway. For the southern part, via Edrom road and on forestry roads.

Accommodation
In Eden. Basic camping sites in the southern part of the park at Saltwater Creek and Bittangabee; no caravans.

Facilities
Picnic areas; walking trails, water sports, fishing.

Features
This coastal park, named after Benjamin Boyd, founder of the abortive settlement of Boydtown, was established in 1973. It was formerly a whaling base. From Boyd's Tower, a former lighthouse, there are magnificent views of the reddish sandstone cliffs in the National Park.

Evans Head K 5

Situation and characteristics
Evans Head (pop. 2370), a fishing port and holiday resort on the northern Holiday Coast, lies 108km/67 miles north-east of Grafton and 10km/6 miles off the Pacific Highway. It offers plenty of scope for fishing and water sports.

Accommodation
Hotel, motel, caravan/camping parks.

Bundjalung National Park

Location; area
Immediately south of Evans Head on the north side of the Evans River, extending to the Clarence River; 17,545 hectares/43,335 acres.

Access
For the northern section, south from Evans Head; centre, from Pacific Highway south of Woodburn; southern section, via road to Iluka. Restrictions on cars in park.

Accommodation
Camping sites in park.

Facilities
Water sports throughout the year (mild climate). Beach and coastal walks. Holiday and recreational facilities at the north and south ends of the park, in Iluka (see entry) and Evans Head. Picnic areas in park. No drinking water.

Features
38km/24 mile long coastline with rain forest, heathland, marshland, lagoons and a rich and varied fauna. Rock formations on Esk River. Stretches of the coast damaged by the removal of mineral sands are being regenerated.

Forbes J 6

Situation and characteristics
Forbes (pop. 8500), originally a gold-digging settlement founded in 1860, lies 386km/240 miles west of Sydney on the Newell Highway and on the Lachlan River. At the height of the gold rush the town had a population of over 30,000; its economy now depends mainly on a slaughterhouse and a grain mill and to some extent also on tourism.

Forbes became notorious for the bushranger Ben Hall, who was shot by the police near the town in 1865 and is buried here, as is Kate Foster, sister of the most celebrated of the bushrangers, Ned Kelly.

Accommodation
Numerous hotels, motels and caravan/camping parks.

Surroundings
Near the town is Lachlan Vintage Village, a reconstruction of a town of the gold-digging period. 6km/4 miles away on the Eugowra road is the wine-growing town of Sandhill.

Forster-Tuncurry K 6

Situation and characteristics
The double town of Forster-Tuncurry (pop. 14,540), the two parts of which are linked by a modern bridge, lies 160km/100 miles north-east of Newcastle on both sides of Wallis Lake. It is a popular holiday resort with excellent facilities for water sports and fishing.

Near the town are more than a dozen good beaches. The beautiful Lakes Way runs along the shores of Myalls, Smiths and Wallis Lakes.

Accommodation

Hotels, many motels and caravan/camping parks.

Surroundings

Excursions to Myall Lakes National Park (see Bulahdelah), 30km/19 miles south, and to Booti Booti National Park.

Gilgandra J 6

Situation and characteristics

Gilgandra (pop. 5160), 67km/42 miles north of Dubbo, is a small country town at the junction of the Newell, Oxley and Castlereagh Highways. Its economy is based on timber, wool and grain. Once famed for the windmills which drew up artesian water but have now been replaced by electric pumps.

Accommodation

Several hotels, motels and caravan/camping parks.

Features

The pier which supported the first bridge (1884) over the Castlereagh River can still be seen. The Gilgandra Observatory has a 300 millimetre telescope and an exhibition on space travel.

★ Glen Innes K 5

Situation and characteristics

Glen Innes (alt. 1073m/3521ft; pop. 6140), the centre of a lush farming district with rich deposits of sapphires and zinc, lies in a beautiful setting on the New England tableland, at the junction of the New England and Gwydir Highways. The area was discovered by two cattle-herds around 1830 and the town was founded in 1852.

Accommodation

Numerous hotels, motels and caravan/camping parks.

Features

There is a large Folk Museum in the former hospital (Ferguson and West Streets) with relics of pioneering days (open: Mon.–Fri. 10–11am and

In Glen Innes town centre

2–5pm). The Town Hall dates from 1875, the Courthouse (in which the notorious bushranger Captain Thunderbolt was tried) from 1874, the Great Central Hotel from 1880.

Surroundings

Near Glen Innes are fossicking areas where visitors can hunt for precious stones. Half way between Glen Innes and Grafton on the old road, running through fine mountain and river scenery, is a tunnel hewn from the rock by convict labour.

★Gibraltar Range National Park

Location; area
79km/50 miles east of Glen Innes; 17,273 hectares/42,664 acres.

Access
Via Gwydir Highway.

Accommodation
In Glen Innes. Camping sites in park.

Facilities
Picnic areas, walking trails; visitor centre.

Features
Situated on the New England plateau at an altitude of around 1200m/4000ft, this is a region of wild mountain scenery, with deep gorges containing waterfalls up to 240m/800ft high and huge granite buttresses, and a wide range of vegetation, from arid heath and marshland to rain forest. There is an exhibition of Aboriginal artifacts in the visitor centre.

The Gwydir Highway, which divides the park into two parts, was indirectly the occasion for the establishment of the park in 1963. From the highway a road runs to Mulligan's Hut (picnic areas). The park is the starting-point of many walking trails.

Gosford K 6

Situation and characteristics
Gosford (pop. 129,000), 85km/53 miles north of Sydney, is the tourist centre of the Brisbane Water area and a favourite commuters' town with good rail connections with Sydney.

Accommodation
Several hotels, motels and caravan/camping parks.

Features
Round the town are many attractive picnic areas and a reptile park. In the town itself is a small stone house of 1838, once occupied by the poet Henry Kendall in 1874–75.

Surroundings
★Old Sydney Town

Old Sydney Town, a few miles west of Gosford, is a faithful reconstruction of a settlement of pioneering days (before 1810), with buildings in colonial style. There are regular presentations of events from the colonial past in an open-air theatre. There is also a replica of an old sailing ship dating from the early days of settlement.

In the immediate vicinity of Gosford are two National Parks and a recreation area.

★Brisbane Water National Park

Location; area
9km/5½ miles south-west of Gosford on the north side of the Hawkesbury River, between the Sydney–Newcastle expressway and Brisbane Water; 12,000 hectares/30,000 acres.

Access
The main entrance to the park (established in 1959) is at Girrakool, just off the Pacific Highway, Calga exit. The east park of the park can be reached on the road from Kariong-Woy to Woy-Patonga.

Accommodation
In Gosford, Woy Woy and Patonga. Bush camping in park.

Facilities
Walking trails, picnic areas.

Features
Sandstone hills with wide views and many Aboriginal remains, including rock drawings. Waterfalls. Beautiful spring flowers (including waratahs). Brisbane Water National Park is separated by the Hawkesbury River and Broken Bay from from Ku-ring-gai Chase National Park (see entry).

★Goulburn J 6

Situation and characteristics

Goulburn (pop. 24,000) lies on the Hume Highway 209km/130 miles south-west of Sydney. It is the centre of a wealthy farming district (wool, wheat, stud cattle and horses) at the junction of the Wollondilly and Mulwarry Rivers beyond the Southern Highlands. The area was explored in 1818 by Throsby, Hume and Meehan. Goulburn was originally a pastoral farming centre until the finding of gold at Braidwood, 87km/55 miles south, brought it wealth. The railway reached here in 1869.

Accommodation

Numerous hotels, motels and caravan/camping parks.

Features

Many handsome buildings bear witness to the town's prosperity in the 1870s. Of particular interest are Riversdale House, St Clair House, Garroorigang House, the town hall, the courthouse and two cathedrals. On Rocky Hill is a First World War memorial. On the western outskirts of the town is the Big Merino, a concrete monster 15m/50ft high containing a small shop and a wool museum. In the adjoining Big Merino Tourist Complex there are presentations on sheep farming daily at 10am and noon.

Surroundings

37km/23 miles north-west of Goulburn is an old gold-digging settlement. There were gold-diggers' camps and bushranger hideouts in other villages in the area. 60km/37 miles north of the town on the Bathurst road are the Abercrombie Caves.

The writer Dame Mary Gilmour was born in nearby Coota Walla.

Goulburn River National Park J 6

Location; area

300km/185 miles north-west of Sydney; 70,000 hectares/173,000 acres.

Access

Via gravel road from Merriwa to Bylong (37km/23 miles), or from Muswellbrook via Denman and Sandy Hollow to Bylong.

Sheep farm in the Goulburn area

Accommodation: In Mudgee, Gulgong, Merriwa and Denman. Bush camping in park.

Facilities: Rock-climbing, swimming. No drinking water.

Features: The central feature of this long, narrow park is the Goulburn River, which flows through it from Ulan in the west to Sandy Hollow in the east. In the upper Hunter Valley, to the west of Muswell Brook, is a rugged sandstone plateau with deeply indented valleys.

The park is particularly beautiful in spring, when the flowers are in blossom. There are walking trails along the Goulburn River.

★Grafton K 5

Situation and characteristics: Grafton (pop. 21,020) lies at a bend in the Clarence River 665km/413 miles north of Sydney, at the junction of the Pacific and Gwydir Highways. It is famed for the jacaranda trees which line its broad streets (Jacaranda Festival at the end of October and beginning of November). The settlement was founded around 1830 by loggers, soon followed by stock farmers. When gold was found on the upper course of the Clarence River the town grew rapidly. By 1880 it was a busy river port.

Accommodation: Many hotels, motels and caravan/camping parks.

Features: The town's prosperity at the end of the 19th century is illustrated by a number of well preserved buildings round Victoria Square (police station, post office, courthouse). Other handsome buildings are Christ Church Cathedral, the Post Office Hotel and the CBC Bank. Schaeffer House (190 Fitzroy Street), built in 1903 by an architect of that name for his own occupation, has preserved its original interior decoration and is now a museum. In Prentice House (1880) is the Regional Art Gallery.

Surroundings: Within easy reach of Grafton are six large National Parks – Gibraltar Range National Park (see Glen Innes) and Washpool National Park to the west, Guy Fawkes River National Park, Nymboida National Park, Yuraygir National Park (see below) and, on the coast to the east, Bundjalung National Park (see Evans Head).

Excursions in four-wheel drive vehicles or on horseback to the impressive Clarence Gorge.

Yuraygir National Park

Location; area: 50km/30 miles east of Grafton; 18,200 hectares/45,000 acres.

Access: Via Woolgoolga and, to the south of Grafton, from the Pacific Highway.

Accommodation: Bush camping. Camping site on Sandon River.

Facilities: In the park and in the surrounding area, along the coast, are holiday and recreational facilities (water sports, fishing, coast and bush walking, picnic areas). No drinking water.

Features: The park (established in 1980) takes its name from the Aboriginal tribe which once lived here. It has a 40km/25 mile long coastline, with isolated beaches separated by rivers and streams and a wide variety of vegetation (woodland, heath, marsh plants).

Grenfell J 6

Situation and characteristics: Grenfell (pop. 2300) is a small country town on the Mid Western Highway, 377km/234 miles west of Sydney. A gold-digging camp was established here in the mid 19th century. It was the birthplace (1867) of the poet Henry Lawson, the son of a gold-digger, who is commemorated by an obelisk.

Accommodation: Hotels, motels, caravan/camping park.

Features: Remains dating from the gold-digging period can be seen on Emu Creek. The town has preserved a number of 19th century buildings, notably the hotels with their wrought-iron verandah balustrades. In gold-digging days the town boasted no fewer than 30 bars.

Weddin Mountains National Park

Location; area 18km/11 miles south-east of Grenfell; 8300 hectares/20,500 acres.

Access From Grenfell on the Bimbi road.

Accommodation In Grenfell. Bush camping in park.

Facilities Walking trails, picnic areas.

Features The most striking features in the National Park (established in 1971 to preserve this wilderness area) are the Weddin Mountains, a sickle-shaped chain of hills rising to a height of over 300m/1000ft above the surrounding plains. The park has a rich and varied natural flora and a rich fauna. There are a number of walking trails.

In the mid 19th century there were hideouts in this area (e.g. Ben Hall's Cave) for a gang of bushrangers.

★Griffith J 6

Situation and characteristics Griffith (pop. 13,190), 580km/360 miles west of Sydney, is the main centre in the Murrumbidgee Irrigation Area and accordingly has had a rapid development. It was designed by Walter Burley Griffin, architect of Canberra, and named after Sir Arthur Griffith, first minister of public works in the New South Wales government. Agriculture is practised on an industrial scale (rice, citrus fruits, vegetables, eggs, poultry). The area is also well known for its wines.

Accommodation Several hotels, motels and caravan/camping parks.

Features On the northern edge of the town is the Pioneer Park Museum, an open-air museum, with 25 buildings of the late 19th and early 20th centuries.

Vineyards, Griffith

Cocoparra National Park

Location; area
19km/12 miles north-east of Griffith in the Riverina area; 8356 hectares/20,639 acres.

Access
From Griffith via Yenda and on the Barry Scenic Drive to the south through the National Park to Binya or Rankin Springs. Alternatively the park can be reached on the old (easily negotiable) Whitton Stock Route along its western boundary.

Accommodation
In Griffin and Yenda. Bush camping in the park; short-stay camping in rest area at Woolshed Flat to the north-west.

Facilities
Bush walking, picnic area; no drinking water.

Features
The park (established in 1969) takes in an area of low hills in a plain with deep depressions (e.g. the narrow Ladysmith Glen). The vegetation consists of cypress pines, dry sclerophyllous (hard-leaved) forest and a variety of wattles and wild flowers.

The Riverina area was first explored by John Oxley in 1817. The Witton Stock Route along the western boundary of the park was travelled by coaches in the 19th century.

Gulgong J 6

Situation and characteristics
The well preserved little gold-digging town of Gulgong (pop. 2050), 295km/185 miles north-west of Sydney, is familiar from its appearance on the Australian 10 dollar note. Also featured on the note is the well-known poet Henry Lawson, who lived in the area as a child. During the gold fever of 1870 some 20,000 people came to the town to look for gold, but ten years later they had all gone.

Accommodation
Hotels, motels, caravan/camping park.

Features
Gulgong is a town of narrow winding streets with many old wooden houses and shops, the Prince of Wales Opera House (1871) and the Gulgong Pioneer Museum.

★Gundagai J 6

Situation and characteristics
Gundagai (pop. 2310), 398km/247 miles south-west of Sydney on the Murrumbidgee River, features in many songs and poems. The name of the little town is derived from an Aboriginal word meaning "upstream". The first settlement on the site was destroyed by a flood in 1852 in which 89 people died – a third of the population. The local Aborigines had warned that the river sometimes suddenly burst its banks, but their warning was not heeded. Between 1860 and 1890 the town went through the turmoil of the gold rush and raids by bushrangers. The main products of the area are wool, wheat, fruit and vegetables.

Accommodation
Several hotels, motels and caravan/camping parks.

Features
On Hume Highway is a popular picnic area where Hume and Hovell, Mitchell and Sturt rested on their expeditions. For more than 100 years all the traffic on the Hume Highway went over a 900m/1000yd long timber viaduct, Australia's longest wooden bridge. It is now closed to motor traffic and has been replaced by an 1100m/1200yd long concrete causeway.

There are a number of old buildings in Sheridan Street (hotel, bank, courthouse, St Patrick's Church). The Gabriel Gallery has an excellent collection of turn-of-the-century photographs.

There is an interesting Historical Museum in Homer Street.

Surroundings
8km/5 miles north of the town at Snake Gully, on Five Mile Creek, is the Dog on the Tucker Box monument, commemorating pioneer teamsters and their dogs. The monument was the work of Frank Rusconis, who also made the marble model of a cathedral in the tourist information office in Gundagai. On the other side of the highway are copper statues of two favourite folk characters, Dad and Dave.

Wooden bridge, Gundagai

From the Mount Parnassus Lookout there are good views of Gundagai and the surrounding area.

Hartley Historic Site K 6

Situation and characteristics

The little township of Hartley, 134km/83 miles west of Sydney on the Great Western Highway, at the foot of the Victoria Pass, was one of the first settlements on the road through the Blue Mountains to Bathurst (see entries) and after 1814 an important stopover for settlers on their way west. The road was constructed by convicts, who also built the Courthouse (1837). The area classed as a Historic Site includes the Royal Hotel, St Bernard's Church, two inns and a number of cottages.

Accommodation

For all practical purposes there is none.

★Hawkesbury River K 6

Situation and characteristics

The Hawkesbury River to the north of Sydney, one of the most beautiful rivers in Australia, played an important part in the early days of the colony of New South Wales. The first settlers arrived in the area in 1794, establishing farms which contributed to the survival of the colony, threatened with starvation by the shortage of food. In 1810 Governor Macquarie ordered the foundation of five towns in the upper Hawkesbury valley which became known as the "Macquarie towns" – Windsor, Richmond (see entries), Castlereagh, Wilberforce and Pitt Town (see entry) – which have preserved many historic old buildings.

The surrounding area is still farming country, and the river is still flanked for considerable distances by unspoiled woodland and bush.

The Hawkesbury River offers excellent facilities for water sports, particularly in its lower reaches between Brooklyn and Pittwater, where it becomes very wide. The best way of seeing it is by boat, and boats of all sizes can be hired in Brooklyn, near the Hawkesbury River Bridge, and also at Bobbin Head, Berowra Waters and Wisemans Ferry. The mailboat which sails upstream from Brooklyn, leaving at 9.30am, also takes passengers. There are also organised boat trips on the intricate river system and to Broken Bay.

At Wisemans Ferry the river can be crossed by ferry. A road on the north bank runs along the boundary of Dharug National Park from Wisemans Ferry via Gunderman and Spencer and through the Mangrove valley to Mangrove Mountain (48km/30 miles).

The freeway from Sydney to Newcastle crosses the Hawkesbury and its tributary the Mooney (sheer sandstone cliffs and fascinating views).

The Hawkesbury River is surrounded by four National Parks. It forms the northern boundary of the old-established Ku-ring-gai Chase National Park, to the north of Sydney, and the southern boundary of Brisbane Water National Park (see Gosford). To the north-west is Dharug National Park, famed for its Aboriginal rock drawings, and to the north of Broken Bay (Marine Park) is Bouddi National Park.

Hill End Historic Site — J 6

Situation and characteristics

The township of Hill End lies amid the rugged hills and gorges of the Central Tableland between Bathurst and Mudgee (80km/50 miles north of Bathurst via Sofala). In gold rush days it was a fabulously wealthy town with a population of over 30,000 in 1872, 50 hotels and a mile and a half long row of shops. After 1874, when the gold was worked out, the gold-diggers departed, leaving only ruins and memories. The old hospital has been restored and now houses a museum.

★Hunter Valley — K 6

Situation and characteristics

The Hunter Valley, the largest expanse of lowlands in the coastal regions of New South Wales, was discovered around 1819 and, with its fertile arable land and good grazing, was soon settled. The prosperity of the area depends on coal and wine: the first vines were planted as early as 1832. The town's old houses and mansions have changed little since the 19th century. On the lower course of the Hunter River are a number of half-forgotten river ports.

History

Around 1804 the convict settlement of Coal River, near Newcastle, was established to work the rich deposits of coal under the green grazing land.

Before the construction of a steelworks in 1915 the export of coal was Newcastle's main source of income, and the area became known as the "Ruhr of New South Wales". Extensive opencast mining operations, still continuing and planned for the future, have increasingly eaten up the agricultural land.

Wine-growing

After a period of prosperity round the turn of the century the wine-producing industry suffered a severe setback during the depression of the 1930s, recovering only in the sixties. Although only a small proportion of total Australian wine production comes from the Hunter Valley, the wines made here are of particular quality (Lindeman, McWilliam, Drayton, Tyrell, Tulloch). The best time to visit the area is in February, when the wine harvest is in full swing. There are innumerable opportunities for tasting the local wines, and there are some first-class restaurants in the area (Hungerford Hill, Pokolbin).

On the Illawarra Coast

Illawarra Coast (Leisure Coast) K 6/7

Situation and characteristics

There are magnificent panoramic views from the winding Princes Highway, which runs along the rugged Illawarra coast. The name is a corruption of an Aboriginal word meaning "high and pleasant place by the sea".

Extending south from Sydney for 300km/185 miles to Batemans Bay, the Illawarra coast is bounded on the west by the Southern Highlands. Along the craggy coast are beautiful surfing beaches, with numerous mountain streams and waterfalls. The inlets and lakes are ideal for water sports and prawn-fishing, and there is an abundance of flowers and fauna.

Illawarra Escarpment State Recreation Area

Location; area: 80km/50 miles south of Sydney; 1250 hectares/3110 acres.
Access: Via Princes Highway.
Accommodation: In Wollongong.
Facilities: Picnic areas, walking trails (particularly round Mount Keira and Mount Kembla).
Features: The Illawarra Escarpment State Recreation Area, established in 1980, consists of five separate areas extending from the Bulli Pass on Regent Mountain in the north to the Bong Bong Pass in the south along the Illawarra escarpment, the scenic backdrop to Wollongong. It provides protection for an expanse of natural bush country within a highly industrialised region.

Iluka K 5

Situation and characteristics

Iluka (pop. 1810) is a coastal resort on the estuary of the Clarence River, 70km/45 miles north of Grafton. Opposite it, on the south side of the delta, is the holiday resort of Yamba (see entry). Iluka is known for its fishing, and a deep-sea fishing fleet operates from its harbour. Immediately north of the little town are the Iluka Rainforest Nature Reserve and Bundjalung National Park (see Evans Head).

Accommodation

Motel, several caravan/camping parks.

Inverell K 5

Situation and characteristics

Inverell (pop. 97000, known as "Sapphire City", lies 70km/45 miles west of Glen Innes on the Gwydir River and on the Gwydir Highway, in fertile farming country. Industrial diamonds, zircons, zinc and sapphires are mined in the area. Visitors can hunt for precious stones with a permit obtainable from the tourist information office.

Accommodation

Several hotels, motels and caravan/camping parks.

Features

Courthouse (1868), with clock-tower; Pioneer Village (homestead and other buildings of around 1840); church and inn.

Surroundings

30km/19 miles south is Copeton Dam State Recreation Area (water sports). 57km/37 miles north is the little New England town of Ashford, in the centre of a tobacco-growing area. North-west of Ashford are limestone caves and the Macintyre Falls; to the south is the Pindari Dam (caravan/camping park).

Jerilderie J 7

Situation and characteristics

Jerilderie (pop. 1100), a little settlement on Billabong Creek, 60km/37½ miles north of Tocumwal on the border with Victoria, was founded in the mid 19th century and developed into a staging-point on the Newell Highway. It is now the centre of a large sheep-farming area. In 1879 it was held for two days by the Kelly gang, who captured the police station, cut the telegraph wires and robbed the bank.

Accommodation

Hotel, several motels and caravan/camping parks.

★Jindabyne J 7

Situation and characteristics

Jindabyne (alt. 930m/3050ft; pop. 2000), a new settlement on the shores of Lake Jindabyne, is a holiday resort which attracts skiers in winter and anglers, water sports enthusiasts and bush walkers in summer. The town's original site on the banks of the Snowy River was drowned by the damming of the river under the Snowy Mountains hydro-electric scheme.

Accommodation

Several hotels, motels and caravan/camping parks.

Features

Jindabyne is a good base from which to visit the Snowy Mountains and Kosciusko National Park (see entries). In winter there is a shuttle bus service to Perisher Valley and Smiggin Holes (see Snowy Mountains). After the snow melts it is possible to drive to Charlotte Pass (see Snowy Mountains), from which Mount Kosciusko can be climbed. A chair-lift at Thredbo operates throughout the year.

Kanangra-Boyd National Park J 6

Location; area

190km/120 miles west of Sydney, near the Jenolan Caves; 68,300 hectares/168,700 acres.

Facilities

Bush camping; bush walking, fishing.

Features

There was a nature reserve in this area from 1890; the present National Park was established in 1968, taking in the southern part of Blue Mountains National Park (see Blue Mountains). There are fine views of the Blue

Mountains from Kanangra Walls. There are impressive waterfalls plunging down from the main plateau into the Grand Kanangra Gorge. Limestone caves, still unexplored.

Katoomba J 6

Situation and characteristics

Katoomba (pop. 13,070), 100km/60 miles west of Sydney, is a highly developed tourist centre in the Blue Mountains (see entry) which draws some 3 million visitors every year. Along with the smaller neighbouring towns of Wentworth (see entry) and Leura, Katoomba rapidly developed in the second half of the 19th century from a coal-mining town into a popular holiday resort, easily accessible by rail from Sydney. Centrally situated in Blue Mountains National Park, it is well equipped with galleries, boutiques and good restaurants.

80km/50 miles from the town, on the south-western edge of the Blue Mountains, are Australia's best known caves, the Jenolan Caves (see Lithgow).

Accommodation

Numerous hotels, motels and caravan/camping parks.

Surroundings of Katoomba

★★Three Sisters

Close to Katoomba is the best-known tourist sight in the Blue Mountains, the striking rock formations known as the Three Sisters, which are floodlit at night. Legend has it that they are three sisters who were bewitched and turned to stone.

Scenic Skyway

The Scenic Skyway is a cableway which runs horizontally across the mountain gorge above Cooks Crossing, with impressive views of Katoomba Falls, Orphan Rock and Jamison valley. The cableway was constructed about 1880 for the transport of miners and of coal.

Three Sisters

Scenic Railway

The Scenic Railway runs down into Jamison valley, with an average gradient of 45°.

Cliff Drive

Cliff Drive follows the cliff tops round Katoomba and Leura, with spectacular views and many picnic spots.

Walking trails along the cliff tops and into Jamison valley runs through rain forest and heathland. There are facilities for riding, driving (four-wheel-drive vehicles), cycling and walking.

Explorers' Tree

The Explorers' Tree, west of Katoomba, commemorates Gregory Blaxland, Henry Lawson and William Wentworth, who were the first to travel through the mountains. There are many lookouts with views of the Wentworth Falls, which plunge down 300m/1000ft into Jamison valley.

Lindsay Museum

The house in Springwood occupied by the painter Norman Lindsay from 1912 to 1969 is now a museum, with a collection of the artist's works.

Other sights

From Katoomba the highway continues to Lithgow (40km/25 miles; see entry) by way of Medlow Bath, Blackheath, Mount Victoria and Hartley, an important stopover for travellers in early colonial days which preserves a number of old buildings of around 1830–40 (see Hartley Historic Site). From Lithgow the return to Sydney (150km/95 miles) can be on "Bells Line of Road" by way of Bell and the old settlements of Richmond and Windsor (see entries).

Near Mount Victoria (Historical Museum at station), on Mount York, is a monument to Blaxland, Lawson and Wentworth.

Kempsey K 6

Situation and characteristics

Kempsey (pop. 24,720), 480km/300 miles north of Sydney on the Macleay River and the Pacific Highway, is, after Port Macquarie (see entry), the oldest town in the northern coastal region of New South Wales. It lies between the Dividing Range and the coast.

Accommodation

Many hotels, motels and caravan/camping parks.

Surroundings

Trial Bay Gaol (see p. 113).

Hat Head National Park

Location; area

24km/15 miles north-east of Kempsey; 6400 hectares/15,800 acres.

Access

From Kempsey (off road to South West Rocks).

Facilities

Camping sites, picnic spots; no drinking water. Fishing, swimming (no lifeguards).

Features

This coastal area, declared a National Park in 1972, extends from Smoky Cape to Crescent Head, with sand-dunes, dune lakes and marshland.

Walking trails

There are coastal trails at Hat Head and Smoky Cape.

★Kiama J 6

Situation and characteristics

The best-known attraction of Kiama (pop. 10,960), founded around 1830 in a dairy farming region, is the Blowhole, discovered by George Bass in 1797, which spouts water to a height of 60m/200ft and is floodlit in the evening. There is also a Little Blowhole. At Jones Beach are the striking Cathedral Rocks. Good beaches for water sports and fishing.

Accommodation

Several hotels, motels and caravan/camping parks. Accommodation also in Gerringong.

Features

Kiama has some fine old 19th century houses (e.g. the Coach-House Gallery of 1858 and the Terrace), built in 1885 to house workers but now occupied by shops and small restaurants.

Surroundings

11km/7 miles south of Kiama on the Illawarra coast is Gerringong, a holiday resort with beautiful beaches of white sand. To the south is Seven Mile Beach National Park, with a monument to the aviation pioneer Charles Kingsford Smith (also commemorated in the name of Sydney's airport), who in 1933 flew from Seven Mile Beach to New Zealand.

★★Kosciusko National Park J 7

Location; area

20km/12½ miles west of Jindabyne; 690,000 hectares/1,704,000 acres (one of the world's largest National Parks).

Access

On Snowy Mountains Highway. In summer all roads into the mountain region are open; on some roads within the park snow chains must be fitted from June 1st to October 10th. Some roads may be closed between May and October.

Accommodation

In tourist and winter sports areas in the Snowy Mountains.

Facilities

Visitor centre on Sawpit Creek near Lake Jindabyne.

Features

Kosciusko National Park takes in the highest peaks in Australia (five summits over 2100m/6890ft), and with its extensive snowfields is one of the most popular winter sports areas in the country. In summer the fascinating variety of its flora and fauna attracts bush walkers, climbers, anglers and water sports enthusiasts.

History

Around 1830 James Spencer found his way to this region and settled at Waste Point on the Snowy River. He knew the mountain country well and had driven up sheep and cattle to graze here in summer. He is believed to have named many of the mountains and rivers, and he introduced other explorers and scientists to the region. From the end of the 19th century onwards various reserves were created for the protection of nature and for recreation, and finally the Kosciusko State Park was established; then in 1967 the National Parks and Wildlife Service took over its management and it was renamed Kosciusko National Park. The region was opened up for tourism by the construction of roads under the Snowy Mountains hydro-electric scheme (see Snowy Mountains) in the fifties and sixties of this century.

Mount Kosciusko was given its name by the Polish explorer Paul Edmund de Strzelecki, who climbed the mountains from the west side and named the highest peak after the Polish freedom fighter Tadeusz Koś-

In the Kosciusko National Park

ciuszko because it resembled Kościuszko's tomb in Warsaw. The mountain was also climbed around 1880 by Charlotte Adams, after whom Charlotte Pass (see Snowy Mountains) is named.

Leeton J 6

Situation and characteristics

Leeton (pop. 6900), 560km/350 miles south-west of Sydney, the first of the planned towns in the Murrumbidgee Irrigation Area (1912), was designed by Walter Burley Griffin. The town's economy depends on the intensive culture of fruit, rice and wine grapes, a fruit cannery and a juice factory (open to visitors).

Accommodation

Several hotels, motels and caravan/camping parks.

Surroundings

9km/5½ miles north-west is Koonadan Historic Site, home of the Wiradjuri tribe of Aborigines.

Lightning Ridge J 5

Situation and characteristics

Lightning Ridge (pop. 2670), situated to the east of the Castlereagh Highway 74km/46 miles north of Walgett (see entry) and 60km/37 miles south of the boundary with Queensland, is surrounded by the famous Lightning Ridge opal fields, in which the valuable black opals are found. The veins of opals lie 20m/65ft under the surface, and the landscape is patterned by spoil heaps and abandoned mines. Although the summers are very hot and the winters cool the opal-miners do not live in underground dwellings as they do in White Cliffs (see entry) and the opal fields of Queensland and South Australia.

Accommodation

Several hotels, motels and caravan/camping parks.

Lismore K 5

Situation and characteristics

Lismore (pop. 40,120), 820km/510 miles north of Sydney on the Bruxner Highway, is the largest town in the Northern Rivers district of New South Wales and the centre of an intensively cultivated agricultural region (dairy farming, tropical fruits, beef, fodder plants, timber).

The town was founded by loggers around 1840 and in the 19th century was an important timber-shipping port.

Accommodation

Many hotels, motels and caravan/camping parks.

Features

Wilsons River Heritage Centre, Lismore Regional Art Gallery.

The town is charmingly situated on the Wilsons River, surrounded by hills with rain forest reserves (many picnic areas).

Surroundings

Round Lismore are three nature reserves – Border Ranges National Park and Mount Warning National Park (on both, see Murwillumbah) and Nightcap National Park.

Lithgow K 6

Situation and characteristics

Lithgow (pop. 11,960), 145km/90 miles west of Sydney, is an important coal-mining town on the north-western fringes of the Blue Mountains, in beautiful surrounding countryside.

Accommodation

Several hotels and motels.

Surroundings

The great attraction for railway enthusiasts is the Zig Zag Railway (10km/6 miles east of Lithgow on the road to Bell), built in 1869 through breathtaking scenery and now partly restored.

5km/3 miles south of Lithgow, just off the Great Western Highway, is the Hassan Walls Lookout, with wide views of the mountains.

Hartley Historic Site

9km/5½ miles south-east is Hartley Historic Site (see entry), with an interesting courthouse built by convict labour.

★★Jenolan Caves

The Jenolan Caves, 60km/37 miles south of Lithgow, are the best-known karstic caves in Australia. The caves with their glittering stalactites and stalagmites in the form of columns and waterfalls were first explored in 1866 and are open daily to visitors. A system of footpaths leads to the eight caves which can be entered; parts of the complex are still unexplored.

The caves are best reached from Hartley or from South Bowenfels on the Great Western Highway.

Surroundings

In the surrounding area is a nature reserve with good walking trails and picnic facilities; superb view to the south of the hills in the Kanangra Boyd National Park, which merges into the southern part of the Blue Mountains National Park (see Blue Mountains).

Maitland J 6

Situation and characteristics

Maitland (pop. 33,440) lies on the Hunter River, 28km/17 miles from Newcastle (see entry) on the New England Highway. The first settlement on the site was established in 1818, when convicts were set to felling timber in the area. Around 1840 it developed into a thriving town and is now the commercial centre of the Hunter Valley (agriculture, coal, industry, shopping centre). Many people commute to Newcastle from here.

Accommodation

Hotels, motels.

Features

The winding High Street and Regent Street in the town centre have been declared a conservation area by the National Trust, since almost all the buildings date from the 19th century. The most interesting features are Grossman House (1860–62), Brough House (1870) and St Mary's Church (Anglican; 1867).

Menindee H 6

Situation and characteristics

Menindee (pop. 800) is a small township on the Darling River in which Burke and Wills established a base camp on their ill-fated expedition to the north in 1860. The Menindee Lake, upstream from the township (excellent facilities for water sports), supply water to Broken Hill (see entry), an artificial oasis in the arid outback 110km/70 miles north-west of Menindee.

The transcontinental railway line from Perth to Sydney runs via Menindee.

Accommodation

Hotels, motel, caravan/camping parks.

Kinchega National Park

Location; area

On the west bank of the Darling River 2km/1¼ miles west of Menindee; 44,182 hectares/109,130 acres.

Access

From Menindee or Broken Hill (111km/69 miles, asphalted road). All other roads are gravel roads or tracks.

Facilities

Simple camping sites; swimming, fishing, bush walking trails, animal- and bird-watching; visitor centre 15km/9 miles south-west of Menindee; picnic spots on banks of Darling.

Features

Kinchega National Park was established in 1967 by the New South Wales government in co-operation with the Broken Hill mining companies. In the mid 19th century the red sandy plains and expanses of black earth once formed the huge Kinchega station, one of the first grazing farms in the Darling valley, an area explored by John Mitchell in 1835 which was frequently a staging-point for other expeditions (Sturt, Wills and Burke).

★Merimbula · Pambula J 7

Situation and characteristics

Merimbula and its sister village Pambula (joint population 425) are popular holiday resorts famed for their beautiful beaches and excellent fishing (boat hire). The only relic of the former little port is the old school (1870), now a museum.

Accommodation

Numerous motels and caravan/camping parks.

Surroundings

To the south, on the coast, is Ben Boyd National Park (see Eden).

Merriwa K 6

Situation and characteristics

The little township of Merriwa (pop. 960) in the western Hunter region is noted for its many old buildings (churches, police station, courthouse, museum).

Accommodation

Motel, caravan/camping park.

Surroundings

Round Merriwa there are many rock formations and a petrified forest. 27km/17 miles south-west is a gem-fossicking area.

Mittagong K 6

Situation and characteristics

Mittagong (pop. 4970), situated on the Hume Highway between Sydney and Goulburn, is the gateway to the Southern Highlands and the birthplace of Australia's iron and steel industry. The town was founded in 1850 by steel-workers from Sheffield (hence its other name of New Sheffield), but its ironworking industry proved unsuccessful and was closed down around 1880. Mittagong was discovered in 1798 by explorers who encountered koalas and lyrebirds here. As a busy stopover on the way to Goulburn in the 19th century the town is well equipped with hotels and inns, including some historic old buildings

Accommodation

Hotels, motels and caravan/camping parks.

Wombeyan Caves

Situation

60km/37 miles north-west of Mittagong in the Southern Highlands are the Wombeyan Caves. Five caves in this extensive cave system (Wollondilly, Kooringa, Fig Tree, Mulwaree and Junction Caves) have an excellent network of paths for visitors.

Access

On side road to Wombeyan and a narrow winding road through impressive mountain scenery. The obligatory route for caravans is via Goulburn, Taralga and Richlands.

Molong J 6

Situation and characteristics

Molong (pop. 1540), situated on the Mitchell Highway 90km/56 miles north-west of Bathurst, is famed for its wool and its wheat. It was founded in 1845 as a State cattle station, and a copper mine was opened in the same year.

Accommodation

Hotels, motel, caravan/camping park.

Features

Museum, housed in an old inn. 4km/2½ miles east, marked by trees with Aboriginal carvings, is the grave of Yuranigh, the Aboriginal guide who accompanied Sir Thomas Mitchell on his expedition to Queensland in 1845–46 (Historic Site).

Surroundings

21km/13 miles south is a monument to Mitchell, on the spot where he pitched his base camp on many journeys of exploration.

★Mootwingee National Park H 6

Location; area
1300km/800 miles west of Sydney and 130km/80 miles north-east of Broken Hill; 68,912 hectares/170,213 acres.

Access
On tracks from Broken Hill, Tibooburra and White Cliffs (possible only in dry weather).

Facilities
Camping sites, picnic spots; no drinking water, no provisions.

Features
Mootwingee National Park, centred on Mootwingee Historic Site (485 hectares/1200 acres; Nootumbulla Creek, with many Aboriginal remains), is one of the youngest of the National Parks, a semi-arid region with rugged sandstone hills and water-holes in narrow gorges. Many Aboriginal rock paintings and drawings, and evidence of early white settlement and exploration.

From the peaks in the Bynguano Range there are good views of the surrounding plains. The mountain kangaroo can be seen here, particularly in the late afternoon.

Moruya K 7

Situation and characteristics
320km/200 miles south of Sydney on the Moruya River and the Pacific Highway, only 6km/4 miles from the sea, is Moruya (pop. 2530), once the gateway to the goldfields of Braidwood (see entry) and Araluen. The town's economy now depends on dairy farming, timber and oyster culture. The granite used in the construction of Sydney Harbour Bridge came from this area.

Accommodation
Several hotels, motels and caravan/camping parks.

Moss Vale K 6

Situation and characteristics
Moss Vale (pop. 5690) lies 153km/95 miles south-west of Sydney in the hinterland of the Illawarra coast, on a site granted to Charles Throsby in 1819. It is now the agricultural and industrial centre of the Southern Highlands.

Accommodation
Several hotels, motels and caravan/camping parks.

Features
On the Illawarra Highway is Throsby Historic Site, with a number of interesting old farmhouses.

Morton National Park

Location; area
19km/12 miles south-east of Moss Vale; 162,400 hectares/401,100 acres.

Access
Northern part of the park: via the road from Moss Vale, or from the Illawarra Highway via Avoca. Southern part: from Braidwood to Nerriga; coming from the Princes Highway via Nowra to Sassafras.

Facilities
Camping sites at Fitzroy Falls and Gambells Rest; visitor centre at Fitzroy Falls; picnic spots, walking trails and many viewpoints.

Features
Parts of this National Park were declared recreation areas and nature reserves in 1938; the park itself was established in 1967. The dominant feature of the park is a sandstone plateau, with steep rock faces, deep gorges, river valleys, waterfalls and patches of subtropical rain forest. Metamorphic rocks lying under the sandstone have been carved into jagged shapes by erosion. The park's main attraction is the Fitzroy Falls.

The Fitzroy Falls in Morton National Park ▶

Mudgee J 6

Situation and characteristics
Mudgee (pop. 7440), 264km/164 miles north-west of Sydney, is one of the oldest towns to the west of the Blue Mountains. Laid out in 1838 to the design of Robert Hoddle, who later planned Melbourne, it lies in a beautiful setting on the Cudgegong River.

Accommodation
Several hotels, motels and caravan/camping parks.

Features
Many old buildings have been preserved in the town centre (churches, railway station, Town Hall, Colonial Inn Museum, police station, post office).

Surroundings
To the west of the town is Burrendong Dam (artificial lake), to the east Windamere Dam (water sports, fishing, camping).

Mulwala J 7

Situation and characteristics
Mulwala (pop. 1750) lies 85km/53 miles west of Albury-Wodonga on the shores of Lake Mulwala, an artificial lake created by the damming of the Murray River in 1939 to provide water for irrigation. The neighbouring town of Yarrawonga, developing faster, has now outstripped Mulwala.

Accommodation
Hotels, motels.

Features
Mulwala is a popular water sports centre, and there are cruises on Lake Mulwala. The trunks of trees drowned by the lake were left standing to break the waves in a storm. The Mulwala Canal is an important element in the Murray River irrigation project, conveying water 120km/75 miles north and irrigating more than 2000 farms.

★Mungo National Park H 6

Location; area
1150km/715 miles west of Sydney; 27,800 hectares/68,700 acres.

Access
Via Mildura, Buronga and the road to Arumpo, 114km/71 miles (track).

Facilities
Camping sites; good facilities for visitors; bush walking trails, observation of nature, picnic spots.

Features
Mungo National Park was established in 1979 on the old Mungo sheep station, which had been bought by the National Parks and Wildlife Foundation. The area was part of an old water system which dried up after the last Ice Age, some 15,000 years ago.

Round the shores of the former lake are white sand-dunes known as the Walls of China. Archaeological finds suggest that the Lake Mungo area was occupied by man 40,000 years ago.

Murrurundi K 6

Situation and characteristics
Murrurundi (pop. 980) lies 94km/58 miles south of Tamworth (see entry) on the New England Highway, set in a lush valley in the Liverpool Ranges, in the north of the Hunter region. The area was first settled around 1820.

Accommodation
Motels, caravan/camping park.

Features
Handsome old buildings: White Hart Hotel (1842), Courthouse, St Joseph's Church (*c.* 1860).

Surroundings
43km/27 miles east are the Timor limestone caves.

Murwillumbah K 5

Situation and characteristics
Amid the banana and sugar-cane plantations near the boundary with Queensland, on the Tweed River 32km/20 miles above its mouth at Tweed

Heads, is the town of Murwillumbah. The Condong sugar mill can be visited between June and December, after the sugar-cane harvest.

Accommodation: Several hotels, motels and caravan/camping parks.

★Mount Warning National Park

Location; area: 30km/19 miles west of Murwillumbah 2200 hectares/5400 acres.

Access: From Murwillumbah on the road to Kyogle via Dum Dum.

Facilities: Camping site on access road, on banks of river; picnic area on Breakfast Creek; bush walking trail.

Features: This area was declared a nature reserve in 1928, centred on Mount Warning (so named by Captain Cook), which dominates the whole of the Tweed valley. Mount Warning (1156m/3793ft) is the remnant of a lava plug in the magma chamber of a huge former volcano, the Border Ranges being the last remains of its side walls. On the lower slopes of the mountain the vegetation consists of subtropical rain forest; higher up it is temperate rain forest with many species of birds.

★Nambucca Heads K 6

Situation and characteristics: The beautifully situated little town of Nambucca Heads (pop. 6250) at the mouth of the Nambucca River, 552km/343 miles north of Sydney on the Pacific Highway, is a popular holiday resort (boating, fishing, swimming).

Accommodation: Numerous hotels, motels and caravan/camping parks.

Features: Breathtaking views from local viewpoints, particularly Yarrahapinni Lookout.

The harbour, Nambucca Heads

Narooma K 7

Situation and characteristics

The fishing port and holiday resort of Narooma (pop. 3450), 360km/225 miles south of Sydney on the Princes Highway, lies at the mouth of the Wagonga River and has beautiful beaches.

Accommodation

Numerous hotels, motels and caravan/camping parks.

Surroundings

Montague Island, 8km/5 miles off the coast, is a wild life sanctuary in an area favoured by deep-sea anglers.

Near Narooma are a number of beautiful lakes and inlets.

Tilba Tilba, 15km/9 miles south on the Princes Highway, is a little settlement which has remained almost unchanged since the 19th century. It has been classified by the National Trust as an "unusual mountain village".

Narrabri J 6

Situation and characteristics

Narrabri (pop. 7440) lies on the Newell Highway 280km/175 miles north of Dubbo (see entry), near the Nandewar Range (Mount Kaputar National Park). It is an old-established agricultural town, though in recent decades cotton (now covering over 50,000 hectares/125,000 acres) has been displacing wheat. Near the town are a solar observatory and a station for measuring cosmic radiation.

Accommodation

Several hotels, motels and caravan/camping parks.

Features

A good base for visiting Mount Kaputar National Park (see below).

The Nandewar Range, Narrabri

Mount Kaputar National Park

Location; area
53km/33 miles east of Narrabri; 36,800 hectares/90,900 acres.

Access
From Narrabri on a road which is sometimes steep and narrow (41km/25 miles an unsurfaced track unsuitable for caravans). Access to northern and central areas from Narrabri–Bingara road and Narrabri–Terry Hie Hie track. No access from Barraba.

Facilities
New camping site at Bark Hut; bush walking, rock-climbing, observation of nature. At Dawsons Spring, at the end of the access road, there are picnic areas and camping sites; no provisions. Visitor centre at Dawsons Spring (32km/20 miles east).

Features
Mount Kaputar National Park, named after the hill of that name (1524m/5000ft), is part of the Nandewar Range and, like the rest of the range, was formed by ancient volcanic activity.

The first European in this area was an escaped convict who came here and lived with the Aborigines. When he was recaptured in 1830 he told Thomas Mitchell about a river named Kindur, and in the following year Mitchell set out to look for the river and found the curiously shaped hills which he called the Nundawar (later Nundewar) Range. The region was settled in the second half of the 19th century. In 1925 an area of 777 hectares/1919 acres was declared a nature reserve, and in 1958 this was extended to form the present National Park. Numerous viewpoints which can be reached by car. Swan Rock is a 40m/130ft high basalt formation resembling organ-pipes.

Walking trails
There are walking trails in different degrees of difficulty, running through rich and varied vegetation (dry eucalyptus forest, wild flowers in spring, snow gums on summits, areas of wet forest and ferns in valleys), with magnificent panoramic views. Rich wild life, in particular numerous birds.

Narrandera J 6

Situation and characteristics
Narrandera (pop. 5000), one of the oldest settlements in the Riverina area, lies 580km/360 miles south-west of Sydney and 430km/265 miles north of Melbourne at the junction of the Newell and Sturt Highways.

Accommodation
Several hotels, motels and caravan/camping parks.

Features
The town has been declared an urban conservation area by the National Trust on account of its many 19th century buildings. There is a monument to Charles Sturt, who camped here in 1826 on his journey to Lake Alexandrina in South Australia.

★Nelson Bay J 6

Situation and characteristics
This beautiful bay is the main anchorage of Port Stephens (see entry), 60km/37 miles north of Newcastle, with excellent fishing waters. Rich flora and wild life in the surrounding area.

Accommodation
Hotel, motels and caravan/camping park.

★New England K 5/6

Situation
New England is a beautiful highland region, with magnificent mountains and many waterfalls, in the hinterland of the Holiday Coast, which extends northward from Port Macquarie to the border with Queensland. Its rivers, streams and artificial lakes (Pindari and Copeton Dams) offer good fishing and excellent facilities for water sports. Its fertile black soil produces wheat and, particularly to the west, cotton, and its excellent grazing nourishes sheep and cattle. It is a good area for gem fossicking (hunting for precious stones). At Glen Innes and Inverell (see entries) there are "sapphire

reserves" where the necessary equipment can be hired; a permit is required and can be obtained from tourist information offices.

New England National Park

Location; area
576km/358 miles north of Sydney, 67km/42 miles east of Armidale; 29,900 hectares/73,900 acres.

Access
From the west by way of the Armidale–Grafton road, 15km/9 miles south of Ebor, then access road to park entrance (11km/7 miles).

Accommodation
In Ebor, Dorrigo, Armidale and Guyra. Camping sites immediately outside park, and some huts in park (previous booking necessary).

Facilities
Picnic areas, mountain huts.

Features
The New England National Park extends over the steep slopes rising from the Bellinger River to the New England plateau (over 1400m/4600ft). Declared a National Park in 1931 and enlarged in 1983, it contains one of the largest surviving areas of rain forest in New South Wales. Three different zones can be distinguished: sub-alpine flora with snow gums at the upper levels, temperate rain forest below this and subtropical rain forest with numerous ferns and orchids in the depressions. There are breathtaking views from Point Lookout of the almost vertical escarpment; in good weather the view extends as far as the Pacific.

Walking trails
There are walking trails along the foot of the escarpment to the areas of rain forest and bush trails through the wilderness. Climbing trips are for experienced climbers only.

★ Newcastle K 6

Situation and characteristics
Newcastle (pop. 432,600 with suburbs), 158km/98 miles north of Sydney, is the second largest city in New South Wales, an important industrial centre

Town centre, Newcastle

(steelworks established 1915) and one of Australia's busiest ports. The area was settled at an early stage, with a penal colony established in 1804, and coal-mining began soon afterwards. It enjoyed a great upsurge of prosperity after becoming the principal port in the Hunter area in the mid 19th century (steel, coal, wheat, wool).

Accommodation

Many hotels, motels and caravan/camping parks.

Features

Historic buildings extend from the waterfront up the hill, bearing witness to the town's prosperity at the end of the 19th century (customs house, railway station, Christ Church Cathedral, courthouse, post office). The Historical Museum (Brown and Pitt Streets) illustrates the history of the town, Hunter Valley and the Newcastle region. The Art Gallery has a good collection of Australian art, particularly of the 19th century.

At the tip of the peninsula (Nobby's Road) is Fort Scratchley, built in 1880–86 to counter a possible Russian attack, from which there are wide views. Queen's Wharf is the centre-point of the foreshore redevelopment programme designed to clean up the coastal zone, disfigured in the past by port and industrial activities, and to provide a walkway to the city centre and scenic walks along the foreshore. The process of redevelopment was helped on by an earthquake in 1990 which caused damage in the business district. Spacious parks and gardens in the city centre; good surfing beaches on the coast. Visitors can see round the BHP steelworks at Port Waratah, the foundation of the city's industry.

Surroundings

Excursions: to Lake Macquarie, a large coastal lagoon 27km/17 miles south, and to the Hunter Valley (see entry), the well-known wine-producing region north-west of the city.

★North Coast · Holiday Coast K 5/6

Situation and characteristics

To the north of Newcastle, behind a narrow coastal strip, the hills of the Great Dividing Range rise to the New England highlands (see entry). On the long northern coasts are a number of well-known bathing resorts and a string of smaller holiday settlements, with long and often empty beaches and at some points good surfing seas.

The Pacific Highway runs for part of the way at some distance from the coast, with coastal roads serving the beaches and holiday resorts.

★Nowra K 6

Situation and characteristics

Nowra (pop. 22,300), 162km/101 miles south-west of Sydney, began life around 1850 as a little settlement on the Shoalhaven River and developed into the centre of an agricultural area. Along with Bomaderry on the north bank of the river, it is now the farming and commercial centre of the region and a popular tourist resort.

Accommodation

Several hotels. Bomaderry has a hotel/motel and a caravan/camping park.

Features

There are numbers of 18th century houses in the town and surrounding area. The Shoalhaven River offers excellent facilities for water sports, and there are a number of beautiful beaches within a radius of 30km/20 miles. The old police station now houses a historical museum.

Surroundings

18km/11 miles north of the town, in a prosperous dairy farming area, is Berry, which has preserved many old buildings. Coolangatta, 18km/11 miles east, was the first settlement in the area, with a row of convict-built cottages which have been restored to make a museum village. 20km/12½ miles north is Kangaroo Valley, a fertile region surrounded by steep wooded hills which was settled from 1831 onwards (Pioneer Farm Museum). 37km/23 miles from the town by way of Kangaroo Valley are the Fitzroy Falls in Morton National Park (see Moss Vale).

Nyngan J 6

Situation and characteristics

The little town of Nyngan (pop. 2500) lies rather more than 600km/370 miles north-west of Sydney at the junction of the Mitchell and Barrier Highways. Here Thomas Mitchell camped in 1835, when his companion Richard Cunningham, a botanist, was killed by Aborigines. The town was founded about 1880, when the railway to Bourke was built. It is famed for its wool.

Accommodation

Several hotels, motels and caravan/camping parks.

Surroundings

64km/40 miles north are the Macquarie Marshes, a bird sanctuary.

Orange J 6

Situation and characteristics

Orange (pop. 33,000), 264km/164 miles north-west of Sydney on the Mitchell Highway, is an old-established town in an agricultural district. This is the principal apple-growing area in New South Wales; other products are lambs, pigs and fodder plants. 27km/17 miles north are the Ophir goldfields, where the first gold in Australia was found in 1851, bringing wealth and prosperity to the town.

Accommodation

Many hotels, motels and caravan/camping parks.

Features

Many buildings survive from the gold-digging period, notably the Courthouse, the Post Office and St Joseph's and Trinity Churches. In Cook Park are handsome old trees.

An obelisk commemorates the town's most famous son, the poet Andrew Paterson ("The Banjo"; b. 1864).

Surroundings

14km/8½ miles south-west of Orange is Mount Canabolas (1395m/4577ft), an extinct volcano with a tree-covered crater and a bird and animal sanctuary. A road runs up to the summit on the route followed by Mitchell in 1835.

Lake Canabolas offers excellent facilities for water sports.

Parkes J 6

Situation and characteristics

364km/226 miles west of Sydney on the Newell Highway is Parkes (pop. 9500), often called the "gateway to the stars" because of the giant radio-telescope 24km/15 miles north of the town (with visitor centre). Founded in 1862, Parkes is now a commercial and industrial centre. It is named after Sir Henry Parkes, prime minister of New South Wales, who visited the town in 1873 and arranged that the most important railway in the western part of the state should pass this way.

Accommodation

Many hotels, motels and caravan/camping parks.

Features

Interesting relics of the past are preserved in the Motor Museum (veteran and vintage vehicles) and the Pioneer Park Museum. From the Shrine of Remembrance on Memorial Hill there are fine panoramic views. On the northern outskirts of the town, on the Newell Highway, is the Kelly Reserve (picnic and barbecue areas in a bush setting; visitor centre).

Surroundings

48km/30 miles north of the town, on Peak Hill, is an opencast gold-mine (picnic areas).

Penrith K 6

Situation and characteristics

57km/35 miles west of Sydney on the Great Western Highway is Penrith (pop. 33,910), a historic old town on the Nepean River, a pleasant stopover in the Sydney–Blue Mountains–Hawkesbury River region.

Accommodation

Hotel, motels, caravan/camping park.

Features

After the construction of the road through the Blue Mountains (1815) a courthouse and a small gaol were built here. There are occasional boat races on the Nepean River.

★Port Macquarie J 6

Situation and characteristics

Port Macquarie (pop. 27,720), the largest town on the northern coast of New South Wales, lies at the mouth of the Hastings River, 430km/265 miles north of Sydney and some 600km/370 miles south of Brisbane. Founded in 1821 as a convict settlement, it has become since the 1970s a popular tourist and holiday centre.

Accommodation

Many hotels, motels and caravan/camping parks.

Features

The most notable of the town's historic buildings is St Thomas's Church, one of the oldest churches in Australia, built by convict labour in 1824–28. Opposite the Courthouse (1869) is the Historical Museum, housed in a commercial building of the 1830s. Other features of interest are a lighthouse of 1879 and an observatory. Good facilities for water sports and fishing.

Surroundings

20km/12½ miles west, inland, is Wauchope (see entry), with Timbertown, a re-creation of a loggers' settlement of the 1880s.

★Port Stephens J 6

Situation and characteristics

Port Stephens Is a large and beautiful bay, 25km/15 miles long, some 240km/150 miles north-east of Sydney. Beaches of white sand, natural bush country and deep blue water give this large natural harbour enclosed by two volcanic headlands something of a tropical look. The main holiday resorts are Nelson Bay (see entry), Shoal Bay, Soldiers Point, Fingal Bay, Lemon Tree Passage, Tea Gardens and Hawks Nest.

In spite of the many thousands of holidaymakers who come here in summer there are still quiet stretches of coast. The deep-water port, less than an hour's drive from Newcastle, is the base of a fleet of fishing boats. Game fishing, water sports of all kinds; boats of all sizes for hire.

Surroundings

Myall Lakes National Park (see Bulahdelah)

Richmond J 6

Situation and characteristics

Richmond, sister town to Windsor (see entry), only 8km/5 miles away, was founded in 1810 during the governorship of Lachlan Macquarie (see Famous People). Both towns do well out of their relative nearness to Sydney, only 60km/37 miles away.

Accommodation

Hotel, motels.

Features

Hobartsville, a mansion in Castlereagh Road; St Peter's Church (1841); graveyard in which some notable pioneers are buried.

Surroundings

South of Richmond is the University of Western Sydney (founded 1895). The RAAF station is the oldest air force establishment in Australia.

Sawtell K 6

Situation and characteristics

Sawtell (pop. 10,840) is a popular holiday resort on the North or Holiday Coast, 8km/5 miles south of Coffs Harbour (see entry). Water sports, walking; beach, safe for children; entertainments.

Accommodation

Hotels, motels, caravan/camping park

Scone K 6

Situation and characteristics
Scone (pop. 4300), 280km/175 miles north of Sydney on the New England Highway, is famed as a horse-breeding centre.

Accommodation
Several hotels, motels and caravan/camping parks.

Surroundings
80km/50 miles north-east is Barrington Tops National Park (see Dungog), with beautiful scenery and good walking trails.

Shellharbour K 6

Situation and characteristics
100km/65 miles south of Sydney is the little town of Shellharbour (pop. 2710), one of the oldest settlements in the region. A thriving port in the 1830, its importance declined after the construction of the south coast railway. It is now an attractive holiday resort with good beaches (particularly on the Windang peninsula) and a favourite residence for commuters to Wollongong (see entry).

Accommodation
Motels, caravan/camping parks.

Surroundings
20km/12½ miles south-west are the Jamberoo Falls, amid beautiful scenery.

Singleton K 6

Situation and characteristics
Singleton (pop. 12,000), 80km/50 miles north-west of Newcastle (see entry), is one of the oldest settlements in the Hunter Valley (see entry). A settlement was established here around 1820, and 16 years later it was declared a town. It is named after Benjamin Singleton, owner of the first inn in the region. It is now a market centre and industrial town in a fertile agricultural area producing milk, meat, wine and vegetables. A major contribution to the town's economy is made by its extensive opencast coal-mines, much of whose output goes to the nearby Bayswater power station.

Accommodation
Several hotels, motels and caravan/camping parks.

Features
The old courthouse and gaol now houses a historical museum. George Street has preserved its 19th century style (Caledonian Hotel, banks, Old Post Office).

★★Snowy Mountains J 7

The Snowy Mountains in south-eastern New South Wales, near the boundary with Victoria, are the state's most popular winter sports area; but the combination of easily accessible mountains, alpine heathlands, lakes, streams and dams (artificial lakes) also attracts great numbers of bush walkers, climbers, anglers, water-skiers and boating enthusiasts in summer.

Snowy Mountains Hydro-electric Scheme
The object of the Snowy Mountains Hydro-electric Scheme of the 1950s and 60s was to divert water from the eastward-flowing Snowy River to irrigate the interior (the Murrumbidgee irrigation scheme) and generate electric power. This involved the construction of many artificial lakes and power stations in Kosciusko National Park (see entry), as well as the building of roads through previously inaccessible mountain country, thus opening up the region for recreation and tourism.

Winter sports
All the winter sports resorts in the Snowy Mountains are within Kosciusko National Park. They are easily accessible, and the larger resorts have excellent winter sports facilities.

Winter in the Snowy Mountains

On the upper course of the Snowy Mountains

Season

The winter sports season usually begins towards the end of May or beginning of June and lasts until the middle or end of October.

The following are the principal skiing areas:

Charlotte Pass

Charlotte Pass is 8km/5 miles from the summit of Mount Kosciusko and 98km/61 miles from Cooma (see entry). It is a good base for ski tours to the highest peaks in the Australian Alps and the venue of many skiing competitions.

Mount Blue Cow

Mount Blue Cow is another popular skiing area. It can be reached only by the Skitube underground railway, which runs from Bullocks Flat Terminal near Jindabyne (see entry) up to Perisher Valley (see below) and on to Mount Blue Cow. Ski hire and instruction, but no overnight accommodation.

Mount Selwyn

This skiing area at the northern end of Kosciusko National Park has been designed for beginners, families and school groups. It is also one of the main centres for cross-country skiing. Ski hire and instruction, but no overnight accommodation.

Perisher Valley

Perisher Valley is one of the highest and most popular resorts (both downhill and cross-country skiing) in the area, with reliable snow cover. Ski hire and instruction.

Smiggin Holes

89km/55 miles from Cooma. Linked with Perisher Valley by ski-lifts and a shuttle bus. Ski hire and instruction.

Thredbo Village

96km/60 miles from Cooma at the foot of the Crackenback Range is Thredbo Village, a world-class resort with the only giant slalom course in Australia approved by the world skiing control board. Runs in all grades of difficulty.

The chair-lift to the summit of Mount Crackenback operates throughout the year. Thredbo Village is well equipped with facilities for visitors, restaurants and entertainment. Ski hire and instruction.

South Coast J/K 7

Situation and characteristics

The South Coast of New South Wales, from Batemans Bay (see entry) to the Victorian border, is a fisherman's paradise. This stretch of coast offers an attractive variety of scenery against a backdrop of the dark summits of the Great Dividing Range – gentle hills, lakes, inlets and forests. The climate is mild throughout the year. Strung along the coast are a series of small holiday resorts offering a wide range of accommodation (much in demand during the main holiday seasons: advance booking advisable).

The most southerly places on the coast are the old fishing village of Eden (see entry) and the almost depopulated settlement of Boydtown, both once prosperous whaling stations.

★ ★Sydney K 6

Capital of New South Wales

Situation and characteristics

Sydney (pop. about 4 million), the oldest, largest and handsomest of Australian towns, lies amid a unique intermingling of land and water on Jackson Bay, its intricately ramified natural harbour, on the south-east coast of the Australian continent.

Origin of name

In 1770 Captain Cook named the natural harbour to the north of Botany Bay Port Jackson in honour of the secretary to the British Admiralty, Sir George Jackson. Eighteen years later, on January 26th 1788, Captain Arthur Phillip, commander of the First Fleet, declared a narrow inlet within Port Jackson a British colony, calling it Sydney Cove after Viscount Sydney, then secretary of state.

Olympia 2000

See Baedeker Special, pp. 174–175

Public transport

Sydney has an efficient public transport system, including suburban and underground railway lines, a monorail system, a comprehensive bus network and numerous ferries and hydrofoils. The networks, especially the underground, are being further extended with Olympia 2000 in mind. An express railway line to the airport is also in course of construction.

Accommodation

Sydney has a wide range of hotels in the first-class to luxury categories, which during the week are often fully booked but at the weekend usually offer price reductions. In addition to moderately priced hotels there are youth hostels (including the world's largest youth hostel with 532 rooms) and other cheap accommodation, mostly in the Kings Cross area. For a longer stay there are service apartments and bed and breakfast houses at reasonable prices. Visitors arriving in Sydney without a booking can apply to the Travellers' Information Service at the airport, which will try to find them a room.

Sightseeing

Sydney Pass

The Sydney Pass, valid for three days, permits travel on all forms of public transport. Also included in the price of the ticket are tours of the harbour, journeys on the City Express bus, the Bondi & Bay Explorer and the Airport Express Bus, as well as journeys within the City Rail Red Zone.

Monorail

Since 1988 the monorail has linked the city with the attractions of Darling Harbour; it operates from 8am–9pm daily.

Explorer Bus

The best introduction to the sights of Sydney is a trip on a red Sydney Explorer Bus, which travels on a circular route with stops near the major sights in the city centre and the harbour area. The buses run daily from 9.30am to 5.30pm. With a day ticket passengers can get off and on the bus as often as they please.

Sightseeing flights

The sights of Sydney can also be seen from the air. Sightseeing flights in light aircraft are run by Red Baron Scenic Flights from Bankstown Aerodrome, south-west of the city. There are also helicopter flights over the harbour, the beaches and the city centre.

Information

Information and maps can be obtained from:
Rocks Visitors Centre, 104 George Street.; tel. 247 4972;
open daily 9am–5pm
Convention & Visitors Bureau, Martin Place; tel. 235 2424;
open Mon.–Fri. 9am–5pm, Sat. noon–4pm.
Travel Centre of New South Wales, 19 Castlereagh; tel,231 4444;
open Mon.–Fri. 9am–5pm
InfoStar, Circular Quay West (computerised information system)

Sights in Sydney

Highlights

Sydney's principal landmarks are the Harbour Bridge, Sydney Tower (at 305m/1000ft the tallest building in the southern hemisphere) and the world-famous Opera House, but the city's core is its huge natural harbour, with an area of over 55sq.km/21sq.miles and arms reaching out in all directions – the remnants of a drowned valley system. The city centre is bounded on the north and west by water, on the east by the green expanses of the Royal Botanic Gardens, the Domain and Hyde Park and on the south by the Central Station.

Layout of the city

In contrast to the regular and spacious layout of the younger Australian cities, Sydney has a complicated and irregular street pattern resulting from its gradual development from the original colonial settlement to the city's present area of over 12,400sq.km/4800sq.miles, resembling in this the old-established cities of Europe. Arthur Phillip, the first governor of the colony, had ambitious plans for his settlement, with spacious squares, broad streets and imposing public buildings; but his successors did not carry out these plans, and Sydney grew up with narrow streets and buildings adapted to the contours of the site. As a result the city's streets were too narrow and irregular even in the days of coach travel.

City centre

Sydney's long, narrow city centre is traversed longitudinally by two main streets, George Street and Pitt Street. All the important businesses, offices

Sydney 2000: with its bay, its inlets and islets and its magnificent architecture, Sydney is not only Australia's most beautiful city but one of the most breathtaking metropolises in the world. It is not surprising that the Olympic Committee decided that the 17th Summer Olympics should be held here in 2000

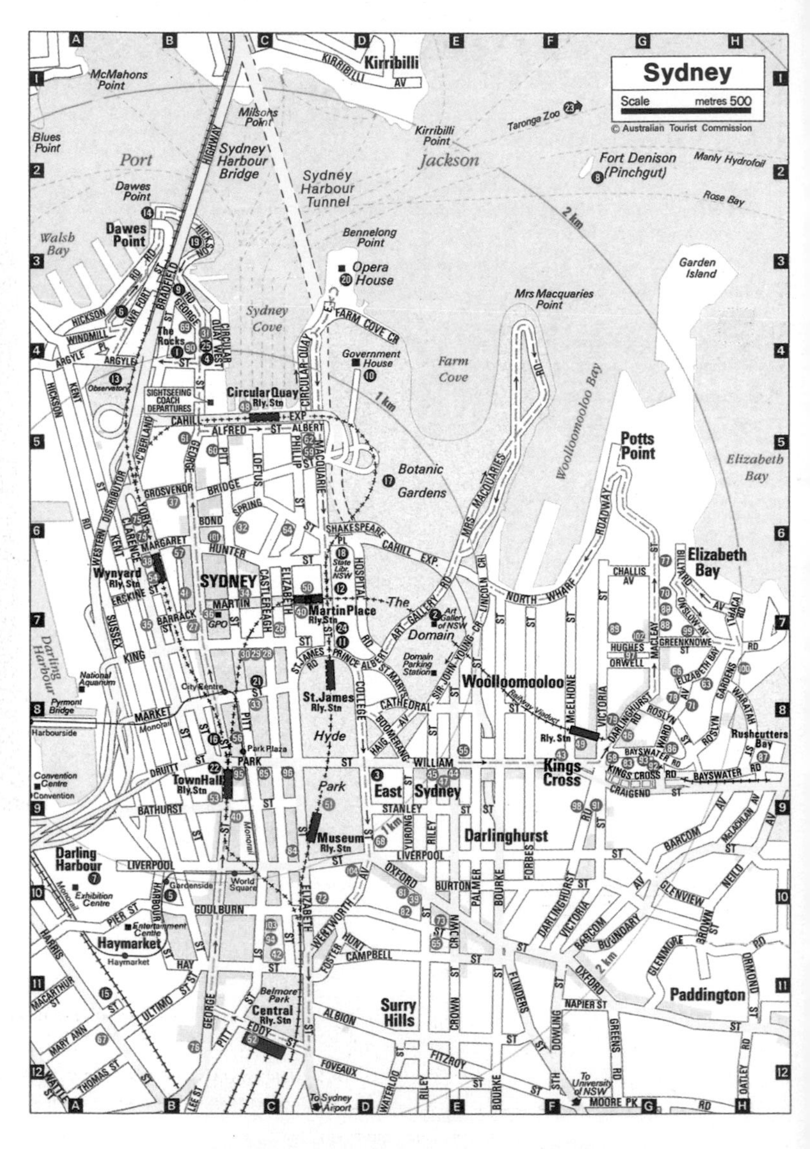

and shops are situated near these two streets, between the Rocks, the area fringing the harbour, in the north and Central Station in the south.

The Rocks is now magnificently restored, and is linked by the Harbour Bridge (opened 1932) with North Sydney. Here too, on the harbour, is Sydney's principal sight, the new Opera House. On the west side of the

Sights and useful addresses in Sydney

Places of Interest

Name	No.	Grid
Argyle Centre	1	B4
Art Gallery of NSW	2	E7
Australia Museum	3	D9
Cadman's Cottage	4	B4
Chinatown	5	B10
Colonial House Museum	6	A4
Darling Harbour	7	A10
Fort Denison	8	G2
Geological,Mining Museum	9	B3
Government House	10	D4
Hyde Pk. Barracks Museum	11	D7
NSW Parliament House	12	D7
Observatory	13	A4
Pier One	14	B2
Powerhouse Museum	15	A11
Queen Victoria Building	16	B8
Royal Botanic Gardens	17	D5
State Library of NSW	18	D6
Sydney Harbour Bridge—Pylon Lookout	19	B3
Sydney Opera House	20	D3
Sydney Tower	21	C8
Sydney Town Hall	22	B9
Taronga Zoo	23	F1
The Mint Museum	24	D7
The Rocks	25	B4

Tourist Information

Name	No.	Grid
Canberra Tourist Bureau	26	C7
NT Govt. Tourist Bureau	27	B7
Qld. Govt. Tourist Bureau	28	C7
South Aust. Travel Centre	29	C7
Tas. Govt. Tourist Bureau	30	C7
The Rocks Visitors Centre	31	B4
The Travel Centre of NSW	32	C6
Vict. Tourism Commission	33	C8
WA Tourist Centre	34	C7

Motoring Association

Name	No.	Grid
NRMA	35	B7

Post Office

Name	No.	Grid
GPO Sydney	36	B7

International Airline

Name	No.	Grid
Qantas Airways	37	B6

Bus Information Centre

Name	No.	Grid
Urban Transit Auth.of NSW	38	B6

Travel and Tours Centre

Name	No.	Grid
State Rail Auth. of NSW	38	B6

Airline—Domestic

Name	No.	Grid
Air New South Wales	39	E10
Ansett Airlines of Aust.	39	E10
Australian Airlines	40	C7 & C9
East-West Airlines	41	B7

Coach Terminals

Name	No.	Grid
Ansett Pioneer	39	E10
Greyhound	39	E10
Deluxe Coachlines	42	C11

Rent-a-Car Offices

Name	No.	Grid
Avis	43	F9
Budget	44	E9
Hertz	45	E9
Letz	46	G8
Thrifty	47	E9

Ferries and Overseas Shipping

Name	No.	Grid
Circular Quay	48	C5

Railway Stations

Name	No.	Grid
Circular Quay	48	C5
Kings Cross	49	F8
Martin Place	50	C7
Museum	51	D9
Sydney Central (Interstate & Country)	52	C12
Town Hall	53	B9
Wynyard	54	B7

Accommodation

Deluxe

Name	No.	Grid
Boulevard	55	E8
Hilton	56	C8
Holiday Inn Menzies	57	B6
Hyatt Kingsgate	58	G9
Intercontinental	59	C5
Ramada Renaissance	60	B5
Regent	61	B5
Ritz Carlton	62	C5
Sebel Town House	63	H8
Sheraton Wentworth	64	C6

Premier

Name	No.	Grid
Cambridge Inn	65	E11
Gazebo Ramada	66	G8
Golden Gate Pk. Plaza	67	A12
Hyde Park Plaza	68	D9
Old Sydney Parkroyal	69	B4
Olims Sydney Hotel	70	G7
Seventeen	71	G8
Southern Cross	72	D10
Waratah Inn	73	E10
Wynyard Travelodge	74	B6
York Apartments	75	B6

Moderate

Name	No.	Grid
Central Plaza	76	B12
Chateau Sydney	77	G6
Clairmont Inn	78	G8
Crest	79	G8
Dorchester Inn	80	G7
Greetings Oxford Koala Hotel	81	D10
Greetings Oxford Towers Motel	82	D10
Hampton Court	83	G9
Hyde Park Inn	84	C10
Koala Park Regis	85	C9
Metro Plainsman Motor Inn	86	G8
Rushcutter Travelodge	87	H9
Sheraton	88	G7
The Jackson Hotel	89	G7
The Russell Hotel	90	B4
Top of the Town	91	F9

Budget

Name	No.	Grid
Backpackers Headquarters	92	G9
Barclay Hotel	93	G9
CB Private Hotel	94	C11
Coronation Hotel	95	C9
Criterion Hotel	96	C9
Down Under Hostel	97	G7
Kirketon	98	F9
Manhattan	99	G7
Roslyn Gdns. Motor Inn	100	H8
The Grand Hotel	101	B6
The Macquarie Hotel	102	G7
Westend	103	C10
YWCA	104	D10

Sydney Explorer Bus Route .... — — —

Shopping ....

central area is Darling Harbour, also finely restored in recent years. To the east, beyond a chain of beautiful parks, are the city's oldest and most interesting suburbs: Woolloomooloo, Kings Cross and Paddington. Farther east and to the south are numerous other suburbs, interspersed with parks, gardens and lakes, extending to the most favoured suburbs directly

East Sydney

on the Pacific and to Botany Bay, with the airport. Visitors arriving in Sydney by air – by far the majority – are landing at almost the same place as Captain Cook two and a quarter centuries ago.

North Sydney

North Sydney with its numerous suburbs and satellite towns and its beautiful beaches on the Pacific, separated from the city centre by the harbour, has developed independently in the last few decades into an important administrative and commercial centre. The eight-lane Harbour Bridge can no longer cope with the heavy volume of traffic at certain times, and in 1992, after long planning, it was supplemented by a tunnel under the harbour.

★★The Rocks

Sydney's Old Town

Immediately after the landing in 1788 the first white settlement was built on the tongue of land projecting into Port Jackson from which the Harbour Bridge now spans the harbour. The name of the Rocks no doubt comes from the rocky coast on the west side of Sydney Cove, where the first tents for the convicts were pitched. Cadman's Cottage (Historic Site) is Sydney's oldest surviving house, once occupied by John Cadman, a convict who later earned his living as a coxswain. In the course of the 19th century the harbour area was occupied by customs depots and warehouses, and the area gained an evil reputation for its disreputable inns and bands of thugs. An outbreak of plague around the turn of the century carried the process of decline further, when whole streets of houses were pulled down. And finally around 1930 the construction of the massive piers of the Harbour Bridge led to further demolition of old houses.

Since the 1970s the surviving remains of old buildings have been restored, and the former slum area has become a new city attraction with its narrow paved streets, restaurants and colonial-period houses (visitor centre near Cadman's Cottage; Explorer Bus stop). The existence of this lively assemblage of shops, galleries, restaurants and pubs and the preservation of more than a hundred of Sydney's oldest buildings are due to the efforts of the action groups of the '60s and '70s, when the government planned to demolish the Rocks and built high-rise blocks on the site.

George Street

George Street, the oldest street in Australia, was originally a nameless track trodden by convicts fetching supplies of water; it was named, after King George III, in 1810. Among old buildings in George Street are the Russell Hotel, the Ox on the Rocks restaurant and the Old Police Station. Around the middle of the 19th century a Chinese quarter grew up in this area and round Argyle Street. Later the Chinese community moved farther south to the Campbell Street/Haymarket area, now Sydney's Chinatown.

Argyle Street

In Argyle Street (Explorer Bus stop), which runs at right angles to George Street, are the Rocks Police Station (1879), the Orient Hotel (1844) and the Argyle Centre, with new shops modelled on old ones. The Argyle Cut is a tunnel through the rock (begun 1843, completed 1859) linking Sydney Cove with Millers Point (Explorer Bus stop). In this area are some well-preserved 19th-century houses and the Garrison Church of 1844. On the south side of Argyle Place is Observatory Hill, with the Observatory (1858) and the National Trust Centre (built in 1815 as a military hospital). In Kent Street (corner of Argyle Street) is the Lord Nelson Hotel (1834).

Argyle Place

Argyle Place, a stretch of gardens within the city centre, was so named by Governor Macquarie in 1810 after his home area of Argyll in Scotland. The surrounding houses, built around 1830 and later, are typical of the period. There are also some Victorian terraced houses dating from the end of the 19th century. In Lower Fort Street, opposite the Garrison Church, are well-restored detached and terraced houses in a mixture of colonial, Georgian and Regency styles, of a kind that may be seen in 19th-century streets in

London. At the corner of Lower Fort Street is the Hero of Waterloo Hotel (1845), with a pointed gable.

Dawes Point

At the northern tip of the promontory on the west side of Sydney Cove is Dawes Point, now a small garden in the shadow of the Harbour Bridge, with good view of the Opera House and Circular Quay. In 1788 William Dawes, a naval officer who was also an astronomer, built an observatory here and a battery protected by earth ramparts. A later stone-built fort was destroyed during the construction of the piers for the Harbour Bridge. The cannon of 1843 and 1844 at the foot of the south-east pier mark the site of Dawes's battery.

The curving bay between Dawes Point and Millers Point, to the west of the Harbour Bridge, was an anchorage for whalers and sailing ships between 1790 and 1840. After the outbreak of plague around 1900 all the landing-stages were rebuilt. In 1912 the first Ocean Passenger Terminal was built, and thereafter hundreds of thousands of immigrants entered Australia here. The terminal was closed down in 1963 and Pier 1 (Explorer Bus stop) became the site of a shopping, entertainment and restaurant complex, while the buildings on Piers 4 and 5 were converted into a theatre.

★★ Harbour Bridge

Before the construction of the Opera House the Harbour Bridge had been for almost fifty years Sydney's best-known landmark, familiarly known to the inhabitants as the Coathanger. The bridge was completed in 1932 after eight years' work, with a work force at times of up to 1400 men. Supported by massive double piers at each end, the bridge spans the 500m/550yd between the north and south sides of the harbour in a single arch rising to 134m/440ft above the water, with a clearance of 49m/160ft for shipping. It carries two railway lines and eight lanes for road traffic, the direction of

The Harbour Bridge, one of Sydney's landmarks

which can be varied according to traffic requirements. There are also walkways for pedestrians. From the bridge there are magnificent views of the city and the harbour. An average of over 170,000 vehicles cross the bridge every day, but increasing traffic forced it to be supplemented by a tunnel under the harbour which was opened in 1992.
In the south-eastern pier is a museum illustrating the history of the bridge's construction (open: daily 10am–5pm). There is a wonderful view of the city from the pier's viewing platform.

★ ★Circular Quay

The landing-place of the First Fleet (Explorer Bus stop) was at the mouth of the Tank River, which has long since been canalised and built over. The south end of the V-shaped inlet at the point where Pitt Street and Alfred Street now meet silted up under the action of the tides, and hundreds of convicts laboured for years to fill it in with stones and rubble and construct a horseshoe-shaped harbour wall known as the Circular Quay. At the beginning of the 20th century this was rebuilt in rectangular form, but the old name was retained. New wharves were built in the 1960s and then cleared in 1987 to make way for a promenade along the waterfront. From the top of the large Overseas Passenger Shipping Terminal (1960; reduced in size in 1987) there are good views, particularly of the Opera House.
The Ferry Wharves on Circular Quay are the busiest part of the harbour. Every morning thousands of commuters from the northern districts of Sydney are discharged from the ferries, and in the late afternoon there is an equally heavy traffic in the other direction. From here too there are harbour tours which show Sydney at its best.

★Museum of Contemporary Art

The Museum of Contemporary Art, housed in an Art Deco building of 1930–50 on Circular Quay, was opened in 1991 thanks to the munificence of J. W. Powen, who bequeathed his fortune to Sydney University for the

Sydney's most famous sight, the Opera House

purchase and exhibition of contemporary art (open: daily except Tue. 11am–7pm).

★★ Opera House

The Opera House (Explorer Bus stop) is without doubt Sydney's principal tourist attraction. The situation is magnificent, and the Opera House itself is breathtaking with its complex of roofs shaped like huge shells or billowing sails. It is surrounded on three sides by water and on the fourth by the Royal Botanic Gardens. Bennelong Point, the site selected by the government in 1957 for a cultural centre, bears the name of an Aborigine who travelled to Britain with Governor Arthur Phillip in 1792 and was wondered at as a noble savage but returned to Sydney in 1795, drink-sodden and rootless. An international competition for the design of the Opera House was won by a Danish architect, Jørn Utzon. From the outset there were controversies and technical problems; construction was delayed and costs mounted. In 1966 the architect, disappointed in his hopes, withdrew from the project. Finally the Opera House was completed in 1973, ten years later than planned, and was formally opened by the Queen. The cost of the building, originally estimated at 10 million Australian dollars, had multiplied tenfold, but the money was raised by a series of Opera House lotteries.

The Opera House is much more than an opera house, with three theatres and studios, a concert hall, a cinema, exhibitions, rehearsal and reception rooms, a library, restaurants and bars.

Seats for particular performances must be booked well in advance. There are daily conducted tours, starting in the foyer of the Exhibition Hall, and the two restaurants are open to the public at large. Visitors can walk round the Opera House above the water of the harbour and continue along the Waterfront Promenade and round Circular Quay. To the south of Circular Quay is the Cahill Expressway, carrying traffic to and from the Harbour Bridge. Under it can be heard the rumble of the underground line which surfaces at the Circular Quay station. There too is the most northerly of Sydney's three large city centre bus terminals; the others are at Wynyard Station, to the west, and Central Station, to the south.

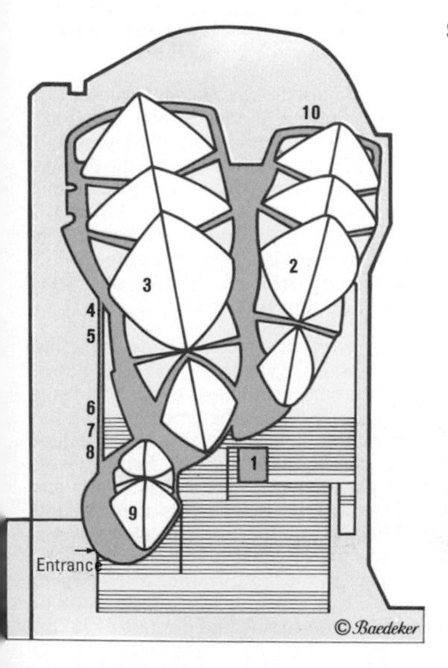

Sydney Opera House
Designed by Jørn Utzon
(1956; completed 1972)

1 Box office
Entrance to foyer
2 Opera Theatre
(1547 seats)
3 Concert Hall
(2690 seats)
4 Drama Theatre
(544 seats)
5 Broadwalk Theatre
(288 seats)
6 Playhouse Cinema
(419 seats)
7 Exhibition Hall
8 Library of the
Performing Arts
9 Bennelong Restaurant
10 Harbour Restaurant

Parks in the City Centre

The city centre is bounded on the east by a string of parks – the Royal Botanic Gardens, the Domain, Hyde Park – extending south from Farm Cove, on the east side of the Opera House, so called because the colony's first farm and vegetable gardens were here. These 70 hectares/175 acres of open space, divided by the expressway into the Botanic Gardens and the Domain Park, were originally the Governor's Domain. It was laid out in 1810 with public footpaths and riding tracks by Governor Macquarie's wife, in whose honour the north-eastern tip of the promontory is called Mrs Macquarie's Point (Explorer Bus stop).

★Fort Denison

A kilometre or so off Mrs Macquarie's Point is the little island of Fort Denison, known as Pinchgut, where convicts used to be imprisoned on a diet of bread and water. It was fortified in 1855–57 as a precaution against a possible Russian attack.

★ Royal Botanic Gardens

The Royal Botanic Gardens (Explorer Bus stop), established in 1816, have an area of 30 hectares/75 acres, mainly devoted to exotic and native trees, with orchids and ferns in hothouses. Open: daily 6.30am–6.30pm, to 8pm in summer.

Tropical Centre

Most of the major native plants are housed in an ultra-modern and very attractive hothouse.

Government House

Government House, the official residence of the governor of New South Wales, can be visited only by special arrangement. The present building was erected between 1836 and 1845 to a design sent from London.

There are good views of Government House from some points in the Botanic Gardens, from the steps of the Opera House and from Government House Gate, near the Conservatorium of Music.

Conservatorium of Music

The historic building occupied by the Conservatorium of Music (founded 1913) was originally built by Francis Greenway in 1816–19 to house the Governor's horses and servants, a project criticised by London as extravagant. It is now used to train musicians.

★ Domain

The Domain, to the south of the Cahill Expressway, is a popular place to relax during the lunch break. At the weekend it becomes Sydney's Speakers' Corner.

★★ Art Gallery of New South Wales

Within the Domain is the Art Gallery of New South Wales (Explorer Bus stop; also free bus 666 from Wynyard Station/George Street). Originally built in 1885, it acquired a new façade and colonnaded forecourt in 1896–1909. It was further extended in 1968–72 and again within the last few years. The Gallery (open: Mon.-Sat. 10am–5pm, Sun. noon–5pm; guided tours Mon. 1 and 2pm, Tue.–Fri. 11am and 1 and 2pm, Sat. and Sun. 1, 2 and 3pm; admission free) has collections of Australian, European and Asian art of the 19th and 20th centuries. There is a good bookshop.

Only a few minutes' walk from the city centre are other collections and exhibitions, particularly in the Paddington district.

★ Hyde Park

Hyde Park (6.5 hectares/16 acres), with its lawns, shady benches, flowerbeds, fountains, statues and the Anzac War Memorial, is Sydney's most central park, just on the edge of the central business district, and consequently draws many visitors, particularly during the lunch break. It lies between Queens Square, Elizabeth Street, Liverpool Street and College Street. Sydney's first underground railway line, the City Railway, was opened in 1926, running under the park between St James Station and Central Station. Before the white settlement this was an area of marshland, the source of the Tank River which flowed into Sydney Cove. Later it was drained and became a riding track and then Sydney's first cricket ground (1803). It was declared a public open space by the first governor, Arthur Phillip, in 1792, and given its present name by Governor Macquarie in 1810. Among the many features in the park is the Archibald Fountain (1932), a

Art Gallery of New South Wales Sydney

LEVEL 5

1 Photographs
2 Library
3 Administration
4 Restaurant

WC Toilets

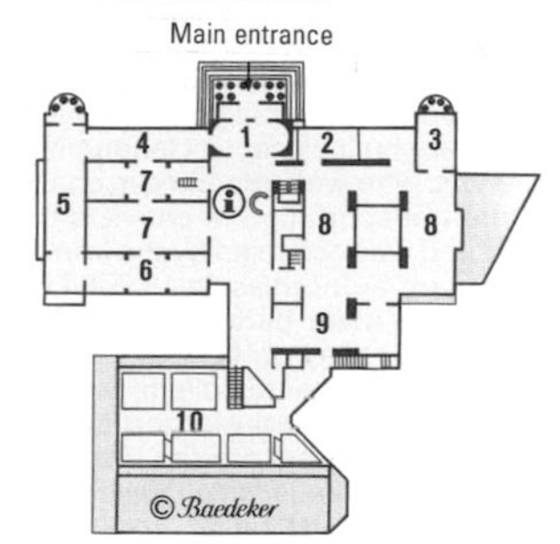

LEVEL 4 (MAIN FLOOR)

1 Cloakroom
2 Shop
3 Administration
4 European art of 15th–18th centuries
5 European art of 18th–19th centuries (Victorian art in Britain)
6 European art of 19th century
7 Australian art of 19th and early 20th centuries
8 Australian art of 20th century
9 Special exhibitions
10 Sculpture Terrace

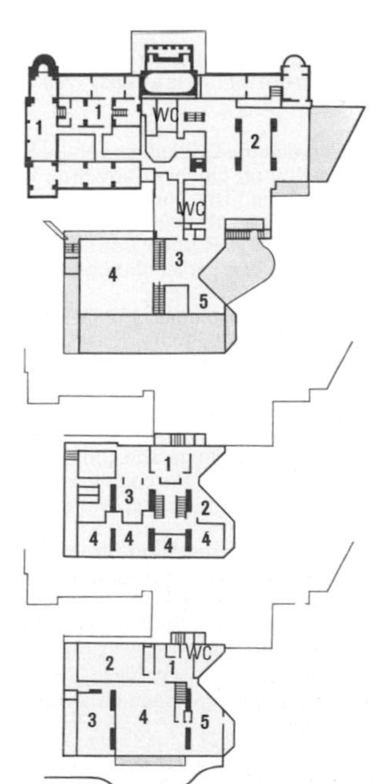

LEVEL 3

1 Aboriginal and Melanesian art (access from Court 8, Old Wing, Level 4)
2 Major exhibitions
3 New acquisitions
Shop
4 Asian art (China, Japan, Korea, India, South-East Asia)
5 Café

LEVEL 2

1 British art of 18th century
2 Impressionism and European art of 20th century
3 Prints, drawings, water-colours
4 Contemporary art

LEVEL 1

1 Foyer
2 Domain Theatre
3 Public programmes
4 Special exhibitions
Education Gallery
5 Art Gallery Society

bronze group with Apollo in the centre, Diana goddess of hunting and Theseus fighting the Minotaur. The fountain was presented to the city by J. F. Archibald to commemorate Australia's alliance with France in the First World War.

Anzac War Memorial

The Anzac War Memorial, in the southern half of the park, was erected in 1934 to commemorate the dead of the First World War. In geometric Art Deco style, it stands 30m/100ft high on a podium with an area of 1200sq.m/13,000sq.ft.

At the north end of Hyde Park, in Queens Square (Explorer Bus stop), are three fine Georgian buildings, masterpieces of the convict architect Francis Greenway: the Hyde Park Barracks, St James's Church and the Supreme Court. In the centre of the square is a statue of Queen Victoria, originally set up here in 1888 and now returned to its site after some comings and goings.

★Hyde Park Barracks

The former Hyde Park Barracks (Queens Square and Macquarie Street), is today part of the Musuem of Applied Arts & Science, a three-storey brick building with a sandstone pediment like that of a Greek temple. Governor Macquarie was so pleased with the building that he gave Greenway his freedom. The barracks were built by convict labour in 1817-19 and housed 800 or more male convicts, who were marched in chains from here to their place of work. After the transportation of convicts to New South Wales ceased in 1848 the building was occupied by the immigration department and later (1887) by the court authorities. In 1975-84 it was restored to its original condition, and the main part of the building now houses a museum on the history of Sydney portraying the lives of early settlers.

★Australian Museum

On the east side of Hyde Park (corner of College Street and William Street) is the Australian Museum, which has the largest natural history collection in the country. Of particular interest are the displays on the life of the Aborigines and the natives of Papua New Guinea. There are also many specimens of animals (particularly birds), rocks, minerals and fossils (open: daily 10am-5pm; guided tours daily at 10.30am, noon, 2 and 3pm; admission free).

From the Australian Museum it is a short distance to St James Station, now also a museum, and from there it is an easy walk along William Street to Kings Cross.

★St Mary's Cathedral (R.C.)

St Mary's Cathedral, between the Domain and Hyde Park, is a neo-Gothic building (1868-82) modelled on Lincoln Cathedral, with a faáade in the style of Notre-Dame in Paris. The south towers are unfinished. The stained glass windows admit a subdued light to the interior. The site for a church was given to the first Roman Catholic clergy in Sydney by Governor Macquarie in 1821. Two earlier churches were destroyed by fire.

St James's Church

St James's Church is Sydney's oldest church (1822). Situated at the corner of King Street and Queens Square, it is dwarfed by the 22-storey Law Courts building. With its double brick arches, subdivided windows and contrasting stone porticoes it is a fine example of colonial Georgian. The tower was formerly a landmark for ships in the spacious harbour basin. Governor Macquarie had originally, in 1819, wanted to build a courthouse on the site, but John Bigge, the commissioner sent out from Britain to enquire into the finances of the colony, insisted on a church, and Francis Greenway had to alter his plans accordingly.

Supreme Court

The Supreme Court (Elizabeth Street/King Street, adjoining St James's Church) was built between 1820 and 1828. Greenway originally designed a rectangular two-storey brick building, but it underwent so much later alteration that little is left of the original. The columned portico was demolished to widen Elizabeth Street.

★Macquarie Street

Macquarie Street, running north from Queens Square, was Sydney's most popular and most fashionable street, particularly in the second half of the

St Mary's Cathedral

19th century, when two- and three-storey verandahed houses in the Italian style, with views of the Domain and the harbour, were built here. In Macquarie Street are two relics of the early days of the colony, the Mint and Parliament House, both occupying wings of the old "Rum Hospital" (see below). The original track through the bush was named after Governor Macquarie in 1810, and thirty years later it was continued northward to Fort Macquarie, now Bennelong Point, the site of the Opera House. Since the building of Sydney Hospital in 1894 Macquarie Street has had strong medical associations.

Mint

Sydney Mint (Macquarie Street/Queens Square) occupies the south end of the old Rum Hospital and has preserved much of its original aspect. After the discovery of gold in 1851 the building was converted into the Mint, which continued to mint gold coins until 1927. Since 1982 it has housed a collection of jewellery, coins as well as many gold objects. (Open: daily except Wed. 10am–5pm, Wed. noon–5pm.)

Rum Hospital

The long middle section of the Rum Hospital was pulled down in 1879, and the present building, in Victorian neo-classical style, was erected in 1894. Plans for its demolition and replacement by a square surrounded by high-rise buildings were under consideration in the 1960s but were not carried out. The foundation stone of the Rum Hospital (architect unknown), was laid by Macquarie in 1811, and the building was completed in 1816. It is so called because Macquarie granted the profitable rum monopoly to the builders, who then built the hospital, using convict labour, at no cost to the colony.

Parliament House

Parliament House (Macquarie Street; Explorer Bus stop) is open to the public Monday to Friday 9.30am–4pm; seats in the visitors' gallery when the New South Wales Parliament is in session must be booked in advance. Parliament has occupied this building (the north wing of the Rum Hospital) since 1827, with extensions on the north and south sides in 1843 and 1856.

State Library of New South Wales

On the east side of Macquarie Street, near Parliament House, is the State Library, an eleven-storey building (though only four of them are above ground) erected in 1988 and linked with the old State Library by a glassed-in bridge. The old Library is an imposing two-storey building in Italian Renaissance style. The core of the Library was the collection of D. S. Mitchell, who spent a lifetime assembling books and documents on Australia and the Pacific (61,000 volumes, now enlarged to 365,000 volumes and 35,000 manuscripts), supplemented by William Dixson's collection of Australian material. Among the Library's treasures are the journals of Captain Cook and Joseph Banks and Captain Bligh's log from the "Bounty". The collection also includes early 19th century photographs.

Opposite the State Library is Shakespeare Gate, leading to the Royal Botanic Gardens (see above).

Museum of Sydney

Museum of Sydney (corner of Bridge and Phillip Streets). This is a new museum, constructed on the site of the first Government House which was pulled down in the 1840s; the foundations have been preserved and can be seen. The Museum displays Sydney's history from its earliest, Aboriginal days up to the 1850s, by means of modern technology such as videos and computer displays.

BMA House

BMA House (headquarters of the Australian Medical Association, formerly a branch of the British Medical Association) is a 13-storey building of 1930 in Art Deco style with a richly decorated façade (Australian flora and fauna, medical symbols).

History House

Adjoining is History House, a three-storey building in Victorian classical style which is the headquarters of the Royal Australian Historical Society.

Martin Place

Martin Place, opposite Parliament House (Explorer Bus stop), is a spacious pedestrian precinct between Macquarie Street and George Street lined by massive bank premises with colonnaded fronts, shady trees, fountains, sculpture and newspaper kiosks. Originally it was only a square in front of the General Post Office (1874), but after a fire in 1891 it was extended eastward.

General Post Office

The General Post Office, an imposing building in Venetian Renaissance style, has colonnades on three sides (George Street, Pitt Street and Martin Place). The clock-tower above the centre of the Martin Place front was added in 1886; as a precaution against air raids it was taken down in 1942 but re-erected in 1964.

The Cenotaph (1929) in front of the Post Office commemorates Australian war dead. This is the scene of Sydney's Anzac Day parade on April 25th.

★★Sydney Tower

The Sydney Tower above the Centrepoint shopping centre, built in 1981, is 325m/1067ft high and a major tourist attraction. From the viewing platform 305m/1000ft above the ground (express lifts Sun–Fri. 9.30am–9.30pm, Sat. to 11.30pm) there are wide panoramic views of Sydney and the surrounding area. In the tower there are two revolving restaurants and a café with bar.

Pitt Street

Between King Street and Market Street is Pitt Street, which since 1987 has been a pedestrian zone.

State Theatre

The State Theatre (49 Market Street) is a huge cinema of 1929 with a lavishly decorated interior modelled on the Palace of Versailles. The annual Sydney Film Festival takes place here.

★Strand Arcade

The Strand Arcade (193–195 Pitt Street to 408–410 George Street), built in 1891, is the only survivor of five large shopping arcades erected in Sydney in the last two decades of the 19th century. After suffering damage in a fire in 1976 it was rebuilt in its original form.

The Sydney Hilton Hotel (1973) at 259 Pitt Street has in its basement the famous marble bar (1893) of the Adams Hotel which previously occupied the site. The Royal Arcade of 1882, which was pulled down in 1969, has also been re-erected here, extending to George Street.

★Queen Victoria Building

The new high point of the shopping quarter, opposite the Hilton, is the Queen Victoria Building, now linked by underground shopping arcades with Town Hall Station. Originally built as a market hall between 1893 and 1898, the Queen Victoria Building is 200m/655ft long 24.30m/80ft across,

Sydney Tower

Telecommunications Tower above Centrepoint Shopping Centre

VIEW TO NORTH
1 The Rocks
2 Sydney Harbour Bridge
3 Circular Quay
4 Sydney Opera House
5 Fort Denison
6 MLC Centre
7 North Sydney
8 Taronga Zoo
9 Middle Harbour
10 Manly
11 Beaches to north
12 North Head

VIEW TO EAST
13 Farm Cove
14 Royal Botanical Garden
15 Domain
16 NSW Art Gallery
17 Parliament Building
18 State Library
19 Mint, Hyde Park Barracks
20 Garden Island
21 Sydney Harbour National Park
22 Watson Bay, The Gap
23 South Head
24 Bondi, eastern suburbs
25 Kings Cross
26 St Mary's Cathedral

VIEW TO WEST
39 Parramatta
40 Darling Harbour
41 Monorail
42 Powerhouse Museum
43 Chinese Garden
44 Leisure Centre
45 Darling Harbour Sports Centre
46 Port installations
47 National Maritime Museum
48 Pyrmont Bridge
49 Sydney Aquarium
50 Goat Island

VIEW TO SOUTH
27 Victoria Barracks
28 Sydney Football Stadium & Cricket Ground
29 Centennial Park
30 Randwick Racecourse
31 Anzac War Memorial
32 Australian Museum
33 Sydney Town Hall
34 St Andrew's Cathedral
35 Queen Victoria Building
36 Central Station
37 Botany Bay
38 Mascot Airport

Total height
304.80m/1000ft

Shaft of tower
46 tube elements (each 5m/16ft long and 6.70m/22ft in dia., weighing 32 tons) 56 cables (each weighing 7 tons), of 2135 strands 7mm/¼in. in dia.

Lifts
Three two-storey express lifts conveying 2000 people an hour to summit in 40 sec.

Summit structure
on nine levels:
1 Restaurant
2 Revolving restaurant (self service)
3 Café, bar
4 Observation deck (telescopes, info., souvenirs
5,6 Air-conditioning
7 Fire extinguishing equipment (water tank holding 162,000 litres/35,600 gallons
8,9 Telecommunications equipment

Aerial mast
30m/100ft high

Pellini
BONZ
façade
SHEPHERDS
JAG
JAG

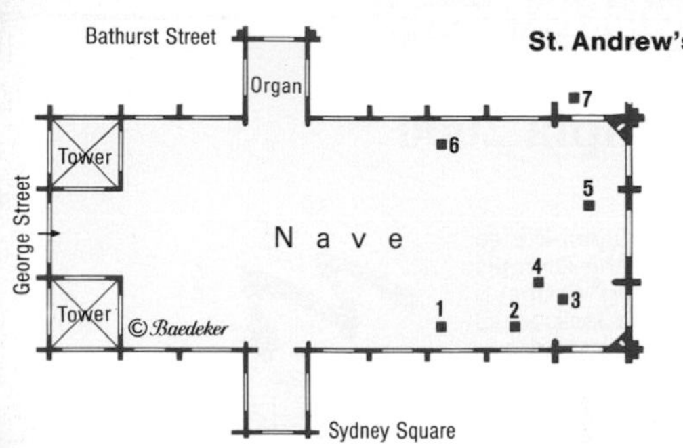

St. Andrew's Anglican Cathedral · Sydney

Australia's oldest cathedral
(founded 1819, consecrated 1868)

1 Font
2 Changi flag from Second World War
3 Flag from Gallipoli campaign (1915)
4 Archibishop's throne
5 Chair of Bishop Broughton, first bishop of Australia
6 Pulpit
7 Monument to Edmund Blacket, architect of the Cathedral

with a 57.50m/190ft high central dome surrounded by 20 smaller domes. After decades of neglect and even plans for demolition, this imposing sandstone building was restored to its original state in 1980–86 and occupied by 200 elegant shops open seven days a week – just in time for the celebrations of Sydney's 200th birthday. It is worth a visit, even if you don't want to do any shopping, as an example of successful restoration and for the sake of its beautiful stained glass windows and mosaic floors.

Town Hall

The Town Hall (1869), at 483 George Street, is a medley of different architectural styles which has been compared to a richly decorated wedding cake. The Centennial Hall (1889), a large concert hall seating an audience of 2500, has one of the largest organs in the world.

Near the Town Hall are three Georgian-style buildings dating from the first half of the 19th century: the School of Arts (*c.* 1836), a predecessor of the University of Technology (277 Pitt Street, near Park Street); the Pitt Street Uniting Church (1846; 264 Pitt Street), with two columns as in an Ionic temple; and the Judge's House (1826; 531 Kent Street), which was let to a judge in the 1830s.

St Andrew's Cathedral (Anglican)

To the south of the Town Hall is the neo-Gothic St Andrew's Cathedral. Begun in 1837, it was completed and consecrated only in 1868.

These three 19th century buildings – the Town Hall, the Queen Victoria Building and St Andrew's Cathedral – formerly gave the George Street and Park Street area its distinctive character, but in recent years they have been overshadowed by high-rise office blocks.

Chinatown

A short distance south of the Town Hall is Sydney's Chinatown, centred on Dixon Street (pedestrian zone), with lion gates at each end on Goulburn Street and Hay Street. The area bustles with activity all week long, day and night, with different Chinese regional cuisines to choose from, shops and markets, a temple and offices, all labelled in Chinese script. Over the years Chinatown has spread beyond George Street towards Haymarket, covering a much larger area than the early 20th century quarter in the Rocks.

In the first half of the 19th century some 2000 Chinese came to Sydney to work as coolies, but during the gold rush they came in their tens of thousands. A magnificent spectacle in Chinatown is the celebration of the Chinese New Year on the first full moon after January 21st.

★★ Darling Harbour

South-west of the Rocks is Darling Harbour, best seen from the water in all its new splendour. From Chinatown, or from the Town Hall or Central Station, it is only a short walk to the varied attractions of this recently restored and rehabilitated area of 54 hectares/133 acres, formerly occupied

◄ *In Queen Victoria Building*

Olympia 2000

Australian enthusiasm for the Olympic idea – Australia has taken part in all the Olympic Games of modern times – and Sydney's uniquely beautiful situation on Port Jackson, its large and intricately ramified natural harbour, must have been decisive considerations leading the International Olympic Committee to decide on September 23rd 1993 that Sydney should have the responsibility of organising the 27th Summer Olympics in the year 2000. After some of the contenders for the honour (Brasilia, Milan and Tashkent) had withdrawn Sydney was left with Istanbul, Manchester, Beijing (Peking) and Berlin as competitors, but finally emerged victorious.

The Olympic Committee's decision was greeted with great enthusiasm not only in Sydney but throughout Australia. It did not take the Sydney authorities by surprise, for by the time their bid was put in more than half the venues for the various events were already built or under construction – though critics feared that the city might have taken on too much. At any rate the dates of the Games are now fixed: from September 16th to October 1st 2000.

The Games are planned to take place in two main areas: Sydney Olympic Park, round Homebush Bay at the west end of Sydney Harbour, and round Darling Harbour, near the city centre. These two areas are linked by arms of the harbour on which ferries will provide fast transport for competitors and spectators. Homebush Bay can also be easily reached by bus or rail.

The climate in the second half of September should be ideal for the Games. During the mild spring of eastern Australia day temperatures are around 20°C/68°F.

In addition to the facilities already in place, there remain to be provided between 1995 and 1999 an Olympic Stadium with seating for 80,000 spectators, a sports hall with seating for 15,000, a velodrome (cycling stadium), sports centres for archery, riding, baseball and tennis and a covered training stadium.

For the first time in the history of the modern Olympics all the athletes and officials (altogether some 15,000 people) will be housed in a single central Olympic Village, in the planning of which the environmental protection organisation Greenpeace is actively involved. It is the declared aim of all concerned in the planning of Olympia 2000 that it shall be "the world's first green Olympics".

Provision has also been made for the media. An estimated 6000 sports journalists will be accommodated in "media villages" at Darling Harbour and Homebush Bay.

Already there are conducted bus tours (the Homebush Bay Shuttle, departing three or four times daily from Strathfield Station, Bicentennial Park and the State Sports Centre) which give Sydney people and visitors a chance to see for themselves the work going on in the Olympic Park. For information on timetables tel. 131 315; advance booking advisable (tel. 334 1070).

Sydney is also hosting the Paralympics (the Olympics for the disabled) in 2000 (October 21st to November 1st).

Olympic Games organisers have designed Olympic Arts Festivals during September and October of each year up to 2000. Their themes include the evolution of Australia's multicultural society and focus on indigenous performances by touring artists.

Baedeker Special

Sydney Olympic Plan

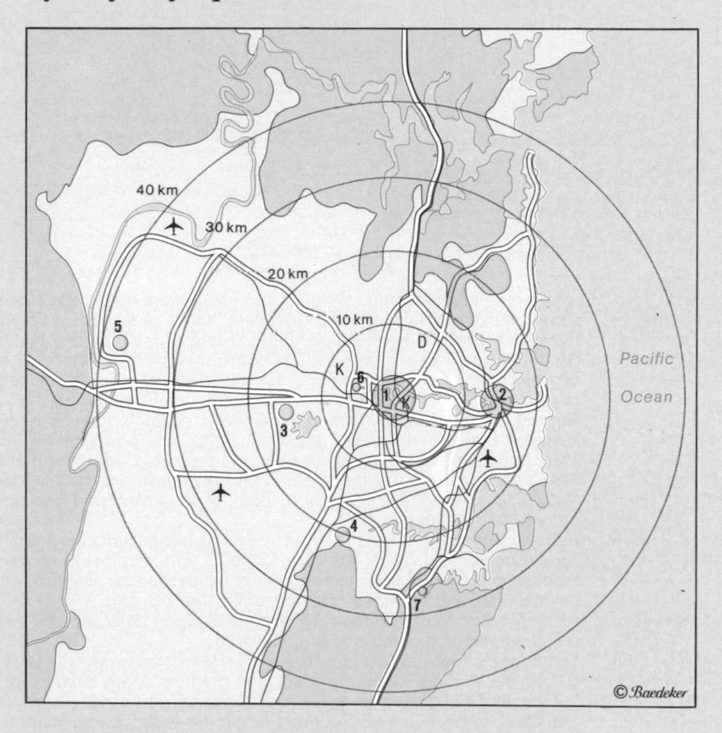

1 SYDNEY OLYMPIC PARK (Homebush Bay)
Archery. athletics, badminton, baseball, cycle racing, fencing, football, gymnastics, handball, hockey, modern pentathlon, swimming, tennis and volleyball.
Olympic Village, main press centre, media village, officials' village.

2 SYDNEY HARBOUR ZONE (Darling Harbour, Moore Park, Rushcutters Bay
Basketball, boxing, football, judo, sailing, table tennis, weightlifting and wrestling
International Broadcasting Centre (IBC), media village, officials' village
Hotels

3 EASTERN CREEK
Cycle racing (time trials), riding

4 HOLSWORTHY: shooting

5 PENRITH LAKES: canoein, kayaking, rowing

6 PARRAMATTA
Football and water polo (heats)

7 AUDLEY (Royal National Park)
Cycle racing (road)

Model of
Sydney Olympic park
on Homebush Bay
see pp. 178–179

D Drug testing laboratory
H Olympic Hospital

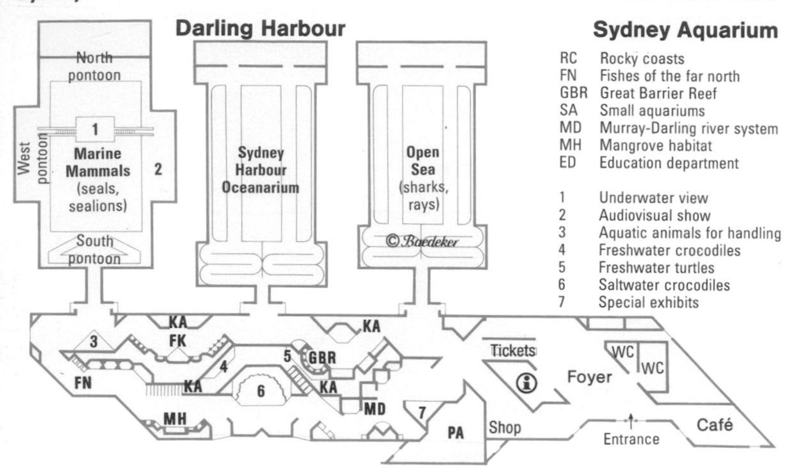

by dilapidated docks and railway lines. These have now given place to a huge waterfront leisure and tourist park, with a great variety of entertainments and amusements, exhibitions and museums, reached and circled by by a monorail system (TNT Harbour Link Monorail; main station on Haymarket, near the Entertainment Centre) running at a height of 5.50m/18ft and often almost grazing historic old buildings.

Among the park's attractions are the Chinese Garden, the Exhibition Centre, the Powerhouse Museum, the Harbourside Festival Marketplace, Tumbalong Park and the magnificent Sydney Aquarium, which gives visitors the impression that they are under the sea (open: daily 9.30am–9pm, last admissions 8pm; Marine Mammal Sanctuary: daily 9.30am–4.30pm).

National Maritime Museum

A palm-fringed promenade runs round Darling Harbour from the Aquarium to the National Maritime Museum with displays of ships and articles on those whose livelihood depends on the sea; also on explorers, convicts and immigrants (open: daily 10am–5pm).

Pyrmont Bridge

At the end of Market Street is Pyrmont Bridge (1902), an old swing bridge which gives access to the monorail.

Sydney Entertainment Centre

The Sydney Entertainment Centre on the Haymarket was built in 1982, before the Darling Harbour project was planned. With seating for an audience of 12,000, it is used for rock concerts, and other events.

★Chinese Garden

The Chinese Garden links Sydney Chinatown with Darling Harbour. It was designed by gardeners from Guangdong, the Chinese province which is twinned with New South Wales (open: Mon.–Fri. 9.30am–7pm, Sat. and Sun. 9am–7pm).

★Powerhouse Museum

The Powerhouse Museum was opened in 1988 after the reconstruction of an old power station and tram depot; at least three hours should be allowed for a visit. There are more than two dozen exhibition areas covering science, technology, everyday items and outstanding works of art (open: daily 10am–5pm).

Sydney Exhibition Centre

To the north of the museum is the Sydney Exhibition Centre in which art exhibitions are held.

★Sega World, IMAX Theatre

A little way to the north-east is a magnificent high-tech leisure park, opened in 1996 and popular with locals and tourists alike. There is a Sega super multi-media computer games centre and an IMAX theatre with an eight-storey high film screen. Disaster and action movies shown here provide the ultimate experience.

Convention Centre, Festival Market Place

Opened in 1995/6, the new Convention Centre and the Festival Market Place lie close to Darwin Harbour and on the far side of the highway which is here partially supported on stilts. Various musical and cultural events are held here all the year through. The Market Place has now become a favourite meeting place for young people.

★Harbourside Shopping Centre

Close to the sea lies the Harbourside Shopping Centre (1996), generally regarded as being currently the best shopping centre in the city. There are some 200 shops selling the latest fashions as well as expensive jewellery and duty-free goods (open: daily 10am–9pm).

★National Maritime Museum

North of Pyrmont Bridge, opposite the Sydney Aquarium, the National Maritime Museum (open: daily 10am–5pm) is worth a visit. It provides much of interest about Australia's eventful maritime history.

Casino

Further north-west, by Pyrmont Bridge, the new Sydney Casino offers keen gamblers the chance to try their luck at blackjack, roulette and two-up.

Fish Market

Along Gipps Street stretches Australia's largest fish-market, which is particularly lively early in the morning. There are some good fish restaurants to be found in the nearby Waterfront Shopping Arcade.

Kings Cross

It is a half-hour walk east on William Street, which cuts across Hyde Park, to Kings Cross, at the point where Darlinghurst Road, Victoria Street and Bayswater road join William Street. Previously known as Queens Cross, the junction was given its present name in 1905 in honour of King Edward VII.

Around 1920 the area round Kings Cross was an artists' and writers' quarter. Then around 1950 it became the haunt of beatniks and later of hippies. It degenerated into a red light district mainly during the Vietnam War, when large numbers of American troops came here on "rest and recreation" leave. To see the two faces of this district it should be visited both during the day and at night. In daylight it seems quiet enough, but after dark it really comes to life.

In stark contrast to the gambling and porno activities of night-time Kings Cross are two Regency-style mansions in the north of the area, in the direction of Potts Point, built by the architect John Verge around 1830 for wealthy citizens of Sydney: Tusculum (1832) at 3 Manning Street (well restored and open to the public since 1988) and the very fine Elizabeth Bay House (1835) in Onslow Avenue (Explorer Bus stop). From Elizabeth Bay House there are fine views northward over the harbour, but its principal charm lies in its staircase hall and its interior decoration and furnishings. Originally it stood in 23 hectares/57 acres of grounds.

Victoria Street

In Victoria Street, which runs through the Kings Cross district, is a well preserved terrace of three-storey Victorian houses.

Elizabeth Bay/ Mackay Street

On Elizabeth Bay and in Mackay Street are a number of interesting Art Deco apartment blocks of the 1930s and 40s. The "good" suburbs of Sydney lie to the north-east on the inlets opening off Port Jackson.

Immediate Surroundings of Sydney

Balmain

Balmain, one of Sydney's nearer suburbs, lies on an inlet to the west of Darling Harbour. Like Paddington (see below) it has well preserved Victorian houses and is the home of many artists.

Glebe

Glebe, south of Balmain, has become a very popular residential area in recent years. In this area is Sydney University, the oldest in Australia.

Liverpool

Liverpool, 32km/20 miles south-west of central Sydney, was founded by Governor Macquarie in 1810, but until the Second World War remained a

The model of Sydney Olympic Park, on Homebush Bay, shows

secluded rural settlement. It has since developed into an independent industrial centre within the Sydney conurbation. It has preserved many historic buildings of the early 19th century, among them St Luke's Church and Liverpool Hospital, both designed by Francis Greenway.

Manly

The well-known suburb of Manly, on the north side of the harbour entrance (North Head), can be reached by ferry or hydrofoil. Its principal tourist attraction is Marineland, a large aquarium with shark-feeding and other shows. The beach is well equipped with facilities for holidaymakers, including a large water slide.

how Olympia 2000 is to be "the world's first green Olympics"

To the north of Manly is a string of popular beach resorts extending up to Palm Beach and Barrenjoey Head, on Broken Bay, the estuary of the Hawkesbury River.

Paddington

The best-known of Sydney's inner suburbs is Paddington, familiarly known as Paddo, only a 2km/1¼ mile walk along Oxford Street from the south-east end of Hyde Park. Thanks to the efforts of local people many of the old terraced houses lining the steep streets have been saved from demolition.

Many young artists have made their homes in Paddington, which has interesting art galleries and craft shops as well as some very attractive restaurants.

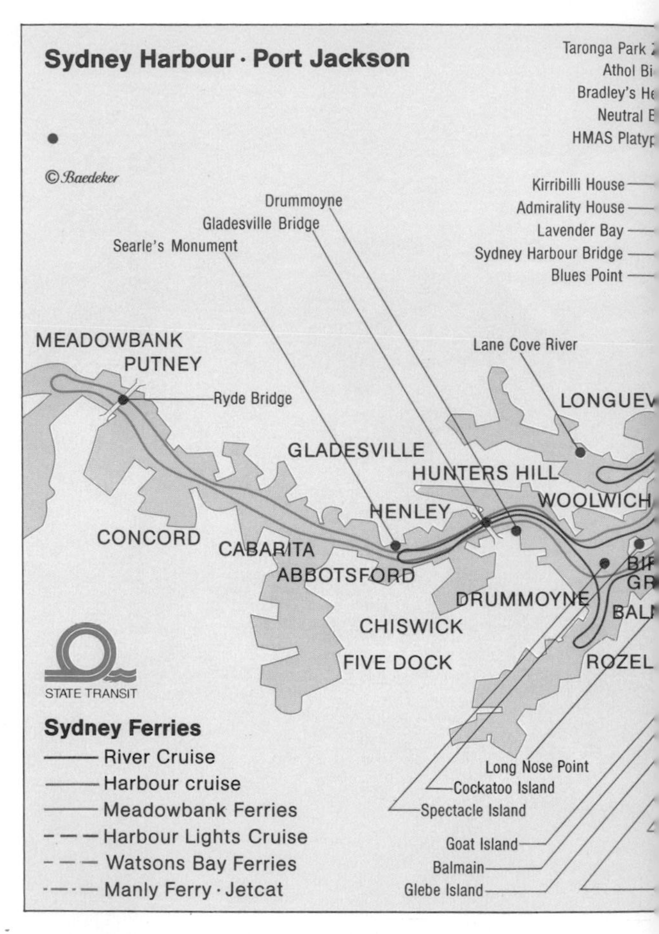

The main feature of interest in Paddington is the Victorian Barracks, on the south side of Oxford Street. Built by convict labour between 1841 and 1847, they are the best preserved large complex of colonial Georgian architecture in Australia. The main block – 225m/740ft long, two-storied, simply and clearly articulated by columns and terraces – housed a British regiment of 800 men. The barracks have remained in use since 1848. Part of the building is now occupied by a Military Museum. Visitors can watch the changing of the guard every Tuesday morning at 10.30 (except in December and January), after which the museum opens.

★Port Jackson

Port Jackson (Sydney Harbour) separates Sydney from its northern districts and suburbs. In addition to the Sydney Harbour Bridge there are other bridges spanning the harbour farther west (Gladesville Bridge, Ryde Bridge). It can also be crossed by ferry from Circular Quay. A cruise round the harbour by boat or ferry is a good way of seeing Sydney from its best side; there are various departure points round the harbour.

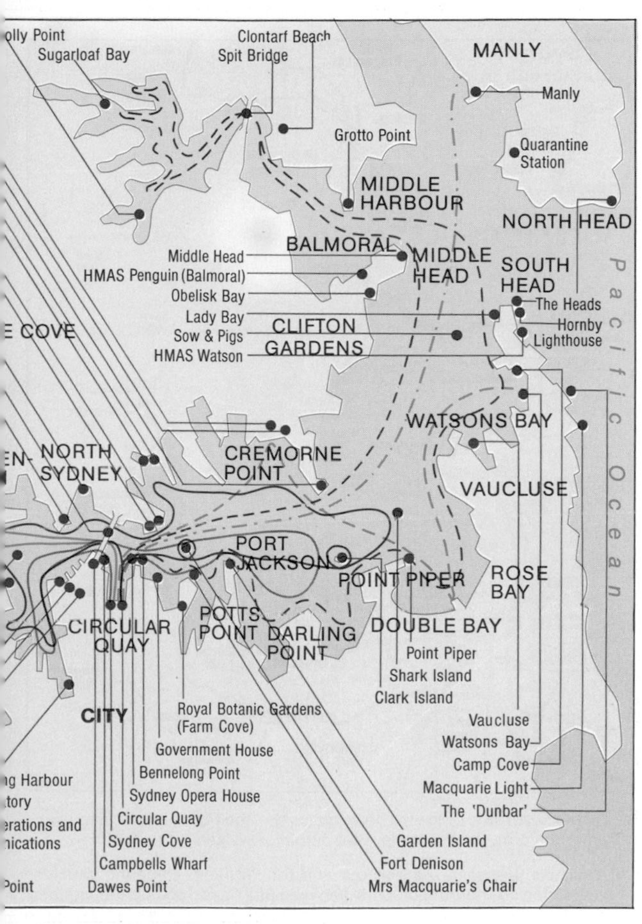

Taronga Park Zoo

From Circular Quay there are also boats to Taronga Park Zoo, beautifully situated on a large tongue of land on the north side of the harbour.

Redfern

The outlying district of Redfern, to the south of Central Station, is a rather depressing quarter of the city, almost a slum, occupied by rootless half-breed Aborigines and the unemployed, often living in degrading conditions.

Suburbs

Farther west extends an endless succession of suburbs, for the most part consisting of detached houses with gardens, with only the occasional district (e.g. Parramatta) more densely built up with houses (flats) and apartment blocks. Even in a large city Australians like to have a house of their own with a garden, however tiny.

On Saturdays there are often yacht races in the harbour, with much betting on the results – a further opportunity to satisfy the Australian passion for gambling.

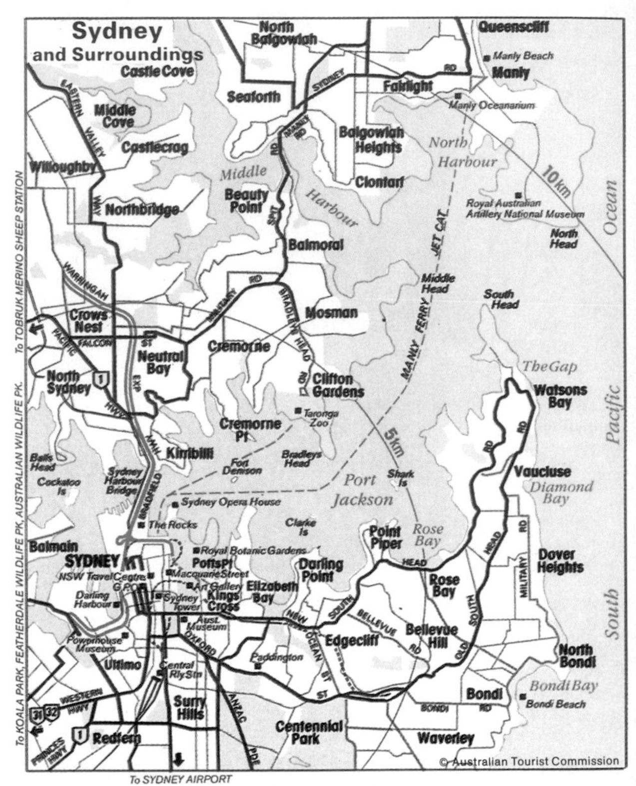

On the north side of the harbour, below the Zoo (Ashton Park) and round Cremorne Point, there are pleasant paths for walkers.

Vaucluse

In Vaucluse, between the harbour and the Pacific, is romantic Vaucluse House (open to the public), built between 1827 and 1850 by the explorer and politician William Wentworth for himself and his large family, set in beautiful gardens.

Watsons Bay

From Watsons Bay there are good views of the South Head, the harbour entrance and Sydney.

★Parramatta

Situation and characteristics

Parramatta, the second British settlement in Australia, was founded in 1788 and was originally known as Rose Hill. Situated 24km/15 miles west of Sydney, it is almost completely surrounded on the west side by the city's suburbs. It was originally planned to make Parramatta the seat of government of the colony, leaving the town with Australia's oldest public building, Old Government House, a fine specimen of colonial Georgian architecture begun in 1790.

Elizabeth Farm House (well restored) was built in 1793 by John MacArthur and his wife Elizabeth, making it probably the oldest surviving

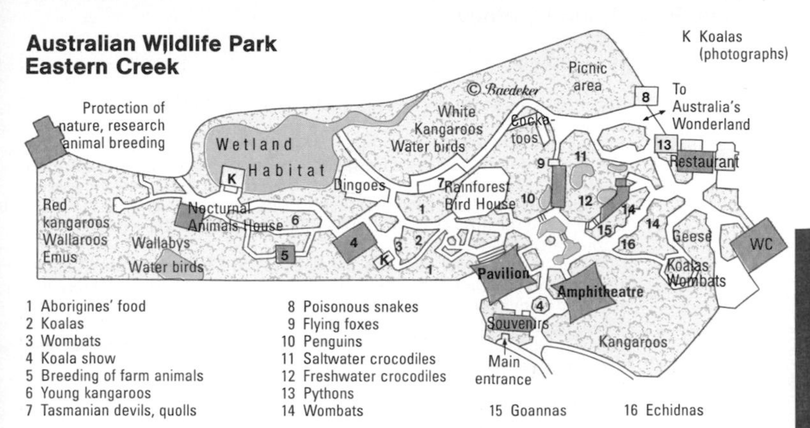

private house in Australia. Other interesting buildings are St Patrick's Cathedral, Roseneath House (*c.* 1834) and some restored terraced houses in Phillip Street. Also of interest is the old cemetery of Parramatta, with the graves dating from the end of the 18th century.

The Lancer Barracks (1818) are the oldest barracks in Australia.

★Australian Wildlife Park

Australia's Wonderland

20km/12½ miles west-north-west of Parramatta, at Eastern Creek (Wallgrove Road), is Australia's largest theme park (200 hectares/500 acres), Australia's Wonderland. Within this Australian equivalent of Disneyland is the fine Australian Wildlife Park (open: daily 9am–5pm), which introduces visitors to the very interesting flora and fauna of Australia.

Beaches Round Sydney

Bathing and surfing

Water sports are among the most popular Australian leisure activities, and the very fine beaches round Sydney give plenty of opportunity for practising them. Within the harbour area there are many sheltered beaches, and outside it, on the Pacific, surfers are catered for by more exposed beaches with high surf (and also with sharks). Bathing within Port Jackson is safe, but the water is badly polluted, since much of the city's sewage is discharged into the sea, inadequately treated, near bathing beaches.

Among the most popular beaches are Farm Cove (near the harbour entrance), Watsons Bay, Lady Bay Beach and Nielson Park, Vaucluse. On the Pacific there are a string of fine beaches extending south from the harbour entrance to Botany Bay.

★Bondi

Bondi is undoubtedly Australia's best known beach, with terraces of Victorian houses as a backdrop. Take the Easton Suburbs line to Bondi Junction, then catch a bus.

Tamarama, Bronte, Coogee, Maroubra

Tamarama, farther south, Bronte, Coogee and Maroubra are also good surfing beaches. Botany Bay, with its sharks, is more suited to boating and sailing than to swimming.

The surfing beaches on the Pacific are patrolled during the long summer season by volunteer lifeguards, who also run very popular lifesaving competitions. Swimmers should keep within the marked areas, which are designed to protect swimmers from surfers as well as from sharks.

National Parks Round Sydney

Botany Bay National Park

Location; area 16km/10 miles south of city centre; 460 hectares/1140 acres.

Facilities Picnic areas.

Features Botany Bay National Park extends over the two tongues of land enclosing the bay, protecting the coast from Little Bay to La Perouse and the Kurnell peninsula. The old cable station was converted in 1987 into a museum commemorating the French discoverer La Pérouse, who arrived in Botany Bay at the same time as Captain Arthur Phillip and was shipwrecked on his homeward voyage.

Within the National Park are the beaches in Congwong Bay, Captain Cook's landing-place at Kurnell (with picnic areas and a museum devoted to Cook's voyages) and the coastal fortifications of around 1880 (Henry Head, Bare Island). Botany Bay was given its name by Joseph Banks, the botanist who accompanied Cook on his voyage and found numerous new species of plants here.

★Ku-ring-gai Chase National Park

Location; area 30km/19 miles north of Sydney; 14,700 hectares/36,300 acres.

Access From Pacific Highway at Mount Colah, or via Turramurra to Bobbin Head, from Church Point or Terrey Hills to West Head, at the northern tip (fine panoramic views).

Facilities Picnic areas and kiosks, boat hire; exhibitions; nature trail for the blind and handicapped. Kalkari visitor centre, Bobbin Head.

Features The park gets its name from the Gurringai tribe who lived in this area. This area of much eroded Hawkesbury sandstone is bounded on the north by the lower course of the Hawkesbury River and its estuary, Broken Bay. The sandstone plateau, dissected by an intricate network of drowned valleys (Cowan Water, Pittwater), has 112km/70 miles of shoreline, with ideal conditions for water sports. Rich flora and fauna; Aboriginal rock paintings and drawings.

Walking trails A number of walking trails have been laid out in the Bobbin Head and West Head areas.

★★Royal National Park

Location; area 36km/22 miles south of Sydney; 15,000 hectares/37,000 acres.

Access By car from the Princes Highway via Loftus, Waterfall and Stanwell Tops.

There is also a direct train service (Illawarra line) to the park.

Facilities Camping site at Bonnie Vale, to the north-east; bush camping, with permit. Good roads through the park, with picnic spots and viewpoints. Good facilities for water sports (fishing, boat hire) amd walking (many tracks within park closed from sunset to 7am).

Visitor centre at Audley, with exhibitions and rest area.

Features The park is bounded on the north by Port Hacking and on the west by the railway line to the south, while to the east are 21km/13 miles of surfing beaches and an almost unspoiled cliff-fringed coast. The Hacking River flows through almost the whole length of the park, a sandstone plateau with a covering of heathland and deeply indented valleys. On the upper course of the river there are still patches of forest. In spring the park is carpeted with flowers.

Before the arrival of European settlers the area was occupied by the Dharawal tribe, who have left rock drawings as evidence of their presence. The area was declared a nature reserve in 1879 and was renamed the Royal National Park in 1955 on the occasion of a visit by Queen Elizabeth II. The felling of timber ceased in 1922.

Walking trails

There are walking trails from all railway stations (Royal Park, Loftus, Engadine, Heathcote, Helensburgh, Lilyvale, Otford, Waterfall). Ferry service over Port Hacking between Cronulla and Bundeena.

The Royal National Park was devastated at the turn of the year 1993–94 by one of the worst bush fires in the history of Australia and almost completely destroyed; but only a few months afterwards there was evidence that Australian bush vegetation had in the course of centuries adapted to the frequent fires. Grasses whose seeds had been hidden in the earth grew again; plants and shrubs sprouted again, in striking contrast to the lunar landscape around them; and trees budded as if there had never been a fire.

The park has remained open during the period of regeneration, and the facilities for visitors are being steadily re-established.

★Sydney Harbour National Park

Location; area

In Port Jackson, east of the city centre; 388 hectares/958 acres.

Facilities

Picnic spots, walking trails, water sports.

Features

The Sydney Harbour National Park has been developed in stages since 1975. It takes in the promontories and islands round the entrance to the harbour, parts of North Head, South Head, Dobroyd Head, Grotto Point, Georges Head, Bradleys Head, Nielson Park and Rodd Island, opening up all these areas to the public. The 19th century fortifications and quarantine station can also be visited.

There is only limited public access to Clark Island and Shark Island. Authority for a visit must be obtained in advance (Park Headquarters, Greycliffe House, at Nielson Park, Vaucluse).

Tamworth J 6

Situation and characteristics

Tamworth (pop. 35,100), commercial and cultural centre of northern New South Wales, lies 280km/175 miles north of Newcastle at the junction of the Oxley and New England Highways. It is also known as the "capital of Australian country music", to which thousands of fans flock in January for the annual Australian Country Music Festival.

Accommodation

Many hotels, motels and caravan/camping parks.

Features

Tamworth City Gallery has a fine collection. From the Oxley Lookout in 400 hectare/1000 acre Oxley Park there is a fine view of the town with its many parks and gardens.

Surroundings

Excursions: Scenic Drive, 63km/39 miles; Nundle, an old gold-digging town, south-east; Lake Keepit (water sports), 57km/35 miles north-west; Chaffey Dam (sailing), 45km/28 miles south-east; Warrabah National Park, 80km/50 miles north-east.

Taree J 6

Situation and characteristics

Tree (pop. 15,700), 320km/200 miles north of Sydney on the Pacific Highway, is the manufacturing and commercial centre of the Manning River district. Dairy farming and timber working in Manning valley.

Accommodation

Many hotels, motels and caravan/camping parks.

Features

The town has a number of fine 19th century buildings (churches, courthouse, school).

Surroundings

Excursions to the Bulga Plateau (50km/31 miles north-west), with the Ellenborough Falls, and Crowdy National Park (40km/25 miles east; see below). Near the town are good surfing beaches. Trout-fishing in dammed streams.

In the green hills of Tamworth (see page 185)

Crowdy Bay National Park

Location; area
25km/16 miles north of Taree; 8000 hectares/20,000 acres.

Access
From Pacific Highway via Moorland and Coral Ville or, farther north, via Laurieton.

Facilities
Fishing, surfing, walking. Picnic areas, but no drinking water.

Features
The attractions of Crowdy Bay National Park, established in 1972, are its wide variety of scenery (forest, heath, marshland, sand-dunes) and large numbers of birds and reptiles. The National Park was previously grazing land. In the dispute between the protection of nature and the exploitation of natural resources (mineral sands) in this area the decision was in favour of the environment, with only restricted working of the mineral sand. In spring there is a brilliant show of flowers.

Tathra J 7

Situation and characteristics
Tathra (pop. 1570) is a popular holiday resort on the South Coast, 18km/11 miles east of Bega between Merimbula and Bermagui. It is best reached from Wagga Wagga, Albury and Griffith on the Snowy Mountains Highway. Good sandy beaches; the estuary of the Bega River is suitable for children.

To the north is Mimosa Rocks National Park, to the south Bournda National Park (on both see Bega).

Accommodation
Motels, caravan/camping parks.

Tenterfield K 5

Situation and characteristics
Tenterfield (pop. 3300), situated amid hills at an altitude of 860m/2820ft, lies close to the border with Queensland, 793km/493 miles from Sydney and

95km/60 miles north of Glen Innes on the New England Highway. Originally this was grazing land, with fruit plantations, timber-working, sawmills and mines (silicates, gold). The landscape is a glory of colour in autumn.

Accommodation
Several hotels, motels and caravan/camping parks.

Features
Tenterfield is famed as the place where Sir Henry Parkes, prime minister of New South Wales, made a speech while visiting the School of Arts here (now a museum) in 1889 calling for the unification of Australia and thus launched the movement for federation.

★Bald Rock National Park

Location; area
29km/18 miles north of Tenterfield in the Northern Tableland; 5400 hectares/13,300 acres.

Access
From Tenterfield north on Mount Lindesay Highway, then 6km/4 miles west through the park on a gravel road to the rest area north of Bald Rock.

Accommodation
In Tenterfield.

Facilities
Short-term camping permitted. Bush walking trails, rest areas with picnic facilities.

Features
The dominant feature in the park is the huge granite dome of Bald Rock (750m/820yd by 500m/550yd, 200m/650ft high), surrounded by bush country. From the summit of the rock, which can be climbed on the north-east side, there are fine panoramic views, extending as far as the Tweed valley. Large numbers of kangaroos, wallabies, wombats and birds live in the park. The area round Bald Rock was known to the Aborigines as Boonoo Boonoo. The area round the rock was declared a protected zone in 1906; in 1971 it became a State Park and in 1974 a National Park.

Walking trail
There is a trail to the summit of Bald Rock (2km/1¼ miles).

Boonoo Boonoo National Park

Location; area
22km/14 miles north-east of Tenterfield in the Northern Tableland; 2692 hectares/6649 acres.

Access
From Tenterfield north on Mount Lindesay Highway, then side road (gravel; 14km/8½ miles).

Accommodation
In Tenterfield.

Facilities
Bush camping. Visitor facilities limited. Bush walking, swimming; some picnic spots.

Features
The main feature of the park is the wild Boonoo Boonoo River, with a 210m/690ft high waterfall and a gorge containing an expanse of rain forest.

Terrigal J 6

Situation and characteristics
Terrigal, a popular holiday resort on the Central Coast, lies 100km/62 miles north of Sydney within the built-up area of Gosford (see entry). Good surfing beaches. To the south is Bouddi National Park (see Gosford): water sports, bush walking, camping.

Accommodation
Hotel, motels and caravan/camping park.

The Entrance J 6

Situation and characteristics
This attractive holiday resort lies on an arm of the sea between Lake Tuggerah and the Pacific, within the built-up area of Gosford (see entry). It is well equipped with amenities for holidaymakers (shops, sports facilities, entertainment). The first inn here was opened in 1895. It attracts many campers, day trippers and other visitors from Sydney, particularly in the holiday seasons.

Accommodation
Many hotels, motels and caravan/camping parks.

Features Good lake and ocean fishing and water sports; daily lake cruises.

Thirlmere Lakes National Park J 6

Location; area 105km/65 miles south-west of Sydney and 10km/6 miles south-west of Picton; 627 hectares/1549 acres.

Access From Thirlmere–Buxton Road; from Hume Highway on road to Couridjah.

Accommodation Hotel and caravan/camping park in Picton.

Facilities Bush camping. Canoeing, swimming. Picnic spots.

Features The park contains a chain of five lakes, the Thirlmere or Picton Lakes, which are the last natural freshwater biotopes; the reeds are important nesting areas for waterfowl.

Tibooburra H 5

Situation and characteristics 337km/209 miles north of Broken Hill, surrounded by granite crags, is the old gold-mining settlement of Tibooburra (pop. under 200), one of the loneliest places in New South Wales amd in summer one of the hottest.

Accommodation Hotels, motel, caravan/camping park.

Features This little township has preserved a number of buildings of the gold-digging period, notably the Courthouse, the Family Hotel and the Tibooburra Hotel. The tourist information office and the offices of the National Park and Wildlife Service are now housed in the Courthouse.

Surroundings Tibooburra is a good base for visiting Sturt National Park (see below). There are still goldfields in the surrounding area.

Sturt National Park

Location; area 23km/14 miles north of Tibooburra; 310,600 hectares/767,200 acres.

Best time to visit Between April and September, during the Australian winter.

Access From Tibooburra.

Facilities Camping (Dead Horse Gully); water and food supplies must be taken. Visitor centre; picnic spots.

Features Sturt National Park, at Cameron Corner in north-western New South Wales (where New South Wales, Queensland and South Australia meet), is the remotest nature reserve in the state. It was established in 1972 after the National Park and Wildlife Service had bought the old sheep stations in the area. It is named after Charles Sturt, who camped here in 1845, during a period of intense drought and heat, while looking for the large lake there was believed to be in the centre of Australia.

This is the most arid area in New South Wales, with semi-desertic vegetation. It is the home of red kangaroos, emus amd lizards, a region of red sand-dunes, great stony plains and tabular hills, the "jump-up country". All the roads in this area, including the Silver City Highway, are unsurfaced and may become impassable after sudden showers of rain. The road from Bourke via Wannaring to Tibooburra, however, is negotiable by ordinary cars. After rain the semi-desert becomes a sea of flowers. With its remains of former grazings and the relics of gold-mining round Tibooburra, this is an ideal area for experiencing the real Australian outback.

Tingha K 5

Situation and characteristics Tingha (pop. 840) is a little New England settlement, 28km/17 miles south-east of Inverell (see entry), where large deposits of tin were discovered in 1870. In the town's heyday there were 6000 men working in the mines. A few mines are still being worked.

Accommodation
Hotel, caravan/camping park.

Features
On Copes Creek is a museum containing a collection of minerals and Aboriginal works of art.

Tumbarumba J 7

Situation and characteristics
Tumbarumba (pop. 1600), an old gold-mining settlement, lies in the western foothills of the Snowy Mountains (see entry), 504km/313 miles south-west of Sydney and 440km/273 miles north-east of Melbourne.

Accommodation
Hotels, motel, caravan/camping parks.

Features
Tumbarumba is a good base for day trips to the Snowy Mountains and the winter sports area on Mount Selwyn. In this beautiful mountain country there are attractive walking trails and bridle-paths and good fishing.

Tumut J 7

Situation and characteristics
Tumut (pop. 6300) lies 424km/263 miles south-west of Sydney on the Snowy Mountains Highway, in a spectacular mountain setting which takes on brilliant colouring in autumn. There are extensive state forests in the area in which timber is felled for the sawmills.

Accommodation
Several hotels, motels and caravan/camping parks.

Surroundings
To the south of the town is Blowering Lake (water sports, fishing), created by a dam on the Tumut River built under the Snowy Mountains hydro-electric scheme to store water for irrigation in the Murrumbidgee valley.

Tweed Heads K 5

Situation and characteristics
The tourist and holiday resort of Tweed Heads (pop. 5440) lies directly on the border with Queensland, and over the years has joined up with the town of Coolangatta on the other side of the state line.

Accommodation
Several hotels, motels and caravan/camping parks.

Features
This little town at the south end of the Gold Coast is well supplied with entertainments for visitors. At Point Danger, directly on the state boundary, is the Captain Cook Memorial and Lighthouse, erected in 1970, on the 200th anniversary of Cook's landing in Australia. Point Danger was so named by Cook because he was almost wrecked here. Evidence of earlier settlement can be seen in the Historic Site and Minjungbal Aboriginal Cultural Centre (on Kirkwood Road, which branches off the Pacific Highway to the south of Tweed Heads).

Surroundings
From the hills round the town there are fine panoramic views of the Tweed valley and the Gold Coast (Razorback Lookout).

Ulladulla K 7

Situation and characteristics
Ulladulla (pop. 9960) is an attractive fishing town on the Illawarra Coast, 148km/92 miles south of Wollongong. Along with nearby Milton it lies at the northern end of a stretch of beautiful coastal lakes and lagoons with white sandy beaches. In the 1930s Italian fishermen built up a fishing fleet which is now based in an extended harbour. The port was already being used by shipping around 1820.

Accommodation
Hotel, several motels and caravan/camping park.

Features
Ulladulla's beautiful beaches and facilities for water sports attract many holidaymakers. There is good bush walking and climbing on Pigeon House Mountain, in the southern part of Morton National Park (see Moss Vale).

Uralla J 6

Situation and characteristics

Uralla (pop. 2300) lies between Armidale and Tamworth on the New England Highway. This little settlement was established in the 1850s after rich discoveries of gold in the area.

Accommodation

Several hotels, motels and caravan/camping parks.

Features

Visitors can hunt for treasure in the fossicking area at the Old Rocky River diggings.

The notorious bushranger Captain Thunderbolt was shot dead by the police in Uralla in 1870 and was buried in the local cemetery.

★Wadbilliga National Park K 7

Location; area

400km/250 miles south of Sydney; 76,400 hectares/188,700 acres.

Access

From the east: from Cobargo via Yowrie on the Wadbilliga Track, which runs through the park; difficult crossing of Tuross River. From west: track from Kybeyan to Countegany, skirting the park.

Accommodation

Bush camping.

Features

Established in 1979, along with Deua National Park, as the southern continuation of a chain of parks (Morton–Budawang–Deua), Wadbilliga National Park takes in one of the largest unspoiled river catchment areas (Brogo and Wadbilliga Rivers).

In the north-west of the park are beautiful waterfalls and an impressive gorge on the Tuross; the western part is a region of tall eucalyptus forest and great expanses of heathland. Bush walking and bush camping in the Brogo and Wadbilliga valleys; good places for swimming.

Wagga Wagga J 7

Situation and characteristics

Wagga Wagga (pop. 54,400), the largest town in the Riverina area, lies on the Murrumbidgee 470km/290 miles from Sydney and 435km/270 miles from Melbourne, close to the Hume Highway. It is a major centre for industry, commerce, education and agriculture. The first settlement here was established around 1832.

Accommodation

Many hotels, motels and caravan/camping parks.

Features

In Fitzmaurice Street are the Historical Museum (just off Lord Baden Powell Drive), the Courthouse (1900), with a tower, the Post Office (1886–88), the CBC Bank (1885) and two 19th century churches, St Andrew's and St Michael's. There are also a botanic garden, a zoo and a college, with a vineyard.

Surroundings

Round Wagga Wagga are two important military bases and the Charles Sturt University. Within easy reach is the historic old gold-mining town of Adelong (see entry).

Walcha K 6

Situation and characteristics

Walcha (pop. 1700), on the eastern slopes of the Great Dividing Range, 70km/43 miles south of Armidale (see entry) on the Oxley Highway, was first settled in 1832. John Oxley camped here on his 1818 expedition. The wooded hills and valleys were the first part of the New England Tableland to be explored.

Accommodation

Hotels, motels, caravan/camping park.

Surroundings

20km/12½ miles east is Oxley Wild Rivers National Park, with its spectacular waterfalls and viewpoints (see Armidale). Woko and Werrikimbe National Parks are also within easy reach.

Werrikimbe National Park

Location; area
66km/41 miles west of Walcha; 35,200 hectares/86,900 acres.

Access
From Oxley Highway between Walcha and Wauchope; tracks from Walcha along eastern boundary of park.

Accommodation
In Wauchope and Walcha.

Facilities
Bush camping.

Features
Werrikimbe National Park, on the eastern edge of the New England Plateau, was established in 1976 and extended in 1982. The plateau is deeply indented by the valleys of the Hastings River and its tributaries. It is an impressive wilderness area, with waterfalls, gorges and expanses of rain forest.

Walking trails
Attractive trails for bush walking.

Wauchope J 6

Situation and characteristics
Wauchope (pop. 4280) lies on the Oxley Highway, 19km/12 miles above the mouth of the Hastings River at Port Macquarie, in a timber-working and dairy farming area.

Accommodation
Hotels, motel, caravan/camping park.

Features
Wauchope's main tourist attraction is Timbertown (3km/2 miles west), a re-creation of a typical timber town of the 1880s.

Wellington J 6

Situation and characteristics
360km/225 miles north-west of Sydney, at the junction of the Macquarie and Bell Rivers, is the little town of Wellington (pop. 5440), famed for the Wellington Caves, 9km/5½ miles south of the town. One of the caves is noted for its giant stalactite, another for its rare cave coral. South and south-west of the town are vineyards; some of the wineries can be visited by appointment.

Accommodation
Several hotels, motels and caravan/camping parks.

Surroundings
20km/12½ miles south-east is Burrendong Dam, an artificial lake with excellent leisure facilities.

Wentworth H 6

Situation and characteristics
The historic old settlement of Wentworth (pop. 1300) lies at the junction of the Murray and Darling Rivers, on the border with Victoria. For many years a busy river and customs port, it was the third largest port in New South Wales (after Sydney and Newcastle) in the heyday of shipping traffic on the Murray River. It is now a quiet holiday resort and tourist centre (Sunraysia).

Accommodation
Several hotels, motels and caravan/camping parks.

Features
Historic buildings: Old Gaol, Courthouse, churches of St John and St Francis Xavier (*c.* 1870).

West Wyalong J 6

Situation and characteristics
Once a gold-mining settlement, West Wyalong (pop. 3800), situated at the junction of the Mid Western and Newell Highways, is now the business centre of a prosperous wheat, wool and mixed farming area. It has an interesting museum with a scale model of a gold-mine.

Accommodation
Several hotels, motels and caravan/camping parks.

Surroundings
48km/30 miles north-east of the town is Lake Cowal, one of the largest lakes in New South Wales and an important waterfowl sanctuary.

★White Cliffs H 6

Situation and characteristics
100km/60 miles north-west of Wilcannia, in the outback, is White Cliffs (pop. 210), with the oldest commercially developed oilfield in Australia – a lunar landscape with over 50,000 craters, the legacy of over 90 years of opal mining. Most of the inhabitants live in underground dwellings to escape the heat of summer and the cold of winter.

Accommodation
Hotel, underground motel, caravan/camping park.

Features
In the town's heyday it had a population of 5000 and five hotels. From that period there still survive a few old buildings (police station, post office, school).

Surroundings
150km/95 miles west of White Cliffs is Mootwingee National Park (see entry), with Aboriginal rock drawings.

Wilcannia H 6

Situation and characteristics
Wilcannia (pop. 900), proclaimed a town in 1864, was once known as the "queen city of the west". It lies on the Darling River and on the Barrier Highway, 196km/122 miles east of Broken Hill. It was once an important river port, shipping wool from the distant north-west of New South Wales, but the end of shipping on the river led to a sharp fall in population, and the town declined. There is a small museum with interesting exhibits on the great days of the paddle-steamers (open: daily 9am–noon and 1–4pm; admission charge). Wilcannia is now mainly the service centre for the thinly populated surrounding area.

Accommodation
Hotels, motels, caravan/camping park.

Features
Wilcannia has preserved a number of 19th century buildings to bear witness to its past.

★Willandra National Park H/J 6

Location; area
730km/455 miles west of Sydney in the Riverina district; 19,400 hectares/47,900 acres.

Access
Hillston–Mossgiel road (track), side road to Trida.

Accommodation
In former workmen's cottages, hotels and motels in Hillston. Camping sites in park.

Facilities
Walking trails, wildlife viewing, picnic spots, fishing, boating.

Features
The old Willandra sheep station was declared a National Park in 1972. The area was first settled in the mid 19th century, and in 1912 one of the largest merino farms in Australia, with over 90,000 sheep, was established here. The old homestead (farmhouse) has been preserved as an interesting museum (stables, sheep-shearing huts). It stands on the shores of the Willandra billabong (water-hole), which marks the northern boundary of the park and extends from the Lachane River in the east to an expanse of marshland in the west.

A road runs over the plain from the old homestead and circles round to return along the shores of the billabong. In the early morning and late afternoon large numbers of animals can be seen by driving slowly round the road.

Windsor K 6

Situation and characteristics

Windsor (pop. 9420), 56km/35 miles north-west of Sydney in the Hawkesbury valley, is one of the oldest towns in Australia, with many buildings dating from its early days. The first settlers came to the area in 1794, and the town, one of the five "Macquarie towns", was founded by Governor Macquarie in 1810. The well-known convict architect Francis Greenway was employed to design and build St Matthew's Church (1817). The Courthouse was also his work.

Accommodation

Hotel, motels.

Surroundings

6km/4 miles from the town is the Hawkesbury Museum, in the old Daniel O'Connell Inn (*c.* 1840). Also of interest is the Australiana Pioneer Village at Wilberforce, with old houses, a coal-mine and demonstrations of sheep-shearing and games of the pioneering era. In the neighbouring village of Ebenezer are a church of 1809, an old cemetery and a schoolhouse.

Windsor is a good starting-point for visits to the other four Macquarie towns – Richmond (see entry), Wilberforce, Pitt Town and Castlereagh.

Cattai National Park

Location; area

13km/8 miles north of Windsor on the Hawkesbury River, in the western outer districts of the Sydney conurbation, 70km/45 miles from the city centre; 364 hectares/900 acres.

Access

Via the Cattai Road, 300m/330yds north of Cattai Creek Bridge.

Accommodation

In Windsor.

Facilities

Picnic spots, boat hire, swimming, walking, riding.

Features

The main feature of interest is the historic Caddie Homestead (1821). The land was acquired by Thomas Arndell, a doctor with the First Fleet, in 1804, and the house remained in the family until 1981.

Wisemans Ferry K 6

Situation and characteristics

Wisemans Ferry (pop. under 200), on the south bank of the Hawkesbury River 66km/41 miles north-west of Sydney, is a popular recreation area (water sports). There are two car ferries across the river.

Accommodation

Caravan/camping parks.

Features

The main feature of interest is the old Wisemans Ferry Inn, named after the founder of the original ferry service and innkeeper. On the north bank of the river is Dharug National Park (see below).

Along the MacDonald River runs the Great Northern Road, built by convict labour.

★Dharug National Park

Location; area

North-east of Wisemans Ferry; 14,800 hectares/36,600 acres.

Access

From Gosford or the Pacific Highway: road to Central Mangrove and from there to Spencer. From Sydney: via Windsor or Glenorie to Wisemans Ferry. By ferry over the river, 4.5km/3 miles east of landing-stage on road to Spencer. The park cannot be reached by public transport.

Accommodation

Hotels and caravan/camping parks at Wisemans Ferry and Gunderman.

Features

Features of the National Park (established in 1967) are sandstone cliffs rising above the windings of the Hawkesbury River, impressive waterfalls, a rich flora and fauna and numerous old Aboriginal rock drawings. Along the northern and western boundary of the park runs the Old Great North Road, the first road from Sydney to the Hunter Valley, constructed by convict labour from 1826 onwards.

Pleasure craft on the Hawkesbury River

Walking trails

From the valley of the Mill Creek there are walking trails into various side valleys. The park also offers ample scope for bush walking and bush camping.

★ Wollemi National Park K 6

Location; area

100km/60 miles north-west of Sydney in the Colo and Hunter valleys; 500,000 hectares/1,235,000 acres.

Access

The road from Windsor to Singleton (see entries) runs along the eastern boundary of the park. There are no roads within the park itself.

Accommodation

In Windsor, Wilberforce and Singleton.

Facilities

Bush camping. The areas round the periphery of the park are to be developed as picnic areas and camping sites, but the centre is to be left unspoiled.

Features

Wollemi is one of the largest National Parks in New South Wales. Adjoining it on the north is the Kanangra Boyd National Park (see entry). The most striking features of the park are the stretches of wild, unspoiled country along the Colo and Wollemi Rivers, with deep sandstone gorges and basalt peaks rising to over 1200m/3900ft. There are expanses of rain forest on the hills and in the deep valleys. Bush and hill walking (strenuous); rock-climbing; canoeing.

Wollongong K 6

Situation and characteristics

Wollongong (pop. 239,600), 82km/51 miles south of Sydney, is the third largest city in New South Wales and the main centre of its heavy industry. It lies in an area of spectacular beauty, with a whole range of beautiful beaches, below the Illawarra escarpment, from which there are fine views of the city and the coast. Founded in 1815 round Lake Illawarra, it remained a small farming town until the middle of the 19th century. Many little places along the coast have been swallowed up by the expanding city.

Accommodation

Hotels, motels, many caravan/camping parks.

Features

In the suburb of Dapto is the Horsley Homestead (built about 1850), one of the few surviving farmhouses of the colonial period. Round Port Kembla, the city's man-made harbour, is a concentration of heavy industry: the largest steelworks in Australia (guided visits) and a copperworks with a chimney almost 200m/650ft high. The harbour, a coal-exporting port, can take ships of over 100,000 tons.

Surroundings

In Mount Kembla Village, to the west of the city, is a historical museum with a reconstruction of a mining disaster in 1902 in which 95 men died.

Lake Illawarra, which extends from the Pacific to the foothills of the Illawarra Range, with an area of 4200 hectares/10,400 acres, is a paradise for anglers, sailing enthusiasts and motorboat fans.

One of the best-known viewpoints in the area is Bald Hill Lookout. This was the site of Lawrence Hargrave's first attempt at flight in the early 1900s; it is now a favourite spot for hang-gliding.

There are rewarding excursions into the hills which rise steeply above the city, and westward on the Illawarra Highway over the Macquarie Pass and through the Macquarie Pass National Park to Moss Vale (see entry), a distance of 70km/45 miles. In the hinterland of Wollongong there are numerous artificial lakes and waterfalls.

Woolgoolga K 6

Situation and characteristics

25km/15½ miles north of Coffs Harbour on the Pacific Highway is the seaside resort of Woolgoolga (pop. 3660), with a good surfing beach and excellent fishing.

Accommodation

Several hotels, motels and caravan/camping parks.

Features

An unusual feature is a Sikh temple, a place of worship for the town's Indian population, who originally worked on Queensland's sugar-cane plantations and later moved south to grow bananas.

Surroundings

10km/6 miles north is Yuraygir National Park, with unspoiled beaches and dunes (see Grafton): walking, fishing, swimming, camping.

★Yamba J 7

Situation and characteristics

At the mouth of the Clarence River, between Grafton and Lismore, is the little town of Yamba (pop. 3700), which offers sea, lake and river fishing. On the other side of the estuary is Iluka (see entry), with a harbour protected by rocks which act as a breakwater. Houseboats for hire; cruises on river.

Accommodation

Hotel, motels, caravan/camping parks.

Surroundings

5km/3 miles south is Yuraygir National Park (see Grafton).

Yarrangobilly Caves J 7

Situation and characteristics

113km/70 miles north of Cooma, just off the Snowy Mountains Highway, are the Yarrangobilly Caves. There are something like 60 caves, but only four of them are open to the public (Glory Hole, North Glory, Jersey and Jillabenan). An additional attraction is a pool of mineral water which is warm all year round. The Reserve round the caves is still relatively unspoiled.

Northern Territory

General

Outback Australia
Area: 1,346,200sq.km./519,800sq. miles
Population: 168,000
Capital: Darwin

Flag

Coat of Arms

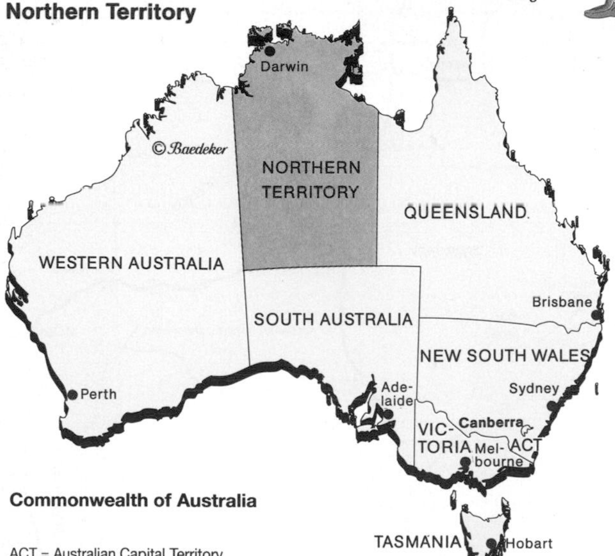

Commonwealth of Australia

ACT = Australian Capital Territory

Symbolic animals: red kangaroo, wedge-tailed eagle

Symbolic plant: Sturt's desert rose

The Northern Territory has always stood apart from the rest of the continent. The "Red Centre" of Australia and the "Top End", the tropical north with its monsoon rains and cyclones, resisted white penetration longer than any other part of the country. The Northern Territory still has a remarkably high proportion of Aborigines in its population; and here, in this great expanse of territory, they have been able to preserve more of their traditional way of life than anywhere else. The relics of their culture combine with the unique landscape to give the Northern Territory its particular attraction.

Administration

In 1863 administrative responsibility for the "Northern Territory of South Australia" was transferred from New South Wales to South Australia. In 1911 the territory was made the direct responsibility of the federal government in Canberra. Between 1926 and 1931 it was divided along the 20th parallel into North Australia and Central Australia.

◀ *The "Amphitheatre" in Finke Gorge National Park*

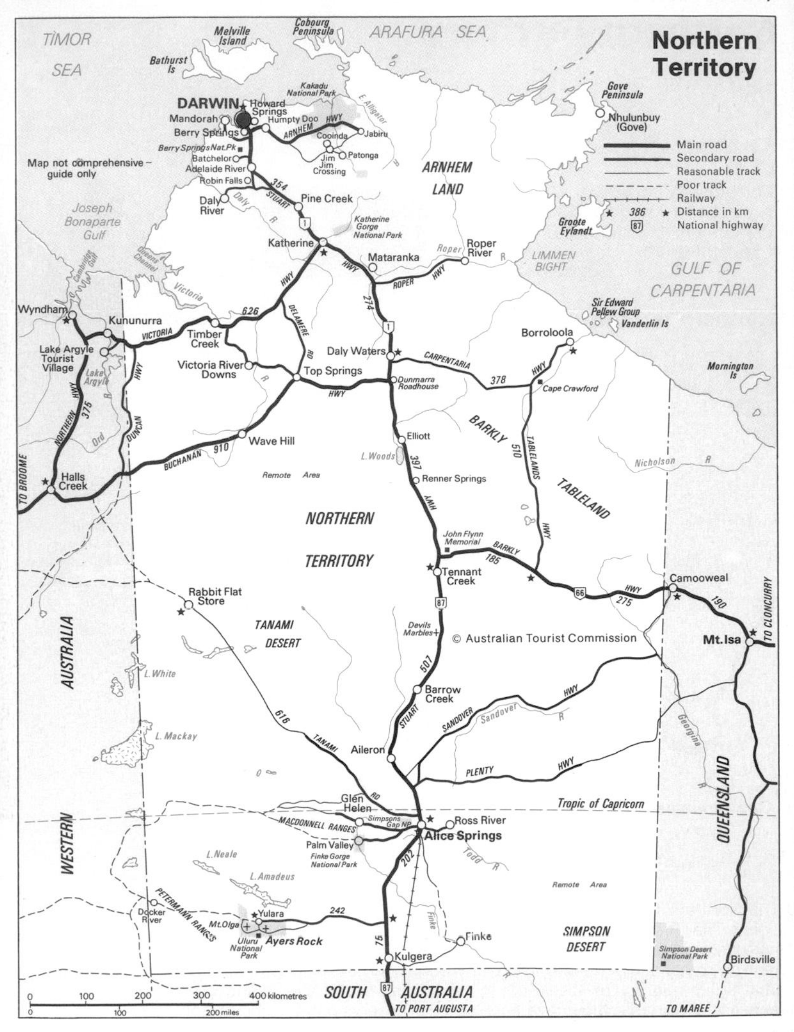

Self-government

Since 1978 the Northern Territory has had a limited degree of self-government. Under the Aboriginal Land Act of 1976 something like a third of the whole territory was returned to Aboriginal ownership.

Tourism

The enormous size of the Northern Territory – extending for over 900km/560 miles from east to west and over 1600km/1000 miles from north to south – means that it presents two very different aspects, the sun-drenched and arid centre with its gorges and valleys carved out by erosion in past ages and the coastal plains of the north, subject to flooding in summer and dominated by the escarpment with its spectacular waterfalls and rock formations. It presents a contrast, too, between the ancient culture of the Aborigines and the amenities of modern civilisation. With the development of mining and pastoral farming and the growth of tourism travel in the Northern Territory now presents no difficulties.

Visitors to Aboriginal lands, however, must obtain a permit from the Aboriginal authorities – the Central Land Council in Alice Springs for the area south of a line between Kununurra and Mount Isa, the Northern Land Council in Casuarina for land north of that line and the Tiwi Land Council for Bathurst and Melville Islands. A permit is not required for travelling through Aboriginal land on a public road.

Aboriginal culture tours

A good way of getting to know the Aboriginal way of life is to take one of the Aboriginal culture tours which are offered in Darwin, Katherine and Alice Springs under the slogan "Come share our culture". The tours are led by Aborigines, who take visitors round their ancestral territories and explain their ancient traditions.

Camels

Characteristic of the Red Centre are the camels – descendants of the camels brought in during the 19th century, mainly from Pakistan, along with their drivers (Afghans, familiarly "ghans"), to provide an essential means of transport for travel in the hot and arid interior. Nowadays camels bred on camel farms can be seen in long caravans conveying visitors along dusty and stony tracks to the regular tourist sights. Another tourist attraction is provided by camel races, for example at Alice Springs.

Railway

The Northern Territory's first railway line, opened in 1889, ran from Darwin to Pine Creek and was extended southward to Birdum/Larrimah in 1929, bringing its total length to 233km/145 miles. It was closed down in 1976 because of damage caused by heavy rain and cyclones and its unprofitability. The railway line from South Australia, construction of which started in 1878, reached Oodnadatta in 1891 but took another 40 years to reach Alice Springs.

Ghan routes

After the old Ghan line (as the railway was called after the Afghan camel-men) was closed down most of the track was taken up, and a new line was laid farther to the west between Tarcoola (SA) and Alice Springs. Nowadays the Ghan takes 24 hours to cover the 1559km/969 miles between Adelaide and Alice Springs; from Tarcoola there are connections to Sydney and Perth. There is a motorail train twice a week during the winter tourist season, once a week in summer.

Old trains

The Ghan Preservation Society in Alice Springs has saved a section of the old Ghan line through the MacDonnell Ranges to Ewaninga from demolition and now runs steam trains or diesel engines as a tourist attraction.

Stuart Highway

Since the mid-eighties the Stuart Highway between Adelaide and Darwin has been asphalted all the way, making the transcontinental journey much easier than it used to be. The problems, however, are still the enormous distances to be covered, the heat and the monotony of the landscape, which adds to the tiring effect on drivers.

Roadhouses

The roadhouses along the rail routes provide something of a diversion. Some of them have a certain nostalgic character, and in a number of such houses visitors can admire collections, some of them quite amusing, including automobile signs and banknotes from all over the world.

Roads and tracks

Before the asphalting of the Stuart Highway was completed a journey on the old track was still an adventurous undertaking. Improvements in the road system have enabled tourism to develop, but there are some who fear that the wilderness will lose its last secrets. But the Northern Territory is so vast that there is still plenty of scope for enterprising drivers who want to push themselves and their vehicle to the limit.

4WD tracks

In addition to "normal" tracks there are also tracks suitable only for jeeps or other four-wheel-drive (4WD) vehicles, following long-abandoned routes to remote cattle stations or mining areas or the old drove-roads, some of which extend beyond the boundaries of the Northern Territory. The Northern Territory Government Tourist Commission publishes a short guide to such 4WD tracks.

Trips in the outback on 4WD tracks call for good equipment, sufficient supplies (water, food, fuel) and a good driver. Before setting out it is essential to enquire about the state of the roads and the supply situation. It is foolish to set out on your own: travelling in convoy makes it easier to cope with breakdowns or other hazards. And if you plan to travel in Aboriginal territory (except for transit on a public road), remember to apply in plenty of time for the necessary permit.

A less hazardous way of seeing the remoter outback areas is to join an organised outback safari, which will still be a great travel experience.

A selection of tracks in the outback:

Gulf Track
From Mataranka via Roper Bar, Borroloola and Wollogorang to Burketown (QLD).

Plenty Highway
The Plenty Highway branches off the Stuart Highway 68km/42 miles north of Alice Springs and runs east to Boulia (QLD).

Simpson Desert Loop
From Alice Springs via Santa Teresa and Andado into South Australia (Mount Dare Station); then south via Oodnadatta to Birdsville (QLD), or back via Finke (side trip to Chambers Pillar) to Alice Springs.

Gunbarrel
Follows the old road from Yulara (Ayers Rock Resort) via Docker River to Wiluna (WA).

Central Ranges Loop
From Alice Springs via Hermannsburg, with side trip to Palm Valley and Finke Gorge National Park (the only access to this park), to Kings Canyon.

Tanami Track
From Alice Springs north-west through the Tanami Desert via Rabbit Flat to Halls Creek (WA); at Lajamanu a track branches off and runs into the northern part of the Northern Territory (4WD not essential).

The Big Run
From Katherine south-west via Timber Creek, the old Victoria River Downs station (once the largest cattle station in the British Empire), Top Springs and Kalkaringi to Halls Creek (WA).

The Cannonball Race

Taking advantage of the fact that in the Northern Territory there are no speed limits on roads outside built-up areas, the Cannonball car race is held every two years (1996, 1998, etc.) on public roads – mainly the Stuart Highway – from Darwin to Ayers Rock and back, a distance of some 3800km/2360 miles. The entrance fees are extremely high and maximum speeds of up to 300km/185 miles an hour are reached. The idea of this breakneck race came from the Hollywood film "Cannonball" (with Burt Reynolds) about an illegal private race across the United States.

Places of Interest from A to Z in the Northern Territory

Adelaide River F 2

Situation and characteristics

Adelaide River is a small settlement on the Stuart Highway, 110km/68 miles south of Darwin.

The river Adelaide was discovered in 1839 by the "Beagle" expedition and named in honour of Queen Adelaide the Queen Mother.

A military base was established at this strategic site during the Second World War and has left its mark in the form of the old arms depot on Snake Creek.

Accommodation

Motel, caravan/camping park.

★Litchfield National Park

Location; area

60km/37 miles north-west of Adelaide River; 65,700 hectares/162,300 acres.

Best time to visit

All the year round.

Access

From Darwin on Stuart Highway, turning off into Cox Peninsula road, or via Batchelor (gravel road, not suitable for caravans; in wet season often flooded). However, a new bridge over the Finniss River now provides access to the particularly impressive waterfalls even during the rainy season.

Accommodation

Camping sites (no electric power) at Wangi Falls, Florence Falls and Tjaynera Falls (Sandy Creek Falls). Motels and caravan/camping parks in nearby Batchelor.

Facilities

Picnic areas and camping sites; bathing in ponds at camping sites. Litchfield Park Road provides a circuit round the park; there are also tracks for 4WD vehicles.

Features

The particular attractions of Litchfield National Park, established only within the last few years, are the numerous waterfalls and springs on the escarpment of the Table Top Range. There are patches of tropical monsoon forest round the waterfalls and ponds; elsewhere there are great expanses of open woodland. The park is named after Frederick Litchfield, who first explored the region on an expedition into the Northern Territory in 1864.

Characteristic features of the park are the "magnetic" termite mounds, which rise like standing stones out of the level black earth. The north-south orientation of the mounds acts as a temperature control mechanism, since only their narrow edges are exposed to the full heat of the midday sun.

Lost City

The Lost City is a formation of large free-standing sandstone columns near the Tolmer Falls in the west of the park, under the Table Top escarpment.

This large protected area, due to be extended eastward to Adelaide River, offers ample scope for bush walking, with the dominating sandstone plateau of the Table Rop Range and the areas of monsoon rain forest and tropical open woodland.

Daly River Nature Park

Location; area

85km/53 miles south-west of Adelaide River; 60 hectares/150 acres.

Best time to visit

Autumn, winter and spring.

Access

From Darwin on Stuart Highway to Adelaide River or Hayes Creek (partly unsurfaced track, suitable for normal vehicles).

Facilities

Bush camping, picnic spots.

Daly River was named by Stuart in 1862 after Dominic Daly, governor of South Australia 1862–68. It is popular with anglers and boating enthusiasts; swimming is not recommended (crocodiles).

★★Alice Springs F 4

Situation

Apart from Canberra (ACT) Alice Springs (alt. 550m/1805ft; pop. 25,000) is the only important town in the interior of Australia. It lies in the geographical centre of the continent, close to the Tropic of Capricorn, 1500km/930 miles from Darwin and 1700km/1060 miles from Adelaide.

History and development

This arid desert region was from time immemorial the home of the Aranda tribes. In 1871 a repeater station on the Overland Telegraph Line was established to the north of the Heavitree Gap in the rocky MacDonnell Ranges, close to a water-hole in a normally dry riverbed. The site was selected by the surveyor William Mills and the water-hole was named after Alice Todd, wife of Charles Todd, postmaster-general of South Australia, and the river became the Todd River. Charles Todd was responsible for carrying out the project for a transcontinental telegraph line to provide faster communication between Britain and eastern Australia.

The town itself grew up 4km/2½ miles south of the telegraph station and until 1933 was called Stuart Town in honour of John McDouall Stuart, who was the first to find his way through the Red Centre of Australia to the north coast in 1862.

At first the place attracted few settlers, and the railway line from Adelaide which had been promised reached only as far north as Oodnadatta. Numerous expeditions, herds of stock and prospectors made a stopover at Heavitree Gap on their journey along the track which later became the Stuart Highway. The little settlement was wholly dependent for supplies on the camel caravans led by Afghan and Indian camel-men until the coming of the railway in 1929 marked the beginning of a new era.

During the brief period when the Northern Territory was divided into North and Central Australia (1926–32) Stuart Town was the seat of government for Central Australia, and the number of white inhabitants increased steadily. The economy of the Red Centre now depended on extensive cattle grazing and mining. During the Second World War Alice Springs became an important military base, and after the bombing of Darwin the seat of government of the Northern Territory.

A major contribution to the development of Alice Springs and the outback was made by the Anglican missionary the Rev. John Flynn (d. 1951; see Famous People), the moving spirit in the establishment of the Flying Doctor Service (see Baedeker Special, p. 275) and the Inland Mission with its hospitals and welfare centres. The first hospital in the centre of Australia was built in 1920–26.

Neville Shute's novel "A Town like Alice" (1950) and its filming made Alice Springs – familiarly known to Australians as "the Alice" – famed throughout the world.

The new Alice Springs

After the Second World War the tourist development of Alice Springs and the Red Centre began, stimulated by the enthusiastic accounts by ex-soldiers fascinated by the outback. As a result the town has been completely transformed, and little is left of the dusty outback settlement that it once was. It is now a town of restaurants, luxury hotels and caravan parks, entertainments of all kinds (including a casino) and innumerable shops and galleries. The development of the town's administrative and supply functions is reflected in many new buildings within the town and on its ever-spreading outskirts.

Access

Alice Springs can be readily reached by air, road or rail (car sleeper service). The airport is 20km/12½ miles south of the town, with a regular bus service to the town centre.

Alice Springs is an important "base camp" for tours (either by independent travellers in a hired car, 4WD vehicle or camper van or by organised groups, to the fascinating natural beauties of central Australia – Ayers Rock, the western and eastern MacDonnell Ranges, Kings Canyon (see entries) or the boundless expanses of the outback.

Accommodation

The varied range of accommodation in and around Alice Springs is listed in the "Holiday Planner" produced annually by the Northern Territory

Government Tourist Bureau, which also gives particulars of events and tours available in the area.

Entertainments

The town offers a variety of entertainments. One popular attraction is Lasseter's Casino on Barrett Drive (on the east bank of the Todd River, to the south of the golf course), with poker machines (daily from 1pm) and gaming tables (daily from 7pm).

Events

The camel races at the end of April and beginning of May are an important annual event. The Bangtail Muster in May, with a street parade and sports carnival, commemorates the herding together and counting of the cattle which took place in earlier days. The great event of the year, however, is the Henley on Todd Regatta at the beginning of October, in which the boats are either carried or trundled along the dry river bed and the day ends with a beer festival.

Sights in Alice Springs

Anzac Hill

From Anzac Hill, to the north of Alice Springs, there are good views of the town with its rectangular grid of streets, the carefully tended gardens and rows of trees, supplied with water by irrigation, and the MacDonnell Ranges to the south, with the Todd River, the Stuart Highway and the railway line finding their way through the narrow Heavitree Gap.

The river is normally dry, but after heavy rain it can turn into a raging torrent, making the roads impassable for days.

Adelaide House

In Todd Mall (pedestrian zone) is Adelaide House, built in 1920–26 under the direction of John Flynn, which since 1980 has been a museum displaying early radio equipment (open: Mon.–Fri. 10am–4pm, Sat. 10am–noon; admission charge).

In a hut behind the hospital Flynn and Traeger installed the pedal powered radio transmitter which made possible the development of the

Camel race, Alice Springs

Royal Flying Doctor Service (established 1929). Adjoining the former hospital, in Todd Mall, is the Flynn Memorial Church (1956). John Flynn's grave is under a large boulder on the fringes of the hills west of the town (Flynn's Grave Historical Reserve).

Royal Flying Doctor Service base

In Stuart Terrace, near the south end of Hartley Street, is the regional base of the Service, with displays illustrating its beginnings and development and its technical equipment (open: Mon.–Sat. 9am–3.30pm, Sun. 1–4pm; admission charge).

Gillen and Spencer Museum

The Gillen and Spencer Museum (Ford Plaza, Todd Mall) is devoted to the natural history of the outback, the culture of the Aborigines and white settlement in the Red Centre (open: daily 9am–5pm; admission charge).

Historic buildings

In Hartley Street, which runs parallel to Todd Street, and Parsons Street, which runs between the two, are other relics of the past, the Old Courthouse and the Residency, both built for Alice Springs' short period as a seat of government in 1926–31, now a museum on the development of the Northern Territory (open: daily 9am–5pm). Hartley Street School (1929, with later extensions) was the first school established by the government. It now houses the regional tourist office and the National Trust.

Panorama Guth

Also in Hartley Street is Panorama Guth, a panoramic view by the Dutch artist Henk Guth of the landscape of the Red Centre of Australia.

Stuart Town Gaol

Stuart Town Gaol (1907–09) in Parsons Street, a solid stone structure, is the oldest building in Alice Springs. The prison was closed down in 1938 and now belongs to the National Trust (open: Tue., Thur. and Sat. mornings; admission charge).

Cemeteries

The old late 19th c. cemetery, with weathered tombstones, is in George Crescent, near the railway station. In Memorial Avenue, which goes off Larapinta Drive to the west of the railway, lies a cemetery containing the graves of the painter Albert Namatjira (1902–59) and the prospector Harold Lasseter, who died in the desert in 1931 while seeking a fabled seam of gold.

Central Australian Aviation Museum

On the old flying strip near the cemetery visitors can see aviation equipment from the pioneering days of desert flying. The Flying Doctors' Museum is also of much interest (open: Mon.–Fri. 9am–4pm, Sat., Sun. 10am–2pm).

★Strehlow Research Centre

Nearby, on Larapinta Drive, is a very informative exhibition of Aboriginal culture. The items were collected by the ethnologist Strehlow who lived with the Australian aborigines for a long period (open: daily 10am–5pm).

Araluen Art Centre

Also in Larapinta Drive is the modern Araluen Arts Centre which puts on art exhibitions, concerts and theatrical performances.

Old Telegraph Station

3km/2 miles north of the town lies the Old Telegraph Station, now a protected building. There are guided tours.

School of the Air

Located to the north-west of Alice Springs, the School of the Air was established in 1951 to provide teaching by radio for children in the remote outback (see Baedeker Special, p. 40). Visitors can listen to children being taught during school hours (Mon.–Fri. 1.30–3.30pm).

Olive Pink Flora Reserve

An interesting feature on the east bank of the Todd River is the Olive Pink Flora Reserve, a botanical garden displaying the vegetation of the Red Centre of Australia (open: daily 10am–6pm; access from Tunk Road).

Surroundings of Alice Springs

Todd River Reserve

In the area of 580ha/1508 acres on the banks of the Todd River, a popular spot for picnics, lies the water-hole where the history of Alice Springs began in 1871. A number of old buildings have been restored and there is an exhibition of relics from earlier days (guided tours by appointment; access on road branching east from Stuart Highway).

Stuart Auto Museum

Lovers of old cars and motoring technology should visit the Stuart Auto Museum on Palm Circuit (Emily Gap Rd., Rose Highway; open: daily 9am–4pm).

★Frontier Camel Farm and Arid Zone

8km/5 miles south-east of the town, with the mighty MacDonnell Range in the background, lies a very special animal park. Camels and dromedaries are bred here near an extensive plantation of date-palms, and visitors are invited to ride on some of these animals.

Reptile Display

Also on display are some native species of snakes and other reptiles which are very dangerous when in the wild (open: daily 9am–5pm).

Pitchi Ritchi Sanctuary

To the south of Alice Springs, at Heavitree Gap, is the interesting Pitchi Ritchi Sanctuary, a combination of bird park and open-air museum with Aboriginal artifacts and clay sculptures by William Ricketts (open: daily 9am–4pm; access from Stuart Highway).

★Ghan Railway, MacDonnell Siding

10km/6 miles south of Alice Springs the Ghan Preservation Society has restored a stretch of the old Ghan Railway which ran through the Australian outback, and rebuilt an old station, MacDonnell Siding. On this stretch travel old-style trains drawn by steam or diesel. The station is open daily 10am–4pm; information about timetables can be obtaining by telephoning (089) 555 047.

Château Hornsby Winery

Before the access road to the airport, Colonel Rose Drive turns off Stuart Highway and leads east to the Château Hornsby Winery, the only winery in the Red Centre; wine tastings and evening entertainment .

Desert Park

The latest attraction is Desert Park, about ten minutes by car to the west of the town. Here visitors can study the flora and fauna of the Australian outback and learn something of the Aboriginal culture.

★Mereenie Loop Road

From Alice Springs it is now possible to drive along Mereenie Loop Road, a circular stretch of several hundred kilometres providing an opportunity to see a number of the major features of the outback, such as King's Canyon and Ayers Rock (see entries). As the road passes through Aboriginal territory a special pass must be obtained from the Central Australian Tourist Information in Alice Springs (Hartley St./Gregory Terrace).

★Corroboree Rock Conservation Reserve

Location; area: 48km/30 miles east of Alice Springs; 7 hectares/17 acres.

Best time to visit: Throughout the year.

Access: From Alice Springs on Ross Highway.

Features: The Corroboree Rock, a striking limestone crag, is a place of great significance to the Aborigines. It is a cult site where initiation rites are performed and sacred stones are kept with which the Aboriginal myths are handed down to the younger generation by the telling of stories about the Dreamtime. Corroboree means a meeting-place for ceremonial, ritual or warlike occasions, usually accompanied by dances. The term is now also applied to the performances of Aboriginal dances organised for tourists. A short walking trail runs through the area.

Emily and Jessie Gaps Nature Park

Location; area: 13km/8 miles east of Alice Springs; 695 hectares/1717 acres.

Access: Via Ross Highway.

Facilities: Bathing, walking trails, rock climbing, rest area.

Features: The Emily and Jessie Gaps are two gorges 4km/2½ miles apart in the eastern MacDonnell Ranges. Here, in the shadow of the steep rock faces, there is water even during the dry season, attracting many birds. On the east wall of Emily Gap are Aboriginal rock paintings.

★Simpsons Gap National Park

Location; area: 18km/11 miles west of Alice Springs; 30,950 hectares/76,450 acres.

Best time to visit: Throughout the year.

Access: On Larapinta Drive; the eastern boundary of the National Park almost reaches the outskirts of Alice Springs. The road to the main gorge is asphalted.

Facilities: The visitor centre at the near end of the access road has intereresting displays and informative material. There are rest areas (gas barbecues), toilets and drinking water. Swimming is not permitted. The park is open only during the day.

Features

Simpsons Cap was discovered in 1871 by a surveyor called Gilbert McMinn. The origin of the name (spelt earlier in this century Simsons Gap) is unclear: it has no connection with the Simpson Desert. Until the establishment of the National Park in 1970 the area was a huge cattle station which had suffered from overgrazing. The balance of nature has now been stabilised.

A visit to Simpsons Gap National Park is a good introduction to the topography of the western MacDonnell Ranges. Deep gorges, carved by prehistoric watercourses through the sandstone of the ancient hills, with permanent waterholes and remains of earlier vegetation, form a striking contrast to the wide desert-like plains and dunes. Areas of white sand, huge river eucalyptuses Band white-barked ghost gums lead to a permanent water-hole in the shelter of rugged cliffs, which are particularly impressive in the slanting sun of late afternoon. To the Aranda tribes who live here the gorge is the home of their giant goanna ancestors.

Immediately beyond the access road, on Larapinta Drive, are two huge ghost gums – a favourite theme of the Aboriginal painter Albert Namatjira.

Walking trails

Walking trails lead to quiet spots where rock wallabies can be seen in the early morning and late afternoon. There are unmarked paths (total length 20km/12½ miles) to other gorges and water-holes.

From Cassia Hill (reached on a road branching off 2km/1¼ miles south of the ranger station) there is a good general view of the Larapinta valley.

Situated so near Alice Springs, the park attracts many visitors and is sometimes overcrowded.

Arltunga Historical Reserve F 4

Location; area

111km/69 miles east of Alice Springs; 5506 hectares/13,600 acres.

Access

Via Ross Highway and branch road 75km/47 miles east of Trephina Gorge (track not always negotiable).

Features

Gold was found here in 1887 and was worked systematically until 1916. Little is left of this isolated mining settlement – mine shafts, rusty machinery, ruins of stone-built houses (the police station and prison have been restored). There is a visitor centre with documentation and an interesting old cemetery. Walkers should be wary of disused mine shafts and wells. Visitors can look for gold in Paddy's Creek, on the south side of the access road. In Arltunga itself digging and the use of metal detectors are prohibited.

★ ★Ayers Rock/Uluru F 5

Situation

Ayers Rock, the most celebrated landmark in the centre of Australia, lies 450km/280 miles south-west of Alice Springs in the centre of Uluru National Park which covers an area of 126,132 hectares/311,546 acres.

Access

There are daily scheduled flights to Connellan Airport, 6km/4 miles from Ayers Rock Resort. Country buses and excursion buses from Alice Springs. For individual travellers access is on the Stuart and Lasseter Highways, turning off at Erldunda. The road is asphalted all the way; even the notorious corrugated track between Ayers Rock and the Olgas has been straightened and asphalted.

Discovery

In 1872 a surveyor called Ernest Giles became the first white man to see the rock. A year later it was more thoroughly surveyed and climbed by William Gosse, who named it after Henry Ayers, prime minister of South Australia.

Until the end of the Second World War only a few curious visitors came here on camel-back, guided by local cattle-drovers. In 1948 it became accessible by road; the influx of tourists grew and a number of motels and camping sites were opened close to the rock. In 1984 these were

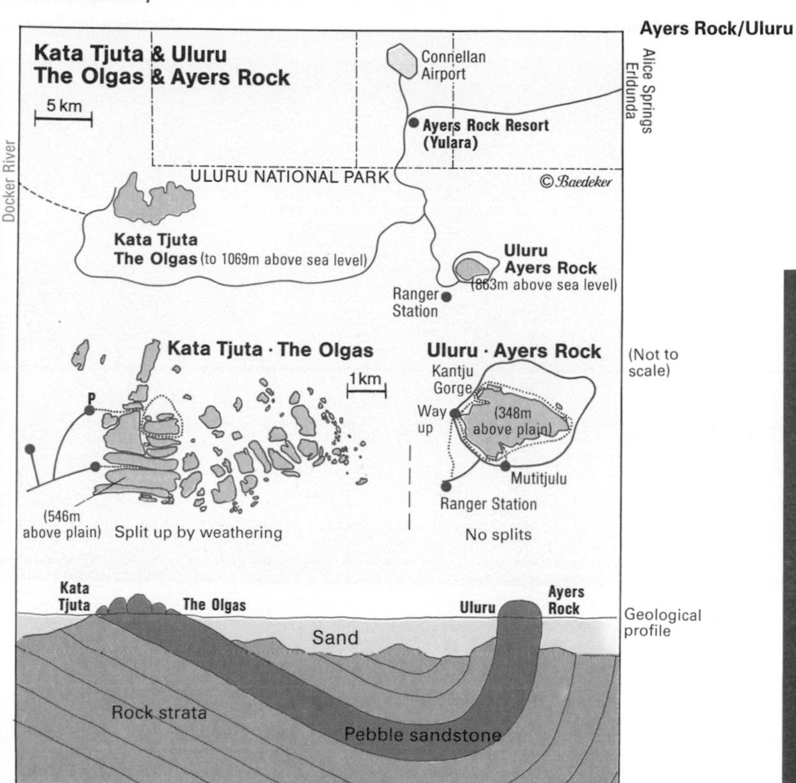

demolished and a new tourist centre with its own airstrip, Ayers Rock Resort, was established 20km/12½ miles away.

The rock

This huge rock, some 3½km/2 miles in length and rising to a height of 348m/1142ft above the surrounding plain, with a circumference of almost 9km/5½ miles, consists of sandstone and conglomerate strata steeply tilted by earth movements. Weathering as a result of extreme variations in temperature and by water and wind erosion produced the gullies and scars, and the oxidation ("rusting") of iron in the rock gave it its red colouring.

The play of colour on Ayers Rock is fascinating, varying according to the position of the sun. It is at its most striking at sunset and sunrise (Sunset Viewing Point). Occasionally it may be shrouded in rain clouds or may take on a black metallic sheen under rain, when it is almost equally impressive.

Ayers Rock plays an important part in Aboriginal myth and ritual. The Aborigines call it "Uluru" which means the "shadowy place". Today, it is the centrepiece of the Uluru National Park, which also includes the equally imposing rock formations known as the Olgas.

Climbing Ayers Rock

The distance to the top is 1.6km/1 mile, but it is a steep ascent at some points; the climb takes about 2 hours there and back. A chain to the top helps climbers and shows the way. You should attempt the climb only if you are sufficiently fit: there are occasional deaths on the rock, from a heart attack or a fall. And you should be sure to take enough water with you.

Ayers Rock, one of Australia's best known landmarks

Circuit of Ayers Rock

A walk round the rock is less strenuous, but is still a memorable experience (3–4 hours). Designated Aboriginal "sacred sites" must be respected. A good way of seeing the park is on one of the guided tours led by Aboriginal guides and rangers.

★Ayers Rock Resort

Situation and characteristics

The Ayers Rock tourist centre, 20km/12½ miles from Ayers Rock and 35km/ 22 miles from the Olgas (Kata Tjuta), was designed by Philip Cox. It is laid out on an S-shaped plan, with a luxury hotel at each end and shops, a visitor centre, restaurants, an amphitheatre, a motel and a large caravan/camping park as well as sports and leisure facilities. The long, low buildings, ochre-coloured, fit well into the surrounding landscape.

The visitor centre has displays and audiovisual presentations on the culture and mythology of the Aborigines and the wild life, landscape and geology of Uluru National Park. It also organises tours of the resort and various tours led by rangers of the ANPWS. There are also bus trips and helicopter flights to Ayers Rock.

★ ★Uluru National Park

Location; area

450km/280 miles south-west of Alice Springs; 126,132 hectares/311,546 acres.

Features

Uluru National Park, established in 1958, is one of Australia's most widely famed tourist attractions and in 1987 was included in UNESCO's World

Heritage List. The park was returned to the local Aborigines in 1985 and is managed jointly by them and the ANPWS in Canberra.

The climate is continental, with hot summers and cold winters. The average annual rainfall is only 200mm/8in., only a tenth of the rate of evaporation.

The great desert-like sandy plain bears only a scanty vegetation of spinifex grass with occasional bushes and trees (desert oaks), but in the sheltered areas at the foot of the rocks, where rainwater gathers, there are trees, river gums and bloodwood trees. When, usually in summer, there is an unexpected shower of rain the desert is covered with a carpet of flowers, including Sturt's desert rose, the heraldic flower of the Northern Territory. Most of the animals, particularly birds, are seen early in the morning or in the late afternoon. The play of colour on Ayers Rock and the Olgas is seen at its finest at sunset, and "sunset viewing areas" are sign-posted to the west of the rocks.

The Olgas · Kata Tjuta

The 36 rock domes of the Olgas (Kata Tjuta, "many heads") cover a much larger area and the highest of them is considerably higher than Ayers Rock (546m/1791ft above the surrounding plain and 1069m/3507ft above sea level). The Olgas are thought to have been originally a single huge rock, larger than Ayers Rock, which as a result of its coarser grain was split up by erosion. The first white man to see them was again Ernest Giles, who named them Mount Olga after a Russian princess.

Walking trails

There are three parking places, each the start of a walking trail. From the western car park the trail runs east into the narrowest part of Mount Olga Gorge, returning by the same route (about 1 hour); from the one on the south side the trail leads to the Kata Tjuta Lookout (1½ hours there and back); and from the one on the north the trail leads to the Valley of the Winds (2 hours for the circuit). It is also possible to walk between the Olgas, but at some points it is a stiff climb and the paths are not marked.

The weathered domes of the Olgas

Barrow Creek F 4

Situation and characteristics

On Barrow Creek, 286km/177 miles north of Alice Springs, is an old roadhouse hotel dating from the time when the Stuart Highway was still a mere track. The bar runs a "bush bank": visitors pin on to the wall behind the counter a banknote with their signature and the date of their visit, and if they ever return to this remote spot they can "cash" their note in the form of drink (with no interest on their investment!).

The area was explored by Stuart, who named it after a South Australian politician, John Henry Barrow. In 1872 a repeater station on the Overland Telegraph Line was established here, with a large cattle-grazing area to provide for the subsistence of the telegraph station, as at other stations on the line. In 1874 the two telegraph officials on duty here were killed by Aborigines. There is a shop and a filling station.

Accommodation

Hotel, caravan/camping park.

Bathurst Island · Melville Island F 2

Situation and characteristics

Bathurst and Melville Islands lie 80km/50 miles from Darwin off the north coast of Australia, separated from the mainland by the Clarence and Dundas Straits. Between the two islands is the narrow Apsley Strait.

Melville Island is, after Tasmania, Australia's largest island. Both islands are Aboriginal territory and are inhabited by Tiwi tribes who had little contact with the mainland Aborigines until the end of the 19th century and have preserved their own distinctive culture and art. Tiwi means "men". The main centre of these very progressive Aborigines is Nguiu (pop. 1200), at the south-eastern tip of Bathurst Island.

History

The first Europeans in this area were the Dutch, who passed the islands on their way to Batavia. In 1824 Britain established a military post at Fort

Dundas, near the present-day settlement of Pularumpi, to discourage French interest in the area, but the fort was abandoned only five years later. Indonesian fishermen had established contacts and trading relations with the Tiwi at an early stage. The Tiwi had steel axes and were therefore able to construct proper canoes, while the mainland Aborigines had only bark canoes. A Roman Catholic mission was established at Nguiu in 1911.

Features

The chief places in the north of Melville Island are Milikapiti and Pularumpi. Barra Base Lodge and Putjamirra are high-class holiday centres.

Organised tours to the holiday resorts run by the Tiwi, beautifully situated on the tropical sea, are an interesting introduction to the way of life and culture, the hunting and fishing of the Aborigines.

Individual travellers by boat or light aircraft must obtain a permit in advance from the Tiwi Land Council in Darwin or Bathurst.

All alcohol is banned on the islands.

Berry Springs Nature Park — F 2

Location; area

65km/40 miles south of Darwin; 405 hectares/1000 acres.

Access

The park can be reached at any time of year on asphalted roads (Stuart Highway, branching off into Cox Peninsula road).

Facilities

Picnic spots, barbecue sites, toilets, walking trails.

Features

Berry Springs Nature Park attracts many visitors, particularly at weekends. Bathing in lakes supplied by springs and surrounded by beautiful tropical forest inhabited by large numbers of birds.

Territory Wildlife Park

Near Berry Springs Nature Park is the Territory Wildlife Park (area 400 hectares/1000 acres), in which both native Australian animals and imported species live in near-natural conditions in large enclosures (open: daily 9am–4pm).

Chambers Pillar Historical Reserve — F 4

Location; area

165km/103 miles south of Alice Springs; 340 hectares/840 acres.

Access

On the Old Southern Road and via Ewaninga and Maryvale (4WD vehicle essential).

Accommodation

None.

Features

Chambers Pillar is a striking sandstone column rising to a height of 50m/165ft out of the white sandy plain. The first white man to see it, in 1860, was John McDouall Stuart, who named it after his sponsor James Chambers (whose daughter's name was given to the Katherine River). Chambers Pillar served as a landmark for travellers in the Red Centre. It played an important part in Aboriginal mythology, which held that Itirkawara, the gecko ancestor, was turned into the rock.

There are no organised tours from Alice Springs to Chambers Pillar. Within the park area there is no water and no shade.

★ Cobourg Peninsula — F 2

Situation

The Cobourg Peninsula, 200km/125 miles north-east of Darwin, is the second most northerly point on the Australian continent (after Cape York in Queensland). It lies within the territory of the Gurig, as the various Aboriginal clans in the area call themselves.

Gurig National Park

Location; area

570km/355 miles east of Darwin by road (only 200km/125 miles by air); 220,000 hectares/543,400 acres.

Best time to visit
Autumn to spring (April to November).

Access
Accessible only by boat (permit required). The approach is on the Arnhem Highway through Kakadu National Park and on via Oenpelli and Murgenella through Arnhem Aboriginal Land (only 4WD vehicles and only during dry season). There are organised tours by air from Darwin.

Accommodation
Camping site in park at Smith Point, near Black Point ranger station. Luxury accommodation in Wilderness Habitat, Seven Spirit Bay (on north coast), with 24 hexagonal huts (reached from Darwin by light aircraft or boat).

Facilities
Ranger station at Black Point in north-east of Port Essington Bay, with visitor centre: displays on history of Cobourg Peninsula (Aborigines, Indonesian trepang fishers, white settlers). Hunting safaris on water buffaloes are organised.

Features
Gurig National Park is an area of Aboriginal territory taking in the Cobourg Peninsula and small neighbouring islands with coral reefs, impressive inlets and beautiful beaches (beware of crocodiles!). This wilderness area, much of which is inaccessible, is flat or gently undulating, with tropical eucalyptus forest, monsoon forest, areas of marshland and mangrove swamps. In spring the park is a resting-place for migratory birds (jabiru storks, brolga cranes, etc.), and the fauna also includes manatees, turtles, crocodiles, wild horses, buffaloes and pigs. Rich fishing grounds.

Supplies of fuel and provisions must be taken with you. The number of vehicles entering the park is restricted by the Aboriginal Land Council.

★ ★Darwin F 2

Capital of the Northern Territory

Situation and characteristics
Darwin is the youngest of the Australian capitals, with an interesting multi-cultural mix of immigrants from all the major countries of the world. The town's favourable situation on the Indian Ocean, within the wider region of South-East Asia and Australia, suggests that it may develop into one of the continent's major centres and a hub of air and sea traffic – an Australian Singapore. It is the only seaport in the Northern Territory. The Darwin Metropolitan area extends to 303sq.km/117sq.miles.

Development
On Christmas Day 1974 Cyclone Tracy swept over Darwin and, with wind speeds of up to 280km/175 miles an hour, laid waste almost the whole town, with the loss of 66 lives. In a magnificent rescue effort most of the 45,000 inhabitants, drenched by the monsoon rains, were evacuated by air.

At first the government was disinclined to rebuild Darwin, since it lay in the main path of tropical cyclones; but the inhabitants returned spontaneously to the town and began the task of rebuilding. Only a few of the stilt houses common in tropical Australia had survived. The ruins of public buildings were incorporated in new structures and many new buildings were erected. It is now obligatory to use cyclone-proof building techniques in both public and private buildings.

Population
In recent decades the population of Darwin has risen to over 80,000, including a considerable Chinese minority. Extension of the town is planned to house an eventual population of 500,000.

Lying as it does within easy reach of South-East Asia, Darwin has, not surprisingly, taken in large numbers of South-East Asian refugees ("boat people").

Tourism
Tourism has played a major part in the growth and prosperity of Darwin. Visitors now number over 500,000 a year. The main season is in the warm and dry winter months.

The excellent system of surfaced roads makes many of the region's sights easily accessible even in the sultry heat, and the wet season has its own particular attractions in the spectacular tropical storms and abundantly flowing waterfalls (though this season may be trying for people with circulatory problems). Unusually heavy falls of rain may sometimes flood the all-weather roads.

Transport

There are regular flights to Darwin from all parts of the Australian continent. The airport for both international and domestic flights lies 8km/ 5 miles north-east of the town amid the suburbs.

Interstate bus services link Darwin with other Australian states. Buses are the cheapest means of overland travel; they are reliable and fast.

There are bus terminals on the south side of Darwin City in Mitchell Street (Darwin Transit Centre) and Harry Chan Avenue, at the south end of Smith Street Mall (local and regional services). The Darwin Bus Service, based in the Harry Chan Avenue terminal, runs regular services in the city and suburbs.

Specially designed for visitors is the "Tour Tub", an open-sided mini bus which runs round the city and inner suburbs, passing most features of interest. With a daily ticket passengers can get on and off the bus as often as they like.

Accommodation

Darwin has a wide choice of hotels in all categories. Thanks to Cyclone Tracy, there are no old hotels in the town. The finest (and most expensive) hotels are on the Esplanade, but there are also reasonably priced hotels and, for young people, youth hostels in the city and the inner suburbs. A government tax is added to the price of a room; this tax does not apply to caravan/camping parks (most of which are at some distance from the centre). The Northern Territory Government Tourist Bureau issues an annual "Holiday Planner" which lists accommodation in Darwin, and the National Road and Motorists Association (NRMA) in Sydney produces a list of caravan/camping parks. During the high season, in winter, many sites are occupied by permanent campers, and advance booking is therefore advisable.

Entertainment

Darwin has numerous night clubs, cinemas and theatres. The Performing Arts Centre in Mitchell Street can seat an audience of over 1000; at the other extreme is the tiny theatre in historic Brown's Mart (Smith Street). There are open-air performances in the Gardens Amphitheatre in the Botanical Gardens (Gardens Street).

A popular attraction is the Diamond Beach Casino, which is part of a large new pyramid-shaped complex with a hotel, restaurants, discothèques, sports facilities and conference rooms just off Mindil Beach, near the Botanical Gardens.

Events

Information about events and festivals in Darwin is given in the free brochures issued by the Top End Tourist Association and the free weekly publication "This Week in Darwin".

In April is the City to Surf race. In June there is the Bougainvillea Festival, which lasts several weeks, with parades, open-air theatre and a fair. The high spot for horse-racing enthusiasts is the Darwin Cup Carnival on Fannie Bay racecourse in July and August. In June the yacht race from Darwin to Ambon in Indonesia attracts large numbers of spectators. August is the big festival month, with the Darwin Rodeo and – perhaps the craziest event of all – the Beer Can Regatta, a race in the harbour between boats made from empty beer and soft drink cans. The Festival of Flaming Arrows also takes place in the harbour – a combination of fireworks and bizarrely decorated and illuminated boats.

Shopping

Darwin has numerous shops, including souvenir shops and craft shops, particularly in Smith Street. Typical Top End products are leather goods (e.g. the leather hats worn by the men of the outback) and Aboriginal craft products such as bark paintings, pictures reproducing sand paintings, woodcarving, basketwork and didgeridoos (tubular wind instruments).

The markets of Darwin, which because of the great heat take place in the evening, show strong Asian influence (spices, foodstuffs), offering an exotic experience. There is a food market every Friday evening at the Bus Transit Centre in Mitchell Street, and every Thursday evening there is a market at Mindil Beach. Markets are also held on Saturdays in the suburbs of Parap and Winnellie and on Sundays in Rapid Creek and Palmerston.

Information

The Darwin Tourist Promotion Association, which has an office at the airport, can arrange accommodation and book tours and give advice and information about events in Darwin.

Sights in Darwin

There are numerous features of interest in and around Darwin. Large numbers of both Australian and foreign visitors are drawn to Kakadu National Park (see entry) in Arnhem Land, with its fascinating scenery and Aboriginal culture, the islands in Tiwi territory (Melville and Bathurst) and on the Cobourg Peninsula, the Red Centre (see entry) and outback safaris through tropical rain forest, flood plains and semi-deserts.

Sightseeing tours

Visitors are offered a wide range of city sightseeing tours, half-day tours, whole-day excursions and harbour cruises (see below). For information consult the "Holiday Planner" published by the Tourist Association and their numerous brochures and leaflets.

There is also a variety of cruises, e.g. day trips, night fishing cruises and weekend excursions, or evening cruises with traditional dancing and dinner on board. Ferries sail from Stokes Hill Wharf (south-east of the City) to Mandorah on the opposite side of the Cox Peninsula.

Sightseeing on foot

On a walk round the city centre visitors can see most of the sights and at the same time experience the relaxed atmosphere of Australia's youngest capital. Because of the tropical heat in the middle of the day it is advisable to take your walk in the early morning or late afternoon.

Darwin City

In spite of the destruction wrought by bombing and cyclones the central area of Darwin – the City – has preserved the regular rectangular layout devised by Surveyor-General George Goyder in 1869, similar to that of the other state capitals (except Sydney).

Civic Centre

In the south-east of the City, near the Harry Chan Avenue bus terminal, is the Civic Centre, a low rectangular building. In the courtyard is the Tree of Knowledge, a handsome old banyan tree.

Christchurch Cathedral

Nearby, at the south-east end of the Esplanade, is the rebuilt Christchurch Cathedral (Anglican). The original church was damaged by Japanese bombing during the Second World War and destroyed by Cyclone Tracy. The new building was consecrated in 1977 in presence of the Archbishop of Canterbury.

The narrow porch and the adjoining wall, which survived the cyclone, were incorporated in the new octagonal church. The waves and fishermen's nets in the stained glass windows commemorate those who died at sea in the cyclone. The heavy altar consists of a single massive piece of jarrah wood.

Police Station Old Courthouse

Along the Esplanade from the Cathedral is the building (by J. K. Knight, 1884) occupied by the Police Station and the Old Courthouse, also known as the Old Naval Headquarters because it was occupied by the Australian Navy during the Second World War. Rebuilt after suffering severe damage in the cyclone, it now houses government offices.

Overland Telegraph Memorial

Nearby is the Overland Telegraph Memorial, commemorating the men who installed the telegraph line from Adelaide to Darwin, a distance of more than 3000km/1850 miles, in 23 months (1872).

Government House

At the south-east end of the Esplanade is Government House, an imposing white building in colonial style which stands 70m/230ft above the sea, with a fine view of the harbour. It is also known as Seven Gables because of the gables on all sides.

◀ *Cliffs at East Point, near Darwin*

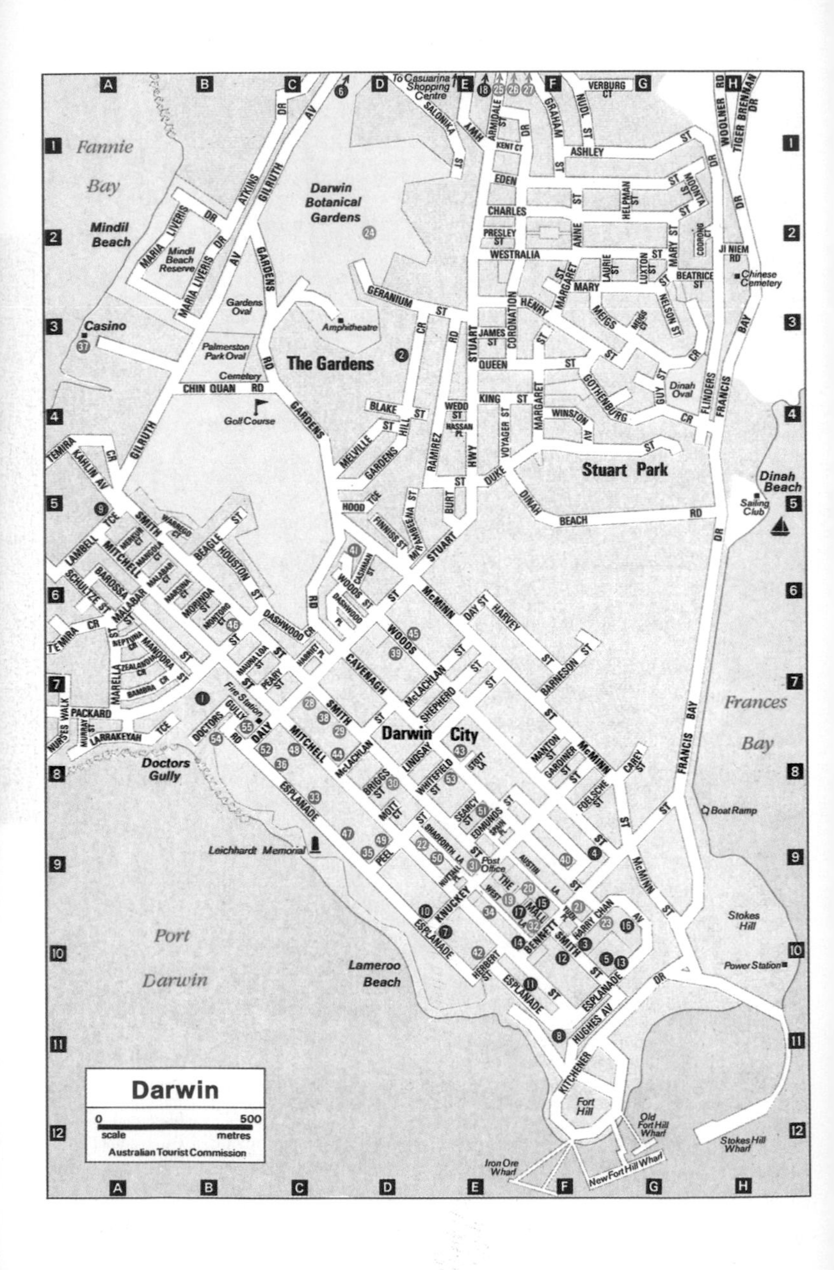
Darwin
0 500
scale metres
Australian Tourist Commission
Fannie Bay
Mindil Beach
Mindil Beach Reserve
Casino
Darwin Botanical Gardens
Gardens Oval
Palmerston Park Oval
Cemetery
Amphitheatre
The Gardens
Golf Course
To Casuarina Shopping Centre
Stuart Park
Dinah Beach
Sailing Club
Chinese Cemetery
Dinah Oval
Frances Bay
Darwin City
Doctors Gully
Fire Station
Leichhardt Memorial
Post Office
Boat Ramp
Stokes Hill
Power Station
Port Darwin
Lameroo Beach
Fort Hill
Old Fort Hill Wharf
Stokes Hill Wharf
Iron Ore Wharf
New Fort Hill Wharf
CHIN QUAN RD
GILRUTH AV
GARDENS RD
GERANIUM ST
STUART HWY
SMITH ST
MITCHELL ST
CAVENAGH ST
WOODS ST
McMINN ST
ESPLANADE
KNUCKEY ST
DALY ST
BENNETT ST
FRANCIS BAY DR
DINAH BEACH RD
HUGHES AV
KITCHENER DR

Places of Interest
Aquascene 1 B7
Aviation Museum 2 D3
Browns Mart 3 F10
Chinese Temple(Joss House) 4 F9
Christ Church Cathedral ... 5 G10
East Point War Museum ... 6 D1
Former Admiralty House ... 7 E10
Government House 8 F11
Indo Pacific Marine 9 A5
Lyons Cottage 10 D10
National Trust Headquarters 10 D10
Old Post Office 11 F10
Old Town Hall 12 F10
Police Station,
Old Court House 13 G10
The Commercial Bank 14 E10
The Star Village 15 F9
The Tree of Knowledge 16 G10
The Victoria Hotel 17 E10
Yarrawonga Park Zoo 18 E1

Tourist Information Centre
NT Tourist Bureau 19 E9

Ansett 20 F9
Ansett NT 20 F9
Australian Airlines 21 F10

Bus & Coach Terminals
Transit Centre 22 D9
Public Bus Terminal
Tel: 089 89751 .... 23 F10
Bus Australia
Deluxe
Greyhound
Pioneer

Parks
Botanical Gardens 24 D2

Rent-a-Car Offices
Avis 25 E1
Budget 26 E1
Cheapa Rent-A-Car 27 E1
Hertz 28 C7
Thrifty 29 C8

Motoring Association
Automobile Assoc. of NT .. 30 D8

Post Office
GPO 31 E9

International Airline
Qantas 32 F10

Accommodation
Deluxe
Beaufort International Hotel 33 C8
Sheraton Darwin 34 E10

Premier
Atrium Hotel Darwin 35 D9
Darwin Travelodge 36 C8
DiamondBeachHotelCasino 37 A3
Marrakai Apartments 38 C7

Moderate
City Gardens 39 D7
Don Hotel 40 F9
Four Seasons Darwin 41 D6
Hotel Darwin 42 E10
Mirambeene Tourist Resort 43 E8
Poinciana Inn 44 C8
Ti-Tree Holiday Apartments 45 D6

Budget
Asti Motel 46 B6
Cherry Blossom 47 D9
Darwin Motor Inn 48 C8
Darwin YHA Hostel 49 D9
Larrakeyah Lodge 50 E9
Tiwi Lodge 51 E8
Top End Frontier Htl./Mtl... 52 C8
Windsor Tourist Lodge 53 E8
YMCA 54 B8
YWCA 55 B8
Main Shopping Area ☐☐☐☐

Government House

Government House was built between 1870 and 1878 by J. K. Knight, who designed most of the official buildings in Darwin's early years. In front of the building are low projecting blocks with movable louvres for ventilation.

Government House is so solidly built that it has survived all cyclones: even Cyclone Tracy only damaged its roof. The building in its tropical gardens is still occupied by the government and is not open to the public.

Old Admiralty House

The Esplanade, which was already designated in the 1869 plan as a public park, runs north from Government House to Old Admiralty House, one of the few surviving buildings dating from around 1920. It is now occupied by an art gallery and a tearoom.

Lyons Cottage

At the corner of Knuckey Street and the Esplanade is Lyons Cottage, a massive bungalow-style house built by the British-Australian Telegraph Company for their head man in Darwin, the first building in the town to have electric light. It is named after a John Lyons, a lawyer who bought the house in 1952 and occupied it during his term of office as mayor of Darwin. After his death it was due to be demolished and replaced by a high-rise hotel, but Cyclone Tracy put an end to the plan. The original stone house was then rebuilt and is now a Telegraphic Museum (open: daily 10am–5pm.

Stuart Memorial

Along Knuckey Street, at the intersection with Smith Street, is the Stuart Memorial, erected to commemorate John McDouall Stuart, who at his third attempt successfully crossed the continent from south to north and prepared the way for the opening up of the country. The Overland Telegraph followed a year later.

Post Office

At the same intersection is the Post Office, incorporating stones from an old mail-coach station of 1872. The previous Post Office in Mitchell Street was destroyed by Japanese bombs in 1942.

Smith Street Mall (pedestrian zone)

From the Stuart Memorial and the Post Office Smith Street Mall, a pedestrian zone, runs south. The Victoria Hotel, familiarly known as the "Vic", was badly damaged by cyclones in 1897, 1937 and 1974 but on each occasion was restored in all its colonial splendour and is now a popular pub. South of the hotel is the Commercial Bank, rebuilt after its destruction by Cyclone Tracy, with a handsome colonnade.

Old Town Hall

The Old Town Hall was built in 1883, when the gold rush at Pine Creek was at its peak. Cyclone Tracy left only ruins, which have been converted into an open-air theatre.

Brown's Mart

Brown's Mart, opposite the ruins of the Old Town Hall at the intersection of Smith Street

and Harry Chan Avenue, is another relic of Darwin's early days. This plain stone building was erected in 1885, damaged several times by cyclones and successively used as a shop, government offices and police headquarters. After the repair of damage by Cyclone Tracy it now houses a small theatre. Farther east is the Chinese Temple, with which this walk through the City ends.

Chinese Temple

The Chinese Temple (corner of Woods Street and Bennett Street) was originally built in 1887 for Darwin's sizeable Chinese community

Sights Outside the Central Area

Aquascene

At the north end of the Esplanade (Doctors Gully) is Aquascene, where at high tide the fish eat out of visitors' hands and play with them (admission charge; for information about time of high tide tel. 81 7837).

★Botanic Gardens

The Botanic Gardens, in the north of the city above Fannie Bay, are well worth a visit (open: daily 7am–7pm, hothouses 7.30am–3.30pm). They were laid out for the government in the 1890s by a Russian immigrant. Particularly impressive are the tropical palm-trees, a miniature rain forest with a waterfall and pond, and the orchid collections.

Amphitheatre

In an amphitheatre in the southern part of the gardens concerts, Aboriginal dances and folklore presentations take place.

★Indo Pacific Marine

The Indo-Pacific Marine in now housed in new premises in the south-east of the city, at the start of Stokes Hill Wharf. Visitors can observe living coral and numerous other denizens of tropical seas (open: June–Sept. 9am–6pm, Oct.–May 10am–5pm).

Australian Pearling Exhibition

Nearby is an exhibition of Australian pearl-fishing.

Museums

Museum and Art Gallery of the NT

This Museum of Arts and Sciences in Conacher Street (Fannie Bay) has an excellent collection of Aboriginal and South-East Asian art and works by

Australian painters. A different kind of attraction is a stuffed crocodile, one of the largest ever killed in northern Australia (open: Mon.–Fri. 9am–5pm, Sat. and Sun. 10am–6pm).

Fannie Bay Gaol Museum

In East Point Road, to the north, is the Fannie Bay Gaol Museum, with a cell block of 1833 and the gallows on which the last execution was carried out in 1952. The gaol contains an interesting exhibition showing Darwin before and during Cyclone Tracy, and in course of reconstruction (audiovisual presentations; open: daily 10am–5pm).

Ross Smith Memorial

Near the museum, to the west of East Point Road, is the Ross Smith Memorial, commemorating the brothers Ross and Keith Smith, who landed here in 1919 after a flight from Britain.

East Point War Museum

The East Point War Museum or Royal Australian Artillery Museum is in the East Point Nature Reserve, in beautiful tropical gardens surrounded by the sea. It documents Darwin's role during the Second World War as an important naval base which was frequently attacked by Japanese bombers from February 1942 onwards. Within the grounds are a coastal battery, observation towers, bunkers and gun positions dating from that period (open: daily 9.30am–4.30pm).

Darwin Aviation Museum

Near the airport, on the Stuart Highway, is the Darwin Aviation Museum, with displays and relics (including a B 52 bomber of the US Air Force and a shot down Japanese Zero fighter) illustrating the development of aviation in the Northern Territory since the Smith brothers' landing (open: daily 9am–5pm).

Parks and Sports Facilities

Darwin is well provided with public open spaces. In addition to the East Point Reserve and the Botanic Gardens there are – particularly along the coast – numerous areas for water sports, cycle tracks, a golf course, a cricket ground, tennis courts and picnic and barbecue areas (Vesteys Beach, Mindil Beach, Bicentennial Park on the Esplanade, with the Leichhardt Memorial). There is good fishing from Stokes Hill Wharf, in the harbour.

To the north-east there are beaches on Nightcliff Drive and Casuarina Beach, which attract many water sports enthusiasts. During the summer (October to May) swimming in the sea is best avoided because of the danger from sharks and box jellyfish; but compensation is offered by the large Olympic Pool in Ross Smith Avenue and public swimming pools in the suburbs. Local people prefer inland waters for bathing in summer. Swimmers in rivers have to beware of crocodiles.

Surroundings of Darwin

There are many attractive parks, nature reserves and zoos in the immediate surroundings of Darwin. They are very popular with local people as well as with visitors, and some of them tend to be crowded at weekends and on public holidays. It is best, therefore, to go there during the week.

Casuarina Coastal Reserve

Location; area

15km/9 miles north of Darwin; 1180 hectares/2910 acres.

Access

Via Trower Road.

Facilities

Picnic area, play area.

Features

In the outer northern suburbs, extending from Rapid Creek to Lee Point, is the Casuarina Coastal Reserve, with expanses of tropical rain forest and mangrove swamp and beautiful beaches (including a section for nude bathing). Off the coast is the Old Man Rock, a sacred place to the Aborigines. Here too can be seen Second World War artillery positions.

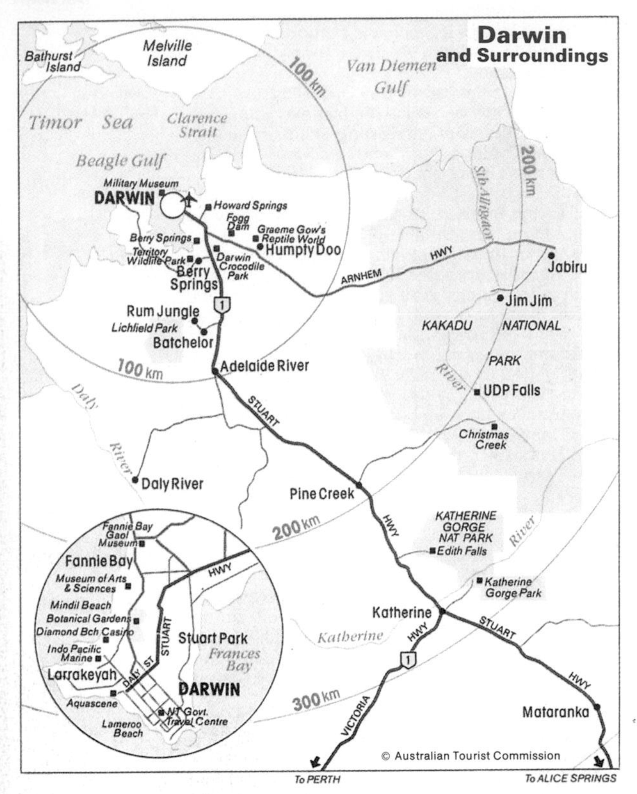

Howard Springs Nature Park

Location; area — 35km/22 miles east of Darwin; 1009 hectares/2492 acres.

Access — Via Stuart Highway.

Facilities — Caravan/camping grounds nearby; rest areas.

Features — Ponds (bathing); rest areas; large numbers of birds. On the road are the oldest surviving houses in the tropical architectural style of 1913.

Adjoining the nature park is the Howard Springs Hunting Reserve, a flood plain and expanse of marshland near the mouth of the Howard River in which ducks and geese can be shot (permit required; shooting seasons must be strictly observed).

Zoos and Wildlife Parks

Yarrawonga Zoo — Yarrawonga Zoo, 20km/12½ miles east of Central Darwin, provides a good introduction to the flora and fauna of the Top End (open: daily 9am–5pm).

Crocodile Farm — In the Crocodile Farm, 40km/25 miles south of Darwin, visitors can observe thousands of crocodiles, large and small (open: daily 9am–5pm; conducted tours daily at 1 and 2pm; feeding time 2pm, on Sundays also 11am; admission charge).

Territory Wildlife Park — To the south of the Crocodile Farm a road branches off the Stuart Highway to Berry Springs Nature Park (see entry). Near here is the Territory Wildlife

Park, in which animals native to the Northern Territory can be seen in their natural surroundings; there is also a large nocturnal animals house (open: daily 9am–4pm). The park is a project of the Conservation Commission of the Northern Territory.

★Devil's Marbles Conservation Reserve F 4

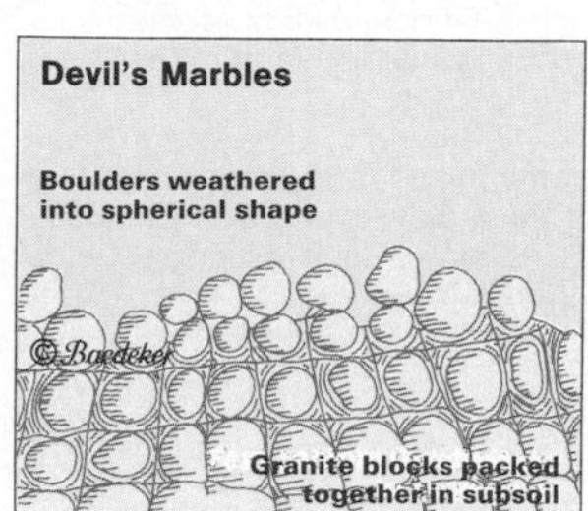

Location; area: 390km/240 miles north of Alice Springs; 1828 hectares/4515 acres.

Access: On Stuart Highway (which runs through the Reserve).

Facilities: Accommodation in Wauchope and Tennant Creek. No facilities for visitors.

Features: These huge granite boulders, worn down and split up by weathering, lying tumbled on the ground or piled on top of one another, are a striking landmark in a featureless sandy plain. In Aboriginal mythology they are the eggs of the rainbow serpent. The shade they provide and the dew which settles round them provide a habitat for low-growing plants and many birds. The Devil's Marbles are a favourite target for photographers; they are seen at their best just before sunset.

Douglas Hot Springs Nature Park F 2

Location; area: On the Douglas River, 200km/125 miles south of Darwin; 3107 hectares/7674 acres.

The Devil's Marbles

Access Off Stuart Highway at Hayes Creek (good gravel road, 42km/26 miles).
Facilities No accommodation. Good walking, swimming and fishing.
Features Within the park are a number of ponds fed by hot springs. The most popular is the Hot Springs Lagoon.

Butterfly Gorge Nature Park

Location; area 17km/10½ miles east of Douglas Springs; 256 hectares/632 acres.
Access The access roads are suitable only for four-wheel-drive vehicles; in the rainy season they are impassable.
Facilities No accommodation. Picnic area.
Features In Butterfly Gorge Nature Park (named after the countless butterflies to be seen here) the Douglas River has carved a way for some 300m/330yd through a sandstone escarpment, forming large, deep rock pools, small waterfalls and a gorge enclosed by high rock faces.

Ewaninga Rock Carvings Conservation Reserve F 4

Location; area 35km/22 miles south of Alice Springs; 6 hectares/15 acres.
Access Via the Old South Road (sandy and dusty in places but negotiable, with care, by conventional cars). The track to the south of Ewaninga (to Chambers Pillar, Maryvale Station) is possible only for four-wheel-drive vehicles.
Features This small reserve in a red sandy plain was established mainly to protect the strange prehistoric carvings on a group of sandstone outcrops. They show a great variety of symbols and patterns – circles, spirals, snakes, animal tracks, etc. The origin and significance of the carvings are unknown: they mean nothing even to the local Aranda tribes. The carvings are badly weathered, and are best seen and photographed in the slanting light of early morning or late afternoon.

At Ooraminna (3km/2 miles south of Ewaninga, road to east; 4WD vehicles only) are rock paintings of a later period.

Ewaninga is at the end of the stretch of the old Ghan railway line on which old-time trains are run as a tourist attraction.

★ Finke Gorge National Park F 4

Location; area 138km/86 miles south-west of Alice Springs; 45,856 hectares/113,264 acres.
Access Larapinta Drive to Hermannsburg; then a difficult track (4WD vehicles only) along the dry and rocky bed of the Finke River; a rare fall of rain may make it impassable.
Facilities Camping ground.
Features Finke Gorge National Park extends along the Finke River between the Krichauff Range in the west and the James Range to the south-east. The imposing rock formations in the park are of ritual significance to the Aborigines. The prehistoric red cabbage palms (*Livistona mariae*), extinct elsewhere, seen here are relics of a much wetter period. They grow in the valley of Palm Creek, a tributary of the Finke River. From the earliest times the bed of the Finke was used by the Aborigines as a route through the hills, and in 1872 Ernest Giles, on the first of his five expeditions through the Red Centre, followed the Finke valley upstream from Chambers Pillar. At the mouth of Ellery Creek he found a number of palms which Ferdinand von Müller, director of the Botanic Gardens in Melbourne, identified on the basis of Giles's specimens and sketches as the ancient *Livistona mariae* species. The river was named by Stuart in 1861 after his sponsor, Finke.

Palm Valley was probably also discovered by the German missionaries of Hermannsburg (see entry), an interesting example of early European settlement in central Australia which was handed over to Aboriginal administration in 1982.

The road to Palm Valley

Because of its inaccessibility, Finke Gorge National Park drew few visitors until a camping ground was established on Palm Creek, near Palm Valley, around 1960.

For visitors without a 4WD vehicle there are organised tours from Alice Springs (information from Northern Territory Government Tourist Bureau).

Fogg Dam · Humpty Doo F 2

Situation and characteristics

Fogg Dam, on the Arnhem Highway 45km/28 miles south-east of Darwin, is the supply and services centre of the rural hinterland of Darwin.

Access

Asphalted all-weather road.

Surroundings

4km/2½ miles west is Graeme Gow's Reptile World (signposted by a huge figure of a crocodile with gleaming red eyes, wearing boxing gloves), with a large collection of snakes and other reptiles (open: daily 8.30am–5pm; admission charge).

On Fogg Dam, an artificial lake 11km/7 miles east of Humpty Doo, are large numbers of water birds, particularly in the morning and evening. During the dry season the water of this reservoir attracts huge flocks of birds.

★Visitor centre

Nearby is a visitor centre of an entirely new type, "Windows of the Wetland", opened in June 1994, which offers an excellent introduction to the local flora and fauna.

Glen Helen F 4

Situation and characteristics

Glen Helen lies on Namatjira Drive, 133km/83 miles west of Alice Springs. A cattle station and stud farm was established here in the 1870s. Near the original homestead is Glen Helen Lodge (restaurant, filling station).

Accommodation: Motel, hostel, caravan/camping ground.

Features: Glen Helen is a good base for trips to Mount Sonder and the western MacDonnells. Within easy reach are Redbank Nature Park, Ormiston Gorge and Pound National Park (see entries) and Glen Helen Gorge Nature Park (see below).

Glen Helen Gorge Nature Park

Location; area: At Glen Helen; 386 hectares/953 acres.

Access: On Namatjira Drive (asphalted as far as Glen Helen).

Accommodation: In Glen Helen; Glen Helen Lodge.

Facilities: Picnic area; no camping. There are tourist facilities at Glen Helen Lodge, which also offers helicopter flights.

Features: Glen Helen Lodge Nature Park consists mainly of an impressive gorge with a deep water-hole, cut through the rock by the very ancient Finke River. The Aranda tribes believe that the water-hole is the home of a gigantic water snake and that the first formless beings of the Dreamtime emerged from its depths. There are interesting rock formations in the park, the Window in the Rock to the east and the Organ Pipes to the west.

Walking trail: A walking trail runs along the old dry river bed.

Gosse Bluff Scientific Reserve F 4

Situation: 200km/125 miles west of Alice Springs.

Access: With four-wheel-drive vehicle on Hermannsburg–Redbank road (permit required for travelling through Aboriginal territory).

Features: Gosse Bluff Scientific Reserve, the gigantic crater left by a comet which hit the earth well over 100 million years ago, was discovered by Ernest Giles in 1872 and named after Harry Gosse, a telegraph operator in Alice Springs. It has yielded much valuable scientific information, particularly by satellite photographs. The crater and its rim have been much worn down by weathering.

Gove Peninsula G 2

Situation and characteristics: Gove Peninsula, one of the remotest parts of the Northern Territory, lies in the far north-east of Arnhem Aboriginal Land, very much off the tourist track. It can be reached only by four-wheel-drive vehicles, and a permit is necessary for travelling in Aboriginal territory.

The reward for the long and difficult journey lies in the wild coastal scenery, the beautiful empty beaches, the tropical vegetation and the excellent fishing in the rivers. The little town of Nhulunbuy is now a holiday resort and a bauxite-mining centre. Visitors arrive by air; supplies come by sea (deep-water harbour).

★Gregory National Park F 3

Location; area: 270km/170 miles south-west of Katherine and 580km/360 miles south of Darwin; 1,333,600 hectares/3,294,000 acres.

Access: On Victoria Highway.

Facilities: Camping grounds, walking trails, boat ramp, fishing.

Features: Gregory National Park is an expanse of highland country with striking gorges, in a zone of transition between tropical and semi-arid regions. There are many remains of Aboriginal culture. The best approach to the park is from the Victoria Highway at Timber Creek and Victoria River Crossing. The unsurfaced road to Top Springs, 30km/19 miles east of

Timber Creek, leads to Jasper Gorge and is negotiable by ordinary cars; all the other tracks in the park are for four-wheel-drive vehicles only. During the wet season all roads and tracks may be flooded. There are organised boat trips on the Victoria River from Victoria River Crossing and Timber Creek.

Bathing is prohibited in the park because of the danger from crocodiles.

★Henbury Meteorites Conservation Reserve F 4

Location; area
147km/91 miles south-west of Alice Springs; 16 hectares/40 acres.

Access
From Stuart Highway, 11km/7 miles along road to Kings Canyon (Watarrka National Park).

Facilities
Picnic areas (no drinking water), simple toilets. There is a walking trail, signposted, round the craters. There are few trees to give shade.

Features
The Henbury Meteorites Conservation Reserve, a kind of lunar landscape, contains twelve craters left by a meteorite which exploded some 5000 years ago. The largest crater is 180m/200yd across and 15m/50ft deep; the smallest, barely perceptible, has a diameter of 6m/20ft and is only a few centimetres deep. The park has only a scanty covering of vegetation except in the crater basin, where water collects and growth is lusher. The fragments of the meteorite which have been found are very heavy, consisting as they do almost solely of metal (90% iron, 8% nickel). It is not worth looking for further fragments; in any case this is prohibited. The craters are seen at their most impressive in the sun of early morning or late afternoon.

★Hermannsburg F 4

Situation and characteristics
Hermannsburg (pop. 500) is on the Larapinta Drive 125km/80 miles south-west of Alice Springs (the last 30km/20 miles on a gravel road; no special permission required). In 1880 German Lutheran missionaries arrived in the Finke River plain to bring the Bible, medical aid and education to the Aranda people, after an arduous 20 months' journey from Bethany in South Australia with horses, sheep and herds of cattle. Their settlement, the first mission station in the Northern Territory, was named after a Lutheran seminary in Hannover.

Some 100 Aborigines lived in the mission in the 1880s, and the present mission buildings were erected around 1890 by Carl Strehlow. There were vegetable gardens, fruit plantations and date palms. The missionaries recorded the language and vocabulary of the Aranda.

Among those who lived here was Albert Namatjira (see Famous People), the best known Aboriginal painter. He is commemorated by a monument in the form of a tall stone column on the Larapinta Drive (10km/6 miles east of Hermannsburg).

Since 1982 the Aranda have been owners of the mission and a wide surrounding area, in which most of the Aborigines live in traditional groups in outlying stations.

There is a similar settlement, with a school for the children of nomadic cattle-herds, at Ipolera, to the west of Hermannsburg, where the Aborigines give tourists an introduction to their way of life.

Accommodation
None.

Features
The historic buildings in Hermannsburg – the church (1880), the schoolhouse, a number of dwelling houses and a smithy – are maintained with assistance from the National Trust. Two of the houses have been converted into a museum (open: daily except Tuesday 8am–5.30pm).

Visitors can see the historic buildings in the main street but not the area with the homes of the Aborigines. Photography is, officially, allowed only with a permit.

There are numerous tours from Alice Springs, often combined with a visit to Palm Valley in Finke Gorge National Park (see entry).

Hermannsburg, a German settlement in Australia

Jabiru F 2

Situation and characteristics

The mining settlement of Jabiru (pop. 1410) lies 250km/155 miles east of Darwin on the Arnhem Highway, within Kakadu National Park (see entry), near the Ranger uranium mine. The popularity of the National Park has made Jabiru an important supply and services centre.

Accommodation

Hotel, caravan/camping park.

Features

The main feature of the little town is the Four Seasons Kakadu Hotel, built in the form of a crocodile 250m/820ft long by 30m/100ft wide (best seen from the air). The crocodile is the totem animal of the Gagudju people, after whom Kakadu National Park is named. The circular layout of Kakadu Frontier Lodge and the caravan/camping park also recalls the circle motif common in Aboriginal art. There is safe swimming in the large artificial bathing lakes. Golf course.

There are conducted tours of the nearby Ranger uranium mine (starting from Jabiru East Airport). Kakadu Air runs sightseeing flights over the steep Arnhem Land Escarpment and other sights in the area.

★★Kakadu National Park F 2

Location; area

250km/155 miles east of Darwin; 1.75 million hectares/4.32 million acres.

Access

Coming from the south, the Kakadu Highway, which branches off the Stuart Highway at Pine Creek, crosses the Mary River to enter the park (206km/128 miles on a road which presents no difficulties in the dry season). An advantage of this road is that it runs close to the escarpment of the Arnhem Plateau. From Darwin, the Arnhem Highway runs over the plain. It is a good idea to take this route to the park (170km/105 miles) and to leave it on the Kakadu Highway, heading south, so as to take in two other sights in the north of the Northern Territory, Katherine Gorge (see Nitmiluk National

Water meadows in Kakadu National Park

Park) and Mataranka (see entry). This route is suitable also for visitors coming from the Red Centre or from Mount Isa in Queensland. In the wet season, when the highway through the park is closed, it is necessary to use the Arnhem Highway in both directions.

Accommodation

Within the park, in addition to the caravan/camping parks at points of particular scenic beauty, there is also accommodation in hotels and caravan/camping parks associated with them: Four Seasons Hotel at Cooinda, with camping ground; Kakadu Holiday Village on the Arnhem Highway (hotel, camping site); Four Seasons Kakadu Hotel (Jabiru); Kakadu Frontier Lodge and caravan/camping park (Jabiru). The youth hostel at Jabiru is open only May–October. For all these places early booking is advisable.

Facilities

At the Rock Art Galleries are car parking, a rest area with drinking water and toilets and an information kiosk.

In the park headquarters and visitor centre there are audiovisual presentations, informative displays and publications on natural history, flora and fauna and the Aborigines and their traditions and culture.

Distances in the park are considerable, and plenty of time should be allowed for seeing it. Three or four days at least are required for anything more than a superficial flying visit.

The best way of seeing the park is in a hired car (car rental firms in Darwin and Jabiru; advance booking advisable). There are no means of public transport within the park. Fuel and provisions can be bought in Jabiru, Cooinda, Kakadu Holiday Village and the Border Store.

There are organised tours from Darwin, but excursions can also be booked in the hotels and at Jabiru airport. There are also sightseeing flights from the airport (8km/5 miles east of the park headquarters).

To enter Aboriginal Arnhem Land (Border Store, Oenpelli) it is necessary to obtain a permit from the Land Council. Information about Kakadu National Park can be obtained from ANPWS in Canberra or its office in Darwin (Smith Street), the park administration in Jabiru or the Northern Territory Government Tourist Bureau.

Origin of name

The name of Kakadu National Park comes from Gagadju, one of the languages spoken by the tribes living in the area of the park. Archaeological evidence has shown that Aborigines have been living in this region for at least 25,000 years; but it seems probable that they have been here much longer than that, according to their myths about the beginnings of all existence in the Dreamtime.

Features

Kakadu National Park has been included in UNESCO's World Heritage List in virtue of its exceptional cultural importance (e.g. Aboriginal rock paintings) and its unspolled natural beauty. As with Ayers Rock (see entry) and the Great Barrier Reef in Queensland, it is necessary to reconcile the constantly increasing numbers of visitors with the strictest protection of the natural landscape and the evidence of native culture. For this purpose the National Park is administered jointly by the traditional owners of the land, the Aboriginal tribes of Arnhem Land, within which the park lies, and the Australian National Park and Wildlife Service (ANPWS) in Canberra.

Much of the successful Australian film "Crocodile Dundee" was shot in Kakadu National Park, providing an excellent advertisement not only for the park but for the whole of the Top End.

Area and characteristics

Kakadu National Park extends for over 200km/125 miles from north to south and over 100km/62½ miles from east to west, taking in almost the whole catchment area of the Crocodile River – making it the largest National Park in Australia and the third largest in the world. Its varied beauties can be seen by road, on foot, from a variety of viewpoints or by boat.

On the north coast is the tidal zone, with river estuaries, mangrove swamps and tall monsoon rain forests, and inland from the coast are the flood plains through which rivers pursue a winding course to the sea. During the dry season salt water and crocodiles advance anything up to 80km/50 miles inland, while during the rest of the year large expanses of wetlands are under water, the flooding varying according to the duration and intensity of the rain. These areas are important staging-points for migratory birds and home to countless water birds – the magpie goose, the brolga (a species of crane), and the jabiru (black-necked stork).

Farther inland is the gently undulating upland country which occupies the greater part of the park. All the main roads run through this area, so that visitors see mainly expanses of open tropical woodland. At the beginning of the dry season small areas of dry grassland, are deliberately burned so as to reduce the danger of large-scale fires at the peak of the dry season.

The escarpment of the Arnhem Land plateau runs diagonally through the park from south-west to north-east. The plateau is dry, and after heavy rain, water pours over its bare rocks and down the escarpment in magnificent waterfalls to join the rivers and wetlands of the north.

The vegetation, consisting of shrubs and grass, is similar to that of Australia's arid interior. During the dry season the waterfalls and rivers dry up, leaving only rock pools and billabongs (water-holes in the river beds) to which many animals come to drink. Erosion has eaten away at the sandstone of the plateau, with projecting formations of harder stone such as Nourlangie Rock, famed for its rock paintings. Scattered patches of monsoon rain forest are found in the gorges and on shady hillsides where there is water.

In the south of the park, in stony upland areas with scattered crags of granite, plants and animals from the wetter north and the arid interior are found side by side. Much of the catchment area of the South Alligator River lies in this stone country.

Seasons

The alternation of the seasons in the tropical Top End is highly dramatic. The Aborigines, living close to nature, divide the year into six seasons, differentiated according to weather conditions and their effect on their hunting and gathering activities.

Nourlangie Rock, Kakadu National Park ▶

In the pre-monsoon period at the end of the hot, dry time of year, with storms and the first rain (the season they called gunumeleng, from October to mid-December), they used to leave the lowland country and seek shelter from the heavy rain and flooding in caves and under rock overhangs.

Then follows the season of heavy rain, storms and flooding, when animals, fleeing into the trees, are easy to catch and goose eggs can be collected (gudjewg, from mid-December to March). Then the rain becomes less heavy and the floods subside, plants bear fruit and animals have their young, and the last storms sweep over the tall spinifex grass in the open woodland (bangerreng, in April).

After this is a time of morning mists and drying winds; carefully controlled fires "clean" the land, still damp under the surface, and stimulate new growth, so that, it is said, many animals can be taken ready roasted (yegge, May to mid-June).

The cool season (days 30°C/86°F, nights 17°C/63°) with less moisture leads to the drying up of watercourses and flood plains; geese must share the remaining water-holes with flocks of waterfowl and are easy to catch (wurrgeng, mid-June to mid-August).

The following weeks are dry, hot and windless; all life seems asleep. Geese can still be caught, but now snakes and tortoises as well. The first storm clouds and lightning announce the coming of a new rainy season (gurrung, mid-August to end September).

Although the wet season (November to March) can be trying, a visit at this time is an impressive experience, with thunderstorms, flooded water-holes, tumbling waterfalls and tumultuous rivers – but also with many roads, tracks, camping grounds and picnic areas closed by flooding.

Wildlife

There are walking trails in the park which enable visitors to observe its wildlife. The innumerable water birds (including the jabiru stork) and crocodiles are best seen by boat (Yellow Water at Four Seasons Hotel, Cooinda, and Kakadu Holiday Village on South Alligator River).

★★Aboriginal rock painting

The two easily accessible rock formations with Aboriginal rock paintings, the Ubirr (Obiri) Rock and the Nourlangie Rock, are a must for all visitors. The Ubirr Rock, in the north-east of the park, is frequently inaccessible during the wet season because the unsurfaced road is flooded.

From the park headquarters (visitor centre) it is 40km/25 miles to the Nourlangie Rock in the south, with the two sites of Anbangbang to the south and Nanguhiwur to the north (footpath, 2km/1¼ miles), 30km/19 miles on an asphalted road branching off the Kakadu Highway. In addition to these two famous sites there are many other cave entrances and rock overhangs with rock paintings in the park and in the rest of Arnhem Land, but these are not easily accessible and are known only to a few specialists.

Along with the Nourlangie Rock to the south of Jabiru, the Ubirr Rock has the most important assemblage of Aboriginal art in Australia. Side by side, and sometimes on top of one another, are very ancient naturalistic representations, followed by symbolic stylisations with mythological figures (e.g. the rainbow serpent). In addition there are fascinating "X-ray" pictures, showing the skeleton and internal organs of the animals depicted (barramundis, crocodiles, turtles). The latest groups of pictures are related to the Aborigines' encounter with Indonesian trepang fishers and white settlers, with representations of boats, guns, horses and buffaloes. Radiocarbon dating has shown that the oldest paintings are more than 20,000 years old.

From the viewpoint there are magnificent views of the flood plains below.

★Waterfalls

The Jim Jim Falls, the Twin Falls (to the south-east) and the Maguk Falls (to the south), which are at their most impressive in the wet season, can be reached only on four-wheel-drive vehicles; there are organised tours from Jabiru and Cooinda in May–October. Gunlom (Waterfall Creek) can be

Aboriginal rock painting on Nourlangie Rock

reached on a track from Mary River Roadhouse (suitable for normal cars but sometimes closed during the wet season).

Bush walking

Bush walks in the park should never be done alone, and proper preparation is essential; a bush camping permit must be obtained before setting out. Even on an ordinary walk visitors should take with them drinking water, sun protection cream and mosquito repellent.

Water sports

Fishing with bait is permitted, but netting is prohibited; there are catch limits on barramundis. There are slips for private boats.

When fishing, boating, etc., a watch should be kept for crocodiles. Swimming is prohibited in the park because of the danger from crocodiles.

Katherine F 2

Situation and characteristics

Katherine (pop. 6000), 314km/195 miles south of Darwin on the Stuart Highway, is the chief place in the "Never Never Country", the third largest town in the Northern Territory and the centre of a large cattle-farming area. Experiments are being made in the growing of fruit and vegetables on irrigated land.

The Katherine River was discovered by Stuart in 1862 on his third expedition to the north and named after the daughter of his sponsor. The coming of the Overland Telegraph led to the foundation of a settlement at Knotts Crossing, and in the late 1870s the first cattle stations were established (Springvale Homestead, 1879). The railway line from Darwin to Pibe Creek was extended to Katherine in 1926, serving mainly for the transport of cattle to Darwin.

During the Second World War there were numerous airfields between Katherine and Birdum. The Tindal Airbase, named after an officer killed in Darwin, was later extended.

Accommodation

Several hotels, motels and caravan/camping parks.

Features — The terminal building of the first airfield, in Giles Street, now houses the Katherine Museum, with a Historical Park. Nearby is the School of the Air (see Baedeker Special, p. 00); guided visits during school terms Mon.–Fri. at 11am. In the old railway station is an exhibition on the "Never Never Railway". The National Trust office, also in the station, can supply a Heritage Trail brochure.

Surroundings — Katherine is a good base for visits to the gorges on the Katherine River in Nitmiluk National Park (see entry), 32km/20 miles north-east, and Cutta Cutta Caves Nature Park.

★Cutta Cutta Caves Nature Park

Location; area — 24km/15 miles south-east of Katherine and 338km/210 miles south-east of Darwin; 1499 hectares/3703 acres.

Access — Via Stuart Highway access road may be almost impassable after heavy rain.

Accommodation — In Katherine.

Facilities — Visitor centre, picnic areas.

Situation and characteristics — The park takes its name from a series of limestone caves with stalactites and stalagmites, inhabited by bats and snakes. The surrounding terrain has much weathered karstic formations. Beware of snakes.

The Cutta Cutta caves are included in many organised tours to the Katherine Gorges. (see Nitmiluk National Park)

★Keep River National Park E 3

Situation — 470km/290 miles south-west of Katherine, 780km/485 miles south-west of Darwin, 36km/22 miles east of Kununurra (WA). The state border with West Australia is also the western boundary of the National Park.

Area — 59,700 hectares/147,500 acres.

Best time to visit — May to end of August. At other times of year the gravel roads in the park may be closed because of flooding.

Access — On Victoria Highway.

Facilities — Two bush camping grounds. Many walking trails. Visitor information centre at park entrance (3km/2 miles east on Victoria Highway). Drinking water only at park entrance.

Features — The recently established Keep River National Park is an area of impressively weathered sandstone formations with a complicated geological structure (glacial and volcanic actiivity, marine sediments). Striking features in the landscape are the massive baobab trees. The old Auvergne Stock Route, a drove road to the Kimberley in West Australia, runs through the park 6km/4 miles north of the Victoria Highway. There are Aboriginal rock paintings on the steep rock faces of the Keep River gorge.

★Kings Canyon • Watarrka National Park F 4

Location; area — 323km/201 miles south-west of Alice Springs, at the west end of the George Gill Range; 72,200 hectares/178,300 acres.

Access — From Alice Springs on Stuart Highway, turning off west at Henbury, then past Wallara Ranch to Kings Canyon; 200km/125 miles on gravel road suitable for ordinary cars. Filling station at Kings Creek camping ground. Alternative route: from Lasseter Highway on Luritja Road (track) to Wallara Ranch.

Lost City, Watarrka National Park

Facilities

Camping ground and lodge (Kings Canyon Frontier Lodge) on Kings Creek; picnic spots, walking trails.

Features

Kings Canyon has the deepest gorge in the Red Centre, with sandstone walls rising to a height of 270m/885ft, sometimes looking as if cut with a knife. On the bottom of the canyon are water-holes which never dry up. In the upper part of the gorge is the "Garden of Eden", with a lush growth of vegetation, including plants which are relics of earlier climatic conditions (e.g. palm ferns).

To the Aborigines this area was a sacred site, and their dwellings and places of assembly were decorated with rock paintings. The National Park borders directly on Aboriginal land, and the Luritja tribe has three settlement areas within the park, to the east at Bargot Springs, in the centre at Lilla and to the north of the new tourist centre. Their traditional name for the area is Watarrka.

Ernest Giles was the first white man to see the dry river bed (though not the canyon itself, 30km/19 miles farther north-west), in 1872, and named it after his principal sponsor, Fieldon King. His favourable report brought many cattle farmers into the area.

The area has been accessible only since 1960, when Jack Cotterill, on his own initiative, built a track to Kings Canyon.

On the plateau above the canyon is the "Lost City", an area of red sandstone rocks weathered into the semblance of ruined houses and streets. The rock is brittle and not safe for rock-climbing.

Walking trails

A steep walking trail leads up to the plateau, along the top of the canyon walls and down through the Lost City to the Garden of Eden, then across to the south wall of the canyon, down to the bottom of the gorge, passing Aboriginal rock paintings, and so back to the car park (6km/4 miles, 3–4 hours; water, head covering and stout footwear essential). There are no safety rails on the steep rock faces. The shorter Kings Creek Walk (1.5km/1 mile) takes about an hour.

MacDonnell Ranges F 4

Situation and characteristics

The MacDonnell Ranges round Alice Springs (see entry) are the most easily accessible hills in central Australia. A series of separate ranges running east–west extend over an area of 400km/250 miles from east to west and 160km/100 miles from north to south. They consist of much eroded quartzite and sandstone. The sandstone has rounded forms, but jagged ridges of limestone strata can be seen on Namatjira Drive.

The highest peaks are in the most northerly ranges (Mount Liebig, 1524m/5000ft; Mount Zeil, 1510m/4954ft; Mount Sonder, 1380m/4528ft). The southern ranges extend to Kings Canyon (George Gill Range) and Rainbow Valley in the east (James Range). These ancient hills, originally over 3000m/10,000ft high, have been worn down to stumps by erosion, and now rise only 500–600m (1650–2000ft) above the surrounding country, which itself lies at around 600m/2000ft above sea level. Seen from above, the steep-sided parallel ridges and deeply indented valleys look like a series of waves with furrows between them.

The sparse arid vegetation on the hills allows their contours and the varied colours of the rock to be clearly seen. The charm of the landscape lies in the contrast between the sharply outlined chasms and gorges, carved out by the force of water in the remote past, and the blue of the sky.

John McDouall Stuart, the first white man to travel through the centre of Australia in 1860, named the hills after the then governor of South Australia, Richard MacDonnell. His route, however, did not take him through the Heavitree Gap to the south of Alice Springs, where the Todd River, the Stuart Highway and the Ghan railway now run; instead he followed the course of the Hugh River, which flows through the Chewing Range (50km/30 miles west of Alice Springs) in what is now known as Stuart Pass.

The Aranda people call their territory Altijra, the "eternal land".

The visitor centre in Simpsons Gap National Park, 24km/15 miles west of Alice Springs, has much informative material on the MacDonnell Ranges.

Mataranka F 2

Situation and characteristics

Mataranka (pop. 150), a supply point for local cattle stations and passing tourists, lies on the Stuart Highway 110km/70 miles south-east of Katherine. Near here is Elsey Station, the setting in 1902–03 of Jeannie Gunn's famous book "We of the Never Never", which depicts life in the remote outback. Her husband, the station manager, died in 1903 and was buried in the Never Never cemetery, after which his widow returned to Melbourne and wrote her book, which became the subject of a film, shot here in 1981.

Surroundings

The replica of the Elsey Homestead and the Mataranka Pool Nature Park (13,840 hectares/34,185 acres), 9km/5½ miles east of the village, are Mataranka's two tourist attractions. The Mataranka Pool, supplied with water from hot springs at a constant temperature of 34°C/93°F and surrounded by tall palms and eucalyptuses, with countless birds, bats and flying foxes, is an enchanting oasis in the hot, arid wilderness.

The pool was "discovered" only during the Second World War, and thereafter developed into a holiday and recreation resort, with motels, a youth hostel, a caravan/camping park, entertainments, a restaurant, shops, a petrol station, an air strip and agencies offering a variety of excursions. The pool and surrounding area are now part of the recently established Elsey Nature Park.

The Never Never cemetery is 20km/12½ miles south-east of Mataranka.

In thc MacDonnell Ranges

★ Mount Connor F 5

Situation and characteristics

20km/12½ miles south of the Lasseter Highway, within Curtin Springs cattle station, is Mount Connor, known to the Aborigines as Atila. It was discovered in 1873 and named after the South Australian politician M. L. Connor.

This tabular hill comes in sight some 130km/80 miles after the Lasseter Highway branches off the Stuart Highway and is often confused with Ayers Rock. It rises to a height of 350m/1150ft above the plain, with a steeply scarped north side and a summit plateau. The south side has a very different aspect, sloping down more gently in a series of depressions.

From the Mount Connor Lookout rest area on the Lasseter Highway there are views of a number of salt lakes.

★★ Nitmiluk (Katherine Gorge) National Park F 2

Location; area

30km/19 miles south-east of Katherine; 180,352 hectares/445,469 acres.

Access

Asphalted road from Katherine. During the wet season it may be temporarily closed because of flooding and there may also be restrictions within the park.

Facilities

Visitor centre at entrance to park (video presentations). Nearby are a picnic area, a caravan/camping park, a boat ramp and a bathing area. Helicopter flights are also on offer.

Features

Katherine Gorge ranks with Kakadu National Park (see entry) and Uluru National Park (see Ayers Rock/Uluru) as one of the three great tourist magnets of the Northern Territory.

Katherine Gorge

Under the Aboriginal land rights legislation the area north-east of Katherine (see entry) was returned to its original native owners, and was then leased back to the government. The National Park is managed jointly by the Conservation Commission and the Aborigines.

The main scenic attraction is the series of gorges, up to 100m/330ft deep, which the Katherine River has cut through the soft sandstone of the southern Arnhem Land plateau. During the dry months the Stuart River carries little water, leaving a series of pools separated by rocks and boulders.

The river is at its most impressive during the wet season, when it surges tumultuously through the narrow gorges. The difference in water level between the wet and dry seasons is more than 10m/33ft.

The system of canyons with their side gorges has a total length of 12km/7½ miles; farther upstream the valley opens out. The perennial flow of the Katherine River nourishes a luxuriant growth of vegetation, in contrast to the dry sandy and stony soil of the Arnhem Land plateau. The park has an abundance of birds (more than 160 species have been recorded) and numbers of freshwater crocodiles (shy creatures which are best seen in the early morning). The tall rock walls of the gorges are at their most impressive when seen from a boat (two-hour, half-day and whole-day trips; hire of canoes).

Walking trails

In addition to boat trips through the gorges (much in demand: book early) there are ample opportunities for seeing the park on walking trails (starting from visitor centre).

The possibilities range from a walk to the viewpoint above the first gorge (4.5km/3 miles; about 2 hours) to a five-day hike to the Edith Falls in the north-west of the park. A very beautiful and impressive trail is the Butterfly Gorge Walk, a 4-hour walk up a side valley in the Katherine Gorge, the home of a host of colourful tropical butterflies. There are also a number of more strenuous walks, to be undertaken only by experienced and properly equipped walkers.

Surroundings

The Edith Falls lie to the north-west of the park. These falls on the Edith River (perennial water-holes) are reached on a surfaced road which branches off the Stuart Highway 40km/25 miles north of Katherine (rest area, toilets). From the foot of the falls there is a track (2km/1¼ miles) to a viewpoint above them.

★Ormiston Gorge and Pound National Park F 4

Location; area

132km/82 miles west of Alice Springs; 4655 hectares/11,498 acres.

Access

Via Namatjira Drive and a good gravel road (8km/5 miles) negotiable by all types of vehicle.

Facilities

Camping ground, ranger station, visitor centre, campfire sites, toilets, showers, beautiful bathing area. Bring your own drinking water.

Features

The Ormiston Gorge and Pound National Park is the largest of the National Parks in the MacDonnell Ranges, most of which are quite small.

The main attraction is the gorge carved out by the Ormiston River. At its south end, some 500m/550yd from the visitor centre, is a water-hole which hardly ever dries up, shaded by mighty river gums and the high rock walls of the gorge, which shimmer in the sunshine in varying colours, depending on the minerals in the rock.

Walking trails

In Ormiston Pound, a wide valley 10km/6 miles across framed by ranges of hills, there are a number of walking circuits (drinking water, sun protection and sturdy footwear essential).

The Ghost Gum Way from the visitor centre to the gorge (2.5km/1½ miles; 1–3 hours there and back) is waymarked in white, the Pound Walk (7km/4½ miles; 3–4 hours) in yellow.

A longer bush walk (several days) leads north through the Pound to Mount Giles (1283m/4210ft).

The Ormiston Gorge: wild and romantic

★Pine Creek F 2

Situation and characteristics

Pine Creek (pop. 390), an interesting little settlement of gold-mining days with well preserved and restored old buildings, lies on the Stuart Highway 230km/145 miles south-east of Darwin and 90km/55 miles north-west of Katherine.

Gold was found here in 1870 by men working on the Overland Telegraph Line, and it is still worked here by opencast methods. During the gold rush of the 1870s Chinese coolies were brought in for the hard work in a hot climate, and Pine Creek became almost a Chinatown, with 1500 Chinese to only 100 whites. Anxiety about Chinese numerical preponderance led to legislation which banned further Chinese immigration from 1888. A railway line from Darwin to Pine Creek was opened in 1889 but closed down in 1976.

Pine Creek has shops, a police station, a filling station and a bank. Fishing, gold-fossicking and shooting trips are on offer.

Accommodation

Hotel, motel, youth hostel, caravan/camping park.

Features

A number of zinc-roofed prefabricated iron buildings have survived from the early 20th century – the railway station, the Overland Telegraph repeater station and the Playford Club House. There are also some remains of the Chinese settlement.

Surroundings

The Kakadu Highway runs north-east to Kakadu National Park (see entry). There is good fishing in the Mary River.

Rainbow Valley Nature Park F 4

Location; area

97km/60 miles south of Alice Springs; 2483 hectares/6133 acres.

Access

Via Stuart Highway, branching off 75km/47 miles south of Alice Springs into a track running east (22km/13½ miles; 4WD vehicle recommended).

There is only one road to and through the park, which cars must not leave.

Facilities

Camping ground; barbecue areas (bring your own firewood); no drinking water. Take away your rubbish!

Features

The most striking features in this valley in the James Range are the rugged free-standing sandstone cliffs and rock formations which glow in rainbow-like bands of colour in the slanting sun of early morning or late afternoon. To the north-west are expanses of sandy country covered with spinifex grass and occasional clay-pans and stands of desert oaks (*casuarinas*). To the south are sandstone hills and crags dissected by erosion, with Aboriginal rock engravings and ochre paintings. The dark red sandstones containing iron oxides are much harder and more resistant to erosion than the soft light-coloured sandstone, which is very fragile and easily destroyed.

There are organised tours from Alice Springs and camel trips from the nearby Virginia Camel Farm.

Red Centre F 4/5

Situation and characteristics

The Red Centre is the heart of Australia, an arid outback region which in spite of its sparse vegetation attracts steadily increasing numbers of visitors with its fascinating colours, ancient rock formations and deep gorges. Its main features of interest are Alice Springs, the largest and best known outback town, the MacDonnell Ranges, Kings Canyon, Finke Gorge National Park, with Palm Valley, Hermannsburg and above all Ayers Rock, with the Olgas and the new tourist centre of Ayers Rock Resort (formerly Yulara).

Roughly a quarter of the population are Aborigines, and the remains of their ancient culture have been better preserved in the thinly populated hot, dry outback than anywhere else.

In the Red Centre, the heart of Australia

The climate is extreme. Hot summers with maximum day temperatures of over 45°C/113°F are followed by warm winter days with nights which are sometimes frosty. Rainfall is very low (average 280mm/11in.), often taking the form of violent showers after long drought.

Redbank Nature Park F 4

Location; area

161km/100 miles west of Alice Springs; 1295 hectares/3200 acres.

Access

From Glen Helen a natural track (improved) for 20km/12½ miles, then side road to park, followed by 4km/2½ miles on a difficult track. A track negotiable only by four-wheel-drive vehicles then runs west (17km/10½ miles) to the Gosse Bluff Scientific Reserve (see entry) and east through Aboriginal territory to Hermannsburg (see entry). Conventional cars would do better to return along Namatjira Drive to Iwupataka and from there take the asphalted Larapinta Drive to Hermannsburg (no permit required for a day trip to see the historic mission station).

Facilities

Bush camping permitted; picnic area, campfire site.

Features

Redbank Nature Park, centred on an impressive gorge with a number of perennial water-holes, lies in a beautiful setting under Mount Sonder.

From the car park it is a half-hour walk to the gorge, at one point only a metre wide, with sheer walls 40m/130ft high. The water in the rock pools is ice-cold.

Ross River F 4

Situation and characteristics

The tiny settlement of Ross River, 85km/53 miles east of Alice Springs on the Ross Highway, grew up at the end of the 19th century round the homestead of the Loves Creek Station. Since 1959 it has been developed as a tourist centre for excursions into the MacDonnell Ranges (see entry).

Ross River is named after John Ross, who along with Harvey and Giles surveyed the route of the Overland Telegraph in 1871, following in the footsteps of John McDouall Stuart.

Access
Easily reached from Alice Springs on the Ross Highway (75km/47 miles asphalted, then a good natural track).

Surroundings
Interesting excursions into the eastern MacDonnell Ranges: N'Dhala Gorge Nature Park (8km south-west; organised tours from Ross River); Arltunga Historic Reserve (44km/27 miles north-east; see entry), with the partly restored remains of an old gold-mining settlement; Ruby Gorge Nature Park (via Arltunga).

Serpentine Gorge Nature Park F 4

Location; area
107km/66 miles west of Alice Springs; 18 hectares/44 acres.

Facilities
Bush camping; picnic area, toilets.

Features
The park takes its name from a narrow winding gorge with water-holes at each end. The first water-hole usually dries up; if it does not, the gorge can be entered only by swimming (the water is cold, and an airbed would be a help). In the park there are many palm ferns (cycads), relics of an earlier vegetation pattern.

Surroundings
11km/7 miles west of the park (road off Namatjira Drive, then narrow, stony path 500m/550yd long) are ochre pits from which the Aborigines got their body paint, in shades ranging from yellow to dark ochre.

Standley Chasm F 4

Situation and characteristics
Standley Chasm, perhaps the most impressive gorge in the MacDonnell Ranges (see entry), lies 50km/30 miles west of Alice Springs in the territory of the Iwupataka Aboriginal Community (no permit required; open: 8.30am–4pm; admission charge). The quartzite walls of the chasm, almost 100m/330ft high, are only a few metres apart, so that only when the sun is directly overhead at midday do its rays reach the bottom of the gorge, bathing its walls in a red glow. A track lined by cycads (palm ferns) and river gums runs along the dry bed of the Hugh River, which has created the chasm by eroding an intrusion of softer rock between the hard quartzite on either side, into the narrow cleft.

The chasm is named after Ida Standley, the first schoolmistress in Alice Springs, who taught Aboriginal children in Jay Creek. Before the area was returned to the Aborigines it was part of a huge cattle station.

Access
Via Larapinta Drive; the 10km/6 mile long side road to near the chasm is asphalted.

Surroundings
6km/4 miles west of the turn-off to the chasm is the junction with Namatjira Drive. Larapinta Drive continues to Hermannsburg (see entry), while Namatjira Drive runs north-west to the other gorges in the western MacDonnell Ranges. After passing through Glen Helen (see entry) it continues as a track to Redbank Gorge Nature Park (see entry). A round trip via Gosse Bluff (see entry) and so back to Hermannsburg is only practicable in a four-wheel-drive vehicle.

Tennant Creek F 3

Situation and characteristics
Tennant Creek (pop. 3500) lies on the Stuart Highway 507km/315 miles north of Alice Springs, 675km/420 miles south of Katherine and 978km/608 miles south of Darwin. It is the only place of any size apart from Katherine on the 1500km/930 mile stretch between Alice Springs and Darwin.

History
In 1860 John McDouall Stuart named the river 10km/6 miles north of the present town after the South Australian cattle-owner John Tennant. In 1872

Pure outback country near Tennant Creek

a repeater station on the Overland Telegraph Line was established here, and this was followed by a few houses. Local people like to tell another story about the origin of the town. It is said to have been founded when a camel caravan carrying beer for the telegraph station broke down on the site of the town. The real reason for the development of the town, however, is likely to have been the discovery of gold here in 1932. Tennant Creek was thus the scene of Australia's last gold rush. After the yield of the gold workings declined, large deposits of copper were found, as well as silver and bismuth; there is also still some gold-working.

Accommodation

Several hotels and motels, youth hostel, caravan/camping parks.

Features

In Schmidt is the Museum of the National Trust, housed in a former military hospital (open: May-October daily 4–6pm). The Roman Catholic church in Windley Street, originally built in Pine Creek in 1904, was taken down in 1935, transported to Tennant Creek and rebuilt.

The best view of the town is to be had from One Tank Hill Lookout (2km/1¼ miles east on Peko Road).

Surroundings

The old telegraph repeater station, situated on the creek 10km/6 miles north of the town, has been restored and is now a museum (open: May–October daily 9am–4pm).

The Government Stamp Battery (built 1958), where haematite quartz ore is crushed, is a "working museum" (1.5km/1 mile east on Peko Road; guided tours 9am–4pm; admission charge).

16km/10 miles east on Peko Road is Nobles Nob Mine, discovered in 1934, later closed down, reopened in 1967 as an opencast mine after the collapse of the roof and finally closed down in 1985.

11km/7 miles north-west of the Stuart Highway are the Devil's Pebbles, a smaller edition of the famous Devil's Marbles (see Devil's Marbles Conservation Reserve): a jumble of rounded granite boulders scattered over a considerable area, in colours varying according to the minerals in the rock. The Aborigines revere them as the eggs of the rainbow serpent.

Mary Ann Dam, an artificial lake 6km/4 miles north of the town, is a favourite recreation area (swimming, water sports; boats for hire).

At Three Ways, 25km/15½ miles north of Tennant Creek, the Barkly Highway, coming from Mount Isa (QLD), runs into the Stuart Highway. Here there is a tall column commemorating the Rev. John Flynn, founder of the Flying Doctor Service (see Famous People and the Baedeker Special on p. 275). Three Ways Roadhouse, motel, cabins, caravan/camping park.

Top End F/G 2

Situation and characteristics

The "Top End" of Australia is the north coast with the offshore islands of Melville and Bathurst, which along with large territories on the mainland (Arnhem Land, Cobourg Peninsula, Daly River) were given back to the Aborigines under the Aboriginal land rights legislation.

The charm of this region lies in its variety of landscape (flood plains, tropical rain forest, the Escarpment, eroded by rivers and waterfalls), its rich flora and fauna and, particularly in Kakadu National Park (see entry), the remains of ancient Aboriginal culture.

Trephina Gorge Nature Park F 4

Location; area

80km/50 miles east of Alice Springs; 1771 hectares/4374 acres.

Access

Via Ross Highway; the last 10km/6 miles are not asphalted. Normally the 9km/5½ miles to Trephina Gorge can be negotiated in an ordinary car; the track to John Hayes Rock Hole, littered with rock fragments, calls for a vehicle with high clearance, preferably with four-wheel-drive.

Accommodation

In Ross River Resort, 21km/13 miles east.

Facilities

Beautiful rest areas and camping grounds. Rock-climbing, bush walking (no waymarked trails).

Features

The park, in an area of great scenic beauty, contains two gorges very different from one another. Trephina Gorge, flanked by sandstone walls, is relatively open, with a broad sandy riverbed, tall river gums and perennial water-holes. John Hayes Rock Hole is narrow and shady; with its many wedge-tailed eagles the area under Mount Hayes is known as the Valley of the Eagles. At the entrance to the gorge there are colonies of bats. The park was formerly part of a large cattle station, which has left a legacy in the form of horses, donkeys and cattle which have gone wild.

Victoria River F 3

Situation and characteristics

The Victoria River roadhouse, 200km/125 miles south-west of Katherine, is beautifully situated at a crossing of the Victoria River, which is noted for its rugged sandstone gorges.

Accommodation

Motel, caravan/camping park.

Surroundings

Excursions to the recently established Gregory National Park (see entry), in the eastern part of which is the gorge of the Victoria River (best seen from a boat). Swimming is not possible because of the danger from crocodiles. Fishing. Boat trips, helicopter flights and safari tours in 4WD vehicles are on offer.

Wallara Ranch F 4

Situation and characteristics

225km/140 miles south-west of Alice Springs, on Ernest Giles Road (near the turn-off for Angus Downs), is this outback inn, which until the completion of the new Kings Canyon Frontier Lodge was an important tourist stopover. From here it is 95km/60 miles to Kings Canyon/Watarrka

National Park (see entry). The inn was once on the huge Angus Downs cattle station.

Wauchope F 4

Situation and characteristics

Wauchope, 113km/70 miles south of Tennant Creek and 393km/244 miles north of Alice Springs, is a convenient stopover on the Stuart Highway. It began life as a supply centre for workers in the wolfram mines discovered in 1914, who included many Chinese. In 1923 the post office was converted into an inn.

Accommodation

Motel, caravan/camping park. Motel and caravan/camping park at Wycliffe Well, 18km/11 miles south of Wauchope.

Surroundings

10km/6 miles north, on the Stuart Highway, are the Devil's Marbles (see entry).

Wildman Reserve F 2

Location; area

170km/106 miles east of Darwin; 23,000 hectares/56,800 acres.

Access

Via Arnhem Highway; side road to Point Stuart (closed in wet season).

Facilities

Boat slipways

Features

The Wildman Reserve (named after Wildman Station) is an area of flood plains and water-holes round the Mary River.

The most popular water-hole is Rock Hole (good fishing). Here water birds and crocodiles can be observed. Along the winding Mary River are monsoon rain forests and paperbark trees.

Warning

Swimming is prohibited because of the danger from crocodiles.

Surroundings

At the end of Point Stuart Road (60km/37 miles) is Point Stuart, on Van Diemen Gulf. It was here that Stuart reached the north coast on his third expedition in 1862, completing the first south–north crossing of the continent.

Queensland

General

Sunshine State
Area: 1,727,000sq.km./667,000sq. miles
Population: 3.037 million
Capital: Brisbane

Flag

Coat of Arms

Queensland

Commonwealth of Australia

ACT = Australian Capital Territory

Symbolic animal: koala

Symbolic plant: Cooktown orchid

Australia's holiday country

The whole of Queensland, the "Sunshine State", lies within the tropical and subtropical zones of Australia; and since most holidaymakers seek sunshine and heat, Queensland is Australia's holiday country *par excellence*. With a coastline of 7400km/4600 miles, it offers endless scope for water sports of all kinds.

Queensland is the second largest of the Australian states (after Western Australia). Of its 1,727,000sq.km/667,000sq.miles more than half lie in the tropics, north of the Tropic of Capricorn.

Topography

The Great Dividing Range, which extends from northern Queensland through New South Wales to Victoria, forms a picturesque backdrop to the coastal regions, reaching close to the coast in the north and south of Queensland. To the west of the Great Dividing Range is a hilly plateau, beyond which are the endless expanses of the outback.

Off the coast, like a gigantic breakwater, is the Great Barrier Reef, a complex of coral reefs which in character and scale is unique in the world. It

◀ *A green landscape against the backdrop of the Glass House Mountains* extends from the Torres Strait, to the north of Cape York, where it comes close to the land, for almost 2000km/1250 miles and ends, 300km/185 miles off the coast, in the latitude of Bundaberg and Gladstone, following the escarpment of the continental shelf. Within the area of the Great Barrier Reef are some two dozen islands equipped to cater for holidaymakers.

Tourist attractions

Queensland's principal attractions, both for Australians and for visitors, are its magnificent beaches. Along its 2000km/1250 miles of coast (measured as the crow flies) a number of different regions can be distinguished – south-eastern, central and northern Queensland and the far north – with numerous holiday places along the coast and road and rail links with their hinterland in the Great Dividing Range. From these various resorts the islands off the coast and on the Great Barrier Reef can be visited. There are, too, over 300 National Parks and other reserves (some of them very small) established to protect endangered areas, in particular expanses of rain forest and the Great Barrier Reef.

South-East Queensland

South-eastern Queensland, with Brisbane in the centre, the Gold Coast to the south and the Sunshine Coast to the north, is a particularly popular holiday area. The hinterland extends by way of Toowoomba and the fertile Darling Downs to Charleville. Offshore are the South and North Stradbroke Islands and Moreton, Bribie and Fraser Islands.

Central Queensland

The central region, with Rockhampton as its principal town, extends from Bundaberg in the south by way of Gladstone to beyond Mackay in the north. Rockhampton lies exactly on the Tropic of Capricorn, and the area reaching inland on both sides of the Tropic is known as Capricornia. Off the coast are the Capricorn Islands. One of the southerly islands on the Great Barrier Reef is Heron Island. Within easy reach of Rockhampton is Keppel Island (Great Keppel). North of Mackay are the Newry Islands and Cumberland Islands.

North Queensland

Northern Queensland, with Townsville as its centre, extends from Proserpine in the south to beyond Cardwell in the north. From Townsville there are road and rail links with the hinterland by way of Charters Towers, extending far west to the mining town of Mount Isa in the outback.

Gloucester Island, Middle Island and the Whitsunday Islands, with Hamilton as the chief tourist centre, are easily reached from Shute Harbour. Magnetic Island is within easy reach of Townsville. Orpheus Island and Hinchinbrook Island, a large tropical island which has been declared a National Park, lie north of Townsville off Ingham and Cardwell. Then between Cardwell and Tully are Dunk Island, Brook Island, Family Island and Goold Island.

Far North

The tropical far north of Queensland, with Cairns as its principal centre, takes in the beautiful Atherton Tableland and the Cape York peninsula, a relatively undeveloped area for more adventurous travellers, with Cooktown, where Captain Cook was forced to beach his ship for repair. Lizard Island is the most northerly island with facilities for tourists on the Great Barrier Reef. In the extreme north, off Cape York, are Possession Island and Thursday Island.

Cairns, beautifully situated on the Marlin Coast 1766km/1097 miles north of Brisbane, with a warm winter and spring, is a good base for excursions. There are boat trips to Green Island or to uninhabited islands in the northern part of the Great Barrier Reef. The highlands to the west and south of Cairns (Atherton Tableland) offer dense tropical rain forest, waterfalls and crater lakes, and magnificent views of their varied landscape. Other attractive excursions are to Kuranda with its steep scenic railway and the historic mining village of Herberton. In a region of tropical heat the agreeable temperatures of the highlands are very welcome. The Bruce Highway ends at Cairns, but an asphalted road, the Cook Highway, continues north for another 80km/50 miles by way of Port Douglas to Mossman,

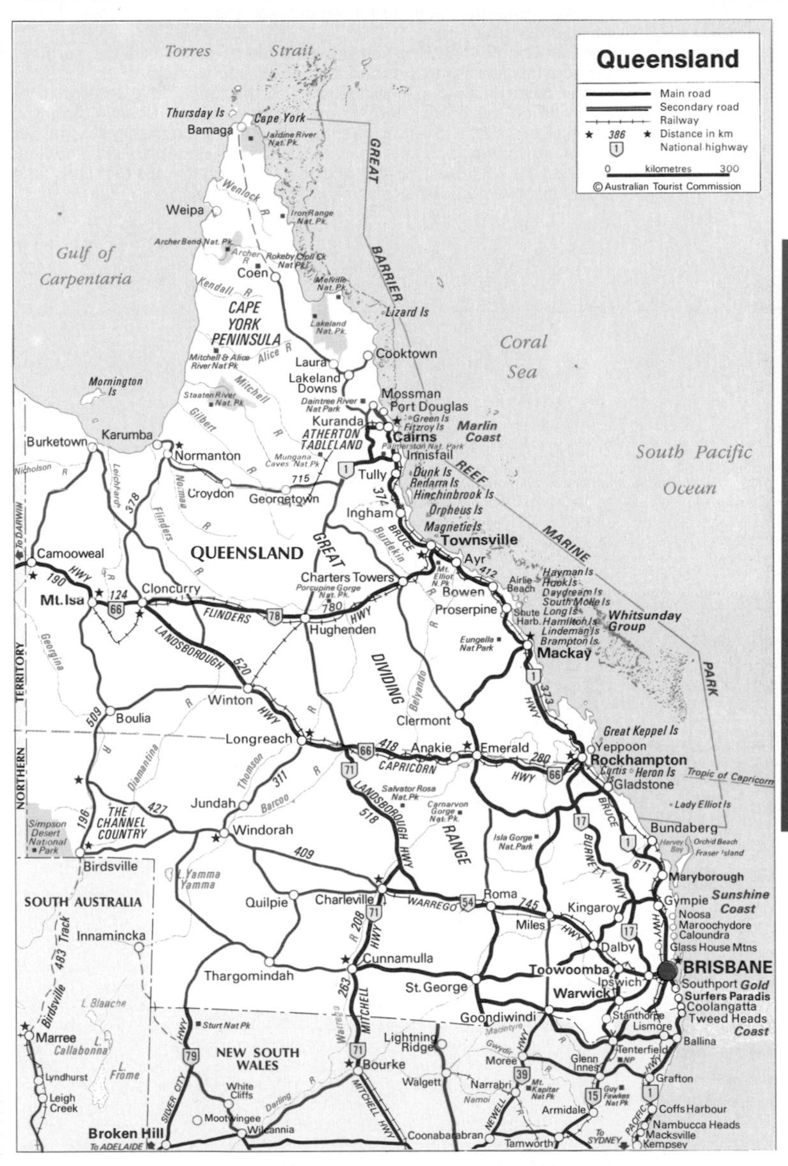

in the sugarcane-growing region. The Cape York peninsula extends north of Cairns for some 1000km/630 miles. Trips into the almost unpopulated "last frontier" area, with its poor tracks, should only be undertaken by travellers properly equipped for the outback and with experience of four-wheel-drive vehicles.

Gulf Country

The Gulf Country between Karumba and the boundary with the Northern Territory has few attractions and few facilities for visitors.

Channel Country

To the south of this, extending down to the lonely little settlement of Birdsville on the border with South Australia, is the Channel Country, which also has little to tempt visitors: hot and dusty in the dry season, hot and muggy in the rainy season, with roads often impassable by flooding. Between the Channel Country and the Gulf Country are Cloncurry and Mount Isa, two outposts of civilisation in the outback.

Places of Interest from A to Z in Queensland

Airlie Beach — J 4

Situation and characteristics

Airlie Beach (pop. 1500) is part of the town of Whitsunday (see entry), a holiday resort on the Whitsunday coast with numerous restaurants and tourist facilities. It has its own marina and a beautiful beach and is a good base for boat trips to the Whitsunday Islands (see entry) and the outer reefs.

Accommodation

Several hotels, motels and caravan/camping parks.

★Conway National Park

Location; area

8km/5 miles east of Airlie Beach and 310km/193 miles south-east of Townsville; 23,800 hectares/58,800 acres.

Best time to visit

Spring.

Access

From Bruce Highway via Proserpine. Bus service from Proserpine to Shute Harbour.

Facilities

Camping ground at Shute Harbour, at north end of park. Bush camping is also possible (permit obtainable in park). Picnic area.

Features

The coastal hills (up to 500m/1650ft) fall steeply down to the Whitsunday Passage. From high viewpoints on the road between Mount Rooper and Swamp Bay there are superb views of the Whitsunday Islands. Rich vegetation (rain forest, mangroves) and wildlife.

Atherton — J 3

Situation and characteristics

Atherton (pop. 4640), south-west of Cairns, is the chief place on the Atherton Tableland. It lies in a productive agricultural area, with good soil and high rainfall (dairy farming, maize plantations) and patches of rain forest. The town grew up round a logging camp and took its name from John Atherton, a farmer who settled here around 1870.

Accommodation

Several motels and caravan/camping parks.

Surroundings

Round Atherton are crater lakes with dense rain forest (Eacham and Barrine, Mount Hypipamee), waterfalls (see Millstream Falls National Park, Millaa Millaa) and magnificent views. At Yungaburra (see entry) is the famous Curtain Fig Tree.

The road over the Atherton Tableland, an area of ancient rock, is an interesting alternative to the Bruce Highway along the coast.

Mount Hypipamee · Crater National Park

Location; area

24km/15 miles south of Atherton (beside road to Ravenshoe); 360 hectares/890 acres.

Access

From Atherton or Ravenshoe on Kennedy Highway.

Facilities

Walking trails to crater; picnic spots; tourist centre.

Features

The crater which gives the park its name was the result of an explosion of volcanic gases in the granite. 70m/77yd in diameter, its granite walls fall steeply down 60m/200ft to the crater lake.

Ayr — K 5

Situation and characteristics

Ayr (pop. 8320), 80km/50 miles south-east of Townsville, is the chief place in the sugarcane-growing area north of the Burdekin delta. Rice is also

A waterfall in the Atherton Tableland

grown in irrigated fields. John Drysdale, the engineer who was responsible for this development, is commemorated by a clock-tower in the town.

Accommodation — Several hotels, motels and caravan/camping parks.

Features — Courthouse, St Francis's Church, Ayr Nature Display (butterflies, beetles, shells), Burdekin Cultural Complex.

Surroundings — 80km/50 miles south-east of Ayr is Cape Upstart National Park (no visitor facilities). Imposing granite crags, long sandy beaches.

Beaudesert K 5

Situation and characteristics — Beaudesert (pop. 5030), on the Mount Lindesay Highway 70km/43 miles south-west of Brisbane, near the border with New South Wales, is an agricultural centre (beef cattle, dairy farming, arable farming).

Accommodation — Some hotels and motels, caravan/camping park.

Features — St Mary's Church (timber-built), Royal Hotel, Old Post Office (19th c.), interesting Pioneer Museum.

Surroundings — Beaudesert is a good base for excursions to the Gold Coast (see entry) by way of Tamborine and to Lamington National Park.

★Lamington National Park

Location; area — 40km/25 miles south of Beaudesert; 20,000 hectares/50,000 acres.

Best time to visit — Throughout the year. The waterfalls are at their most impressive after the summer rain (March and April); in spring (September and October) there are wild flowers; in winter the weather is at its best (dry and sunny).

Access — From Brisbane on Pacific Highway or Mount Lindesay Highway. There are excursion buses from Brisbane.

Accommodation — There are two privately run tourist centres, O'Reilly's Green Mountains in the west and Binna Burra in the east (lodges and camping ground). Camping grounds in Green Mountains (often full at holiday times; advance booking advisable).

Facilities
Picnic spots, walking trails.

Features
Lamington National Park (established 1915), with excellent visitor facilities, is one of the state's most popular National Parks. It was named after Lord Lamington, governor of Queensland.

The park lies in hilly country (the Border Ranges) in the extreme south-east of Queensland, with a plateau (900–1200m/3000–4000ft) extending along the McPherson Range, which falls steeply down on the south side in cliffs and gorges. The hills are remnants of the ancient Mount Warning shield volcano.

The part contains over 500 waterfalls, tropical and subtropical rain forest and beech forests in the higher regions, with a very varied fauna (more than 190 species of birds).

Walking trails
There is an excellent network of walking trails in the park, with a total length of over 150km/95 miles. The best views are to be had from trails in the south of the park.

Bedarra Island J 3

Access
There are daily flights from Cairns and Townsville to Dunk Island; continue from there by water-taxi

Accommodation
An exclusive holiday centre for 30 guests. Children under 15 and day visitors are not welcome

Situation and characteristics
Bedarra Island, one of the Family Islands (see entry), lies off the coast opposite Tully, some 30km/20 miles north-east of Cardwell. Within the last few years this little island with its great variety of fauna and flora and superb beaches has become a very exclusive holiday destination. Guests stay in romantic villas with a view of the sea.

Bellenden-Ker National Park J 3

Location; area
60km/37 miles south of Cairns and 5km/3 miles west of Babinda; 31,000 hectares/76,600 acres.

Best time to visit
Winter.

Access
From Bruce or Gillies Highway.

Facilities
Picnic area and walking trail at Josephine Falls, at south end of park. Swimming.

Features
Bellenden-Ker National Park is an almost completely unspoiled area containing Queensland's highest hills, Mount Bartle Frere (1611m/5286ft) and Mount Bellenden-Ker (1591m/5220ft). Different types of rain forest can be seen at different heights.

Notable features of the park are Josephine Falls and the rich fauna. There is good bush walking and rock-climbing (for experienced climbers only).

Biggenden K 5

Situation and characteristics
Biggenden (pop. 800), an old gold-mining town surrounded by picturesque wild hills, lies 100km/60 miles south-west of Bundaberg. The Chowey Creek is spanned by a rare early example of a concrete bridge (1905). Other features of interest are the old Mount Shamrock goldmine and the opencast magnetite mine.

Accommodation
Hotels, caravan/camping park.

Mount Walsh National Park

Location; area — 7km/4½ miles south of Biggenden; 2987 hectares/7378 acres.

Best time to visit — Throughout the year.

Access — On foot from Biggenden; there is no road to the park.

Features — Mount Walsh National Park is one of a group of wild and romantic National Parks, largely unspoiled and undeveloped for tourism. Bush walking and climbing on the rugged peaks of Mount Walsh and the Bluff are to be recommended only for experienced climbers. The dominant features of the landscape are eucalyptus forests on the hillsides and dense groves of palms in the valleys.

Accommodation — Bush camping.

★ Birdsville G 5

Situation and characteristics

The little settlement of Birdsville (pop. under 200) is an important stopover on the journey through the interior of Queensland to or from Mount Isa and through the Simpson Desert. It lies in the Channel Country outback, 2000km/1240 miles west of Brisbane.

The little township lies on the Birdsville Track, the long and toilsome route along which herds of cattle were driven to Marree in South Australia to be loaded on to trains. The track, which was used from 1880 onwards, runs through the most arid region in the Australian interior between the Simpson Desert and Sturt's Stony Desert.

The track can be negotiated by four-wheel-drive vehicles, properly equipped and provisioned, between May and October. It is advisable not to drive alone.

At the end of the 19th century Birdsville, originally called Diamantina Crossing because of its situation at a crossing of the (often dry) Diamantina River, was a busy little township thanks to the cattle-droving traffic and its

Bottle trees, characteristic features of the Queensland landscape

function as a customs post near the border with South Australia. In those days it had three hotels, three shops, offices and even a doctor.

After the establishment of the Commonwealth of Australia in 1901 the duty on the export of cattle was abolished and the town's income disappeared. Most of the houses fell into disrepair, and the decline was accelerated by a drought lasting several years.

Birdsville's water comes, almost at boiling point, from a well 1200m/4000ft deep and is brought down to a normal temperature in cooling ponds.

Accommodation

Hotel, caravan/camping park.

Features

The ruins of the Royal Hotel are a reminder of the town's heyday. The local pub, however, still survives and does great business during the annual Birdsville Races in August or September, one of Australia's most famous race meetings, which attract thousands of visitors.

Blackwater J 4

Situation and characteristics

Blackwater (pop. 8000) lies 200km/125 miles west of Rockhampton on the Capricorn Highway. The population consists largely of miners working in the Blackwater Mines to north and south of the town. The coal is conveyed to Gladstone (see entry) by train and either exported or used in the production of energy (particularly for aluminium smelting). Visitors can see round the Utah Mine.

Accommodation

Motels and caravan/camping parks.

Blackdown Tableland National Park

Location; area

55km/34 miles south-east of Blackwater; two sections with a total area of almost 24,000 hectares/59,000 acres.

Best time to visit

Spring and autumn.

Access

From Capricorn Highway, forestry road 11km/7 miles west of Dingo (unsuitable for trailer caravans). In rainy weather or when there is a high fire risk the access road may be closed.

Facilities

Camping (permit required, obtainable in Rockhampton or from ranger in park). Picnic spots; 20km/12½ miles of walking trails.

Features

Blackdown Tableland National Park lies on a gently undulating sandstone plateau 800–950m/2600–3100ft above sea level. At this altitude it is usually anything up to 15°C/27°F cooler than in the surrounding plains. It is an area of dense forests with deep gorges, carved out by the Mimosa Creek and its tributaries, and waterfalls. Many species of ferns flourish in the park, and in general the flora and fauna is very distinctive as a result of the park's isolation, with steep scarps up to 600m/2000ft high cutting it off from the plains below. In winter there is often frost and, in the event of rain, dense mist.

Warning

Rock-climbing is prohibited because of the unstable nature of the rock.

Boulia G 4

Situation and characteristics

The little township of Boulia (pop. 300) lies on the Burke River in the Channel Country outback. Originally established in 1876 as a supply base for an explorer named Henry, it soon developed into an important stopover on the cattle-droving route.

Accommodation

Hotel, caravan/camping park.

Features

Stone Cottage Museum (1880).

N.B.

During the wet season in summer, when the broad winding watercourses are swollen by the monsoon rains, all tracks in the area become impassable.

Bowen J 3/4

Situation and characteristics

Bowen (pop. 8250) was founded in 1861–62, the first town in northern Queensland, and named after the state's first governor. It has a fine sheltered situation on Port Denison, to the north of the Whitsunday Islands and roughly half way between Mackay and Townsville on the Bruce Highway. The climate is very agreeable, with an average of eight hours of sunshine per day. Beautiful beaches. Day trips to Stone Island.

In the interior, round Collinsville, are large opencast coal-mines. The coal is brought to Bowen by rail and shipped from the new coal terminal at Abbot Point.

Accommodation

Several hotels, motels and caravan/camping parks.

Brampton Island National Park J 4

Situation and characteristics

Brampton is one of the Cumberland Islands, named by Captain Cook after the Duke of Cumberland in 1770. Lying to the south of the Whitsunday Islands, they are often called the southern Whitsundays. The nearest place on the mainland is Mackay (see entry), 35km/22 miles away, from which Brampton Island can be reached either by air or by ship.

Brampton is a hilly and densely wooded island with an area of 4.6sq.km/1.8sq.miles, rising to 219m/719ft at its highest point. Like the Whitsunday Islands, it is surrounded by coral reefs, with the outer reef lying some 40km/25 miles away. On the coasts are mangrove swamps and in the interior are coconut palms, originally planted at the end of the 19th century. Walking trails.

Accommodation

Resort complex for 240 guests run by Australian Airlines.

Surroundings

At low tide it is possible to walk over a sandbank to Carlisle Island and to tiny Pelican Island.

Most of the other islands of varying sizes in the Cumberland Group, some 70 in all, have been declared National Parks. There are no holiday settlements, and camping is possible only on some of the islands; a permit is required (obtainable from the QNPWS information bureau in Mackay) and campers must take their own provisions.

★Bribie Island K 5

Situation and characteristics

Bribie Island, still largely unspoiled, offers excellent facilities for water sports (boating, fishing). Some 30km/19 miles long, it lies 70km/45 miles north of Brisbane, separated from the mainland by the Pumicestone Passage. It is connected with Caloundra (see entry) by a bridge.

On Bribie Island are the little settlements of Bongaree (facing the mainland, to the south of the bridge) and Woorim (near the surfing beach on the east side of the island). On the west side of the island is Pumicestone National Park (no roads in park).

Accommodation

Several hotels, motels and caravan/camping parks.

★★Brisbane K 5

Capital of Queensland

Situation and characteristics

Brisbane, Australia's third largest city and capital of Queensland since 1859, lies on both sides of the Brisbane River, with a total area of

Modern architecture, Brisbane ▶

Paddle-steamers, Brisbane

1220sq.km/470sq.miles. It is bounded on the east by the sea and on the west by the Great Dividing Range. Its suburbs extend north and south to merge into the endless string of holiday resorts along the Sunshine Coast and Gold Coast (see entries).

The people of Brisbane call their city "big, bold and beautiful"; and it must be agreed that this sea of houses reflected in the river is of highly impressive effect. Visitors are attracted by its sunny climate, its luxuriant parks and gardens and its more relaxed life-style in contrast to the hectic activity of the cities of the south-east.

History and development

Like Sydney, Brisbane was originally a convict colony, established in 1824; but some farmers and cattle-breeders also established themselves in the town's hinterland, and when transportation came to an end in 1839 it began to attract numbers of free settlers.

In 1859 Queensland was separated from New South Wales, and Brisbane became capital of the new state. Its early years were difficult, and even a hundred years later the town was often dismissed as "provincial". Queensland differed from the other Australian states in having a number of centres, each with its own sphere of influence.

An important event in the recent history of the city was the international exhibition held in Brisbane, Expo 88.

Population

The population of Brisbane increased in successive stages. After the transportation of convicts ceased in 1839 the young colony rapidly grew to 20,000 people, of whom around 5000 lived in Brisbane. The Brisbane conurbation now has a population of more than 1.5 million.

Economy

Brisbane is the commercial and financial capital of Queensland, with its most important seaport and largest airport. Industry is well developed round the city, with the processing of foodstuffs (canning) playing an important part. A number of large commercial concerns have offices in the city centre. Tourism is now making an increasingly important contribution to the city's economy. Brisbane is also the gateway to the "Gold Coast" perhaps the most popular holiday region in Australia.

Transport

Brisbane has excellent links with the regional and national transport system. In Roma Street, in the north-west of the city, is the Brisbane Transit Centre (Australian Railways), the terminus for state and interstate services, and close by is the central bus station.

The new national and international airport lies 12km/7½ miles north-east of the city centre in the direction of Moreton Bay, with frequent daily flights from all parts of Australia and abroad.

Public transport within the city (buses, suburban train services), run by the Metropolitan Transit Authority, is also well developed. Information about services and fares can be obtained from the Public Transport Information Centre at the corner of George and Ann Streets.

The ferries on the Brisbane River are a convenient way of getting to know the inner suburbs. The two main landing-stages are at Edward Street and the Customs House (Queen Street).

Excursions

The Golden Mile Ferry Service runs one-hour cruises. One of Brisbane's best known tourist attractions is the "Kookaburra Queen", an old paddle steamer based at Pier 9 which runs cruises on the Brisbane River several times daily (with lunch, tea or dinner). The Brisbane Paddlewheeler company (Cameron Street, West End) runs Sunday cruises with jazz music. The ships of the Koala Cruises company sail upstream as far as Ipswich.

Accommodation

Brisbane offers a wide choice of accommodation for all requirements and in all price categories – luxury hotels, old-style mansions converted into hotels, motels, guesthouses, youth hostels. The tourist information offices in City Hall, at the corner of Adelaide and Edward Streets and in the Riverside Centre in Eagle Street will help visitors looking for accommodation. Caravan parks and camping grounds are to be found at some distance outside the city; the nearest are at Aspley (13km/8 miles north), Durack (16km/10 miles south-west), Eight Mile Plains (15km/9 miles south), Rochedale (19km/12 miles south), Taigum (14km/8½ miles north) and Wacol (19km/12 miles south-west).

Events

The Warana Festival takes place in September, with numerous musical, dance and dramatic performances; the culminating point is a great parade through the city streets. The Ekka is an agricultural show in the Exhibition Grounds in Fortitude Valley, with riding events and a fair. In September there is the Spring Hill Fair in Leichhardt Street and in October the Colonial George Street Festival.

Entertainment

There is a wide choice of evening and after-dark entertainment in numerous discos and jazz clubs and in many pubs and night spots. There are theatrical performances and concerts in the Performing Arts Centre in South Brisbane (Concert Hall, Lyric and Cremorne Theatres). Detailed information on events can be obtained in the press, particularly in the Saturday "Courier Mail" under the heading "What's On In Town".

Shopping

Brisbane offers a tempting range of large department stores, specialised shops and boutiques. There are nine large shopping arcades, including the new Myer Centre, the Wintergarden on the Mall, the Brisbane Arcade and the Rowes Arcade (open: Mon.–Thu. 8.15am–5.30pm, Fri. 8.15am–9pm, Sat. 8.15am–4pm, Sun. 10am–4pm).

Sport

Perhaps the best known sports grounds are the Gabba cricket ground and the dog-racing track in Woolloongabba, on the south side of the Brisbane River. Brisbane has four racecourses (Albion Park, Doomben, Eagle Farm and Bundamba). The Queen Elizabeth II Jubilee Sports Centre in Nathan and the Aquatic Centre in Chandler (both to the south-east of the city centre) were built for the 1982 Commonwealth Games.

Sights in Brisbane

Information

Town plans and brochures can be obtained from the Sunmap Centre (Anzac Square), the Queensland Government Travel Centre (196 Adelaide Street), Brisbane City Council (in the pedestrian zone) and the City Hall.

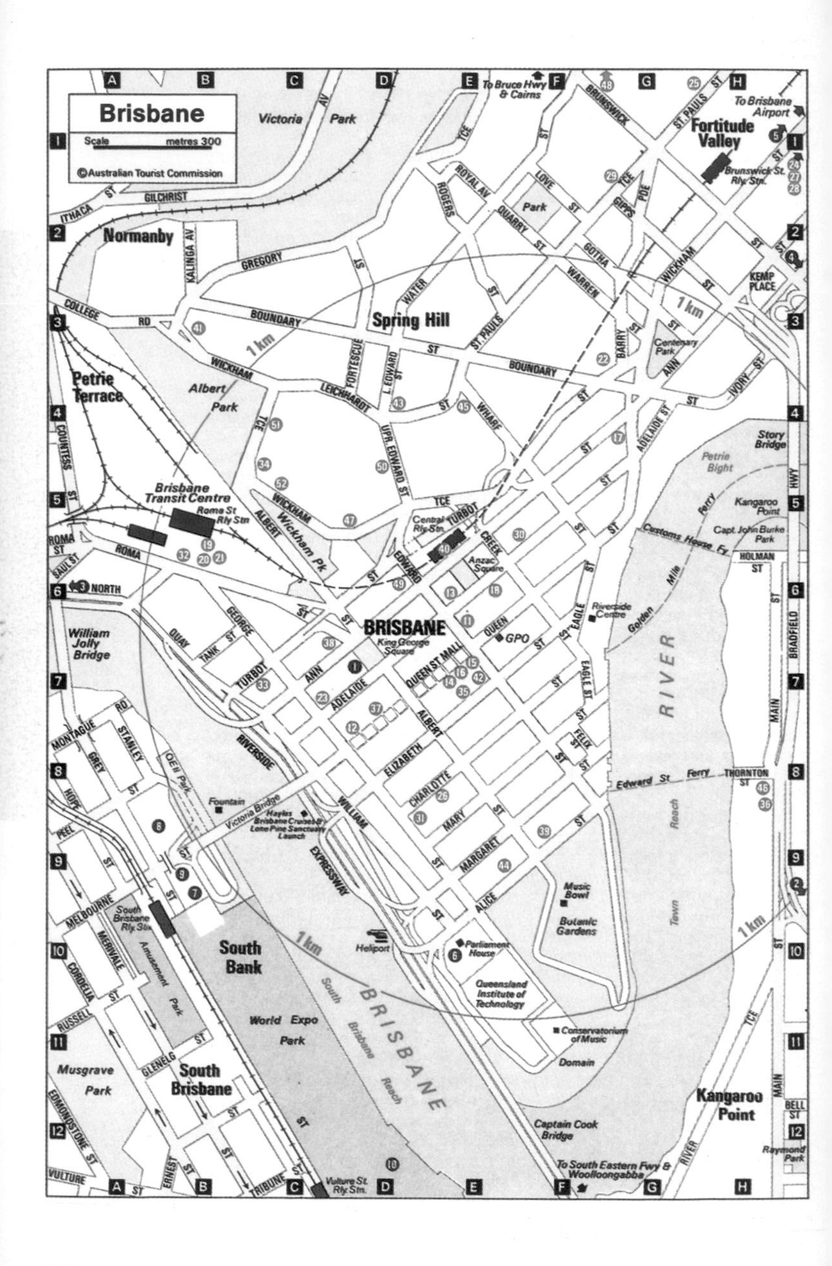
Brisbane
Scale metres 300
©Australian Tourist Commission
Victoria Park
Normanby
Spring Hill
Fortitude Valley
Petrie Terrace
Albert Park
Brisbane Transit Centre
Roma St Rly Stn
Central Rly Stn
Anzac Square
BRISBANE
King George Square
GPO
Riverside Centre
William Jolly Bridge
Wickham Pk
Victoria Bridge
Fountain
QE II Park
Hayles Brisbane Cruises & Lone Pine Sanctuary Launch
Heliport
Parliament House
Queensland Institute of Technology
Conservatorium of Music
Domain
Music Bowl
Botanic Gardens
South Bank
World Expo Park
Amusement Park
South Brisbane Rly Stn
South Brisbane
Musgrave Park
Kangaroo Point
Captain Cook Bridge
To South Eastern Fwy & Woolloongabba
Vulture St. Rly Stn.
To Bruce Hwy & Cairns
To Brisbane Airport
Brunswick St. Rly Stn.
Centenary Park
Story Bridge
Petrie Bight
Kangaroo Point
Capt. John Burke Park
Customs House Fy
Golden Mile Ferry
Edward St Ferry
Town Reach
South Brisbane Reach
BRISBANE RIVER
Raymond Park
1 km

Sights and useful addresses

Places of Interest

Name	No.	Grid
Brisbane City Hall	1	D7
Brisbane Civic Art Gallery & Museum	1	D7
Early St. Historical Village	2	H9
Lone Pine Koala Sanctuary	3	A6
New Farm Park	4	H2
Newstead House	5	H1
Parliament House	6	E10
Performing Arts Centre	7	B9
Queensland Art Gallery	8	B9
Queensland Cultural Centre	9	B9
Qld. Maritime Musuem	10	D12

Tourist Information Centres

Name	No.	Grid
Holiday W.A. Centre	11	E6
N.T. Govt. Tourist Bureau	12	C8
Qld. Govt. Travel Centre	13	E6
Tas. Govt. Tourist Bureau	14	E7
Travel Centre of N.S.W.	15	E7
Victour Travel Centre	16	E7

Airlines– City Departure Terminals

Name	No.	Grid
Ansett Airlines of Australia	17	G4
Australian Airlines	18	E6

Coach Terminals

Name	No.	Grid
Pioneer	19	B5
Greyhound	20	B6
McCafferty's	21	B6
Skennars	22	G3

National Parks

Name	No.	Grid
Nat. Pks. & Wildlife Service	23	C7

Rent-a-Car Offices

Name	No.	Grid
Avis	24	H1
Budget	25	G1
Hertz	26	E8
Manx	27	H1
Thrifty	28	H1

Major City Railway Stations

Name	Grid
Brunswick Street	H1
Central	E5
Roma St.(B'bane Transit Centre)	B5

Ferry Wharfs

Name	Grid
Hayles Brisbane Cruises	C9
Lone Pine Sanctuary Launch	C9

Motoring Association

Name	No.	Grid
Royal Automobile Club of Qld.(R.A.C.Q.)	29	G1

Post Office

Name	Grid
G.P.O.	E7

International Airline

Name	No.	Grid
Qantas Airways	30	F5

Accommodation

*Facilities for the handicapped.

Premier

Name	No.	Grid
Bellevue Hotel	31	D9
Brisbane City Travelodge	32	B6
*Gateway Hotel	33	C7
Gazebo Ramada Hotel	34	C5
Hilton International	35	E7
Kangaroo Point Travelodge	36	H8
Lennons Brisbane Hotel	37	D7
Mayfair Crest	38	C7
Parkroyal Brisbane	39	F9
Sheraton Brisbane Hotel	40	E5

Moderate

Name	No.	Grid
Albert Park Motor Inn	41	B3
Embassy Hotel	42	E7
Farquhars Metro Motor Inn	43	D4
Parkview	44	E9
Ridge All-Suites Inn	45	E4
Story Bridge Motor Inn	46	H8
Tower Mill Motor Inn	47	D5

Budget

Name	No.	Grid
Brisbane Youth Hostel	48	G1
Capital Hotel	49	D6
Dorchester	50	D5
Marrs Town House	51	C4
Soho Budget Hotel	52	C5

Shopping

Central Area

The city centre, in a sharp bend on the Brisbane River, is laid out on a rectangular plan which makes it easy for visitors to find their way about. Streets running south-east/north-west are named after British kings and princes (William, George, Albert, Edward), the cross streets after queens and princesses (Ann, Adelaide, Elizabeth, Charlotte, Mary, Margaret, Alice). While in the 19th century most of the private houses in central Brisbane were built on stilts to adapt to the subtropical climate (though this is often concealed by later façades), the public buildings of the period were designed to impress, reflecting the increasing self-confidence of their Victorian builders.

The surviving 19th century buildings are in sharp contrast to the high-rise buildings of reinforced concrete and reflective glass which tower heavenwards in the centre of Brisbane as in the other Australian capitals.

★City tour

The distances in central Brisbane are not great, and it is perfectly possible to see the principal sights on foot. A convenient starting-point for a sightseeing tour is Central Station (built 1900; suburban services) in Ann Street, opposite Anzac Square.

Shrine of Remembrance

In Anzac Square is the Shrine of Remembrance, in the form of a circular Greek temple, which commemorates the Australian dead in the two world wars and other wars.

Old Windmill

A short distance north-west of Anzac Square, in Wickham Terrace, is the Old Windmill (or Old Observatory), the oldest building in the city. It was originally intended for grinding grain, but the mechanism did not work and it was converted into a treadmill for prisoners (16 to 25 at a time), becoming known as the "tower of torture". From the middle of the 19th century it was used as a signal and weather station.

King George Square

Returning south, we cross Turbot and Ann Street and come to King George Square, the centre of municipal administration.

★City Hall

The west side of the square is occupied by the City Hall (1920–30), a building in neo-classical style with a tall tower in Florentine style and a colonnaded façade and portico.

Although the tower has been overtopped by the modern high-rise blocks it still offers an impressive view of the city from the platform at the top (lift; not open on Sundays). Within the City Hall is the Civic Art Gallery, with a collection which includes historical documents, photographs, ceramics and furniture as well as pictures, mainly 19th century works (outback scenes by Richard J. Randall).

Petrie Tableau

In front of the City Hall is the Petrie Tableau, a piece of metal sculpture by Stephen Walker set up here on the 200th anniversary of white settlement in Australia. It depicts Petrie, one of the earliest free settlers, setting out to explore the interior.

Queen Street Mall

From here Albert Street continues south to Queen Street Mall, a pedestrian zone with boutiques, department stores, shopping arcades, pavement cafés and cinemas.

★Treasury Casino

Queen Street Mall runs south-west to the Treasury Building (1885–1928), which occupies an entire block between George, William, Queen and Elizabeth Streets. In the convict settlement this was the site of the military barracks. Built in the style of an Italian palazzo, the Treasury has recently been completely renovated and now houses a luxury hotel with several restaurants and bars as well as a casino.

★South Bank Parklands

On the opposite bank of the Brisbane River lies the extensive area where the EXPO '88 international exhibition was held; it has now been converted into the South Bank Parklands (16 hectares/40 acres, open: daily 10am-10pm), with restaurants and cafés and beautifully laid-out picnic areas. From here there is a splendid view of the city skyline.

★Queensland Culture Centre

In the north of this area and near Victoria Bridge will be found the Queensland Culture Centre. This ultra-modern complex contains the Queensland Art Gallery, the Queensland Performing Arts Centre, the State Library of Queensland and the Queensland Museum.

The art gallery is large and light, and its main strength lies in its collection of European and Australian art of the 19th and 20th centuries (open: daily 10am-5pm). The State Library of Queensland (open: Mon.–Thur. 10am-8pm, Fri.-Sun. 10am-5pm), which includes the John Oxley Library, gives a broad insight into the history of Queensland. The main emphasis of the Queensland Museum is on the natural history of eastern Australia, together with the "Avian Cirrus", the plane in which Bert Hinkler made the first solo flight from Britain to Australia in 1928. The Queensland Performing Arts Centre (guided tours Mon.–Fri. between 10am and 4pm) houses a theatre with seating for an audience of 2000, a small experimental theatre and a magnificent concert hall. It is home to the Queensland Theatre Company and the Queensland Symphony Orchestra.

★Gondwana Rainforest Sanctuary

A popular attraction is the Gondwana Rainforest Sanctuary, an artificially created rainforest with large butterfly and insect houses (open: daily 8am–5pm; high admission charge),

Queensland Maritime Museum

To the south of South Bank Parklands stands the Queensland Maritime Museum, with a dry dock of 1871 and the Second World War frigate "Diamantina".

Queens Garden

Returning across Victoria Bridge to the Treasury Building, turn south to Queens Garden, in the centre of which stands a statue of Queen Victoria.

Sciencentre

To the south-east, in William Street, is the Sciencentre, a hands-on museum of science and technology.

Old Commissariat Stores

Also in William Street are the Old Commissariat Stores, built by convict labour in 1828. The upper floor was then used as a grain store. The top storey was added in 1913, even though the tablet giving the date 1828 is on this floor. After the end of the convict period the building was used as a hostel for immigrants and for the storage of records. It is now a museum and the headquarters of the Royal Historical Society of Queensland (Queen's Wharf Road).

George Street Mansions

Farther south are the George Street Mansions (1890), six well restored terraced houses with handsome façades in dark-coloured brick and arcading in light-coloured sandstone, now occupied by shops.

Parliament House

Facing these houses is Parliament House, an imposing sandstone building in French Renaissance style designed by Charles Tiffin, winner of a national architectural competition, and built in stages between 1865 and 1891. There are conducted tours of the building, and when Parliament is sitting visitors are admitted to the public gallery.

Botanic Gardens

North-east of Parliament House are the Botanic Gardens, on a site occupied by a farm in the days of the convict colony. It is beautifully laid out with displays of exotic flowers, huge bunya pines and palms.

★Old Government House

To the west of the Botanic Gardens is Old Government House, built in 1860–62 for the first governor of the new colony. This handsome building with its gracefully rounded portico and arcading remained in government hands until 1910, when it became the home of the University of Queensland. It is now part of the Queensland Institute of Technology, and also houses the headquarters of the National Trust, the body responsible for the protection of ancient monuments (bookshop, information centre).

Eagle Street

From here the riverfront promenade runs north to Eagle Street, with a number of modern high-rise buildings in concrete and glass.

General Post Office

We now turn west and after passing the neo-Gothic St Stephen's Cathedral (R.C.) come to the General Post Office (1872–79), a magnificent building in neo-classical style. It has a small museum with old telephones and radios.

St John's Cathedral/ Deanery

From here it is a short distance back to the starting-point of the tour. Those who want to extend the tour a little should follow Ann Street north-east to St John's Cathedral (Anglican) and the Deanery (No. 417). The Deanery, built in 1853, was reckoned the handsomest house in the town, and from 1859 to 1862 was the seat of the governor of Queensland pending the

Post Office Square

completion of his official residence. Since 1910 it has been the deanery of St John's Cathedral (begun in 1901 but still not completely finished).

Outside the City Centre

★Newstead House

Newstead House (Breakfast Creek Road, in the northern district of Newstead), built in 1846, is Brisbane's oldest surviving private house. Now a museum, it is beautifully situated above the Brisbane River and Breakfast Creek. On the corner of this road is the Boardwalk, comprising a group of speciality shops, restaurants, viewing tower and water clock.

The Boardwalk

Breakfast Creek Hotel

Across the river from Newstead House is the richly decorated Breakfast Creek Hotel (1889) with its famed beer-garden (Kingsford Smith Drive, Breakfast Creek).

Temple of Holy Triad/ Joss House

Nearby, in Higgs Street (Newstead), is the Temple of Holy Triad or Joss House (1885), the only Chinese temple in Brisbane, a small but graceful building which has been carefully restored.

Chinatown

From the city centre Ann Street leads to the northern district of Fortitude Valley, with many shops and Brisbane's Chinatown (Asian restaurants).

New Farm Park

South-east of Fortitude Valley, in the New Farm district (Brunswick Street), is New Farm Park, situated on the banks of the river. Here from September to November there is a magnificent display of over 12,000 rose-bushes, with jacaranda trees and many colourful shrubs.

★Earlystreet Historical Village

In the Norman Park district, 6km/4 miles south of the city centre, is the Earlystreet Historical Village, in the beautiful gardens of the Villa Eulalia, with reconstructed buildings of the colonial period, furnished in th style of the time (open: daily).

Government House

In the Bardon district, to the west of the city centre, is Government House, originally built in 1865 for Johann Heussler, who brought many farm workers from Germany to Queensland. It became the official residence of the governor in 1920, when Old Government House was handed over to the University of Technology.

In Brisbane Botanic Gardens

The new Botanic Gardens (Mount Coot-tha Botanic Gardens) lie 8km/5 miles west of the city centre in the suburb of Toowong (Mount Coot-tha Road). A gigantic glass dome houses over 2000 species of trees and bushes (open: daily 8am–5pm). In the grounds there is also the Sir Thomas Brisbane Planetarium.

★ Mount Coot-tha Botanic Gardens

Surroundings of Brisbane

North Stradbroke Island

The islands in Moreton Bay, reached by car ferry, are pleasant places for holidays within easy reach of the city. North Stradbroke Island offers a variety of scenery – beautiful beaches, mangrove swamps, lakes, wilderness areas in the bush – and has accommodation for visitors at Point Lookout, Amity Point and Dunwich (see Stradbroke Islands).

★ Moreton Island

Moreton Island, much of which is a National Park, has beautiful sandy beaches, with dunes, expanses of heathland and an abundance of bird life. Mount Tempest is the highest coastal sand-dune (280m/920ft). On the east side of the island is a 30km/19 mile long surfing beach; on the sheltered west side are three small settlements, anchorages and a resort complex at Tangalooma, which until 1962 was the only whaling station in Queensland. Now you can feed dolphins there, by hand. There are signposted tracks for 4WD vehicles and walking trails. The lighthouse at the northern tip of the island was built in 1857.

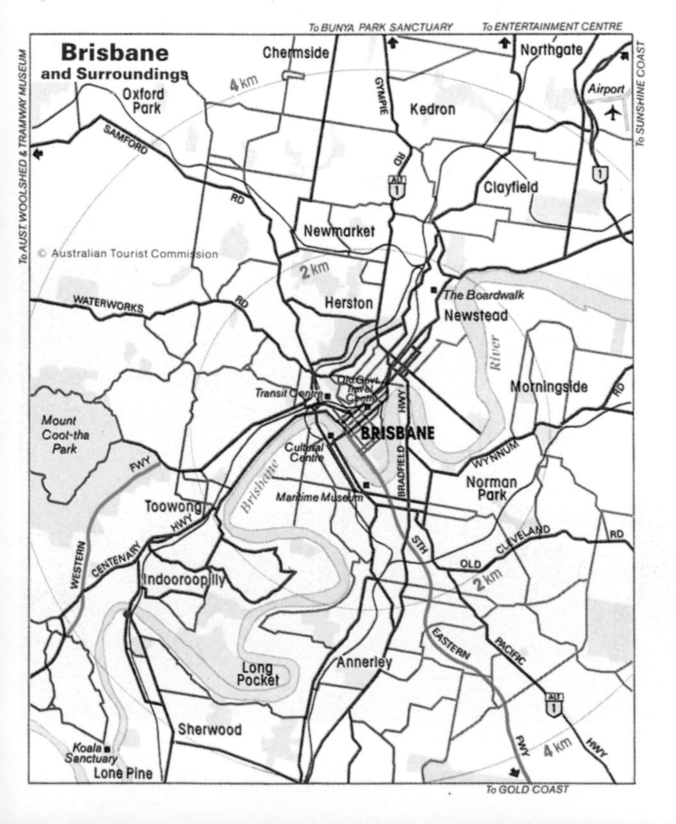

★Bunya Park Wildlife Sanctuary

An attractive excursion from Brisbane is to Bunya Park Wildlife Sanctuary (reached by way of Bunya Park Drive, Eatons Hill, 14km/8½ miles north-west of the city centre on Highway 28 at Cash's Crossing). In the park is a research station on the life and behaviour of koalas (see Baedeker Special, p. 23).

Australian Woolshed

The Australian Woolshed (148 Samford Road, Ferny Hills, 14km/8½ miles north-west of city centre) gives a picture of sheep-farming life in the interior of Queensland, with demonstrations of sheep-shearing and wool-spinning (open: daily 9am–5pm).

★Lone Pine Koala Sanctuary

The Lone Pine Koala Sanctuary, on the Brisbane River 11km/7 miles south-west of the city centre, is best reached by boat (Lone Pine Cruises, departing from Hayles Wharf, North Quay, daily at 1pm). This wildlife park (open: daily 9am–5pm) is the oldest of its kind in Australia. Here visitors can see over 80 types of native Australian animals and birds, cuddle koalas and feed kangaroos, which particularly appeals to children.

Brisbane Forest Park

Brisbane Forest Park (area 25,000 hectares/62,000 acres), 30km/19 miles west of the city centre (The Gap, Mount Nebo Road, via Highway 31) offers the possibility of excursions into the D'Aguilar Range. Within this great expanse of wild bush country and eucalyptus forests are Maiala National Park and Manorina National Park (camping ground, picnic spots, nature trail).

Maiala National Park, also known as D'Aguilar Range National Park, with excellent visitor facilities, is a favourite day trip from Brisbane. From the wooded hills there are magnificent views of the coastal plain.

Scenic Rim

Further away from Brisbane are three of the most interesting National Parks in Queensland, extending in an arc (the "Scenic Rim") 100km/ 65 miles south and south-west of the city: Springbrook National Park, Tamborine National Park (see entries) and Lamington National Park (see Beaudesert).

Tame kangaroos in Lone Pine Koala Sanctuary

★Bundaberg K 4

Situation and characteristics

Bundaberg (pop. 32,740), 380km/235 miles north of Brisbane at the north end of Hervey Bay (see entry), is famed for the production of Bundaberg rum, made from the sugar-cane grown on the flat and fertile plains round the Burnett River. Other important local products are timber and vegetables (particularly tomatoes).

Accommodation

Numerous hotels, over 30 motels, youth hostels, many caravan/camping parks.

Features

Bundaberg is a town of broad tree-lined streets and beautiful parks. A number of sugar mills and the famous rum distillery are open to visitors.

The huge storage and bulk terminal faciliity at Port Bundaberg, 16km/10 miles north-east, can store over 300,000 tons of sugar. From the Hummock, a 100m/330ft high hill, there is a good view of the green irrigated sugar-cane plantations. In the town itself there are a number of handsome Victorian buildings (the School of Arts, the Post Office, the Customs House, Christ Church and the Holy Rosary Church).

Bundaberg was the birthplace in 1892 of the aviation pioneer Bert Hinkler, who made the first solo flight from Britain to Australia in 1928. He made his first attempt to fly in a glider on Mon Repos Beach in 1912. There is a monument to him on the Hummock, and the Hinkler family house in Mount Perry road is now a memorial museum. Bert Hinkler was killed in an air crash in the Italian Alps in 1933.

The large (and strictly protected) loggerhead and other turtles come to lay their eggs on Mon Repos Beach.

Bundaberg is the most southerly gateway to the Great Barrier Reef (see entry). There are cruises from the town to the uninhabited Lady Musgrave Island (see entry) and flights to Lady Elliot Island (with resort complex; see entry).

Caboolture K 5

Situation and characteristics

Caboolture (pop. 8900), 50km/30 miles north of Brisbane just off the Bruce Highway, is the centre of a dairy farming area in which tropical fruits are also grown. Lying so near the Brisbane conurbation, its population has increased considerably in recent years.

The area round the Caboolture River ("Snake" in the Aboriginal language) was settled about 1860.

Accommodation

Several motels and caravan/camping parks.

Features

The reconstructed Caboolture Historical Village is a living open-air museum.

Surroundings

Caboolture is a good base for excursions to the nearby Glass House Mountains National Park, Bribie Island and Moreton Bay (see entries).

★★Cairns J 3

Situation and characteristics

Cairns (pop. 68,000), the most northerly town in Queensland, was founded in 1876 as a supply port for the Hodgkinson goldfields and the tin-mines in the interior. It has grown rapidly in recent years.

Cairns has a superb location between the Great Barrier Reef (see entry) and the dark hills of the Atherton Tableland, with numeous beautiful beaches extending along Trinity Bay to Port Douglas (see entry). The lush tropical vegetation, the varied scenery and the relaxed life-style in this tropical climate all contribute to the charm of the town.

Originally called Trinity Bay after the bay in which it lies (discovered by Cook on Trinity Sunday in 1770), it was later renamed Cairns after the then governor of Queensland, William W. Cairns.

Best time to visit

May to October. The summer, with its heavy rainfall and tropical heat, is not to be recommended.

Esplanade and Pier Marketplace in Cairns

Transport

The Bruce Highway runs along the coast to end at Cairns (1719km/ 1068 miles). The railway line also ends at Cairns. A tarred road, the Captain Cook Highway, continues north to Port Douglas, Mossman and Daintree (see entries), but beyond this there are only tracks and rivers with no bridges.

Cairns Airport handles regular services from many other Australian towns and also from Tokyo, Bangkok, Singapore, the United States and Europe.

Economy

The economy of Cairns and the surrounding area depends mainly on sugarcane cultivation, but tourism is now of increasing importance. In recent years, thanks to the international airport, large numbers of visitors have come to Cairns, particularly from Japan.

Accommodation

Cairns has a wide range of accommodation for visitors. Round the Esplanade are a number of old hotels, as well as modern establishments of international standard, over 40 motels and more than 20 caravan/ camping parks.

Events

Mareeba Rodeo (July); Cairns Amateur Horserace Meeting (September); Fun in the Sun, a week-long festival in October.

Information

The tourist information office is at the corner of Sheridan and Aplin Streets.

Sights in Cairns

The oldest parts of this "capital of the Far North", which in its early days had to compete with Port Douglas, 70km/43 miles farther north, are close to the seafront (Barbary Coast, Wharf Street, Esplanade).

Cairns is a town of palm-fringed streets and parks brilliant with tropical flowers. The park-like Esplanade runs along the bay for 5km/3 miles. The old town of Cairns round Wharf Street and the Esplanade can be explored with the help of a brochure issued by the National Trust.

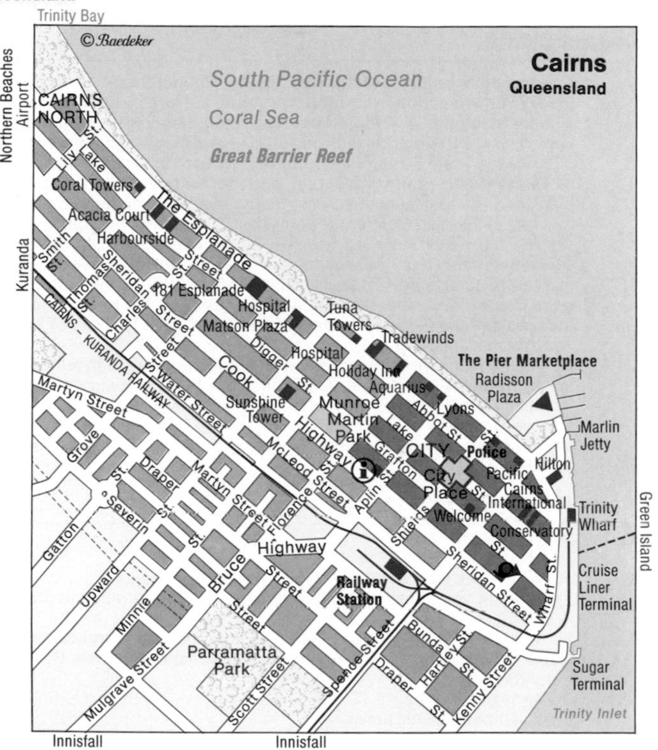

The town's principal attraction is the Flecker Botanic Gardens on Collins Avenue (open: daily 7.30am–5.30pm). Originally laid out in 1886, they contain large numbers of tropical plants, including over 100 species of palm. Footpaths through the gardens lead to the patch of rain forest on Mount Whitfield, from which there are magnificent views of the town and the coast. The Centenary Lakes (Greenslopes Street, Cairns North) were created in 1976, the town's 100th anniversary, as an extension of the Botanic Gardens.

★★ Flecker Botanic Gardens

At the corner of Lake and Shield Streets is Cairns's Cultural Centre, consisting of the Cairns Museum and Art Gallery, and the Library, all housed in the former School of Arts (1907), a building in the style characteristic of the Australian tropics.

Cultural Centre

The House on the Hill (Kingsford Street, Mooroobool, a few kilometres north of the town) was built in 1895 by Mayor R. A. Kingsford, grandfather of the aviator Charles Kingsford Smith. This handsome building on a hillside amid tropical forest was used during the Second World War as a military headquarters. It is now a restaurant, with superb views.

House on the Hill

A popular meeting-place for both local people and visitors is the Pier Marketplace, with fine views of Trinity Bay and a wide choice of shops with long opening hours. Here too is the landing-stage used by most of the boats to the Great Barrier Reef (see entry).

★ Pier Marketplace

At 1 Junction Street, Edge Hill, is the Royal Flying Doctor Base, where visitors can see exhibitions and presentations illustrating the history and the work of the Royal Flying Doctor Service (see Baedeker Special, p. 275).

Royal Flying Doctor Base

Surroundings of Cairns

Cairns is an excellent base for day trips and longer tours in the highlands to the south-west (Atherton Tableland, with rain forest reserves, waterfalls and fine viewpoints). A trip on the steep old-time railway line through the Barron Gorge to Kuranda (see entry) is a memorable experience.

Since the Great Barrier Reef runs very close to the coast in the far north of Queensland, making the reef and its islands (Green, Fitzroy and Frankland Islands) easy of access, Cairns is a favourite jumping-off point for visits to the reef. A variety of boats, fast catamarans, hydrofoils and helicopters ferry hosts of day trippers, holidaymakers, scuba divers and snorkellers every day. There are also cruises to Cooktown (see entry) in the inaccessible north and Thursday Island (see entry), off the northernmost tip of Queensland. Also on offer are adventurous tours to Savannah Gulf, the coasts of the Gulf of Carpentaria and the rugged territory of the Cape York Peninsula (see entry).

N.B. During the summer cyclones, heavy monsoon rain and high temperatures are of frequent occurrence. A trip into the thinly populated Cape York Peninsula is still an adventure which calls for careful preparation. The risk-free way to travel in territory of this kind is to join one of the safari-style tours run by agencies in Cairns. Beware of salt-water crocodiles on many of the beaches.

National Parks Round Cairns

Barron Falls National Park

Location; area: 30km/19 miles west of Cairns; 2780 hectares/6870 acres.

Best time to visit: Throughout year; best from January to March; heavy rain and great heat in summer.

Access: By rail (old-style trains) from Cairns to Kuranda (see entry) or by Skyrail (cable railway) from Smithfield (north of Cairns) to Kuranda. By road via Kuranda Highway.

Accommodation: In Cairns or Kuranda.

Facilities: Bush camping; picnic areas.

★★Rainforest: The beautiful rainforest with the romantic waterfalls on the Barron River and its tributaries has recently been included in the UNESCO list world heritage sites. The waterfalls are particularly high during and after the rainy season (January to March). The way to see the countryside is by taking a trip on the Kuranda vintage railway or by Skyrail (see above). A particularly striking feature is the waterfall on the Barron River, which pours down from a height of 260m/850ft into the gorge.

Green Island National Park

Location; area: 29km/18 miles north-east of Cairns; 13 hectares/32 acres.

Best time to visit: April to November.

Access: Fast catamarans (expensive) or by the "Big Cat" (cheaper) from Cairns (not during cyclones in summer).

Accommodation: Coral Cay Hotel; lodges.

Facilities: No camping; no visitor facilities.

Features: Although this tiny flat island has an area of only 13 hectares/32 acres, the island and its surrounding reefs cover an area of 3000 hectares/7500 acres. It is covered with dense tropical rain forest vegetation. There are walking trails round and through the island, from which many sea birds can be observed.

A good way of seeing the beauties of the coral reefs and the colourful tropical fish is on a trip in a glass-bottomed boat. There are an underwater observatory and an aquarium.

Surroundings: The neighbouring coral island, Michaelmas Cay, is the nesting-place of many thousand sea birds – one of the largest colonies of birds on the Great Barrier Reef.

Caloundra K 5

Situation and characteristics

Caloundra (pop. 20,000) is a popular holiday resort at the south end of the Sunshine Coast (see entry), 96km/60 miles from Brisbane on a turn-off from the Bruce Highway. The shipping lane to Brisbane lies directly off the coast. The name Caloundra comes from an Aboriginal word meaning "beautiful place".

Accommodation

Numerous hotels, motels and caravan/camping parks.

Features

Caloundra has two good beaches suitable for families with children, Bullock Beach and Golden Beach, a sheltered harbour and ideal facilities for water sports on the long Pumicestone Passage between Bribie Island (see entry) and the mainland to the south of Caloundra.

From the cliffs above Caloundra there are fine views of Moreton Bay (see entry) and the large ships on their way to Brisbane.

Surroundings

At Wickham Point is a small coastal park commemorating the crew of the hospital ship "Centaur", which was sunk by Japanese aircraft off Cape Moreton during the Second World War.

At Seafarer's Wharf is a small-scale replica of Cook's "Endeavour".

Caloundra is within easy reach of the Glass House Mountains National Park.

Cape Tribulation National Park J 3

Location; area

140km/185 miles north of Cairns, 64km/40 miles north of Mossman; 17,000 hectares/42,000 acres.

Best time to visit

Winter.

Access

From Mossman in four-wheel-drive vehicle; ferry over Daintree River.

Facilities

Bush camping; bush walking; no visitor facilities.

A rugged coastal landscape, Queensland

Features

Cape Tribulation National Park consists of a hilly expanse of rain forest wilderness rising to 1300m/4265ft and a stretch of impressive coastal scenery. It has a particularly rich flora and fauna. Declared a National Park in 1981, it now also takes in the older Thornton Peak National Park. Although the park itself has no facilities for visitors there are a number of holiday settlements on the coast.

Cape York Peninsula H/J 2/3

Situation and characteristics

A gigantic triangle larger in area than the whole state of Victoria, the Cape York Peninsula is the most northerly part of Queensland. The base of the triangle extends from Normanton and Karuba, on the Gulf of Carpentaria, in the west to Cairns in the east, while at the apex is Thursday Island (familiarly, "TI") off the northern tip of the peninsula in the Torres Strait.

Apart from a few isolated cattle stations, Aboriginal villages and little settlements along the line of the old Overland Telegraph the peninsula is practically uninhabited. June to September is the best time to visit.

Features

Little has changed in the landscape of the Cape York Peninsula over the last 150 years. This wild territory with its heavy tropical rains, cyclones and untameable rivers has resisted all attempts at cultivation. It is thus a natural wildlife reserve for the native flora and fauna (orchids, insect-eating plants, crocodiles).

Transport

In the whole of the north there are practically no asphalted roads or bridges, which would be likely to survive the heavy rains. During the wet season in summer no traffic goes by land and the only way to get about is by plane or by boat. In normal weather conditions it is possible between the end of May and the beginning of November to travel in a four-wheel-drive vehicle from Cairns via Mareeba or Cooktown (see entries), Laura and Coen to Bamaga at the northern tip of the peninsula. Between Coen and Bamaga

Anthills on Cape York Peninsula

there are no petrol stations, and on the journey north a number of rivers have to be forded.

The Royal Automobile Club of Queensland has produced excellent maps and informative material on this route. Experienced local agencies run tours which offer adventure and a memorable experience without risk. It is also possible to sail from Cairns to Thursday Island. After a long period of drought it is possible to drive in a sturdy normal car as far as Coen and Weipa, on the west coast; but most car rental firms do not allow their cars or camper vans to be taken farther north than Mossman, Port Douglas and Dauntree, where the surfaced roads come to an end.

Aboriginal settlements

All over the Cape York Peninsula there are independent Aboriginal territories and settlements, which can be visited only with a permit from the Aboriginal administration. The most important settlements are Lockhart River and Portland Roads on the east coast, Edward River, Weipa South and Aurukun on the Gulf of Carpentaria and Bamaga at the northern tip of the peninsula. No permit is necessary for travelling on public roads.

Capricorn Islands K 4

Situation and characteristics

The Capricorn Islands are an attractive group lying on the Tropic of Capricorn in the southern part of the Great Barrier Reef (see entry), north of the Bunker Islands. The best known of the islands, and the one best equipped to cater for visitors, is Heron Island (see entry).

Masthead, Erskine, Wilson, Wreck, North West and Tryon Islands are wildlife reserves. Day visits and camping are permitted, subject to some restrictions, and visitors must have regard to the function of the islands as nesting-grounds for sea birds. There are boat trips to the coral islands and the reef from Rosslyn Bay/Yeppoon (Capricorn Reefseeker), and from Great Keppel Island (see entry).

Cardwell J 3

Situation and characteristics

Half way between Townsville and Cairns on the Bruce Highway is Cardwell (pop. 1280), now a quiet little coastal town. It is set against a backdrop of rugged hills and sheltered on the east by Hinchinbrook Island (see entry), with the largest island National Park (magnificent bush walking through tropical forest).

Cardwell offers good fishing and attractive boat trips. In the past it was of importance as a gateway to the interior, for before the foundation of Cooktown in 1873 Cardwell was the only port between Bowen, far to the south, and the northern tip of the Cape York Peninsula, from which supplies were conveyed to the Etheridge goldfields.

Accommodation

Several hotels, motels and caravan/camping parks.

Dunk Island National Park

Location; area

30km/19 miles north of Cardwell; 10sq.km/3.9sq.miles, of which 7.3sq.km/2.8sq.miles are a National Park.

Best time to visit

May to November; there is heavy rainfall during the rest of the year.

Access

By ferry from Clump Point and Mission Beach; also flights from Cairns and Townsville.

Facilities

Camping is permitted in the National Park for a maximum of three days (permit must be obtained in Cardwell); picnic spots, walking trails.

Features

Dunk Island, 5km/3 miles offshore and 30km/19 miles north-east of Cardwell, is the largest of the Family Islands (see entry). The island was named by Cook after the First Lord of the Admiralty. Snorkelling, scuba diving and fishing.

The highest point on the island, most of which is covered by tropical rain forest, reaches a height of 271m/889ft. There are large resort complexes run by Australian Airlines, with a wide range of leisure activities, which can accommodate 400 visitors. There are beautiful walking trails all over the island; panoramic views from Mount Kootaloo.

Surroundings — South of Dunk are the privately owned islands of Timana (Thorpe) and Bedarra (Richards; see entry) and five smaller islands scheduled as National Parks, all within the Family Islands group.

Edmund Kennedy National Park

Location; area — 12km/7½ miles north of Cardwell; 6200 hectares/15,300 acres.

Best time to visit — Autumn and spring.

Access — From Bruce Highway, track 4km/2½ miles north of Cardwell (impassable after heavy rain).

Facilities — Camping grounds; picnic areas. No drinking water.

Features — In 1848 Edmund Kennedy set out on his ill-fated expedition from Rockingham Bay to Cape York. Inexperienced, poorly equipped and with misleading maps, the party found no way north and Kennedy was killed by Aborigines. The National Park takes in a stretch of country typical of the wet tropics, with rain forest, open woodland, palms, marshland and mangrove swamps along the coast and the numerous rivers. There are boardways through the mangrove swamps.

Warning — Swimming is inadvisable because of the danger from crocodiles.

★Carnarvon National Park J 4/5

Location; area — 460km/285 miles south-west of Rockhampton; 223,000 hectares/551,000 acres.

Best time to visit — April to October. In summer it is too hot. Wild flowers in spring.

Access — From Gladstone via Rolleston to Carnarvon Gorge; from Brisbane via Roma. After heavy rain the tracks to the park may be impassable even by four-wheel-drive vehicles.

Facilities — Camping and caravan sites at near end of gorge; picnic spots, walking trails; information centre. Visitors must take their own food and water: neither is available in the park.

Features — The Carnarvon National Park, first designated as a reserve in 1932, is one of the most important National Parks in Australia. The area was discovered in 1844 by Ludwig Leichhardt, who called it Ruined Castle Valley. The original park was later enlarged by the addition of the Salvator Rosa area (to the west), with eroded sandstone pinnacles, and the wilderness area of Ka Ka Mundi, with Mount Moffatt (an arid region with isolated sandstone cliffs and Aboriginal sites; Kenniff Cave). These areas are wild and without any tourist facilities – for experienced bush walkers only.

The most interesting feature is the 30km/19 mile long Carnarvon Gorge, with sheer sandstone walls rising to heights of up to 200m/650ft. In the main gorge, with a perennial flow of water, there are tall trees (eucalyptuses, casuarinas, palms). The park has an extraordinarily rich fauna: no fewer than 172 species of birds and 28 species of mammals have been recorded. The hills in the park are part of Queensland's central sandstone belt. Thanks to the permeability of the sandstone rainwater feeds the large Artesian Basin in the interior. Bathing is possible in some of the rivers.

Walking trails — A network of walking trails leads from the camping ground at the downstream end of the park to all the features of interest, crossing the river several times. The complete route takes a full day to cover. The high spots are the extraordinary natural beauties to be seen in Moss Gardens (with a waterfall which plunges down in several steps), the Amphitheatre, Ward's Canyon and the Art Gallery, the most accessible of the caves with Aboriginal rock paintings (including some in the "stencil" technique). From the Kenniff Lookout on Mount Moffatt there are spectacular views of the gorges on the Consuelo tableland.

Unspoiled wilderness, Carnarvon National Park ▶

Charleville J 5

Situation and characteristics

Charleville (pop. 3600), situated in the dry Mulga Country 750km/465 miles west of Brisbane, lies in the centre of a rich pastoral district with hundreds of thousands of sheep and cattle. It is the terminus of the Westlander rail service.

Accommodation

Several hotels, motels and caravan/camping parks.

Features

Both the Royal Flying Doctor Service (see Baedeker Special, p. 275) and the School of the Air (see Baedeker Special, p. 40) have bases in Charleville, which visitors can see round (the School of the Air only during the school "terms").

Also of interest is the Historical Museum in the old Queensland National Bank Building (*c.* 1880) in Albert Street, a wooden building which has preserved its original internal arrangement. An unusual exhibit is a "vortex cannon" used in unsuccessful rain-making experiments in 1902.

★Charters Towers J 4

Situation and characteristics

Charters Towers (pop. 9000), situated 135km/84 miles south-west of Townsville on the Flinders Highway to Mount Isa, is the commercial centre for the cattle farms and citrus fruit plantations in the surrounding area and also a school centre. Many handsome 19th century buildings bear witness to the town's great days as the first gold-mining town in Queensland. On Christmas Day in 1871, it is said, an Aboriginal boy named Jupiter made the first strike in the hills along the Burdekin River while looking for cattle which had bolted during a thunderstorm. The owner of the farm, Hugh Mosman, staked his claim; the gold rush began, and soon the population of the little settlement had risen to 30,000. Mosman thereupon adopted and educated the boy Jupiter. The town took its name from a mine overseer named Charters, with the addition of Tors (hills), which became Charters Towers.

In its heyday Charters Towers claimed to be the second largest and the wealthiest town in Queensland, and the inhabitants referred to their town as "the world". In those days it had 90 hotels and a stock exchange open every day, including Sundays (which can still be seen). After the alluvial goldfields were worked out, around 1880, underground mining continued for another 30 years, yielding large quantities of gold. The mine finally closed in 1910 and many of the prospectors left the town.

Accommodation

Several hotels, motels and caravan/camping parks.

Features

Many fine examples of classic Queensland architecture, with deep verandahs, roofed balconies, colonnades and rich wrought-iron ornament, have been preserved: e.g. Ay-Ot Lookout (a private house at the corner of Hodgkinson Street and High Street), the City Hall (corner of Gill and Mosman Streets), the Civic Club (Ryan Street), the Excelsior Hotel (Church and Gill Streets), the former Australian Bank and Lyall's Jewellery Store in Mosman Street, the former Bank of New South Wales (Gill Street), Pfeiffer House (which belonged to a German mine-owner of that name; now a Mormon temple) in Paull Street, the Post Office (corner of Gill and Bow Streets), with a clock-tower, and above all the Stock Exchange Arcade in Mosman Street, now occupied by the offices of the National Trust and the Gold-Mining Museum.

Surroundings

At Millchester, 5km/3 miles from the town, is the Venus Battery, where gold-bearing ore was crushed and processed; restored to working order, it is now open daily to visitors. 70km/43 miles is Ravenswood (see entry) which a century ago was also an important gold-mining town.

Childers K 5

Situation and characteristics

Childers (pop. 1850), 50km/31 miles south of Bundaberg, is the centre of a fertile region of red soil on which sugar-cane is grown. In its tree-lined

Baedeker Special

Flying Doctors

If only Bill hadn't broken his leg he would have been pretty sure of living beyond the age of 24. The accident happened far out in the Australian outback, somewhere on Innamincka Station, a cattle farm well away from any kind of civilisation. And the result was inevitable: Bill, the 24-year-old cattleman, had to be transported to the nearest hospital, more than 300 miles away, where he arrived more dead than alive. Even an emergency amputation could not save him, and he died a few days later. This was in the year 1878 – and it was by no means the only tragedy of this kind in these regions of Australia so hostile to man.

Exactly half a century later an idea – a life-saving idea – came to John Flynn, a Presbyterian missionary in the outback. He had a vision of an emergency medical service which should cover the whole Australian continent. Flynn was aware of the technical developments that had taken place since pioneering days in Australia. It was 25 years since the Wright Brothers had successfully accomplished the first motorised flight in aviation history; and while in faraway Italy Guglielmo Marconi was pondering over his experiments with short waves a few enterprising spirits in Australia were preparing to launch a regular air service, the Queensland and Northern Territory Air Services (the initials of which were later to make up the name of Australia's national airline, Qantas).

It must surely be possible, Flynn thought, to build up a service for providing emergency medical care covering large areas of territory which could be called up by radio. And had he not heard about an Australian called Edward Traeger who was developing radio equipment which would make land–air communication possible?

Flynn set to work: he brought together a group of pilots, radio operators, doctors and nurses, and within a short space of time, on May 15th 1928, the first specially equipped plane of the Aerial Medical Service took off from the little airfield at Cloncurry in Queensland.

The "flying doctors" are still active in providing prompt medical aid in case of need. They now have a fleet of 33 aircraft which can cope with conditions in the Australian outback. A short runway, or no runway at all, presents no problems for the experienced pilots of the Flying Doctor Service. Since the service started they have logged more than 4 million nautical miles and tens of thousands of patients have been transported to the nearest hospital.

The headquarters of the Royal Flying Doctor Service (RFDS) are now in Alice Springs, and can be inspected by visitors. In addition there are 13 bases spread over the whole country. The RFDS serves an area of over 2 million sq. miles and is thus by far the largest air rescue service in the world. The most frequent cases it has to deal with are car and motorcycle accidents, followed by snakebites and other ailments. The RFDS aircraft are equipped to deal with (almost) any emergency: their cabins are like miniature intensive care wards, in which even minor surgical procedures can be carried out.

Not every illness, however, needs a flying doctor to call. Each farm in the outback has a medicine chest containing the most essential medicines, all numbered, and every day, at a set time, the RFDS runs a radio outpatient department. On receiving a call from the outback, the RFDS base gets in touch with a doctor in the hospital, who after hearing the patient's symptoms can make his diagnosis and prescribe the necessary medicine, giving the number of the drug and the dosage.

The Flying Doctor Service provides medical aid free of charge to the patient. It is financed by donations and government subsidies.

streets are richly decorated house fronts bearing witness to its 19th century prosperity.

Accommodation — Several hotels, motels and caravan/camping parks.

Features — The Halls of Memory commemorate the dead of the Second World War. During the sugar-processing season (August to November) visitors can see round some of the local sugar mills (e.g. the Central Sugar Mill, Cordalba). Two other features of interest are the Pharmacy Museum in Churchill Street and the Olde Butcher Shoppe in North Street.

Surroundings — On the coast, a short distance from the town, is the popular Woodgate Beach. In Woodgate National Park (see Maryborough) there are beautiful walking trails though swamp country and many opportunities for watching birds.

Chillagoe H 3

Situation and characteristics — Chillagoe (pop. 220), 210km/130 miles west of Cairns in the outback of northern Queensland, was once an important mining town (copper, silver, lead, gold, wolfram). It can be reached from Dimbulah only on unsurfaced tracks.

Accommodation — Hotel, motel, caravan/camping park.

Features — Chillagoe has a small museum with relics of old mining days.

Chillagoe-Mungana Caves National Park

Location; area — At Chillagoe; 1876 hectares/4634 acres (in nine separate parts).

Best time to visit — April to November, during the dry winter.

Access — Via Mareeba and Dimbulah. The track from Chillagoe is often impassable in the rainy season, and at all times is unsuited to trailer caravans.

Accommodation — In Chillagoe. Camping grounds in park.

Facilities — Camping grounds, picnic areas.

Features — The most striking features of the Chillagoe-Mungana Caves National Park are the limestone cliffs, up to 70m/230ft high, containing stalactitic caves, some of them very large. In some of the caves are Aboriginal rock paintings. Visitors are allowed to enter a few of their caves on their own (pocket torch essential); others can only be seen on a conducted tour.

Cleveland K 5

Situation and characteristics — With its excellent situation on the coast, 35km/22 miles south-east of Brisbane in Redland Shire, Cleveland (pop. 6580) had a fair prospect of becoming the principal port and ultimately capital of the colony; but unfortunately when the governor of the day, George Gipps, paid an official visit to the town it was low tide, and the governor was so put off by the mud flats over which he had to trudge that the choice fell on Brisbane. And so Cleveland has remained a quiet little town to which people come for a restful holiday.

Accommodation — Motels.

Features — There remain a number of historic buildings from the time when Cleveland had great plans for the future, including the Grand View Hotel (1849), the Old Courthouse (1853), now a restaurant, and Cleveland Lighthouse (1847–64).

Surroundings — There are a number of handsome old mansions round Cleveland, notably Whepstead Manor at Wellington Point (1874), now a restaurant, and Ormiston House (1862).

Cloncurry H 4

Situation and characteristics — Cloncurry (pop. 2800) lies in the outback of northern Queensland, 124km/77 miles east of Mount Isa. Copper-mining was of great importance in the surrounding area from the 1860s until after the First World War. In the early 1920s Cloncurry was the destination of the first regular flights by the Queensland and Northern Territory Air Services (now Qantas). The world-famed Royal Flying Doctor Service was founded in Cloncurry by the Rev. John Flynn in 1928 and a museum displays its history.

Accommodation

Hotels, motels, caravan/camping park.

Features

The Afghan and Chinese cemetery is a relic of copper-mining days, as are the old mine workings in the surrounding hills.

The Flying Doctor Service has a very interesting museum in Cloncurry illustrating the work of the service (open: Mon.–Fri. 7am–4pm, Sat. and Sun. 9am–3pm; admission charge).

There is also a museum displaying other relics of the copper-mining period and some of the equipment used by Burke and Wills on their ill-fated expedition.

★Cooktown J 3

Situation and characteristics

Cooktown (pop. 1300), situated 350km/215 miles north of Cairns on the Cape York Peninsula (see entry) and accessible only on unsurfaced tracks, was the first – though very temporary – white settlement on the east coast of Australia. In 1770 Captain Cook had to beach the "Endeavour" here for repair after running aground on a coral reef, and the crew lived ashore in tents for seven weeks.

In 1872 gold was found on the Palmer River, and within a short time Cooktown became the port for the Palmer goldfields, with almost a hundred bars, hotels and a main street 3km/2 miles long. By 1900 the gold was worked out, and the town in its remote situation on the Cape York Peninsula sank almost into oblivion.

Nowadays the steadily increasing tourist interest in the far north of Queensland has reached Cooktown. The town has accommodation for visitors and can be reached by boat, by air or, in dry weather, overland. Tourism is slowly but steadily becoming an important element in the town's economy. There are now organised trips to Cooktown by boat from Cairns and Port Douglas (see entries).

Accommodation

Several hotels, motels and caravan/camping parks.

Features

Most of the buildings of the gold-mining period have disappeared. The James Cook Historical Museum in Helen Street, a richly decorated brick building of 1887–88, has interesting displays on Cook's life and voyages.

A Chinese shrine commemorates the many Chinese who died in the goldfields. In the cemetery in Charlotte Street is the grave of Mrs Mary Watson, an early settler who recorded her tragic flight from the Aborigines on Lizard Island in her diary.

The Discovery Festival held annually in June celebrates Cook's landing with a re-enactment.

Surroundings

From Grassy Hill there are good views of the surrounding country and the reefs. In 1988, Australia's bicentennial year, a 5000km/3100 mile long Bicentennial National Trail for walkers and riders from Cooktown to Healesville in Victoria was inaugurated.

Cooktown is a good base for trips to Black Mountain National Park (see below), Lakefield National Park (see entry) and the Aboriginal cave paintings at Laura.

Black Mountain National Park

Location; area

30km/19 miles south of Cooktown; 780 hectares/1930 acres.

Best time to visit

In autumn, when the waterfalls are at their most impressive, and in winter.

Access

From Cooktown on the Cairns road.

Facilities

Bush camping is possible. No tourist facilities.

Features

This is an area of granite boulders, bare rocky peaks and hillsides covered with rain forest vegetation. The highest point is the Black Mountain

In Black Mountain National Park

(475m/1558ft). The hill and the park take their name from the dark-coloured lichens which cover the bare granite. The park is a rock wallaby reserve.

Surroundings — Outside the park there are tracks leading to the waterfalls on the Annan River and Mumgumby Creek.

Warning — Beware of snakes!

Cedar Bay National Park

Location; area — 50km/31 miles south of Cooktown; 5650 hectares/13,955 acres.

Best time to visit — Winter.

Access — From Cooktown via Blomfield; the rough track goes through the park. The coastal region of the park is more easily accessible from the sea.

Facilities — Bush camping possible; no visitor facilities.

Features — The Gap Creek valley divides the park into two parts. The Bloomfield Track, a dusty road suitable only for four-wheel-drive vehicles, runs through the valley.

Endeavour National Park and Mount Cook National Park

Location; area — 5km/3 miles west and 2km/1¼ miles south of Cooktown; both parks together 1840 hectares/4545 acres.

Best time to visit — Winter.

Features — While Cook was having the "Endeavour" repaired in this area in June 1970 his companion, the botanist Joseph Banks, recorded the flora and fauna. The larger of the two National Parks, to the west of Cooktown, is named after Cook's ship and fine examples of Aboriginal rock art are found here. Mount Cook (432m/1417ft), after which the smaller park (500 hectares/1250 acres) is named, lies on the southern outskirts of Cooktown.

Croydon H 3

Situation and characteristics

Croydon (pop. 220), once an important gold and silver town, lies in the Gulf Country 560km/350 miles south-west of Cairns. Gold was discovered here in 1883, and in spite of its remote situation the settlement grew rapidly. But when the mines (the best known of which was the Golden Gate) were worked out in the 20th century the population declined equally rapidly. Some buildings and machinery of gold-mining days have survived, and much restoration work is being done with a view to establishing an open-air museum.

Another relic of the past is the rail bus which travels once a week along the isolated line (155km/95 miles) betwen Croydon and Normanton (see entry), near the coast of the Gulf of Carpentaria.

Accommodation

Hotel.

Daintree J 3

Situation and characteristics

Daintree (pop. under 200) lies 120km/75 miles north of Cairns in the valley of the Daintree River, surrounded by hills covered with rain forest.

Accommodation

Caravan/camping park.

Features

The country round Daintree is a Natural Park, listed as a World Heritage Area, with superb wildlife, rich tropical flora and fauna (birds, butterflies and freshwater crocodiles in the mangrove swamps on the Daintree and its tributaries). Boat trips on the Daintree River.

Surroundings

Cape Tribulation National Park (see entry), where rain forest and the Coral Sea meet.

Dalby K 5

Situation and characteristics

Dalby (pop. 10,000), 83km/52 miles north-west of Toowoomba in the fertile Darling Downs, is the centre of a rich grain-growing area in which there is also much stock farming. It is well situated at the junction of the Warrego, Bunya and Moonie Highways.

Accommodation

Several motels and caravan/camping parks.

Features

In Edward Street is an obelisk marking the spot where the explorer Henry Dennis camped in 1841. Pioneer Park Museum (early buildings, household and agricultural items).

Surroundings

Excursions to Lake Broadwater (29km/18 miles south-west) and Bunya Mountains National Park (60km/37 miles north-east; see Kingaroy).

Emerald J 4

Situation and characteristics

Emerald (pop. 6000), an agricultural centre (cattle, grain, oilseeds, soya beans, cotton), lies in the Central Highlands of Queensland, 266km/ 165 miles west of Rockhampton, at the junction of the Capricorn and Gregory Highways.

Accommodation

Several motels and caravan/camping parks.

Features

The town's streets are lined with shady fig-trees. Handsome railway station of 1901.

Surroundings

To the north are the Gregory coalfields (conducted tours), with the mining town of Capella. 20km/12½ miles south is Fairbairn Dam, an artificial lake with picnic spots and water sports.

Warning

Great care is required when driving after dark: there have been many accidents with kangaroos and emus.

Emu Park K 4

Situation and characteristics — Emu Park (pop. 1530) is an attractive little holiday resort on Keppel Bay, 40km/25 miles north-east of Rockhampton. Thanks to the offshore islands, particularly Great Keppel Island (see entry), it has sheltered beaches.

Accommodation — Several motels and caravan/camping parks.

Features — On a headland overlooking the bay is the "Singing Ship", a monument to Captain Cook in the form of a sailing ship, with hidden pipes which create musical sounds when the wind is blowing. In 1770 Joseph Banks, the botanist with Cook's expedition, studied the plants in Keppel Bay.

★Eungella National Park J 4

Location; area — 430km/265 miles north-west of Rockhampton, 80km/50 miles west of Mackay; 50,000 hectares/125,000 acres.

Best time to visit — May to November. Occasional cold spells at higher altitudes in winter; in summer it can be hot, with heavy rain (drier in the western part of the park).

Access — From Mackay through the Pioneer River valley via Finch Hatton.

Accommodation — Three camping grounds in park (Finch Hatton Gorge, Crediton Creek and Broken River). There are also privately run camping grounds and lodges on the outskirts of the park at Broken River and Eungella.

Facilities — Walking trails, picnic areas; information centre at Broken Hill camping ground.

Features — Eungella National Park lies in the rugged Clark Range, with hills up to 1200m/3900ft in height. At the higher levels there are expanses of rain forest, often shrouded in cloud or mist; lower down there is tropical rain forest. Towards the drier west side of the park there is open woodland.

Family Islands J 3

Situation and characteristics — The Family Islands group, off the Tully coast, 30km/19 miles north-east of Cardwell, includes the main island, Dunk (National Park; see Cardwell), and the smaller islands (also reserves) of Wheeler, Combe, Smith, Bowden and Hudson (combined area 1.2sq.km/300 acres), on which camping is allowed (permit required). Timana (Thorpe) Island, between Dunk and Bedarra, is another small island, privately owned.

The islands are covered with dense tropical forest.

Accommodation — There are resort complexes on Dunk Island and Bedarra.

Fitzroy Island J 3

Situation and characteristics — Little Fitzroy Island (4sq.km/1½sq.miles) lies near the coast, 26km/16 miles south of Cairns, with hills rising to over 260m/850ft. It was named by Captain Cook in 1770 after Augustus Fitzroy, Duke of Grafton. The island is a popular destination for day trips from Cairns (diving on banks of coral, walking, fishing). There is a striking lighthouse.

Accommodation — Small resort complex run by Great Adventures, with a hostel, villas and a camping ground.

★Fraser Island K 5

Situation and characteristics — Fraser Island, lying off the coast between Bundaberg and Brisbane, was formerly called Great Sandy (it is Australia's largest sand island). Over

120km/75 miles long and between 7km/4½ miles and 25km/15½ miles across, it was formerly occupied by Aborigines of the Butchulla tribe. On the east side of the island there are numerous Aboriginal ceremonial sites.

In the interior of the island there are numbers of freshwater lakes, either "window lakes" of clear ground-water or "perched lakes" of brownish water in depressions in the dunes over impermeable rock strata. There is a very varied flora and fauna (mangrove forests, subtropical rain forests and forests managed for timber; wild horses, dingoes and over 200 species of birds, including migratory birds in passage). The sand of which the island consists, apart from a few volcanic formations and layers of sedimentary rock, was formed over many millions of years from detritus eroded from the Great Dividing Range, carried down to the sea by rivers and deposited and piled up in dunes up to 250m/820ft high by the prevailing south-easterly trade winds. The dunes have been stabilised by vegetation. The minerals (iron oxides) in the sand have given the sandstone cliffs on the east coast (Cathedral Sandcliffs) their variegated colouring.

Access
Ferry and boat services from Rainbow Beach, Hervey Bay and River Heads.

Climate
The climate is maritime subtropical, with rain (up to 1800mm/70in. annually) falling mainly between December and May. July is the coldest month (14–21°C/57–70°F); in summer the temperature rarely rises above 30°C/86°F.

Economy
In the last few decades timber-felling and the extraction of mineral sand have made important contributions to the island's economy. In recent years there has been some controversy over the working of sand.

Tourism is now of increasing importance. There are numerous resort complexes and motels, as well as camping grounds in Great Sandy National Park and in the state-owned forests.

Facilities
Boating harbour in Wathumba Creek, on west side of island; good fishing at Waddy Point, on the east side. To camp or drive a car on the island a permit must be obtained from the Queensland National Parks and Wildlife Service (QNPWS). Some beach areas are closed to allow the vegetation to recover. Organised tours are on offer.

Warning
The beautiful white sandy beaches can be treacherous.

Woody Island/ Little Woody Island
Between Fraser Island and Hervey Bay are Woody Island and Little Woody Island, the two together forming a National Park with an area of 660 hectares/1630 acres. Bush camping on Woody island (with permit); campers must take all their supplies, including water, with them.

Great Sandy National Park

Location; area
At the north end of Fraser Island; 52,000 hectares/130,000 acres.

Best time to visit
In spring for the wild flowers; in summer for the migrant birds.

Accommodation
Camping grounds at Dundubara, in the south-east of the park, where the park offices are.

Features
The National Park (established in 1971) contains areas of eucalyptus forest and bush, heathland, lagoons and marshland. Good walking. Fresh water is scarce.

Gladstone K 4

Situation and characteristics
Although Matthew Flinders discovered the deep-water harbour of Port Curtis during his reconnaissance of the Australian coasts in 1802, Gladstone (pop. 35,300) remained an unremarkable little town until the second half of the 20th century. Its boom years began in the 1960s with the development of the harbour into one of the best-equipped and busiest in Australia.

The main reason for this growth was the opening up of the immensely rich coalfields of central Queensland, worked by opencast methods. The coal supplies a huge power station in Gladstone and the surplus is exported, mainly to Japan. Gladstone also processes the bauxite worked at Weipa on the Cape York Peninsula (see entry), producing aluminium oxide at Parsons Point and then aluminium on Boyne Island. Since aluminium production is highly energy-intensive, the easy accessibility of coal supplies make Gladstone an ideal site for the industry.

Accommodation — Numerous hotels, motels and caravan/camping parks.

Features — A number of old buildings in the modern town bear witness to Gladstone's past, for example the Grand Hotel (1897) and the church of Our Lady Star of the Sea, in a mingling of different styles.

Surroundings — Of particular interest to holidaymakers are Tannum Sands, from which there is a bridge to Boyne Island, the site of a large aluminium smelting plant. Quoin Island, in the harbour, has a number of resort complexes. To the south-east is the Agnes Water "Town of 1770" area, where Cook landed in 1770. The coastal region round Gladstone is known as Reef Adventureland, since from here the southern part of the Great Barrier Reef (see entry) can be most easily reached by boat or helicopter.

Glass House Mountains National Park K 5

Location; area — 65km/40 miles north of Brisbane, in the hinterland of the Sunshine Coast (see entry); 698 hectares/1724 acres (in four sections).

Best time to visit — Throughout the year. Wild flowers in spring (September to November).

Accommodation — In Caboolture (see entry) and the tourist resorts on the Sunshine Coast (see entry).

Facilities — Picnic areas at Beerwah and Tibrogargan.

Features — The unmistakable landmark of the Glass House Mountains National Park is a group of nine volcanic plugs rising abruptly out of the coastal plain. The mountains were so named by Captain Cook in 1770, perhaps because of their glass-smooth sides. The individual hills bear names from the language of the Aborigines. The four most striking crags are Coonowrin, Beerwah, Ngungun and Tibrogargan; the highest is Mount Beerwah (738m/2421ft). Some of them can be climbed (experienced rock-climbers only).

★★Gold Coast K 5

Situation and characteristics — It is claimed that nowhere else in Australia are there so many luxury hotels, resort complexes, motels, apartments, guesthouses and youth hostels, such a range of entertainments and sports facilities, such opportunities for enjoying yourself or for shopping, as on the Gold Coast. Particularly during the holiday season the resorts on the Gold Coast, with over 3 million visitors a year, are in a constant bustle of life and activity: booking in advance, therefore, is essential. The Gold Coast has a mild climate, with average maximum temperatures of 22°C/72°F in winter and 28°C/82°F in summer and over 300 days in the year with sunshine.

The Gold Coast is one of Australia's best known holiday regions. During the last few decades it has been involved in a massive tourist development and building boom, extending along the beaches from Southport in the north to Coolangatta in the south and reaching into the green hinterland. After some years of recession the economy was given a fresh boost by the Bicentennial celebrations and Expo 88 in Brisbane, only 70km/45 miles away, and development is again going full steam ahead. One problem has been the washing away of sand from the beaches, which has made extensive protective measures necessary.

The green grazing country immediately inland from the coast reaches into the hilly landscape of the Great Dividing Range, with hills rising to above 1000m/3300ft. There is an excellent network of roads running up the valleys and leading to viewpoints in the hinterland, and the rain forests in the National Park are within easy reach. Possible excursions, for example, are to the Numinbah Valley immediately north of the border with New

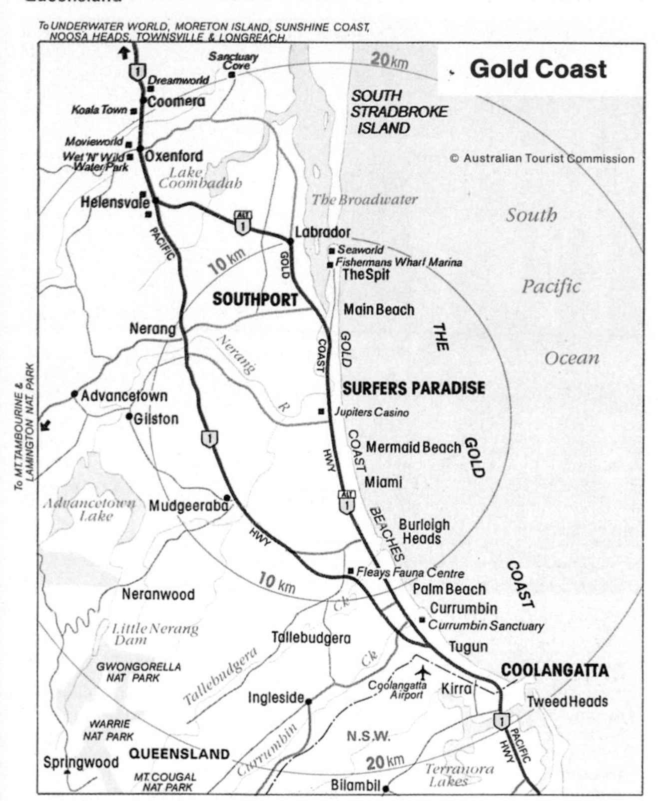

South Wales, to the Natural Arch Bridge National Park (see Nerang), Lamington National Park (see Beaudesert) or Mount Tamborine.

To the south can be seen Mount Warning, the lava plug of a former giant volcano which impressed Captain Cook.

All Australian domestic airlines fly to Coolangatta. There are trains (including motorail trains) from Sydney to Murwillumbah, from where visitors can continue by car or bus. The Gold Coast can be reached from Sydney by car on the Pacific Highway (No. 1; 900km/560 miles); from Brisbane it is only 79km/49 miles to Southport and 100km/62 miles to Coolangatta (South-East Freeway, Pacific Highway and Gold Coast Highway). There are buses from Brisbane (Roma Station) or direct from the airport to the Gold Coast.

Coolangatta

Situation and characteristics

Coolangatta is the most southerly resort on the Gold Coast, situated directly on the New South Wales border. This area, which was settled at an early stage, has plantations of tropical fruit ("Avocado Land") and has all the tourist facilities (restaurants, hotels in all price categories, shops) typical of this commercialised holiday coast. Here too is the Gold Coast's airport.

Sun, surf and sand in Surfers Paradise

Coolangatta is separated from Tweed Heads in New South Wales, which is similarly equipped to cater for holidaymakers, by the estuary of the Tweed River. Its development into a holiday resort began in 1903, when the railway line from Nerang was built, though there was a guesthouse on Marine Parade as early as 1885.

Cook gave the name Point Danger to the cape, falling sheer down to the sea, on the north side of the Tweed estuary, from which there are magnificent views of the coast and the ocean. On the boundary between Queensland and New South Wales is a monument to Cook which is also a lighthouse, erected in 1970 on the 200th anniversary of Cook's passage this way.

Currumbin

Situation and characteristics

6km/4 miles north of Coolangatta, at the mouth of the Currumbin Creek, is Currumbin, noted mainly for the Currumbin Sanctuary, a wildlife reserve owned by the National Trust. It is the home of many thousand brightly coloured rainbow lorikeets, which will eat from visitors' hands and even perch on their heads. In and around the town there are a wide range of entertainments and opportunities for wildlife viewing, as well as hotels, motels and caravan/camping parks.

Southport

Situation and characteristics

Southport, the first settlement on the Gold Coast, was founded in 1875. It is now the business and commercial centre of this busy holiday area, with every conceivable facility for leisure activities, entertainment, sport and shopping. Its situation at the outflow of the Nerang River into the Broadwater, sheltered by the offshore island of South Stradbroke, makes it ideal for every kind of water sport.

Sea World

To the north of Southport is Sea World, the largest commercial marine park in Australia, with numerous shows (performing dolphins and sealions, a water-ski ballet) and sideshows and a monorail offering fine views of the park.

Fisherman's Wharf

Immediately south of Sea World is Fisherman's Wharf, a shopping and entertainment centre in the style of a fishing village, with restaurants and a large boating harbour. From here boats sail to South Stradbroke Island, to Sanctuary Cove with its resort complexes and to Dreamworld, a theme park at Coomera, with a goldrush town, Koala sanctuary and fun rides.

Surfers Paradise

Situation and characteristics

Surfers Paradise – "Surfers" for short – is Australia's best known seaside holiday centre. The place takes its name from the Surfers Paradise Hotel which was established here in 1923. After the Second World War it enjoyed a great boom, based on its three alliterative assets, "sun, surf and sand". This led to tremendous building activity, and the seafront, with its beautiful beach of fine sand, is now lined with high-rise hotels and apartment blocks. Surfers Paradise attracts its visitors with an immense range of entertainments, sporting and leisure activities and its active night life (a casino is among its many attractions).

To the south of Surfers Paradise is Broadbeach, whose great array of shops and hotels is linked by monorail with Jupiters, Australia's largest casino. 18km/11 miles north at Oxenford, is Movie World, where old film sets have been recreated by Warner Bros.

Also on the Gold Coast is Beaudesert (see entry), with the Lamington and Mount Barney National Parks.

Goondiwindi K 5

Situation and characteristics

The little country town of Goondiwindi (pop. 4390) lies 360km/225 miles south-west of Brisbane on the Cunningham Highway (named after the explorer Allan Cunningham). The name of the town is derived from an Aboriginal word meaning "resting place of the birds". The economy of the area is based on cattle-raising and the growing of grain in irrigated fields (huge grain silos).

Accommodation

Several motels and caravan/camping parks.

Features

The old Customs House, in use until the establishment of the Commonwealth of Australia in 1901, is now a museum. The Victoria Hotel dates from 1898.

The Spring Festival is celebrated in October.

Gordonvale J 3

Situation and characteristics

The little town of Gordonvale (pop. 2300) lies 24km/15 miles south of Cairns, just off the Bruce Highway, in a sugar-growing area. Previously known as Mulgrave and as Nelson, its present name comes from an early settler called Gordon.

Accommodation

Several hotels, caravan/camping park.

Surroundings

To the west of the town the Gillies Highway runs up to the Atherton Tableland in a succession of several hundred bends. Nearby is the Bellenden-Ker National Park (see entry).

★★Great Barrier Reef H–K 1–4

Situation and characteristics

The Great Barrier Reef, the world's largest coral reef, is often ranked as one of the wonders of the world. It is not a single continuous reef but a complex

See Baedeker Special, pp. 288–89

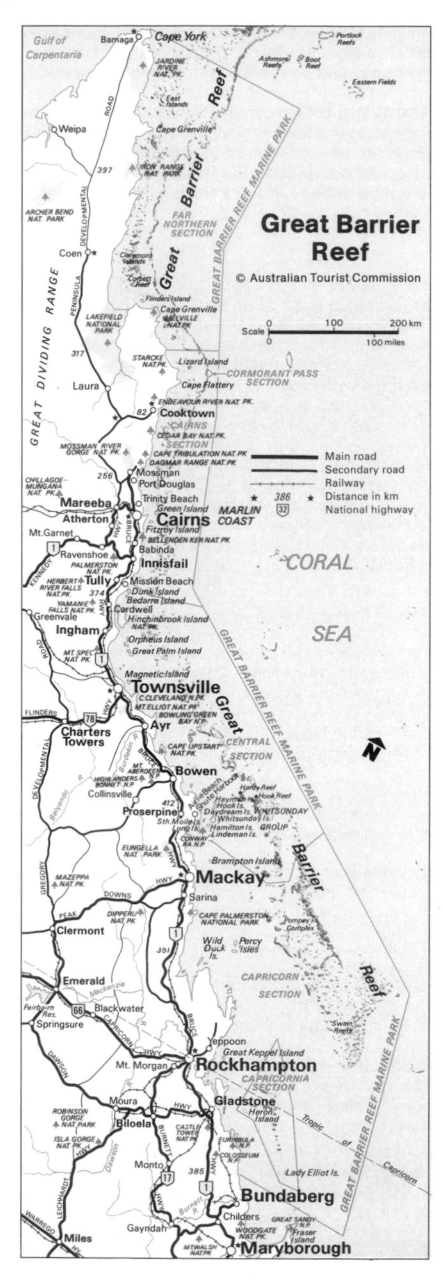

of almost 3000 separate coral reefs extending off the northern coast of Queensland from latitude 24° south to beyond the 10th parallel and reaching beyond the north-eastern corner of Australia to Papua New Guinea. The outer string of reefs, built up on Australia's continental shelf and falling steeply down on the outside, is around 250km/155 miles from the mainland at the south end, off Mackay, but only 30km/20 miles away at the north end.

The National Park authorities make strenuous efforts, through conducted visits, brochures and exhibitions, to teach both children and adults the importance and interest of the Great Barrier Reef and to secure their co-operation in preserving it. For some years now they have followed a middle course: they "sacrifice" some of the islands nearer the coast in order to allow visitors to see something of the wonders of the reef; but most of the islands (other than those in private ownership) are under statutory protection. Camping is allowed only to a very limited extent and with a permit; and in considering applications for a permit the authorities will have regard to the interests of nesting birds and other environmental considerations.

Access

Just under 20 of the islands within the area of the Great Barrier Reef have resort complexes of greater or lesser size, which can be reached by sea or air. Hamilton Island has an airstrip which can take jet aircraft.

In planning a visit to the Great Barrier Reef it is better to avoid, if possible, the main holiday periods, when holiday accommodation and seats in boats and planes are at a premium. During these periods, too, permits for camping on islands in the National Park are difficult to get.

In earlier years there was little concern about possible dangers to the ecology of the Great Barrier Reef. Some islands were damaged by overgrazing by goats; in the 19th century great quantities of sea cucumbers (bêche-de-mer) – a special Chinese delicacy – were gathered from the reefs; and around the turn of the century the islands' deposits of guano (seabirds' droppings, used in dried form as a fertiliser) were worked on a large scale. Around 1970 plans for the large-scale quarrying of limestone and drilling for oil were frustrated by the action of environmental interests. Finally the governments in Brisbane and Canberra agreed to give the Great Barrier Reef statutory protection as a National Park, to be managed by the Great Barrier Reef Marine Park Authority.

Excessive numbers of visitors are one threat to the reefs, but there are other factors more difficult to influence. The widespread pollution of the sea, fertilisers, pesticides and oil residues are all harmful to the creatures who create the banks of coral. At one time the crown-of-thorns starfish, which appeared in great numbers and ate up whole banks of coral, was thought to be a danger to the reef, but the threat seems now to be receding and the corals recover rapidly.

The coral reefs have their hazards for human visitors, who should beware of the poisonous stonefish and the equally poisonous cone shell. Shoes with stout soles should be worn when walking on the reef, and in the water a lookout should be kept for the poisonous and very inquisitive sea snakes. In summer (November to March) box jellyfish with their stinging tentacles are a serious danger off the coasts if the water is not clear.

Islands in the Great Barrier Reef

Bedarra Island, Capricorn Islands (see entries), Dunk Island (see Cardwell), Fitzroy Island, Great Keppel Island, Heron Island, Hinchinbrook Island, Lady Elliot Island, Lizard Island (see entries), Magnetic Island (see Townsville), Orpheus Island, Whitsunday Islands (see entries).

★Great Keppel Island K 4

Situation and characteristics

Great Keppel Island (area 14sq.km/5½sq.miles) is the largest of the 18 islands off Keppel Bay, none of them more than 20km/12½ miles from the Capricornia coast. The other islands, lacking drinking water, have little in the way of facilities for visitors.

The hills on Great Keppel rise to heights of up to 175m/575ft. The island can be reached by boat from Rosslyn Bay (north of Rockhampton) or from Yeppoon, to the south. It is possible also to fly from Rockhampton.

Facilities

On Great Keppel Island is a large resort complex run by Australian Airlines. It is designed mainly for young people, with a wide range of entertainments. There are also a youth hostel and a camping ground, and facilities for a variety of sports (diving, snorkelling, riding, hang gliding, etc.), beaches of fine sand and walking trails. The island is popular with families and with day trippers.

Halfway Island
Humpey Island
Barren Island
Middle Island

On Middle Island there is an underwater observatory. Halfway Island and Humpey Island can be visited from Great Keppel Island. There are good diving grounds off the islands, particularly Barren Island. North Keppel, Miall, Middle, Halfway and Humpey Islands are National Parks, with facilities for camping (permit required, obtainable from ranger at Rosslyn Bay or Rockhampton; campers must take their own supplies, including water).

Baedeker Special

A Natural Wonder Under Threat

When the alarm call came it was not unexpected, and the cause of the approaching catastrophe was soon identified: the hundreds of thousands of crown-of-thorns starfishes which were threatening a natural wonder unique in the world, the Great Barrier Reef. With their poisonous spines they were breaking through the vulnerable calcareous shell of the coral polyps and sucking out its contents.

The reason for the sudden proliferation of these "coral-killers" is still not clear. It has been suggested that they multiplied because man had almost exterminated their natural enemy, the triton snail, but this has not been proved. Wherever the crown-of-thorns starfish appeared, however, it left traces of its destructive appetite in the form of dead, ghost-like branches of coral extending over a distance of more than 300 miles. Curiously, it appeared in such large numbers only on the Great Barrier Reef: elsewhere, for example in the Maldives, the coral islands in the Indian Ocean, there was no similar invasion.

And then the unexpected happened. The crown-of-thorns starfish disappeared; and the marine biologists who had feared that by the end of the century this unique and colourful world of coral would be no more, discovered to their astonishment that these tiny creatures were able to resist the attacks of their worst enemy and, after a period of regeneration, to survive.

The coral polyp is a species of invertebrate less than half an inch long. Feeding on the plankton which floats in the sea, it ingests lime, which it then excretes to form a hard protective coating. To live and grow – by a fraction of an inch each year – it needs warm, clear water rich in oxygen which lets in plenty of light. It does not thrive in poor light, in water carrying alluvium at the mouths of rivers or in water temperatures below 20°C/68°F.

Over the centuries the skeletons of uncountable generations of corals have built up the innumerable individual reefs of the Great Barrier Reef to form a tremendous breakwater sheltering Australia's coastal waters and a habitat for a colourful world of flora and fauna which have adapted to the special conditions of the reef. Divers exploring the Great Barrier Reef have identified no fewer than 4000 species of molluscs, 400 species of coral and 1500 species of fish as well as many species of crabs. Nowhere else on earth is there such a finely balanced ecological system within such a (relatively) small area.

The crown-of-thorns starfish is not the only enemy of the corals off the Australian coast. They are also threatened by the activities of man. Every year thousands of tons of heavy metals, including such highly poisonous ones as cadmium and lead, are carried by marine currents from Papua New Guinea, only a few hundred miles away, to the Great Barrier Reef. It is feared that the full extent of the damage caused by these poisonous substances has not yet been revealed. A further danger facing the corals is the global warming of the seas, which threatens to upset the very delicate balance, built up over many millions of years, of this underwater world, which the experts believe is not in a position to adjust so rapidly to the new conditions confronting it.

In the Great Barrier Reef there are over 700 coral and continental islands (i.e. islands on the continental shelf). The continental islands were at one time coastal ranges of hills which were drowned by a rise in sea level. These continental islands, mostly lying close to the coast, often have their own coral reefs. In contrast to the coral islands, which are low and often quite small, most of the continental islands have quite considerable hills, which offer good walking and magnificent views over other islands and reefs and the magically

Colourful corals on the Great Barrier Reef

blue sea. Only a few of the islands in the Great Barrier Reef are inhabited, and frequently they have no fresh water.

The variety of underwater life on the reefs, which are estimated to be 20 million years old, is fascinating. A great range of corals in all the colours of the rainbow (when broken off they quickly lose their colour), the colourful fish in all shapes and sizes and the many species of shellfish nestling in the reef form an eco-system which is one of Australia's greatest tourist attractions. The great influx of tourists, increasing from year to year, also constitutes a danger to the ecological balance of the reefs. The innumerable coral islands and continental islands with their fringing reefs provide nesting-places for great numbers of seabirds and beaches where turtles lay their eggs. In 1981, therefore, the Great Barrier Reef was designated a statutorily protected marine park under the control of the federal government, and it was also included in UNESCO's list of World Heritage sites.

Measures have been taken to reduce the conflict between tourism and the protection of the environment by regulating the tourist traffic. Although it is not possible to keep divers and reef walkers away from the reefs altogether the streams of visitors can be canalised and threatened areas closed off. Visitors to this underwater wonder of the world must be brought to realise their responsibility for its preservation. Apart from the fact that breaking off pieces of coral is an offence subject to a substantial fine, scuba divers and snorkellers must resolve to confine themselves to looking and not touching. We must all contribute to ensuring that the ecological catastrophe which would destroy the Great Barrier Reef will never happen.

Tropical fish, Great Barrier Reef (see page 285)

Gympie K 5

Situation and characteristics

Gympie (pop. 11,700) lies 180km/110 miles north of Brisbane on the Bruce Highway. Gold was found here in 1867, and the rich goldfields helped the young colony to survive. After the gold petered out in the 1920s the town depended for its continuing prosperity on dairy farming and agriculture.

Accommodation

Numerous hotels, motels and caravan/camping parks.

Features

The annual Gold Rush Festival in October harks back to gold-mining days and commemorates James Nash, who first found gold here.

Surroundings

Gympie lies to the north of Cooloola National Park (see Noosa Heads). Excursions to Tin Can Bay and Rainbow Beach (50km/31 miles east), from which there is a ferry to Fraser Island (see entry).

★Heron Island K 4

Situation and characteristics

Heron Island lies in the Great Barrier Reef (see entry) 70km/43 miles from Gladstone and 100km/62 miles from Rockhampton. It is one of the finest diving grounds in the world, easily accessible from Gladstone (see entry) by helicopter or boat.

This tiny coral island, with an area of only 42 hectares/105 acres, lies on the outer reef, surrounded by the huge Witari Reef. It is a favourite haunt of underwater photographers, with an extraordinary concentration of reef life, with over 800 species of coral and 1150 species of fish. Among them are two giant moray eels known as Harry and Fang who have no fear of man and approach visitors to beg for food.

In addition to its fascinating underwater world the island is also frequented by large numbers of birds and by turtles, which lay their eggs here between October and February. The young hatch out between December and May. Visitors can watch the young emerging but must not of course interfere with them (conducted tours are on offer).

Accommodation

The area outside the resort complex (which can accommodate a maximum of 500 visitors) has been declared a National Park, in which camping is not permitted.

Features

On the island is a Marine Biological Research Station run by the University of Queensland which carries on research on the reefs and islands. Visitors can see round the station.

Other attractions are guided reef walks, fishing trips, diving excursions, diving instruction and cruises in glass-bottomed boats.

Hervey Bay (Sugar Coast) K 5

Situation and characteristics

The town of Hervey Bay (pop. 15,000) lies between Maryborough and Bundaberg (see entries) within the shelter of Fraser Island. This is one of the most popular holiday areas on the Queensland coast, with quiet beaches suitable for small children. The mild climate draws many visitors from the colder south of Australia during the winter months. The town consists of a string of beach resorts round the bay (Gatakers Bay, Pialba, Scarness, Torquay, Urangan, Burrum Heads, Toogoom, Howard, Torbanlea).

Accommodation

Many hotels, motels and caravan/camping parks.

Features

Urangan has a pier 1km/½ mile long much favoured by anglers, from which there is a good view of Fraser Island (see entry). In Scarness is a museum with relics of early settler days.

Surroundings

Excursions to Fraser Island (boat to the island, then tour in 4WD vehicles) are popular, as are whale-watching tours (boat trips to observe the humpback whales which call in here on their way back to the Antarctic between August and the middle of October). The season begins with a Whale Festival in August.

★Hinchinbrook Island J 3

Situation and characteristics

Hinchinbrook Island lies 100km/60 miles north-west of Townsville and 6km/4 miles east of Cardwell. With an area of 39,000 hectares/96,000 acres, it is the largest island off the Queensland coast and the largest island National Park in the world. It is separated from the mainland only by the narrow but deep, mangrove-fringed Hinchinbrook Channel. Cook, sailing this way in 1770, did not realise that he was passing an island.

The island extends for 34km/21 miles from north to south, with Mount Bowen (1121m/3678ft) as its highest peak. It is an island of sandy beaches, partly unexplored wilderness, dense rain forest of milky pine and palm fig trees, and mangrove swamps.

Best time to visit

Winter and spring.

Access

There are day trips from Cardwell to the north end of the island (resort complex) and from Lucinda to the south end (George Point, end of coastal walk). On the outer side of the island, facing the ocean, access for boats is difficult.

Accommodation

At the northern tip of the island (Cape Richards) there is a small resort complex (accommodation for 60); also camping sites. Bush camping is also possible (permit required, obtainable from QNPWS, Cardwell).

Features

This is an island for nature-lovers: there is little in the way of entertainment but plenty of scope for walking and water sports. There is a very rewarding walk (30km/19 miles) along the coast from Ramsay Bay on the east side of the island to George Point in the south. Walkers must be in good condition and take plenty of water with them. The Queensland National Park and Wildlife Service (QNPWS) issues a brochure on this coastal walk.

Surroundings

To the north of Hinchinbrook are the National Park islands of Goold (camping permitted; no drinking water) and the four small Brooks Islands with their huge colonies of Torres pigeons. Farther north are the Family Islands (see entry), with the main island of Dunk (see Cardwell). Opposite Hinchinbrook Island, on the mainland, is Hinchinbrook Channel National Park, 5600 hectares/13,800 acres of marshland, dunes and mangroves along the coast.

Hughenden H 4

Situation and characteristics

Hughenden (pop. 1900), the commercial centre of an extensive pastoral district, lies on the Flinders River 250km/155 miles west of Charters Towers. It is on the Flinders Highway and the railway from Townsville to Mount Isa. Its economy is based on wool, cattle and grain.

The first white men in this area were William Landsborough and his companions, who camped here in 1862 while unsuccessfully searching for the missing Burke and Wills expedition. A large cattle station was established here only a year later.

Accommodation

Several hotels, motels and caravan/camping parks.

Features

Dinosaur Display Centre, with life-size models of dinosaurs.

Surroundings

From Mount Walker, south of the town, there is a good general view of the town and surrounding area.

★Porcupine Gorge National Park

Location; area

50km/30 miles north of Hughenden; 2938 hectares/7257 acres.

Best time to visit

Autumn, winter and spring.

Access

Access north of Hughenden on Kennedy Developmental Road (unsurfaced track for most of the way; impassable after heavy rain).

Facilities

Bush camping; no facilities for visitors.

Features

Porcupine Gorge National Park consists of an impressive gorge with rock walls up to 150m/500ft high, cut by Porcupine Creek (a perennially flowing river) through a layer of basalt into softer sedimentary rock below. A striking feature is the play of colour on the walls of the gorge. There is an abundance of wildlife to be seen in the gorge, particularly during the dry season, when there is still water in the river.

The pyramidal rock formations to the north of the gorge, near the entrance, are favourite spots for bush camping.

Ingham J 3

Situation and characteristics

The little town of Ingham (pop. 5700), named after W. B. Ingham, an early settler and sugar-cane planter, lies on the lower course of the Herbert River in a large sugar-growing area. Graves in the churchyard point to the Mediterranean origins of the early settlers. The Victoria Mill is one of the largest sugar mills in the world; the Macknade Mill has been operating since 1874.

Accommodation

Several hotels, motels and caravan/camping parks.

Surroundings

The sugar produced here is shipped from Lucinda, 29km/18 miles north. Other products of the region are tobacco, timber and cattle

Excursions to the National Parks in the surrounding area, with jungle-like rain forest and waterfalls. In addition to the parks described below there are Herbert River Falls National Park, with an impressive gorge and high, steep rock faces, Mount Fox, an extinct volcano, and the offshore islands of Dunk (see Cardwell), Orpheus and Hinchinbrook (see entries).

Jourama National Park

Location; area
20km/12½ miles south of Ingham; 1100 hectares/2700 acres.

Best time to visit
Autumn and spring.

Access
On gravel road which branches off Bruce Highway between Townsville and Ingham.

Facilities
Camping grounds, picnic areas, walking trails.

Features
The main scenic attractions of Jourama National Park are its waterfalls and the beautiful valley of Waterview Creek, covered with dense vegetation and scattered with granite boulders. From the access road there are short walking trails to the waterfall and the viewpoint above the falls. There are also some steeper trails; but rock climbing is inadvisable because of the many loose bits of rock. Good bathing in the park.

Wallaman Falls National Park

Location; area
50km/30 miles west of Ingham; 600 hectares/1500 acres.

Best time to visit
Autumn or spring for camping; the falls are at their most impressive in late summer.

Access
Track from Trebonne, 8km/5 miles west of Ingham.

Facilities
Camping grounds (permit required, obtainable from QNPWS in Ingham); picnic areas, walking trails.

Features
The most impressive feature in Wallaman Falls National Park is the waterfall on Stony Creek, a tributary of the Herbert River, where the water plunges down 279m/915ft (greatest flow of water at end of summer).

Above the falls are expanses of luxuriant rain forest. There is a good general view from a lookout reached on a track which takes off from the road. Walking trails; bathing areas.

Surroundings
To the north of Wallaman Falls National Park are a number of other National Parks, areas of inaccessible wilderness round the Herbert River and its tributaries, with smaller waterfalls. These parks are only for fit and experienced rock climbers: Herbert River Falls National Park (2400 hectares/6000 acres), Yamanie Falls (9700 hectares/24,000 acres), Herkes Creek Falls (500 hectares/1250 acres), Sword Creek Falls (500 hectares/1250 acres), Garrawalt Falls (5000 hectares/12,500 acres), Broadwater Creel Falls (500 hectares/1250 acres).

Innisfail J 3

Situation and characteristics
92km/57 miles south of Cairns, near the mouth of the Johnstone River, is Innisfail (pop. 8159), where sugar-cane has been grown and processed since 1880, when the first plantation was established by the bishop of Brisbane. After the Second World War many immigrants from the Mediterranean area, particularly from Italy, settled here.

Accommodation
Several motels and caravan/camping parks.

Features
In Owen Street is a handsome Chinese temple. The Sugar Festival is celebrated in August, and in December is the Opera Festival.

Surroundings
At Nerada, 28km/17 miles west, is a large tea plantation. On the Johnstone River is a crocodile farm, and in the surrounding area are a number of waterfalls. Excursions to Palmerston National Park (see Millaa Millaa) and to the Atherton Tableland on the well made Palmerston Highway.

There are beautiful, clean beaches to north and south of the town. Innisfail is also a good base for trips to the Great Barrier Reef (see entry).

Sugar-cane plantation, Innisfail (see page 293)

★Ipswich K 5

Situation and characteristics

Ipswich (pop. 73,300), the gateway to the fertile Darling Downs, lies 40km/25 miles south-west of Brisbane, of which it is now virtually an outer suburb. It was founded in 1827 as a convict settlement, and limekilns here supplied lime for the building of Brisbane. Known until 1842 as Limestone Hills, it was then renamed after the English town of Ipswich.

Accommodation

Numerous hotels, motels and caravan/camping parks.

Features

Ipswich has preserved many houses and public buildings of the colonial period, notably Claremount House, a Georgian mansion in Milford Street (1858); the Courthouse in East Street (1859), designed by Charles Tiffin, later the architect of Old Government House, the Customs House and Parliament House in Brisbane; the railway station in Bell Street (1892); and St Paul's Church (corner of Nicholas and Brisbane Streets), built in 1858, when it was considered one of the finest churches in Queensland, The School of Arts (1861) was dignified by the addition of a classical-style faáade in 1864 and became the Town Hall.

Kingaroy K 5

Situation and characteristics

Kingaroy (pop. 7000) is famed as the "Peanut Capital of Australia". Peanuts flourish in the red soil of the area, and over 50,000 tons are harvested annually and stored in giant silos. Other local crops are beans and grain. There are conducted tours of the peanut and baked beans processing factories.

Accommodation

Several motels and caravan/camping parks.

★Bunya Mountains National Park

Location; area
50km/30 miles south of Kingaroy; 12000 hectares/30,000 acres. Throughout the year, but particularly beautiful from September to November, with orchids in the rain forest and a profusion of wild flowers.

Access
Via Kingaroy, Jondaryan or Dalby.

Facilities
Camping grounds, picnic areas, walking trails.

Features
Bunya Mountains National Park was established in 1908 to prevent further felling of the forest. It is part of the Great Dividing Range, with hills rising to 1100m/3600ft (Mount Kiangarow, Mount Mowbullan), forests of bunya pine, expanses of rain forest, impressive waterfalls and areas of grassland. From some points there are magnificent views. Many kangaroos and wallabies.

★Kuranda J 3

Situation and characteristics
Kuranda (pop. 750) is a popular tourist centre on the Atherton Tableland. It lies among tropical forest on the escarpment of the Macalister Range, 27km/17 miles north-west of Cairns.

Access
The most beautiful way to get to Kuranda is by the Kuranda Scenic Railway from Cairns; Skyrail from Smithfield (to the north of Cairns), by road along the Kuranda Highway.

Accommodation
Several hotels and motels, caravan/camping park.

Features
Kuranda's main attraction is its colourful local market (Wed., Thur., Fri. and Sun. 9am–2.30pm). Large numbers of rare butterflies can be seen flying around in the Butterfly Sanctuary (open: daily 10am–3pm) and in Birdworld many species of birds from the tropical rainforest (open: daily 9am–4pm). Walks can be arranged on request from Kuranda to the wildly romantic Barron Falls (see Cairns – Barron Falls National Park).

Tjapukai Aboriginal Cultural Park
Tjapukai Aboriginal Cultural Park by the Caravonica Lakes near Smithfield (open; daily 9am–5pm) is well worth a visit. It provides an excellent insight into Aboriginal culture, and in the Dance Theatre native dance performances are given from time to time.

★Kuranda Scenic Railway

★Skyrail Rainforest Cableway
Exploring the rainforest by taking the Kuranda Scenic Railway and the Skyrail Rainforest Cableway, the longest of its kind in the world, is a unique experience. For the journey through the mountains the Scenic Railway (initial construction of which commenced in 1881; numerous bridges and tunnels) is recommended, parts of which run near to the Barron Gorge with its roaring waterfalls. The journey ends in the little station at Kuranda which is almost hidden by tropical plants and palms.

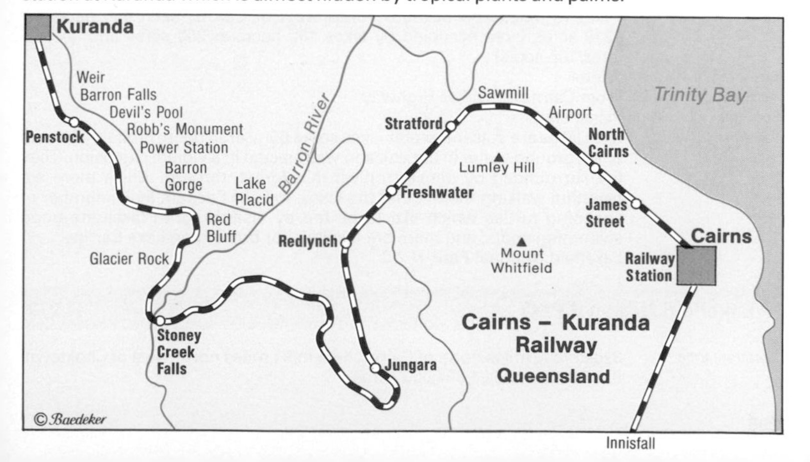

Davies Creek National Park

30km/20 miles south of Kuranda lies Davies Creek National Park (480 hectares/1200 acres), which is best visited in winter. The approach road is off Kennedy Highway between Kuranda and Mareeba. Features include the Davies Creek Waterfall, together with huge blocks of granite, eucalyptus groves and grassland with termite mounds.

★Lady Elliot Island K 4

Situation and characteristics

Lady Elliot Island, a tiny coral island (42 hectares/105 acres) with a small airstrip for light aircraft (coming from Bundaberg, 80km/50 miles away), lies at the south end of the Great Barrier Reef (see entry). It is named after the "Lady Elliot", a ship which ran aground on the reef off Hinchinbrook Island (see entry) in 1812.

Accommodation

There is a small resort complex (maximum 120 guests), originally a camp for scuba divers.

Features

Lady Elliot Island is a happy hunting ground for experienced divers, with many wrecks to be explored. The underwater world can be seen, less strenuously, from a glass-bottomed boat. Also over 50 species of birds.

Lady Musgrave Island K 4

Situation and characteristics

This tiny coral island (15 hectares/38 acres), one of the Bunker Islands, lies 40km/25 miles north of Lady Elliot Island and 100km/60 miles north-east of Bundaberg.

Access

There are day trips from Bundaberg in a fast catamaran. The island lies at the west end of a large lagoon with a safe entry and good anchorage.

Accommodation

Lady Musgrave Island is a National Park, with no holiday accommodation. Camping is possible (permit required, obtainable from QNPWS; campers must take all supplies, including water and fuel).

Features

The vegetation suffered from over-grazing by goats which had been released on the island to provide sustenance for shipwrecked seafarers, but has recovered since 1971. Around the end of the 19th century damaged was caused on the island, as on many islands in the Great Barrier Reef, by the extraction of guano. Lady Musgrave Island is an important nesting-place for birds, and turtles come here to lay their eggs. There are good diving grounds all round the island.

Lake Barrine National Park and Lake Eacham National Park J 3

Location; area

70km/43 miles and 60km/37 miles west of Cairns; each 490 hectares/1210 acres (area occupied by lakes 100 hectares/250 acres and 40 hectares/100 acres).

Best time to visit

Winter.

Access

From Cairns on Gillies Highway.

Facilities

Picnic areas.

Features

Both lakes are volcanic crater lakes some 65m/215ft deep, probably formed when ground-water in the volcano was ejected in a violent explosion. They are surrounded by dense tropical rain forest, through which there are beautiful walking trails round the lakes. In Lake Eacham live a number of snapping turtles which like to be fed by visitors. Both lakes are good swimming spots, and there are facilities for boating on Lake Barrine.

Lakefield National Park H 2/3

★Lakefield National Park H 2/3

Location; area

320km/200 miles north of Cairns, 146km/91 miles north-west of Cooktown; 528,000 hectares/1,304,000 acres.

A lagoon in Lakefield National Park

Best time to visit: Because of the heavy rain and high temperatures in summer the park should be visited only in the dry season (June to October).

Access: Via Laura (4WD vehicles only), passing the former Old Laura cattle station; or from Cooktown via Battle Camp.

Facilities: Areas for bush camping along the rivers and lagoons; three ranger stations. No supplies.

Features: The very varied landscape of Lakefield National Park includes savannas and plains with open woodland which are flooded in the rainy season, wide rivers and expanses of marshland, lagoons with rich flora and fauna, particularly water birds and crocodiles, mangrove swamps and rain forest. It is the most accessible National Park on Cape York Peninsula north of Cooktown (see entries).

N.B. The ranger stations can give information about where bush camping and canoeing are possible. In the tidal reaches of rivers beware of crocodiles. Proper equipment for travel in the outback is essential.

Lawn Hill National Park G 3

Location; area: 1100km/685 miles west of Townsville, 410km/255 miles north of Mount Isa; 12,000 hectares/30,000 acres.

Best time to visit: Winter and spring.

Access: From Burketown–Camooweal road at Gregory Downs, 117km/73 miles south of Burketown (track impassable after rain).

Facilities: Camping and picnic areas.

Features: The central feature of the park is a gorge up to 60m/200ft deep cut through the Barkly Tableland by Lawn Hill Creek. In the bare rock faces are Aboriginal paintings. Archaeological evidence shows that the area was settled more than 30,000 years ago. The perennially flowing river has created an oasis with a rich flora and fauna (kangaroos, emus, many birds, freshwater crocodiles).

There are 20km/12½ miles of walking trails in the park.

★Lizard Island J 2

Situation and characteristics

Lizard Island (area 21sq.km/8sq.miles; highest point 368m/1207ft) is a remote and isolated island some 270km/170 miles north of Cairns, the most northerly island in the Great Barrier Reef with many facilities for visitors. It lies only 15km/9 miles from the outer reef. The island was given its name in 1770 by Joseph Banks, the botanist with Cook's expedition, after the large but harmless monitor lizards he found here. After running aground on a coral reef Cook stayed near present-day Cooktown for some weeks while the "Endeavour" was being repaired and then spent a day on Lizard Island looking for a passage out of the reefs to the open sea.

Access

There are flights to the island from Cairns. There are no regular boat services from the mainland, but boats sailing from Cairns to Thursday Island (see entry) also take passengers.

There are good anchorages on Lizard Island for boats of all kinds (Watson's Bay, Blue Lagoon).

Accommodation

There is a resort complex on the island with accommodation for 64 guests (expensive; no children). Camping is possible (permit required, obtainable from QNPWS, Cairns; campers must take all supplies).

Features

There are magnificent beaches, excellent for swimming, snorkelling and scuba diving, in this almost completely unspoiled part of the reef. Lizard Island was scheduled as a National Park in 1939, as were the other small islands in the group in 1987. Camping (with permit) is allowed almost everywhere. The Lizard Island Research Station (conducted visits Mon. and Fri. at 4pm) was established by the Australian Museum in Sydney in 1974, with finance from private foundations. It has accommodation for visitors, mainly scientists and students.

There are a number of walking trails on the island, including one to Cook's Look, from which there are superb panoramic views extending to the outer reef. Big-game fishing enthusiasts from far and wide come to Lizard Island between September and December to fish for black marlin.

Logan City K 5

Situation and characteristics

Logan City (pop. 132,000), a rapidly growing town some 30km/20 miles south of Brisbane, now forms part of the Brisbane conurbation. Declared a shire in 1978, it became a city in 1981. Its situation between the state capital and the City of Gold Coast holiday region has made it a much sought-after residential town.

The town is named after Captain Patrick Logan, one of the founders and much feared commandant of the Moreton Bay penal settlement, who organised the exploration of the region and discovered the Logan River.

Accommodation

Numerous motels and caravan/camping parks.

★Longreach H 4

Situation and characteristics

At the end of the Capricornia Highway, which runs along the Tropic of Capricorn (see entry), and on the railway line from Rockhampton to Winton is the little town of Longreach (pop. 3800), the centre of a huge sheep and cattle region in west central Queensland, on the fringes of the outback. The site on the Thomson River was from an early stage a favourite camping site and stopover for cattle drovers and adventurers on their way to the wild

Australian west. In Australia's bicentennial year these daring heroes of the outback were commemorated by the establishment of the Stockman's Hall of Fame and Outback Heritage Centre (exhibitions, theatre, library, etc.).

Opposite is the old airfield of the Queensland and Northern Territory Air Services. The airline which was to become world-famous as Qantas carried out its first experimental flights at Winton (see entry), 170km/105 miles north of Longreach, but soon afterwards moved to Longreach. The first hangar of 1912 is still standing.

Australia's first aircraft factory was also in Longreach, and the DH-50 biplane was assembled here in the 1920s. Regular air services began in Longreach, and light aircraft soon became the most important means of transport to the inhospitable expanses of the west and north.

The Flying Surgeon Service, conveying surgeons to remote hospitals in the outback, started from Longreach in 1959.

Accommodation

Several hotels, motels and caravan/camping parks.

★Mackay J 4

Situation and characteristics

Mackay (pop. 40,000), situated on a monotonous stretch of the Bruce Highway, is often called the sugar capital of Australia. It has a good claim to the title, for the five sugar mills processing sugar-cane from the plantations which pattern the landscape of this region supply a third of the country's total output of sugar. The first sugar-cane plantation was established in 1866, and soon afterwards the first sugar mill was built and Mackay was declared a town.

As a port, Mackay ships not only huge quantities of sugar but also coal from the opencast mines in central Queensland (Hay Point). Its large harbour was created by the construction of a breakwater in 1939. Alongside sugar, coal, beef, dairy farming, timber-working and the growing of tropical fruits an increasingly important contribution to the town's economy is now being made by tourism.

Accommodation

Many hotels, motels and caravan/camping parks.

Features

A number of handsome buildings – the Town Hall, the Commonwealth and National Banks, the Courthouse, the Police Station, the Customs House – have been preserved from Mackay's early days. The town's streets are lined with palms. Queens Park has a beautiful array of flowers, tropical trees and shrubs and an orchid house.

Surroundings

From Mackay, boats ply to the Great Barrier Reef and to the Whitsunday Islands (see entry) and other islands. To the north of the town are a string of beautiful beaches. For nature-lovers there is Cape Hillsborough National Park (see below).The best approach to Eungella National Park (see entry) is from Mackay via Marian, Mirani and Finch Hatton: a beautiful road (80km/50 miles) which runs through tropical rain forest with numerous waterfalls and walking trails.

Information

The tourist information office in Mackay is housed in a replica of an old sugar mill in Nebo Road.

Cape Hillsborough National Park

Location; area

45km/28 miles north-east of Mackay; 800 hectares/2000 acres.

Best time to visit

Autumn and spring.

Access

From Bruce Highway on side roads at Mount Ossa and Yakapari.

Facilities

Camping ground at Smalleys Beach; picnic areas, walking trails.

Features

The promontory on which Cape Hillsborough National Park lies is dominated by steeply scarped hills rising to around 300m/1000ft. The park, with dunes, expanses of coastal scrub, rainforest and grassland and eight viewpoints, also takes in the Andrews Point peninsula and little Wedge Island, which can be reached on foot at low tide. A nature trail runs up the Hidden

Valley. There is an excellent network of walking trails, and there are also beautiful beaches; but during the summer, because of the danger of the box jellyfish, it is better to bathe inland in Cascade Creek.

Main Range National Park K 5

Location; area
On Cunningham Highway, 120km/75 miles south-west of Brisbane (main access road at Cunningham Highway ranger station); 11,500 hectares/28,400 acres.

Best time to visit
Spring and autumn.

Facilities
Camping ground; picnic spots (at Cunningham's Gap, Spicers Gap and Governor's Chair Lookout); ranger station; bush walking trails.

Features
The park extends for 40km/25 miles along the Great Dividing Range. It has an extensive network of walking trails through woodland and rain forest and over unspoiled bush country, with magnificent views.

Surroundings
North-west of Main Range National Park is Mount Mistake National Park (area 5560 hectares/13,735 acres), another expanse of wild unspoiled country. Before visiting this park it is advisable to contact the ranger station.

Mareeba J 3

Situation and characteristics
Mareeba (pop. 8000), 68km/42 miles west of Cairns, is the largest town on the Atherton Tableland and the centre of Australia's principal tobacco-growing region. Another crop grown in the area between Mareeba and Dimbulah, irrigated with water from Lake Tinaroo (an artificial lake formed by a dam on the Barron River), is rice.

The Mareeba Rodeo in July draws large numbers of visitors.

Accommodation
Several hotels, motels and caravan/camping parks.

★ Maroochydore K 5

Situation and characteristics
Maroochydore (pop. 21,000), 110km/68 miles north of Brisbane, is the oldest beach resort in Queensland and the business centre of the Sunshine Coast (see entry). The town grew up in the 1880s round a sawmill near the mouth of the Maroochy River. Situated as it is on the beautiful surf beaches of the Sunshine Coast and in the estuary of the river (water birds, safe bathing beaches), it has developed into a popular holiday centre.

The name of the river and the town comes from an Aboriginal word meaning "place with black swans".

Accommodation
Numerous hotels, motels and caravan/camping parks.

Features
North of the town, near the airport, is a Pioneer Village, and at Bli Bli is a Fairytale Castle. Underwater World has a huge tank of seawater with a glass-walled passage through it, giving visitors a close-up view of the variety of the underwater world off the Australian coast (open: daily 9am–5pm; admission charge).

Mooloolaba

Situation and characteristics
Mooloolaba, a very popular holiday resort with beautiful sandy beaches and excellent facilities for visitors, lies to the south of Maroochydore. The harbour at the mouth of the Mooloolaba River is sheltered by the rocky coasts of Alexandra Headland and Port Cartwright, providing a safe anchorage for fishing boats and pleasure craft. From here pilots take large vessels to Brisbane along the shipping lane running close to the coast.

Mooloolaba is the finishing line of the annual yacht race from Sydney and the starting-point of the race to Gladstone.

Accommodation

Several hotels, motels and caravan/camping parks.

★Maryborough K 5

Situation and characteristics

Maryborough (pop. 23,000), 260km/160 miles from Brisbane, in its day an important river port on the Mary River from which wool, sugar and building timber were shipped, was settled at an early stage, and its role as a supply centre for the goldfields round Gympie (90km/55 miles south; see entry) from 1867 brought further prosperity. Nowadays the port installations have disappeared and Maryborough has become an industrial town (sawmills, sugar factory). It has preserved so many late 19th century buildings that it is known as Queensland's Heritage City.

Accommodation

Many hotels, motels and caravan/camping parks.

Features

The tourist information centre in Ferry Street, near the bridge over the river, issues a brochure describing a Heritage Walk through the town.

Among the most notable old buildings are the City Hall (1908) in Kent Street; the School of Arts Building (1887), headquarters of the Historical Society, also in Kent Street; the Post Office (1869) in Bazaar Street; Windsor House (1888, Kent Street); the Royal Hotel (1902, Kent Street); the Customs House and Customs House Hotel (1870, Wharf Street), on the river; and St Paul's Church.

There are also many old houses in typical Queensland style, well adapted to the hot weather. Many of them are built on stilts as a protection against heavy rain and to improve ventilation; they have wide roofed verandahs and are richly decorated with wrought-iron railings. The town also has attractive parks and gardens.

Surroundings

Ulula Lagoon, an old reservoir outside the town, is the haunt of many water birds. Attractive excursions are to Rainbow Beach and the Cooloola Coast to the south (90km/55 miles).

27km/17 miles north of Maryborough is Burrum Heads (pop. 900), a holiday resort in Hervey Bay. Near Burrum Heads is Woodgate National Park (area 5490 hectares/13,560 acres; camping grounds, barbecue areas), which is worth visiting at any time of year. There are walking trails through the beautiful coastal region, with sand-dunes and mangrove swamps.

Miles K 5

Situation and characteristics

The little town of Miles (pop. 1500) lies on Dogwood Creek, so named by the explorer Ludwig Leichhardt in 1844 after the shrubs growing along its banks. Originally called Dogwood Crossing, it was later renamed Miles after a local member of parliament. It is an important traffic hub on the Warrego and Leichhardt Highways and the Brisbane–Charleville railway line. The area has always been good sheep country, but nowadays the emphasis is on cattle and wheat. After rain there are a profusion of wild flowers.

Accommodation

Hotels, motels and caravan/camping parks.

Features

The Miles and District Historical Village is a pioneer settlement with many old buildings.

Millaa Millaa J 3

Situation and characteristics

The attraction of Millaa Millaa, 74km/46 miles west of Innisfail on the Atherton Tableland, lies not so much in the town itself as in its surroundings. To the east are the Millaa Millaa, Zillie and Elinjaa Falls, all seen on a gravel road which leaves and rejoins the Palmerston Highway. From a viewpoint to the west of the town there are panoramic views of the Atherton Tableland. At Nerada is a tea plantation, which visitors can see round.

Accommodation
Caravan/camping parks.

★Palmerston National Park

Location; area
30km/19 miles east of Millaa Millaa; 14,200 hectares/35,100 acres.

Best time to visit
May to November. In summer it is hot and rainy.

Access
Via Innisfail or Millaa Millaa.

Facilities
Camping grounds; ranger station; picnic and barbecue areas. Visitor facilities in Innisfail and Millaa Millaa.

Features
A road runs through tall rain forest to the gorges on the Johnstone River; from the road there are walking trails to a number of waterfalls. The narrow, winding road is at some points almost closed by vegetation. The park is named after the pioneer and prospector Christie Palmerston, who discovered this route in 1882. Swimming in lakes; white-water rafting on the North Johnstone River.

Millstream Falls National Park J 3

Location; area
140km/87 miles south-west of Cairns; 370 hectares/910 acres.

Best time to visit
In summer it is very hot, with high rainfall. The waterfalls are at their most impressive in autumn (March to May) after the abundant summer rain.

Access
By way of the Atherton Tableland and Ravenshoe.

Facilities
Camping grounds; picnic areas (above the main falls), walking trails and footpaths.

Features
This relatively small National Park is centred on the Millstream Falls, which are up to 60m/65yd wide and have an abundant flow of water throughout the year. In the water below the falls are platypuses. Swimming is possible.

Mission Beach J 3

Situation and characteristics
Half way between Townsville and Cairns, a few kilometres east of Tully, is Mission Beach (pop. 800), a quiet holiday area with a number of beach resorts. The settlements along the bay are surrounded by expanses of rain forest and hills.

Surroundings
Day trips by boat to Dunk Island (see Cardwell) and the islands in the Great Barrier Reef (see entry), and trips through mangrove swamps and rain forest. White-water rafting on the Tully River.

At the south end of the beach is a cairn commemorating Edmund Kennedy's ill-fated Cape York expedition in 1848.

Accommodation
Several motels and caravan/camping parks.

Moreton Bay K 5

Situation and characteristics
The Brisbane River flows into Moreton Bay, in which there are over 300 islands, large, small and tiny. The larger islands – South and North Stradbroke Islands (see Stradbroke Islands), Moreton Island (see Brisbane) and Bribie Island (see entry) – shelter the mainland coast from the Pacific surf. The southern tip of South Stradbroke Island reaches as far south as Southport, on the Gold Coast (see entry), the northern tip of Bribie Island as far north as Caloundra on the Sunshine Coast (see entries). On the island of St Helena are the ruins of a convict prison.

The history of Queensland began in Moreton Bay in 1824, when the first penal settlement was established at Redcliffe (though it survived only for a short time). Redcliffe has now become a suburb of Brisbane, as has the old beach resort of Sandgate, farther south. The first sugar-cane plantations were established at Ormiston, which has preserved a mansion of 1862.

Mossman J 3

Situation and characteristics

Mossman (pop. 1850), 20km/12½ miles north of Port Douglas and 90km/56 miles north of Cairns on the Cook Highway, is the centre of the most northerly sugarcane-growing area in Queensland. The town is surrounded by hills, the highest of which is Mount Demi (1159m/3803ft).

Accommodation

Several hotels and motels, caravan/camping park.

Features

There are tours of Mossman Central Mill during the cane-crushing season (June to December).

Surroundings

From Port Douglas a steam train, the Bally Hooley Steam Express, runs on a narrow-gauge line through the canefields to the mill. The growing of tropical fruits in this area is increasing (tours of plantations).

Excursions to Daintree National Park (see below) and Cape Tribulation National Park (see entry). Beaches near town, at Cooya, Newell and Wonga.

Daintree National Park

Location; area

5km/3 miles west of Mossman; 56,000 hectares/138,000 acres.

Best time to visit

Winter.

Facilities

Bush camping; walking trails, picnic area.

Features

In the park is a deep gorge cut by the Mossman River through the granite. Other features are coastal hills, waterfalls, various types of rain forest and rich and varied wildlife. The gorge is the entrance to the park, which is largely unspoiled and without tourist facilities.

★Mount Isa G 4

Situation and characteristics

Mount Isa (pop. 24,720), known to local people as "the Isa", is the largest town in the interior of northern Queensland. It is a company town, in which almost all the inhabitants are employed by or dependent on the Mount Isa Mines, but it is also an oasis of civilisation in the hot and inhospitable outback where in the past only a few cattle grazed. Here in 1923 a prospector called James Campbell Miles discovered rich deposits of lead and silver on the western edge of the Cloncurry field. The first tented encampment of the early miners soon developed into an important industrial, commercial and administrative centre. Nowadays copper and zinc as well silver and lead are worked in deep mines. The ore is carried by rail to Townsville (see entry), and from there most of it is exported. The town is notable for its considerable extent; its administrative area covers an area of some 45,000sq.km/17,375sq.miles and extends eastward from the boundary of the Northern Territory for 200km/125 miles.

Access

Mount Isa can be reached by air, rail, overland bus or car (asphalted road). The wet season (December to March) can be disagreeable, although there is much less rain than farther north. The Barkly Highway runs west from Mount Isa by way of Camooweal and through the Northern Territory, with the outback stretching away as far as the eye can see, to Tennant Creek. The Diamantina Developmental Road runs in a wide arc through the Channel Country to Boulia (see entry), from which the Kennedy Developmental Road continues to Winton (see entry).

Accommodation

Numerous hotels, motels and caravan/camping parks.

Features

The Royal Flying Doctor Service (see Baedeker Special, p. 275) and the

The mining town of Mount Isa, an oasis in the outback

School of the Air (see Baedeker Special, p. 40) have bases in Mount Isa (on the Barkly Highway). Visitors can see round the premises (Flying Doctor Service Mon.–Sat. 9am–3pm, School of the Air Mon.–Fri. 10am–noon except during school holidays).

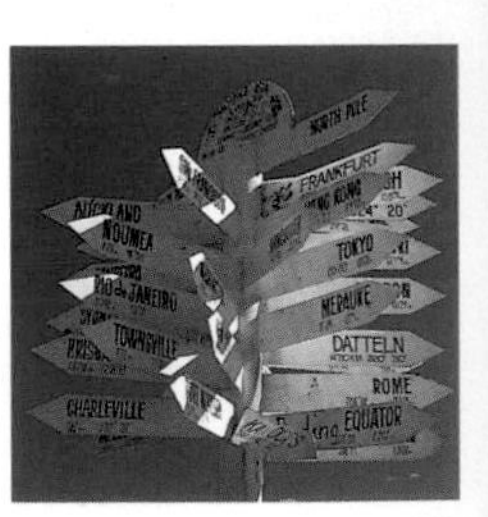

Signpost, Mount Isa

Surroundings

Lake Moondarra, an artificial lake 15km/9 miles north of the town, and the larger Lake Julius, 100km/65 miles north, are good for excursions and water sports. Visitors can tour both surface and underground mines (advance appointment necessary; minimum age 16).

★Mount Morgan K 4

Situation and characteristics

The mining town of Mount Morgan (pop. 2900) lies 38km/24 miles south-west of Rockhampton. Gold and copper have been worked by opencast methods for more than a century, together with silver, lead and zinc. The mine, partly filled with water, is one of the world's largest man-made holes (bus tours; previous booking necessary). When mining was at its peak, at the beginning of the 20th century, the town was many times its present size. With its old mining installations and buildings (Courthouse, Queensland National Hotel, Grand Hotel, railway station, suspension bridge), Mount Morgan is classified as a Heritage Town. It is named after the Morgan brothers, who founded a mining company here in 1882.

Accommodation

Limited.

Mount Spec National Park (Crystal Creek National Park) J 3

Location; area: 70km/43 miles north-west of Townsville; 7224 hectares/17,843 acres.
Best time to visit: Autumn and spring.
Access: Roads to Little Crystal Creek and Big Crystal Creek from Bruce Highway, 67km/42 miles and 69km/43 miles north of Townsville.
Facilities: Camping grounds (also bush camping, with permit from QNPWS, Townsville); picnic area, walking trails.
Features: On the summits and slopes of the Paluma Range are areas of rain forest; Mount Spec itself is 960m/3150ft high. There are a number of good viewpoints in the park, with views extending over the coastal plain to Halifax Bay and the Palm Islands to the north-east. From the picnic area on Big Crystal Creek there is a short walking trail to various viewpoints. Little Crystal Creek offers waterfalls and bathing beaches in a rain forest valley.

Nambour K 5

Situation and characteristics: The area round Nambour (pop. 10,500), 100km/62 miles north of Brisbane on the Bruce Highway, was settled in the 1860s. The first to come were prospectors from the Gympie goldfields (60km/37 miles north-west) looking (unsuccesfully) for gold in this area. Sugar has been the main crop since the 1890s.
Accommodation: Several hotels, motels and caravan/camping parks.
Surroundings: There is evidence in this area of the Australian taste for the gigantic: the 15m/50ft high walk-through Big Pineapple at a pineapple plantation to the south of the town, the Big Cow 6km/4 miles north and the Super Bee advertising a honey factory 14km/8½ miles south.

Within easy reach is the Sunshine Coast, with the resorts of Maroochydore and Mooloolaba (see entries), only 20km/12½ miles away. To the west are the Blackall Ranges, from which there are magnificent views of the coast, and to the south is Glass House Mountains National Park (see entry).

Nerang K 5

Situation and characteristics: Nerang (pop. 10,000), a little town on the Nerang River, lies in the hinterland of the Gold Coast 10km/6 miles west of Southport. Its popularity as a holiday resort has led to a considerable increase in population. Apart from the Gold Coast (see entry) with all its attractions for visitors and holidaymakers the main area of tourist interest is the beautiful Numinbah valley. Other attractions, farther afield, are Springbrook National Park (see entry) with its waterfalls and viewpoints and Natural Arch National Park (see below).
Accommodation: A number of hotels, motels and caravan/camping parks.

Natural Arch National Park

Location; area: 110km/65 miles south of Brisbane, 38km/24 miles south of Nerang; 200 hectares/500 acres.
Best time to visit: Throughout the year.
Access: From Nerang on the Murwillumbah road.
Accommodation: In Nerang.
Facilities: Picnic area, walking trails.
Features: The central feature of this National Park is a waterfall which plunges down into a basalt cave from which the water flows under a natural basalt arch. There are attractive trails from the picnic area to the river through largely unspoiled rain forest and to a viewpoint from which Mount Warning, a lava

Noosa, a holiday centre on the Noosa River

plug which is a remnant of a large shield volcano, can be seen, affording fascinating views of the scenic beauties of this little National Park.

Noosa K 5

Situation and characteristics

Noosa (pop. 12,000), the most northerly and most fashionable of the resorts on the Sunshine Coast (see entry), is beautifully situated on the Noosa River and on coastal lagoons, with Noosa National Park above the steeply scarped coast. The town offers two fine beaches, Sunshine and Sunrise.

Accommodation

Many hotels, motels and caravan/camping parks.

Surroundings

North of the town are the Teewah Coloured Sands and Cooloola National Park (see below). Both are within easy reach either by road (4WD vehicles only) or by boat via the Noosa River, Lake Cooroibah and Lake Cootharaba.

Inland, on the Noosa River, are the quiet settlements of Tewantin and Noosaville.

★Cooloola National Park

Location; area

65km/40 miles north-east of Gympie; 39,000 hectares/96,000 acres.

Best time to visit

Autumn and spring.

Access

From Rainbow Beach or Noosa (four-wheel-drive vehicle).

Facilities

Camping grounds; picnic areas.

Features

High sand-dunes, areas of blown sand and multicoloured sand cliffs are the main features of this park, which can be reached by ordinary vehicles only from the north-east, near the Freshwater and Double Island Point camping grounds. The southern part of the park can be reached by boat from Boreen Point, Elanda and Tewantin.

There are a number of other National Parks within easy reach. Noosa National Park (area 469 hectares/1158 acres) takes in an area of woodland

and marsh on the south bank of the Noosa River, downstream from Lake Cootharaba. Mount Pinbarren National Park (23 hectares/57 acres) contains an expanse of rain forest on the hill of that name. Pipeclay National Park (2 hectares/5 acres) protects an Aboriginal ceremonial site some distance off the road to Rainbow Beach.

Normanton H 3

Situation and characteristics

Normanton (pop. 1150), lies 150km/95 miles north-west of Croydon on the lower course of the winding Norman River, some 80km/50 miles above its outflow into the Gulf of Carpentaria. It can be reached from Cloncurry (378km/235 miles north) on the asphalted Burke Developmental Road. The town, founded in 1868, was at one time an important river port through which prospectors and supplies were conveyed to the goldfields round Croydon.

Accommodation

A number of hotels, motels and caravan/camping parks.

Features

The old Gulflander train, running only between Normanton and Croydon, still operates, though the original steam engines gave place in 1922 to a rail bus which runs once a week.

Surroundings

Round Normanton are many lakes with an abundance of bird life. 70km/43 miles north-west is Karumba (pop. 600), the prawn-fishing centre of the Gulf region.

Orpheus Island J 3

Situation and characteristics

Orpheus Island, the second largest of the Palm Islands, lies 80km/50 miles from Townsville and 20km/12½ miles from Lucinda (near Ingham). Only two islands in the group (Orpheus and Pelorus) can be visited; the other eight (Brisk, Curacao, Eclipse, Esk, Falcon, Fantone, Havannah and Great Palm) are reserves belonging to the Aborigines which can be entered only with a special permit. Orpheus Island has an area of 14sq.km/5½sq.miles and its highest point rises to 172m/564ft above sea level. It comprises open woodland, grassland and, in depressions and sheltered inlets, rain forest, with long beaches of white sand. The reefs round the island are a happy hunting ground for divers and snorkellers, with over 1000 species of fish and over 300 species of coral. Also dolphins and sightings of humpback whales.

Access

The island can be reached from Townsville by seaplane, and there are also flights from Cairns (calling in on Hinchinbrook Island to the north). There are water taxis from Dungeness (near Lucinda) and boats from Townsville (via Magnetic Island).

Accommodation

A resort complex (pleasant but expensive; no children under 12), originally established in 1940 was remodelled in Mediterranean style in 1981. Camping is allowed at Yankee Bay and Pioneer Bay (permit required, obtainable from QNPWS, Townsville).

Port Douglas J 3

Situation and characteristics

Port Douglas (pop. 2100), 60km/37 miles north of Cairns, is reached on the Cook Highway, a scenic coast road which runs between beaches and rain forest-covered hills which reach down almost to the sea.

Port Douglas was founded during the opening up of the far north of Queensland, and in those days was a serious competitor of Cairns as a port for supplying the goldfields on the Palmer and Hodgkinson Rivers; but when a railway was laid from the goldfields to Cairns Port Douglas's great days were over. Its decline was hastened by a devastating cyclone in 1911.

In recent years, however, the increasing numbers of visitors to the far north have given the town a new lease of life and its population has risen sharply. The sleepy little village has now become a luxury holiday resort.

Accommodation
Several resort complexes, many hotels, motels and caravan/camping parks.

Features
All the town's old buildings were destroyed in the 1911 cyclone with the exception of the old Courthouse of 1879 and the Courthouse Hotel (1880) in Wharf Street.

From the Flagstaff Hill Lookout there are breathtaking views of the beach and the Coral Sea. The Shipwreck Museum on Ben Cropp's Wharf displays relics of wrecked ships.

Surroundings
Port Douglas is attractively situated, with a beautiful beach (Four Mile Beach) and a wide range of entertainments and excursions on offer. An old steam train, the Bally Hooley Sugar Train, runs through the canefields to the sugar mill at Mossman (see entry). Other possibilities are tours in the rain forest (visit the Rainforest Habitat), expeditions in four-wheel-drive vehicles to Daintree National Park (see Mossman) and farther north through the rugged landscape of the Cape York Peninsula (see entry), and boat trips to Cooktown and the Great Barrier Reef (see entries).

Quilpie H 5

Situation and characteristics
Quilpie (pop. 760), on the Bulloo River in the Channel Country outback, 180km/112 miles west of Charleville, is a centre for the large sheep and cattle stations in the area. It is chiefly famed for the opals found here (boulder opals).

The little town can be reached by way of the asphalted Diamantina Developmental Road from Charleville or by rail, but to see the opal-mining area involves a drive in a 4WD vehicle. In summer it can be almost intolerably hot.

Accommodation
Hotels, motels, caravan/camping park.

Features
St Finbarr's Church (R.C.) has an altar, font and lectern made from opal-bearing rock.

Ravenshoe J 3

Situation and characteristics
Ravenshoe (pop. 1000) is the highest town in Queensland (alt. 915m/3002ft). It lies on the Atherton Tableland in a magnificent setting amid luxuriant rain forests.

Tully Gorge National Park

Location; area
24km/15 miles south of Ravenshoe; 502 hectares/1240 acres.

Best time to visit
Winter.

Access
Surfaced road from Ravenshoe.

Accommodation
In Ravenshoe.

Facilities
Picnic area, walking trail.

Features
The Tully River carries less water than it used to following the construction of the dam at Koombooloomba to power a hydro-electric station, but the gorge it has hewn through a rain forest-covered plateau shows the force it exerted in the past. There is a walking trail leading to a good viewpoint.

Ravenswood J 4

Situation and characteristics
70km/43 miles east of Charters Towers is Ravenswood, a well preserved old gold-mining town. It is reached on a side road which branches off the Flinders Highway at Mingela and runs south.

Old house fronts, Rockhampton

There are a number of handsome old hotels, still operating. A small museum displays old gold-mining equipment.

★Rockhampton K 4

Situation and characteristics

Rockhampton (pop. 63,000) – "Rockie" to local people – lies on the Fitzroy River some 650km/405 miles north-west of Brisbane on the Bruce Highway 40km/25 miles inland. The Tropic of Capricorn runs through the town. Rockhampton is called the beef capital of Australia, with over 2 million head of cattle in the surrounding area, and huge figures of cattle greet visitors at the north and south entrances to the town. New disease-resistant breeds have been produced by cross-breeding.

Accommodation

Numerous hotels, motels and caravan/camping parks.

Features

Rockhampton has many well preserved 19th-century public buildings, private houses and churches, recalling the one-time importance of the town as a port for central Queensland.

In Quay Street, which runs parallel to the Fitzroy River, there are over 20 buildings under statutory protection as national monuments. One of the finest is the Criterion Hotel (corner of Quay Street and Fitzroy Street), built in 1889 on the site of the old Bush Inn of 1857, the year in which the town was founded. The Customs House (begun 1898) in Quay Street is a fine example of neo-classical architecture with a copper dome and a semi-circular portico. The Heritage Tavern, originally the Commercial Hotel (1898), is a handsome three-storey building with rich wrought-iron decoration.

The Post Office, at the corner of East and Denham Streets, is a striking building with arcading and a clock-tower. Other notable buildings are Archer Park Station in Denison Street and the Supreme Court (1887) in

Fitzroy Street. Among the old churches St Andrew's (1893; Bolsover Street/Derby Street), St Paul's Cathedral (1887–93; Alma Street/William Street) and St Joseph's Cathedral (1899; William Street) are fine examples of Queensland architecture.

Broad, tree-lined streets and parks and gardens gay with flowers add to the charm of Rockhampton. The Botanic Gardens in Spencer Street, established in 1869, are one of the finest subtropical parks in Australia, with the Murray Lagoon, home to countless water birds, orchid and fern houses, walk-through aviaries, a small zoo and a Japanese garden.

Surroundings

On the Bruce Highway, at the turn-off for Yeppoon, is the Aboriginal Dreamtime Cultural Centre, one of the most interesting institutions of its kind in Australia.

Round the town are a number of old farms which have been in the same family for generations: the Glenmore Homestead in Parkhurst, 12km/7½ miles north; the Gracemere Homestead, just off the Capricorn Highway, 11km/7 miles south-west; and St Aubin's Village and Herb Farm, Canoona Road, near the airport.

Other features of interest round Rockhampton are the limestone caves in the Berserker Range (e.g. the Cammoo Caves and Olsen's Capricorn Caverns, 23km/14 miles north) and the old mining town of Mount Morgan (see entry), 38km/24 miles south-west on the Burnett Highway.

40km/25 miles north-east of Rockhampton are the beautiful beaches of Yeppoon and Emu Park (see entries), with the "Singing Ship" monument to Captain Cook at Emu Park. Great Keppel Island (see entry), a popular holiday island, lies 13km/8 miles off the Capricorn Coast.

Roma J 5

Situation and characteristics

Roma (pop. 7000), the largest town in southern central Queensland, lies at the junction of the Warrego and Carnarvon Highways, 260km/160 miles from Dalby and 460km/285 miles from Brisbane. The town was founded immediately after the separation of Queensland from New South Wales, and was named after the wife of the first governor of Queensland, Sir George Bowen. Thereafter it rapidly developed into the centre of a large cattle and sheep farming district.

Accommodation

Several hotels, motels and caravan/camping parks.

Surroundings

A tarred road (250km/155 miles; last 50km/30 miles an unsurfaced track) runs north from Roma by way of Injune to the Carnarvon National Park (see entry).

Shute Harbour J 4

Situation and characteristics

Shute Harbour (pop. under 200), part of the town of Whitsunday (see entry), lies 35km/22 miles north-east of Proserpine in a picturesque bay on the fringes of Conway National Park (see Airlie Beach). From a hill above the bay there are superb views of the Whitsunday Passage and some of the more than 70 Whitsunday Islands (see entry), only seven of which are inhabited. From the landing-stage in the harbour a swarm of catamarans, motorboats and yachts take day trippers and holidaymakers out to the hotels and resort complexes on the inhabited islands and scuba divers, snorkellers, reef walkers and sun-lovers to lonely beaches on uninhabited islands and the banks of coral. Cruises on sailing ships lasting several days and flights to the outer reef (Hardy Lagoon) are also on offer. The colourful corals and fishes on the reef can be observed from glass-bottomed boats or, close-up, by scuba divers and snorkellers.

Accommodation

Motels and caravan/camping parks.

Resort complex, Shute Harbour

Simpson Desert National Park G 5

Location; area
100km/60 miles west of Birdsville, 1550km/965 miles west of Brisbane; 700,000 hectares/1,700,000 acres.

Best time to visit
July to September; in summer it is too hot and too dry.

Access
Via Birdsville (4WD vehicles only).

Facilities
Bush camping (permit required). No facilities for visitors.

Features
Simpson Desert National Park lies in south-western Queensland, on the borders of South Australia and the Northern Territory. It is a region of sandy hills and ranges of dunes up to 30m/100ft high extending for long distances from south-east to north-west. There is a scanty vegetation cover of tussock grassland in which a few desert animals live. After the occasional showers of rain the ground is carpeted with flowers, attracting great flocks of birds.

Warning
For travelling in the hostile environment of the Simpson Desert, proper equipment and outback experience are essential.

Springbrook National Park K 5

Location; area
100km/60 miles south of Brisbane; 2159 hectares/5333 acres.

Best time to visit
Spring and autumn.

Access
Easily reached from Brisbane on the Pacific Highway and from Southport, Surfers Paradise and Burleigh Heads via Mudgereeba.

Facilities
Bush camping; picnic areas, walking trails.

Features
Springbrook National Park is within easy reach for a day trip from the Gold Coast (see entry). It was created by the amalgamation of the smaller reserves of Gwongorella, Warrie, Mount Cougal and Mount Wunburra. The park is dominated by the imposing rock faces (up to 900m/3000ft high) and

gorges of the McPherson Range. There are expanses of rain forest and many orchids, and a rich and varied bird life.

From walking trails in the park there are fine views of the hills and the coasts.

Warning
Mount Cougal and Mount Wunburra should be tackled only by experienced rock-climbers.

Stanthorpe K 5

Situation and characteristics
Stanthorpe (pop. 5000), 225km/140 miles south-west of Brisbane, is the main town in the Granite Belt, the chain of hills running along the boundary between New South Wales and Queensland. Lying at an altitude of over 800m/2625ft, it has the lowest temperatures in Queensland, but the climate and the soil are suitable for the growing of fruit and wine grapes (wineries can be inspected; wine tasting). In spring there is a glorious show of blossom on the fruit-trees, and many species of orchids grow in the area.

Accommodation
Several hotels, motels and caravan/camping parks.

Surroundings
Within easy reach are the Girraween and Sundown National Parks with their impressive granite crags (see below) and Bald Rock National Park in New South Wales (see entry).

Girraween National Park

Location; area
34km/21 miles south of Stanthorpe; 11,000 hectares/27,000 acres.

Best time to visit
Spring (when flowers are in bloom).

Facilities
Camping ground, bush camping; picnic areas, walking trails, visitor centre.

Features
Girraween National Park lies at the north end of the New England plateau, on the borders of New South Wales. The park's average altitude of 900m/2950ft with its winter frosts has led to heavy weathering of the rock, producing bizarrely shaped granite crags and huge oval boulders piled up on one another. The flora of the park is closer to that of the cooler south than to the rest of Queensland. In charming contrast are the eucalyptus forests, the marsh flora and the bushes which cling to clefts in the rock right up to the summit of Mount Norman (1267m/4157ft). In spring there are great expanses of many-coloured wild flowers.

Walking trails
From the visitor centre near the two camping grounds there are a number of walking trails of varying length (Granite Arch Track, Mount Norman).

Sundown National Park

Location; area
85km/53 miles south-west of Stanthorpe, on the border with New South Wales; 11,200 hectares/27,700 acres.

Best time to visit
Spring and autumn.

Access
Via the road from Stanthorpe to Glenlyon (in dry weather only). From the New England Highway via Ballandean, to the north (4WD vehicles only).

Facilities
Camping grounds, bush camping; ranger station, barbecue areas, toilets, showers.

Features
This is an area of rugged gorges on the Severn River and dense forests. There are no roads or trails, but it is possible to walk along the streams in the park (though care must be taken not to lose your bearings).

Stradbroke Islands K 5

Situation and characteristics
South and North Stradbroke Islands were a single island until 1896, when a cyclone swept away the sandbank between the two, leaving a channel which was given the name of Jumpinpin.

Access

There are ferries (cars carried) from Redland Bay and Cleveland to Dunwich on North Stradbroke Island and day trips from Southport to South Stradbroke Island.

Accommodation

Resort complexes, a motel and many caravan/camping parks (only on North Stradbroke Island).

★North Stradbroke Island

North Stradbroke Island, affectionately known as "Straddie", is a popular holiday island on Moreton Bay (see entry), only 40km/25 miles east of Brisbane. The normal population of 3000 is increased at the height of the holiday season by anything up to 40,000 visitors. The landscape, however, is still unspoiled, with mangrove swamps, freshwater lakes (Blue Lake National Park), expanses of bush country and very beautiful beaches. On the island are the three small settlements of Amity Point at the north-western tip, Dunwich (established in 1828 as a quarantine station for immigrants) and Point Lookout (with the only hotel on the island) at the north-eastern corner, where there are cliffs with impressive surf.

Blue Lake National Park

10km/6 miles east of Dunwich is the entrance to Blue Lake National Park, an area of 500 hectares/1250 acres centred on Lake Kaboora, which is surrounded by eucalyptus woodland. From the entrance to the park it is a half-hour walk to the lake and the surf beach (Main Beach). No visitor facilities. Best times to visit: spring and autumn.

South Stradbroke Island

The long and almost uninhabited South Stradbroke Island extends southwards, near to Southport on the Gold Coast (see entry), with excellent facilities for water sports in the sheltered Broadwater.

★Sugar Coast K 4/5

Situation and characteristics

The stretch of Hervey Bay between Maryborough and Bundaberg, sheltered by the 120km/75-mile long Fraser Island (see entries), is known as the Sugar Coast. It is a popular holiday area, particularly for families, with no dangerous surf. There are boat trips to Fraser Island, combined with 4WD tours of the island on its sandy tracks, and a variety of other day trips. The principal places on the Sugar Coast are Maryborough, an important port and industrial town in the late 19th century, and Bundaberg, an important sugar town at the north end of Hervey Bay (see entries).

★★Sunshine Coast K 5

Situation and characteristics

The second great tourist and holiday area in southern Queensland after the Gold Coast (see entry) is the Sunshine Coast, which extends north for more than 50km/30 miles from Caloundra (see entry), 90km/55 miles north of Brisbane, to Noosa (see entry). Long beaches of beautiful white sand are interrupted by stretches of rocky coast. The Sunshine Coast, with a population of around 120,000, is less commercialised, less spoiled and quieter than the Gold Coast. Although there are only occasional high-rise hotel or apartment blocks there is a good deal of building going on, particularly at Noosa. Here, as on the Gold Coast and the Great Barrier Reef, the increasing popularity of the Queensland coasts with holidaymakers is all too obvious. There is impressive coastal scenery, with quiet sheltered waters as well as magnificent surfing beaches but Queensland, with its subtropical climate, has the advantage over Australia's south coast, of making water sports and other outdoor activities possible throughout the year. Average maximum temperatures of over 20°C/68°F in winter make a holiday or retirement home in Queensland an attractive proposition for many Australians.

The landscape of the Sunshine Coast is very varied, with sandy bays bounded by steep cliffs and areas of natural bush country, and quiet coastal waters and rivers offering an alternative to the surf of the ocean.

Twin Waters Hotel, on the Sunshine Coast

The business centre of the Sunshine Coast is Maroochydore (see entry) at the mouth of the Maroochy River. To the north of Maroochydore are the resorts of Coolum Beach, Peregian Beach, Marcus Beach and Sunshine Beach.

Access

There are airfields on the Sunshine Coast at Caloundra, Maroochydore and Noosa. The railway from Brisbane to Gympie runs through the hinterland of the Sunshine Coast via Nambour and direct buses from Brisbane to the various resorts. The road to Caloundra branches off the Bruce Highway, and a coast road leads to Noosa. A new Sunshine Motorway runs from the Maroochy River to Noosa.

Accommodation

The whole coastal region is well equipped with accommodation for visitors in all categories, with numerous caravan/camping parks, youth hostels, motels, holiday apartments and luxurious villas.

Tamborine National Park K 5

Location; area

75km/47 miles south of Brisbane; 630 hectares/1555 acres.

Best time to visit

Spring (for wild flowers) and autumn.

Access

From Brisbane on the Pacific Highway; from the Gold Coast via Oxenford.

Facilities

Picnic areas, walking trails.

Features

Tamborine National Park, a popular destination for day trips from Brisbane, was formed by the amalgamation of a number of smaller separate reserves (Cedar Creek Falls, Joalah, The Knoll, Witches Falls, Macrozamia Grove, McDonald Park and Palm Grove). Witches Falls National Park (area 130 hectares/320 acres), established in 1908, was the first National Park in Queensland; the other seven, on the northern slopes of Mount Tamborine, came later.

The park takes in an area of rain forest vegetation with a number of waterfalls and good viewpoints. At many points there are opportunities for wildlife viewing.

Taroom J 5

Situation and characteristics

Taroom (pop. 750), the centre of a cattle-raising area, lies on the Dawson River, 134km/83 miles north of Miles on the Leichhardt Highway.

Ludwig Leichhardt (see Famous People) passed this way in 1844 on his expedition from Dalby to the north and carved his initials on a tree (still to be seen in the main street). The local Aboriginals put up a bitter resistance to white settlement, launching a raid on Hornet Bank in 1857 which was followed by bloody reprisals.

Accommodation

Caravan/camping park.

Isla Gorge National Park

Location; area

59km/37 miles north of Taroom on the Leichhardt Highway; 7800 hectares/19,300 acres.

Best time to visit

Spring and autumn.

Access

From Theodore or Taroom; the park lies directly on the highway.

Facilities

Camping grounds; picnic areas.

Features

The park takes in an area of deeply indented gorges and sandstone rock walls. On the highway is a rest area, from which there are various walks and bush trails.

Thursday Island H 2

Situation and characteristics

Off Cape York in the Torres Strait, extending across the strait almost to the coast of Papua New Guinea, are numerous islands which belong to Australia but are mainly inhabited by Melanesians (population around 9000). Thursday Island (area 3.5sq.km/1⅓sq.miles), 39km/25 miles off the tip of the Cape York Peninsula (see entry) and 2000km/1370 miles from Brisbane as the crow flies, is the most northerly administrative centre in Queensland. In addition to Melanesians (Torres Strait Islanders) the population includes Aborigines and Asians. In the 19th century the island was a centre of pearl-fishing, the mother-of-pearl industry and trepang-gathering.

Access

There are regular air services between Cairns and Thursday Island; the airfield is on the neighbouring Horn Island. By sea, there are regular cruises from Cairns to Thursday Island and back, and a ferry service from Bamaga at the tip of Cape York, with boats picking up passengers at Pundsand Bay.

Features

There are a number of handsome 19th-century buildings – the Quetta Memorial Church (built in 1893 to commemorate the sinking of the "Quetta" off the island in 1890), the Courthouse (1876) and the Grand and Federal Hotels. In the north of the island is a cemetery containing the graves of many pearl-fishers and Melanesians.

★ Toowoomba K 5

Situation and characteristics

Toowoomba (pop. 80,000), the largest town in the interior of Queensland and an important administrative and commercial centre, lies at a height of 600m/2000ft on the edge of the Great Dividing Range, 130km/80 miles west of Brisbane. It is the gateway to the fertile Darling Downs, an undulating tableland ranging in height between 400m/1300ft and 700m/2300ft. From the 1840s onwards it was an important staging-point for cattle-drovers coming from the great expanses of grazing to the west.

Accommodation

Many motels and caravan/camping parks.

Features

Toowoomba has preserved a number of handsome 19th-century buildings both public and private. The Royal Bull's Head Inn in Brisbane Street was opened in the mid-19th century as an inn and later became the post office of the Drayton district. The Smithfield Homestead, a Victorian villa in Panda Street, is now an elegant restaurant. Side by side in Margaret Street are the Post Office of 1878 and the Courthouse from the same period. In Ruthven Street is the Town Hall (1900), with a clock-tower, which contains the City Art Gallery and a theatre. Clifford House in Russell Street, originally built as a club, is now a restaurant.

Toowoomba also has the Lionel Lindsay Gallery of Australian Art and Literature in Jellico Street. In Parker Street, in the Drayton district, is the Early Settlers Museum. The Cobb & Co. Museum in Lindsay Street traces the history of horse-drawn vehicles. Three notable old churches are St Patrick's Cathedral (R.C.), St Luke's Cathedral (Anglican) and St Matthew's in Drayton.

Surroundings

There are a number of scenic drives into the country round Toowoomba (signposted as Tourist Routes 1 and 2). There are viewpoints at Picnic Point, Webb Park, Prince Henry Drive, Mount Lofty and Mount Kynoch on signposted routes through the town and to the impressive escarpment of the Great Dividing Range.

★Townsville J 3

Situation and characteristics

Townsville (pop. 97,000), the most important town in northern Queensland, lies on Cleveland Bay at the foot of Castle Hill, a granite crag 300m/1000ft high, 1450km/900 miles north of Brisbane. The largest tropical town in Australia, which successfully combines its 19th-century heritage with the achievements and the buildings of the present day, it was founded in 1864 as a port for the shipment of the agricultural produce of the hinterland. The port project was financed by John Black and Robert Towns,

A typical old Queensland house in Townsville

and the town, originally called Cleveland Bay, was renamed Townsville in 1865 after a visit by Robert Towns.

Townsville is now an important industrial town (metal-processing) and commercial centre, with a considerable trade with South-East Asia. It is also an excellent base for excursions and tours, particularly to Magnetic Island (see below).

Access

Townsville has a large airport linking it with all parts of Australia and with countries overseas. It also has good rail and bus connections and a municipal bus service.

After heavy falls of rain in summer some roads may become impassable through flooding.

Accommodation

Large numbers of hotels, motels and caravan/camping parks.

Events

The ten-day Paciific Festival takes place annually in September/October.

Information

Information about what to see and what's on in Townsville can be obtained from the Southern Information Centre on the Bruce Highway, Enterprise House (3 The Strand), and the information kiosk in Flinders Mall. The offices of the Royal Automobile Club of Queensland (RACQ) are in Ross River Road in the Aitkenvale district.

Sights in Townsville

Flinders Street

The town's main street is Flinders Street, which has many handsome buildings of the colonial period; part of the street is now a pedestrian zone (Flinders Mall). Among the most notable buildings are the Australian Bank of Commerce (1888), the Cabaret Restaurant, Magnetic House (1887–88), the National Bank (1880) and the Post Office (1886), whose original clock-tower was pulled down during the Second World War and replaced in 1964 by a tower with a copper dome.

Strand

In the Strand, which runs along the waterfront, are the Criterion Hotel (1904), the Queen's Hotel (1900s; now the Radio and Television Centre) and the Customs House (1900–02). Note also the handsome bandstand of 1913, with rich wrought-iron decoration, in Anzac Park, between the Strand and the boating harbour.

Old districts

In the old districts round the harbour are many old private houses in typical Queensland style, built on stilts to promote the circulation of air and provide shade in the heat of the day but often so covered with a lush growth of vegetation that the open structure of the house is concealed. The deep roofed terraces and ventilation openings in the roof are also designed to mitigate the heat. Many such houses are to be seen in Castling Street.

The former Magistrates' Courthouse (1876) at the corner of Sturt Street and Stokes Street is now a community information centre.

Another handsome relic of earlier times is the Victoria Bridge, a swing bridge over Ross Creek.

At the foot of Castle Hill (Stanley Street) is the brick-built neo-Gothic Cathedral of the Sacred Heart (1902).

Castle Hill

From steep-sided Castle Hill there are magnificent views of the town and the harbour. A good tarred road winds its way up to the summit.

The modern town

Townsville also has a number of handsome modern buildings. On the Western Breakwater (Sir Leslie Thiess Drive) is the Sheraton Breakwater Casino, the only casino in northern Queensland, which offers a variety of other attractions as well as the gaming rooms.

Great Barrier Reef Wonderland

Another magnet for visitors is the Great Barrier Reef Wonderland (open: daily 9am–5pm; admission charge), with an underwater tunnel of acrylic glass which gives visitors a close-up view of the wonderful underwater world of the coral reefs, with a colourful variety of fish (including sharks). In the same complex are the Omnimax Theatre, which shows three-dimensional films, the Museum of Tropical Queensland and ferry terminals to Magnetic Island.

A sandy bay on Magnetic Island

Parks and gardens

The town owes much of its charm to its many parks and private gardens with their luxuriant tropical flowers and fruits. The Queen's Park in Warburton Street is one of the town's oldest public parks. Adjoining are the Queen's Gardens, a botanic garden established in 1870.

Education and research

Townsville is also an important educational and cultural centre. In addition to the Institute of Education to the south of the town there is the impressive complex of the James Cook University, the first in Australia to offer a course of studies in tourism.

The Australian Institute of Marine Science which is attached to the University is one of the world's leading research institutes in the field of marine biology. The head office of the Great Barrier Reef Marine Park Authority is also in Townsville.

Surroundings of Townsville

Excursions

Townsville is a good base for day trips and longer cruises to the Great Barrier Reef, to Hinchinbrook, Orpheus and Bedarra Islands and to Magnetic Island, only 8km/5 miles away.

★Magnetic Island

Situation and characteristics

Magnetic Island has an area of 52sq.km/20sq.miles, about 70% of which is a National Park. Its highest point is Mount Cook (497ft/1731ft). The island has a resident population of just over 2000, but this is multiplied many times during the holiday season. The best times to visit the island are autumn and spring.

The island was given its name by Cook, whose compass went wrong when he sailed past it in 1770. During the 19th century a number of small holiday resorts were established along the east coast; at the end of the century tourists began to come and a ferry service was started.

Access

From the landing-stage in Flinders Street East, near the Great Barrier Reef Wonderland, ferries (including car ferries) take less than half an hour to reach Magnetic Island and its chief town, Picnic Bay. There are so many competing services that it is worth while shopping around for the best price. There are buses between Picnic Bay and Horseshoe Bay.

Accommodation

Magnetic Island has a wide range of accommodation for visitors in all price categories.

Features

The east side of the island is well developed, with tarred roads. From Picnic Bay a road runs along the coast to Horseshoe Bay. The north and west coasts can be reached only on walking trails. Within the National Park itself a huge bird sanctuary, and occupying more than two-thirds of the island, is Mount Cook (497m/1631ft), from which there are superb views. The island can be explored on numerous walking trails. There are beaches and resort complexes on Picnic Bay, Nelly Bay, Arcadia, Horseshoe Bay, Radical Bay and Alma Bay (though bathing is dangerous between October and April because of box jellyfishes). There are also good diving grounds. A particular attraction is Shark World, a salt-water aquarium on Nelly Bay (open: daily 9am–6pm; sharks fed daily at 11.30am and 2pm; admission charge) and there is also a Koala Sanctuary.

Surroundings

The fortifications above Florence Bay date from the Second World War.

From Magnetic Island there are excursions to the outer reef and the Palm Islands.

★Bowling Green Bay National Park

Location; area

30km/19 miles south-east of Townsville; 55,000 hectares/135,850 acres.

Best time to visit

Autumn, winter and spring.

Access

Road to Mount Elliot area off Bruce Highway 24km/15 miles south of Townsville. To Cape Cleveland area, track off Bruce Highway 34km/21 miles south of Townsville (in wet weather only with 4WD vehicle).

Facilities

Camping grounds; bush camping (with permit, obtainable in Townsville); picnic areas.

Features

Bowling Green Bay National Park consists of a rugged, hilly wilderness and a lowland area in the delta of the Burdekin River, with mangrove swamps and salt-pans, extending to Cape Bowling Green. The areas of marsh and deposits of mud are constantly growing, providing nesting sites for large numbers of water birds. There are two granite hills in the park, Mount Elliot in the south and Cape Cleveland in the north. In the wetter areas round the hills there are the most southerly expanses of tropical rain forest in Australia. There is a popular bathing-place on Alligator Creek, from which a walking trail follows the river to a waterfall.

Tropic of Capricorn B–K 4

Situation and characteristics

The Tropic of Capricorn, which runs immediately south of Rockhampton, is marked on the Bruce Highway by a tower.

The Tropic is also a climatic frontier. The territory to the north has warm, dry winters, while to the south winters are usually cool and wet. The whole region is notorious for long periods of drought and for deluges of rain.

The Capricorn Highway and the railway from Rockhampton via Emerald to Longreach (675km/420 miles; see entries) in the interior run roughly parallel to the Tropic.

★Warwick K 5

Situation and characteristics

Warwick (pop. 10,600) lies at the junction of the Cunningham and New England Highways, 160km/100 miles south-west of Brisbane and 80km/50 miles south of Toowoomba.

Accommodation
Many hotels, motels and caravan/camping parks.

Features
Warwick has a number of notable 19th-century buildings – the Courthouse (1886), the Post Office (1891), the Town Hall (1888), with a clock-tower, the National Hotel (1890) and Pringle Cottage (1863), now a museum.

Warwick's situation above the Condamine River at an altitude of 450m/1475ft is good for rose-growing, and thousands of rose-bushes in gardens and parks and along the main road justify its claim to be the city of roses. A rodeo held annually in October attracts many visitors.

Surroundings
Within easy reach of Warwick are the Leslie Dam, an artificial lake 15km/9 miles west and two National Parks on the borders of New South Wales to the south, Main Range National Park (see entry) on the Cunningham Highway in the direction of Brisbane (60km/37 miles) and Queen Mary Falls National Park (see below),

Queen Mary Falls National Park

Location; area
48km/30 miles south-east of Warwick; 333 hectares/823 acres.

Best time to visit
Spring and autumn.

Access
On New England Highway or Cunningham Highway.

Accommodation
In Warwick.

Facilities
No camping; car park, picnic and barbecue area.

Features
Queen Mary Falls National Park takes in a hilly region on Spring Creek, a tributary of the Condamine River. Its particular attractions are the falls from which it takes its name and the gorge on the river. Walking trails with fine panoramic views.

Whitsunday J 4

Situation and characteristics
The name Whitsunday is applied to the resorts of Airlie Beach (see entry), Cannonvale and Shute Harbour (see entry), situated on the mainland opposite the Whitsunday Islands (see entry). Its economy depends mainly on the tourist and holiday trade, which brings over 500,000 visitors annually to the area.

Accommodation
Many hotels, motels and caravan/camping parks.

Surroundings
Excursions to the Great Barrier Reef, the Whitsunday Islands (see entries) and Conway National Park (see Airlie Beach).

Whitsunday Islands J 4

Situation and characteristics
The Whitsunday group consists of some 70 islands lying within a 50km/30 miles radius of Shute Harbour (see entry), the main jumping-off point for trips to the islands, perhaps the best-known group, and the best equipped to cater for tourists, in the Great Barrier Reef area.

The islands were given their name by Captain Cook, who sailed between them (through what is now known as the Whitsunday Passage) at Whitsun 1770. The name is not quite correct, for Cook in writing his log forgot that he had crossed the international date line. He did not at first observe the outer reef, some 60km/37 miles from Shute Harbour – though he had been surprised at the unusually calm sea – and noticed it only when his ship, the "Endeavour", ran aground on the reef off Cooktown which thereafter was known as the Endeavour Reef.

The Whitsunday Islands are continental islands, the summits of a coastal range of hills emerging from the sea which has submerged them. All but five of them have been declared National Parks. On the mainland opposite the islands is Conway National Park (see Airlie Beach).

A paradislac island world: the Whitsunday Islands

Daydream Island

Situation and characteristics

Daydream Island, also known as West Molle, is the smallest island in the Whitsunday group, with an area of only 10 hectares/25 acres. It is covered with dense rain forest vegetation, with hills up to 50m/165ft high.

Accommodation

There is a recently built resort complex. Watersports, coral viewing and reef fishing.

Access

By boat from Shute Harbour or via Hamilton Island.

★Hamilton Island

Situation and characteristics

Although it has an area of only 6sq.km (less than 2½sq.miles), Hamilton is the island in the Whitsunday group best equipped to cater for tourists, with 2500 beds in apartment complexes and two high-rise hotels. In addition there are many day trippers to the island during the holiday season.

Access

Hamilton's excellent communications also contribute to its popularity as a holiday area. Its airport has a runway which can take large jet aircraft, in contrast to the other holiday islands whose airstrips are suitable only for light aircraft. There are flights to Hamilton Island from all the Australian capitals (Ansett and Eastwest Airlines). Negotiations are in progress on landing rights for direct flights from New Zealand, Tokyo and Singapore, and it is to be expected that the island will one day have an international airport.

Hamilton Island is also easily accessible by sea. There are regular services by fast catamarans from Shute Harbour on the mainland; the crossing takes 30 minutes.

Resort complex

In picturesque Catseye Bay with its marvellously beautiful beach is a modern resort complex (children welcome). On the slopes above the water are a white villa belonging to Keith Williams, one of the "discoverers" of the island as a holiday resort, a Polynesian-style house which can be rented and the former holiday home of ex-Beatle George Harrison. Beyond a hill is the harbour area, with shops, boutiques, restaurants, a night club and a supermarket, all designed in typical Queensland style.

Sport

Hamilton Island offers opportunities for every conceivable form of sport. On the main island there are tennis and squash courts, a fitness centre and facilities for all kinds of water sports (swimming, water-skiing, windsurfing, parasailing, etc.). Visitors can hire small dinghies, sailing boats, large yachts, with or without crew, and catamarans, and they can learn to dive. The spacious marina has moorings for 400 boats and yachts.

Excursions

A popular excursion is through the hills in the north of the island to the fauna park on the coast. Apart from the descendants of the goats which in the past were left on the island to provide subsistence for shipwrecked mariners and of the red deer which were formerly raised here the animals are mainly Australian species – kangaroos, koalas, dingoes, crocodiles, Tasmanian devils and innumerable brightly coloured lorikeets and white and yellow cockatoos. The cockatoos have almost become the island's heraldic emblem, and it is because of them that the flower tubs on the balconies of houses have to be protected by wire netting. The two trained dolphins in a large pool are a very popular attraction. It is planned to construct a large walk-through oceanarium in the harbour area which will allow visitors to get a close-up view of the marvellous underwater world of the coral reefs.

There are pleasant walks on the island through almost unspoiled natural surroundings, with steep-sided hills, the highest of which is Passage Peak (230m/755ft), with magnificent panoramic views from the top. For those who would find the ascent in the tropical sun too strenuous there is the One Tree Hill Lookout on the way to the fauna park, from which there are fine views over the island and Catseye Bay.

Near this viewpoint is a small white church in Queensland style, All Saints, to which many young couples, particularly from Japan, come to be married; and indeed the island as a whole is a favourite with young Japanese honeymooners.

Opposite the little church is the Motorcycle Museum, housing the large collection assembled by Keith Williams, who started life as a designer of motorcycle racecourses.

★Hayman Island

Situation and characteristics

This continental island (i.e. an island on the continental shelf), the most northerly of the inhabited islands in the Whitsunday group, has an area of 4sq.km/1½sq.miles, with hills rising to 250m/820ft. Hayman was one of the first islands on the reef to be developed for tourism (from 1935 onwards), originally for fishing holidays. The American writer Zane Grey, who was a keen fisherman, helped to make the island known. In 1950 an attractive hotel was built on Hayman, and in 1985 this was enlarged and remodelled, at great expense, as a highly exclusive and luxurious resort complex set in a magically beautiful landscape.

Access

Hayman Island can be reached from Shute Harbour either by boat or by air; from Hamilton Island the transfer from the airport can be by luxury yacht.

Excursions

Hayman Island offers a wide range of water sports and charming excursions to the outer reef. There are beautiful walking trails through the forest to the Whitsunday Lookout and Cook's Lookout. A number of tiny uninhabited islets off the main island can be reached on foot at low tide.

Hook Island

Situation and characteristics

Hook Island is also a continental island, with an area of 53sq.km/20sq.miles, hills rising to 454m/1490ft and beautiful beaches. There are safe anchorages in two long fjord-like inlets on the south coast, Nara and Macona Inlets.

There are camping grounds on Macona Inlet and elsewhere in the National Park (Stonehaven, Butterfly Bay). At the south-eastern tip of the island is a modest resort complex, with an underwater observatory (open: daily).

Accommodation

Lindeman Island

Situation and characteristics

Lindeman Island, with an area of 8sqkm/3sq.miles and hills rising to 210m/689ft, is popular with families, since it offers a great variety of activities for children, including an adventure playground. Unlike some of the other islands (e.g. Hamilton), it is not overcrowded, being too remote for day trips and cruises. It has facilities for many kinds of sport, particularly water sports, and also has a beautiful golf course. There are 20km/12½ miles of walking trails, all starting from the little island airstrip. The island has a varied flora and fauna and a Butterfly Valley. From the top of Mount Oldfield there are magnificent views.

Access

Lindeman can be reached by light aircraft from Mackay, Proserpine and Townsville and by boat from Shute Harbour and Hamilton Island.

Accommodation

Hotel (resort complex).

Excursions

To the neighbouring islands of Seaforth and Shaw.

Long Island

Situation and characteristics

Long Island, also known as Molle Island, has an area of 12sq.km/4½sq.miles and hills rising to 270m/886ft. This long, narrow island lying close to the coast is separated from the mainland only by a narrow channel (strong currents). There are 13km/8 miles of walking trails. The beaches on the west coast are sandy, on the east coast rocky.

Access

By boat from Shute Harbour or Hamilton Island. There are good anchorages for yachts.

Accommodation

An old holiday village dating from the 1930s has been redeveloped as three comfortable resort complexes known as Kontiki, Palm Bay and Paradise Bay.

Warning

Between November and March bathing in the sea is dangerous because of box jellyfish.

South Molle Island

Situation and characteristics

South Molle is a continental island with an area of 4sq.km/1½sq.miles and hills rising to 198m/650ft. Much of its area has been declared a National Park, and the vegetation has now recovered from earlier over-grazing. It has long beaches of sand and coral and a number of short walking trails. The island lies in the middle of the Whitsunday group, of which there are fine views from Mount Jeffreys, Spion Knob and the Balancing Rock. It was named after George Molle, governor of New South Wales (1815). The island is forest-covered in the north, round the resort complex, and in the extreme south; the centre is largely covered by grassland. It is home to many species of birds. There are facilities for many types of sport, diving instruction and a variety of other leisure activities. The island is well suited for family holidays with children.

Access

Reached most easily by boat or helicopter from Hamilton Island. There are also boats from Shute Harbour.

Accommodation

Resort complex (400 beds) run by Ansett Airlines.

★Whitsunday Island

Situation and characteristics

Whitsunday Island, the uninhabited main island in the group (area 109sq.km/42sq.miles), is separated from Hook Island by a narrow channel. It has good beaches and diving grounds, a network of walking trails and a notably rich flora and fauna.

Access
Regular boat service from Shute Harbour; cruise ships also take passengers to the island.

Accommodation
Bush camping.

Winton H 4

Situation and characteristics
The outback town of Winton (pop. 1200), 340km/210 miles south-east of Cloncurry on the Landsborough Highway, is famed as the birthplace of the Australian national airline, Qantas, which established its headquarters here in 1920, later moving to Longreach (see entry), 180km/112 miles south. It also has associations with "Banjo" Paterson (see Famous People), who wrote his famous ballad "Waltzing Matilda" in 1895 at the Dagworth Station (100km/62 miles north-west of Winton). The song, which has almost become Australia's national anthem, is believed to be based on an actual incident at the Combo water-hole in the Dagworth area.

Winton lies in an extensive sheep-farming area, and it was one of the scenes of the great sheep-shearers' strike in 1891. The wool was formerly carried in ox-carts to Winton for onward transport by rail; nowadays it is mainly cattle from the Channel Country and the Northern Territory that are brought to Winton by huge road trains for loading on to the railway.

The town's water supply comes from deep artesian bores at a temperature of 70°C/158°F.

Accommodation
Hotels, motels, caravan/camping park.

Features
The town's main features of interest are the Quantilda Pioneer Museum (irregular opening hours) and the statue of a swagman near the swimming pool, commemorating the early settlers.

Bladensburg National Park

Location; area
25km/15½ miles south of Winton; 33,700 hectares/83,200 acres.

Best time to visit
Winter and spring.

Access
On private tracks.

Facilities
No visitor facilities.

Features
Bladensburg National Park, established in 1984, has remained undeveloped for tourism in order to protect its low wooded hills and grassland, with patches of denser vegetation round semi-permanent water-holes.

Yeppoon K 4

Situation and characteristics
Yeppoon (pop. 7000) lies in Keppel Bay, 40km/25 miles north-east of Rockhampton. The main street and the road to Rockhampton are lined by shade-giving palms and pines. The beaches between Yeppoon and Rockhampton are known as the Capricorn Coast.

Accommodation
Several motels and caravan/camping parks.

Features
Between Yeppoon and Emu Park is the "Singing Ship" monument to Captain Cook (see Emu Park).

Surroundings
Off the coast is Great Keppel Island (see entry), with a wide range of tourist facilities and entertainments.

Yungaburra J 3

Situation and characteristics
Yungaburra (pop. 770) lies on the Atherton Tableland, 60km/37 miles south-west of Cairns on the Gillies Highway. A particular attraction is the much photographed Curtain Fig Tree, a strangler fig named for the aerial roots which hang down like a curtain (2.5km/1½ miles south).

Accommodation
Caravan/camping park.

Surroundings

Evidence of volcanic activity in the past is provided by two crater lakes, Eacham and Barrine, both declared National Parks (see Lake Barrine National Park and Lake Eacham National Park). Lake Tinaroo, a huge artificial lake created in 1958, supplies water for irrigating the tobacco and rice fields and generating electric power.

South Australia

General

Festival State
Area: 984,377sq.km./380,068sq. miles
Population: 1.459 million
Capital: Adelaide

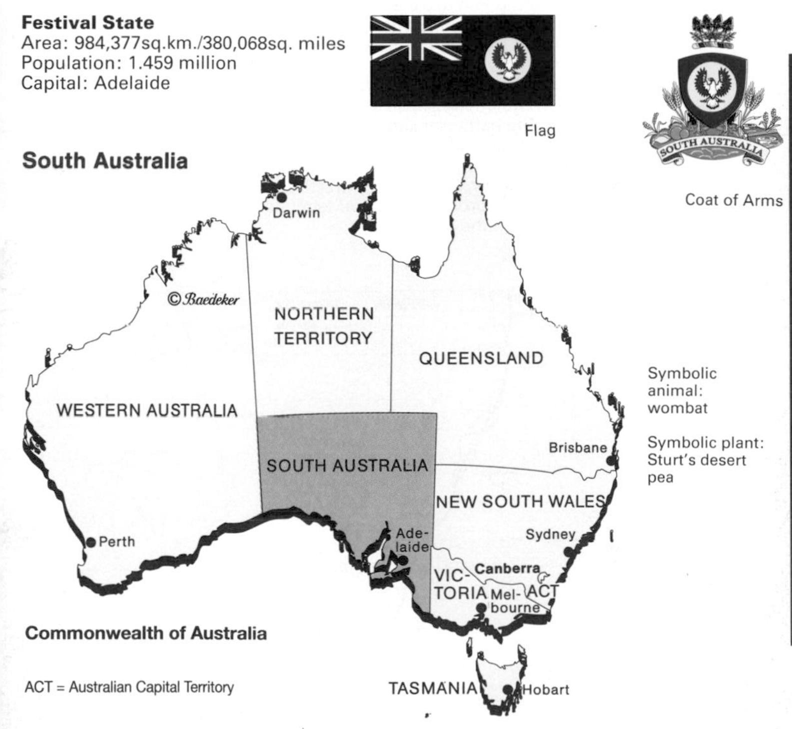

Flag

Coat of Arms

Symbolic animal: wombat

Symbolic plant: Sturt's desert pea

Situation and characteristics

South Australia, a state rich in minerals (iron, coal, uranium, gold, silver, opals, coal, oil, natural gas), occupies a central position in the southern half of the continent. In the arid west of the state are the vast expanses of the Victoria Desert and the Nullarbor Plain; in the dry north-west are the Musgrove Ranges; to the north-east are the Simpson Desert, the Sturt Stony Desert and the Strzelecki Desert, with numerous salt lakes; and to the south-east are the very beautiful Flinders and Mount Lofty Ranges. On the north side of the Flinders Ranges are extensive depressions and salt-pans, the largest of which are Lake Eyre and Lake Torrens. In the coastal region to the east are the wedge-shaped Eyre Peninsula, the boot-shaped Yorke Peninsula and the spur of the Fleurieu Peninsula, off which is beautiful Kangaroo Island. The southern part of the state with its Mediterranean climate produces large quantities of wine and fruit (particularly in the Barossa and Clare Valleys), but wheat is also grown and large areas are given up to extensive pastoral farming.

◀ *Remarkable Rocks, Kangaroo Island*

Tourist attractions

Adelaide, capital of South Australia, is a friendly and attractive city with venerable old 19th-century buildings and extensive parks and gardens. It is ringed by the beautiful Adelaide Hills and Mount Lofty Ranges, and in the surrounding area are the best known wine-growing districts in Australia, the Barossa Valley to the north-east and the "Wine Coast" with McLaren Vale on the Fleurieu Peninsula to the south.

There are sheltered bathing beaches on Gulf St Vincent and good surfing beaches on the south coast of the Fleurieu Peninsula, at the south-western tip of the Yorke Peninsula and on the Eyre Peninsula. Scuba divers can explore the wrecks off Kangaroo Island and the reefs to the south of Adelaide (Port Noarlunga, Aldinga Bay). The best sailing waters are in Gulf St Vincent.

Kangaroo Island, Australia's third largest island, is a very popular holiday destination with many scenic beauties, including fine coastal scenery, and a rich fauna (in particular kangaroos, koalas and seals). The south-eastern part of the state, with Mount Gambier, a former volcano, and its crater lakes, borders on Victoria. This is a region of flat grazing land and fascinating coastal scenery. Particularly attractive, too, are the varied coastal landscapes of the Coorong, a chain of lagoons and salt lakes between Lake Alexandrina and the sea.

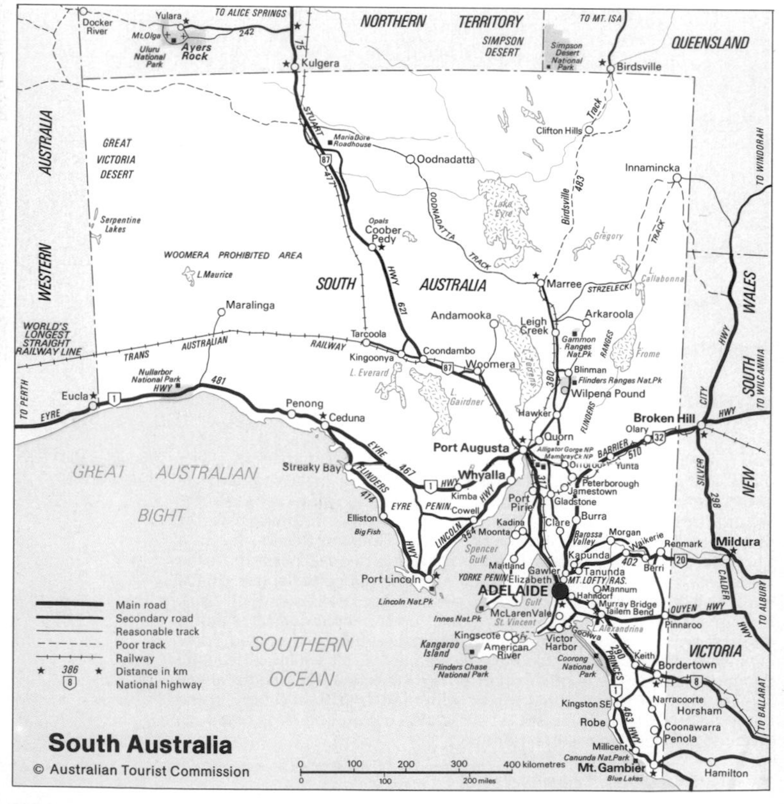

The Murray River, much of which is navigable (paddle-steamers, house boats), flows into Lake Alexandrina, supplying water for the plantations of citrus fruits and vineyards in the otherwise semi-arid plain.

The Yorke Peninsula lies between Gulf St Vincent and Spencer Gulf, with beautiful beaches and Innes National Park at its south-western tip to attract holidaymakers. The area round the three-town triangle of Wallaroo–Moonta–Kadina, once a great copper-mining area, is known as Little Cornwall and preserves some of the traditions of the Cornish miners who flocked here in the 19th and early 20th centuries.

The coastal regions of the Eyre Peninsula have varied attractions for holidaymakers. The beaches on the east coast are sheltered, while on the stormy west coast there are good surfing beaches and rugged cliffs. In the north of the peninsula are the hills of the Gawler Ranges with the rich deposits of iron ore which supply the heavy industry of Whyalla.

At the north end of Gulf St Vincent are the Flinders Ranges, which extend northward for 400km/250 miles into the arid outback. This fascinating mountain world with its changing play of colour, its heavily eroded rock formations and – in spite of its aridity – its rich flora and fauna is a must for all visitors to South Australia. The region was first explored by Matthew Flinders in the early 19th century. In many places there are Aboriginal rock paintings and drawings.

Beyond the Flinders Ranges is a landscape which becomes ever flatter and more featureless, with the endless expanse of Lake Eyre, a salt lake lying below sea level – though this desert-like region is still small in comparison with the immense expanses of the outback in northern Australia. In this almost uninhabited wilderness are a number of Aboriginal reserves, which can be visited only with special permission, and the controversial Woomera weapon-testing range, which is a prohibited area.

Particular attractions in the outback are the opal-mining towns such as Coober Pedy (much of which is underground) and the adventurous roads

View of the Barossa Valley wine-growing region

and tracks leading into New South Wales, Queensland and the Northern Territory.

The endless salt-pans to the north (Lake Torrens, Lake Eyre, etc.), some of them lying under sea level, have now mostly dried up. Only very rarely, when there has been exceptionally heavy rain in the distant hills of the eastern Dividing Range, does sufficient water from their immense catchment areas reach them, converting them briefly into shallow lakes.

To the north of the 32nd parallel, where only 1% of the population of South Australia live in small and sometimes tiny settlements, the country is barren, arid and hostile to man. Endless expanses of desert, dusty and monotonous, blazing hot in summer and uncomfortably cold on winter nights, make up the greater part of the territory of South Australia, and the western part of the state is bounded by desert too.

Places of Interest from A to Z in South Australia

★ ★Adelaide G 6

Capital of South Australia

Situation and characteristics

Adelaide (pop. 1.1 million; city region 1.6 million), Australia's fifth largest city and one of its most gracious, lies on a stretch of coast bounded on the west by Gulf St Vincent and on the landward side by the Mount Lofty Ranges (Adelaide Hills). The city has spread steadily farther eastward towards the wooded slopes of the hills, but further expansion in that direction is held back mainly by the fear of forest fires and bush fires. Only a few years ago large areas of forest and a number of houses on the outskirts of Adelaide were destroyed in a devastating fire.

The town was named after Queen Adelaide, wife of William IV.

History

Like Melbourne (see entry), Adelaide was not established as a penal colony but was founded by free citizens, mainly from Britain. The first settlers, led by Captain John Hindmarsh, landed from HMS "Buffalo" in Holdfast Bay (now Glenelg) on December 28th 1826. The site was chosen by the surveyor-general of the colony, Colonel William Light, who is commemorated by Light's Vision Lookout in North Adelaide. The town's further development confirmed his judgment, and the people of Adelaide are proud of the layout he designed with its wide streets, squares and open spaces.

Economy

In the last twenty years or so Adelaide has become an important industrial centre. Its main industries are construction, cars, engineering and textile manufacture. A high-tech park financed mainly by Japanese investment is being built on the edge of town.

Transport

Adelaide is fully integrated into the Australian transport network. It has an international airport, with a shuttle bus running between the airport and the city centre on weekdays. There are daily express train services to Melbourne, Sydney and Perth. Municipal transport is run by the State Transport Authority (STA; information bureau at corner of King William Street and Currie Street), including the ultra-modern trolleybus system, a close network of bus services and the suburban railways.

Accommodation

Numerous hotels, motels, reasonably priced hostels, caravan/camping parks. Advance booking is strongly advised.

Entertainment

Formerly often regarded as conservative and somewhat prim, Adelaide now has a very active and varied night life, with a wide range of theatres, cinemas, dance halls and night clubs. The leading theatres are in the Festival Centre in King William Road, in the north of the city (the Playhouse, the Space Theatre) and in Grote Street (Her Majesty's Theatre). Most of the night clubs and other night spots are in Hindley Street, the western continuation of Rundle Mall (pedestrian zone). The Australian passion for gambling is catered for by the Casino in a former railway station in North Terrace.

Events

Festival of Arts (in March in even-numbered years; most events in Festival Centre); Come Out Youth Festival (in May in odd-numbered years; Festival Centre); congresses in Adelaide Convention Centre (North Terrace); Adelaide Cup race (third Mon. in May; Morphettville racecourse).

Shopping

The best starting-point for a shopping expedition is Rundle Mall (pedestrian zone), with numerous department stores, shops and boutiques. The most exclusive shops are in Melbourne Street (North Adelaide). On Sundays there is the Adelaide Sunday Market (mainly antiques) in the premises of the Adelaide Market Company, an old building in East Terrace (between Grenfell and Rundle Streets). Near here is the Tandanya National Aboriginal Cultural Institute, where Aboriginal craft products (bark painting, woodcarving, etc,) can be bought. These, along with opals and wine, are among the most popular souvenirs of Adelaide.

Sport

Cricket is played at the Adelaide Oval. There are tennis courts near the Oval, in the Sports Centre in Memorial Drive and in Belair Park. There are a number of excellent golf courses (Belair, North Adelaide, etc.). The great meeting-places for sailing enthusiasts are Brighton, Seacliff, Glenelg, Grange, Henley, Largs Bay, Somerton and Port Adelaide. Swimmers and high divers are catered for by the Adelaide Aquatic Centre (Fitzroy Terrace, North Adelaide).

Information

South Australia Government Travel Centre, 18 King William Street, Adelaide 5000, tel. 08 212 1505.

The City

Adelaide used to have a reputation for being somewhat strait-laced, and it is still a very conservative, quiet and orderly city. It has preserved many of the plain stone houses of the early settlers alongside magnificent private mansions and public buildings built in the heyday of mining and agriculture in the 1870s. The city's skyline has changed drastically in the last few decades, and the buildings and church towers of the 19th century are now overshadowed by high-rise office blocks and banks. Particularly striking – seen from the Torrens River – are the light-coloured tent roofs of the Festival Centre and the post-modern Hyatt Regency Hotel.

Layout

Colonel Light's original plan for the town was a square measuring one mile each way with the streets laid out on a rectangular grid. This layout has been preserved in the older part of the city and has influenced the planning of North Adelaide.

Green belt

The green belt round the city of Adelaide and its suburb North Adelaide was included in Light's original plan of 1832, and the people of Adelaide have shown themselves determined to defend these parks and gardens against any restriction or encroachment by contemporary town planners.

Sightseeing in Adelaide

Many bus companies offer city sightseeing tours and excursions into the surrounding area. Visitors can also do their sightseeing in pedicabs (a kind of bicycle-rickshaw) driven by sturdy young men. But it is also possible to look round central Adelaide on foot. From outside the South Australia Government Travel Centre (at 18 King William St.) the Adelaide Explorer Bus sets off on a 34km/21 mile tour of the city.

King William Street

King William Street, a broad avenue 42m/140ft wide, cuts through the centre of the city from south to north and continues as King William Road, with the same width, over the Torrens River into North Adelaide. The cross streets change their names at King William Street except for South Terrace and North Terrace, which bound the city on the south and north and keep their names for their whole length. Thanks to the far-sighted planning of the city's founder, King William Street is still able to cope with modern traffic, though many of its 19th-century buildings have given place to modern high-rise blocks.

★Edmund Wright House

The preservation of Edmund Wright House (59 King William Street) is due to a campaign by local people in the 1970s against a proposal to demolish it. This richly decorated building in French Renaissance style was built by Edmund Wright in 1875–78 for the Bank of South Australia; it is now used for various official and social functions.

★Victoria Square

In the centre of the city, at the intersection with Grote Street and Wakefield Street, King William Street opens out into Victoria Square, with beautifully laid out gardens. In the shadow of the modern high-rise blocks (among them the Hilton Hotel) a few handsome 19th-century buildings have been preserved. In the centre of the square is a statue of Queen Victoria. On the north side is a charming fountain by John Dowie, with figures representing the three principal rivers of South Australia, the Murray, the Torrens and the Onkaparinga. Nearby are monuments to the explorers Stuart and Sturt.

★Town Hall

A little north of Victoria Square, on the east side of King William Street, is the Town Hall (by William Wright, 1863), in Italian Renaissance style, with a handsome clock-tower commemorating Queen Victoria's husband Prince Albert (d. 1861) which became a city landmark. On the façade are portraits of Italian artists and of Victoria and Albert.

General Post Office

Diagonally opposite the Town Hall is the General Post Office (1867), in a similar style, with a smaller clock-tower. In earlier days the arrival of mail from Britain was indicated by a flag during the day and a red light at night.

Postal Museum

The Postal Museum at 2 Franklin Street (open: Mon.–Fri. 11am–2pm) documents the development of postal services in South Australia from colonial times to the present day. Philatelists will be interested in the rare stamps and special postmarks.

Telecommunications Museum

The Telecommunications Museum at 131 King William Street (open: Sun.–Fri. 10.30am–3.30pm), with mementoes of the legendary postmaster Charles Todd, illustrates the arduous beginnings of communications in the second half of the 19th century and the laying of the overland telegraph line from Port Augusta to Darwin in 1872, later followed by the submarine cable to Java which made possible long-distance communication with Europe.

Treasury Building, St Francis Xavier Cathedral

On the east side of Victoria Square are the Treasury Building, adjoining the Town Hall, and St Francis Xavier Cathedral (1856–1926).

Courthouse

On the south side of the square are the imposing Magistrates' Courthouse (1851), with a Doric colonnade, and the Supreme Court (1868), in neo-classical style.

★Central Market

A few paces west of Victoria Square, on the south side of Grote Street, is the Central Market, which since the second half of the 19th century has supplied the city with fresh fruit, vegetables and culinary delicacies. Market days: Tue. 7am–5.30pm, Thu. 11am–5.30pm, Fri. 7am–9pm, Sat. 7am–1pm.

Tram to Glenelg

From the south side of Victoria Square the city's only surviving tram leaves for Glenelg.

★Rundle Mall

Some distance north of Victoria Square Rundle Mall, a busy shopping street (pedestrian zone), runs east from King William Street, lined with large department stores, boutiques and shops of all kinds (including several bookshops and art shops).

Here too are a number of large shopping arcades – the Rundle Arcade, the Gallery Shopping Centre, the Link Renaissance Centre and Arcade, City Cross, the Regent Arcade, John Martin's Plaza, the Southern Cross Arcade (with the façade of the old Southern Cross Hotel) and the charmingly old-fashioned Adelaide Arcade (1885). For the relaxation of tired shoppers, too, there are numbers of bistros and cafés.

Hindley Street

The western continuation of Rundle Mall beyond King William Street is Hindley Street, in which there are a number of good restaurants and some night spots.

★North Terrace

In North Terrace, a handsome tree-lined boulevard, there are several imposing public buildings, including the State Library, art galleries,

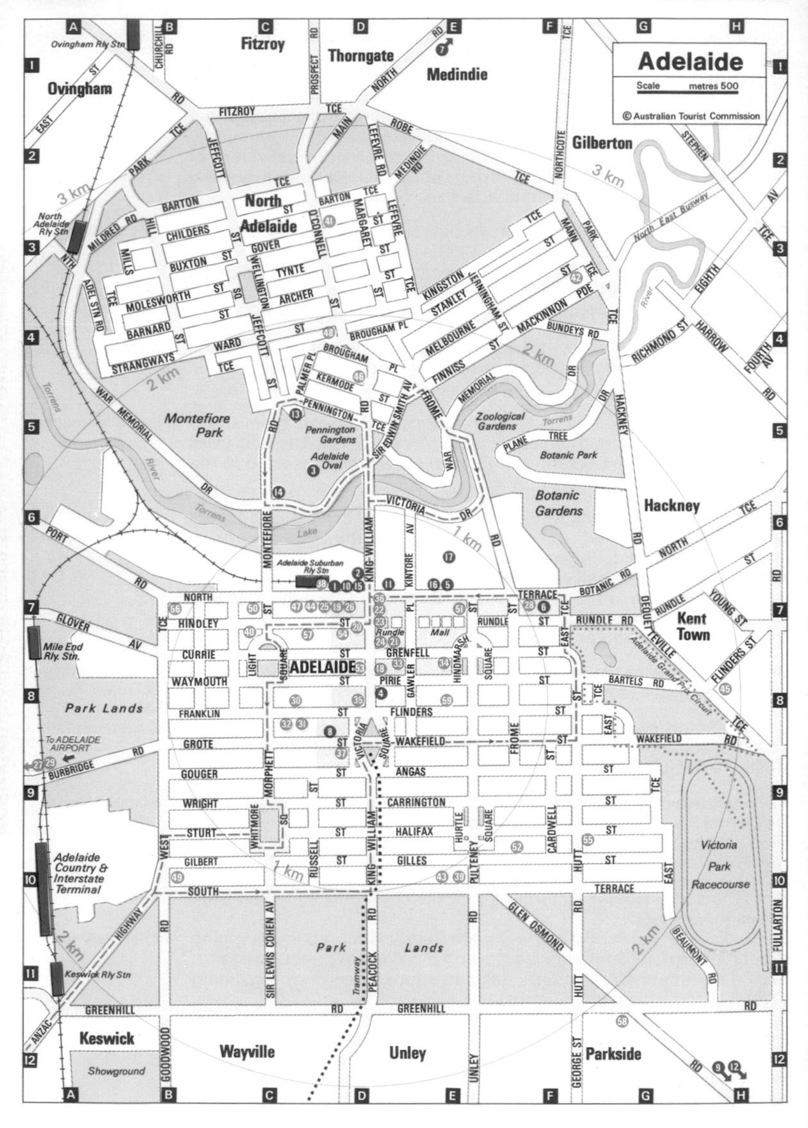

museums and the old railway station, now the Adelaide Casino. Beyond North Terrace, bounded by Torrens Lake, are extensive parks and gardens, with the Festival Centre, Government House, the campus of Adelaide University and the Parade Ground.

Places of Interest
- Adelaide Casino ❶ D7
- Adelaide Festival Theatre ❷ D7
- Adelaide Oval ❸ D6
- Adelaide Town Hall ❹ E8
- Art Gallery of South Aust. ❺ E7
- Ayers House ❻ G7
- Birdwood Mill Museum ❼ F1
- Central Market ❽ D9
- Cleland Conservation Park ❾ H12
- Constitutional Museum ❿ D7
- Government House ⓫ E7
- Hahndorf ⓬ H12
- Lights Vision Lookout ⓭ D5
- Memorial Dr. Tennis Courts ⓮ C6
- Parliament House ⓯ D7
- S.A. Historical Museum ⓰ E7
- University of Adelaide ⓱ E7

Tourist Information Centres
- Holiday W.A. Centre ⑱ E8
- N.S.W. Tourist Commission ⑲ D7
- N.T. Govt. Tourist Bureau ⑳ D8
- Qld. Govt. Travel Centre ㉑ E8
- S.A. Govt. Travel Centre ㉒ E7
- Tas. Govt. Tourist Bureau ㉓ E7
- Victour Travel Centre ㉔ E8

Airline Terminals
- Ansett ㉕ D7
- Australian Airlines ㉖ D7

Rent-a-Car Offices
- Avis ㉗ A9
- Budget ㉘ F7
- Hertz ㉙ A9
- Thrifty ㉚ D8

Railway Station
- Adelaide (Suburban) D7
- Country & Interstate Terminal A10

Coach Terminals
- Ansett Pioneer ㉛ D9
- Greyhound ㉜ C9
- Premier Roadlines ㉜ C9
- Stateliner ㉜ C9

National Parks
- Nat. Parks & Wildlife Serv. ㉝ E8

Motoring Association
- Royal Auto. Assoc. of S.A. ㉞ E8

Post Office
- G.P.O. ㉟ D8

International Airlines
- Qantas Airways ㊱ E7

Accommodation

Deluxe
- Hilton Internat'nal Adelaide ㊲ D9
- Hyatt Regency Adelaide ㊳ D7

Premier
- Adelaide Parkroyal ㊴ E10
- Eden Adelaide ㊵ C7
- Old Adelaide Inn ㊶ D3

Moderate
- Adelaide Meridien ㊷ F3
- Adelaide Travelodge ㊸ E10
- Festival Lodge ㊹ C7
- Flinders Lodge ㊺ H8
- Greenways Apartments ㊻ D4
- Grosvenor ㊼ C7
- Hotel Adelaide ㊽ D4
- South Park Motor Inn ㊾ B10
- The Barron Townhouse ㊿ C7
- The Mansions 51 E7

Budget
- Adelaide YHA Hostel 52 F10
- Ambassadors 53 D8
- City Central Motel 54 D7
- Clarice Motel 55 F10
- Newmarket 56 B7
- Plaza 57 C7
- Powells Court 58 G12
- YMCA 59 E8

Adelaide Explorer Bus

Shopping

Holy Trinity Church

Near the east end of North Terrace is Holy Trinity Church, the oldest Anglican church in South Australia, the foundation stone of which was laid by Governor Hindmarsh in 1838; the church was enlarged in 1845 and again in 1888. Compared with the imposing Victoria Bridge which spans Torrens Lake a little to the north, it looks like a village church. Nearby is a monument marking the site of the first school in the colony, opened in 1838.

Adelaide Station/Casino

The old Adelaide Station (1929), in neo-classical style, is now the elegant Adelaide Casino, with restaurants and bars as well as the gaming rooms. It is open from late morning until the early hours, every day.

Suburban Station

Adjoining the Casino is the terminus of the suburban railway system.

Constitutional Museum

To the east of the Casino, in Old Parliament House, is the Constitutional Museum (open: Mon.–Fri. 10am–5pm, Sat. and Sun. noon–5pm), which documents the political history of South Australia and the city of Adelaide (video show).

***Parliament House**

On the corner of King William Road is the new Parliament House, the most imposing public building in Adelaide, with a monumental colonnade. It was opened in 1939 after five years' building.

***Festival Centre**

To the north of Parliament House is the Adelaide Festival Centre (conducted tours daily at 9.30am), an ultra-modern cultural centre opened in 1977, with a tent-like roof structure slightly reminiscent of the Sydney Opera House. Here in alternate years is held the highly regarded Adelaide Arts Festival (theatre, opera, ballet, exhibitions, readings by writers, lectures). It contains a large theatre (2000 seats), a smaller one (600 seats) which is the home of the South Australia Theatre Company, the experimental Space Theatre (380 seats) and an amphitheatre (800 seats) for concerts and recitals. At two-yearly intervals (1998, 2000 etc), on the occasion of the Adelaide Festival, some top-class theatrical, operatic and ballet performances are put on, as well as poetry-readings. The sculptural decoration of the South Plaza was the work of the German sculptor Otto Herbert Hajek.

Elder Park

To the north of the Festival Centre, extending to the Torrens River, is Elder Park, with an attractive rotunda which is a popular meeting-point. From the Popeye landing-stage there are boat trips on the river.

Government House

To the west of the Festival Centre, beyond King William Road, is the neo-classical Government House (begun 1836), set in spacious gardens. It is the official residence of the governor of South Australia and is not open to the public.

Adelaide Club

Adjoining Government House, at 165 North Terrace, is the select Adelaide Club.

War Memorial

South-east of Government House is the War Memorial commemorating the Australian dead of the two world wars and later wars.

State Library

Farther east is the State Library (1884), which forms an architectural unity with the adjoining

South Australian Museum. It is the largest public library in South Australia, with a special collection of works on the history of the state.

★★South Australian Museum

The South Australian Museum (open: daily 10am-5pm, from noon on Wed.: guided tours Sun. 2.15 and 3pm) occupies a building with a French-style mansard roof and a tower (1914). It contains a large collection of Aboriginal and Melanesian art and Egyptian antiquities. Of particular interest are the prehistoric and natural history collections.

Migration Museum

North of the South Australian Museum and State Library, at 82 Kintore Avenue, is the Migration Museum (open: Mon.–Fri. 10am–5pm, Sat., Sun. and pub. hols. 1–5pm). Housed in a well restored former poorhouse, it traces the history of immigration to South Australia.

Art Gallery of South Australia

Farther east along the North Terrace is the Art Gallery of South Australia, (open: daily 9.30am–5pm, guided tours Sat. and Sun.11 am and 3pm). This magnificent gallery has a fine collection by modern artists, as well as some 17th c. landscape and genre paintings.

★Gallery of South Australian Art

This gallery contains works by South Australian artists. It is housed in a building which has served a variety of purposes (as a church, a police barracks, the state records office, etc.).

University of Adelaide

Between North Terrace and Victoria Drive, which runs along the Torrens River, is the spacious campus of the University of Adelaide. The most notable buildings are the Mitchell Building (1881), Elder Hall and the church-like Bonython Hall.

Royal Hospital

East of the University campus, is the large Royal Adelaide Hospital.

★★Ayers House

At the east end of North Terrace, the north-east corner of the square grid of central Adelaide, is Ayers House, famed as one of the finest examples of Regency architecture in Australia. Originally a modest house built in 1846, it was owned from 1855 to 1878 by Henry Ayers, for many years prime minister of South Australia, after whom Ayers Rock is named. Ayers transformed it into an elegant 40-roomed mansion with a large new dining room and a ballroom. It is now the headquarters of the National Trust of South Australia and also contains two excellent restaurants. Richly appointed in

Ayers House, a fine example of Regency architecture

Victorian style, it is open to the public (Tue.–Fri. 10am–4pm, Sat. and Sun. 2–4pm).

★Botanical Gardens

Beyond the Royal Adelaide Hospital, to the north of Ayers House, are the spacious Botanical Gardens (established in 1855), with a rich display of subtropical and Mediterranean flora. A particular attraction is the old palm-house of 1871 and the Bicentennial Conservatory which contains plants from the Asian Pacific region.

Zoo

Adjoining the Botanical Gardens on the north-west is the Zoo (main entrance in Frome Road; open: daily 9.30am–5pm), established in the late 19th century, in which the animals are kept in as nearly natural conditions as possible. Particular attractions are the aviaries and the anthropoid ape enclosure, as well as a group of yellow-footed rock wallabies, a particularly endangered species.

★Tandanya Aboriginal Cultural Institute

South of Ayers House, near the west end of Rymill Park, is the Tandanya Aboriginal Cultural Institute (Grenfell Street), where visitors can see something of contemporary Aboriginal culture (theatre, dances, arts and crafts).

Rymill Park, Victoria Park, Grand Prix Circuit

South-east of Ayers House, on the eastern edge of the central area, is Rymill Park, beautifully laid out with rose-gardens, a lake and children's play areas. In this park and Victoria Park (with racecourse), immediately south, is the motor-racing circuit on which the annual Formula 1 Grand Prix is run.

North Adelaide

Five bridges over the Torrens River (here dammed to form Torrens Lake) lead to the suburb of North Adelaide, which, like the city centre, is laid out on a regular grid. It was designed, with its surrounding green belt, by William Light. It has preserved a number of handsome 19th-century houses (e.g. Carclew House in Jeffcott Street) bearing witness to the prosperity of their owners as well as some of the closely packed houses occupied by the workers. Many of the old buildings have been restored and now house elegant shops and restaurants. The Old Lion Hotel at 163 Melbourne Street, originally a brewery established in the mid 19th century, is an Adelaide institution.

★St Peter's Cathedral

The neo-Gothic St Peter's Cathedral, an imposing building with tall twin spires, was built between 1869 and 1904. Light filters into the interior through fine stained glass windows. The powerful eight-bell carillon rings only on special festival days.

Montefiore Park Light's Vision

To the east of St Peter's, on the north bank of the Torrens River, is Montefiore Park. On a low hill near the north side of the park is Light's Vision, a monument to William Light, founder and designer of the town.

Bonython Park

Farther west, along the Torrens River, is Bonython Park, which with its pond for sailing model boats and its play and rest areas appeals particularly to families with children.

Surroundings of Adelaide

Elizabeth

30km/19 miles north-east of Adelaide is the new town of Elizabeth (pop. 35,000; several hotels and motels), founded in 1955 and named after Queen Elizabeth II. It is considered a model example of a town designed to cope with the motor-car, with separate pedestrian zones, shopping centres and parks and gardens. In this satellite town on the northern periphery of the Adelaide conurbation is the large General Motors–Holden car factory.

Gawler

Gawler (pop. 14,000; hotel, motel, caravan/camping parks) lies 40km/25 miles north of Adelaide in a thriving agricultural area near the wine-growing Barossa Valley. The town, founded in 1839, was like Adelaide, planned by Colonel William Light. It has preserved some handsome 19th century buildings, including churches, hotels and pubs, a mill, a post office and a telegraph station.

In Montefiore Park

★Adelaide Hills

A few kilometres east of Adelaide are the beautiful Adelaide Hills, the southern part of the Mount Lofty Ranges and a popular recreation area for the people of Adelaide, with a rich and varied Australian flora and fauna.

★Black Hill Conservation Park, Morialta Conservation Park

13km/8 miles north-east of Adelaide on the scenic Old Norton Summit Road are the steep crags – among them the Three Sugarloaves – of the Black Hills (466m/1529ft). The wild and romantic gorges and waterfalls on Fourth Creek draw many nature-lovers from the city.

Athelstone Wildflowers Gardens

In the northern part of the conservation area are the very beautiful Atherstone Wildflowers Gardens, which are seen at their best in spring (open: daily 8.30am–5pm).

★Birdwood Mill

An attractive excursion is through the Adelaide Hills to Birdwood Mill, an old mill 45km/28 miles east of Adelaide idyllically situated on the Torrens River, with play and picnic areas.

★National Motor Museum

At Birdwood Mill is the National Motor Museum (open: daily 9am–5pm), the oldest exhibit in which is a Peugeot of 1897. Every two years is held the Bay to Birdwood Rally, in which veteran and vintage cars cough and splutter their way from Holdfast Bay up into the hills.

Cleland Conservation Park

13km/8 miles east of Adelaide on the north-western slopes of Mount Lofty (726m/2382ft) is Cleland Conservation Park (open: daily 9.30am–5pm), where visitors can see many Australian animals and get a close-up view of koalas (afternoons only).

★Mount Lofty Botanic Gardens

Among the most popular destinations for excursions in this area are Mount Lofty Botanic Gardens (open: daily 10am–4pm), 20km/12½ miles south-east of Adelaide on the eastern slopes of Mount Lofty, in the Piccadilly Valley, where the high rainfall favours the growth of rhododendrons and ferns. Other features are a rock garden and artificial lakes.

★Belair National Park

15km/9 miles south of the city is Belair National Park, established in 1891, the first large nature reserve in South Australia. Within the park is Old Government House, with a ballroom and a swimming pool (open to

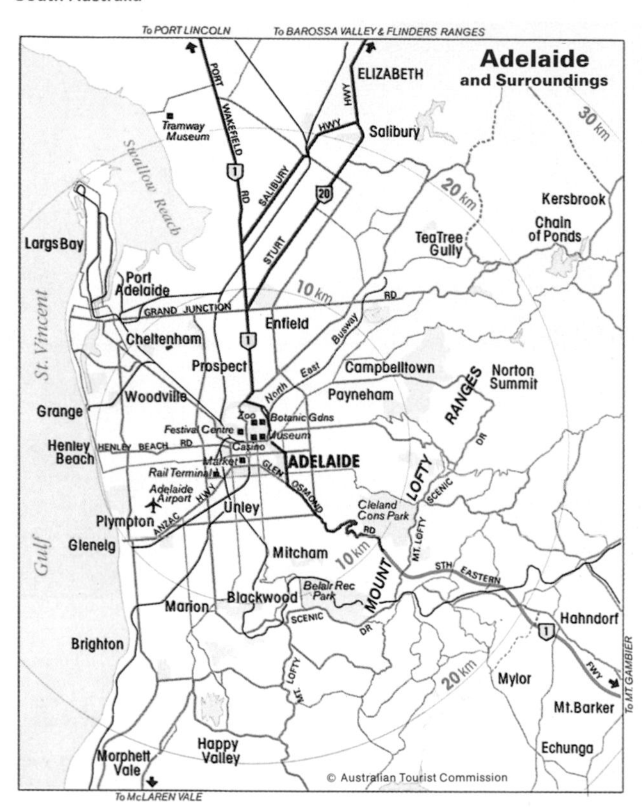

the public only at weekends and during the school holidays, daily 12.30–4pm).

This was the summer residence of the governor of South Australia until 1880, when it gave way to a much grander house, Marble Hill, in a high and secluded situation in the hills 25km/15½ miles east of Adelaide. The new residence was destroyed in a forest fire in 1955 and thereafter was partly restored.

It is open to the public Wed. and Sat. 1–5pm, Sun. 10am–5pm.

Brownhill Creek Recreation Park

Brownhill Creek Recreation Park, 8km/5 miles south of Adelaide at Micham, offers shady picnic spots within easy reach of the city and magnificent panoramic views.

Windy Point

Another attractive excursion is to Windy Point Recreation Park, in the hills 10km/6 miles south of Adelaide. From the Lookout there are superb views, particularly at night.

McLaren Vale

See Southern Vale

★Glenelg

10km/6 miles south-west of Adelaide is the popular bathing resort of Glenelg in sheltered (and surf-free) Gulf St Vincent. The quickest way to reach it is on the Anzac Highway or in Adelaide the old-style trams (one has been refurbished as a restaurant) which leave from Victoria Square. The first group of free settlers disembarked from HMS "Buffalo" here, in Holdfast Bay, and Captain Hindmarsh took possession of the territory in the

The old-time tram from Adelaide to Glenelg

name of the British Crown. There is a replica of the "Buffalo" in Patawalonga Marina (Adelphi Terrace, North Glenelg), open: daily 10am–5pm. In Mosely Square is the old Town Hall (1875). The latest attraction is the Magic Mountain Amusement Centre, with a giant waterslide and a variety of other entertainments.

North of Glenelg, on the Military Road (West Beach), is Marineland, with a large aquarium and displays by performing dolphins and seals.

Grange

10km/6 miles west of Adelaide, on Gulf St Vincent, is Grange, with the Charles Sturt Memorial Museum (open: Wed. to Sat. and pub. hols. 1–5pm) in Grange House, at the corner of Jetty Street and Nepean Drive. This old brick-built house with an attractive interior was the home of Charles Sturt, who explored the course of the Murray River in a whaler.

★Port Adelaide

In 1837 Port Adelaide, 14km/8½ miles north-west of the city centre, was an area of marshland which became known, not without reason, as Port Misery. Gradually, however, it developed into a busy port with a considerable freight-handling capacity. A number of imposing 19th century buildings bear witness to its early prosperity – the Customs House (1879), the Courthouse, the Police Station (1861) and a number of old warehouses, banks and hotels. The South Australian Maritime Museum at 119 Lipson Street (open: Sat.–Wed. 10am–5pm) has an interesting collection of material on ships and the sea, including a lighthouse and a number of old ships. Nearby, in the old Port Dock Station, is the Railway Museum (open: Sun.–Fri. 10am–5pm, Sat. noon–5pm), with a veteran train which runs at certain times.

Semaphore

2km/1¼ miles north-west of Port Adelaide, at Semaphore, is Fort Glanville (open only on Sunday afternoons in summer), South Australia's first fort (never used), built in 1878 when an attack by Russia was feared.

Largs Bay

North of Semaphore, in Largs Bay, is the three-storey Largs Pier Hotel (1883), an imposing building reflecting the prosperity of the late 19th century.

St Kilda

In St Kilda, 26km/16 miles north of Adelaide on Highway 1 (Main North Road), is an interesting Tramway Museum (open: Sun. and pub. hols. 1–5pm), with an old-time tram which runs at certain times.

Hackham

In Hackham, 30km/19 miles south of Adelaide and a few kilometres inland from the beaches round Port Noarlunga, is a Pioneer Village Museum (open: Wed.–Sun. 10am–5pm) which conveys some impression of the life of the early settlers.

Bathing beaches

The much frequented bathing beaches in the Adelaide region extend for 32km/20 miles along Gulf St Vincent from North Haven in the north to Hallett Cove in the south; the finest are Glenelg and Henley Beaches. There are boat slips at Marino, Seacliff, Brighton, Somerton Park, Glenelg, West Beach, Semaphore, Largs North and North Haven. Farther south too, on the Fleurieu Peninsula, the beaches are clean and not overcrowded. There is safe bathing at O'Sullivan, Christies and Sellicks.

Nude bathing

Maslin Beach, a few kilometres south of Port Noarlunga, has been officially declared a nudist beach – the first in Australia.

Surfing beaches

The best surfing beaches are on the south coast of the Fleurieu Peninsula, where there is a perpetual high swell coming in from the ocean.

Andamooka G 6

Situation and characteristics

610km/379 miles north of Adelaide is the little township of Andamooka (pop. 400), on the north-western shore of the saltpan Lake Torres. Opals have been mined here since the 1920s – usually darker in colour than the better known opals of Coober Pedy (see entry). Because of the extreme climatic conditions many people live in underground houses (dugouts).

Accommodation

Hotel, motel, caravan/camping park.

Features

Andamooka has retained much of the character of a pioneer settlement. Its one particular feature of interest is Duke's Bottle Home, made entirely of empty beer bottles.

Surroundings

30km/19 miles west of Andamooka is the mining settlement of Roxby Downs (pop. 2500; motel), in a desert setting. It was built some years ago to house employees of the Olympic Dam Copper Mine, to the north of the little town. There are also rich deposits of uranium in the area.

Ardrossan G 6

Situation and characteristics

The little port of Ardrossan (pop. 1000), situated some 150km/95 miles north-east of Adelaide on a low bluff above the sea, is the most important port for the shipment of grain (particularly wheat and barley) on the east coast of the Yorke Peninsula, with large silos for grain storage.

Accommodation

Hotels, motels and caravan/camping parks.

Features

There is an interesting museum of local history. The "stump jump" plough (with a spring ploughshare which could avoid large stones and other obstacles and made ploughing easier) was invented here in the 19th century.

Barmera G 6

Situation and characteristics

Barmera (pop. 1860), now the centre of an irrigated area growing grapes, apricots, peaches and citrus fruits, was originally established after the First World War as a settlement of ex-soldiers. It lies 230km/145 miles north-east of Adelaide in the Riverland area on the shores of Lake Bonney.

Accommodation

Motels and caravan/camping parks.

Features

Napper's Old Accommodation House (1850), now in ruins, was built to house cattle-drovers on the overland stock route from New South Wales. On the shores of Lake Bonney (fishing, water sports) is an obelisk commemorating Donald Campbell's attempt on the world water speed record in 1964. Also of interest are the Art Gallery and the National Trust Museum. The displays in the Cobdogla Museum vividly illustrate the history of irrigation. There are a number of wineries which can be visited (wine tasting).

★★Barossa Valley G 6

Situation and characteristics

The Barossa Valley, some 50km/30 miles north-east of Adelaide, is famed as a wine-growing district, comparable with the Hunter Valley in New South Wales. It was given its name by Surveyor-General William Light in memory of Barrosa in Spain, where he had fought in a decisive battle in 1811.

The district was settled in the 1840s by British and German immigrants. Some of the original German place-names were replaced during the First World War by English ones.

The flat valley, where the main settlements lie Lyndoch, Tanunda and Nuriootpa (see entry), is traversed by a busy road from Gawler to the Sturt

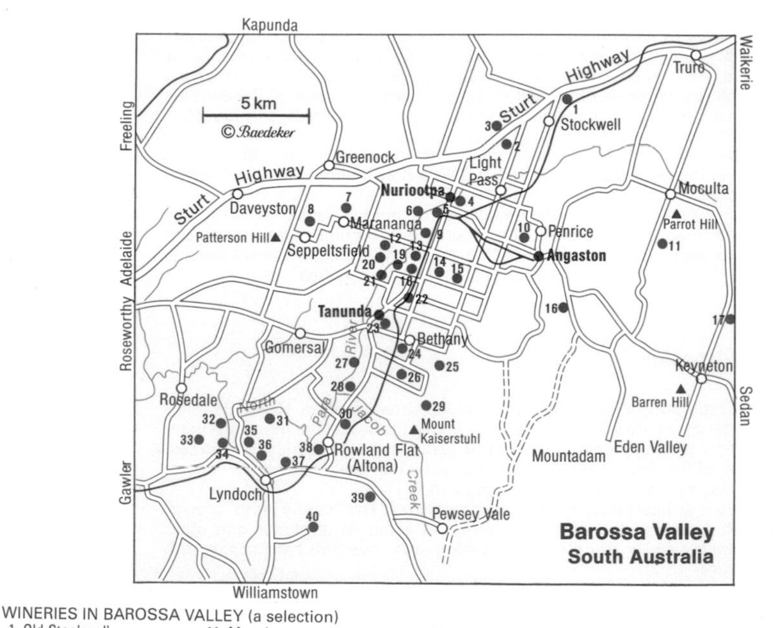

WINERIES IN BAROSSA VALLEY (a selection)

1 Old Stockwell
2 Wolf-Blass
3 Mildara-Blass
4 Elderton
5 Tolley, Scott & Tolley
6 Tarac
7 Gnadenfrei
8 Karl Seppelt
9 Penfolds (Kaiserstuhl)
10 Saltram
11 Moculta
12 Tolleys Pedare
13 Château Dorrien
14 Hardy's Siegersdorf
15 Tarchalice
16 Yalumba
17 Henschke
18 Leo Buring
19 Bernkastel
20 Peter Lehmann
21 Veritas
22 Basedows
23 Château Tanuda
24 High Wycombe
25 Bethany
26 Rockford
27 St Hallett
28 Grant Burge
29 Krondorf
30 Orlando Wyndham
31 Chattertons
32 Château Yaldara
33 Wards Gateway
34 Wilsford
35 Karlsburg
36 Red Gum
37 Kellermeister
38 Liebichs Rovalley
39 Barossa Settlers
40 Karrawirra

A reminder that German wine-makers came here

In the Barossa Valley, one of Australia's best known wine-growing regions

Highway. The attractions it offers to tourists are wine festivals with folk singing and dancing, visits to wineries and wine tastings. There is plenty of accommodation for visitors, but at festival times it is fully booked.

★★Vintage Festival

The Barossa Valley's Vintage Festival is held in March or April in odd-numbered years, with processions, brass bands, maypole dancing and, of course, much wine tasting.

Angaston

Angaston (alt. 381m/1184ft; pop. 2000; hotels, motels) is the highest settlement in the Barossa Valley. It takes its name from George Fife Angas, one of the founding fathers of South Australia, who paid the fares of free settlers and provided them with land. Angaston has preserved a remarkable number of old buildings, including the mansion of Collingrove (1850). In and around the town there are many wineries offering wine tasting.

Springton

In Springton, 26km/16 miles south of Angaston in the Eden Valley, is the ancient Herbig Tree, an enormous hollow gum tree in which a pioneer settler named Herbig is said to have lived with his family.

Nuriootpa

Nuriootpa (pop. 3300; hotel, motel, caravan/camping park), 72km/45 miles north-east of Adelaide, is the largest settlement in the Barossa Valley and its commercial centre. The Kaiser Stuhl winery is a reminder that German settlers introduced wine-making to the valley. Coulthard House (1855), a handsome two-storey settler's house built of bluestone, is now a museum. Round Nuriootpa are a number of wineries which can be visited (wine tasting).

★Lyndoch

60km/37 miles north-east of Adelaide, at the south end of the Barossa Valley, is Lyndoch (pop. 700; hotel, motel, caravan/camping park), which is famed for its wine. At the end of the 19th century this was a wheat-growing area: now the main product is wine, some of it of outstanding quality, made by both small and very large wineries, some of them family-owned. Many wineries are open to visitors, and offer wine tastings. Château Yaldara with its crenellated tower is like a French château, Karlsburg like a German castle. Château Yaldara contains a collection of fine porcelain, pictures and other works of art, mainly by European artists, and a collection of mechanical musical instruments.

★Tanunda

70km/45 miles from Adelaide, centrally situated in the Barossa Valley, is Tanunda (pop. 3100), which grew out of a German settlement called Langmeil. It is now a popular tourist resort (hotel, motels, caravan/camping park) in which German traditions and cuisine are still maintained. The Barossa Valley Historical Museum (open: daily 10am–5pm) has an interesting collection of material on the history of settlement in the valley.

From Mengler Hill there are good views of the surrounding country. The town has three Lutheran churches, including the Langmeil village church, which is approached by a long avenue of cypresses. Round the town are a number of wineries which can be visited and the Kaiserstuhl Conservation Park.

★Kapunda

80km/50 miles north of Adelaide is Kapunda (pop. 2000; hotels, caravan/camping park), the centre of a farming and wine-growing area in the Barossa Valley. In 1842 rich deposits of copper were found in the area, and Kapunda became the first large mining town in Australia, with a population which reached 10,000 at its peak. By 1888, however, the mines had to be abandoned because of flooding. Many buildings have survived from the early days of the settlement and are now protected as national monuments, including the old school, the courthouse and a number of miners' houses. The old Baptist church of 1866 is now a museum on the history of the town (open: daily 1–4pm). The very informative Historic Mine Walking Trail takes visitors round the abandoned copper mine.

Berri H 6

Situation and characteristics

Originally a refuelling stop for paddle-steamers on the Murray River, Berri (pop. 4000) was declared a town in 1911 and is now the commercial centre of the Riverland region, an extensive irrigated wine- and fruit-growing area. At the entrance to the little town is the Big Orange, an enormous reminder of the fact that oranges and lemons are grown here. Opposite the Big Orange is the Riverland Display Centre (old vehicles, Aboriginal arts and crafts).

Accommodation

Hotel, motels, caravan/camping park.

Surroundings

3km/2 miles west of the town is the Berri Estates winery and distillery, the largest in Australia (visits by appointment). A number of fruit-processing factories round Berri can also be visited.

Bordertown H 7

Situation and characteristics

Bordertown (pop. 2300) lies on the Dukes Highway 300km/185 miles south-east of Adelaide, near the borders of Victoria. In the mid 19th century it was an important supply centre for the goldfields of western Victoria. It is now the centre of an agricultural area (wool, wheat, milk).

From nearby Mount Monster there are fine views.

Accommodation

Hotels, motels, caravan/camping park.

★Burra G 6

Situation and characteristics

From 1845 to 1877 copper-mining brought prosperity to the area round Burra (pop. 1200), which has preserved evidence of its past in the form of miners' cottages, mine buildings, chimneys, etc. Burra is now the centre of a sheep-farming area.

Accommodation

Hotels, caravan/camping parks.

Features

Courthouse; police lockup; Bon Accord Mine buildings, now a museum.

Surroundings

To the north-east, at Mongalata, are the remains of old gold workings. To the west is the Clare Valley (see entry), a well-known wine-growing area.

Ceduna F 6

Situation and characteristics

800km/500 miles north-west of Adelaide, at the junction of the Eyre and Flinders Highways, is the little town of Ceduna (pop. 3000), the last settlement of any size before the crossing of the inhospitable Nullarbor Plain in Western Australia. The port at Thevenard, 3km/2 miles east, ships grain, gypsum and salt and is the base of a fishing fleet. Its situation in Denial Bay, with its sheltered beaches and offshore islands, makes it an ideal place for a beach holiday.

Accommodation

Motels, caravan/camping parks.

Surroundings

13km/8 miles from Ceduna are the ruins of McDonald, a settlement founded in the 1840s. Day trips to beaches in Decres Bay, Laura Bay and Davenport Creek. 34km/21 miles north is the Overseas Telecommunications Earth Station (open for visits: Mon.–Fri. 10am–3pm), which links Australia with countries in Asia, Africa and Europe. North-east of Ceduna is the Yumbarra Conservation Park, with bizarrely shaped granite crags rising out of low sandy hills.

★Clare Valley G 6

Situation and characteristics

140km/85 miles north of Adelaide is the Clare Valley with its chief town, Clare (pop. 2600). Old documents show that there was a settlement here, named after County Clare in Ireland, as early as 1832. Clare is now best known as the centre of a wine-making area, in which the first vines were planted by a group of Jesuit priests at Sevenhill in 1848. There is a large wine festival in May.

Accommodation
Hotels, motels, caravan/camping parks.

Features
The mid-19th-century courthouse is now a museum of local history. The Sevenhill Cellars, still run by priests, can be visited (wine tasting).

★Mintaro
15km/9 miles east of Clare is Mintaro, now classified as a Heritage Town. In the past a staging-point for the transport of copper from Burra (see entry) to Port Wakefield, it declined after the construction of the railway. Features of particular interest are Robinson's Cottage, an old settler's house, and Martindale Hall, a neo-classical mansion which is now a hotel.

★★Coober Pedy F 5

Situation and characteristics
The opal-mining town of Coober Pedy (pop. 2500) lies in the heart of the South Australian outback some 850km/530 miles north of Adelaide on the Stuart Highway. The name of the town comes from an Aboriginal phrase meaning "white fellows in a hole" – most of the inhabitants live in underground dwellings (dugouts) to escape the fierce heat of summer and the extreme cold of winter.

Accommodation
Desert Cave (the world's first underground hotel), 2 motels, caravan/camping park.

Features
The activities of opal-miners over many years, since gold prospectors found valuable white opals here in 1911, have converted the desolate countryside round Coober Pedy into a kind of lunar landscape. Visitors can still try their luck after obtaining a prospecting permit from the Mines Department in Coober Pedy. The Mine Museum has interesting displays on

An underground kitchen/living-room, Coober Pedy

the history of prospecting for precious stones and demonstrations of opals being cut and polished. Also worth a visit is the Catacomb Church.

Surroundings

240km/150 miles on the Stuart Highway, at Marla, are the Mintabie opal-fields.

Coonawarra H 7

Situation and characteristics

The area round the little settlement of Coonawarra is the most southerly wine-growing region in South Australia. Although the high quality of the terra-rossa soils in this area was recognised in the 19th century and there were ambitious plans for developing wine production, it was only in the '50s and '60s of the 20th century that these plans really came to fruition. The Coonawarra vineyards, covering an area only 13km/8 miles long and 1km/¾ mile across, now produce grapes of the highest quality and award-winning wines. Wineries can be visited and the wines tasted.

★★Coorong National Park G 7

Location; area

Two hours' drive from Adelaide, to the south of Lake Alexandrina (at the mouth of the Murray River); 300sq.km/116sq.miles.

Best time to visit

September to May.

Access

From Adelaide on the Princes Highway (Highway 1), going south-west, to Meningie (160km/100 miles) or Kingston, then south along the coast.

Facilities

Camping grounds; picnic areas.

Features

Coorong National Park was established mainly to protect its rich bird life and fascinating coastal scenery. A long, narrow lagoon, never wider than 3km/2 miles, and shallow saltpans are sheltered from the surf by the high sand-dunes on the long Younghusband Peninsula. The area is frequented by cormorants, pelicans and ibises.

Meningie

The little township of Meningie (pop. 800; hotel, motel, caravan/camping park) is a good base for excursions in Coorong National Park and for exploring the shores of Lake Albert and Lake Alexandrina.

Kingston S.E.

At the south end of the Coorong coast is the little holiday resort of Kingston S.E. (pop. 1500; not to be confused with Kingston on the Murray River). Originally called Maria Creek after a ship wrecked in the bay, it was given its present name after Governor G. S. Kingston built a hostel here in 1840. It is now a lively holiday resort (hotels, motels, caravan/camping park) and a good base from which to explore Coorong National Park. There is an interesting Pioneer Museum run by the National Trust.

Cape Jaffa

South-west of Kingston, extending into the Southern Ocean, is Cape Jaffa, with a prominent lighthouse, which attracts many visitors.

★Eyre Peninsula F/G 6

Situation and characteristics

Half way along the south coast of Australia the Eyre Peninsula projects like a broad triangular spur into the Southern Ocean, separating the Great Australian Bight to the west from Spencer Gulf to the east. At the corners of the triangle are Ceduna in the west, Port Lincoln in the south and Whyalla and Port Augusta in the east (see entries). The northern boundary of the peninsula is formed by the Gawler Ranges in the arid north. The east coast, on Spencer Gulf, has safe and sheltered beaches and good fishing waters. The peninsula is named after the explorer John Edward Eyre, who in 1840–41, starting from Adelaide, surveyed the coastal regions on the Great Australian Bight. After travelling north as far as the huge salt lake which bears his name he turned west and south to cross the Nullarbor Plain close to the coast and reach Albany in Western Australia.

In the interior of the Eyre Peninsula the Koppio hills in the south give way farther north to great flat expanses of farming land, and in the thinly inhabited far north the horizon is bounded by the Gawler Ranges. To the west is the desolate, treeless Nullarbor Plain, ending on the coast in cliffs of dangerously friable sandstone. Between June and October whales can be seen passing along the coast close to the land.

West Coast

Elliston

In Waterloo Bay on the west coast of the peninsula is the popular holiday resort of Elliston (hotels, motels, holiday apartments, caravan/camping parks), with safe bathing beaches and beautiful wild coastal scenery. There are fine views from Mount Wedge (250m/820ft).

Flinders Island

30km/19 miles west of Elliston, in the Great Australian Bight, is Flinders Island (diving, water sports, etc.).

Streaky Bay

130km/80 miles north-west of Elliston is the little resort and fishing port of Streaky Bay (pop. 1000; hotel, motel, caravan/camping park), with good sandy bays, little inlets and high cliffs. In the hinterland is wheat-growing country. There is an interesting local museum in the old schoolhouse. Along the beautiful coasts nearby can be seen many pelicans.

Point Labatt

40km/25 miles south of Streaky Bay is Point Labatt, a nature reserve with a large colony of sealions.

Ceduna

See entry

Coffin Bay

See Port Lincoln

East Coast

Cowell

110km/68 miles south of Whyalla (see entry) is the old settlement of Cowell (pop. 700; motel, caravan/camping park), where Franklin Harbour, a large coastal lagoon, offers safe, sheltered beaches for bathing and fishing. The economy depends on the deposits of jade in the area, fishing and farming as well as on tourism (hotels, motels, caravan/camping parks). South of Cowell is Franklin Harbour Conservation Park (good fishing). Visitors can join a "jade safari" which will take them into the beautiful Minbrie Ranges and give them an opportunity of prospecting for a piece of jade for themselves.

Arno Bay

50km/30 miles south of Cowell is the popular little resort of Arno Bay.

Tumby Bay

Tumby Bay (pop. 1200), 50km/30 miles north-east of Port Lincoln (see entry) on the south-east coast of the Eyre Peninsula, has developed in recent years into a popular holiday resort (hotels, motels, camping ground), with a semicircular bay of white sand. The old police station now houses a museum of local history. Beautiful coastal scenery.

The offshore islands to the east have been designated as the Sir Joseph Banks Group Conservation Park (sealions, dolphins, many species of birds).

Port Lincoln

See entry

★Fleurieu Peninsula G 7

Situation and characteristics

The Fleurieu Peninsula, a spur of land projecting south-west from the South Mount Lofty Ranges, extends from O'Halloran Hill (south of Adelaide) to Cape Jervis on the west coast and the vast expanse of Lake Alexandrina in the east. It has a good network of main and secondary roads and a range of beaches for every taste – sheltered sandy inlets in Gulf St Vincent, mighty cliffs and thundering surf in the south. Victor Harbor, in Encounter Bay to the south-east, is a popular beach and holiday resort linked with Granite Island by a long causeway.

Sights on the Fleurieu Peninsula

★Goolwa

The popular and rapidly growing resort of Goolwa (pop. 3000; motels, caravan/camping parks) on the south-east coast of the peninsula lies on the narrow channel at the outlet of Lake Alexandrina, into which the Murray River flows. In the days when there was a busy shipping traffic on the Murray River Goolwa was an important port, with a number of shipyards. In its heyday – from which it has preserved a number of handsome old buildings – it was known as the New Orleans of Australia, mainly because of the numerous paddle-steamers plying on the river. An old paddle-steamer, the "Mundoo", still offers cruises on the river. The first public horse-drawn railway (1854) ran between the river harbour on the Murray and Port Elliot, on the coast. To the east of Goolwa are the Barrages, which prevent seawater from reaching the Murray.

Off Goolwa (ferry service) is Hindmarsh Island, a favourite haunt of bird-watchers.

Victor Harbor

See entry

Granite Island

See Victor Harbor

Spring Mountain

To the south of the road from Aldinga (see below) to Victor Harbor is Spring Mountain, on which the Boundy River rises. On its southern slopes is a conservation park in which visitors can see the rich flora of southern Australia, and on its east side is a wildlife reserve containing many species of Australian animals whose numbers elsewhere have been decimated.

Hindmarsh Falls

A few kilometres east of Spring Mountain are the romantic Hindmarsh Falls.

Port Elliot

North-east of Victor Harbor is Port Elliot (pop. 1200), the oldest port in Encounter Bay. Situated within easy reach of the Adelaide conurbation, it is now a popular holiday resort (hotels, motels, caravan/camping park). It has preserved a number of 19th century buildings, including a hotel of 1852 and Heathfield House. In the bay there are both sheltered beaches for bathers and good surfing beaches. From Port Elliot there are fine views of the mouth of the Murray River and Lake Alexandrina.

★Deep Creek Conservation Park

At the south-western tip of the peninsula is Deep Creek Conservation Park, with a rich variety of flora and fauna and an imposing cliff-fringed coast on the Southern Ocean.

Cape Jervis

From Cape Jervis, at the tip of the peninsula, there is a ferry service to Kangaroo Island (see entry).

Aldinga

The little town of Aldinga (pop. 3600) lies near the bay of the same name on the north-western coast of the Fleurieu Peninsula, only 45km/28 miles south of Adelaide. Evidence of its 19th century prosperity is provided by churches built in the 1860s and old mills and inns. The Aldinga Inn is one of the oldest in South Australia. 4km/2½ miles west of Aldinga is a very popular bathing beach. Farther north, at Maslin, is Australia's first nudist bathing beach. Within easy reach of Maslin is the wine-growing district of McLaren Vale.

McLaren Vale

See entry

★Flinders Ranges G 6

The Flinders Ranges, the gradually rising northward continuation of the Mount Lofty Ranges, run from north to south through the eastern part of South Australia for several hundred kilometres. They are named after Matthew Flinders, who explored much of southern Australia in 1801–03. The hills are rich in minerals (particularly copper and uranium) and of great scenic beauty, especially in the South Flinders Ranges north-east of Port Augusta (see entry) and in Flinders Ranges National Park to the north of Hawker.

★★Flinders Ranges National Park

Location; area
470km/290 miles north of Adelaide, 55km/34 miles north of Hawker; 80,578 hectares/199,028 acres.

Best time to visit
Spring to autumn.

Access
There are good roads from Port Augusta over the Pichi Richi Pass to Hawker and via Wilpena through the park to Blinman and Parachilna.

Accommodation
In Hawker.

Facilities
Bush camping; ranger stations at Wilpena and Oraparinna; walking trails.

Features
The most scenic part of the Flinders Ranges is the area north-east of Hawker which has been designated as a National Park, taking in the grandiose Wilpena Pound, with St Mary's Peak (1188m/3898ft) as its highest point. The sheltered valleys have a rich growth of vegetation, in striking contrast to the arid surrounding area. In spring the ground is carpeted with wild flowers. The varied forms and colours of the hills have inspired many painters, among them Hans Heysen.

Hawker
Hawker (pop. 300; hotel, motel, camping ground), a typical outback settlement in the centre of the northern Flinders Ranges, 400km/250 miles north of Adelaide, was once the prosperous centre of a large wheat-growing area, served by a railway line. Following a series of long droughts wheat-growing was abandoned, and Hawker is now a popular base for excursions into the impressive mountain scenery of the Flinders Ranges.

North of Hawker, in the Yourambulla Caves and on the Arkaroo Rock, are Aboriginal rock paintings.

★★Wilpena Pound
60km/37 miles north-east of Hawker is one of Australia's great natural wonders, Wilpena Pound. This is an elevated basin, 17km/10½ miles long by 7km/4½ miles across, enclosed by sheer cliffs over 1000m/3300ft high, which can be entered only through a narrow gorge. The name Wilpena comes from an Aboriginal term meaning the bent fingers of a closed hand. The rock walls of Wilpena Pound, shaped by erosion, were formed in the Palaeozoic period. The whole area occupies an important place in Aboriginal mythology. A trek round the Pound, with the ascent of St Mary's Peak, takes a full day of strenuous walking, with breathtaking views.

Wilpena
The little settlement of Wilpena (pop. 200; motel, caravan/camping park) is beautifully situated in a natural amphitheatre surrounded by hills, with a fascinating play of colour, changing over the course of the day. The only entrance is through a narrow gorge. In 1900 a wheat farmer built a homestead within the Pound, but flooding compelled him to abandon it.

The impressive mountain landscape draws many climbers and bush walkers. At some points there are rock paintings and drawings and other evidences of Aboriginal culture, some of them very ancient.

Blinman
The hamlet of Blinman, which now has only a few dozen inhabitants, lies 480km/300 miles north of Adelaide in the Flinders Ranges. From 1860 to 1890 it was a thriving copper-mining centre. It is now a small tourist resort (hotel, caravan/camping park) catering for visitors attracted by the natural beauties of the National Park.

Possible excursions from Blinman are to the Aroona Valley, in which there is an old settlement, Mount Hayward and the Brachina Gorge to the south.

★Great Wall of China
10km/6 miles south of Blinman is the Great Wall of China, a striking ridge of hills. Beltana, now almost a ghost town, is protected as a Historic Reserve. There are remains of copper-mining in the area.

★Arkaroola
The remote settlement of Arkaroola, with only a few dozen inhabitants, lies in an impressive outback setting in the Flinders Ranges, an area of jagged quartzite ridges and deep rugged gorges with rare plants and animals and a

◄ *In Flinders Ranges National Park*

variety of minerals. At Bolla Bollana Springs are the ruins of an old coppermine. The area round Arkaroola was settled by man at an early stage, as is shown by Aboriginal rock drawings and traces of settlement; it also features in Aboriginal mythology. There is accommodation for visitors in hotels, motels and caravan/camping parks.

South of Arkaroola are the Big Moro, Chambers and Italowie Gorges. Within easy reach is Mount Painter. There are breathtaking views from Freeling Heights over the Yudnamutana Gorge, and from Siller's Lookout over Lake Frome, a salt lake. 30km/19 miles north are the hot springs of Paralana.

★Gammon Ranges National Park

Arkaroola is also a good starting-point for wilderness tours in Gammon Ranges National Park (area 1000sq.km/386sq.miles), at the north end of the Flinders Ranges; the best times for a visit are spring and autumn. Tracks suitable for four-wheel-drive vehicles, with impressive views of the hills, lead into this rugged and little frequented wilderness in which bush camping offers the only overnight accommodation.

★Hahndorf G 7

Situation and characteristics

30km/19 miles south-east of Adelaide, in a beautiful upland region, is Hahndorf (pop. 1700), a settlement originally established in 1839 by German immigrants, with tree-lined streets, typically German half-timbered houses and Lutheran churches with steeples. In 1988 Hahndorf, the second oldest German settlement in Australia, was declared a State Heritage Area. The town takes its name from one Captain Hahn who helped the new settlers to find land.

Hans Heysen

Hahndorf is famed for its association with Sir Hans Heysen (1877–1968), a German-born artist who came to Australia in 1883 and later built himself an Alpine-style house on the outskirts of Hahndorf. He liked to paint the landscapes of the Adelaide Hills and Flanders Ranges. There are examples of his work to be seen in many places, including the Hahndorf Academy.

Features

Among the town's handsome old buildings are the Old Mill (1864; now a restaurant and motel), the Old Windmill (1842; renovated 1966), the German Arms Hotel (established 1839; present building *c.* 1868), St Michael's Church (1856) and the Hahndorf Inn (1858). The Clock Museum has a collection of old clocks and the German Train Village will appeal to railway enthusiasts. In the old schoolhouse (1857) is the art gallery of the Hahndorf Academy (open: daily 10am–5pm).

★Schuetzenfest

A German-style Schuetzenfest (originally a marksmen's festival) is celebrated every January, with German food and drink, music and entertainment.

Innamincka H 5

Situation and characteristics

The tiny settlement of Innamincka (motel) lies on the Strzelecki Track near Coongie Lake and Cooper Creek. There is a monument commemorating the tragic end of Burke and Wills's expedition in 1861. Here in the 1920s John Flynn, founder of the Flying Doctor Service (see Baedeker Special, p. 275), began to build up a radio communications network.

Cordillo Downs

North of Innamincka is the Cordillo Downs Station (originally a sheep-farm, now cattle), the only human settlement on the Strzelecki Track.

Moomba Oilfield

Near Innamincka is the rich Moomba Oilfield.

Warning

The Strzelecki Track is only for drivers with outback experience and a four-wheel-drive vehicle. There are no supplies or petrol between Lyndhurst and Innamincka.

★★Kangaroo Island G 7

Situation

Kangaroo Island, Australia's third largest island, lies south-west of the Fleurieu Peninsula (see entry), 120km/75 miles from Adelaide, separated from the mainland by the narrow Backstairs Passage.

Access

There are ferries between Cape Jervis (the south-western tip of the Fleurieu Peninsula) and Penneshaw on Kangaroo Island and between Adelaide and Port Lincoln (on the Eyre Peninsula) and Kingscote on Kangaroo Island. There are also air services from Adelaide (Air Kangaroo Island, Lloyds Aviation). There is no public transport on the island itself.

N.B.

Distances on Kangaroo Island are fairly great, and only a few sections of road are asphalted. To explore the island properly, therefore, several days should be allowed.

History

The first European settlers arrived on the island in 1838, but lack of water, food and building timber led many of them to leave again and settle round Adelaide instead.

Features

Kangaroo Island has many tourist attractions – varied coastal scenery with bizarre rock formations, stalactitic caves and beautiful beaches. It has a rich variety of fauna (including a colony of sealions in Seal Bay) and a total of 16 nature reserves, including the very interesting Flinders Chase National Park at the west end of the island, Cape Gantheaume on the south-east coast and Kelly Hill Conservation Park on the south-west coast. The rugged cliffs on the south coast have been eaten away by the fierce surf. On Cape Borda, at the north-western tip of the island, is an old lighthouse.

★Flinders Chase National Park

The western end of the island is occupied by Flinders Chase National Park (area 590sq.km/230sq.miles), which is best visited in spring, summer or autumn. It can be reached either by boat or by bush aircraft. Camping is permitted. The park has a notably rich flora and fauna (particularly birds). On the west coast are the Remarkable Rocks (bizarrely shaped granite boulders) and Admirals Arch, a limestone arch which is apparently the last relic of a stalactitic cave.

Kingscote

The main centre and principal port of Kangaroo Island is Kingscote (pop. 1500), where European settlers established their first base before moving

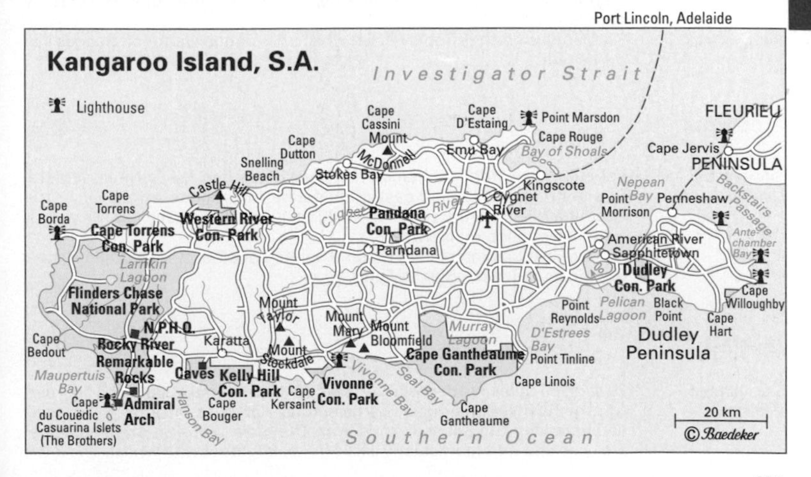

on to the southern mainland of Australia. The National Trust Museum illustrates the history of the island. The town has hotels, motels and caravan/camping parks.

American River

The fishing village of American River, now a holiday resort, lies at the east end of the island, near the isthmus leading to the Dudley Peninsula. It takes its name from the American seamen who built a boat here in 1803–04.

★Lake Eyre National Park G 5

Location; area

Lake Eyre National Park takes in an area of 12,880sq.km/4975sq.miles round Australia's largest salt lake in the hot and arid country of east central South Australia.

Best time to visit

In the winter months, after the region's rare falls of rain.

Warning

The exploration of this National Park is only for travellers with outback experience and a suitable four-wheel-drive vehicle. There are no service facilities.

Features

Lake Eyre National Park has a vegetation typical of the arid regions of Australia. The lake, named after the great explorer of Australia John Eyre, has had water in it on only three occasions since its discovery. Normally it consists merely of a layer of salt up to 3m/10ft deep. This salt lake provided almost ideal conditions for Donald Campbell's attempt on the world land speed record in 1964. On July 17th in that year he achieved a speed of 690km/429 miles an hour in his turbine-driven "Bluebird" and established a new world record.

Leigh Creek G 6

Situation and characteristics

Leigh Creek (pop. 1400; caravan/camping park), 520km/325 miles north of Adelaide in the Flinders Ranges, is the largest settlement north of Port Augusta (see entry). The town's economy is based on a large opencast coalfield which eventually swallowed up the original settlement, forcing the inhabitants in 1982 to move to a new site 13km/8 miles to the north.

Leigh Creek now sends 2 million tons of coal annually to the large power station in Port Augusta. Visitors can see round the coal workings by appointment.

Surroundings

8km/5 miles north is Copley, from which the rugged Gammon Ranges can be visited.

Lobethal G 6

Situation and characteristics

Lobethal, like Hahndorf (see entry), was founded by German settlers. Situated 40km/25 miles east of Adelaide in a sheltered valley in the Adelaide Hills, it is the centre of an agricultural area. In the 19th century it also had woollen mills (tweed).

There is much interesting material in the Lobethal Archives and Historical Museum (open: Sun. 2–5pm).

★Loxton H 6

Situation and characteristics

250km/155 miles north-east of Adelaide is Loxton (pop. 3300), the "garden city" of the Riverland region. Large numbers of ex-servicemen were resettled here after the Second World War. The main crops, in irrigated fields, are wine and fruit (particularly citrus fruits), together with wheat. The town was originally called Loxtons Hut, after a boundary rider of that name who built a primitive hut here.

Accommodation

Hotel, motel, caravan/camping parks.

Features

On the banks of the river is the Historical Village, with some two dozen faithfully re-created turn-of-the century buildings (open: Mon.–Fri. 10am–4pm, Sat., Sun., pub. hols. and during school holidays 10am–5pm). There are a number of galleries showing work by local artists.

★Berri Estates Winery

Outside the town is the Berri Estates Winery, the largest wine-making establishment in the southern hemisphere, which can be visited by appointment.

Mannum G 6

Situation and characteristics

Mannum (pop. 2000), in the centre of a mainly agricultural area (wool, beef, cereals, etc.), is one of the oldest settlements on the Murray River. It is the starting-point of the water-supply pipeline to Adelaide. "Mary Ann", the first paddle-steamer on the Murray River, 18m/60ft long was built here in 1853. Its huge square boiler stands in the riverfront park, along with a replica of the whaler in which Sturt sailed down the Murray in 1830. The "Marion", another old paddle-steamer built in 1898, is now a museum. Others – the "Lady Mannum", "Proud Mary" and "Murray Explorer" – operate cruises on the river. House boats on the Murray can be hired.

Accommodation

Hotels, motel, caravan/camping park.

Marree G 5

Situation and characteristics

The little outback town of Marree (pop. 400; hotel), situated at the junction of the notorious Birdsville Track and the Oodnadatta Track, was an important station on the overland telegraph line in the 19th century. A monument commemorates the surveyor John McDouall Stuart (see Famous People), who camped here during his 1859 expedition. For many years Marree was a staging-point for the Afghan-led camel trains of the 19th century. Of the camel-men's settlement, known as Ghan Town, only ruins remain. The Ghan railway which later followed the old trade route also passed through Marree, and the cattle which had been driven from Queensland on the Birdsville Track were loaded on to the train here. After the line was interrupted by flooding, however, it was moved farther west towards Tarcoola.

★McLaren Vale · Wine Coast G 7

Situation and characteristics

The gentle western slopes of the Mount Lofty Ranges to the south of Adelaide and the narrow coastal plain are famed for their wine. This whole area is known as the Wine Coast. The main wine-making towns are Clarendon, Reynella and above all McLaren Vale.

McLaren Vale

25km/15½ miles south of Adelaide is McLaren Vale (pop. 1500; motels), the main centre of the wine-growing region south of the capital (Wine Coast). The Barn, an old coaching station, now houses a restaurant and an art gallery. Round the town are dozens of wineries, most of which can be visited by appointment.

The Bushing Festival, a light-hearted wine festival, is held annually in October.

Old Noarlunga, Port Noarlunga

32km/20 miles south of Adelaide, in the Wine Coast region, are Old Noarlunga and Port Noarlunga, which has excellent bathing beaches, particularly Christies, Moana and Maslin Beaches, with accommodation for holidaymakers (hotel, motel, caravan/camping park).

A vineyard in the McLaren Vale

Hackham

At Hackham, 8km/5 miles farther north, is the interesting Pioneer Village Museum.

In this area, too, there are many wineries which can be visited.

Willunga

On the edge of the wine-growing area, 50km/30 miles south of Adelaide, is the little town of Willunga (pop. 1200), which was settled at a very early stage. It has a number of handsome old 19th-century buildings of bluestone with slated roofs. The Police Station, the Courthouse and the historic Bush Inn are under statutory protection.

The country round Willunga is famed for its almond-trees and the Almond Blossom Festival is held in July.

Morgan G 6

Situation and characteristics

170km/105 miles north-east of Adelaide, on the Murray River, is the little township of Morgan (pop. 440), which in the past was an important river port. It is the starting-point of the important water-supply pipeline to Whyalla (see entry).

Accommodation

Hotels, motels, caravan/camping park.

Features

The 12m/40ft high wharves of 1878 are well preserved. Other fine old buildings are the customs house, courthouse and railway station.

Mount Gambier H 7

Situation and characteristics

In the extreme south-east of South Australia, on the slopes of an extinct volcano, is the town of Mount Gambier (pop. 22,000), the commercial centre of an agricultural region (wheat, dairy farming, sheep) in which there are also large pine forests. Mount Gambier is easily reached from

Blue Lake, Mount Gambier

Adelaide on the Princes Highway. The Henty family settled here around 1834 and began to develop the fertile land round the town.

Accommodation

Many hotels, motels and caravan/camping parks.

★Mount Gambier

The town's main tourist attraction is Mount Gambier itself, an extinct volcano with four crater lakes. A curious natural phenomenon can be observed on the Blue Lake (maximum depth 197m/646ft) annually in November, when the colour of the lake changes from dull grey to brilliant blue, changing back at the end of summer. A scenic drive, with wide views, runs round the crater.

Excursions

Penola

52km/32 miles north of Mount Gambier is Penola (pop. 1200; hotel, motel, caravan/camping park), which preserves some hewn-timber cottages of the pioneering period. The mansion of Yallum Park dates from 1880. The old post office now houses a museum of local history.

Coonawarra

15km/9 miles north-west is Coonawarra, famed as a wine-making town (visits to wineries, wine tastings).

Millicent

50km/30 miles north-west is Millicent (pop. 5000; hotels, motels, caravan/camping park), an important commercial and industrial town with a large paper mill. The marshland surrounding the town was drained in the 19th century to provide land for pastoral farming and the growing of wheat. In the old schoolhouse of 1873 is a museum (open: Mon.–Sat. 10am–noon and 1–4pm) with interesting material on life in pioneering days. There is also an attractive Shell Garden (open: daily 9am–5pm), with fuchsias and begonias.

Tantanoola Caves

At Tantanoola, half way between Millicent and Mount Gambier, are a number of interesting limestone caves.

★Canunda National Park

10km/6 miles south-west of Millicent is the main entrance to Canunda National Park (area 90sq.km/35sq.miles; best visited in spring and autumn), with travelling dunes, rare coastal vegetation and many species of birds.

★Beachport

32km/20 miles north-west of Millicent, on the Southern Ocean, is Beachport (pop. 410), which in earlier days was an important whaling station. Its sheltered beaches have now made it a popular holiday resort with a variety of accommodation for visitors (hotel, motels, caravan/camping parks, etc.).

From the Bowman Scenic Drive there are fine views of the Southern Ocean. Between Lake George and the sea is Beachport Conservation Park.

Offshore is Penguin Island, to which there are excursions in summer.

★Mount Remarkable National Park G 6

Location; area
65km/40 miles north of Port Pirie; 8500 hectares/21,000 acres.

Best time to visit
Autumn and spring.

Access
Best via Port Pirie.

Facilities
Camping grounds. No drinking water.

Features
This very beautiful National Park is centred on Mount Remarkable (959m/3146ft), the most striking hill in the southern Flinders Ranges (see entry), which was given its name by the explorer Edward Eyre in 1839.

Magnificent panoramic views, wild gorges and rich wildlife (particularly birds) are the attractions for visitors – who must, however, have had some experience of bush walking and be properly equipped.

Melrose
Under the east side of Mount Remarkable lies Melrose (pop. 200), the oldest settlement in the southern Flinders Ranges, now a rising holiday resort (hotels, caravan/camping park). It preserves a number of old buildings, including the Police Station, the old Courthouse (1862; now a museum of local history), the North Star Hotel and the Mount Remarkable Hotel.

Murray Bridge G 7

Situation and characteristics
Murray Bridge (pop. 13,000), the largest town on the Murray River, has grown considerably over the last ten years or so. It lies 80km/50 miles east of Adelaide, with which it is linked with the fine South Eastern Freeway. After its foundation in the mid-19th century, Murray Bridge played an important part as a crossing-place for the herds of cattle driven from the east. A bridge built in 1879 is still in use. In the heyday of shipping on the Murray the town was also an important port.

Features
Among buildings of historical interest are the old mill, the railway station and the Murray Bridge Hotel. Also of interest is the Captain's Cottage Museum. Round the town are market gardens and farming country, with numerous glasshouses and a large milk-processing factory.

From Murray Bridge there are short excursions and longer cruises on the Murray River.

Accommodation
Hotels, motels, caravan/camping parks, house boats.

Naracoorte H 7

Situation and characteristics
Naracoorte (pop. 4800), founded in the 1840s, is one of the oldest inland settlements in South Australia. The local economy is based on cattle- and sheep-farming and wheat-growing. Wine is produced in the surrounding area.

Accommodation
Hotels, motels, caravan/camping parks.

★ Naracoorte Caves
11km/7 miles south-east of the town are the famous Naracoorte Caves. Of the 60 caves so far explored three are open to the public. The Alexandra and

Blanche Caves have spectacular stalactites and stalagmites, while the Victoria Fossil Cave, also containing stalactites and stalagmites, is famous for the fossils of giant Ice Age marsupials and the skeleton of a giant wombat which were found here in 1969. The Bat Cave is the home of a large colony of bats. There are conducted visits of the show caves daily between 9.30am and 4pm.

Nullarbor National Park F 6

Location; area

1100km/685 miles west of Adelaide and 300km/185 miles west of Ceduna; 2300sq.km/890sq.miles.

Best time to visit

Autumn, winter and spring.

Access

The Eyre Highway runs through the park.

Facilities

Bush camping.

Features

This vast monotonous plain with no trees (as its name indicates, from Latin "nullus arbor") is covered only with low-growing salt scrub. It is only after abundant winter rains that multi-coloured flowers and many varieties of grass bring a touch of life to the landscape. Rough tracks lead to the imposing cliffs which fringe it on the south.

Warning

Beware of the friable rock on the edge of the cliffs!

Oodnadatta G 5

Situation and characteristics

The tiny settlement of Oodnadatta (pop. 230) on the edge of the Simpson Desert is reached on the Oodnadatta Track (4WD vehicles only), following the route taken by John McDouall Stuart (see Famous People) on his crossing of Australia in 1861–62. Later the same route was followed by the overland telegraph.

The Ghan railway from Port Augusta to Alice Springs ran by way of Oodnadatta until the line was moved farther west to avoid flooding.

The name Oodnadatta comes from an Aboriginal term for the blossom of the mulga, a shrub which grows in these arid conditions.

Accommodation

Hotel, caravan/camping park.

Witjira National Park

200km/125 miles north of Oodnadatta is Witjira National Park (see entry).

Peterborough G 6

Situation and characteristics

Peterborough (pop. 2200) is a place of interest to railway enthusiasts. In the past it was the junction of three different railway systems, and it is still a railway town, on the (relatively) busy line from Port Pirie to Broken Hill. There is a very interesting Railway Museum, and at weekends and on public holidays the local railway preservation society runs steam train excursions on a narrow-gauge line.

Accommodation

Hotels, motels, caravan/camping park.

Pinnaroo H 7

Situation and characteristics

Pinnaroo (pop. 750) lies on the Ouyen Highway, only 6km/4 miles from the Victorian border. It has a museum of agricultural machinery and a research institute concerned among other things with developing resistant and productive cereal strains.

Accommodation

Hotels, motel, caravan/camping park.

Surroundings

Round Pinnaroo are a number of protected areas of the endangered mallee

Historic old houses in Port Augusta

scrub vegetation (Biliatt Conservation Park, Scorpion Springs and Mount Saugh).

★Port Augusta G 6

Situation and characteristics

The port and industrial town of Port Augusta (pop. 14,600) lies 320km/200 miles north of Adelaide at the northern tip of the Spencer Gulf. It is a supply centre for the outback areas of the state and the large sheep stations in the area and an important railway junction, with direct connections to Perth, Sydney and Alice Springs. The economy of the town was given a great boost when the State Electricity Trust built a number of large power stations here. These are fuelled by coal from the opencast mines at Leigh Creek, 300km/185 miles north, and generate more than a third of the state's electricity.

Accommodation

Motels, caravan/camping parks.

Features

On a Heritage Walk round the town visitors will see a number of fine old buildings, including the Town Hall (1887), the Courthouse (1884) and above all St Augustine's Church, with beautiful stained glass. The Cudnatta Art Gallery is housed in the old railway station.

★Homestead Park Pioneer Museum

A particular tourist attraction is the Homestead Park Pioneer Museum in Elsie Street, which re-creates the life of pioneering days, with a blacksmith's shop, the pine-log Yudnappinna Homestead and an old steam train.

Wadlata Outback Centre

The Wadlata Outback Centre presents a picture of the outback, with its attractions and its hazards, which will be of particular interest to adventurous travellers contemplating an outback journey.

Royal Flying Doctor Service

In Vincent Street is the base of the Royal Flying Doctor Service. Sightseeing flights are on offer at the flying school's airfield.

The Australian Arid Lands Botanic Gardens display the surprisingly varied flora of the arid regions of Australia.

★Australian Arid Lands Botanic Gardens

Excursions

★Pichi Richi Pass Scenic Drive

Half an hour's drive north-east of Port Augusta is the Pichi Richi Pass Scenic Drive, which offers a magnificent scenic experience.

★Quorn

During the school holidays an old-time steam train runs from Woolshed Flat to the historic little town of Quorn (pop. 1100), north-east of Port Augusta. The town, now a popular tourist centre (hotels, motels, caravan/camping park), lies in a valley in the Flinders Ranges and was founded in 1878 as a station on the Great Northern Railway, which closed down in 1957. An old mill now houses a museum of local history and an art gallery. North of the town are a number of ruined homesteads, relics of the days when wheat-growing flourished in this area.

★Warren Gorge, Buckaringa Gorge

20km/12½ miles and 30km/18½ miles north of Quorn are the wild and romantic Warren Gorge, a Mecca for rock-climbers, and Buckaringa Gorge.

★Hancock's Lookout

40km/25 miles south-east of Port Augusta is Hancock's Lookout, from which there are breathtaking views.

★Port Lincoln G 6

Port Lincoln (pop. 13,000), at the southern tip of the Eyre Peninsula (see entry), is only 250km/155 miles from Adelaide as the crow flies, but almost 600km/375 miles by road. It was one of the earliest European-style settlements, established in 1839. Shortage of water and a relatively infertile hinterland hampered its early development, but these problems have been dealt with and the area now produces rich crops of wheat. Port Lincoln is the base of a Australia's largest fishing fleet and a busy commercial port, exporting wheat, wool, sheep and frozen fish.

Accommodation

Hotels, motels, caravan/camping parks.

Features

With its sheltered bays, mild climate and beautiful coastal scenery, with rugged cliffs alternating with beautiful beaches, Port Lincoln is becoming an increasingly popular holiday resort. In the town itself there is the interesting Mill Cottage Museum (1867). From elegant Boston House there is a majestic view over the bay. The Lincoln Hotel (1840) in Tasman Terrace is the oldest of its kind on the Eyre Peninsula.

The beginning of the tunny-fishing season is marked by the Tunarama Festival, held annually in January on the weekend after Australia Day.

Excursions

Spencer Gulf, Dangerous Reef

Off the coast are a number of attractive little islands, easily reached by boat. Further out lies the famous Dangerous Reef, in the waters around which live large numbers of white sharks. Boat and diving trips are organised, with the possibility of seeing some sharks.

★Lincoln National Park

10km/6 miles south of Port Lincoln, occupying the southern tip of the Eyre Peninsula, is Lincoln National Park (area 174sq.km/67sq.miles; best visited in summer; camping grounds), with rugged cliffs, mallee scrub vegetation and many species of birds. Good fishing and swimming.

★Coffin Bay National Park

On a spur of land reaching out into the Great Australian Bight on the south-western coast of the Eyre Peninsula, 50km/30 miles west of Port Lincoln, is Coffin Bay National Park (area 300sq.km/115sq.miles; best visited in spring and autumn), a region of granite and limestone crags, with heavy surf thundering against jagged cliffs, heathland with a sparse growth of vegetation and travelling dunes, and sheltered sandy bays for sun worshippers and water sports enthusiasts.

★Coffin Bay (village)

Picturesquely situated on a long sheltered inlet near the south-western tip of the Eyre Peninsula is the little fishing village of Coffin Bay (pop. 340; hotel, caravan/camping park), named by Matthew Flinders after his friend Isaac Coffin. Tourist accommodation includes a hotel and caravan/camping park.

Port Pirie G 6

Situation and characteristics

Port Pirie (pop. 14,000), an important port and industrial town, lies 230km/145 miles north of Adelaide on the Spencer Gulf. The first settlers came here in 1845, and since then wheat-growing has continued to play a major part in the economy of the area, as evidenced by the huge grain silos which dominate the skyline. Lead from Broken Hill (NSW) began to be smelted here in 1889, and Port Pirie now has the largest lead smelters in Australia. Silver and zinc ores from Broken Hill are processed here and fishing also makes a contribution to the town's economy.

Accommodation

Hotels, motels, caravan/camping parks.

Features

The National Trust Museum Buildings in Ellen Street include an old Victorian railway station. Carnbrae, a historic mansion in Florence Street, has well preserved furniture and furnishings and a large collection of dolls.

★Country Music Festival

The Port Pirie Country Music Festival, held annually in October, attracts thousands of visitors from all over Australia.

Excursions

Crystal Brook

25km/15½ miles south-east of Port Pirie is Crystal Brook (pop. 1300; hotels, caravan/camping park), a farming centre (wheat, sheep, cattle) dominated by huge grain silos. It was given its name by John Eyre on his expedition to the north in 1838. It has an animal park and other tourist facilities and is a good base for trips into the southern Flinders Ranges (see entry).

20km/12½ miles north-east of Crystal Brook, in the beautiful valley of the Rocky River, is Gladstone, once an important railway junction.

Mount Remarkable

See Mount Remarkable National Park

Renmark H 6

Situation and characteristics

Renmark (pop. 4260) lies in the centre of the oldest irrigation area in Australia, 260km/160 miles north-east of Adelaide in the Riverland area on the Murray River, near the point where the states of South Australia, New South Wales and Victoria meet. The first irrigation system was installed by the Chaffey brothers from Canada in 1887, and now huge plantations of citrus and other fruits and vineyards are supplied with water from the Murray. The fruit is processed in local canneries and juice factories. Wheat, sheep and dairy farming also make their contributions to the local economy.

Accommodation

Hotels, motels, caravan/camping parks.

Features

Olivewood, the former Chaffey homestead, is now a National Trust museum. The town is attractively laid out with gardens and beds of roses. The Renmark Hotel is an imposing three-storey building at a bend in the river.

Cruises are run on the Murray River, and house boats can be hired.

★Robe G 7

Situation and characteristics

340km/210 miles south of Adelaide, on Guichen Bay, is the attractive little town of Robe (pop. 740), which has many well preserved old buildings. In earlier days it was an important wool-exporting port, and in 1857 over 10,000 Chinese disembarked here on their way to the goldfields in Victoria. Robe is now an increasingly popular holiday destination.

Accommodation

Hotels, motels, caravan/camping parks.

Features

Some two dozen buildings in the town are under statutory protection. Karatta House was the summer residence of the governor of South Australia in the 1860s. The old Customs House now contains an interesting museum of local history. Other notable old buildings are the Lakeside and Caledonian Inns.

The coast round the town is particularly beautiful. There are safe beaches in Guichen Bay and also stretches of rugged cliffs carved into bizarre shapes by the fierce surf from the Southern Ocean. On the numerous lagoons and coastal lakes large numbers of birds can be observed.

★Southern Vales • Wine Coast G 7

Situation and importance

The western slopes of Mount Lofty Ranges to the south of Adelaide and the narrow coastal plain are a well-known wine-producing region of South Australia, and are colloquially known as the "Wine Coast". The main towns associated with viniculture are Clarendon, Reynella and, in particular, McLaren Vale.

McLaren Vale

40km/25 miles south of Adelaide lies McLaren Vale (pop. 1500; motels). No fewer than four dozen wineries are to be found here, and many are open to visitors, offering conducted tours and wine-tasting.

The Barn, a former coaching inn, now houses a well-known restaurant with an art gallery. The Bushing Festival, a merry wine-festival which attracts large numbers of visitors, is held here every October.

Old Noarlunga, Port Noarlunga

The town of Old Noarlunga and its harbour lie 32km/20 miles south of Adelaide in the Wine Coast region. Port Noarlunga boasts some excellent bathing beaches, the main ones being Christian Beach, Moana Beach and Maslin Beach. Tourist accommodation includes a hotel, motel and caravan/camping park.

Hackham

The Pioneer Museum in Hackham, 8km/5 miles further north, is of interest. Some wineries in the area are also open to visitors.

Willunga

On the edge of the Southern Vales wine-producing region and only 50km/30 miles south of Adelaide lies the historic little town of Willunga (pop. 1200; motel), with some old 18th c. buildings in bluestone with slate roofs. The police station, court buildings and the old Bush Inn are listed buildings. The almond trees nearby are a wonderful sight when in bloom in July/August.

Strathalbyn G 6

Situation and characteristics

The inland town of Strathalbyn (pop. 2600), 60km/37 miles south-east of Adelaide on the Angas River, was founded in 1839. As its name indicates, it has Scottish associations.

Accommodation

Caravan park.

Features

The town has preserved a number of old buildings, including the police station, the courthouse, St Andrew's Church and an old grain mill. There is an interesting Pioneer Museum.

Swan Reach G 6

Situation and characteristics

The little settlement of Swan Reach (pop. 230) lies on the Murray River, 100km/62 miles east of Gawler. The beautiful surrounding country and good fishing are attracting increasing numbers of holidaymakers. House boats can be hired for excursions on the river, and the "Murray

Accommodation

Explorer" offers longer cruises, for example to Mannum.
Hotel, caravan/camping park.

Tailem Bend G 7

Situation and characteristics

Tailem Bend (pop. 1500), 110km/68 miles south-east of Adelaide, is an important traffic hub. It lies at the junction of the Dukes Highway (Hwy 8), Princes Highway (Hwy 1) and Ouyen Highway (Hwy 12), and is also an important railway junction.

Accommodation

Hotels, motel, caravan/camping park.

Features

5km/3 miles north of Tailem Bend is the Old Tailem Town Pioneer Village, an interesting open-air museum (open: daily 10am–5pm).

Victor Harbor G 7

Situation and characteristics

The very popular holiday resort Victor Harbor (pop. 6000; hotels, motels, caravan/camping parks) lies 84km/52 miles south of Adelaide on the south-east coast of the Fleurieu Peninsula, looking out over Encounter Bay, where in 1802 the explorer Matthew Flinders encountered his French rival Nicolas Baudin. The bay is sheltered from the surf of the Southern Ocean by Granite Island. In the past Victor Harbor was an important whaling and sealing station.

Accommodation

Hotels, motels, caravan/camping parks.

Granite Island

Granite Island is linked to the mainland by a causeway on which a horse-drawn tram still runs. A chair-lift goes to the highest point on the island, on which there is a wildlife reserve (kangaroos, dwarf penguins, seabirds).

Waikerie G/H 6

Situation and characteristics

The little town of Waikerie (pop. 1800), 170km/105 miles north-east of Adelaide, is a kind of oasis in the otherwise arid mallee scrub in which fruit, wine grapes and vegetables are grown with the aid of irrigation. It has been called a gliders' paradise, with a gliding club 4km/2-1/2 miles east of the town.

The Murray River is lined by high sandstone cliffs and tall eucalyptus trees. There are house boats available for hire. In the mallee scrub of the surrounding area, along the river and in the irrigated area are many species of birds.

Accommodation

Motel, caravan/camping parks.

Pooginook Park

12km/7-1/2 miles north-east of Waikerie is Pooginook Conservation Park, with typical mallee vegetation and fauna (including the mallee fowl).

Whyalla G 6

Situation and characteristics

Whyalla (pop. 26,000) lies 390km/240 miles north-west of Adelaide at the north-eastern corner of the Eyre Peninsula (see entry). It is the second largest town in South Australia, with a deep-water port, and an important centre of heavy industry processing iron ore from Iron Knob and Iron Baron in the nearby Middle Back Ranges. The town itself has no particular features of interest.

History

The origins of Whyalla go back to a little 19th century settlement called Hummock Hill which was given a tremendous boost when the industrial giant BHP established a large steelworks. From 1939 to 1978 the town also had a large shipyard.

Accommodation

Hotels, motels, caravan/camping parks.

Features

The principal attraction of the town's Maritime Museum is the "Whyalla", a ship built here in 1941. There are very interesting conducted tours of the BHP steelworks, which also include an excursion to the Iron Knob iron mines.

★Witjira National Park G 5

Location; area

1400km/870 miles north-west of Adelaide; 7800sq.km/3000sq.miles.

Best time to visit

July to September. A visit in summer, with its intense heat, is not to be recommended.

Access

From Oodnadatta (4WD vehicles only; 200km/125 miles). This is a journey for experienced and properly equipped outbackers only.

Features

Witjira National Park is famed for its hot artesian springs, which provide a habitat for a very varied fauna (particularly amphibians and birds). Of special interest are the Dalhousie Thermal Ponds, 180km/110 miles north of Oodnadatta (see entry).

The arid region with artesian springs extends from the stony plains in the west to the sand-dunes of the Simpson Desert. It features prominently in Aboriginal mythology.

Yorke Peninsula G 6/7

Situation and characteristics

The boot-shaped Yorke Peninsula to the west of Adelaide lies between Spencer Gulf in the west and Gulf St Vincent in the east. Around 1860 rich deposits of copper were found at Wallaroo, Moonta and Kadina and a mining boom developed, during which many Cornish miners came to the area. Mining was abandoned in the 1920s, and only a few ruins remain as reminders of past activity. This is now a grain-growing region.

The east coast of the peninsula is particularly beautiful. There are safe bathing beaches on the west coast.

Little Cornwall

Situation and characteristics

The three-town triangle of Kadina, Moonta and Wallaroo on the north-west coast of the Yorke Peninsula where the rich deposits of copper were discovered is often called Little Cornwall. The many thousands of Cornish miners who settled here have left a legacy of Cornish tradition, given expression in the festival, Kernewek Lowender, held in May in odd-numbered years.

Kadina

The largest town on the Yorke Peninsula and its commercial centre is Kadina (pop. 3700), which lies some 10km/6 miles inland from the north-west coast. Its history is closely bound up with the 19th century copper boom, and it preserves a number of old-established hotels and inns with verandahs and wrought-iron balcony railings. The Kadina Museum illustrates the history of the Matta Matta copper-mine and displays old agricultural machinery.

Moonta

A large deposit of copper was discovered at Moonta (pop. 3000) in 1861 and continued to be worked until the 1920s. Part of the mining installations is now a museum of industrial history.

Wallaroo

In a wide bay on the north-west coast of the Yorke Peninsula is Wallaroo (pop. 2500), which in recent decades has developed into a busy grain-exporting port. The deposits of copper found near here in 1859 continued to be worked until the price of copper in world markets fell in the 1920s. A number of buildings dating from the period of the copper boom have been preserved, and the old post office now houses an interesting National Trust museum of local history.

Coastal scenery in the south-west of the Yorke Peninsula

Tourism now also makes a contribution to the economy of Wallaroo (hotels, motels, caravan/camping park), largely because of its relatively safe beaches.

Other Excursions on the Yorke Peninsula

Maitland

South-east of Little Cornwall, in the centre of the peninsula, is Maitland (pop. 1100), which has an interesting National Trust museum, mainly devoted to the history of agriculture.

Port Victoria

Half way down the west coast of the peninsula is Port Victoria (pop. 250), which in the days of the windjammers was an important grain port. Its heyday is recalled in the Maritime Museum. Round the little settlement are a number of sheltered bathing beaches.

Minlaton

Minlaton (800), in the centre of the southern half of the peninsula, was the birthplace of the aviation pioneer Harry Butler, whose plane is displayed in the aviation museum which bears his name. Within easy reach of Minlaton are bathing beaches at Port Vincent (25km/15½ miles east), Bluff and Port Rickaby (20km/12½ miles west). There is some accommodation (motel, camping ground) for visitors.

Yorketown

Yorketown (pop. 800), in an extensive grain-growing area, is the supply centre for the south end of the peninsula (the heel and toe of the "boot"). Round the town are a number of salt lakes, some of which have taken on a curious pink colouring. The rugged coastal scenery is highly impressive.

In recent years, thanks to its proximity to Innes National Park, Yorketown has developed into a popular holiday resort (hotel, motel, caravan/camping park).

★Innes National Park

At the southern tip of the peninsula is Innes National Park (area 90sq.km/35sq.miles), a region of mallee and heath vegetation, salt lakes, marshland and sand-dunes. This is a place for bird-watchers, with many protected species, including the rare western whipbird. There are good surfing beaches in Pondalowie Bay.

Edithburgh

15km/9 miles east of Yorketown is the little township of Edithburgh (pop. 450), on the cliff-fringed south coast of the peninsula. Thanks to its beautiful situation it is a popular tourist resort (motels, caravan/camping park). From Edithburgh there are superb views of Gulf St Vincent and the Troubridge Shoals, a chain of tiny islands. There is an interesting local museum. The jetty dates from 1873. There are an idyllic rock swimming pool at the foot of the cliffs, a good bathing beach in Sultana Bay, to the south, and good diving grounds in the coastal waters, including the wreck of the "Clan Ranald", which sank in 1934.

Tasmania

General

Holiday Island
Area: 68,000sq.km./26,250sq. miles
Population: 471,000
Capital: Hobart

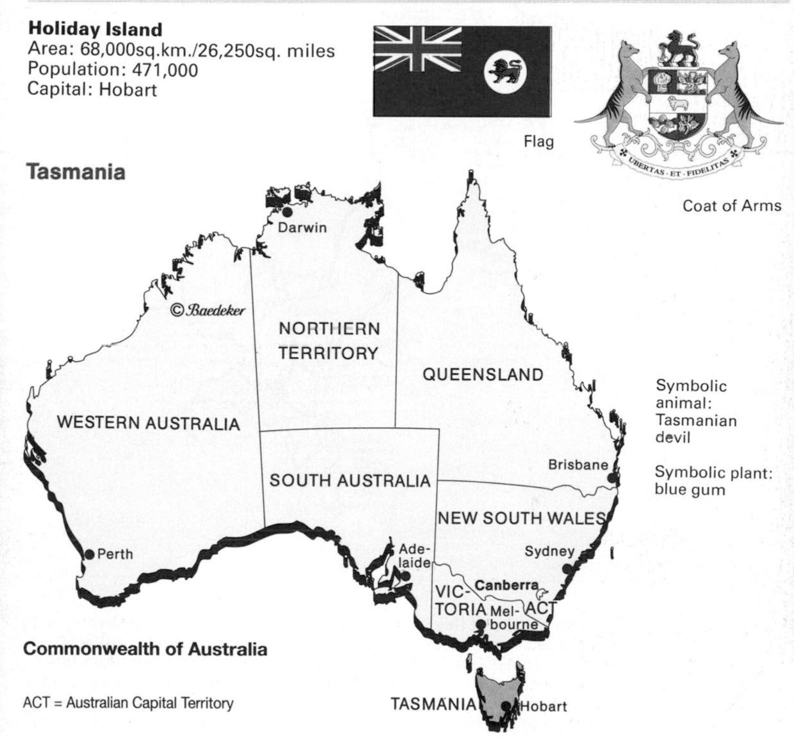

Symbolic animal: Tasmanian devil

Symbolic plant: blue gum

Situation and characteristics

The heart-shaped island of Tasmania lies some 300km/185 miles south of the Australian mainland, separated from it by the usually stormy Bass Strait. The smallest of the Australian states, it has an area of only 68,000sq.km/26,000sq.miles and measures only just over 300km/185 miles from east to west and rather less than that from north to south. Lying as it does in the relatively cool Australian south, it cannot offer the attractions of coral reefs and all-year-round bathing; but immigrants from Britain must have been reminded of the climate they had been used to at home. During the summer months many mainlanders (inhabitants of the Australian mainland) like to spend their holidays in the temperate climate of the "Holiday Island", with its scenic beauty and range of facilities for leisure activities.

Tasmania was known in the 19th century as a convict island on which prisoners transported from Britain were condemned to hard labour, breaking stone, hewing coal, felling timber, building roads and bridges.

◀ *Tasman's Arch, a striking natural feature in Tasmania*

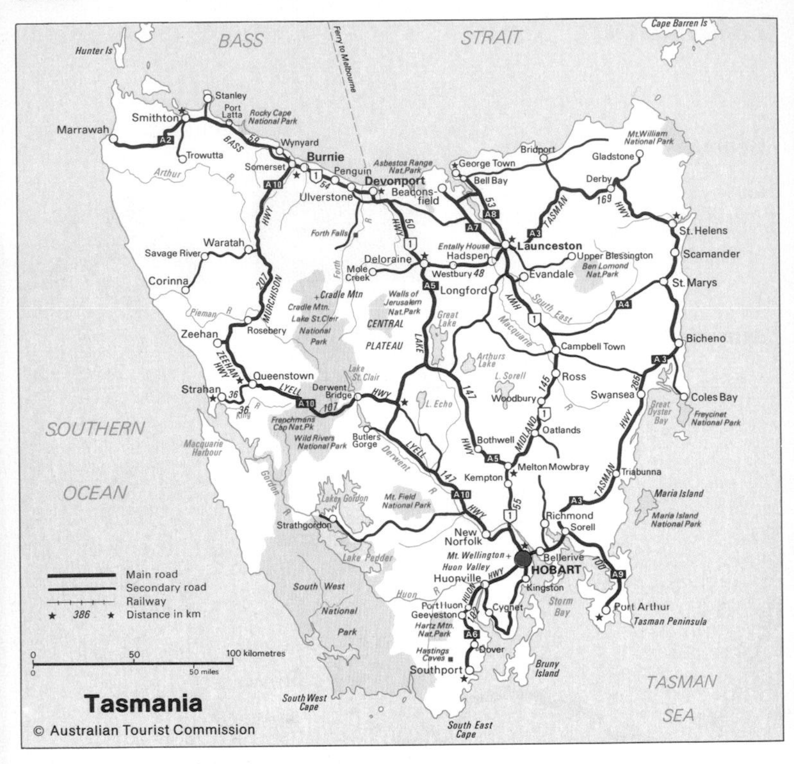

Topography

The topography of this hilly island in the cool temperate west-wind zone was shaped by glacial action during the Ice Age. Its highest peak is Mount Ossa (1617m/5305ft). In the west of the island are temperate rain forests and, here and there, expanses of moorland; in the drier east eucalyptus forests predominate.

The island is comparatively rich in minerals – auriferous copper ore, tin, iron ore, wolfram and coal. Ample power is available from the island's vast hydro-electric potential, and over the last few decades an elaborate system of artificial lakes has been built up, particularly in western Tasmania, to pound water for powering hydro-electric stations.

Tourist attractions

Tasmania has more hills than any other Australian state. Roughly two-thirds of its area is covered by plateaux bounded by escarpments ("tiers"). In the south-east, round the capital city of Hobart, the landscape is friendlier, and the early settlers were attracted by its fertile soil. Particularly attractive parts of the island are the Tasman Peninsula, with Port Arthur, and Huon Valley, the "apple valley". Along the north coast, too, Tasmania has the appearance of a well-cared-for garden. The volcanic soil and mild climate produce good grazing land and rich crops of fruit, potatoes and other vegetables. Important towns on the north coast, in addition to Launceston, are George Town, Devonport, Burnie, Wynyard and Stanley. The east coast has quiet fishing ports and beautiful sandy beaches, with such holiday resorts as Swansea, Bicheno and St Helens. In the hilly Midlands, so green and English that the early settlers at once felt at home, are a

Baedeker Special

The Tasmanian Devil and its Cousins

The Tasmanian devil who features in the Bugs Bunny cartoon films is not a Hollywood invention but a very real animal which is found only on the remote island of Tasmania. Like many other Australian mammals, it is a marsupial: that is, the females have a pouch containing mammary glands on their belly in which the young live until they are able to live on their own.

The Tasmanian devil differs from those other marsupials, the kangaroo and the koala, in both appearance and habits. It is a carnivore, a squat little animal somewhat similar to a fox with four sturdy legs, a hard skull and immensely strong teeth and jaws. Dark grey or black in colour, with a white stripe across the chest, it does its hunting by night. Its main diet consists of small birds and mammals, but it also eats carrion and sometimes catches fish. When it is irritated it has a fierce whining growl. The Tasmanian devil is Tasmania's mascot and emblem, and can be seen in many Australian zoos.

The largest carnivorous marsupial is the Tasmanian tiger or Tasmanian wolf, which is now thought to be extinct. The last time a Tasmanian tiger was seen in the wild was in the 1930s and the largest in captivity died in 1936, in Hobart Zoo. There remains the possibility that a few may have survived in the inaccessible primeval forests of south-western Tasmania. It is called the Tasmanian tiger because of the light-coloured stripes on its back.

The only rodent among Tasmania's marsupials is the wombat, found mainly in the south of the island. It is a solitary, nocturnal animal, not unlike a beaver in appearance, with a grey or dark-coloured coat and short legs, between 30 and 50 inches long. It eats mainly grasses, roots and mushrooms and lives in underground burrows which it excavates with its strong front legs. Interestingly, the female's pouch is on its back, making it that much easier for the young to find their way to their warm nest. The wombat is now an endangered species.

Tasmanian devils – funny but fierce

number of old settlements (Ross, Evandale, Richmond, New Norfolk, Oatlands), living museums which recall the early days of the colony. The central plateau reaches out towards the inaccessible south and west in imposing ranges of hills. The eastern part is known as the "land of a thousand lakes", after the innumerable glaciated valleys and barrier lakes. Lake St Clair, 17km/10½ miles long and 200m/650ft deep, is a relic of the Ice Age. Almost the whole of the south-west – a unique expanse of undisturbed wilderness – is on UNESCO's World Heritage list and under strict statutory protection. The South West National Park, with an area of 605,000 hectares/150,000 acres, occupies a tenth of Tasmania. The damming of Lake Pedder to supply a hydro-electric station led to a sharp conflict between environmentalists and the electricity authorities. One benefit for visitors is that the construction of a road to the reservoir made the National Park more easily accessible. The wild storm-lashed west and south coasts are still unspoiled. Apart from Strahan, on Macquarie Harbour, there is no good sheltered harbour.

Places of Interest from A to Z in Tasmania

Avoca J 8

Situation and characteristics

The little township of Avoca (pop. 220) lies 80km/50 miles south-east of Launceston (see entry) in the beautiful valley of the South Esk River, which flows through the foothills of Ben Lomond.

Features

In colonial times Avoca was a place of some consequence, as a number of fine old buildings show. The neo-Romanesque St Thomas's Church was built in 1843 to the design of James Blackburn; the parish hall is also a notable 19th century building.

Surroundings

To the north of the town is Bona Vista (1848), one of the finest mansions in Tasmania. A few kilometres east of Avoca is a prominent hill, St Paul's Dome (1027m/3370ft).

Beaconsfield J 8

Situation and characteristics

Beaconsfield (pop. 1100), lying to the west of the river Tamar 46km/29 miles north-west of Launceston (see entry), was founded early in the colonial period and was originally known as Cabbage Tree Hill. After the discovery of rich deposits of gold in 1877 it grew rapidly to become the third largest town in Tasmania, but in 1914 the mine was closed down because of flooding. There are now plans to reopen it.

Features

The Grubb Shaft Museum, housed in one of the brick pithead buildings of 1904, contains the old steam-driven winding gear and an exhibition on gold-mining. It is planned to restore the old pump-house. A notable feature of the town is Holy Trinity Church, with decorative gables and a handsome tower. North of the town, on the road from Kelso to Greens Beach, is a monument marking the site of the early settlement of York Town (1804). To the south-east of Beaconsfield is the modern Batman Bridge spanning the Tamar. Opposite Beauty Point is the deep-water harbour of Bell Bay.

Asbestos Range National Park

Location

17km/10½ miles north-west of Beaconsfield on the north coast of Tasmania.

Best time to visit

Spring to autumn.

Access

From Beaconsfield there are reasonably negotiable roads and tracks to the eastern and western part of the National Park.

Facilities

Camping grounds; picnic areas, walking and riding trails, ranger station.

Features

The Asbestos Range National Park lies on the coast to the west of the natural harbour of Port Dalrymple, between Port Sorell and Greens Beach. Inland from the coast is an unspoiled tract of country which offers good walking. The park has a very varied pattern of coastal, dune and heath vegetation and a rich wildlife (including wombats, opossums, wallabies and Forester kangaroos, which became extinct in the 19th century but were successfully bred in captivity and reintroduced). Bakers Beach is popular with water sports enthusiasts, though there is a dangerous current at its western end. Inland from the beach is a freshwater lagoon on which many water birds can be observed.

★ Bicheno J 8

Situation and characteristics

On the north-eastern coast of Tasmania, some 200km/125 miles from Hobart, is the old fishing port of Bicheno (pop. 700), which now attracts many holidaymakers with its beautiful beaches and good fishing. Originally Bicheno was a whaling station established about 1803. In the mid 19th century coal was shipped from here. Along with tourism, crayfishing is a major source of income.

Accommodation
Hotel, motel, caravan/camping park.

Features
7km/4½ miles north is the East Coast Bird Life and Animal Park. From the Twin Hills there are fine views.

There is a picturesque foreshore walkway from Redbill Point, north of the town, to the Blowhole, to the south.

Douglas-Apsley National Park

Location; area
15km/9 miles north-west of Bicheno; 16,080 hectares/39,700 acres.

Access
A track from Bicheno runs north through the park to the Apsley Gorge. From Launceston (see entry) it can be reached on the Midland Highway and Esk Main Road.

Accommodation
In Bicheno.

Facilities
Bush camping; walking trails, rest areas.

Features
The Douglas-Apsley National Park, established in 1990, lies inland from the north-east coast of Tasmania. It is an almost untouched area of dry sclerophyll (hard-leaved) forest, forest-clad ridges and patches of rain forest, with impressive waterfalls and wild gorges. Also very beautiful, but difficult of access, are the valleys of the Apsley River and Douglas River. There are spectacular views on the rugged north-east coast, shaped by the surf of the Tasman Sea.

Bothwell J 8

Situation and characteristics
Bothwell (pop. 360) lies on the Clyde River 75km/47 miles north-west of Hobart in a sheep and cattle farming district. It is the gateway to the rugged central highlands and the lake district. The town was founded in 1824 by Governor Sir George Arthur, and Scottish immigrants soon laid out what is believed to be Australia's earliest golf course. In the surrounding area there are excellent trout-fishing waters (Arthurs Lake, Penstock Lagoon, Lake Echo, etc.).

Accommodation
Camping/caravan park.

Features
This quiet little country town has more than fifty fine 19th century buildings. The Castle Hotel in Patrick Street dates from 1829, with an 1860 extension. St Luke's Uniting Church (built by John Leo Archer in 1831) is Australia's second oldest Presbyterian church; the figures over the doorway were carved by the convict sculptor Daniel Herbert. The Georgian-style Slate House (High Street) was built in 1835. The "Coffee Palace" in Dalrymple Street is now a museum. Wentworth House (1833) belonged to a brother of William Wentworth, one of the team who found a passage through the Blue Mountains. The old Post Office, a timber building of 1891, originally housed the Van Diemen's Land Bank.

Surroundings
Round Bothwell there are a number of other interesting old buildings, for example Thorpe Mill (2km/1¼ miles north) with its large water-wheel.

Central Plateau Conservation Area

Location; area
North of Bothwell; 89,200 hectares/220,300 acres.

Features
The central plateau of Tasmania is often called the "land of a thousand lakes". The largest of the lakes are the Great Lake, Lake Echo, Lake Sorell, Arthurs Lake and Lake St Clair. The plateau rises from the Clyde Valley in the south (alt. 300m/1000ft) to 1000m/3300ft at the Great Lake. To the north it is bounded by the hills of the Great Western Tiers. In spite of a climate which is raw even in summer the lake district is very popular with bush walkers and anglers.

The Central Plateau is traversed by the 150km/95 mile long Lake Highway (gravel surface at some points).

Lake Highway

★Bruny Island (North Bruny Island · South Bruny Island) J 8

Situation and characteristics

The thinly populated North and South Bruny Islands, off the south-east coast of Tasmania, are linked by a very narrow isthmus. There is a ferry between Kettering on the mainland and Roberts Point on North Bruny Island. The island was visited in the second half of the 18th century by a number of well-known navigators (Furneaux in 1773, Cook in 1777, Bligh in 1788 and 1792), and Captain Bligh is said to have planted the first apple-trees in Australia here. Bruny Island is named after the French Admiral Bruny d'Entrecasteaux, who surveyed this area in 1792 and is also commemorated in the name of the channel between Tasmania and Bruny Island.

Accommodation

Guesthouses, caravan/camping parks.

Features

In the south-east of the northern island, near Cape Queen Elizabeth, is a memorial to the early European navigators who passed this way. From the lookout (viewpoint) at the near end of the isthmus between Isthmus Bay and Adventure Bay there are magnificent panoramic views.

On the south island visitors can see the spot where Cook landed. In Adventure Bay is the Bligh Museum. There are good bush walks in Labillardiére State Reserve, to the summit of Mount Bruny (506m/1660ft) and to Tasman Head, at the southern tip of the island. A prominent landmark on Cape Bruny (the south-western tip of the island) is an old lighthouse of 1836.

Burnie J 8

Situation and characteristics

150km/95 miles west of Launceston (see entry), on Blackmans Point, is Burnie (pop. 20,500), the fourth largest town in Tasmania. Founded in 1829 and named after the director of a land development company, it originally consisted only of a few huts, a warehouse and a blacksmith's shop. It was given a great boost by the opening of a tin-mine on Mount Bischoff (75km/47 miles south-west), the ore from which was shipped from Burnie's deep-water harbour. In 1938 a large paper mill was established in the town, using wood from the great expanses of forest round the town. Burnie is still an important industrial town, with foodstuffs factories (milk products, chocolate, etc.) as well as the paper mill.

Accommodation

Hotels, motels and caravan/camping park.

Features

In Burnie Park is the mid 19th century Burnie Inn, one of the town's oldest buildings, restored and re-erected here. The town's principal attraction is the Pioneer Village Museum in the Civic Centre Plaza, which carries visitors back to the early days of the settlement. A number of handsome old houses with wrought-iron ornament bear witness to Burnie's prosperity in its heyday, for example the richly decorated police office in Wibon Street, built in 1908 as a doctor's house.

Carnival

Burnie holds a Carnival, with a full programme of sporting and other events, annually on January 1st.

★Campbell Town J 8

Situation and characteristics

Campbell Town (pop. 900), named after Governor Macquarie's wife, lies on the Midland Highway 70km/43 miles south of Launceston (see entry) and 130km/80 miles north of Hobart. A garrison was installed here around 1820, and the country round the town soon developed into a large sheep-farming area. The main sources of income are now wool, cattle and timber.

Accommodation
Hotels (also in Lake Leake).

Features
There are numerous old houses amid uniform modern buildings. In the Grange, a brick house in 17th century style with pointed gables, Dr William Valentine made the first telephone call in Australia in 1874. Other notable buildings are Balmoral Cottage (*c.* 1840; Bridge Street), Howley Lodge (1845; Bridge Street) and three churches, St Luke's (1835; Anglican) at the corner of Bridge Street and Pedder Street, St Michael's (1857; R.C.) in King Street and St Andrew's (Presbyterian). Three inns dating from pioneering days are the Campbell Town Inn (1840) at the corner of High Street and Queen Street and Powell's Hotel (1834) and the Foxhunter's Return Inn (1833) in High Street. The brick bridge over the Elizabeth River was built by convict labour in 1836–38.

Surroundings
★Ross
10km/6 miles south of Campbell Town is the little settlement of Ross (pop. 300), with a number of historic old buildings, which has developed in recent years into a holiday resort with excellent "colonial accommodation" for visitors. There is also a popular caravan/camping park.

Ross was originally established in 1812 as a military post to protect the road from Launceston to Hobart, and became an important coaching station. Round the little town is a sheep-farming district famed for its high-quality wool.

The bridge over the Macquarie River was designed by John Lee Archer and built by convict labour. The convict stonemason Daniel Herbert was granted a free pardon for his work on the bridge. Among statutorily protected buildings are the Man o' Ross Hotel (1817), the town's oldest bar, and the Old Barracks, which bear a coat of arms and the date 1836. The Scotch Thistle Inn, a coaching inn built in 1826, preserves its old courtyard, coach shed and blacksmith's shop. The Elms Inn has a collection of militaria. Other fine colonial-era buildings are St John's Church (Anglican) of 1869 and the United Church of 1885 on the hill beside the bridge. European trees along the main street contribute to the atmosphere of colonial times.

Round Campbell Town and Ross there are excellent trout-fishing waters (Lake Sorell, Lake Crescent, Tooms Lake, Lake Leake), and there is duck-shooting in the nearby hills.

★★Cradle Mountain/Lake St Clair National Park J 8

Location; area
Western Tasmania (160km/100 miles north-west of Hobart); 161,000 hectares/398,000 acres.

Best time to visit
Summer (November to March).

Access
To Lake St Clair: Lyell Highway (A 10) to Derwent Bridge, where a side road goes off to the lake. To Cradle Valley: Murchison Highway (A 10) and C 132; 60km/37 miles north-east of Rosebery side road to Cradle Valley Lodge. In winter some stretches of road may be closed.

Facilities
Camping/caravan grounds, huts (advance booking essential in main holiday season); rest and picnic areas; long-distance walking trail, the Overland Track; information centre.

Topography
Cradle Mountain/Lake St Clair National Park takes in the highest regions in Tasmania, with a number of rugged peaks covered with dolerite, including Mount Ossa (1616m/5302ft), the highest point on the island. The park occupies the northern part of the Tasmanian Wilderness World Heritage Area listed by UNESCO in 1982. To the south is Franklin Lower Gordon Wild Rivers National Park (see entry). The topography of the area, with its Alpine aspect, was mainly formed during and more particularly at the end of the last Ice Age, when the retreating glaciers left behind precipitous peaks, U-shaped valleys and barrier lakes. The first section of the National Park was established in 1922 after an exploration of the area by an immigrant Austrian scientist, Gustav Weindorfer.

Mount Cradle,
Cradle Valley
The northern part of the park, round Mount Cradle (1545m/5069ft), is particularly beautiful. Cradle Valley is well equipped to cater for tourists,

Jagged peaks in Cradle Mountain National Park

with Cradle Valley Lodge and Waldheim Chalet, built in 1912 on the initiative of Gustav Weindorfer. The visitor centre offers an abundance of information on the natural history of Tasmania.

Lake St Clair

The chief attraction in the southern part of the park is Lake St Clair (alt. 730m/2395ft; 17km/10½ miles long and up to 200m/650ft deep; fishing and boating), a barrier lake formed by a moraine.

Overland Track

The famous Overland Track, 80km/50 miles long, runs south from Cradle Valley (Waldheim Chalet) past Cradle Mountain to Cynthia Bay on Lake St Clair. This is an extremely strenuous walk for which at least five days should be allowed. Walkers must inform the ranger station (Waldheim Chalet or Cynthia Bay) before setting out on the walk and after completing it. There are small camping grounds and mountain huts along the route.

Other walks

There are a number of shorter (one-day) walks from Cradle Valley. The Weindorfer Walk, a nature trail for part of the way, is a 6km/4 mile circuit through beautiful forest country. The Lake Dove Walk runs round the lake, with magnificent views. There is a rewarding climb to the summit of the Little Horn (1300m/4265ft). From the summit of Cradle Mountain (12km/7½ miles, from Waldheim Chalet via Marion Lookout, returning by Crater Peak Lookout) there are breathtaking views. There is also a very attractive walk on the Cuvier Valley Track (17km/10½ miles), with wide views. The Watersmeet Nature Walk runs from Cynthia Bay close to the shores of Lake St Clair to the junction of the Hugel and Cuvier Rivers. From Cynthia Bay there is an 18km/11 mile circuit (whole day) to Mount Rufus and the Hugel Lakes.

★Deloraine J 8

Situation and characteristics

Deloraine (pop. 2100), lies on the Meander River 50km/31 miles west of Launceston (see entry) in the centre of a farming district (particularly dairy farming), near the intersection of the Bass and Lake Highways. It has a beautiful setting between the north coast of Tasmania and the hills of the Great Western Tiers to the south.

Accommodation
Hotels; beautiful caravan/camping park on the banks of the Meander.

Features
A few buildings survive from the original village, established about 1840, among them Bonney's Inn (1831), now a restaurant, and Bowerbank Mill (*c.* 1853), a water mill built by William Archer which was converted to steam power in 1871 and now houses an art gallery. Other notable buildings are the Deloraine Folk Museum, in the former Family and Commercial Inn (1864), St Mark's Church (*c.* 1860; Anglican), the Roman Catholic church (*c.* 1880) and a small military museum.

Surroundings
There is good trout fishing in the Meander and Mersey Rivers. On the Lake Highway is Calstock, an old stud farm. There are attractive excursions to a number of waterfalls in the area – Liffey Falls, Meander Falls (half an hour's drive south), Montana Falls – to the central plateau by way of Golden Valley (Lake Highway) and to the Marakoopa and King Solomon Caves (see Mole Creek).

Westbury
16km/10 miles east of Deloraine is the little town of Westbury (pop. 1300; tourist hotel), founded in 1828. The White House (*c.* 1840), built round an inner courtyard, now houses a collection of 17th and 18th century furniture and art and old toys. The Olde English Inn (1833) is now occupied by an antiques shop. Holy Trinity Church (R.C.), with a fine bell-tower, is one of the largest in the district.

★Devonport J 8

Situation and characteristics
Devonport (pop. 25,400), Tasmania's third largest town, lies on the north coast, at the mouth of the Mersey River, and is the starting-point of the Bass Highway. For many visitors it is the gateway to Tasmania, since the "Spirit of Tasmania", the car ferry from Melbourne, puts in here. It is an important industrial centre and port, shipping agricultural produce. It has its own airport, which has promoted its development as a tourist centre.

Accommodation
Several hotels, motels, caravan/camping park.

Features
Devonport has a number of interesting museums, including the Maritime Museum, the Early Motoring and Folk Museum, the Wheel House Museum (an old coach-builder's workshop) and the Taswegia Printery Museum (an old printing office).

★Tiagarra Aboriginal Art Centre
The Tiagarra Aboriginal Culture and Art Centre (open: daily except in July) has an informative exhibition on the Aboriginal inhabitants of Tasmania, who were wiped out in the 19th century. The Centre is situated on Mersey Bluff, a rocky promontory on the Bass Strait which to the Aborigines was a sacred place. On the cliffs along the coast there are Aboriginal rock drawings.

Don River Tramway
The Don River Tramway was constructed in 1854 to transport timber from the Don Valley to the west. In 1916 a railway line was built to carry stone from the limestone quarries. The line was closed down in 1963, but five years later was reopened as the Don River Railway, with a railway museum displaying a large collection of old rolling stock. A veteran train runs on the line daily in summer and on Sundays at other times of year.

Home Hill
Home Hill (1916; open: Tue.–Thu. and Sun. afternoons) was the home of Joseph Lyons, prime minister of Tasmania 1923–28 and of Australia 1932–39. After his death, in 1943, his widow was elected to the Australian Parliament, the first woman member.

Surroundings
Latrobe
13km/8 miles south-east of Devonport is the little town of Latrobe (pop. 2600), on the Mersey River, which flourished in the late 19th century. In the main street are a number of Victorian buildings. The former Courthouse in Gilbert Street now houses a museum of regional history.

Every year at Christmas the biggest cycle race in Australia is run here. It is organised by the Latrobe Bicycle Race Club, which was founded in 1896.

Frogmore
Just outside Latrobe is Frogmore, a historic old homestead of around 1880 in neo-classical style, now a farm guesthouse.

Port Sorell

20km/12½ miles east of Devonport is Port Sorell (pop. 1400), at the mouth of the Rubicon River. Founded in 1822 and named after Governor Sorell, it is the oldest settlement on the north-west coast of Tasmania. Many of its old buildings were destroyed in a great bush fire at the beginning of the 20th century. Port Sorell is now a popular holiday resort (water sports, fishing, walking).

Asbestos Range

To the east of Port Sorell is the Asbestos Range National Park (see Beaconsfield).

Sheffield

30km/19 miles south of Devonport, in the northern foothills of the Great Western Tiers, is the rising tourist resort of Sheffield (pop. 1000; hotel, motel, caravan/camping park). A farming town, it lies in an area of impressive gorges, forests, waterfalls and rivers well stocked with fish. An interesting feature of the town is the paintings of historical scenes on house walls. Within easy reach are the artificial lakes of the Mersey-Forth hydro-electric scheme. On Lake Barrington are a number of attractive picnic areas. A winding road leads to Cradle Mountain/Lake St Clair National Park, 60km/37 miles south-west.

Ulverstone

20km/12½ miles west of Devonport, near the mouth of the Leven River, is Ulverstone (pop. 12,000), a relatively late foundation, situated in a thriving agricultural area of fertile volcanic soil of which it is the commercial centre. In Anzac Park is a large war memorial borne on three pillars. There are a number of fine old houses round the town. Westella (1886), 3km/2 miles east on the Bass Highway, is now occupied by an art and antiques dealer. Lonah, on the old road to Penguin, was built in 1870 for a British general; it has fine old trees of European origin. There are excellent facilities for water sports and angling on the beaches to the east of the town and on the river and its estuary to the west.

Penguin

40km/25 miles west of Devonport on the north coast of Tasmania, at the foot of the forest-clad Dial Range, is the little town of Penguin (pop. 2800), founded about 1860. In the period of prosperity after the finding of gold in Victoria Penguin became an important port for the shipment of building timber. It has two fine churches, St Stephen's (Anglican; built 1874, enlarged 1896) and the interesting timber-built Uniting Church of 1903. From the summit of Mount Montgomery (471m/1545ft) there are wide views.

Dover J 8

Situation and characteristics

The old timber town of Dover (pop. 400) lies 80km/50 miles south of Hobart at the outflow of the Esperance River into the D'Entrecasteaux Channel, opposite Bruny Island (see entry). Now an attractive little fishing port, it was originally a convict settlement. The original Commandant's Office still stands. Many old cottages and English trees recall the time in the 19th century when the processing and exporting of timber was the town's major industry. Its main sources of income nowadays are fishing and fruit-growing. There has been a sharp decline in population since the early eighties, though it seems well suited for tourist development, with excellent facilities for water sports, fishing and bush walking.

Accommodation

Hotel, caravan/camping park.

Surroundings

Cockle Creek, in Recherche Bay (50km/31 miles south of Dover near the southern tip of Tasmania), is the starting-point of a long-distance walking trail along the unspoiled south coast and through the South West National Park to Scotts Peak Dam, at the south end of Lake Pedder. Organised tours are on offer.

Hastings

20km/12½ miles south-west of Dover, just off the Huon Highway, is Hastings (pop. under 200).

★ Hastings Caves

16km/10 miles north-west of Hastings are a number of karstic caves with spectacular stalactites and stalagmites. There are regular conducted tours of Newdegate Cave. Nearby is a thermal pool.

Lune River

A few kilometres south of Hastings is Lune River, where both professionals and amateurs hunt for precious stones.

Stalactites in the Hastings Caves

Ida Bay

The main attraction of the little settlement of Ida Bay, farther south, is the old Ida Bay Railway, originally built to transport limestone to the coast.

Fingal J 8

Situation and characteristics

Fingal (pop. 450) lies in the beautiful Esk Valley in north-eastern Tasmania, on the Main Esk Road. To the north-west of the little town, the centre of a coal-mining area, is Ben Lomond National Park (see Launceston). The first considerable finds of gold in Tasmania were made near here in 1852.

Accommodation

Hotel.

Features

Fingal has two fine 19th century houses, Malahide and Killymoon, and two churches, St Peter's and St Joseph's (R.C.). The Fingal Hotel was built during the convict period. Round Fingal is the largest coalfield in Tasmania.

Flinders Island J 7/8

Situation and characteristics

Flinders Island, the largest island in the Furneaux Group, lies in Bass Strait off north-eastern Tasmania. It is named after Matthew Flinders, who sailed through Bass Strait in 1797.

The Furneaux Islands are named after Captain Furneaux, commander of Cook's supply ship "Adventure", who discovered the group of 42 islands. They are probably a remnant of a land bridge linking Tasmania with the Australian mainland. Seal-hunters established settlements on the islands at an early stage. Off the rocky coasts are numerous wrecks.

In the 1830s Flinders Island was used as a place of internment for the last Tasmanian Aborigines on the main island, whose numbers thereafter fell sharply. The last survivors were finally removed to Oyster Cove, south of

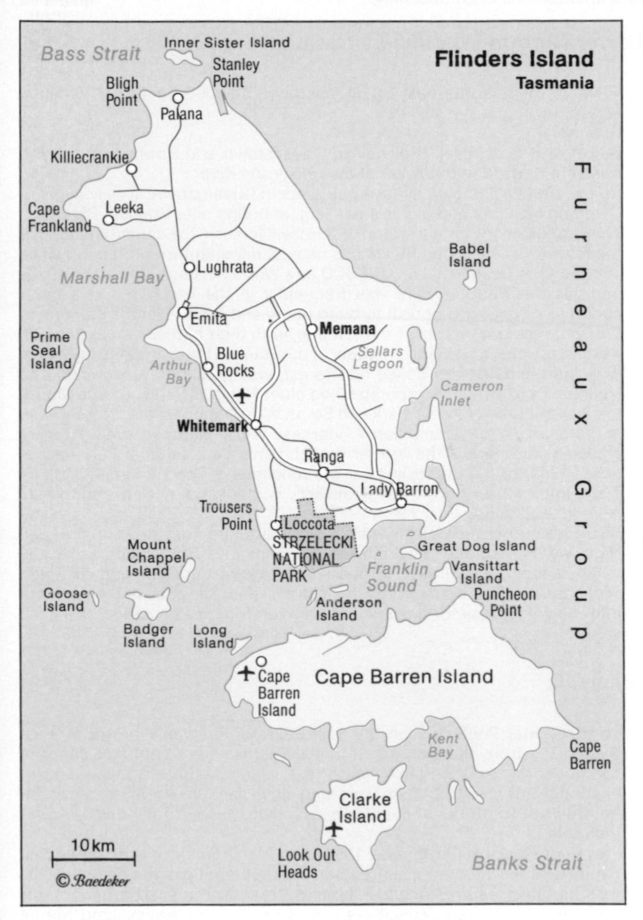

Hobart, in 1874, and a few years later the Aborigines of Tasmania were extinct. At Emita, on the west side of Flinders Island, are a cemetery and a chapel marking the site of the Aboriginal settlement (Wybalenna Historic Site). The main centre on the thinly populated island, which was developed for agriculture after the Second World War, is Whitemark, also on the west coast. Native fauna abounds, especially muttonbirds, and the beaches are excellent.

Access

Flinders Island can be reached by air from Devonport, Hobart or Launceston and by boat from Devonport, George Town or Hobart.

Accommodation

Hotels, guesthouses; farmhouse holidays.

★Strzelecki National Park

At the south-western tip of Flinders Island is Strzelecki National Park, named after the explorer Paul Edmund de Strzelecki (see Famous People). This unspoiled region is good walking country, particularly round the Strzelecki Range, from which there are magnificent views over the island, reaching as far as Cape Barren Island, home to a protected species of geese.

★★Franklin Lower Gordon Wild Rivers National Park J 8

Location; area 40km/25 miles south-east of Queenstown; 440,000 hectares/1,087,000 acres.

Best time to visit Summer.

Access By car or bus on Lyell Highway to Queenstown and Strahan; excursion boats from Strahan to lower course of Gordon River.

Accommodation Hotels, motels and caravan/camping park in Queenstown.

Facilities Camping grounds and picnic areas (e.g. at bridge over Franklin River).

Topography This grandiose mountain region of primeval forest in the catchment area of the Franklin and Gordon Rivers has been under statutory protection since 1981 and has been listed by UNESCO as a World Heritage site. In the 1970s and 80s the National Park was frequently in the news during a bitter controversy over a proposal to build dams and hydro-electric stations in the area. The opponents of the scheme, with their battlecry "No dams!", were victorious, and the wild beauty of the Franklin River and its tributaries, with their expanses of dense rain forest, was preserved unspoiled. The National Park, which incorporates two older National Parks, Cradle Mountain/Lake St Clair National Park and South West National Park (see entries), is the heart of the Tasmanian Wilderness World Heritage Area. Also included in the park is the former Frenchman's Cap National Park (established 1941) round the rocky peak of Frenchman's Cap (1443m/4734ft).

White-water rafting The tumultuous Franklin River attracts white-water rafting enthusiasts from far and wide.

Walking trails There are numerous walking trails starting out from rest areas on the Lyell Highway. Particularly rewarding is the Donaghys Hill Wilderness Walk, which leaves the highway on the south side of the Collingwood River. Along the western boundary of the National Park it is possible to push out into the wilderness for a few kilometres (on foot or in a canoe or a 4WD vehicle).

★Freycinet Peninsula J 8

Situation and characteristics The Freycinet Peninsula on the east coast of Tasmania protects Great Oyster Bay from the heavy surf of the Tasman Sea. With its variety of scenery and relatively safe beaches (e.g. Nine Mile Beach) this quiet bay has long attracted holidaymakers and now has an excellent tourist infrastructure (motels, caravan/camping parks, beach facilities, walking trails, etc.).

Freycinet National Park Freycinet National Park (area 100sq.km/39sq.miles), one of the oldest nature reserves in Australia, occupies the southern tip of the peninsula. Its most notable features are the Hazards, three striking red granite crags rising out of the sea; Wineglass Bay, with its high waves; and Mount Freycinet (614m/2015ft). Also within the park is Schouten Island, which lies off the peninsula to the south.

Coles Bay At the entrance to the park is the little holiday resort of Coles Bay, whose main attraction is its beautiful beaches. It is also a good base for walks and climbs in the hills. It has a motel and several caravan/camping parks; advance booking is advisable, particularly in the main holiday seasons (high summer, Easter).

Geeveston J 8

Situation and characteristics 60km/37 miles south-west of Hobart on the Huon Highway is Geeveston (pop. 750), an important timber town with a large paper mill. The timber comes from the hardwood forests in the Arve and Weld valleys to the west of the town, with trees up to 87m/285ft high. Geeveston is a good base for excursions to Hartz Mountains National Park (see below). A 23km/14 mile long track leads to Waratah Lookout.

There are boat trips on the Huon River and the nearby D'Entrecasteaux Channel.

Accommodation

Hotel; camping in National Park.

★Hartz Mountains National Park

20km/12½ miles west of Geeveston is Hartz Mountains National Park (area 7140 hectares/17,640 acres; bush camping, picnic areas, walking trails). The park, originally scheduled as a scenic reserve in 1939, is part of the Tasmanian Wilderness World Heritage Area. The access road from Geeveston runs up the Huon Valley into an area of moorland. The National Park is a popular destination for weekend excursions, and in winter it attracts large numbers of cross-country skiers. The area is subject to sudden showers of rain, storms and mist, and warm clothing and protection against rain are advisable even in summer.

A chain of high dolerite peaks runs through the park from north to south between the Arve and Picton river systems. The highest point is Hartz Peak (1255m/4118ft). At the foot of the hills are barrier lakes formed by Ice Age moraines. There are superb views from Waratah Lookout, near the Picnic Hut. Near the park entrance, amid beech rain forest, are the Keogh and Arve Falls. There are also expanses of eucalyptus forest which give place to Alpine moorland with heath vegetation and snow gums. At various points there are fine views of the wild highlands of Tasmania, extending eastward to Bruny Island.

George Town J 8

Situation and characteristics

George Town (pop. 5500) lies on the east side of the natural harbour of Port Dalrymple (the estuary of the Tamar), 50km/31 miles north-west of Launceston (see entry). There was a settlement here as early as 1811, named after King George III. George Town is now a busy industrial town, with the large Comalco aluminium plant (which can be visited).

Accommodation

Hotel, caravan/camping park.

Features

A monument on the Esplanade commemorates an involuntary landing by Col. William Paterson and his crew when HMS "Buffalo" ran aground in 1804. The Grove is an elegant house of the 1820s (restored), now occupied by a restaurant. Directly on the harbour is the venerable Pier Hotel. The old pilot station now houses the local Maritime Museum.

Surroundings

George Town lies in a fruit-growing area (particularly strawberries and apples). There are boat trips to the islands of the Furneaux group (see Flinders Island).

Low Head

On Low Head, 5km/3 miles north of George Town, are both a good surfing beach and a sheltered bathing beach.

Lefroy

20km/12½ miles east of George Town are the ruins of the gold-mining town of Lefroy, which flourished around 1870.

Pipers Brook

Pipers Brook, 30km/19 miles east of George Town, is famed for its excellent wines.

Bell Bay

A few kilometres south of George Town is the industrial port of Bell Bay, which has recently gained added importance as the destination of the fast catamaran service from Victoria over the Bass Strait (the "Sea Cat", a rival to the "Abel Tasman").

★★Hobart J 8

Capital of Tasmania

Situation and size

The most southerly city in Australia is Hobart, the Tasmanian capital. It is beautifully situated at the foot of Mount Wellington (1270m/4167ft), straddling the estuary of the Derwent River, which here flows into the Tasman Sea. The city covers an area of 70sq.km/27sq.miles and has a population of some 200,000. The wider catchment area of Hobart extends over almost 1000sq.km/385sq.miles, adding some tens of thousands to the population of the city itself.

View from Mount Nelson of Hobart, one of the world's finest harbours

History and development

When the French navigator Nicolas Baudin was encountered cruising off the coast of Tasmania in 1802, the British authorities in the young colony of New South Wales, suspecting a French intention to found a settlement in the area, despatched Lieutenant John Bowen with an expedition to the south of Van Diemen's Land to establish a foothold on the island ahead of the French. The site in Risdon Cove, on the east bank of the Derwent, where Bowen set up his encampment in September 1803 was not well chosen: it lacked drinking water, and was abandoned a few months later. Finally Col. David Collins established a settlement farther down the Derwent River in February 1805, naming it after Lord Hobart, secretary for war in the British government. Hobart was proclaimed a town only in 1842.

In 1811 Lachlan Macquarie, governor of New South Wales, visited the site and settled the layout of the new town, fixing the line of seven main streets, ordering the construction of the Anglesea Barracks and the signal station on Mount Nelson and deciding the site of the seat of government of Tasmania. It was many years, however, before these plans were put into effect: Government House, for example, was not completed until 1858. In course of time Hobart developed into an important port and supply centre for whalers. The excellent deep-water harbour, the abundance of high-quality building timber (slow-growing Huon pine) in the immediate neighbourhood and the availability of cheap convict labour provided the basis for the steady growth of the young town. Nowhere else in Australia were so many ships built, and nowhere else in Australia have so many buildings of the pioneering period been preserved.

When Van Diemen's Land was separated from New South Wales in 1825 Hobart had a population of 5000. In the 1850s many of the inhabitants left to try their luck in the goldfields of Victoria, and from 1870 onwards intensive mining activity led to the growth of new centres in Tasmania, particularly in the north and west. Nevertheless Hobart continued to grow, thanks in particular to considerable influxes of population after the two world wars.

Transport

Hobart's international airport lies 22km/13½ miles south-east of the city and has excellent connections with the Australian domestic air network (in many cases via Melbourne and Sydney) and with Christchurch in New Zealand.

In view of the relatively short distances within Tasmania itself regional air services, apart from special cases (e.g. tourist flights into the interior), are of minor importance.

The car ferry, "Spirit of Tasmania", sails from Melbourne three times a week (Mon., Wed., Fri. at 6pm, reaching Devonport 14½ hours later. The return journey is on the other weekdays. Flights to Hobart go from all Australia's main airports.

The bus services run by the Metropolitan Transport Trust (MTT) link the city with its widely scattered outer suburbs.

There are special "Day Rover" tickets which are of particular interest to visitors.

Information about services can be obtained from the MTT desk in the Tasmanian Travel Centre (TTC) at 80 Elizabeth Street.

From Hobart there are overland buses to all places of any size in Tasmania. The Tasmanian Redline Coaches have a dense network of services; their "Super Tassie Pass", for either one or two weeks, is a good buy. Information: 96 Harrington Street.

A wide range of city tours and sightseeing excursions in the surrounding area are on offer. During the main holiday season (December to the end of April) there is a wide choice of package tours to Port Arthur (see entry), Mount Wellington, Richmond, Launceston (see entries), the Hastings Caves, the Huon valley, the Derwent valley, Lake Pedder and the Russell Falls.

Cars and mobile homes are available for hire in large numbers, but should be booked in plenty of time.

Accommodation

Two luxury hotels, several middle-category hotels, numerous smaller hotels and motels, "colonial accommodation" (in 19th-century houses and

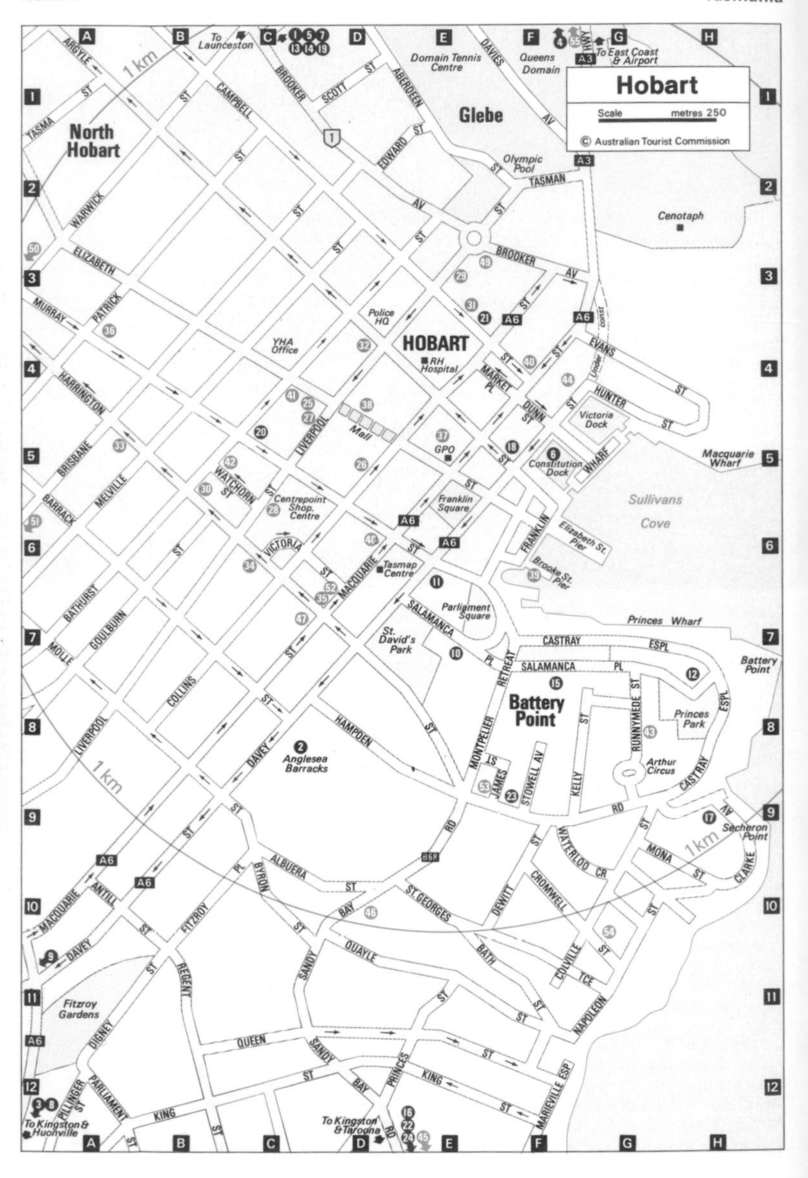

Hobart
Scale metres 250
© Australian Tourist Commission
North Hobart
Glebe
HOBART
Battery Point
To Launceston
To East Coast & Airport
Domain Tennis Centre
Queens Domain
Olympic Pool
Cenotaph
Police HQ
YHA Office
RH Hospital
Mall
GPO
Victoria Dock
Constitution Dock
Macquarie Wharf
Sullivans Cove
Franklin Square
Centrepoint Shop. Centre
Tasmap Centre
Elizabeth St. Pier
Brooke St. Pier
Parliament Square
Princes Wharf
St. David's Park
Battery Point
Princes Park
Arthur Circus
Anglesea Barracks
Secheron Point
Fitzroy Gardens
To Kingston & Huonville
To Kingston & Taroona
1 km

Places of Interest
Alpen Rail (model railway) . 1 C1
Anglesea Barracks 2 C8
Antarctic Division H.Q. 3 A12
Botanical Gardens 4 F1
Cadbury Confectionary Fcty. 5 C1
Constitution Dock 6 F5
Lady Franklin Gallery 7 C1
Mt. Nelson Signal Station . . 8 A12
Mt. Wellington Lookout . . . 9 A11
National Trust Office 10 E7
Parliament House 11 E6
Postal & Teleg. Museum . . . 12 H7
Risdon Cove Historic Site . . 13 C1
RunnymedeNatTrustHome 14 C1
Salamanca Pl.(Sat. Market) 15 F7
Shot Tower 16 E12
Tas. Maritime Museum 17 H9
Tas. Museum & Art Gallery . 18 F5
Tas. Transport Museum 19 C1
The Allport Library & Museum of Fine Arts 20 C5
Theatre Royal 21 E3
The State Library of Tas. . . . 20 C5
Tudor Court (Model Village & Dolls House) 22 E12
Van Diemans Land Memorial Folk Museum 23 F9
Wrest Point Federal Casino 24 E12

Tourist Information Centres
Tasbureau 25 C4
Victorian Tourist Comm. . . . 26 D5
N.T. Govt. Tourist Bureau . . 27 C5

Airlines– City Departure Terminals
Ansett Airlines of Aust. 28 C6
Australian Airlines 29 E3

Rent-a-Car Offices
Auto Rent–Hertz 30 B5
Avis 31 E3
Budget 32 D4
Thrifty 33 A5

Coach Terminal
Tas. Redline Coaches 34 C6

National Parks
Lands, Pks. & Wildlife Depot 35 D7

Motoring Association
Royal Auto. Club of Tas. . . . 36 A4

Post Office
G.P.O. 37 E5

International Airlines
Qantas Airways 38 D4

Ferries and Cruises
Brooke Street Pier 39 F6

Metropolitan Bus Info.
MTT City Depot 40 F4

Accommodation
* Facilities for the handicapped

Premier
Four Seasons Downtowner 41 C4
* Four Seasons Westside 42 C5
Innkeepers Lenna of Hobart 43 G8
Sheraton Hotel 44 F4
Wrest Point Federal Casino 45 E12

Moderate
Blue Hills 46 D10
Four Seasons Town House . 47 C7
Hadleys 48 D6
Hatchers Hobart Motor Inn 49 E3
Hobart Pacific Motor Inn . . 50 A3
Marquis of Hastings 51 A6

Budget
Astor 52 D6
Barton Cottage 53 E9
Cromwell Cottage 54 G10
Hobart Youth Hostel 55 F1

Helpful Telephone Numbers
Emergency 000
Tasbureau 300211

Shopping

cottages), rooms in private houses, a youth hostel, four caravan/camping parks near the city.

Food and drink

Numerous restaurants in all price categories; very popular fish restaurants on waterfront.

As regards drinks, the beer which has been brewed for generations in the Cascade Brewery and cider made from locally grown apples are to be recommended. Some very drinkable wines are now produced in Tasmania.

Events

Casino at Wrest Point, with night club, discothèque and dinner theatre; evening performances in the well-reputed little Theatre Royal in Campbell Street; Playhouse, 106 Bathurst Street; ABC Odeon, 163 Liverpool Street. Many pubs in the central area have live music in the evening.

Shopping

In addition to the shopping arcades and department stores in the city centre (in particular Liverpool Street, Murray Street, Elizabeth Street, Collins Street with the Centrepoint Arcade and the Cat and Fiddle Arcade, Elizabeth Mall) there are many shops and galleries on the waterfront selling craft objects (particularly of Huon pine), glass and jewellery. A Tasmanian speciality is leatherwood honey (from the flowers of the leatherwood tree).

Sport

The most popular sports in Hobart are water sports (particularly sailing), fishing, golf, cricket and above all tennis. "Real tennis" is played at the Royal Tennis Club at 45 Davery Street (the only other place where it is played in Australia is Melbourne). Cycling and jogging are also very popular.

There is plenty of scope for adventurous bush walkers on nearby Mount Wellington.

Popular spectator sports are football (Australian rules), rugby, association football, cricket (November to March) and horse-racing (particularly on Elwich racecourse).

Sights in Hobart

Central Hobart, between Battery Point in the south-east and the Domain in the north-east, has a clear and regular layout, based on Governor Macquarie's plan of 1811. The main shopping and business streets are Liverpool and Collins Streets and two cross streets, Elizabeth Street (with the pedestrian zone, Elizabeth Mall) and Murray Street. In the central area many 19th century buildings have been preserved.

Sightseeing walks

Every Saturday morning the National Trust runs sightseeing walks in the harbour quarter led by knowledgeable local people, starting from Franklin Square at 9.30am.

★Battery Point

The old harbour quarter of Battery Point with its warehouses and small dwelling-houses (Salamanca Place, Arthur Circus) is like an open-air historical museum. The buildings were erected by convicts, among whom were evidently some first-rate craftsmen.

In the Galleria Salamanca (33 Salamanca Place) is the National Trust information centre, which can supply a wealth of informative material on the history of Hobart.

Tasmanian Maritime Museum

The Tasmanian Maritime Museum (open: daily) in Secheron Road occupies Secheron House, built in 1831 for George Frankland, surveyor-general of the colony. It commands a fine view of the bay. Inside is a good collection of nautical artefacts showing Tasmania's close links with the sea.

Salamanca Place

Salamanca Place, built between 1835 and 1860, is a busy street of handsome warehouses now occupied by restaurants and pubs, antique dealers and souvenir shops (street musicians; craft market on Saturday). It is named after the battle of Salamanca (1812).

The oldest building in the harbour area is the Guard House (1818) on Battery Point. The site of the gun battery which once stood here is now occupied by Princes Park. Here too there was a signal station which could communicate visually with the one on Mount Nelson, to the south.

Post Office Museum

The Post Office Museum on Castray Esplanade occupies a government building dating from 1838. It has on display an exhibition on the history of postal services and a collection of old telephone apparatus.

Kelly Steps

From Salamanca Place a steep flight of steps named after Captain James Kelly (who surveyed the west coast of Tasmania) leads up to Kelly Street.

★Van Diemen's Land Folk Museum

The Van Diemen's Land Folk Museum in Hampden Road (open: daily 9am–5pm), is in a house built in 1834, and finished in period style to show how early settlers lived.

The picturesque harbour of Hobart

Particularly notable among the historic old buildings in the harbour quarter are Mure's Fish House (1849; 5 Knopwood Street), now a quality restaurant, and Lenna House (*c.* 1880; 20 Runnymede Street), a handsome Italian-style mansion (now a hotel and restaurant called Alexander's).

Historic buildings

Elegant "colonial accommodation" for visitors is available in Colville Cottage (1880; 32 Mona Street).

Also of interest are the little mid-19th-century cottages round Arthur Circus (formerly the village square).

St George's Church

The neo-classical St George's Anglican Church (1836; tower 1847) in Cromwell Street was built by two of Tasmania's most prominent colonial architects, John Lee Archer and James Blackburn.

Parliament House

Parliament House (overlooking Parliament Square) was originally built by convict labour in 1835–40 as the Customs House and converted to its present function in 1856, when Tasmania became an independent state. The tiny Legislative Council Chamber has been preserved almost unaltered (entrance in Murray Street; public admitted to gallery when Parliament is in session).

St David's Park

To the south-west is Hobart's first cemetery, now a public park. The founder of the town, David Collins, is buried here.

Anglesea Barracks

The Anglesea Barracks in Davey Street, built in 1814 (open: Mon.–Fri.; conducted tours Tue. at 11am), is the oldest military establishment in Australia still in use. Outside it are two 18th century cannon. A pillar commemorates the soldiers stationed here who died in the Maori War in New Zealand in 1840.

★Constitution Dock

Davey Street runs north-east along the harbour, which was and still is the hub of the city's life. Constitution Dock, now a boating harbour, attracts many visitors in the first week in January, when it is crowded with smart yachts after the annual Sydney to Hobart race.

Customs House

At the intersection of Davey Street and Dunn Street, close to the harbour, is the imposing Customs House (1902), with a neo-classical façade.

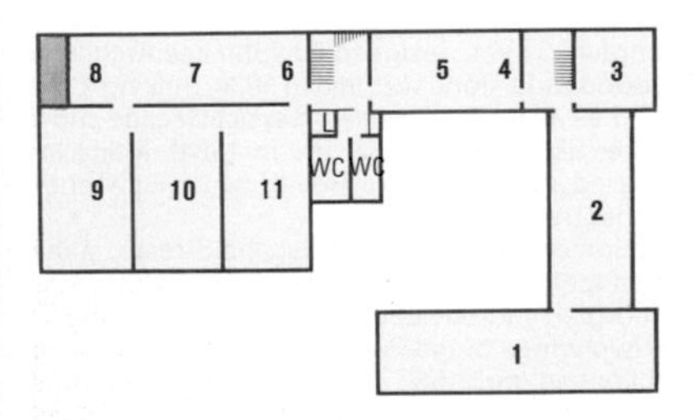

FIRST FLOOR
1 Colonial art
2 Decorative art
3 History of the convicts
4 Antarctica
5 Peoples of the Pacific
6 Medals
7 Money
8 Applied science
9 History of seafaring
10 Special exhibitions
11 Aboriginal population of Tasmania

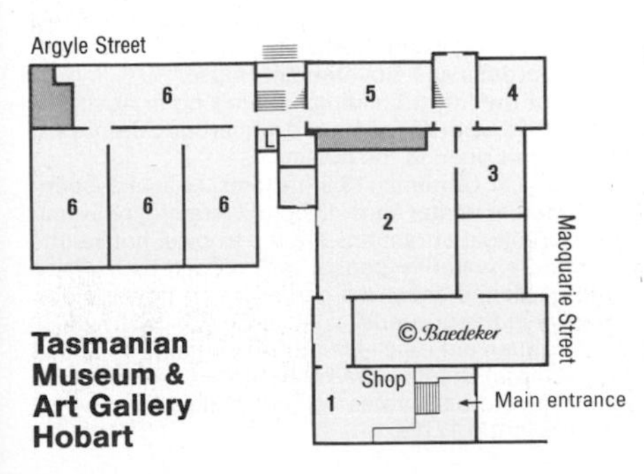

Tasmanian Museum & Art Gallery Hobart

GROUND FLOOR
1 Foyer
2 Zoology
3 Geology
4 Fauna
5 Special art exhibitions
6 20th century Australian art

L Lift
WC Toilets

★Tasmanian Museum and Art Gallery

A little way north-west of Constitution Dock is the Tasmanian Museum and Art Gallery (40 Macquarie Street; open: daily 10am–5pm). Part of the museum has extensive collections illustrating the history of seafaring in the southern hemisphere and the development of whaling, Aboriginal culture and relics of the convict settlement. The art gallery displays mainly 19th-century art as well as rare prints of different periods.

Franklin Square

A short distance south-west is Franklin Square, a trim public garden.

Town Hall

On the north-east side of the square, at the corner of Elizabeth Street and Macquarie Street, is the Town Hall, built in 1864 to the design of Henry Hunter, an architect much influenced by Italian architecture. It occupies the site of a house built in 1804 by David Collins, founder of the town, as his official residence.

St David's Cathedral

South-west of Franklin Square, in Macquarie Street is St David's Cathedral (Anglican). The foundation stone of this handsome neo-Gothic sandstone building was laid in 1868. It has beautiful stained glass.

Cat and Fiddle Arcade

A little way north-west of the Cathedral is the Cat and Fiddle Arcade, one of Hobart's busiest shopping streets. On the walls of the arcade are figures from nursery rhymes. Many tourists are attracted by the gem-cutting workshop, where attractive jewellery is on sale.

Elizabeth Street Mall

To the north-east is Elizabeth Street Mall, another street full of temptations for shoppers.

State Library, Allport Library and Museum

North-west of the Cat and Fiddle Arcade, in Murray Street, is the State Library, with the Allport Library and Museum (open: Wed.–Fri. 9am–5pm). The collection (art, furniture, silver, books and writings on Asia) was presented to the state by Henry Allport, whose ancestors had come to Tasmania in 1831. The State Library also contains the State Archives.

Tourist information

Close by are the tourist information office, the Tasmanian Travel Centre and a small but elegant theatre.

St Andrew's Church

To the north-east is the architecturally interesting St Andrew's Church (1836). The adjoining Scots Church Hall, built 13 years earlier, is one of the oldest religious buildings in Tasmania.

Synagogue

The Oriental-style Synagogue in Argyle Street, built in 1843, is Australia's oldest synagogue.

★ Theatre Royal

The Theatre Royal at 29 Campbell Street, designed by John Lee Archer, is an architectural jewel. The foundation stone was laid in 1834, making it the earliest theatre in Australia. It has an impressive neo-classical façade and a charming interior (rebuilt after its destruction by fire in 1984). Many international stars have appeared in the Theatre Royal, which Lawrence Olivier rated "the best little theatre in the world".

Penitentiary Chapel, Criminal Courts

Farther north, at the intersection of Campbell and Brisbane Streets, is the former Penitentiary, with a chapel built by John Lee Archer in 1831, now thoroughly restored. Few Georgian church buildings are as well preserved as this little chapel. In 1860 two wings of the Penitentiary were converted into the Criminal Courts, still in use until 1983. There are conducted tours (daily between 10am and 2pm) of the cell blocks and the execution court.

In the north-east of the city is Queen's Domain, a large public open space which was part of Macquarie's 1811 plan, with a variety of sports facilities (tennis centre, Olympic pool, cricket ground, athletic centre), an adventure playground, the Botanical Gardens and Government House.

★ Government House

Government House is one of the finest buildings of the kind in Australia. Built in sandstone in Tudor style, with 70 rooms and numerous chimneys, it was completed in 1858. It is not open to the public.

★ Royal Tasmanian Botanical Gardens

The Royal Tasmanian Botanical Gardens (13.5 hectares/33 acres; open: daily in summer 8am–6.30pm, in winter 8am–4.45pm) were originally laid out in 1818. Among their principal attractions are the tropical house, the fern house, the rose-garden, a waterlily pool, a rock garden with native Australian plants, a herb garden, a Japanese garden and a flower clock. There is also an observatory in the grounds.

Antipodean Voyage Fountain

The Antipodean Voyage Fountain or French Memorial Fountain (1972) was carved by the Tasmanian sculptor Stephen Walker from the weather-resistant wood of the Huon pine. It commemorates the French expedition which surveyed Tasmanian waters in the 1770s.

Arthur Wall

The Arthur Wall was built in 1829, with a heating system for tropical plants.

Runnymede House

Runnymede House (61 Bay Road), north-west of Queen's Domain, is an elegant two-storey mansion of the mid 19th century set in a beautiful garden, with a view over New Town Bay. It was built around 1837 for a lawyer named Robert Pitcairn who had campaigned for the ending of the transportation of convicts. In 1850 it became the residence of the Anglican bishop, who added the music room, used for receptions and religious services. In 1864 it passed into the hands of a sea-captain, who named it Runnymede after his ship. Finally in 1967 it was acquired by the state and handed over to the management of the National Trust. It has since been restored to its 19th century state.

★ Tasman Bridge

One of Hobart's landmarks is the Tasman Bridge (1964), which spans the Derwent River in a bold arch, borne on numerous piers, linking Queen's Domain with the suburb of Montagu. Eleven years after its construction a cargo vessel rammed one of the piers, threatening the bridge with collapse, and a replacement bridge was built a few kilometres north. The Tasman Bridge is now once again operating normally.

Holy Trinity Church

Holy Trinity Church (17 Church Street, North Hobart) has a fine peal of bells (1847).

St Mary's Cathedral

In the grounds of St Mary's College and St Virgil's College (Harrington Street, West Hobart) is St Mary's Cathedral (R.C.). It was built in the 1860s on the site of Tasmania's first Roman Catholic church.

Lady Franklin Gallery

A few minutes' drive west, in Lenah Valley, is the Lady Franklin Gallery, named after the art-loving wife of Governor Sir John Franklin, who took a major part in the planning of Australia's first public museum. But the gallery, built in 1843 in the style of a Greek temple, did not live up to its founders' expectations. The collections were neglected and the building was used for many years as a warehouse, until in 1936 the Arts Society of Tasmania took it over and restored it to its original function (open: Sat. and Sun. 2–4.30pm).

Surroundings of Hobart

Glenchory

In the suburb of Glenchory, 10km/6 miles north of the city centre, there are a number of old settlers' houses, including Pitts Farm (1806), Lowestoft and Summerholme. Nearby is the factory of the Electrolytic Zinc Company, which can be visited. In Anfield Street is the Tasmanian Transport Museum (open: Sat. and Sun. 1–5pm).

Claremont

The main attractions of Claremont (12km/7½ miles north of Hobart) are the Cadbury-Schweppes chocolate factory and Alpenrail, a large model railway layout at 82 Abbotsfield Road W.

Granton

Farther north, in Granton (south bank of Derwent River), are two relics of the convict colony, the Old Watch House (Main Road), now a filling station, with the smallest prison cell in Australia (50cm/20in. square, 2m/6½ft high), and the Black Snake Inn (1833).

Bridgewater

20km/12½ miles north of Hobart, at the most important crossing of the Derwent River, is Bridgewater (pop. 8700), once a considerable market town but in recent years a residential suburb of Hobart, with a rapidly increasing population.

The 1.3km/¾ mile long causeway over the Derwent was built in the early 1830s by 200 convicts. The first bridge was opened in 1849; the present one dates from 1946.

Brighton

5km/3 miles north of Bridgewater is the village of Brighton (pop. 650), which grew out of a military post established in 1826 and named by Governor Macquarie after Brighton in Sussex. The Brighton army camp is still the main military base in Tasmania.

Bonorong Park

South-east of Brighton is Bonorong Park, a wildlife sanctuary which attracts many visitors.

★ Pontville

A few kilometres north-east of Brighton is the historic township of Pontville (pop. 900), founded in 1830 as a bridgehead on the Jordan River. Many of its old buildings are under statutory protection. For the purposes of restoration work two abandoned sandstone quarries were reopened. The neo-Romanesque St Mark's Church (Anglican) was built by James Blackburn in 1841. Behind the church is the Sheiling, formerly the police station (1819). The old post office, originally the officers' mess, dates from around 1824. The five little houses in the "Row", beside the bridge of 1824, were built about the same time for soldiers guarding the convicts.

Risdon Cove

From the Goodwood district the Bowen Bridge crosses the Derwent to Risdon Cove, where the first settlement – later moved south to Sullivan Cove on the other side of the river – was established. On the Risdon Cove Historic Site (open: daily 9.30am–4.30pm) is an interesting exhibition on the history of the settlement.

Bellerive

The Tasman Bridge leads from Hobart to the suburb of Bellerive, on the east bank of the Derwent. On Kangaroo Bluff is an old fort from which there is a fine panoramic view of Hobart against the mighty backdrop of Mount Wellington. There are a number of good bathing beaches round Bellerive.

Rokeby

South-east of Bellerive, on the south side of the Derwent estuary, is Rokeby (pop. 3500), which was founded in 1809. Here the settlers grew their first wheat and harvested their first apples. Two interesting old buildings are St Matthew's Church and the old Courthouse. Rokeby lies on the way to the water sports centre of South Arm, 20km/12½ miles farther south. Clifton Beach, 10km/6 miles south, is popular with surfers.

Sorell

26km/16 miles east of Hobart is Sorell (pop. 3200), founded in 1821 and named after a former governor of Tasmania. This area provided grain not only for Tasmania but at certain times also for New South Wales, which threatened to go hungry because of its less productive agriculture. Many Hobart families have holiday homes on the extensive sweep of coast between Carlton and Dodges Ferry. A notable landmark in Sorell is the neo-Romanesque Scots Uniting Church (1842). The 3.3km/2 mile long causeway on the Hobart–Port Arthur road was completed in 1872 after eight years' work.

Richmond

See entry

Sandy Bay, Wrest Point ★Casino

To the south of Hobart, in Sandy Bay, is Wrest Point, on which the first legal casino in Australia was opened in 1973. Attached to the Casino is a luxury hotel with a congress centre and a night club.

Tudor Court

Tudor Court (827 Sandy Bay Road; open: daily 9am–5pm) is a faithful replica of an English village.

University of Tasmania

To the west of the Casino is the campus of the University of Tasmania (founded 1890). On the campus is the John Elliot Classic Museum (open: February to November Mon.–Fri. 10am–4pm).

★Mount Nelson

From Wrest Point Nelson Road runs south, with many bends, up Mount Nelson (340m/1116ft). Although it is small compared with Mount Wellington, it affords a splendid panoramic view of Hobart, its harbour and the mouth of the Derwent. The old signal station is now occupied by a tearoom.

Taroona

Under the south side of Mount Nelson, 10km/6 miles from Hobart, is Taroona, a select old residential district with beautiful beaches and views of the Derwent. The Shot Tower, built by convict labour, was used to produce perfectly rounded lead shot; it is now occupied by a small museum and an art gallery.

Kingston, Blackmans Bay

12km/7½ miles south of Hobart is the suburb of Kingston (pop. 11,000), which has an excellent tourist infrastructure (hotels, motels, caravan/camping parks). The beaches round Kingston and farther south (Blackmans Bay, Tinderbox, Howden) are ideal for water sports. The Kingston Beach Regatta is held in January. The neighbouring coasts are of great scenic beauty.

Commonwealth Antarctic Division

To the south of Kingston is the headquarters of the Commonwealth Antarctic Division, an outstation of the Department of Science and Technology which carries out Antarctic research. There is an exhibition (open: on weekdays 9am–4pm) explaining and illustrating the work of the station.

The Huon Valley, a famed fruit-growing area

Kettering

30km/19 miles south of Hobart on the Channel Highway is Kettering (pop. 320), in the centre of a large fruit-growing area. From here there is a ferry over the D'Entrecasteaux Channel to Bruny Island (see entry).

Cascades

In Cascades, a south-western suburb of Hobart, are the imposing premises of the Cascade Brewery (156 Collins Street), built in 1832, which illustrate the importance of hop-growing and brewing to the economy of Tasmania.

★Mount Wellington

To the west of Hobart is the massive presence of Mount Wellington (1270m/4167ft). A narrow mountain road winds its way up from the Huon Highway to the summit (12km/7½ miles), from which there are breathtaking views over Hobart, the Derwent valley and the D'Entrecasteaux Channel. In the pavilion on the top is a display of old photographs of Hobart and Mount Wellington. Safe boardways lead to the very edge of the precipitous escarpment.

Huonville

40km/25 miles south-west of Hobart is Huonville (pop. 1300), the commercial centre of the Huon valley, a large fruit-growing area (mainly apples). In early colonial days the settlers felled great quantiities of the slow-growing Huon pine, whose fine wood was then much in demand. The beautiful country round Huonville, with the little townships of Ranelagh (Motor Museum), Grove (Apple Museum) and Glen Huon, is a favourite recreation area with the people of Hobart.

Franklin

8km/5 miles south-west of Huonville is Franklin (pop. 450), the earliest European settlement in the Huon valley, founded in 1804. Its economy is based on timber-working (sawmills), fruit-growing and dairy farming. It has two interesting old buildings, the Franklin Tavern (1851) and the Anglican church (1863).

Cygnet

20km/12½ miles south of Huonville, in a wide bay in Port Huon, is Cygnet (pop. 830), the centre of a large fruit-growing district. It was originally named Port de Cygne by the French admiral Bruny d'Entrecasteaux because of the number of swans in the bay. It is now a popular holiday resort, with beautiful beaches.

Lymington

Round the village of Lymington, farther to the south, visitors may, if they are very lucky, find agates.

King Island H 7/8

Situation and characteristics

King Island lies in the Bass Strait off the north-western tip of Tasmania. Although the climate of the island is fairly raw, its wildlife draws many visitors. Every spring millions of muttonbirds can be observed here in their breeding colonies. The sea elephants which were formerly numerous here have now been almost exterminated, but it is still possible to observe other species of seal.

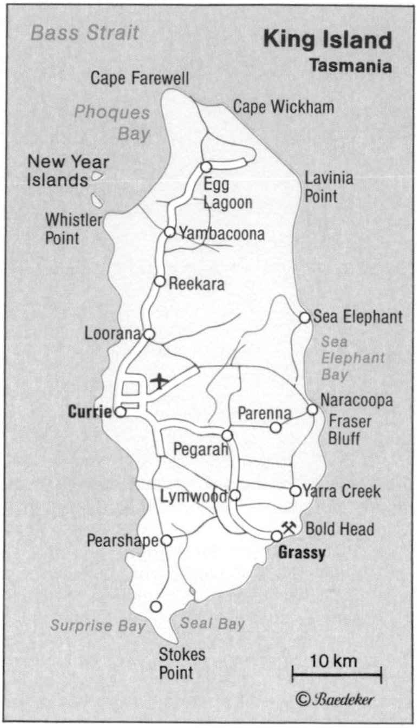

The inhabitants of the island live mainly by dairy farming and mining scheelite for its wolfram content. Seaweed is also harvested.

Access

There are regular flights to from Melbourne and from Wynyard in northern Tasmania to Currie, on the west side of King Island.

Accommodation

Several small hotels and camping grounds.

Features

40km/25 miles north of Currie is the Lavina Nature Reserve (area 6800 hectares/16,800 acres), established to protect the coastal vegetation. There are a number of wrecks off the island for scuba divers to explore. The lighthouse on Cape Wickham, at the north end of the island, is one of the tallest in Australia. At both the north and the south ends of the island there are beautiful beaches and bathing places.

★ Launceston J 8

Situation and characteristics

Launceston (pop. 66,000), the second largest town in Tasmania, lies in the north-east of the island at the head of the Tamar River, which is formed by the junction of the North and South Esk and after a winding course of 64km/40 miles flows into the Bass Strait. With the immediately surrounding area it has a population of 88,000.

History and development

The sheltered harbour in the estuary of the Tamar was surveyed by Bass and Flinders during their circumnavigation of Tasmania in 1798 and was named Port Dalrymple after the Admiralty hydrographer. In 1804 William Paterson founded the present settlement of George Town on Port Dalrymple. A year later Paterson founded another settlement farther upstream which he called Patersonia. It was renamed Launceston in 1907 in honour of Governor Philip King, who came from Launceston in Cornwall. In 1835 a party of settlers led by John Batman sailed from here to Port Phillip in Victoria and founded Melbourne.

The town prospered thanks to the productive agriculture of the surrounding area and to its mills and breweries. By the 1820s it was already the most important town in northern Tasmania, with extensive port installations and warehouses along the waterfront.

Transport

From the airport 16km/10 miles south of the town centre there are connections with Hobart and Melbourne. Launceston lies at the junction of five important highways – the Midlands Highway from the south, the Tasman Highway from the east, the West and East Tamar Highways from the north and the Bass Highway from the west.

Accommodation

Launceston has a number of hotels and motels, including the Penny Royal motel complex, Launceston Country Club Casino (Prospect Vale, 8km/5 miles south-west, in a large park, with golf courses and a casino) and the Grindelwald Swiss Village (West Tamar Highway, 18km/11 miles north of Launceston); caravan/camping park at 94 Glen Dhu Street, Hadspen Camping Park.

Sights in Launceston

Pedestrian zones

In the town centre there are two pedestrian zones, the Brisbane Street Mall between Charles Street and St John Street and the curving Quadrant Mall between St John Street and Brisbane Street. Most of the town's historic buildings are in St John Street and George Street.

St John's Church, Princes Square

St John's Anglican Church (157 St John Street), built in 1824 and later enlarged, gives Princes Square, between Frederick, St John, Elizabeth and Charles Streets, its particular character. The square was originally a claypit and later became a parade ground and place of assembly. From the mid-19th century onwards it gradually developed into a park with tall oak-trees. The elaborate fountain came from the 1855 Paris Exhibition.

Baptist Christ Church

In Frederick Street is the brick-built neo-Gothic Baptist Christ Church (1885), next to a little neo-classical chapel of 1842.

Synagogue

The Synagogue at 126 St John Street, built in 1844, is the second oldest in Australia.

Town Hall

The imposing Town Hall (corner of St John and Cameron Streets), in neo-classical style, was built in 1864 by a local architect, Peter Mills.

Post Office

Opposite the Town Hall is the Post Office, a red brick building of the 1880s with a later, rather ill-matched, tower.

Macquarie House

Macquarie House, in Civic Square (behind the Town Hall) was originally a warehouse, built in 1830. Later it was used as a barracks and as government offices. After restoration it now houses a branch of the Queen Victoria Museum (open: Mon.–Sat. and on Sunday afternoons), with an exhibition on the history of the town.

George Street

In George Street, which runs parallel to St John Street, are a number of notable buildings.

Colonial Motor Inn

The main wing of the Colonial Motor Inn (corner of Elizabeth and George Streets) is the former Grammar School of 1847, one of the earliest private schools in the country. The hotel complex also includes the former St John's Parish Hall of 1842.

Albion House

Albion House (153–155 George Street), built in 1837, is an elegant Regency building.

Union Bank

The former Union Bank (*c.* 1860; corner of George and Paterson Streets), with Doric columns, now houses the Tasmanian headquarters of the National Trust (open: daily 9am–5pm).

Old Umbrella Shop

At 60 George Street is the Old Umbrella Shop, a fine 1860s building which has remained almost unchanged since the end of the 19th century. It now belongs to the National Trust and contains an umbrella museum and a souvenir shop (open: Mon.–Fri. 9am–5pm, Sat. 9am–noon).

Batman-Fawkner Inn

The Batman-Fawkner Inn at 35 Cameron Street dates from the town's early years (*c.* 1820). Its first owner, John P. Fawkner, along with John Batman, crossed Bass Strait to Victoria in quest of new grazing land and founded Melbourne.

Customs House

On the Esplanade flanking the North Esk is the imposing neo-classical Customs House of 1885, fronted by a colonnade. Its magnificence reflects the town's 19th century prosperity.

Staffordshire House

Staffordshire House (1833; 56 Charles Street), with shops on the ground floor, apartments above and an associated warehouse, has recently been restored by the National Trust.

City Park

Cameron Street runs north-east to the City Park (12 hectares/30 acres), with old elms and oaks, a small monkey and wallaby enclosure, a conservatory and a richly decorated fountain.

Albert Hall

On the west side of the City Park, in Tamar Street, is the Albert Hall, built for the Tasmanian International Exhibition of 1891. It is now a cultural centre, used for concerts, exhibitions, etc.

Royal Park

To the west of the town centre, at the point where the North and South Esk join to form the Tamar, is the Royal Park, with the Queen Victoria Museum and Cenotaph.

★Queen Victoria Museum and Art Gallery

The Queen Victoria Museum and Art Gallery in Wellington Street (on the west side of the town centre), built in 1891, is a good example of late 19th-century public architecture. It has collections of material on the early days of settlement and the convict colony and on the natural history of Tasmania. Its principal attraction is a splendid Chinese joss house decorated with gold leaf, originally built by Chinese miners in northern Tasmania.

Ritchie's Mill

In Kings Park, to the south-west, where the West Tamar Highway is carried high over the outflow of the South Esk River, is Ritchie's Mill, a four-storey grain mill of 1845 which now houses a craft shop and a tearoom.

"Lady Stelfox"

Nearby is the landing-stage used by the old paddle-steamer "Lady Stelfox", which still takes visitors on river cruises (e.g. to Cataract Gorge).

★Cataract Gorge

To the south-west of the town is the wild and romantic Cataract Gorge, carved out over many centuries by the South Esk. On both sides of the gorge are daringly engineered walking trails. There is also a chair-lift over the gorge. At its south end are the remains of an old hydro-electric station. There are fine views into the gorge from the Kings Bridge and the Gorge Restaurant.

Zig Zag Reserve

Above the gorge, to the south, is the Zig Zag Reserve, a recreation area commanding wide views.

★Penny Royal World

One of Tasmania's most popular attractions is Penny Royal World, an entertainment park which is also an open-air museum and incorporates a large motel complex. The central features of the park are a re-erected windmill and a reconstructed watermill dating from the 1820s which originally stood to the south of Launceston. Other highlights are the Royal Gunpowder Mill, a bullet-casting shed in a quarry by the cataract, and a smithy and a coachbuilder's workshop where craftsmen can be watched at work.

Surroundings of Launceston

Hadspen

A few kilometres south-west of the town centre is Hadspen (pop. 1100), founded in the early 1820s. It has preserved numerous small Georgian buildings, including the Red Feather Inn (1845), the town gaol and the church.

★Entally House

18km/11 miles south-west of Launceston, reached by way of the Bass Highway, is Entally House, one of the oldest mansions owned by the National Trust. It was built about 1820 by Thomas Reibey, whose mother had been transported to New South Wales as a convict at the age of 13 and had risen to become a successful businesswoman in Sydney. Thomas Reibey's son became prime minister of Tasmania in 1866–67. The house has an elegant Regency interior and valuable silver and is surrounded by beautiful grounds, with a greenhouse, stables, a coach-house and a chapel. Opening times: daily 10am–noon and 1–5pm.

In Penny Royal World

Waverley Woollen Mills

The Waverley Woollen Mills (1874), 5km/3 miles south of Launceston (St Leonards, Waverley Road), are still operating with the original machinery (can be visited).

Franklin House

Franklin House, 6km/4 miles south of Launceston (access via Kings Meadows), was built in 1838 for a brewer and innkeeper and in 1842 became a boys' school. The house has been restored by the National Trust and furnished in period style (open: daily 9am–5pm, 9am–4pm in winter).

★Evandale

Evandale (pop. 850), 20km/12½ miles south of Launceston, was founded in 1829. It has been classed as a Historic Village, and the whole village is under statutory protection. It is a unique example of a complete and unspoiled Georgian settlement.

Situated on high ground above the South Esk River, it was originally called Collins Hill but was later renamed in honour of G. W. Evans, the first surveyor-general of Tasmania. John Kelly, father of the notorious bush-ranger Ned Kelly, worked here as a convict, and John Batman, founder of Melbourne, and the well-known English landscape painter John Glover lived near the town.

The High Street, with its Georgian and Victorian buildings, is very attractive. The Clarendon Arms Hotel has been in business since 1847. Two notable churches are the Anglican church of 1871, with 300 nameless convicts' graves in the churchyard, and the Uniting Church of 1840, famed as the most beautiful village church in Australia. The massive water-tower on the outskirts of the village was built at the end of the 19th century.

To the west of Evandale is the oldest merino sheep station in Australia, established in 1809. The homestead of Pleasant Banks Farm was built in 1838.

★Clarendon House

30km/19 miles south of Launceston by way of Evandale, on the banks of the South Esk, is Clarendon House, built in 1838 for the very wealthy wool and grain dealer James Cox. This elegant Georgian country house with its pillared portico is one of the finest of its kind in the whole of Australia (open: daily 10am–5pm, in winter 10am–4pm).

★Longford

Longford (pop. 2000), 22km/13½ miles south-west of Launceston in a pastoral farming district (dairy products, high-quality merino wool), has been classed by the National Trust as a Historic Town, the whole of which is under statutory protection. The first settlers came here around 1813. The main streets of Longford with their old shops and inns have the air of a small town in 19th century England. The oldest buildings in the town were built by convict labour. Christ Church (1839) has beautiful stained glass from Newcastle (England) and a graceful tower; there are many graves of early settlers in the churchyard. The Racecourse Hotel (1845) was originally designed as a railway station and later became an old people's home; it is now a popular tourist hotel furnished in colonial style. Jessen Lodge (1827) is also a hotel. Other notable old buildings are the Queen's Arms Hotel, the Blenheim Inn and the Roman Catholic and Methodist churches.

★Brickendon House

Brickendon House, 2km/1¼ south of the town, was built by William Archer in 1824 for his family and is still owned by his descendants. The Archer brothers played a major part in the development of northern Tasmania, and William Archer, who was born in Tasmania, ranks as the first native Tasmanian architect.

Perth

5km/3 miles north-east of Longford is the little township of Perth, once an important coaching station on the Midland Highway to Hobart, with a number of historic old buildings.

Cressy

Cressy, in a sheep-farming district 10km/6 miles south of Longford, also preserves a number of old buildings.

Poatina

20km/12½ miles south-west of Cressy is Poatina (pop. 210), a new settlement on the Central Plateau established to house construction workers employed on the nearby hydro-electric scheme and the staff of the large power station, much of which is underground (can be visited). From a lookout above Poatina, to the west, and from Bradys Lookout (1371m/4498ft), to the south, there are fine views over the plateau towards Launceston and Ben Lomond.

Deddington

40km/25 miles south-east of Launceston is the little settlement of Deddington. The English landscape painter John Glover settled here in 1830, naming the place after his home village in the Lake District. A chapel built here in 1840 is believed to have been designed by Glover, who is buried in the nearby churchyard. Other old buildings are an inn and the ruins of the police station.

Kingston

14km/8½ miles south is Kingston, a house built by convict labour in 1825 for John Batman, founder of Melbourne, who was a friend of John Glover's. Along with a number of others they were the first white men to climb Ben Lomond (1833).

★Ben Lomond National Park

50km/31 miles south-east of Launceston is Ben Lomond National Park (area 165sq.km/64sq.miles), which attracts large numbers of hill walkers and nature-lovers and is one of the most popular winter sports areas in Australia. A steep road, with many bends, leads up to the summit plateau, on which there are a number of mountain huts. During the winter sports season the Northern Tasmanian Alpine Club runs a "ski village" (overnight accommodation, restaurants, shops) on the slopes of Legges Tor (1573m/5161ft), Tasmania's second highest mountain. Striking features of Ben Lomond National Park are the dolerite columns, carved out by Ice Age glaciers and further dissected by frost. The slopes of the hills are covered with great expanses of scree, almost devoid of vegetation, and area of Alpine moorland with characteristic moorland vegetation. In spring and summer there are large numbers of wild flowers.

Lilydale

30km/19 miles north-east of Launceston, under the north-west side of Mount Arthur (1187m/3895ft), is Lilydale (pop. 360), in a beautiful setting which has made it a popular excursion and holiday destination (caravan/camping park; accommodation in farms).

3km/2 miles north-east of the village are the wild and romantic Lilydale Falls.

Lavender farms

The lavender farms at Nabowla, 25km/15½ miles north-east of Lilydale, and Bridestowe, 40km/25 miles north-east, attract many visitors when the lavender is in bloom (end of August to beginning of January).

Macquarie Harbour J 8

Situation and characteristics

This large natural harbour, the only one on the wild west coast of Tasmania, was discovered in 1815 by James Kelly. It is named after Lachlan Macquarie, governor of New South Wales (see Famous People), for until 1825 Tasmania was part of that state. The harbour, into the south-east end of which the Gordon River flows, is protected from the storms of the Southern Ocean by Cape Sorell and Wellington Heads. Convicts sent to work here called the narrow entrance to the harbour Hell's Gates.

The harbour gained in importance in the 1880s, when tin and copper mining began on the west coast of Tasmania, and this led to the development of Strahan, in an inlet at the north end of Macquarie Harbour.

★Sarah Island

From Strahan a boat can be taken to Sarah Island (now scheduled as a Historic Site), on which a penal settlement was established in 1822. The convicts sent here worked in the harshest conditions, felling the Huon pines which were valued for their tough timber, and breaking stone in the Franklin and Gordon Rivers. The penal settlement was abandoned in 1833 following the development of the large convict colony of Port Arthur (see entry) in south-eastern Tasmania.

★Gordon River

From Strahan there are boat and seaplane trips to the lower course of the Gordon River, where there are still unspoiled expanses of rain forest, with idyllic waterfalls and Huon pines. There is a very rewarding Rainforest Walk. The tracts of dense and impenetrable rain forest and the tumultuous rivers Franklin and Gordon, untrammelled by any dams, are particularly impressive when seen from the air. There are also sightseeing flights to the

Strahan Harbour

junction of the Franklin and the Gordon at Sir John Falls, over Frenchmans Cap and to Queenstown.

Strahan

The only port on the inhospitable west coast of Tasmania is Strahan (pop. 600), 35km/22 miles south-west of Queenstown (see entry) at the north end of Macquarie Harbour. Originally it shipped the high-quality timber of the Huon pine, and then enjoyed a boom when copper-mining began on Mount Lyell, near Queenstown. The construction of the railway line from Strahan to Zeehan in 1892 also brought increased prosperity. Nowadays Strahan is mainly a fishing port, since large vessels cannot make their way through the narrow Hell's Gates. From the water-tower there are good views of the town and harbour.

★Ocean Beach

6km/4 miles west, on the open sea, is Ocean Beach with its tall dunes and tremendous surf.

Maria Island National Park J 8

Location

Maria Island, originally a penal colony and now a National Park, lies 15km/9 miles south-east of Triabunna (see entry) in the Tasman Sea.

Access

There is a passenger ferry between the resort of Louisville and Darlington, and there are air taxis between Triabunna and Darlington.

Accommodation

Accommodation in penitentiary; camping grounds. During the main holiday season advance booking is advisable. There are no shops on the island.

Topography

The sheltered beaches on the west coast of the island (Mercury Passage) are popular with swimmers, snorkellers and scuba divers. The hills rise sharply up from the coast, and on the summits it can be disagreeably cool. The hillsides are covered with dry eucalyptus forest, and there are expanses of heathland and depressions full of ferns. There is a rich fauna, including the rare Cape Barren geese, Forester kangaroos and even wallabies. On Mount Maria (709m/2326ft) there are beautiful walking trails and good climbing routes. From the tops of the hills there are fine views of the island and the east coast of Tasmania. There are interesting caves in the rock faces with ancient marine sediments.

Darlington

There are remains of the penal village to which prisoners convicted of serious offences and particularly troublesome convicts were sent before the establishment of the penal colony of Port Arthur (see entry). Later this became a probation centre. No further convicts were sent to Maria Island after the middle of the 19th century.

A few ruined buildings dating from around 1880 are relics of 19th century attempts to develop wine-growing, silk production and cement manufacture on the island.

Mole Creek J 8

Situation and characteristics

Under the north-east side of the Great Western Tiers, some 70km/45 miles west of Launceston (see entry), is the little settlement of Mole Creek (pop. 250; camping park), a good base for excursions in the surrounding area with its interesting flora and fauna. Mole Creek itself is the centre of a forestry, farming and beekeeping district.

A local speciality is leatherwood honey, garnered by the bees from the blossom of the leatherwood trees which grow only in the rain forests of western Tasmania.

★Maracoopa Cave

A few kilometres west of Mole Creek, at Maybery, is the Maracoopa Cave, a marvellous stalactitic cave inhabited by a species of glowworm found nowhere else.

★King Solomon Cave

15km/9 miles west of Mole Creek, near the Mersey River, is the King Solomon Cave (protected site), one of the finest show caves in Australia, with spectacular stalactites and stalagmites.

★Mount Field National Park J 8

Location; area
75km/47 miles west of Hobart; 16,257 hectares/40,155 acres.

Best time to visit
Throughout the year.

Access
Via Lyell Highway and Maydena Road; snow chains required in winter. Bus service from Hobart.

Accommodation
Camping ground at park entrance (advance booking advisable in summer).

Features
Mount Field is one of Australia's oldest National Parks, with magnificent rain forests, Alpine moorland and fine waterfalls. On the high moorland snow lies until summer, and there may also be heavy rain and cold spells in summer. The last Tasmanian tiger was caught in this area in 1930.

Walking trails
There are a variety of beautiful walking trails in the National Park; one of them, the short Russell Falls Nature Walk, is suitable even for wheelchair-users. There is an easy walk round Lake Dobson, and experienced bush walkers have a choice of attractive routes.

Winter sports
Mount Field National Park is a popular skiing area in winter, with downhill skiing on Mount Mawson and langlauf elsewhere.

Mount William National Park J 8

Location; area
North-eastern tip of Tasmania; 140sq.km/54sq.miles.

Best time to visit
Summer.

Access
Tasman Highway, then road running east from Herrick via Gladstone; only tracks within park.

Facilities
Camping grounds; picnic areas, ranger station, walking and riding trails.

Features
Mount William National Park is of interest particularly as the home of the rare Forester kangaroo. Above the dunes and heathland along the coast rise forest-covered hills. In the north of the park, on both sides of Cape Naturaliste, are long open bays, good for swimming and surf fishing. Extensive eucalyptus forests cover the slopes of Mount William (216m/709ft) and Bailey's Hill. There is a varied fauna including seabirds and land animals, mostly nocturnal. With a bit of luck visitors may even see a Tasmanian devil (see Baedeker Special, p. 371).

Gladstone
A few kilometres east of the entrance to Mount William National Park is Gladstone (pop. under 200; hotel), once an important mining town and now a good base for excursions to the park. In the 1870s this was a flourishing gold- and tin-mining area, and round Gladstone are many ghost towns (abandoned mining settlements), among them Boobyalla and Moorina.

★New Norfolk J 8

Situation and characteristics
New Norfolk (pop. 6200) lies an hour's drive north-west of Hobart in the beautiful valley of the Derwent. The first inhabitants came from the settlement of Norfolk Island after its abandonment in 1807: hence the name of the town. With many fine old buildings, it has been listed by the National Trust as a Historic Town under statutory protection.

Accommodation
Hotel, motel, caravan/camping park.

Features
St Matthew's Church (Anglican) in Bathurst Street, built in 1823, is Tasmania's oldest church. In Montague Street are the Old Colony Inn (1835) and the Bush Inn, twenty years older, which received its liquor licence in 1825. Nearby is the landing-stage used by passenger boats on the Derwent. In the Oast House in Hobart Road hops were dried from 1867 to 1969; it now houses a museum (hop-growing, etc.) and an art gallery.

Surroundings
The neighbouring township of Boyer, on the north bank of the Derwent, is dominated by a large paper mill.

Rewarding excursions from New Norfolk are to the Plenty Salmon Ponds (11km/7 miles west), where the first trout hatchery in Australia was established in 1864, to Mount Field National Park (30km/19 miles; see entry), with the Russell Falls, and to Lake Pedder, at the north end of the large South West National Park (see entry; access on Gordon River Road via Maydena).

Oatlands J 8

Situation and charactaristics

Oatlands (pop. 510), scheduled as a historic town, lies on the shores of Lake Dulverton, 90km/56 miles north of Hobart on the Midland Highway. The settlement was founded in the 1830s and was given its name by Governor Macquarie. For many years it was the main settlement in the Midlands of Tasmania, but more recently its population has fallen sharply.

Accommodation

Hotels and guesthouses.

Features

A number of buildings have survived from the early years of the settlement. The Courthouse in Campbell Street was built by convict labour in 1829. A notable building in the High Street is Holyrood House (1840), which was successively a coaching inn, a doctor's house and a schoolhouse and is now a restaurant furnished in the style of the 1840s. There are a number of other old buildings in the High Street. St Peter's Church (Anglican) was built in 1838. Callington Flour Mill continued to operate until 1890. This old windmill was restored a few years ago.

Surroundings

There is good fishing in the surrounding area, for example on Lake Dulverton, Lake Sorell and Lake Crescent. 13km/8 miles south-west of Oatlands is the little township of Jericho, with the interesting Mud Walls.

★★Port Arthur J 8

Situation and characteristics

In spite of – or perhaps because of – their infamous past the remains of the old convict settlement of Port Arthur have become one of the most visited

Ruins of Port Arthur: relics of an infamous past

tourist attractions in the whole of Australia. A lantern-lit "ghost tour" of the ruins at night is an eerie experience.

In daylight and sunshine, however, visitors can enjoy the scenic beauty of this coastal region with its wild cliffs, sheltered inlets and fascinating natural features.

Port Arthur lies in the south of the Tasman Peninsula (see entry), two hours' drive from Hobart. Here in 1830 Governor Sir George Arthur established a penal settlement to which the inmates of several smaller penal stations (including Sarah Island in Macquarie Harbour and Maria Island off the east coast) were transferred. The convicts sent here were put to hewing coal in the coal-mines and felling timber. The Port Arthur convict colony was not closed down until 1877, twenty years after the transportation of convicts had ceased.

Access

By car from Hobart on Arthur Highway; regular bus services from Hobart to Port Arthur; coach excursions from Hobart.

Accommodation

Fox and Hounds Old English Inn, with motel annexe; youth hostel; caravan/camping park.

Features

In spite of a devastating fire in 1897 there are impressive remains of the old penal settlement: the guard tower, the church, the model prison (with a circular layout and the guard house in the middle) and the hospital. A major programme of restoration and conservation was completed in 1986. The old lunatic asylum and the commandant's house are now in private ownership. The museum displays documents and relics of the penal settlement.

The settlement is open to the public daily 9am–5pm. There are conducted tours every hour from 9.30am to 3.30pm.

Island of the Dead

In Port Arthur Bay is the Island of the Dead, with 1769 nameless convict graves and 180 named graves of prison staff and the military.

Convict tramway

Beside the modern road can be seen remains of the convict tramway between Taranna and Oakwood, constructed to short-circuit the time-consuming voyage round the southern tip of the peninsula. The carriages were pushed and pulled along the tracks by convicts.

Queenstown J 8

Situation and characteristics

Queenstown, with a population of just under 4000, is the largest town in western Tasmania. Gold and other minerals were found here in 1856, and practically overnight Queenstown became a boom town. Mining (mainly copper, silver and gold) has been continuous here since the 1880s.

As a result of this mining activity the land round the town has been turned upside down, and the forests have been stripped bare to supply fuel for the smelting of copper; and the regeneration of the forest has been hampered by acid rain combined with the heavy local rainfall, atmospheric pollution and the resultant erosion. Nevertheless it is planned to replant the bare hillsides, littered with boulders which produce a changing play of light and colour, depending on the mineral content of the rock and the position of the sun.

In spite of modern development Queenstown has preserved something of the atmosphere of the 19th century. Wide streets and venerable old buildings bear witness to a time when Queenstown had a population of over 5000 and no fewer than 14 hotels.

Accommodation

Hotels, motels, caravan/camping park.

Features

The Empire Hotel (1901) is a representative example of the town's architecture in its heyday. The former Imperial Hotel (1898) now houses a museum which among much else has a collection of old photographs illustrating the development of the region. The Mount Lyell Mine and Mining Museum at 10 Garner Road (open daily; conducted visits) traces the history of mining in the Queenstown area. The town's main employer is the Mount Lyell Company on the eastern outskirts of the town, whose mine can be visited.

Surroundings

The Lyell Highway runs east from Queenstown, passing through the former mining settlement of Gormanston and the ghost town of Linda, and

then, on a boldly engineered mountain road, with wide views, climbs up into the forest-covered hills in the Franklin River area, with Frenchman's Cap (see Franklin Lower Gordon Wild Rivers National Park). The beautiful mountain forests in the National Park are in stark contrast to the lunar landscape round Queenstown.

★★ Richmond J 8

Situation and characteristics

25km/15½ miles north-east of Hobart is the much visited town of Richmond (pop. 700), which is a kind of living open-air museum. The town was founded soon after the landing of the first settlers in Risdon Cove in 1803 (see Hobart), and in 1824 it was officially recognised as a township. It soon developed into the commercial centre of a very fertile grain-growing district, though only one of the old grain mills has survived.

Richmond was also an important military post, and there was also a penal colony here, whose inmates constructed many of the town's buildings, as well as the oldest bridge in Australia.

Of all the early settlements in Tasmania Richmond presents the most complete and most homogeneous picture of a town of the colonial period.

Accommodation

Hotel, caravan/camping park.

Features

The town's best known feature is the bridge over the Coal River, built by convict labour in 1825. A short distance to the north is the neo-Gothic St John's Church (by Frederick Thomas, 1837–59), the oldest Roman Catholic church in Australia. The best view of the much photographed bridge shows in the background St Luke's Church (Anglican; by John Lee Archer, 1834–36). The timber roof structure was so well constructed that the convict carpenter responsible was given a free pardon. The church also has very fine stained glass.

Richmond Gaol (1825) is also well preserved. In Bridge Street are a whole string of fine old buildings. The Old Bakehouse (now a souvenir shop) still has its old ovens. The Bridge Inn (1834) houses a complex of shops, Saddler's Court (*c.* 1848) an art gallery. The Courthouse (1826) still serves its original purpose.

The Richmond Arms Hotel, with rich wrought-iron ornament, was built in 1888 on the site of an earlier building of 1827 which was destroyed by fire, leaving only its stable (now restored). The three-storey Granary was built in 1832 by James Bushcombe, who along with his brother Henry was one of the wealthiest men in the town. Beside it is Bushcombe's General Store; the dwelling-house dates from 1826, the shop with its neo-classical façade from 1829. From 1832 to 1972 the shop housed the oldest post office in Australia; it is now occupied by a small museum of photography.

Ashmore's shop (1850) is now a tearoom. The old Richmond Hotel (*c.* 1830) still bears over the door the name of the licensee in 1838, Lawrence Cotham. On the southern outskirts of the town is Prospect House, built by James Bushcombe in the 1830s for his family and now occupied by a restaurant (specialising in game dishes). Oak Lodge was built for Henry Bushcombe.

★ Rocky Cape National Park J 8

Location

North-west coast, on Bass Strait.

Access

Bass Highway; then side road to Sisters Beach or Rocky Cape, 12km/7½ miles and 30km/19 miles west of Wynyard.

Accommodation

In Boat Harbour.

Facilities

Water sports; picnic area, ranger station.

Features

Rocky Cape National Park, established in 1967 to protect the prehistoric caves, is a rugged stretch of coast with reefs and small offshore islands.

◀ *Australia's oldest bridge, built by convict labour, at Richmond*

Scenery at Boat Harbour, in Rocky Cape National Park

The caves, occupied by the aboriginal inhabitants of Tasmania over thousands of years, are of great archaeological interest for the great heaps of animal and fish bones, shells, etc., which throw light on the life of the Aborigines. Rock shelters which provided protection from the weather can be seen at the west end of Sisters Beach and on Flagpole Hill at Rocky Cape. Along the coast are little hidden beaches sheltered by promontories of quartzite rock reaching out into the Bass Strait.

Walking trails

Well marked walking trails run east along the coast from Rocky Cape to Sisters Beach and up the hills (fine views of coast).

Boat Harbour

A few kilometres east of Rocky Cape National Park, just off the Bass Highway, is the little settlement of Boat Harbour (pop. 300). Here rocky promontories alternate with little sickle-shaped beaches. There is good bathing on Boat Harbour Beach and Sisters Beach (which is within the National Park). Acommodation is available in motels and on a camping ground. Excursions to Sisters Island and to Birdlife Park (rare species of birds). Inland is a fertile agricultural area.

Wynyard

73km/45 miles west of Devonport (see entry), at the mouth of the Inglis River, is Wynyard (pop. 4600), the commercial centre of a rich dairy and mixed farming area, with a large dairy factory. Lying within easy reach of Melbourne and with many attractions for holidaymakers (bathing beaches, golf courses, water sports), it is now a popular tourist centre.

Fossil Bluff

7km/4½ miles north of Wynyard is Fossil Bluff, where the oldest marsupial fossils in Australia were found.

Rosebery J 8

Situation and characteristics

The little mining town of Rosebery (pop. 2100) lies at the foot of Mount Murchison in north-western Tasmania, an hour's drive north of Queenstown (see entry). Gold was found in Rosebery Creek in 1892. The town is now dominated by the large plant of the Electrolytic Zinc Company, to which ore is transported by cableway from a mine at Williamsford, 7km/4½ miles south.

Accommodation

Hotels, caravan/camping park.

Features

The most striking features in the hills round Rosebery are Mount Murchison (1275m/4183ft) to the east and the Montezuma Falls to the south-west. There are a number of artificial lakes and hydro-electric stations, among them the long (60km/37 miles), narrow Pieman Lake to the west of Rosebery. North-east of the town is Lake Mackintosh, fed by rivers flowing down from Cradle Mountain National Park (see entry). To the south of Rosebery a multi-stage dam is under construction.

St Helens J 8

Situation and characteristics

St Helens (pop. 1200), a resort famed for its fish restaurants which is particularly popular in summer, lies on the north-east coast of Tasmania. Originally a convict colony and a whaling station, it later developed into the most important fishing port on the east coast. Round the town are a number of good, safe beaches, including Georges Bay. Some of them are popular with surfers.

Accommodation

Hotels, caravan/camping parks (advance booking essential in summer).

Surroundings
Bay of Fires

To the north of St Helens is the beautiful Bay of Fires. Some sections of coast in this area are nature reserves. Camping; walking.

Scamander

20km/12½ miles south of St Helens is the little resort of Scamander (pop. 700), in a beautiful setting at the mouth of the Scamander, a river famed for its abundance of fish.

Savage River J 8

Situation and characteristics

In the wild and rugged country of north-western Tasmania, 73km/45 miles west of the Murchison Highway, is the mining town of Savage River, with Tasmania's only opencast iron-mine. The deposits of iron ore were discovered around 1870, but they could not be worked until means were devised for transporting the ore from this inaccessible region. It took almost a hundred years until a solution was found in 1967. The ore is now formed into a slurry which is pumped through an 85km/53 mile long pipeline to Port Latta on the north-west coast, to the west of Rocky Cape National Park (see entry), where it is processed and exported, mainly to Japan.

Accommodation

Hotel.

Surroundings
Corinna,
Pieman Gorge

30km/19 miles south-west, in a beautiful setting, is the old gold-mining settlement of Corinna. From here there are rewarding walks south-east to the dam forming Lake Pieman and north-west to the wild and romantic Pieman Gorge.

Luina

20km/12½ miles east of Savage River is Luina, once an important mining town, with a tin-mine and large deposits of copper.

Waratah

40km/25 miles east of Savage River is Waratah (pop. 330), the scene of Tasmania's first mining boom. Large deposits of tin were discovered on Mount Bischoff, north of the town, in 1872, and by 1900 Waratah had a population of 2000. The mine was closed down in 1935, but consideration is now being given to the restarting of mining operations on the Que River. Waratah has preserved a few buildings from the days of the tin-mining boom, including the Courthouse, the Atheneum Hall and the old church.

Scottsdale J 8

Situation and characteristics

Scottsdale (pop. 2000), charmingly situated amid green hills, is the most important town in north-eastern Tasmania, situated 70km/43 miles north-east of Launceston (see entry). It is the commercial centre of a rich agricultural and forestry area producing large crops of vegetables (frozen foods). In recent years the population of the area has been declining.

Accommodation

Hotels, caravan/camping park.

Surroundings
Bridport

20km/12½ miles north of Scottsdale, in Anderson Bay, is the little fishing town of Bridport (pop. 1200; caravan/camping park), whose beautiful beaches and good fishing (particularly trout) are now attracting increasing numbers of holidaymakers. From Waterhouse Point there are superb views.

Branxholm

25km/15½ miles east of Scottsdale on the Tasman Highway is the old mining settlement of Branxholm (pop. 260), with a number of old timber houses. The main sources of income in this area are a tin-mine and extensive pine forests. From Mount Horror (686m/2251ft; fire watch-tower) there are wide views.

Lavender farm

20km/12½ miles west of Scottsdale, at Nabowla, is a large lavender farm (seen at its best in summer, when the lavender is in flower).

Derby

The little tin-mining town of Derby (pop. 200) lies 30km/19 miles east of Scottsdale on the Tasman Highway. In its 19th century heyday it had a population of over 3000. In 1929, after a period of heavy rainfall, the Briseis Dam was breached and water poured down through the town, killing 14 people. This was a severe setback to mining activity. Features of interest are the Derby Tin Mine Museum (history of tin-mining) and the Dorset Hotel (1915). At Winnaleah, on the Tasman Highway, is a modern cheese factory which can be visited.

South West National Park J 8

Location; area

160km/100 miles west of Hobart; 605,000 hectares/1,494,000 acres.

Best time to visit

Spring, summer and autumn.

Unspoiled natural beauty in South West National Park

Access

Via Lyell Highway, Gordon River Road and Scotts Peak Road (tolls payable at Maydena Gate).

Facilities

Camping ground; in summer wilderness camps; sightseeing flights and boat trips from Bathurst Harbour/Port Davey.

Topography

The South West National Park is the largest and remotest National Park in Tasmania. It is the southern part of the Tasmanian Wilderness World Heritage Area and occupies the whole of the south-west of the island. It is a region of bare quartzite and dolerite mountains (Arthur Range, Frankland Range, etc.), densely wooded valleys and expanses of grassland, bounded on the south by grand coastal scenery, with the impressive drowned valley system of Port Davey.

In the 1970s a large reservoir, Lake Pedder, was formed on the eastern slopes of the Frankland Range to power a large hydro-electric station, and the construction of the Gordon River and Scotts Peak Roads gave easy access to the north-western and south-eastern shores of the lake. Lake Pedder is now a paradise for anglers and boating enthusiasts, though the water is usually too cold for swimmers.

Walking trails

The few poorly waymarked long-distance trails through the lonely expanses of the National Park are for experienced bush walkers only. From Scotts Peak Dam, at the south-east end of the lake, there are paths to the wild and very lonely south coast. Walkers are required, for their own safety, to report to the ranger station before undertaking and after completing their walk.

Roads

There are spectacular views of the rugged landscape of south-western Tasmania from the Gordon River Road (a gravel track for part of the way) and Scotts Peak Road.

★Stanley J 8

Location and importance

The little town of Stanley (pop. 600), founded in 1826, lies in the north-western corner of Tasmania on a headland jutting out into the Bass Strait. Here could be found the headquarters of the "Van Diemen's Land Company", set up with the object of clearing land and rearing merino sheep. During the gold-rush in the newly-formed state of Victoria Stanley became an important port to which ships brought supplies for the prospectors. Today Stanley is home to a sizeable fishing fleet, shrimps and sharks being among the main catches.

Because of its well-maintained buildings Stanley is under the protection of the National Trust.

Accommodation

Hotel, caravan park and camp-site

Sights

The town's emblem is "The Nut", a massive volcanic hill standing 135m/443ft high. The softer material was eroded away long ago. Matthew Flinders, who viewed it in 1798, was reminded of a Christmas cake. There is a chairlift to the top.

At the foot of the hill stands "Pets' cottage", once the residence of the architect John Lee Archer, who designed what are probably the most beautiful of Tasmania's older buildings. However, the town's most famous son is Joseph A. Lyons, who was prime minister of Australia fro 1932 to 1939. The house in which he was born stands in Alexander Terrace. Around the old landing stages where whalers and sailing ships once berthed are grouped a number of attractive old buildings, included a massive grain store and the old customs house. The very popular Union Hotel on Church Street, with its vaulted cellars and narrow staircases, was built in 1847 and has since been restored. The Plough Inn on the same street has also been restored and is furnished in 19th c. style. Also worth a visit is the Discovery Centre, with displays of folk-art and a shell collection (open: daily).

On the outskirts of the town lies Highfield, an estate with a period house, remains of a chapel and various outbuildings including farm cottages, stables and barns. The Van Diemen's Land Company representative lived here in the 19th c.

Surroundings
Smithton

Smithton (pop. 3500), the main township in the far north-west of Tasmania, lies on the Bass Highway 22km/14 miles south-west of Stanley. It is the centre of a rich agricultural region specialising in dairy farming and vegetable growing. Forestry (large saw-mill) and fishing also flourish here.

Mella

When draining farmland near the township of Mella, a few miles further west, the fossilised remains of giant marsupials were discovered.

Marrawah

The north-west coast of Tasmania lies a good 50km/30 miles west of Smithton. Marrawah boasts some excellent surfing beaches.

Swansea J 8

Location and importance

Swansea (pop. 210) is an old settlement lying on Great Oyster Bay in eastern Tasmania. In the 19th c. it gained importance as the administrative centre of Glamorgan, the oldest rural district in Australia.

Accommodation

Hotel, caravan park and camp-site

Sights

On Franklin Street stands Morris' General Store. This three-storey building dates from 1838 and contains a small museum. Bark Mill, built in the 1870s, houses the East Coast Museum. Also of interest is the restored bark-grinding mill, which once produced tannin for use in preparing leather. In the old schoolhouse dating from 1869 can be seen memorabilia from the Pioneering days.

Surroundings
"Spiky Bridge"

The Tasman Highway leads southwards from Swansea along the coast to Spiky Bridge 8km/5 miles away. Its unique buildings include bridges edged with pointed stones to prevent cattle from falling off.

From the coast there is a fine view of the Freycinet Peninsusla (see entry).

★ Nine Mile Beach

North-east of Swansea, at the end of Great Oyster Bay, lies Nine Mile Beach, which is very popular with holidaymakers and water sports enthusiasts.

The Tessellated Pavement, created by nature

Tasman Peninsula · Forestier Peninsula J 8

Situation and characteristics

Two hours' drive east of Hobart are the Tasman and Forestier Peninsulas, linked by a narrow isthmus, Eaglehawk Neck. On the east side of both peninsulas are storm-lashed cliffs and crags; the coast is particularly wild round Eaglehawk Neck.

Accommodation

Caravan/camping park on Garden Point (reached from Hobart on Arthur Highway).

Features

The famous Tessellated Pavement is a natural rock platform which has been broken up into the appearance of square tiles. There are other striking rock formations at the Blowhole, Tasman's Arch and the Devil's Kitchen. In the north-west of the Tasman Peninsula is Lime Bay Nature Reserve with its sandy beaches and rugged cliffs. Inland are areas of heathland.

Also in the north-west of the peninsula is Coal Mine Historic Site, where convicts from Port Arthur (see entry) hewed coal.

Eaglehawk Neck

Eaglehawk Neck (motel), less than 100 metres wide, links the Tasman and Forestier Peninsulas. When Port Arthur became a penal settlement soldiers and tethered guard dogs were posted on this narrow strip of land to prevent escapes. There is now a quiet fishing village and holiday resort here. On the rugged coast of the isthmus and the Tasman Peninsula are a number of curious rock formations – Tasman's Arch, the Devil's Kitchen, the Blowhole and the Tessellated Pavement, etc.

Port Arthur

See entry

Dunalley

The fishing village of Dunalley (pop. 200) lies in Blackman Bay, on the narrow strip of land linking the Forestier Peninsula with the mainland. The Denison Canal (2.2km/1½ miles long; swing bridge) cuts across the isthmus, shortening the passage to Hobart for small ships by 60km/37 miles. On Cape Paul is the Tasman Memorial, commemorating the first landing by Europeans on December 2nd 1642.

Copping

At Copping, on the mainland just north of the Forestier Peninsula, is the Colonial and Convict Exhibition, with many interesting relics of the convict period, including old tools and machinery.

Tasmanian Wilderness World Heritage Area J 8

Location

The Tasmanian Wilderness World Heritage Area includes a number of National Parks in western and south-western Tasmania with a total area of 1.4 million hectares/3.5 million acres. The most important constituents of the area are Cradle Mountain/Lake St Clair National Park, South West National Park and Franklin Lower Gordon Wild Rivers National Park (see entries), which were included in UNESCO's World Heritage list in 1982. Walls of Jerusalem National Park (see entry), the Central Plateau Conservation Area and Hartz Mountains National Park (see Geeveston) were added in 1989.

Topography

The Tasmanian Wilderness World Heritage Area takes in an immense expanse of almost unchanged natural landscape, with mighty rivers and rugged mountains, which reflects the whole course of the earth's history. This dramatic landscape, with its grandiose peaks of schist and quartzite (Frenchman's Cap, Federation Peak), its columnar dolerite formations (Precipitous Bluff, Mount Ossa) and its tumultuous rivers (Franklin, Gordon), came into being during and after the last Ice Ages. With the melting of the ice the level of the sea rose several metres, drowning the broad estuaries of the rivers and giving rise to such beautiful natural harbours as Port Davey and Bathurst Harbour in south-western Tasmania.

The vegetation of the Tasmanian Wilderness World Heritage Area includes Alpine heathland, great open forests of eucalyptus and expanses of cool temperate rain forest and moorland. The Huon pines found here are among the oldest plants on earth – anything up to 2000 years old.

In this area too are traces of early human existence (caves and Ice Age occupation sites of the Aborigines, ancient rock paintings) and remains of the convict period in the 19th century.

Given its relatively high altitude, this land of rocks and lakes is subject to sudden bouts of bad weather. The unpredictable weather conditions (a high annual rainfall of up to 2500mm/100in., strong west winds, cold spells with snow even in summer) complicate the planning of a journey in this area.

The development of this territory and the provision of facilities for visitors should not be prevented but must be so arranged that this unspoiled region can be preserved for the enjoyment of future generations.This has led in recent years to a ban on the construction of any more dams which would drastically alter the natural landscape.

Lyell Highway

The Lyell Highway, constructed in 1932 as a link between the mining town of Queenstown (see entry) and Hobart, is the main access route to the central and northern parts of the World Heritage Area.

Gordon River Road

The Gordon River Road runs from Hobart by way of Maydena to Lake Pedder, which before the area was put under statutory protection was enlarged by the construction of dams. From this road there are magnificent views.

Scotts Peak Road

The Scotts Peak Road is the starting-point of a number of long bush and mountain walks (Mount Anne Track, Western Arthurs Peak, Federation Peak, etc.).

Walking trails

From the Lyell Highway there are trails to the rain forests on the banks of the Franklin River, the Nelson Falls and Donaghys Hill Wilderness Lookout (views of Franklin valley and Frenchman's Cap). Recherche Bay is the starting-point of the South Coast Track, which leads to Bathurst Harbour and through South West National Park (see entry) to the south end of Lake Pedder.

The world-famous Overland Track (for which five days should be allowed) runs south from Cradle Valley to Lake St Clair, the deepest lake in Tasmania and the source of the Derwent River.

Only those with much experience of the arts of survival should undertake a cross-country trip through the Tasmanian wilderness, and even they should never go alone. There are organised tours (walking, climbing, in 4WD vehicles, canoeing and boating) which give close-up experience of this great empty territory with less risk.

White-water rafting

There are white-water rafting runs on the Collingwood and Franklin Rivers.

Sightseeing flights

Sightseeing flights, with landings at places of particular interest, are run (weather permitting) from Hobart.

Triabunna J 8

Situation and characteristics

The old garrison town and whaling station of Triabunna (pop. 1000), 90km/55 miles north-east of Hobart in Prosser Bay, is now a fishing port. Thanks to its good bathing beaches and the excellent angling in the surrounding area it has developed in recent years into a holiday resort.

Accommodation

Hotels, caravan/camping park.

Surroundings

Buckland

25km/15½ miles south-west of Triabunna on the Tasman Highway is the little township of Buckland. Its principal sight is the church of St John the Baptist (1846), which has a fine 14th century stained glass window depicting scenes from the life of the Baptist. The window came from Battle Abbey, near Hastings, which was destroyed by Cromwell in the 17th century; it was preserved from destruction and two centuries later was presented to Buckland by the Marquess of Salisbury. The Old Buckland Inn dates from the mid 19th century.

Maria Island

From Triabunna there is a ferry to Maria Island, once a penal colony.

Orford

At the mouth of the Prosser River, easily reached on the Tasman Highway, is Orford (pop. 500; motels, caravan/camping park), a little holiday resort with excellent facilities for water sports, fishing, walking and golf.

★Walls of Jerusalem National Park J 8

Location; area
110km/68 miles west of Launceston (see entry), 115km/71 miles south of Devonport (see entry); 51,800 hectares/127,950 acres.

Best time to visit
Summer (though even in this season there may be sudden changes of weather).

Access
On Bass Highway via Deloraine; via Mole Creek and Mersey Forest Road.

Accommodation
In Mole Creek.

Facilities
Bush camping.

Features
The Walls of Jerusalem National Park is part of the Tasmanian Wilderness World Heritage Area (see entry). Its unusual name comes from the sheer rock walls which enclose the Lake Country on the central plateau with its numerous lakes of glacial origin. The highest peaks are the West Wall (1490m/4889ft) and Mount Jerusalem (1458m/4784ft). Good walking and climbing; in winter cross-country skiing.

★Zeehan J 8

Situation and characteristics
The little town of Zeehan (pop. 1200), 35km/22 miles north-west of Queenstown (see entry), is named after the ship in which Abel Tasman sailed round Tasmania in 1642. The discovery of silver in 1882 brought an economic boom, and by 1900 the town had a population of over 5000 and 26 hotels, making it Tasmania's third largest town. In 1908 mining began to decline, and in 1960 the last mine closed. Zeehan is now only a shadow of its former self.

Accommodation
Hotels, motel, caravan/camping park.

Features
A relic of the town's one-time prosperity is the Gaiety Theatre (1898; 1000 seats), in which such great stars as Enrico Caruso and Dame Nellie Melba once appeared. Another reminder of past splendour is the old Grand Hotel (1898), now used for a variety of functions. The West Coast Pioneers Memorial Museum, housed in the School of Mines (1894) has a magnificent collection of minerals. Beside the museum is a collection of old steam engines and rolling stock.

Surroundings
Renison Bell
The prospects of the town are now looking up with the reopening of the Renison Bell tin-mine, 17km/10½ miles north-east.

Victoria

General

Garden State
Area: 228,000sq.km./88,000sq. miles
Population: 4.458 million
Capital: Melbourne

Flag

Coat of Arms

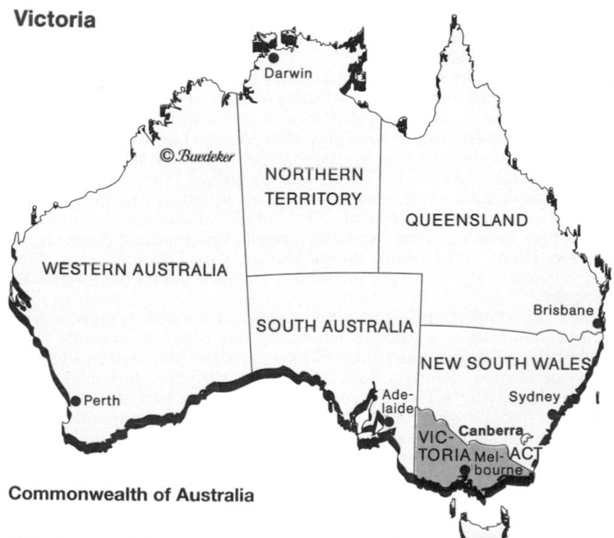

Symbolic animal: honey-eater

Symbolic plant: heath

The Garden State

The state of Victoria lies in the south-east of the continent and includes none of the typical Australian interior territory, the arid, hot, inhospitable outback. Its varied landscape is very similar to that of Europe. In the Australian spring large areas of the state are like one large flowering garden, entitling Victoria to call itself the Garden State. In addition to its great scenic attractions Victoria has preserved many historic old 19th-century buildings and towns.

Topography

The coastal regions of Victoria are divided into two different sections. While the south-east coast – particularly on Ninety Mile Beach – has flat beaches suitable for all kinds of water sports, the south-west coast is fringed by rugged cliffs. Half way along the coast, at the north end of Port Phillip Bay, is the Metropolitan Area of Melbourne, extending into the interior for some 100km/60 miles. On the north and west Melbourne is

◀ *Rugged coastal scenery in Port Campbell National Park*

bordered by the goldfields which extend from the hinterland of the south-west coast to the Murray River in the north, the boundary between Victoria and New South Wales. Extending in a broad swathe to the borders of Western Australia is the Western District, with the magnificent scenery of the south-west coast, forest-clad hills and a fertile hinterland of wide plains – wheat-growing country and grazing land. To the north, this belt of fertile land merges gradually into dry mallee scrub.

To the east of Melbourne, extending along the south-east coast to the boundary with New South Wales, is the territory known as Gippsland. Inland from the long beaches is beautiful hill country, with forests, grassland and numerous lakes, forming the largest system of inland waters in Australia. To the north-east Victoria extends into the Australian Alps, a region still largely unspoiled, to the north of which are the rich fruit-growing and wine-making areas in the Goulburn and Ovens valleys.

Tourist attractions

Victoria's main tourist attractions, in addition to the capital, Melbourne, and the towns associated with the gold rush and the shipping trade on the Murray River, are its numerous National Parks. There are, too, the holiday attractions of the coasts, the lakes and the rivers with their endless scope for water sports and angling.

The coast of Victoria has a total length of 1200km/750 miles. In addition to safe bathing beaches beyond the Ninety Mile Beach and in Port Phillip Bay there are many impressive stretches of surf-lashed coast, particularly towards the west, fringed by mighty cliffs. Victoria has many natural lakes (e.g. Lake Hindmarsh near Warracknabeal in the north-west and many volcanic crater lakes in the south-west) as well as numerous man-made lakes, some quite small, others of vast size, in attractive settings, which have been created since the early 20th century by the construction of dams to supply drinking water, water for irrigation and electric power (Lakes Eildon, Hume and Mulwala on the Murray, Lake Eppalock, etc.). These man-made lakes have many attractions for water sports enthusiasts and anglers.

Melbourne

One of the state's principal attractions is Melbourne with its museums and parks, and also as a base for interesting day trips, for example to the Dandenong Ranges, Healesville, Phillip Island, the Mornington and Bellarine peninsulas, Hanging Rock and Mount Macedon. In winter Mount Buller, Mount Buffalo and the Bogong range, lying within easy reach of the city, are popular winter sports areas, and in summer they are magnificent walking and camping country.

Gippsland South-East

The tourist attractions of the south-east are the Latrobe valley with its lush green meadowland and above all the Gippsland Lakes, with a climate which is mild even in winter, and Wilsons Promontory, Victoria's best known National Park. The favourite holiday places in the Gippsland Lakes area are Paynesville, Metung, Lakes Entrance and Lake Wellington, Lake Victoria, Lake King and Lake Reeve, just inland from Ninety Mile Beach. Other resorts on the coast of Victoria with facilities for water sports are, from the west, Inverloch (in Venus Bay), the sheltered Anderson Inlet and Walkerville in Waratah Bay. Then follows the coast of Wilsons Promotory, the most southerly point on the Australian continent, with caves, beaches and islands (some stretches of coast being accessible only from the sea). Farther east are Port Welshpool, a deep-water harbour with wharves for large ships, and Port Albert, with historic old buildings. To the east of Lakes Entrance is Lake Tyers, which is quieter than the Gippsland Lakes. To the east of Gippsland there are Marlo, at the mouth of the Brodribb River, Bemm River, in Sydenham Inlet, Cape Conran, Tamboon Inlet, at the mouth of the Cann River, and Mallacoota Inlet at the eastern end of Victoria. At the mouth of Mallacoota Inlet, where the Tasman Sea and the Bass Strait meet, it can be too stormy for small boats, but within the inlet there are 322km/200 miles of beaches which offer ideal conditions for water sports and fishing.

North-East

In the north-east of Victoria is the mountain world of the Victorian Alps, with beautiful National Parks which offer excellent skiing in winter and

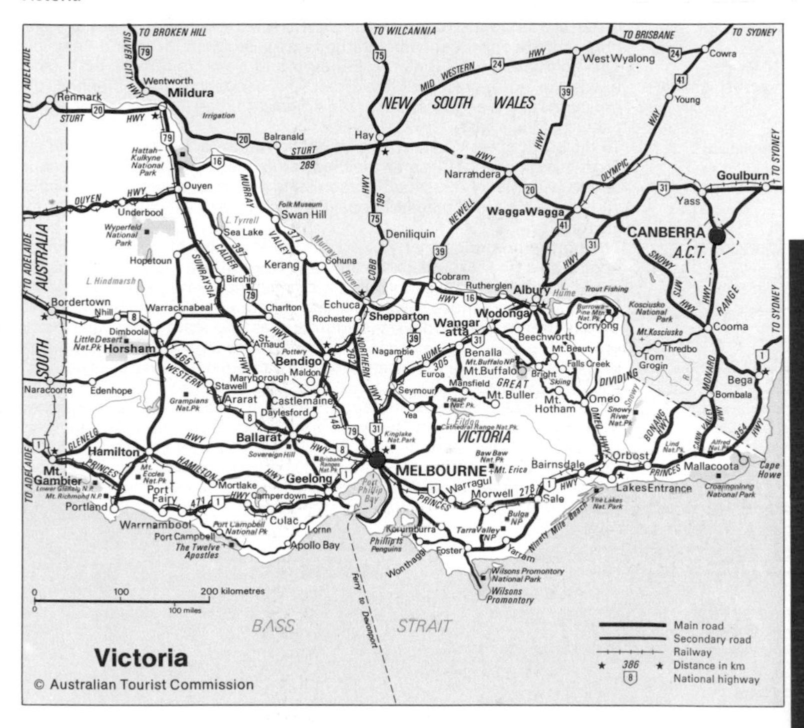

plenty of good walking in summer. In this part of the state, too, are the Kelly Country (Glenrowan, Benella, Beechworth), scene of the exploits of the bushranger Ned Kelly and his gang, and the fruit-growing and wine-producing Goulburn and Ovens valleys.

Western District
South-west coast

The Western District breeds the best cattle and sheep in Australia. The merino wool produced here is of the highest quality, and the main centre of the wool trade is Hamilton, the "wool capital of the world". The wealth of the cattle and sheep farmers was reflected in their elegant mansions and large estates, so that many towns in Victoria have handsome old houses dating from the early years of the colony. The lush flat grazing land in the centre of the Western District gives place in the east to the district of volcanic crater lakes round Camperdown, where there is ample scope for water sports and fishing. To the north the Grampians rise out of the gently undulating landscape. The wild south-west coast from Anglesea to Nelson, near the boundary with South Australia, offers fascinating views, seen from the Great Ocean Road. Most of the places along this stretch of coast attract visitors for the scenery rather than boating enthusiasts. Particularly round Port Campbell, with its numerous rock formations in the sea, its reefs and cliffs and dangerous currents, boating is possible only in good weather and only for the experienced. Port Campbell itself has a small natural harbour enclosed by cliffs and reefs. Apollo Bay is the only refuge for small craft between Queenscliff and Port Fairy. Anglesea, Torquay, Barwon Heads and Ocean Grove, near Geelong, have good surfing beaches and are also suitable for boating. The only sheltered harbours with facilities for water sports on the rugged west coast are Warrnambool, Port Fairy and Portland, the only deep-water harbour between Melbourne and Adelaide.

Goldfields
Central Highlands

The goldfields, with Ballarat, Bendigo and Castlemaine as their chief towns, lie north-west of Melbourne. The handsome old buildings, the museums and the reconstructions in the gold-mining towns present a vivid picture of their past.

Grampians
Wimmera

To the north of the Western District is the Wimmera, Victoria's wheat belt. To the south-east of this area are the Grampians, an impressive mountain region with plenty of scope for interesting excursions, walks and wildlife viewing in the Grampians National Park, which has excellent facilities for visitors.

Murray River

The northern boundary of Victoria is formed by the Murray River, which begins as a clear mountain stream and grows into a massive expanse of water (Lake Hume, Lake Mulwala), with a rich flora and fauna, historic old towns such as Echuca, Swan Hill and Mildura and productive irrigated agriculture. In earlier days the Murray was the state's principal traffic artery: it is now of great economic importance as a source of water for irrigation and a major tourist attraction, in particular because of its perpetually mild climate.

Winter sports

There are seven main winter sports areas in Victoria, all easily reached from Melbourne: Mount Donna Buang (95km/59 miles), Lake Mountain (109km/68 miles), Mount Baw Baw (177km/110 miles), Mount Buller (241km/150 miles), Mount Buffalo (331km/206 miles), Mount Hotham (367km/228 miles) and Falls Creek (379km/235 miles). The short skiing season usually lasts from June to the beginning of October; prices are high.

Places of Interest from A to Z in Victoria

★Alpine National Park J 7

Location; area
150km/95 miles north of Bairnsdale, 50km/30 miles east of Mansfield and 50km/30 miles south of Bright; 646,000 hectares/1,596,000 acres.

Best time to visit
Spring and summer for the wild flowers, winter for winter sports.

Access
From Bairnsdale via Omeo, from Mansfield and from Bright.

Facilities
Winter sports (cross-country skiing), riding.

Features
This National Park was established in 1989–90 by the amalgamation of three existing National Parks (Bogong N.P., Cobberas-Tingaringy N.P. and Wonnangatta-Moroka N.P.) and other reserves, making it the third largest National Park in Victoria. It extends east from Mansfield (see Lake Eildon) by way of the Central Highlands and the Victorian Alps to the borders of New South Wales, where it joins up with Kosciusko National Park (NSW) and Namadgi National Park (ACT).

In Bogong National Park are the two highest peaks in Victoria, Mount Bogong and Mount Feathertop. In Falls Creek and Hotham Heights there are excellent winter sports facilities (cross-country skiing), and in summer the Bogong plateau is good country for walking (with some trails that are extremely strenuous) and riding.

Cobberas-Tingaringy National Park (area 18,000 hectares/45,000 acres) is a region of magnificent mountains, rugged landscape and Alpine forests.

In the north of Wonnangatta-Moroka National Park are the high peaks of the Victorian Alps, a watershed for the rivers and streams which have carved deep valleys and gorges from the plateau.

In these Alpine regions the weather is very changeable, and it is essential to take protective clothing and emergency provisions. In spring and summer the land is carpeted with flowers. During the skiing season there are regular bus services to the skiing areas.

★Apollo Bay H 7

Situation and characteristics
Apollo Bay (pop. 890), 118km/73 miles south-west of Geelong, is a good base for excursions into the Cape Otway hills on roads of great scenic beauty (often unsurfaced and with many bends). The town's economy centres on the fishing industry (fish-freezing plant), and for anglers there is good sport in the sea and the mountain streams. There are excellent surfing beaches on the rugged coast, on which many ships have come to grief. There are fine views from Marriner's Lookout.

Accommodation
Numerous motels and caravan/camping parks.

Surroundings
At Apollo Bay the Great Ocean Road (see entry) leaves the coast and runs inland to the Otway Ranges.

In Melba Gully State Park, near Lavers Hill, there is an area of fern forest (also found in abundance in the rain forest on Cape Otway).

Otway National Park

Location; area
A few kilometres west of Apollo Bay; 12,750 hectares/31,490 acres.

Best time to visit
Spring to autumn.

Accommodation
In Apollo Bay.

Facilities
Good walking trails; water sports on coast.

Features
The Great Ocean Road runs through the park, an area of impressive and varied scenery – deep depressions overgrown with ferns, dense eucalyptus forests, cool temperate rain forest, heathland and a magnificent stretch

of coast between Apollo Bay and Princeton. On Cape Otway, 14km/8½ miles south of the Great Ocean Road, is a lighthouse built by convict labour in 1848.

Ararat H 7

Situation and characteristics

Ararat (pop. 8300) lies on Mount Ararat, 200km/125 miles west of Melbourne. During the 1857 gold rush here, when the population of the town rapidly rose to 20,000, many Chinese prospectors made rich finds on the Canton Lead and were then driven away by white rivals. After the brief gold boom Ararat became the commercial centre of a farming area (wool, wine).

Accommodation

Hotels, motels and caravan/camping parks.

Features

The town has preserved a number of handsome buildings (the Post Office, the Town Hall) from its 19th century heyday. Other features of interest are the Botanical Gardens (fine display of orchids), Alexandra Park and a monument to the Chinese gold prospectors. There are fine views of the town and surrounding area from One Tree Hill.

Surroundings

At Great Western, 16km/10 miles north-west of Ararat, wine has been grown since 1863, when a Frenchman named Jean Trouette planted a small vineyard (Seppelt's Vineyards; famed red and sparkling wines). There are other wineries south and west of Ararat; some can be visited. North of Great Western are the Malakoff goldfields.

Avoca H 7

Situation and characteristics

The gold-digging town of Avoca (pop. 1030) lies in the Central Highlands at the junction of the Pyrenees and Sunraysia Highways, 190km/120 miles north-west of Melbourne. It owes its name to John Mitchell, who explored

Ararat Town Hall, built by gold

this area and gave the name of Avoca (after the river of that name in Ireland) to the river on which the town was founded in 1852.

Accommodation

Caravan/camping park.

Features

Avoca has preserved a number of bluestone buildings from the early days of the settlement, including the old gaol, the powder magazine, the court-house, and one of the oldest pharmacies in the country. There is good fishing in the Wimmera, Avoca and Bet Bet Creek.

Surroundings

Within easy reach of Avoca are many wine-growing districts in the Central Highlands, producing some excellent wines.

Walking trails

There are good walking trails of varying length in the hills of the Pyrenees Range.

Bacchus Marsh H 7

Situation and characteristics

50km/30 miles west of Melbourne on the Western Freeway is Bacchus Marshes (pop. 11,000). It lies in an area of drained marshland on the edge of a fertile valley between the Werribee and Lerderderg Rivers, a fruit- and wine-growing area known as Apple Valley. The town takes its name from Captain W. H. Bacchus, a founder member of the Melbourne Club.

Accommodation

Hotels, motels, caravan/camping park.

Features

There are a number of historic buildings, including the old Manor House, dating from the time when Bacchus Marsh was an important coaching station on the road to the goldfields.

Surroundings

Bacchus Marsh is a good base for excursions to Werribee Gorge State Park, to the south of the Western Freeway, to Brisbane Ranges National Park (see below) and to the Lederderg Gorge to the north of the town.

Brisbane Ranges National Park

Location; area

30km/19 miles south of Bacchus Marsh, between Geelong and Ballan; 7517 hectares/18,567 acres.

Access

On Anakie–Ballan road.

Accommodation

Small camping ground (advance booking advisable).

Features

Lying so near Melbourne, Brisbane Ranges National Park attracts many visitors. In spring it appeals particularly to birdwatchers and flower-lovers, and it has an excellent network of trails for walkers. A favourite picnic spot is the Anakie Gorge. Nearby is Steiglitz Historic Park, with relics of the gold-digging period.

★Bairnsdale J 7

Situation and characteristics

Bairnsdale, situated 280km/175 miles east of Melbourne at the junction of the Princes and Omeo Highways and the road south to the Gippsland Lakes (see entry), is the commercial centre of Gippsland. It is a good base for excursions to the Alpine National Park (see entry).

Accommodation

Several hotels, motels and caravan/camping parks.

Features

The main features of interest are St Mary's Church, with wall and ceiling paintings in Italian style, and the Botanical Gardens.

Surroundings

19km/11 miles west of Bairnsdale, near Mitchell River National Park, is Lindenow, with good walking trails and, in a gorge, an Aboriginal ceremonial site.

To the south of Bairnsdale, at Eagle Point Bluff, the Mitchell River flows into Lake King, with silt jetties 6km/4 miles long. On the shores of the lake is the fishing village of Metung, which preserves some houses dating from pioneering days. The road north on the Omeo Highway, following the valley of the Tambo River, is particularly beautiful when the acacias are in flower.

Tropical rain forest in Mitchell River National Park

Mitchell River National Park

Location; area	60km/37 miles north-west of Bairnsdale; 11,900 hectares/29,400 acres.
Access	Access road 30km/19 miles north of Princes Highway via Fernbank.
Facilities	Restricted facilities for camping (advance booking advisable); canoeing on Mitchell River.
Features	The main features of this National Park are luxuriant rain forest, the gorge on the Mitchell River and the cave known as the Den of Nargun, an Aboriginal cult site. When Woolshed Creek is flowing in summer it covers the entrance to this stalactitic cave with a veil of water 20m/65ft wide. The sheer walls of the gorge shelter the warm temperate rain forest with its abundance of ferns and orchids.

Ballarat H 7

Situation and characteristics

Ballarat (pop. 64,000) lies 110km/70 miles west of Melbourne in the Central Highlands. The town is famed as the scene of the Eureka rising, the only "civil war" in Australia's history, when gold-miners refused to pay government licence fees and barricaded themselves into the Eureka Stockade. The rebellion was repressed by the army on December 3rd 1854, leaving 27 dead and many wounded. The rich finds of gold increased the population of the town to 40,000 within two years. Over 20 million ounces of gold were recovered during the gold boom, which lasted 20 years.

Accommodation

Many hotels, motels and caravan/camping parks.

Features

Ballarat's principal tourist attraction is Sovereign Hill. Here, on a 26 hectare/65 acre site, is a reconstruction of a gold-mining town centred on a real gold-mine, with a Gold Museum, shops, a hotel, a theatre, a Chinese temple and figures in contemporary costume re-creating the life of the town in the 1860s.

In Ballarat's main street (Sturt Street) are numbers of handsome and substantial houses dating from the 1880s. The mixture of architectural styles – neo-Romanesque, neo-Gothic, neo-Renaissance – is characteristic of the Australian gold-mining towns. The prosperity of the town in its heyday is shown by such fine buildings as the post office, the railway station, Montrose Cottage (the first stone house built in the goldfields), Craig's Royal Hotel and the Town Hall.

The Eureka Museum has a collection of relics of gold-mining days. Also of interest are the Doll Museum, the Old Curiosity Shop, the Old Ballarat Pottery and the Ballarat Fine Art Gallery.

The Botanic Gardens (area 40 hectares/100 acres) are famed for their begonias, rhododendrons and azaleas. In a colonnaded gallery are busts of Australian prime ministers. Also in the gardens is a house (*c.* 1860) which was occupied by the poet Adam Lindsay Gordon. Beside the park is Lake Wendouree, an artificial lake on which the rowing events in the 1956 Olympics were staged. Ballarat Wildlife Park in Ballarat East concentrates on Australian fauna such as wombats, koala and Tasmanian devils. (Open: daily 9.30am–5pm.)

On the west side of the town, on the road to Ararat (see entry), are the 22km/13½ mile long Avenue of Honour, lined by 3900 trees, and the Arch of Victory, honouring those who fought in the First World War.

Creswick

Situation and characteristics

18km/11 miles north of Ballarat is Creswick (pop. 2700), whose goldfields in the 19th century were among the richest in Australia, attracting a population of 60,000. In December 1882 the gold-mine was flooded and 22 miners were drowned. Gold-panners are still at work in the many streams in the surrounding area.

Accommodation

Motel, caravan/camping park.

Features

Features of interest are the ornate Town Hall and Creswick Historical Museum (Albert Street), which has paintings by Norman Lindsay.

Daylesford

Situation

Daylesford (pop. 2470) is 27km/17 miles north-east of Creswick, picturesquely situated on Daylesford Lake, is known as Australia's spa centre.

Accommodation

Motel, caravan/camping parks.

Features

Notable features of the town are a number of neo-Gothic churches, the Town Hall and the Post Office. In the Botanical Gardens on Wombat Hill is a lookout tower from which there is a good view of the volcanic crater of Mount Franklin, 13km/8 miles away. A few kilometres north is Hepburn Springs, whose medicinal waters have been famed since the 19th century.

Clunes

Situation and characteristics

Clunes (pop. 820), 40km/25 miles north of Ballarat, was the first gold-mining settlement in Victoria. Gold was discovered here in 1851, and within three months 8000 hopeful prospectors had flocked to the town. A year after the first finds the number had risen to 30,000, and four years later it had reached 100,000. One result of this was that the population of Melbourne and Geelong fell dramatically. The surface deposits of gold, however, were soon exhausted, and the underground seams could be worked only at the expense of backbreaking labour and heavy investment of machinery and capital. Clunes was the birthplace in 1862 of the painter John Longstaff, whose huge painting of the ill-fated explorers Burke, Wills and King hangs in the National Gallery in Melbourne.

Accommodation

Hotel, motel, caravan/camping park.

Features

In the broad main street there are a number of fine old buildings dating from gold-mining days (two schools, hotels, banks, the post office, the Town Hall).

Dunolly

Situation and characteristics

90km/56 miles south of Ballarat is Dunolly (pop. 650), near which the "Welcome Stranger" nugget, the largest ever discovered, was found. During the gold rush in the 1850s there was a huge influx of Chinese and European prospectors and the population of the town rose to 45,000. The rush soon died down, but gold-panning still goes on in the local creeks.

Accommodation

Caravan/camping park.

Features

There are a number of old buildings in the main street. There is an interesting Goldfields and Arts Museum (open: only at weekends).

Baw Baw National Park J 7

Location; area

60km/37 miles west of Moe in western Gippsland; 3300 hectares/8200 acres.

Best time to visit

In winter for skiing, in summer for walking.

Access

Via Yarra Junction and Noojee; via Moe and Willow Grove.

Facilities

Outside the park is the Alpine Village, a tourist centre with accommodation for visitors and supplies. Winter sports facilities (ski-lifts, cross-country skiing); walking trails.

Features

Baw Baw National Park is ideal country for long-distance walks in summer and a good skiing area in winter. The landscape is dominated by the precipitous slopes of Mount Erica (1524m/5000ft) and deeply indented valleys. The vegetation is sub-alpine: forests of snow gums with dense scrub undergrowth reach up to the summit regions of the hills at the south end of the Central Highlands, from which there are fine views.

Outside the National Park is the popular Alpine Village skiing area. There is usually snow until September at heights above 1200m/3900ft. There are numerous ski-lifts to cater for the large numbers of skiers who come here at weekends and during the holidays, although the pistes are not so demanding as those of Falls Creek (see entry) and Hotham Heights.

Walking trails

Some of the trails in the park are strenuous. Within the park is the south end of the long-distance alpine trail from Walhalla to Tom Groggin on Mount Kosciusko (NSW).

★ Beechworth J 7

Situation and characteristics

Beechworth (pop. 3700), once the centre of the Ovens goldfields and now the administrative centre of north-eastern Victoria, lies 270km/170 miles north-east of Melbourne on the Old Sydney Road, between Wangaratta and Myrtleford, in the foothills of the Victorian Alps. The rich Beechworth goldfield was discovered by a shepherd in the 1850s, and in 14 years more than 85 tons of gold were found. During the gold boom the population of the town rose to 8000 and it had 61 hotels and a theatre in which world-famous actors appeared.

Accommodation

Several hotels, motels and caravan/camping parks.

Features

The town is famed for its well-preserved 19th-century buildings, more than 30 of which have been classified by the National Trust as of historical importance. Particularly notable are the powder magazine and the mid-19th-century government buildings, built in the local granite, and a number of museums. The old gaol, in which Ned Kelly (see Baedeker Special, p. 61) was imprisoned, is still in use and some of his memorabilia are in the Burke Museum.

Surroundings

There are a number of scenic roads round the town with rest areas, good viewpoints and waterfalls. On the road to the north is a cemetery with the graves of Chinese gold prospectors.

Bellarine Peninsula H 7

Situation and characteristics

The Bellarine Peninsula is the counterpart to the Mornington Peninsula (see entry) on the west side of Port Phillip Bay (see entry). During the summer holiday season there are ferry services across the "Rip", the narrow entrance (only 2.7km/1⅔ miles across) to the bay, between Queenscliff on the Bellarine Peninsula and Portsea and Sorrento on the Mornington Peninsula. Like the Mornington Peninsula, the Bellarine Peninsula is a favourite holiday area with the people of Melbourne and Geelong, with facilities for water sports of all kinds. During the season the population of the little towns on the peninsula is multiplied many times.

In 1802 Matthew Flinders, one of the first Europeans to pass this way, landed on Indented Head, 6km/4 miles east of Portarlington, and in 1835 John Batman and his companions, coming from Tasmania, landed here in their quest for new grazing land.

Old-time railway

The Bellarine Peninsula Railway runs occasional steam trains across the peninsula from Queenscliff to Drysdale (16km/10 miles) and Swan Bay.

Portarlington

Situation and characteristics

Portarlington (pop. 2270), on the north coast of the Bellarine Peninsula, is a holiday resort with beaches which are safe for children, facilities for a variety of water sports and good fishing. It is named after the little town of Portarlington in Ireland. A four-storey grain mill of 1857 has been converted into a museum.

Accommodation

Hotel, caravan/camping parks.

★ Queenscliff · Point Lonsdale

Situation and characteristics

Queenscliff (pop. 3740), originally a fishing village, is now an elegant summer resort.

Accommodation

Several hotels and caravan/camping parks in Queenscliff; caravan/camping parks in Point Lonsdale.

Features

A number of handsome old hotels (Vuegrand, Royal, Ozone, Queenscliff) bear witness to past grandeur. Beside the post office in Hesse Street is a historical museum. Fort Queenscliff, with a black lighthouse of 1862, was built in 1882, at a time when a Russian attack was feared, to protect the entrance of Port Phillip Bay. The fort is now occupied by the Australian Military College. Below the lighthouse is Buckley's Cave, in which William Buckley, an escaped convict, lived for many years among the Aborigines.

Ocean Grove · Barwon Heads

Situation and characteristics

These two little towns on the south coast of the peninsula, with a joint population of 8920, attract many visitors in summer, since they are the resorts nearest to Geelong (see entry) with good surfing and diving beaches. Barwon Heads also has sheltered bathing beaches in the estuary of the Barwon River. Nearby is Lake Connewarre, with mangrove swamps.

★ Benalla H 7

Situation and characteristics

Benalla (pop. 9200) lies on the Hume Highway 190km/120 miles north of Melbourne and rather more than 100km/60 miles south of Wodonga. Lake Benalla (water sports, bird sanctuary) is an artificial lake created by a dam on Broken River. In the late 1870s Benalla was a frequent target of raids by Ned Kelly's gang (see Baedeker Special, p. 61), who were finally caught in 1880 in the nearby town of Glenrowan.

Accommodation — Hotel, several motels and caravan/camping parks.

Features — Benalla is famed for its rose gardens (Rose Festival in October/November). Benalla Art Gallery displays the Ledger Collection of Australian painting.

★Bendigo J 7

Situation and characteristics — 150km/95 miles north-west of Melbourne (reached on the Calder or McIvor Highway), situated at the junction of a number of major roads, is Bendigo (pop. 70,000), once one of the wealthiest gold towns in Australia. It has preserved many old buildings from its 19th century heyday.

Accommodation — Many hotels, motels and caravan/camping parks.

Features — Although mining for gold, which began here in 1851, ceased in the 1950s, Bendigo's past as a gold-mining town is still very much alive, particularly in the 100-year-old Central Deborah Mine, with a shaft going down 396m/1300ft, which is now a museum. A vintage tram, with a recorded commentary, takes visitors from the Central Deborah Mine through the town centre to the Chinese temple.

Among the most interesting buildings are the Shamrock Hotel, the Cathedral of the Sacred Heart, the Post Office and the Bendigo Art Gallery. Other features of interest are the fountain at Charing Cross, the lookout tower (an old mine winding tower) in Rosalind Park and the police station and gaol. The Chinese temple was built around 1860, when Bendigo had a large Chinese community. During the Easter Fair an enormous Chinese dragon is paraded through the streets.

The Bendigo Pottery at Epsom, 7km/4½ miles from Bendigo on the Midland Highway, is believed to be Australia's oldest pottery.

Round the town are a number of wine-growing areas (Mandurang, Maiden Gully).

Town centre, Bendigo, once one of the wealthiest gold-diggers' towns

★Castlemaine

Situation and characteristics

Castlemaine (pop. 7140) lies 40km/25 miles south of Bendigo at the foot of Mount Alexander. Great quantities of gold were found in this area in the 1850s and 1860s, but disease in the mining camps and falling yields led to a decline in prospecting activity.

Accommodation

Hotels.

Features

A number of old buildings show the town's former prosperity. The Town Market (1862) has been well restored and is now the local museum. Other notable buildings are the Midland Hotel, the Imperial Hotel, the Courthouse, the Town Hall, the Gaol and the Bank.

Surroundings

The Wattle Gully Goldmine at Chewton, after being closed down for many years, is now again being worked. At Vaughan there are mineral springs and a Chinese cemetery. Guildford had at one time the largest camp of Chinese prospectors in the goldfields. Wine is grown at Harcourt, on Mount Alexander.

★Maldon

Situation and characteristics

The area round Maldon (pop. 1250), 18km/11 miles east of Castlemaine, attracted over 20,000 prospectors during the gold rush. Maldon itself has been declared by the National Trust the "First Notable Town" in Victoria in virtue of its well-preserved ensemble of 19th-century buildings and many old European trees. Maldon draws many visitors, particularly when the wild flowers are in bloom.

Accommodation

Motel, caravan/camping park.

Features

Among Maldon's well restored 19th-century buildings are the hospital, the post office, two churches, the courthouse (now a museum), Dabb's general store, a number of restaurants and tearooms and a motel. The deep goldmines on Mount Tarrangower were among the richest in the country. Nearby is a cemetery with the graves of Chinese prospectors.

10km/6 miles north-west is Cairn Curran Lake (water sports, picnic spots). The whole of the surrounding area is of interest for its variety of rock formations.

★Kyneton

Situation and characteristics

65km/40 miles south of Bendigo on the Calder Highway is Kyneton (pop. 4900), which flourished in gold-mining days as a supply centre for the goldfields and as a staging-point on the way there.

Accommodation

Hotels, motels, caravan/camping park.

Features

The old part of the town is well preserved, with many fine bluestone buildings (churches, police station, grain mill). The Historical Centre Collection is housed in a two-storey building of 1855, formerly a bank. The bluestone Hospital has decorative verandah railings. The Botanic Gardens contain many fine old trees.

Surroundings

The Hanging Rock, a massive volcanic rock formation at Woodend (15km/9 miles south), was made famous by the book (by Joan Lindsay) and film "Picnic at Hanging Rock". There are races here on New Year's Day.

10km/6 miles farther south-east is Macedon (pop. 1140), which has a number of handsome 19th-century houses with beautiful gardens, dating from the time when Macedon was a fashionable summer resort for the citizens of Melbourne. From the summit of Mount Macedon (1013m/3324ft), on which there is a memorial cross commemorating those who died in the First World War, there is a fine view over the Gisborne Plains.

Bright J 7

Situation and characteristics

310km/195 miles north-east of Melbourne is Bright (pop. 2000), founded after the discovery of gold in the area. This was the centre of the Buckland

Valley riots on 1857 when white prospectors drove out their Chinese rivals with considerable brutality.

Bright, situated in the Ovens valley at the foot of the Victorian Alps, is the centre of a popular winter sports area and a good base for walks in summer. The area is seen at its most beautiful in autumn, when the European deciduous trees take on their autumn colouring. Bright, well equipped with shops and restaurants, is a supply centre for holidaymakers in the surrounding area.

Accommodation
Hotels, motels, caravan/camping parks.

Features
There are a number of beautiful walking trails leading to good viewpoints (Clearspot Lookout, Huggins Lookout). On the Alpine Road leading to Mount Hotham there are fine views of Mount Feathertop, the Razor Back and Mount Bogong.

Surroundings
Harrietville, a charming little mountain village 18km/11 miles south of Bright, is a good base for ski treks in winter and for walks in Bogong National Park (see Alpine National Park) in summer.

★Burrowa-Pine Mountain National Park J 7

Location; area
430km/265 miles north-east of Melbourne, north-west of Corryong; 17,600 hectares/43,500 acres.

Best time to visit
Spring and autumn.

Access
On Murray Valley Highway via Cudgewa or Walwa.

Facilities
Camping ground; rest areas.

Features
The most striking features of this National Park are its massive granite crags and impressive waterfalls. There are camping sites and rest areas near the Cudgewa Bluff Falls from which there are various walking trails. The isolated granite dome of Pine Mountain (1062m/3484ft) rises steeply out of the Murray plain. It is a fairly stiff climb to the summit, from which there are spectacular panoramic views. To the south is Mount Burrowa (1300m/4265ft).

Drinking water is sometimes scarce in summer.

★Corryong

Situation and characteristics
The little town of Corryong (pop. 1270), 27km/17 miles south-east on the borders of New South Wales, is a good base from which to visit Burrowa-Pine Mountain National Park and the Snowy Mountains (see Jindabyne, NSW). It lies in a region of magnificent mountain scenery, with good trout streams. Jack Riley, the hero of "Banjo" Paterson's story "The Man from Snowy River", came from this area, was a friend of Paterson's and is buried in Corryong.

Accommodation
Several hotels, motels and caravan/camping parks.

Surroundings
There is a good viewpoint 1km/¾ mile south-east of the town. From a viewpoint at Towong, 12km/7½ miles north-east, there are magnificent views extending as far as Kosciusko National Park (see entry, NSW).

★Colac H 7

Situation and characteristics
On the eastern edge of the Western District of Victoria, 150km/95 miles south-west of Melbourne, on the Princes Highway, is Colac (pop. 10,060), which attracts visitors with its situation on Lake Colac (good fishing, water sports). On the shores of the lake are the large Botanic Gardens. The town and surrounding area are fairly densely populated, thanks largely to the fertile agricultural country round Colac.

Accommodation
Several hotels, motels and caravan/camping parks.

Surroundings
From the Alvie Red Rock Lookout, near the town, 20 volcanic lakes can be seen.

To the west of Colac is Lake Corangamite, the largest salt lake in Victoria.
Beautiful winding roads runs south from the town through impressive mountain scenery to join the Great Ocean Road (see entry) and from there farther south to Cape Otway (old lighthouse).

★Croajingolong National Park J 7

Location; area — On the south-east coast of Victoria; 8600 hectares/21,200 acres.
Best time to visit — Spring (for wild flowers).
Access — On Princes Highway, turn-offs at Genoa and Cann River.
Accommodation — In Cann River and Mallacoota.
Facilities — Walking, water sports. There is a tourist centre in Mallacoota.
Features — The recently established Croajingolong National Park takes in the previously existing Captain Cook, Wingan Inlet and Mallacoota Inlet reserves together with the Nadgee nature reserve in New South Wales. A series of lonely, wild beaches and rocky promontories extend for 100km/60 miles from the New South Wales border along the East Gippsland coast to Sydenham Inlet (Bemm River).

Also within the park is Point Hicks (lighthouse), which Cook sailed past in 1770. It is named after the officer of the watch who was the first to sight the Australian mainland. The park preserves the original vegetation of the rain forest, woodland and heath. In spring there is a profusion of wild flowers, and throughout the year rare species of animal may be observed.

★ Mallacoota

Situation and characteristics — The unspoiled natural beauty of the country round the Mallacoota Inlet is making Mallacoota (pop. 830), on the Gippsland coast near the boundary with New South Wales, an increasingly popular holiday place.

Once a small fishing village, it is now the tourist centre of Croajingolong National Park. From Genoa Peak there are panoramic views over the coast.
Accommodation — Several hotels and caravan/camping parks.

Alfred National Park

Location; area — 18km/11 miles east of Cann River; 2300 hectares/5700 acres.
Access — The Princes Highway runs through the park.
Accommodation — Motels and caravan/camping parks in Genoa and Cann River.
Features — The characteristic features of Alfred National Park are its deep, moist depressions, with over 40 species of ferns, and one of the few areas of warm temperate and sometimes subtropical rain forest in Victoria.

★ Echuca H 7

Situation and characteristics — Echuca (pop. 9540), formerly the largest inland port in Australia and a place of considerable economic importance, lies 200km/125 miles north of Melbourne near the junction of the Goulburn and Campaspe Rivers with the Murray. It is now joined up with Moama, across the Murray in New South Wales.
Accommodation — Many hotels, motels and caravan/camping parks.
Features — On the river is a massive wharf of red gum wood (restored). Two old buildings, well restored, are the Star and Bridge Hotels. There are cruises on the river in old paddle-steamers ("Canberra", "Pride of Murray").
Surroundings — Camping, canoeing, water-skiing.

The Barmah Red Gum Forest extends along the banks of the Murray for 190km/120 miles.

Euroa J 7

Situation and characteristics

Euroa (pop. 2730) lies on the Hume Highway 150km/95 miles north of Melbourne. The town enjoyed a period of prosperity after the introduction of merino sheep at Seven Creeks, to the north, in 1851. Near here is the Faithfull Creek station, where the Kelly gang (see Baedeker Special, p. 61) carried out a raid on the National Bank in 1878 – an event re-enacted annually in December.

Accommodation

Motels, caravan/camping park.

Surroundings

Excursions to the Gooram Falls and the Strathbogie Ranges.

Falls Creek J 7

Situation and characteristics

Falls Creek, 380km/235 miles north-east of Melbourne, is one of the most popular winter sports areas in Victoria. The skiing area includes the former Bogong National Park, now part of the Alpine National Park (see entry), and the country round Mount Hotham (see entry).

Access

Falls Creek is reached from the Hume Highway, turning off at Wangaratta (see entry) into the Ovens Highway; then from Bright via Bogong to the Falls Creek holiday village. From the south it is reached by way of Bairnsdale, Omeo and Shannonvale (snow chains essential in winter; during the season there are buses to Mount Beauty and Albury-Wodonga).

Accommodation

The privately run Alpine villages of Falls Creek and Hotham Heights (very expensive at certain seasons) are outside the National Park.

Facilities

In the winter sports area there are numerous well co-ordinated lifts, pistes in all grades of difficulty and cross-country skiing trails. In summer this is a popular holiday region (walking, riding, climbing).

Foster J 7

Situation and characteristics

Foster (pop. 1010) is an attractive little town 170km/105 miles south-east of Melbourne within easy reach of Corner Inlet, Waratah Bay and Wilson's Promontory National Park (see entry). Known during the gold-digging period in South Gippsland as Stockyard Creek, it was renamed in 1871 after W. H. Foster, chief inspector of the goldfields in the region.

Accommodation

Motels, caravan/camping park.

Features

There is a good general view of the area from Foster North Lookout, 6km/4 miles north-west of the town. There are beautiful beaches at Walkerville and in Waratah Bay. 12km/7½ miles south of Walkerville is Cape Lintrap (lighthouse), from which there are superb views of the rocky coast and the Bass Strait.

Surroundings

The richest finds of gold were made at Turtons Creek, 18km/11 miles north. Lyrebirds can sometimes be seen in the tree fern gullies nearby.

★Geelong H 7

Situation and characteristics

Geelong (pop. 152,780), a busy port and industrial centre 75km/47 miles south-west of Melbourne, is the second largest city in Victoria. In 1824 the explorers Hume and Hovell reported that the land round Corio Bay was of excellent quality, and the first permanent settlement was established twelve years later, in 1836. At first it was the centre of an agricultural area; then, during the gold boom, it became the main port for prospectors heading for the diggings and for the shipment of gold. In the early 20th century the town began its rapid development into the industrial centre which it is today. It is also an important traffic hub, situated as it is at the junction of the Princes Highway (Melbourne to Portland and Adelaide), Midland Highway (to Ballarat), Hamilton Highway and Bellarine Highway.

Accommodation

Many hotels, motels and caravan/camping parks.

Features

Geelong has preserved some 160 19th-century buildings, which contrast agreeably with the town's uninspired modern architecture. Particularly notable are the church of SS Peter and Paul and Christ Church (1843; the oldest Anglican church in Victoria); the Customs House (1838), the state's oldest surviving wooden building; the imposing Town Hall; and the Market Hall of 1912, which has taken on a new lease of life as a shopping centre. The Art Gallery is privately owned.

The National Wool Museum

A few minutes' walk from the station on the corner of Moorabool and Brougham Streets, is the National Wool Museum in a former bluestone woolstore. Realistic human models shear sheep, use early machinery and sort bales, providing visitors with an easy-to-follow history of Australia's woollen industry. (Open: daily 10am-5pm.)

Surroundings

There are a number of interesting old settlements in the immediate neighbourhood of Geelong (Fyansford, Batesford, Lara, etc.). Other possible excursions are by way of Batesford to Anakie and Anakie Gorge, to the south of Brisbane Ranges National Park (see Bacchus Marsh), continuing to Steiglitz (old courthouse).

A popular day trip from Geelong is to the Bellarine Peninsula (see entry), with the towns of Queenscliff, Portarlington, Ocean Grove and Barwon Heads. South of Geelong is Torquay with its fine surfing beaches, where the 300km/185 mile long Great Ocean Road begins.

Lorne

Situation and characteristics

73km/45 miles south of Geelong on the Great Ocean Road is Lorne (pop. 940), a little town which is very much in the style of an English seaside resort. Sheltered by the hills of the Otway Range, it has a mild and equable climate, good surfing beaches and walking trails in the Cumberland River Valley, Allenvale and the Lorne-Angahook Forest Park. From Teddy's Lookout there are fine views over Loutit Bay.

Accommodation

Several hotels, motels and caravan/camping parks.

★Gippsland Lakes J 7

Situation and characteristics

The Gippsland Lakes are Australia's largest system of inland waterways, with a total area of 400sq.km/155sq.miles. This complex of lakes, rivers and canals offers endless scope for water sports and angling. Into this area flow the rivers Latrobe, Avon, Perry, Mitchell, Nicholson and Tambo. The lakes – Lake Wellington, Lake Victoria, Lake King and Lake Reeve – are separated from the sea by a long narrow strip of sand-dunes, the best known stretch of which is Ninety Mile Beach.

★Lakes Entrance

Lakes Entrance (pop. 6000) is a very popular holiday resort at the east end of the Gippsland Lakes. The entrance to the lagoon was opened up artificially only a hundred years ago, giving access from the sea to the great complex of lakes at Lakes Entrance. The area round Lakes Entrance was first settled around 1850. During the holiday season the population of Lakes Entrance is multiplied many times. Around Christmas advance booking is necessary and tariffs are high, since many Australians come here for a holiday then.

Accommodation

Many hotels, motels and caravan/camping parks.

Lakes Entrance, giving access to Australia's largest inland waterway system

Features — Features of interest in the town are the Shell Museum on the Esplanade, the Antique Car and Folk Museum and the Riviera Marine Aquarium. Not to be missed however is the Aboriginal Keeping Place in nearby Bairnsdale. There is a good view from Jemmy's Point.

Surroundings — A bridge leads to Ninety Mile Beach which, although popular with surfers and bathers, is somewhat dangerous. It is much safer to bathe in one of the lagoons. A trip through the Gippsland Lakes in a house-boat is an interesting experience. Some of the fishermen who still live in Lakes Entrance offer both short and long fishing trips.

Lakes Entrance is a good base for excursions to the Alpine north, the old mining areas of Omeo and the Buchan limestone caves (57km/35 miles via Nowa Nowa; see Orbost).

★★Grampians National Park H 7

Location — 30km/19 miles north-east of Hamilton (see entry) and 25km/15½ miles west of Stawell (see entry). The park is well served by roads.

Best time to visit — August to November (when wild flowers are in bloom).

Access — Via Halls Gap, to the north-east, or Dunkeld, to the south.

Accommodation — In Halls Gap (motels, guesthouses, holiday apartments, youth hostel, caravan/camping park).

Facilities — Camping grounds; picnic areas, walking trails, roads.

Features — The Grampians are a range of rugged sandstone hills up to 1000m/3300ft high, the last remains of the western foothills of the Great Dividing Range. The highest peak, Mount William (1167m/3829ft) was climbed in July 1836 by Thomas Mitchell, who named the range after the Grampians of his Scottish homeland. The Grampians were declared a National Park in 1984. On one side the hills fall gently away, on the other they have steep rock faces, much eroded by wind and water. In the western Grampians there are Aboriginal rock paintings, and at the visitor centre there is an exhibition of Aboriginal culture. The hills are covered with heath and scrub, the valleys with forest. The park is famed for its wild flowers (over 700 species of flowering plants), and the fauna includes koalas, kangaroos, echidnas, platypuses, opossums, deer and over 100 species of birds.

Surroundings

In the nearby town of Dunkeld is a historical museum with a collection of material on the Aborigines and documents on Thomas Mitchell's journeys of exploration.

★★Great Ocean Road H 7

The Great Ocean Road, built to provide employment during the economic depression of the early thirties, gives access to more than 300km/185 miles of spectacular coastal scenery. Originally completed in 1932, it has since then been upgraded for almost the whole of its length to become Highway 100.

The south-west coast of Victoria is one of the state's great tourist attractions, a succession of dramatic landscapes, with sheer cliffs, idyllic bays and lonely beaches. The Great Ocean Road begins at Torquay, 22km/13½ miles south of Geelong (see entry), and comes in 46km/29 miles to the popular holiday resort of Lome, with substantial hotels and guesthouses which hark back to earlier days. Inland from Lome are the Otway Ranges, extending from Anglesea to Cape Otway, with beautiful walking trails, waterfalls and rest areas. At Apollo Bay (see entry), 39km/24 miles farther south, the road leaves the coast for a time and runs through the Otway rain forest, on slopes covered with ferns. Side roads, usually unsurfaced but negotiable by ordinary cars, lead into the quiet, unspoiled forest. In this area visits can be paid to Melba Gully State Park and the tiny settlement of Lavers Hill, once an important timber-working centre. At Princetown the road returns to the coast, skirting Port Campbell National Park (see entry), the real high point on the Great Ocean Road, on a fascinating stretch of road with breathtaking views. Off the wild, cliff-fringed coast are a number of heavily eroded rock formations, lashed by the surf – London Bridge, the Twelve Apostles (illustration, p. 462), the Arch and Loch Ard Gorge.

London Bridge, a bizarre rock formation on the Great Ocean Road

Less well known are the Bay of Isles and Bay of Martyrs to the west of Peterborough. The Great Ocean Road then turns inland. At Warrnambool (see entry), 53km/33 miles beyond Peterborough, it runs into the Princes Highway, which continues via Portland (see entry) to Mount Gambier in South Australia.

★Hamilton H 7

Situation and characteristics

Hamilton (pop. 11,500), the "wool capital of the world", is the most important town in the Western District of Victoria and a shopping centre for wealthy sheep and cattle farmers. It lies on the Glenelg Highway and can be reached from Melbourne by way of Ballarat or via Geelong and the Hamilton Highway (310km/195 miles).

Accommodation

Several hotels, motels and caravan/camping parks.

Features

In the centre of the town is Lake Hamilton. There is a small zoo in the Botanical Gardens. The Art Gallery, in the Town Hall complex, was built up with the help of private donations.

Surroundings

Hamilton is a good base from which to visit the resorts of Portland (see entry), Port Fairy and Warrnambool (see entry) on the south-west coast and the Grampians National Park to the north, each about an hour's drive away. Other sights within easy reach are the Wannon and Nigretta Falls.

Mount Eccles National Park

Location; area

40km/25 miles south of Hamilton; 400 hectares/1000 acres.

Access

Via the Hamilton–Port Fairy road, turning off at MacArthur.

Facilities

Camping; walking trails, picnic areas.

Features

Mount Eccles is a long extinct volcano with an impressive crater and lava channels, caves and tunnels left by quarrying. Particularly striking are the rock formation known as Stony Rises and Lake Surprise, a crater lake.

Healesville J 7

Situation and characteristics

76km/48 miles east of Melbourne is Healesville (pop. 8930), a popular holiday resort amid mountain forests which has appealed to visitors since the 19th century with its agreeably cool summer climate.

Accommodation

Several hotels, motels and caravan/camping parks.

Surroundings

Round Healesville there are beautiful walking trails and scenic roads. The 5000km/3100 mile long Bicentennial National Trail for walkers and riders runs from Healesville to Cooktown in northern Queensland.

★Healesville Wildlife Sanctuary

Outside the town, on Badger Creek Road, is the famous Healesville Sanctuary, an unspoilt bushland area (32 hectares/80 acres) of ferns, gum trees and wattles where over 200 species of native animals, birds and reptiles live. There is also a platypus research station.

Within easy reach of Healesville are Toolangi State Forest and Myers Creek Reserve (waterfalls). 8km/5 miles south-west, round Gruyere, is a wine-growing area, with fine views.

Marysville

Situation and characteristics

Marysville (pop. 650), 36km/22 miles north-east of Healesville, developed into a large gold-mining settlement after gold was found in the area in the 1860s. Its economy now centres on agriculture and timber-working. Its quiet situation amid forest-covered hills attracts many visitors from Melbourne at weekends. In summer, lying fairly high, it is agreeably cool; in winter the hills are often covered with snow.

Accommodation

Hotel, motels, caravan/camping park.

Surroundings

Within easy reach of Marysville are Lake Eildon (see entry) and Cumberland Valley Forest. On Lake Mountain there is often sufficient snow for skiing. Big River State Forest offers good fishing, shooting, camping and fossicking for gold.

Walking trails

There are walking trails to Keppels Lookout, Mount Gordon and Stevensons Falls, the highest waterfall in Victoria (83m/272ft).

Warburton

Situation and characteristics

Warburton (pop. 2000), 36km/22 miles south-east of Healesville amid extensive forests, grew up in the 1860s as a gold-digging town; it is now a timber-working centre and a popular holiday resort.

Accommodation

Hotels, motels, caravan/camping park.

Features

The Acheron Way is a beautiful scenic road with views of Mount Donna Buang, Mount Victoria and Ben Cairn. 16km/10 miles north-east is the Upper Yarra Lake, with good picnic spots. The country round Warburton is ideal for walking and riding. To the south of the town are many wineries, particularly at Yarra Glen (Yarra Valley Wineries); many of them welcome visitors (wine tasting and sale).

Horsham H 7

Situation and characteristics

300km/185 miles north-west of Melbourne, at the junction of the Western, Wimmera and Henty Highways, is Horsham (pop. 13,000), centre of the Wimmera wheat-growing region, with a cereal research centre. It is also noted for its top-quality merino wool.

Accommodation

Many hotels, motels and caravan/camping parks.

Surroundings

On the Wimmera River and the nearby lakes there is ample scope for fishing and relaxation. Horsham is a good base for visits to Little Desert National Park (see below) and Grampians National Park (see entry), 50km/30 miles east. 27km/17 miles west of Horsham on the Western Highway is Natimuk (pop. 550). Particular attractions here are Lake Natimuk (water sports; water birds) and Mount Arapiles, a 356m/1170ft high sandstone crag known as the Ayers Rock of Victoria. First climbed by Thomas Mitchell in 1836, it still attracts rock-climbers, although there is now a road to the summit.

★Little Desert National Park

Location; area

40km/25 miles west of Horsham; 35,000 hectares/86,500 acres.

Best time to visit

Spring and autumn. In summer it is very hot.

Access

On Western Highway, turning off at Nhill. From Horsham via Natimuk.

Accommodation

In Kiata; motels in Dimboola and Nhill.

Facilities

Camping grounds; picnic areas, short walking trails.

Features

The name of this park is misleading, since it is neither small nor desert-like. It is a region of sandy plains covered with mallee scrub vegetation, with a great range of sand-loving plants and large numbers of birds. Here too can be seen the nest-mounds of the mallee fowl, in which incubation is aided by the warmth of decomposing vegetable matter.

Warracknabeal

Situation and characteristics

Warracknabeal (pop. 2800), 60km/37 miles north of Horsham, is the centre of a huge wheat-growing area.

Features of interest are the Historical Centre, with an exhibition on the history of the region, a number of old buildings (water-tower, gaol, post office, courthouse, hotels) and the North-Western Agricultural Machinery Museum.

Accommodation

Motel, caravan/camping park.

Surroundings

Some 30km/19 miles north of the town can be seen sections of the dingo fence, extending from Swan Hill to the South Australian border, which was constructed in 1883 to keep out these dangerous wild dogs.

Jeparit

Situation and characteristics

The little settlement of Jeparit (pop. 480), situated on Lake Hindmarsh 72km/45 miles north of Horsham, was the birthplace in 1894 of Robert Menzies, prime minister of Australia for many years. There is a monument to him in the town.

Accommodation

Hotel, caravan/camping park.

Features

On Lake Hindmarsh are good sandy bathing beaches and many water birds. South of Jeparit is Wimmera Mallee Pioneers Museum (old agricultural machinery). 20km/12½ miles south is Antwerp, near which is the Ebenezer mission station, founded in 1859 by Czech missionaries and restored some years ago by the National Trust. 44km/27 miles north of Jeparit is Wyperfeld National Park (see entry).

★Korumbarra J 7

Situation and characteristics

116km/72 miles south-east of Melbourne on the South Gippsland Highway, in a rich dairy farming region, is Korumbarra (pop. 2770), where coal was formerly mined for the railway. Coal was discovered in 1872 but began to be worked only in 1890. The last mine closed down in 1958.

Accommodation

Hotel, motel, caravan/camping park.

Features

Coal Creek Historical Park is a faithful reconstruction of a 19th century mining settlement (open: daily 9am–5pm; admission charge).

Surroundings

There is good fishing in Waratah Bay and Corner Inlet. From Cooks Hill there are wide views of Wilsons Promontory National Park (see entry) and the Bass Strait.

★Lake Eildon J 7

Situation and characteristics

Lake Eildon, 150km/95 miles north-east of Melbourne, is Victoria's largest lake, with an area of 138sq.km/53sq.miles and a shoreline of 515km/320 miles. It is a man-made lake, created to provide water for irrigation and the generation of power, and its creation led to the drowning of many farms in the Goulburn and Delatite valleys. The area round the lake, amid the gently rolling foothills of the Victorian Alps, is now a very popular holiday region. There are facilities for water sports in the holiday centres of Eildon and Bonnie Doon, where house boats can also be hired.

Accommodation

Motels and camping grounds in Eildon (advance reservation advisable).

Alexandra

Situation and characteristics

The little town of Alexandra (pop. 2200), 20km/12½ miles west of Lake Eildon, has preserved a number of handsome old buildings (Town Hall, Union Hotel, Courthouse).

Accommodation

Several hotels, motels and caravan/camping parks.

Surroundings

On the west side of Lake Eildon, 17km/10½ miles east of Alexandra, is Fraser National Park (area 3750 hectares/9250 acres; water sports, fishing, walking). Its hills were deforested, first by gold prospectors and later to provide grazing land, but since grazing ceased the forest has been regenerating.

To the south of Alexandra is the McKenzie Nature Reserve, an area of unspoiled bush country with many orchids. There is also good walking country in Cathedral Range State Park and Eildon State Park.

Mansfield

The little holiday resort of Mansfield (pop. 2310) lies 3km/2 miles from the northern arm of Lake Eildon and 40km/25 miles from Mount Buller, a popular winter sports centre, with pistes in all grades of difficulty and an Alpine village with accommodation for visitors and restaurants. In Mansfield itself there is a monument to three policemen shot by Ned Kelly in 1878 (see Baedeker Special, p. 61).

Situation and characteristics

Accommodation

Many hotels, motels and caravan/camping parks.

Surroundings

60km/37 miles north-east on a scenic road is Whitfield. 14km/8½ miles north is Mount Samaria State Park. To the south are the Goulburn and Jamieson Rivers (trout-fishing, gold-panning). Jamieson, on the south side of Lake Eildon, is an old gold-mining town.

Maryborough H 7

Situation and characteristics

On the northern slopes of the Great Dividing Range, 165km/105 miles north-west of Melbourne, is Maryborough, an old sheep-farming town which prospered during the gold rush. The gold-mines were worked out by the early 20th century. Maryborough is now an industrial town (knitwear, engineering) and an agricultural and timber-working centre.

Accommodation

Motels, caravan/camping park.

Features

Maryborough has a fine old railway station with which Mark Twain was very taken during his visit to Australia. Other buildings which bear witness to the town's prosperity in gold-mining days are the Courthouse, the Town Hall and the Post Office in Civic Square. A typical example of 19th century architecture is the Bull and Mouth Hotel in the town centre. In the park is a richly decorated wrought-iron bandstand.

★★Melbourne H/J 7

Capital of Victoria

Situation and characteristics

Melbourne, Australia's second largest city, lies in the south-east of the continent, straddling the Yarra River at the north end of Port Phillip Bay, which shelters it from the stormy Bass Strait. It is the most European, or more precisely the most British, of the Australian capitals.

The total area of the Melbourne conurbation (Greater Melbourne) is 6110sq.km/2360sq.miles, making it one of the world's largest cities in terms of area. To the east it extends into the Dandenong Ranges, in the south on to the Mornington Peninsula. Of its total area, however, just under a third consists of parks, gardens and open spaces, so that Melbourne can truly claim to be a green city.

History and development

Melbourne was founded in 1835 by John Batman, coming from Tasmania, and named after Viscount Melbourne, then British prime minister. The town's prosperity was based on the introduction of merino sheep and above all – in contrast to Sydney – on the involvement of free settlers rather than convict labour. After it was granted the status of a town in 1842 Robert Hoddle was commissioned to plan its further development. When gold was found at Clunes in 1851, prospectors flocked to the goldfields of western Victoria, and banks and mining companies established themselves in Melbourne, which then enjoyed a tremendous boom. This is reflected in the handsome buildings still to be seen in the city centre and in the international exhibition of 1880. In the 1890s, however, the boom collapsed: Melbourne fell into an economic depression and lost ground to Sydney. From 1901 until the move to the new federal capital of Canberra in 1927 it was the official capital of Australia, and until 1965 the Royal Mint in Melbourne produced all Australia's coins.

Population

Since the Second World War a large influx of immigrants, mainly from the Mediterranean area, has made Melbourne a multi-lingual, multi-cultural

Melbourne's business district from the Yarra River

city. The number of immigrants from Greece, for example, is so large that Melbourne has been called the third largest Greek city, after Athens and Salonica. The city's population is now about 3.2 million.

Transport

Melbourne is fully integrated into the Australian transport system. Its airport at Tullamarine is 22km/13½ miles north-west of the city centre and linked with it by the Skybus service which runs at half-hourly intervals.

From Spencer Street Station there are regular rail services to towns in Victoria and in other states. Local services go from Flinders Street Station. Melbourne is the only city in Australia to have preserved its own tramway system, which extends out into the suburbs and is now supplemented by buses and local train services. The new underground system has so far only three stations, Flagstaff and Museum in Latrobe Street and Parliament in Spring Street. A "Met pass" (on sale at Flinders Street and Spencer Street stations) covers a day's travel on all forms of public transport plus admission to certain tourist attractions.

The ferry "Spirit of Tasmania" sails regularly from Station Pier to Tasmania.

Events

In March Melbourne celebrates the Moomba Festival, which lasts ten days and nights, with elaborate parades and other events. Also in March, the Australian Formula 1 Grand Prix motor race is held in Albert Park. In September there is the Royal Agricultural Show; and in the second half of September there is the Arts Festival (music, dance, drama, film, literature, art).

Entertainment

For information about what's on in Melbourne (concerts, theatres, pop and rock) consult the EG (Entertainment Guide) section in the Friday edition of the "Melbourne Age". The city's night life is concentrated mainly in the southern district of St Kilda.

Restaurants

There are listings of Melbourne restaurants in two brochures, "Dining Out in Melbourne" and "Eating Out in Melbourne". In view of the strict liquor laws, Melbourne, like the rest of Victoria, has relatively few licensed restau-

In Central Melbourne ▶

Retail
LEASE
59
Airport West
178
BENEFITS

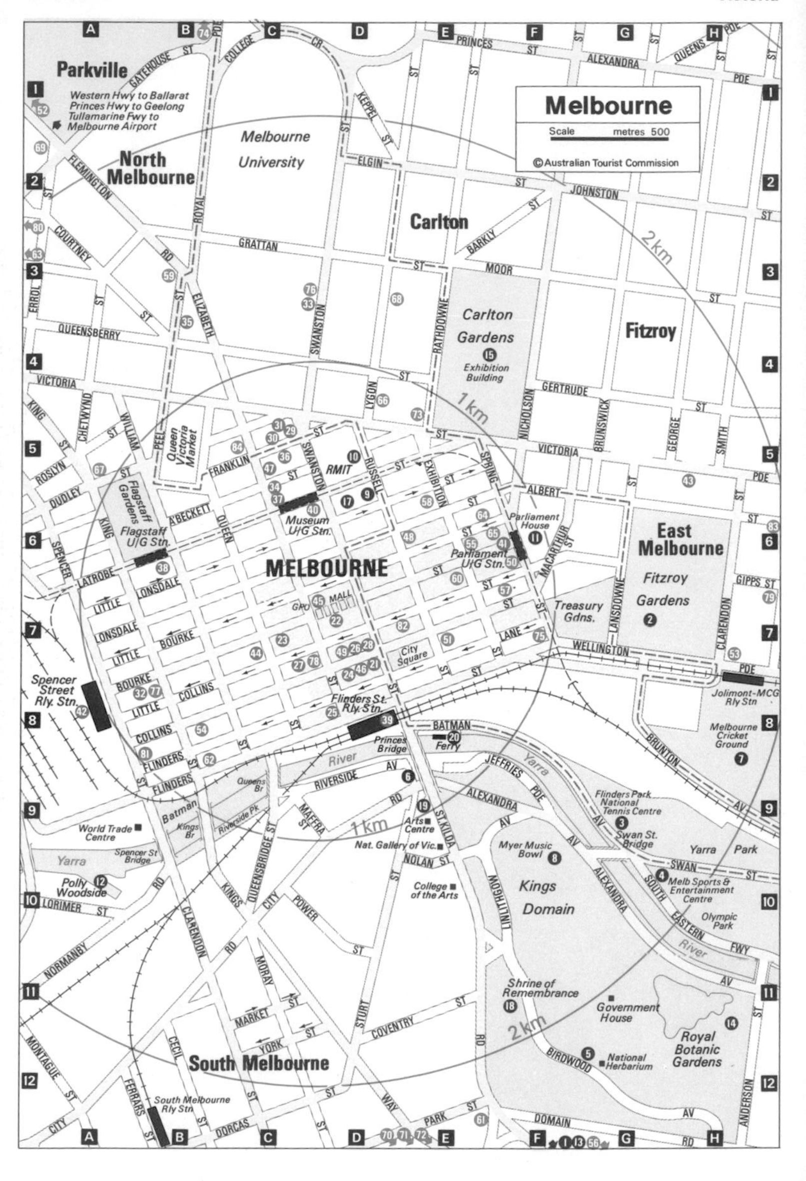
Melbourne
Scale metres 500
©Australian Tourist Commission
Parkville
Western Hwy to Ballarat
Princes Hwy to Geelong
Tullamarine Fwy to
Melbourne Airport
North
Melbourne
Melbourne
University
Carlton
Carlton
Gardens
Exhibition
Building
Fitzroy
East
Melbourne
Fitzroy
Gardens
Treasury
Gdns.
Parliament
House
Parliament
U/G Stn.
MELBOURNE
RMIT
Museum
U/G Stn.
Queen
Victoria
Market
Flagstaff
Gardens
Flagstaff
U/G Stn.
Spencer
Street
Rly. Stn.
City
Square
Flinders St.
Rly. Stn.
Princes
Bridge
Ferry
River
Yarra
Queens
Br
Batman
Kings
Br
Riverside Pk
World Trade
Centre
Spencer St
Bridge
Polly
Woodside
Arts
Centre
Nat. Gallery of Vic.
College
of the Arts
Myer Music
Bowl
Kings
Domain
Flinders Park
National
Tennis Centre
Swan St.
Bridge
Yarra Park
Melb Sports &
Entertainment
Centre
Olympic
Park
Jolimont-MCG
Rly Stn
Melbourne
Cricket
Ground
Shrine of
Remembrance
Government
House
National
Herbarium
Royal
Botanic
Gardens
South Melbourne
South Melbourne
Rly Stn
1 km
2 km
PRINCES
ALEXANDRA
QUEENS
PDE
COLLEGE
CR
GATEHOUSE
ST
KEPPEL
ELGIN
JOHNSTON
FLEMINGTON
RD
COURTNEY
GRATTAN
BARKLY
MOOR
ROYAL
ERROL
QUEENSBERRY
ELIZABETH
SWANSTON
RATHDOWNE
VICTORIA
GERTRUDE
NICHOLSON
BRUNSWICK
GEORGE
SMITH
LYGON
KING
CHETWYND
WILLIAM
PEEL
ROSLYN
DUDLEY
FRANKLIN
RUSSELL
EXHIBITION
SPRING
ALBERT
A'BECKETT
QUEEN
SPENCER
LATROBE
LONSDALE
LITTLE
BOURKE
COLLINS
FLINDERS
MACARTHUR
LANSDOWNE
CLARENDON
GIPPS
WELLINGTON
BATMAN
JEFFRIES
ALEXANDRA
AV
BRUNTON
RIVERSIDE
MAFFRA
ST KILDA
NOLAN
SWAN
SOUTH
EASTERN
FWY
LINLITHGOW
LORIMER
NORMANBY
KINGS
QUEENSBRIDGE
CITY
POWER
MORAY
MARKET
YORK
STURT
COVENTRY
BIRDWOOD
CECIL
MONTAGUE
FERRARS
DORCAS
PARK
WAY
DOMAIN
ANDERSON
GRO
MALL

Places of Interest

Como 1 F12
Cook's Cottage 2 G7
Flinders Park National Tennis Centre 3 G9
Indoor Sports & Entertainment Centre 4 G10
LaTrobe's Cottage 5 G12
Melbourne Concert Hall & Performing Arts Museum 6 E9
Melbourne Cricket Ground 7 H8
Myer Music Bowl 8 F9
National Museum of Vict. 9 D6
Old Melbourne Gaol 10 D5
Parliament House 11 F6
Pollywoodside 12 A10
RipponLea 13 F12
Royal Botanic Gardens 14 H11
Royal Exhibition Building 15 E4
Royal Zoological Gardens 16 B1
Science Museum & Planetarium 17 D6
Shrine of Remembrance 18 F11
State Library 17 D6
Victorian Arts Centre 19 E9
Yarra River Cruises (Ferry Wharves) 20 E8

Tourist Information Centre

Canberra Tourist Bureau 21 D7
Holiday W.A. Centre 22 D7
N.T. Govt. Tourist Bureau 23 C7
Qld. Govt. Travel Centre 24 D8
S.A. Govt. Tourist Bureau 25 D8
Tas. Govt. Tourist Bureau 26 D7
Travel Centre of N.S.W. 27 C7
Victour Travel Centre 28 D7

Airlines – City Terminals

Ansett Airlines of Aust. 29 C5
Australian Airlines 30 C5

Coach Terminals

Ansett Pioneer 31 C5
Greyhound 32 B8

Rent-a-Car Offices

Astoria 33 C3
Avis 34 C5
Budget 35 B4
Hertz 36 C5
Thrifty 37 C6

City Railway Stations

Flagstaff 38 B6
Flinders Street (Some country services) 39 D8
Museum 40 C6
Parliament 41 F6
Spencer Street (Interstate & country) 42 A8

National Parks

National Parks Service 43 H5

Motoring Associations

Royal Automobile Club of Victoria (R.A.C.V.) 44 C7

Post Office

G.P.O. 45 D7

International Airlines

Qantas Airways 46 D7

City to Airport Transfers

Skybus Airport Bus Service– Frequent direct service to and from Spencer St. Station and from city hotels and railway stations. 47 C5

Accommodation

**Facilities for the handicapped*

Premier

*Chateau Melbourne 48 E6
*Hotel Australia 49 D7
Hotel Windsor 50 F8
Hyatt on Collins 51 E7
Melb. Airport Travelodge 52 A1
*Melbourne Hilton 53 H7
*Menzies at Rialto 54 B8
Noah's Hotel Melbourne 55 E6
Parkroyal 56 F12
*Regent Melbourne 57 F7
*Rockmans Regency 58 E6
Settlers Old Melbourne 59 B3
*Southern Cross 60 E6
St. Kilda Rd. Travelodge 61 E12

Moderate

Centre City Travel Inn 62 B8
City Gardens 63 A3
City Limits Inn 64 E6
Crossley Lodge Motel 65 F6
Downtowner Motel 66 D4
Flagstaff City Motor Inn 67 A5
Lygon Lodge 68 D3
*Marco Polo Inn 69 A2
*Palm Lake 70 E12
*President 71 D12
Queenslodge Motor Inn 72 E12
Rathdowne Internat. Motel 73 E5
*Royal Parade Travelodge 74 B1
Sheraton Hotel 75 F7
Town House Hotel 76 C3

Budget

Kingsgate Private Hotel 77 B8
London 78 C7
Magnolia Crt. Private Hotel 79 H7
Melbourne Youth Hostel (members only) 80 A3
The Spencer Motel 81 B8
The Victoria Hotel 82 D7
Treasury Motor Lodge 83 H6
*YWCA 84 C5

Melbourne Explorer Bus

Shopping

rants but innumerable "bring your own" (BYO) establishments, identified by a "BYO" sign at the entrance, to which diners bring their own drinks, paying only corkage and a small amount for the use of glasses.

Accommodation

Melbourne has over 22,000 beds in more than 180 hotels, some three dozen of which are within the central area. Many of them are new, including some luxurious and expensive establishments (Chateau Melbourne, Australia Hotel, The Windsor, Grand Hyatt, Melbourne Hilton, Menzies at Rialto, Noah's Hotel Melbourne, Regent Melbourne). Hotels are listed in the visitors' guide "Hello Melbourne" and other brochures. Camping sites are all some way from the city centre. They include Half Moon Park, Geelong Road/Millers Road, Brooklyn, 11km/7 miles to the west; Big 4 Caravan Park, Elizabeth St., Coburg East, 14km/9 miles north; Northside Leisure Village, c/o Hune Highway and Coopers Road, Campbellfield, 14km/9 miles north; Willowbrook Gardens Caravan Village, Mickleham Road, Westmeadows, 18km/11 miles north-west; Hobsons Bay Caravan Park, 158 Kororoit Creek Road, Williamstown, 17km/10¼ miles south.

Sport

The great event of Melbourne's sporting year is the final of the Australian football tournament, held annually in September.

The National Tennis Centre in Flinders Park is the venue in January of the Australian Open, the first Grand Slam tournament of the year. The Melbourne Cup is run on Flemington Racecourse on the first Tuesday in November.

Sights in Melbourne

Sightseeing tours

At least two or three days should be allowed for seeing the sights of Melbourne and surroundings. A convenient way of seeing the principal sights is to take the double-decker City Explorer Bus which leaves Flinders Street Station (Swanston Street side) hourly from 10am to 4pm every day except Monday. Passengers can get off at any one of the stops and later continue with the next bus. The ticket also gives reductions on admission charges to some museums and the Zoo. There is also the City Circle Tram, a free service with old-time tramcars, introduced in 1994, which runs round the city centre, taking in the main sights (daily 10am–6pm, every ten minutes). Brochures, city plans and information of all kinds can be obtained from the Melbourne Tourist Information Centre, 230 Collins Street: tel. (03) 9650 1522, and from information kiosks in Bourke St. and City Square.

The city

The skyline of Melbourne has altered considerably over the years. Although much of the city's Victorian architecture has been preserved, many handsome bluestone buildings have given place to huge modern high-rise blocks, particularly in the business district. Melbourne's Victorian roots are still visible, however, in the broad streets, the European trees and the 19th-century buildings which have been restored and refurbished in recent years, particularly in the inner suburbs. And a walk in the central area will show that the term "Garden State" applies also to the capital with its numerous parks and gardens. The central area of Melbourne, on the right bank of the Yarra River, is in the form of a regular rectangle bounded on the south by Flinders Street, which runs parallel to the river, on the west by Spencer Street, on the north by Latrobe Street and on the east by Spring Street. Within this area the surveyor and town planner Robert Hoddle laid out a grid of 30m/100ft wide avenues intersecting at right angles every 200m/220yd. The governor of the day disliked the great empty spaces between the main streets running south-west/north-east (Bourke Street, Collins Street and Flinders Street) and inserted narrower streets between them (Little Flinders Street, Little Collins Street, Little Bourke Street, Little Lonsdale Street). Swanston Street and Elizabeth Street cut across these streets, and in the area thus marked out is Melbourne's main shopping district.

North of the Yarra River

*Flinders Street Station

Directly on the banks of the river is Flinders Street Station (1905), the hub of the city's suburban lines and a good starting-point for a tour of the city centre. Here the Princes Bridge spans the Yarra, heading south, while Swanston Street leads north into the central area.

St Paul's Cathedral

Facing the station is St Paul's Cathedral (Anglican), on the site of an earlier parish church of 1850 (the pews from which have been preserved). The foundation stone of the present neo-Gothic church was laid in 1880. It has a richly decorated façade with pointed gables, bell-towers and a massive tower over the crossing.

City Square

To the north of the Cathedral is the re-planned City Square, with a semicircular amphitheatre-like depression, fountains and a monument to Burke and Wills, who set out from Melbourne in 1860 on their unsuccessful attempt to cross Australia from south to north.

***Collins Street**

Town Hall

Swanston Street now cuts across Collins Street. On the right is the Town Hall, originally built in the 1860s, burned down in 1927 and rebuilt with the addition of a large hall which is used for concerts.

In Collins Street – Melbourne's best known street – there are many elegant old buildings. Among them, at the east end of the street, is the Melbourne Club, founded in 1839: the oldest institution in Victoria and still frequented by the Establishment. Collins Street has a number of well preserved neo-Gothic buildings, including Goode House, the Olderfleet Building, the South Australian Insurance Building and, at the west end, the luxury Menzies at Rialto Hotel, whose Victorian façade is in interesting contrast to the glass walls of the surrounding high-rise blocks, the most imposing of which is the 242m/794ft high Rialto Towers. An observation deck at the top (525 Collins Street) gives a bird's-eye view of Melbourne.

St James's Old Cathedral

At the corner of Collins and William Streets is St James's Old Cathedral, a bluestone and sandstone building begun in 1839 which is Melbourne's oldest surviving building. The font, from St Catherine's Church in London, was presented to Governor Charles Latrobe by Queen Victoria.

Princess Theatre

William Street

In William Street are the former Royal Mint and the Supreme Court and Law Courts, built between 1877 and 1884 (not, as originally planned, as a plain brick building but as an imposing sandstone edifice).

Bourke Street
★Royal Arcade

The most notable feature in Bourke Street is the Royal Arcade, an elegant shopping arcade of 1869. The large clock is supported by the two legendary giants Gog and Magog. Also in this street is Myers' huge department store, the largest in the southern hemisphere. Farther east is the Bourke Street Mall, a pedestrian zone (though there are trams running through it: pedestrians must watch out!).

General Post Office

At the near end of the mall, on the corner of Elizabeth Street, is the General Post Office, originally built in 1867; the top storey and the clock-tower were added at the end of the 19th century.

Chinatown

Turning left at the end of the mall into Swanston Street and then right into Little Bourke Street, we find ourselves in Chinatown. In Choen Place is the Museum of Chinese Australian History (history of Chinese settlers in Australia).

Parliament House

At the east end of Bourke Street is Parliament House (1856–92), it is now used for meetings of the Victoria state representatives. Until the move to Canberra in 1929 the building was occupied by the Australian Parliament. When the state council is not in session; Mon–Fri 10 and 11am, 2 and 3pm there are conducted visits.

Windsor Hotel

In Spring Street, opposite the Houses of Parliament, is the Windsor Hotel (1883), one of the last of the old grand hotels, patronised by many celebrities.

Princess Theatre

Near the hotel is the Princess Theatre, with an ornate neo-Baroque façade of 1887, complete with a trumpet-blowing angel over the pediment and wrought-iron crowns topping the roof.

St Patrick's Cathedral

Behind the Houses of Parliament is St Patrick's Cathedral (R.C.; 1858–68), the largest church in Australia.

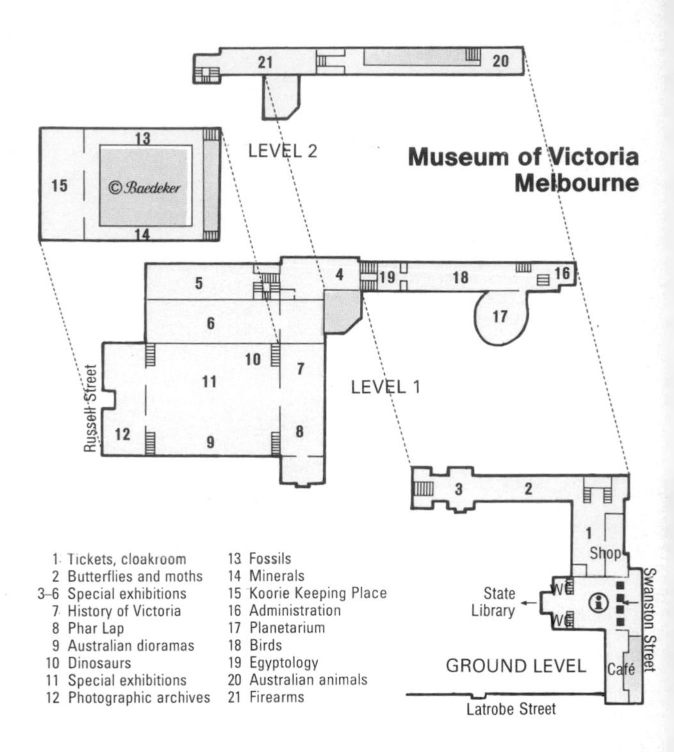

Latrobe Street

★Melbourne Central

National Museum of Victoria and State Library

The features of most interest in Latrobe Street, to the north, are mainly round the intersections with Swanston and Russell Streets. At the corner of Swanston Street lies the imposing and very popular Melbourne Central shopping centre. There is a fine view from the fire-watching tower, a protected building with a glass roof. At the corner of Russell Street is the National Museum of Victoria (open: daily 10am–5pm), devoted to natural history and science in Victoria, and the State Library. The extensive range of museum exhibits will shortly be transferred to new premises neighbouring the restored freighter, the "Polly Woodside" (see p.448). Attached to the Museum is a planetarium.

Old Melbourne Gaol

The Old Melbourne Gaol in Russell Street was built in 1841 and remained in use as a prison until 1929. It contains the gallows on which the notorious bushranger Ned Kelly was hanged in 1880 (see Baedeker Special, p. 61).

Flagstaff Gardens

At the west end of Latrobe Street are the Flagstaff Gardens. In Melbourne's early days this was the highest point in the settlement, with a signal station and a lookout from which a watch was kept for the arrival of ships. The creation of the independent state of Victoria was officially proclaimed from this hill.

★Queen Victoria Market

Covering an area of 6 hectares/15 acres and lying just to the north-east is Queen Victoria Market, which has been selling fruit and vegetables, clothes and handicrafts etc. for more than 100 years (Tue.–Sun. 6am–2pm, Fri. 6am–6pm, Sat. 6am–3pm, Sun. 9am–4pm).

Victorian Arts Centre ▶

in
YONKERS
FROM 23 JULY
PLAYHOUSE
ERICSSON

Fitzroy Gardens/ Treasury Gardens

Fitzroy Gardens and the neighbouring Treasury Gardens, to the east of the city centre near the Hilton Hotel, were the earliest public gardens in Melbourne. The gardens were designed by James Sinclair, who had previously worked for the Tsar in St Petersburg; the paths are laid out in the pattern of the Union Jack. In Fitzroy Gardens are Captain Cook's Cottage (said to be his parents' cottage, brought here from Yorkshire in 1935), which contains an exhibition on the great navigator, and a model Tudor village.

★Melbourne Cricket Ground

To the south of Fitzroy Gardens is the famous Melbourne Cricket Ground, with the Australian Gallery of Sport and Olympic Museum (open: daily 10am–4pm).

South of the Yarra River

★Victorian Arts Centre

Melbourne's status as a metropolis of art and culture is vouched for by the Victorian Arts Centre, on the south bank of the Yarra just beyond the Princes Bridge. An unmistakable landmark is the 115m/375ft high lattice-work spire of steel and aluminium over the largest of the three theatres in the complex, on St Kilda Road, which is of particularly fantastic effect when illuminated at night. The planning of the Arts centre (by Roy Grounds) began in 1956. The following thirty years saw the building of Australia's largest theatre, the Melbourne Concert Hall (with seating for 2500) close to the river, the Performing Arts Museum and the Westpac Gallery. Guided tours: Sun –Fri. noon–2.30pm; occasional evening tours. For programme dtails tel. (03) 9617 8211.

National Gallery of Victoria

The National Gallery of Victoria, with 2000sq.m/21,500sq.ft of exhibition space, displays a collection of works by European and Australian artists of the 19th and early 20th centuries as well as Aboriginal art. The most striking feature of the building is the glass mosaic roof of the Great Hall (by Leonard French), the largest of its kind in the world, which creates a magical play of colour. The National Gallery is open: Mon.–Sat. 10am–3pm.

Queen Victoria Gardens/ Alexandra Gardens

Along the south bank of the Yarra, immediately below the Princes Bridge, are the Queen Victoria Gardens and Alexandra Gardens. Opposite them, on the north bank, are the Ferry Wharves, from which there are cruises on the river offering fine views of the city. There is a good general view of the central area looking across the river from the south end of the Princes Bridge.

★Kings Domain

Immediately south of the Alexandra and Queen Victoria Gardens is the large park known as the Kings Domain, laid out during the economic depression to provide work for the unemployed.

Sydney Myer Music Bowl

Near the north end of the Kings Domain is the Sydney Myer Music Bowl, which was presented to the city by the Russian immigrant and department store magnate Sydney Myer. This is a huge open-air theatre (area 2000sq.m/21,500sq.ft) under a tent-like canopy, which can seat an audience of 2000; but for the free opera performances and symphony concerts given here in high summer, around Christmas, there is a huge overflow audience sitting on the surrounding grass.

★Shrine of Remembrance (see illustration page 448)

Farther south is the Shrine of Remembrance (1934), an imposing memorial to the dead of the First World War. The commemorative marches which start from Swanston Street on Anzac Day (April 25th) end here; and on November 11th at 11am – the time at which the First World War ended – the sun shines through an opening in the roof on to the Stone of Remembrance. From this point there is a good view of the central area of Melbourne.

National Gallery of Victoria Melbourne

© Baedeker

THIRD FLOOR
1 Australian ceramics
2 Education section
3 Administration
4 Lecture room

SECOND FLOOR
1 Decorative art
2 European art
3 Costume Corridor
4 19th century Australian art
5 Contemporary Australian art

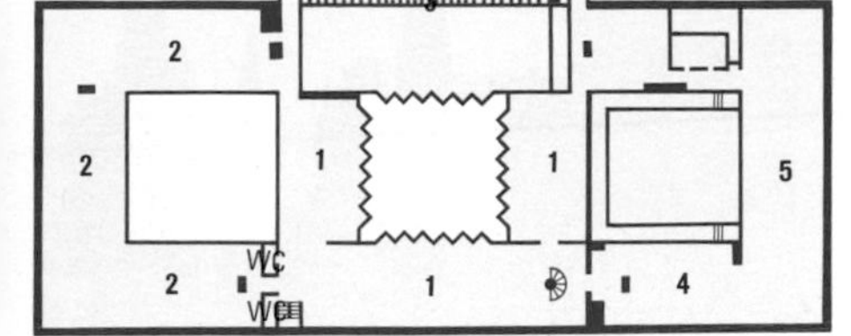

FIRST FLOOR
1 Entrance gallery
2 Tribal art
3 Aboriginal art
4 Library
5 Study room

GROUND FLOOR
1 Australian art
2 Museum Society
3 Prints and drawings
4 New Australian art
5 Photography
6 Special exhibitions

C Cloakroom
WC Toilets
Information

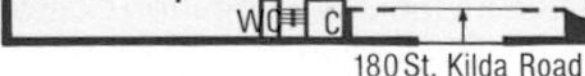

Victoria Barracks

Opposite the Shrine of Remembrance are the Victoria Barracks, where the War Cabinet met during the Second World War. The barracks, built of bluestone, were erected in the 1860s when there were fears of a Russian invasion.

Government House

North-east of the Shrine of Remembrance the white walls of Government House can be seen rising above the trees. It is a copy of Queen Victoria's residence on the Isle of Wight, Osborne House. When Melbourne was the federal capital this was the official residence of the Governor-General of Australia.

Latrobe's Cottage

To the south of Government House is Latrobe's Cottage, built in 1840 for Charles Latrobe, first governor of Victoria, from prefabricated parts imported from Britain.

★★Royal Botanic Gardens

Adjoining the Kings Domain on the east and bounded on the north by the river are the Royal Botanic Gardens, which rank among the finest of their

Shrine of Remembrance, a memorial to the dead of the First World War

kind in the world. Within an area of over 40 hectares/100 acres there are 12,000 different species of plants. The site of the gardens was decided on in 1845, and in 1852 Ferdinand von Müller, a German-born botanist, began to lay them out. The gardens were extended by his successor, William Guilfoyle. Some of the trees on the Oak Lawn are over 100 years old. The Yarra originally flowed through the gardens; then, when the river was straightened to prevent the flooding which had previously occurred every year, the bends which were cut off became lakes. In addition to the flowers and trees the park has its own fauna, with large numbers of birds and even bats. The domed Temple of the Winds and other rotundas in the gardens show the Victorian liking for decoration. The National Herbarium was established in 1935 on the 100th anniversary of the city's foundation. (open: Mon.–Sat. 7.30am, Sun. 9am until sunset. Guided tours daily except Mon. 10am and 11am).

Former docks, Exhibition Centre, "Polly Woodside"

The docks on the south bank of the Yarra River, to the south-west of Spencer Bridge, were until recently rather run-down. The area took on a new lease of life with the building of the Melbourne Exhibition Centre and the equipping of the Marine Museum (Open: Mon.–Fri. 10am–4pm, Sat., Sun. 10am–5pm). Many visitors are attracted to the "Polly Woodside", a sailing freighter built in Belfast in 1885 and now restored. On the opposite bank of the river stand the ultra-modern World Trade Centre and World Congress Centre complexes.

Suburbs of Melbourne

Some of Melbourne's suburbs, which had become rather rundown have now taken on a fresh lease of life with new shops and restaurants, and many of the Victorian houses have been lovingly restored.

Carlton

Carlton, to the north of the city centre is the district with most Victorian houses. It is now the city's Italian quarter, with numerous Italian restaurants, particularly in Lygon Street.

Carlton Gardens

At the north-east corner of the central area, on the north side of Victoria Street, are Carlton Gardens, in the centre of which is the Exhibition Build-

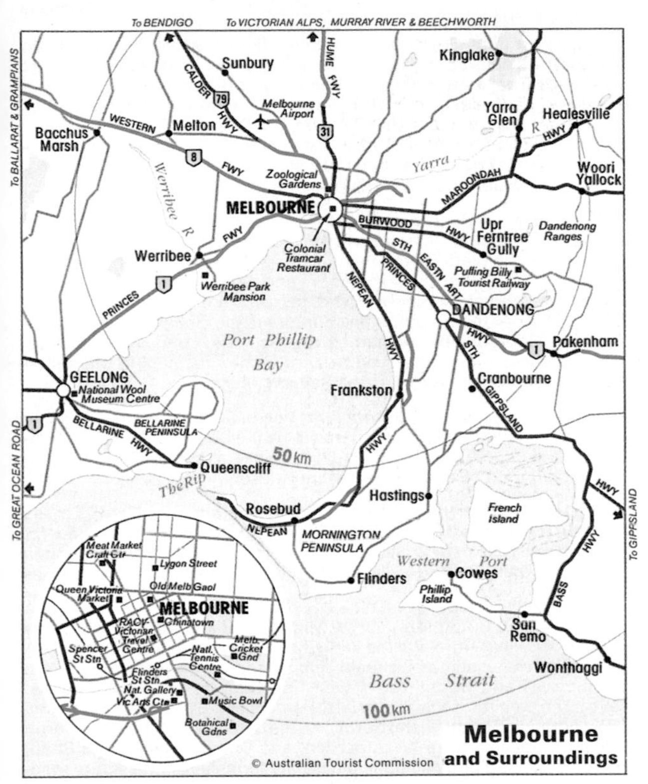

ing, designed by David Mitchell, father of Dame Nellie Melba, for the 1880 international exhibition. It was then the city's largest building, and with its high dome became Melbourne's principal landmark. The Victorian Parliament met here from 1901 to 1927 while the Houses of Parliament were occupied by the Commonwealth Parliament. The building is now used for exhibitions and trade fairs. Of the original complex, which covered 8 hectares/20 acres, only the main hall has been preserved.

University of Melbourne

The core of the University of Melbourne (founded 1853) is a square ivy-clad building in neo-Gothic style. Trinity College was added in 1872, followed by eleven other colleges. Wilson Hall (1950) occupies the site of an earlier building of 1874 which was destroyed by fire.

Parkville/Fitzroy

★Zoo

The neighbouring districts of Parkville and Fitzroy also have many old buildings. In Parkville, adjoining Royal Park, is Melbourne's excellent Zoo, the oldest in Australia, with enclosures for the animals (native and imported) which are as large and as natural as possible. Particular features are the enclosed bridge which runs through the lions' enclosure and the walk-through aviary and butterfly house (open: daily 9.30am–5.30pm). In Royal Park is a monument marking the spot from which Burke and Wills set out in 1860 to cross the continent from south to north. Access by City Explorer Bus.

Royal Park

Richmond

Richmond, to the south-east of the city centre, is a predominantly Greek quarter, with Greek shops and restaurants in its old buildings.

St Kilda

To the south of the Yarra is the St Kilda district, which has long been Melbourne's entertainment quarter, at its busiest in the evening and at weekends. The range of entertainment is wide – numerous restaurants and bars, particularly in Fitzroy Street, Luna Park, a large and noisy amusement centre, the Palais Theatre, the Palais de Danse. There are also pleasant walks along the bay on the two Esplanades. Night life is to be found mainly in clubs and bars; in pubs there is jazz, rock and folk music; and there are numerous discothèques.

Williamstown

Williamstown, at the mouth of the Yarra, is one of the oldest parts of Melbourne, the port having been established at the same time as the town. From the piers there are views over Hobsons Bay (the northern corner of Port Phillip Bay), the docks and container terminals of Port Melbourne, the skyscrapers in the city centre and the arch of West Gate Bridge. At the tip of the promontory is the Gellibrand lighthouse (1852). Moored in Williamstown is the old minesweeper "Castlemaine", now preserved as a maritime museum. In Champion Road, North Williamstown, is the Railway Museum.

Toorak

Toorak, with its elegant old mansions, tree-lined streets and expensive shops and restaurants, is considered to be Melbourne's wealthiest suburb. Toorak House was the residence of several governors of Victoria and served until 1874 as Government House.

Frankston

Frankston is a commuter suburb of Melbourne, situated 40km/25 miles south of the city centre on the Mornington Peninsula, with a beautiful beach almost 60km/37 miles long, numerous caravan/camping parks and good hotels. Ballan House, built in 1845, is one of the oldest houses in the area.

Other suburbs

The suburbs of South Melbourne, Middle Park and Albert Park, to the south of the city centre and the Yarra, have preserved many typical 19th century houses such as Emerald Hill. Armadale, Malvern, Hawthorn, Camberwell and South Yarra, with fine villas set in large gardens, reflect the wealth of their founders. Particularly notable is Rippon Lea (192 Hotham Street, Elsternwick, to the south of St Kilda), a large Victorian house with a large garden, and Como (near Toorak Road, South Yarra), is a large elegant, pleasantly furnished 19th-century mansion.

The suburbs of Heidelberg, Box Hill and Beaumaris are associated with the Heidelberg, the first independent Australian school of painting. The members of the group (Roberts, Streeton, McCubbin, Conder and Abrahams) painted from nature, living in bush camps and huts in Box Hill, Heidelberg (so called by a German purchaser of land because the scenery reminded him of Heidelberg in Germany) and Beaumaris (on Port Phillip Bay, south of Brighton).

Beaches

Because of Melbourne's sheltered situation at the head of Port Phillip Bay (see entry) there are no surfing beaches in the immediate neighbourhood of the city. Surfers have to go farther afield, to the seaward coast of the Mornington Peninsula and the coast south of Geelong (Torquay) (see entries).

Close to the city there are popular (and frequently overcrowded) beaches at Port Melbourne, Albert Park and South Melbourne; farther south are Elwood, Brighton and Sandringham. The finest sheltered beaches are on the bay side of the Mornington Peninsula to the south of Frankston, Melbourne's favourite recreation area, usually overcrowded during the holiday season and at weekends.

National Parks Near Melbourne

Churchill National Park

Location; area — 32km/20 miles south-east of Melbourne; 193 hectares/477 acres.
Access — Via Stud Road, Rowville. There is a bus service to the park.
Facilities — No camping grounds; picnic areas.
Features — Churchill National Park, lying on the outskirts of the city, is a popular recreation area with the people of Melbourne, with attractive picnic spots and walking trails.

In spite of the park's small size the vegetation is characteristic of the natural open woodland on the fringes of the Dandenong Ranges. It is the home of many birds, particularly bellbirds.

★Dandenong Ranges National Park

Location; area — 40km/25 miles east of Melbourne; 1900 hectares/4700 acres.
Access — Via Burwood Highway; bus service.
Facilities — Guesthouses, picnic areas, walking trails, footpaths.
Features — Dandenong Ranges National Park takes in the former Ferntree Gully National Park (the first National Park in Victoria, established 1882) and Doongalla and Sherbrooke Forests. The vegetation pattern, with forests of ferns, numerous species of orchids and many birds, is somewhat similar to that of a subtropical rain forest. The high rainfall and volcanic soils produce a lush growth of vegetation, with tree ferns, tall mountain ashes (giant gums) and many European deciduous trees. With all its natural beauty, the area is densely populated, and the park tends to be overcrowded at weekends. Ferntree Gully is now one of Melbourne's outer suburbs. This has long been a favoured summer holiday region, and many of the handsome old villas have been converted into elegant restaurants and guesthouses

A trip with "Puffing Billy" in Dandenong Ranges National Park

(e.g. Burnham Beeches, Sherbrooke, in the style of the 1920s). In addition to good restaurants there are attractive picnic spots, art galleries, antique shops, tree nurseries and plantations of flowers.

From the summit of Mount Dandenong (633m/2077ft), the highest point in the park, there is a magnificent view of the skyline of Melbourne (particularly impressive at night).

The Dandenong Tourist Road runs through the park from Ferntree Gully to Montrose, and there is a suburban rail line to Belgrave. The road from Belgrave to Kallista runs through the almost unspoiled landscape of Sherbrooke, with many birds (including lyrebirds and rosellas).

One of the attractions of the Dandenongs is "Puffing Billy", a turn-of-the-century narrow-gauge railway, originally built to transport agricultural produce. In summer it runs daily, and during the rest of the year at weekends, between Belgrave and Emerald, drawn by a steam engine (a diesel when there is danger of forest fires). In Menzies Creek, half way along the line, there is a railway museum.

Olinda, 11km/7 miles north of Belgrave, is famed for its rhododendron gardens. Here too is a house which belonged to Edward Henty, one of the first settlers in Victoria; it was erected in Melbourne in 1855, using prefabricated parts imported from Britain, and moved to its present site in 1970.

At Montrose, in the northern Dandenongs (Mount Dandenong Road), is Rickett's Sanctuary, named after the musician and sculptor William Rickett, with many of his sculptures.

Emerald

Emerald (pop. 3610), terminus of the "Puffing Billy" railway, lies 50km/30 miles east of Melbourne in a beautiful upland setting, with wide views. There are many lavender fields in the area. Emerald is a favourite destination for weekend visits and day trips, with excellent shops (including craft shops). Near the little town is Emerald Lake, a good place for picnics and water sports.

Kinglake National Park

Location; area — 65km/40 miles north-east of Melbourne; 11,430 hectares/28,230 acres.

Access — Via Wittlesea, Yarraglen or Yea.

Facilities — The Gums camping ground (advance booking advisable); picnic areas, good walking trails.

Features — The park is a region of hill ridges covered with dry eucalyptus forest and fern gullies. This is the nearest that the Great Dividing Range comes to the city of Melbourne.

Organ Pipes National Park

Location; area — 25km/15½ miles north-west of Melbourne; 85 hectares/210 acres.

Access — Via Calder Highway, turning off at Sydenham; railway station 3km/2 miles from park.

Facilities — No camping grounds; picnic areas, footpaths.

Features — Lying so close to Melbourne, Organ Pipes National Park draws many visitors throughout the year. It takes its name from its 20m/65ft high basalt columns resembling organ pipes. The soil in the valley has been washed away by water. The trees were cleared from the area 130 years ago to provide grazing land, but since the establishment of the National Park the vegetation typical of basalt soils is now beginning to reappear.

★Mildura H 6

Situation and characteristics

Mildura (pop. 20,770), 544km/338 miles north-west of Melbourne on the Sunraysia Highway, developed along with the irrigation of the area initiated towards the end of the 19th century by the Chaffey brothers, two

Paddle-steamers on the Murray River

Canadian-born irrigation experts. After a period of economic depression in the early 20th century Mildura recovered after the First World War, when ex-soldiers were resettled in the town. Public relations men have devised the name Sunraysia for this area, where the sun shines almost all the time. The mild, sunny winters and beautiful situation on the banks of the Murray have made Mildura and its neighbouring towns popular holiday destinations, attracting over half a million visitors annually to this sunny side of Victoria. The equable climate favours intensive wine-growing in the country round Mildura.

The great days of shipping traffic on the Murray are recalled by the paddle-steamer cruises on the Murray and the Darling, departing from Mildura Wharf, which are now a great tourist attraction. House boats can also be hired.

Accommodation

Many hotels, motels and caravan/camping parks.

Features

The town has an attractive main street, 12km/7½ miles long, with a broad strip of flowerbeds, grass and trees in the middle. The former home of the Chaffey brothers is now a museum. The Working Men's Club claims to have the world's longest bar.

Surroundings

From Mildura an excursion (114km/71 miles) can be made on unsurfaced tracks (impassable after rain) to Mungo National Park in New South Wales.

Moe J 7

Situation and characteristics

Moe (pop. 20,000), 130km/80 miles east of Melbourne on the Princes Highway, in Gippsland, is a coal-mining town occupied by workers in the opencast mines of brown coal in the area. Many of its inhabitants came from Yallourn, another mining town which had to be evacuated because it was situated over valuable seams of coal.

Accommodation

Hotels, motels, caravan/camping park.

Features

The Yallourn power station with its three huge cooling towers, using coal from the Yallourn opencast mine, can be visited. On the Princes Highway is Old Gippstown Pioneer Township, an open-air museum in which old buildings of the pioneering period have been brought together.

Surroundings

46km/29 miles north-east of Moe is the old gold-mining town of Walhalla, where gold was worked between 1865 and 1913. In those days Walhalla had a population of 5000: now it is almost a ghost town. Visitors can see the Long Tunnel Mine. A few kilometres east is Baw Baw National Park (see entry).

★Mornington Peninsula H/J 7

Access

The Mornington Peninsula is reached from central Melbourne by way of the Nepean Highway, which runs south-east along the coast from Mordialloc to Frankston and then turns south-west to Portsea.

During the summer there are ferries from Queenscliff (see Bellarine Peninsula) across the Rip, the narrow passage between the Bellarine and Mornington Peninsulas, to Portsea and Sorrento.

Situation and characteristics

The Mornington Peninsula extends between Port Phillip Bay to the west and Western Port to the east. Portsea, at its western tip, is just over 100km/60 miles from Melbourne. It takes its name from the little town of Mornington (founded 1864) half way down its west coast. Most of the settlements in the peninsula are on this coast (Frankston, Mornington, Mount Martha, Dromana, McRae, Rosebud, Rye, Blairgowrie, Sorrento, Portsea); the east side, on Western Port, is much less developed, as is the coast facing the Bass Strait (Flinders, Crib Point, Hastings).

Melbourne's suburban railway line ends at Frankston, 40km/25 miles south of the city centre, from which there are buses to the tip of the peninsula. From Frankston the beaches extend south-west for almost 60km/37 miles, with an endless series of weekend and holiday settlements and camping grounds. Inland from the beautiful beaches are wooded hills and rock formations such as Arthur's Seat at Dromana, from which there are wide views. The hinterland is now an extensive wine-growing area. The narrow southern tip of the peninsula, running west, shows a striking diversity in its beaches: the "front beaches" on its west and north sides, looking on to Port Phillip Bay (see entry) have quiet, safe water, while only a few kilometres away the "back beaches" on its south side, facing the Bass Strait, have high seas which offer ideal conditions for surfing. Near this stretch of coast with its magnificent views are such curious rock formations, eroded by the sea, as London Bridge, off Portsea. Between Point Nepean and Cape Schanck with its lighthouse of 1859 extends Point Nepean National Park. Farther along the coast towards Flinders and West Head are two remarkable rock formations, the Blowhole and Elephant Rock. From Crib Point, at the east end of the peninsula, there are passenger ferries to the almost completely undeveloped French Island, once a penal colony, and the main tourist attraction in the area, Phillip Island (see entry).

The whole of the Mornington Peninsula is a favourite holiday and recreation area for people living in the Melbourne conurbation and is very busy at holiday times, particularly Christmas and Easter. Advance booking is therefore essential.

Point Nepean National Park

Location; area

Along the south-west coast of the Mornington Peninsula; 2200 hectares/5435 acres.

Features

Point Nepean National Park takes in the western tip of the Mornington Peninsula, the coastal strip on the Bass Strait and the bush country at the south end of the peninsula. With its long surf beaches and beautiful coastal scenery, it is perhaps the most interesting of the National Parks in the neighbourhood of Melbourne. Particularly striking is the road from Portsea

Coastal scenery, Mornington Peninsula

to Bushrangers Bay and Main Creek. Access to the tip of the peninsula is subject to some restrictions: for information apply to the local office of the Department of Conservation, Forests and Lands.

Sorrento

Situation and characteristics

The holiday resort of Sorrento, at the tip of the Mornington Peninsula, has preserved something of the atmosphere of the turn of the century, when steamers from Melbourne brought summer visitors to the elegant hotels, some of which have been preserved (e.g. the Continental Hotel). There was a first white attempt at settlement near Sorrento in 1803, when David Collins landed in Sullivan Bay with over 300 settlers and convicts in order to forestall any attempt by the French to take possession of the territory. Only a year later the project was abandoned and Collins moved across the Bass Strait to Tasmania. On the cliffs above Sullivan Bay are the graves of some of the early settlers and a monument to Collins.

Portsea

Situation and characteristics

Portsea, at the farthest tip of the peninsula, is a very popular holiday resort, with quiet, safe water on the "front beaches" in Port Phillip Bay and wild surf on the "back beaches" fronting the ocean. Many beaches are private property and not open to the public. During the holiday season there is a ferry across the "Rip" to Queenscliff on the Bellarine Peninsula (see entry).

Morwell J 7

Situation and characteristics

Morwell (pop. 17,000), 152km/94 miles east of Melbourne, is one of the leading towns in the Latrobe valley. Founded in 1861 under the name of

Maryvale, it prospered as a supply centre for the gold-diggers of Walhalla and Tanjil. The importance of the town and surrounding area now depends on the power stations of the State Electricity Commission (SEC), fuelled by brown coal from the opencast mines in the Latrobe valley, which generate over 85% of the electricity produced in Victoria. Morwell also has some secondary industries such as the Maryvale Paper Mill (10km/6 miles north), the largest in Australia.

Accommodation — Several hotels, motels and caravan/camping parks.

Features — The main sights are the large-scale opencast coal workings, the power stations and the Latrobe Valley Arts Centre.

Morwell National Park

Location; area — 16km/10 miles south of Morwell; 283 hectares/699 acres.

Best time to visit — Spring and early summer for wild flowers.

Access — From Midland Highway between Churchill and Boolara.

Accommodation — Hotels, motels and caravan/camping parks in Morwell.

Facilities — Picnic areas, walking trails.

Features — The steep wooded slopes of the Strzelecki Ranges and the luxuriant growth of ferns along the streams are among the last relics of the Gippsland Forest with its rare butterfly orchids.

Tarra-Bulga National Park

Location; area — 50km/30 miles south-east of Morwell, between Yarram on the South Gippsland Highway and Traralgon on the Princes Highway; 1230 hectares/3038 acres.

Access — From the north on Midland Highway from Morwell, then east on Grand Ridge Road; from the south via Welshpool north on Midland Highway, then Grand Ridge Road to park, or south from Traralgon (35km/22 miles).

Accommodation — Hotels, motels and caravan/camping parks in Morwell or Traralgon.

Facilities — Fine walking trails; some picnic areas.

Features — In the hilly landscape of the Strzelecki Ranges some patches of the old Gippsland Forest and temperate rain forest vegetation have survived – huge mountain ashes (giant gums) and deep gullies with tree ferns and a rich bird life.

Mount Beauty J 7

Situation and characteristics — Mount Beauty (pop. 2100), in the upper Kiewa valley 344km/214 miles east of Melbourne, was originally established in the 1940s to house workers on the Kiewa hydro-electric scheme. Thereafter it developed into a well equipped holiday village at the foot of Mount Bogong (1986m/6516ft), Victoria's highest mountain, the gateway to Bogong National Park, which is now incorporated in the Alpine National Park (see entry). Mount Beauty is an important winter sports centre. A beautiful mountain road leads to Falls Creek (see entry) and the Bogong High Plains. Water sports on the Rocky Valley Dam.

Accommodation — Motels, caravan/camping parks.

★Mount Buffalo National Park J 7

Location; area — 330km/205 miles north-east of Melbourne; 31,000 hectares/77,000 acres.

Best time to visit — Summer for walking and climbing, winter for skiing.

Access — Hume Highway to Wangaratta, then Ovens Highway via Myrtleford, Bright and Porepunkah. Snow chains essential in winter.

Facilities — Camping ground near Lake Catani (closed from end of May to beginning of November); comfortable accommodation in the Chalet and Tatra Inn. Downhill and cross-country skiing; lifts.

In Mount Buffalo National Park

Features

The skiing area in Mount Buffalo National Park has attracted skiers since 1930, making it the oldest winter sports region in Victoria. In summer it appeals to walkers and rock-climbers.

Mount Hotham J 7

Situation and characteristics

On Mount Hotham, 370km/230 miles north-east of Melbourne, is a popular winter sports area which because of its height has reliable snow cover. There are good pistes in all grades of difficulty and excellent cross-country skiing on Dargo High Plains. The skiing village of Hotham Heights straggles along the road, and the ski-lifts are at some distance from one another. The village can be reached on the Hume Highway to Wangaratta, then the Ovens Highway to Bright and the scenic Alpine Way via Harrietville; from Gippsland it can be reached by way of Bairnsdale and Omeo. Like Falls Creek (see entry), Mount Hotham lies within the former Bogong National Park (see Alpine National Park), but Hotham Heights is outside the park in the valley. During the season there is a bus service to Bright (see entry), where cheaper accommodation is available. Mount Hotham is also a popular holiday area in summer (walking, climbing, riding).

Nagambie J 7

Situation and characteristics

Nagambie (pop. 1100), lies on the shores of Lake Nagambie, a man-made lake created in 1890 by the damming of the Goulburn. Although the dam was constructed entirely by human muscle, it was regarded in its day as a masterpiece of technology.

Nagambie, 125km/78 miles north of Melbourne, is reached on the Hume Highway to Seymour, then the Goulburn Valley Highway. The town has

	preserved a number of old houses. There are good facilities for water sports on the lake.
Accommodation	Motels, caravan/camping parks.
Surroundings	In the area are two of Australia's leading wineries, Château Tahbilk and Mitchelton, which can be visited.

Omeo J 7

Situation and characteristics	400km/250 miles north-east of Melbourne, in the heart of the Victorian Alps, is the little township of Omeo (pop. 550), whose name in the language of the Aborigines means "hills". It is within easy reach (55km/34 miles to Hotham Heights) of the winter sports area on Mount Hotham (see entry); in summer there is good walking country and good fishing round the town. Omeo was devastated by earthquakes in 1885 and 1892 and bush fires in 1939. In spite of this there are still many traces of the gold-digging period (abandoned mine-shafts and ruined buildings). Gold panning is still popular in Livingstone Creek, and pans can be hired. Omeo is reached from Melbourne by way of the Princes Highway to Bairnsdale, then the Omeo Highway. It is an extremely beautiful road, but exhausting driving.
Accommodation	Hotel, motel, caravan/camping park.

Orbost J 7

Situation and characteristics	Orbost (pop. 2500), 285km/175 miles east of Melbourne on the Princes Highway, lies on the Snowy River, surrounded by the spectacular coastal and mountain scenery of East Gippsland. Its economy is based on timber-working, dairy farming and vegetable growing. It has an interesting historical museum.
Accommodation	Hotels, motels and caravan/camping parks.
Surroundings	The Bonang Highway runs north from Orbost through the mountains to Delegate and Bombala in New South Wales (164km/102 miles).

14km/8½ miles south-east, at the mouth of the Snowy River, is Marlo, from which it is 33km/21 miles along the coast to Conran, with fine views of coastal scenery and the sea.

57km/35 miles east on the Princes Highway via Cabbage Tree is the fishing village of Bemm River, on Sydenham Inlet (water sports).

45km/28 miles east of Orbost, just off the Princes Highway, is the Bemm River Rainforest Walk, a trail through eucalyptus forest and gullies with dense rain forest which was laid out by the road authorities in co-operation with the army.

★Buchan

Situation and characteristics	Buchan (pop. 400) is a little timber-working township 58km/36 miles north-west of Orbost in the Gippsland mountain country.
Accommodation	Motel, camping grounds.
Features	Buchan is famed for its limestone caves, over 300 in number. The two principal caves, the Royal Cave and the Fairy Cave, are open to the public (conducted tours). Near the caves are a park and a swimming pool fed by a spring.

Errinundra National Park

Location; area	90km/56 miles north-east of Orbost; 25,100 hectares/62,000 acres.
Accommodation	In Orbost.
Facilities	Rest areas being developed.

Sunset over the Hattah Lakes ▶

Features — This recently established National Park contains the largest expanses of cool temperate rain forest and old wet eucalyptus forest. The roads in the park are also used by timber trucks: it is advisable, therefore, before setting out to ask the Department of Conservation, Forests and Lands about the state of the roads.

Ouyen H 6

Situation and characteristics — Ouyen (pop. 1500), 470km/290 miles north-west of Melbourne on the Sunraysia Highway and 100km/60 miles south of Mildura, is a traffic hub and agricultural centre in the huge Mallee wheat belt.

Accommodation — Hotel, motels, caravan/camping park.

Surroundings — Within easy reach of Ouyen are the Hattah-Kulkyne National Park and the recently established Yanga-Nyawi (Murray-Sunset) National Park, with camping grounds on the Pink Lakes.

★Hattah-Kulkyne National Park

Location; area — 34km/21 miles north of Ouyen at Hattah; 48,000 hectares/119,000 acres.

Best time to visit — Spring and autumn; summer is very hot.

Access — From Murray Valley Highway, access road 4km/2½ miles east of Hattah.

Accommodation — In Ouyen.

Facilities — Bush camping (with permission from ranger); rest areas. Bring your own water!

Features — Occasional flooding by the Murray supplies a series of lakes with water, allowing tall river red gums to flourish. Otherwise the vegetation cover is mallee scrub. There are many water birds in the park, and it is also home to the mallee fowl, which deposits its eggs in mounds of decomposing vegetation which serve as incubators.

Yanga-Nyawi (Murray-Sunset) National Park

Location; area — 65km/40 miles west of Ouyen; 63,300 hectares/156,400 acres.

Best time to visit — Autumn to spring; summer is very hot.

Access — Via Ouyen; or from Pinnaroo (South Australia) on Mallee Highway, turning off at Linga.

Facilities — Camping grounds on Pink Lakes, otherwise bush camping; rest areas; roads (unsurfaced tracks).

Features — Yanga-Nyawi National Park (or Murray-Sunset National Park), established in 1991 (previously Pink Lakes State Park), reaches west to the borders of South Australia and north to adjoin Wyperfeld National Park (see entry). It is planned to extend it northward as far as the Murray River, thus bringing an immense area of mallee scrub with its typical flora and fauna under protection. There are many unsurfaced tracks through the park (4WD vehicles advisable).

Phillip Island J 7

Situation and characteristics — Phillip Island (area 10,300 hectares/25,400 acres) lies some 140km/85 miles south-east of Melbourne at the mouth of Western Port bay, linked with the mainland by the Newhaven Bridge.

Access — On South Gippsland Highway to Lang Lang, then Bass Highway via San Remo.

Features — The great tourist attraction is the evening parade by tiny fairy penguins on Summerland Beach. Off the south-west coast is a group of rocks known as the Nobbies, home to a colony of fur seals, which can be observed with binoculars. There are also nesting colonies of muttonbirds in the sand-dunes on Cape Woolamai, at the south-eastern tip of the island. On this stretch of coast facing the open sea there are rugged granite crags, curious rock formations (pinnacles and colonnades), thunderous surf and spectacular views. The koalas in the Koala Conservation Centre have unfortunately been decimated by disease. At Rhyll in the marshy north of the island is a nesting area frequented by rare birds (pelicans, ibises, swans).

The chief place on the island, Cowes (pop. 2400), on the north coast, has sheltered beaches which are safe for children, craft shops, entertainments, restaurants and many motels and caravan/camping parks. (Most of the island's holiday accommodation is on the north coast.)

In the Kingston Gardens Zoo, 5km/3 miles south of Cowes, Australian animals (wombats, kangaroos, wallabies, cockatoos) live in relatively free conditions. On Churchill Island (to the north of Newhaven), which is linked with the main island by a bridge, there are a number of historic old buildings.

★★Penguin Parade

The penguin parade which takes place every evening at Summerland Beach, on the south-west coast of the island, is an unforgettable experience. The little fairy penguins emerge from the sea and waddle up to their nests in the dunes, undisturbed by the floodlighting, the stands for spectators and the crowds of people. Flash photographs are forbidden. Warm clothing is required, since there may be a long wait after sunset.

Western Port

Western Port, the bay to the north of Phillip Island, offers sheltered inlets and harbours for all kinds of water sports. There are good sandy beaches at Hastings, Shoreham, Point Leo, Merricks, Balnarring and Somers, while off Flinders, at the mouth of the bay, there are good diving grounds. In the centre of the bay is French Island, a former penal colony, which George Bass in 1798 thought was a promontory on the mainland. There has been little development on the island, which has therefore preserved unspoiled expanses of bush country and heath and a rich wildlife. There is a regular ferry service between Stony Point, on the mainland, and French Island.

★Port Albert J 7

Situation and characteristics

Port Albert (pop. 300), a tiny but historic township, lies in Gippsland, on the south-east coast, to the south of Yarram and Morwell and some 270km/170 miles south-east of Melbourne. Named after Prince Albert the Prince Consort, it was the first established port in Victoria. Sailing ships from Europe and America once docked at the large timber jetty here, and boats from China brought thousands of prospectors to the goldfields in northern Gippsland. Originally established for trade with Tasmania, Port Albert was the supply port for Gippsland until the railway line from Melbourne to Sale was opened in 1878.

Accommodation

Hotel, caravan/camping parks.

Features

Port Albert has preserved a number of old buildings – government offices, shops, the Bank of Victoria, the Maritime Museum, Christ Church (1858). Close to the waterfront is the Port Albert Hotel, first licensed in 1842, one of the oldest hotels still operating in Australia.

★Port Campbell National Park H 7

Location; area

270km/170 miles south-west of Melbourne; 1750 hectares/4320 acres.

Best time to visit

Late spring to autumn.

The Twelve Apostles, Port Campbell National Park

Access
From Princetown to west of Peterborough the Great Ocean Road runs through the park.

Accommodation
In Apollo Bay and Warrnambool (see entries).

Facilities
Camping ground; viewpoints, rest areas.

Features
Port Campbell National Park takes in the best known and most spectacular stretch of the Great Ocean Road (see entry), with magnificent views of a series of interesting rock formations – the Twelve Apostles, Muttonbird Island, London Bridge, Loch Ard Gorge. Loch Ard Gorge recalls the wreck of the clipper "Loch Ard" which ran aground on a reef in 1878 with the loss of 52 lives; four graves in this narrow gorge carved out by the surf are reminders of the tragedy. Other impressive features are the cliffs to the west of Peterborough, the Bay of Martyrs and the Bay of Islands. The limestone rocks along the coast have been eaten away over millions of years by fierce waves and winds, creating gorges and gullies, arches, blowholes and sheer, rugged cliffs.

Warnnig
Bathers should beware of dangerous waves and currents under the cliffs.

★Portland H 6

Situation and characteristics
Portland (pop. 11,160), 360km/225 miles west of Melbourne, is the only deep-water port between Melbourne and Adelaide and the oldest permanent white settlement in Victoria. Before the Henty family established a farm here in 1834 whalers and sealers had frequently sought refuge in the bay. Portland has preserved over 100 historic buildings (Steam Packet Hotel, Mac's Hotel, Customs House, Courthouse in Cliff Street). Now an important port and commercial centre, it also has attractions for visitors – good beaches for swimming and surfing and beautiful coastal and forest scenery.

Accommodation
Many motels and caravan/camping parks.

Features

Features of interest in the town, in addition to its historic buildings, are the Botanical Gardens (1857), the historical museum in the old Town Hall and a number of historic homesteads round the town (Maretimo, Burswood). Battery Hill offers good views and picnic facilities.

Surroundings

To the south of the town is Cape Nelson State Park, with an impressive stretch of coastal scenery and a lighthouse. At Cape Bridgewater, 21km/13 miles west, are a petrified forest and blowholes. There are pleasant walks to Discovery Bay and Cape Duquesne.

From Portland the Princes Highway runs inland to Mount Gambier in South Australia. The road along the coast to the west leads to the pretty little holiday resort of Nelson. On Lake Condah, 50km/30 miles east of Portland, an old mission station has been rebuilt.

★ Lower Glenelg National Park

Location; area

40km/25 miles west of Portland, along the Glenelg River, north of the road from Portland to Nelson; 27,300 hectares/67,400 acres.

Best time to visit

Spring (wild flowers) to autumn.

Access

South off Princes Highway, north off Portland–Nelson road.

Accommodation

In Mount Gambier (South Australia), Portland and Dartmoor.

Facilities

Camping ground; rest areas, picnic spots, unsurfaced tracks and walking trails.

Features

The principal attraction of this park is the 65km/40 mile long gorge on the Glenelg River, which is up to 50m/165ft deep. Boating, canoeing, wildlife viewing. The Princess Margaret Caves in the north-west of the park (open: daily) can be reached from Nelson or Mount Gambier.

Mount Richmond National Park

Location; area

32km/20 miles west of Portland; 1733 hectares/4281 acres.

Best time to visit

Spring (for wild flowers).

Access

From Portland–Nelson road, turning off at Gorae West.

Facilities

No accommodation in immediate vicinity. Picnic and barbecue areas.

Features

Mount Richmond, an extinct volcano, is covered with layers of sand, with typical coastal vegetation. A road runs up to the summit of the hill (227m/745ft), from which there are good views of the coastline of Discovery Bay. The timber lookout tower offers wider views of the coast and the interior.

★ Rutherglen J 7

Situation and characteristics

Rutherglen (pop. 2250), 270km/170 miles north-east of Melbourne on the Murray Valley Highway, in the centre of the most important wine-growing area in Victoria. In 1830 the first settlers came here from Tasmania, looking for grazing land for their sheep and cattle. The finding of gold in the 1850s brought a great influx of prospectors, bringing the population of the town to around 25,000. At the same time wine-growing was introduced. The wineries in Rutherglen prospered until phylloxera hit the vines at the turn of the century and the area growing wine was drastically reduced. Nowadays there are numerous wineries (wine tastings and sales) round Rutherglen, extending south up the Ovens valley to Milawa.

Rutherglen is a good base for day trips to Yarrawonga on Lake Mulwala, Beechworth, Bright and Mount Buffalo National Park (see entries).

Accommodation

Several hotels, motels, caravan/camping park.

St Arnaud H 7

Situation and characteristics

St Arnaud (pop. 3000), 250km/155 miles north-west of Melbourne on the Sunraysia Highway, lies in beautiful hill country. Founded in 1842 as a

	pastoral farming settlement, it was soon afterwards caught up in the gold rush. The gold-mines continued to be worked until 1926.
Accommodation	Hotels, motels, caravan/camping park.
Features	St Arnaud has preserved many 19th century buildings with rich wrought-iron decoration. There is good fishing in the Avoca River and Teddington Reservoir.
Surroundings	The Melville Caves, 40km/25 miles east of St Arnaud on the road to Inglewood, were the haunt of bushrangers in the 19th century.

Sale J 7

Situation and characteristics	Sale (pop. 14,000), the administrative and commercial centre of Gippsland, developed rapidly after drilling for oil in the Bass Strait began.
Accommodation	Several motels and caravan/camping parks.
Features	The main features of the town are its situation on Lake Guthridge, an attractive pedestrian zone and a number of handsome old buildings, notably the Criterion Hotel with its wrought-iron verandahs. In the tourist information centre there is an exhibition on the extraction of oil and natural gas.
Surroundings	To the south of Sale, near Lake Wellington, is a large gas processing plant. A reminder of Sale's one-time importance as a port is a canal linking it, by way of the Latrobe and Thomson Rivers, with Lake Wellington which was used by steamships until 1920. 5km/3 miles south of Sale is a 60m/200ft long swing bridge over the Latrobe River, built in 1883. 32km/20 miles south is Ninety Mile Beach (see Gippsland Lakes), and 25km/15½ miles away is Marlay Point, on the shores of Lake Wellington. 110km/70 miles north by way of Stratford and Maffra is the old gold-digging settlement of Dargo. 150km/95 miles north-west via Licola and Jamieson is Lake Eildon (see entry; the road may be closed in winter). There are also shorter trips north-westward to the hills round Maffra and Heyfield.

Shepparton · Mooroopna J 7

Situation and characteristics	180km/110 miles north of Melbourne is the double town of Shepparton/Mooroopna (pop. 48,600), the chief place in the Goulburn valley. It has developed out of a ferry station at the junction of the Broken River with the Goulburn into an agricultural and industrial centre with the largest fruit cannery in Australia. In the town centre is the Art Gallery (Australian painting and ceramics).
Accommodation	Many hotels, motels and caravan/camping parks in Shepparton; motels and caravan/camping parks in Mooroopna.
Surroundings	There are numerous wineries in the surrounding area.

★Snowy River National Park J 7

Location; area	135km/85 miles north of Lakes Entrance; 95,400 hectares/235,600 acres.
Best time to visit	Summer and autumn.
Access	On Princes Highway to Nowa Nowa, then via Buchan; or from Orbost via Bonang.
Facilities	Camping ground at McKillops Bridge; walking trails.
Features	Magnificent river scenery with deep gorges, eucalyptus forests on the Rodger River, a very varied vegetation pattern and a rich fauna. The park is popular with climbers and mountain walkers, and also with experienced bush walkers. Canoeing on Snowy River.

Farming country near Stawell, a region of endless space

Stawell H 7

Situation and characteristics

Stawell (pop. 6700), 123km/76 miles north-west of Ballarat on the Western Highway, is a good base for excursions to the northern Grampians and Grampian National Park (see entry). 24km/15 miles west is Halls Gap, another good base for the Grampians. Gold was found on Big Hill in the 1850s, bringing a great influx of prospectors to the town, then known as the Reefs.

Accommodation

Several motels and caravan/camping parks.

Features

Stawell has a number of historic buildings, notably St Matthew's Church. Caspar's World in Miniature displays small-scale models of famous buildings and dioramas depicting episodes in Australian history (open: daily 9am–5pm; admission charge).

Surroundings

3km/2 miles south-east are the granite crags known as the Sisters. 11km/7 miles south is Bunjil's Cave, with Aboriginal rock paintings.

★ Swan Hill H 7

Situation and characteristics

When Thomas Mitchell camped here, on the banks of the Murray, on his 1836 expedition he was kept awake all night by the black swans after which the town was later named. In the 19th century Swan Hill (pop. 9600), 340km/210 miles north-west of Melbourne, was an important river port. The town's great days are recalled in the Swan Hill Pioneer Settlement on the banks of the river, with the "Gem", the largest paddle-steamer on the Murray. Swan Hill is now a popular holiday centre with a mild, sunny climate, good fishing and facilities for water sports.

Accommodation

Many hotels, motels and caravan/camping parks.

Victorian Alps J 7

Access

The Victorian Alps are easily reached from the west and north (via Mansfield, Bright, Mount Beauty and Corryong), but from the south (Gippsland) there are only a few roads through the mountains (via Bonang, Buchan, Omeo or Dargo). The north–south connections are scenically very fine but are sometimes difficult for drivers (some sections unsurfaced; may be closed in winter).

Situation and characteristics

The Victorian Alps – gently rounded foothills of the Great Dividing Range, the counterparts to the Snowy Mountains in New South Wales – extend into the eastern and north-eastern outskirts of Melbourne. They are not high enough to have a permanent snow cover, but during the winter (June–October) they usually have reliable snow, offering good and sometimes excellent conditions for winter sports. In summer they are popular with climbers, riders and walkers; there are good trout streams and lakes with excellent facilities for water sports. In northern Victoria the Alps tail off in gentle hills, a region which is the largest producer of wine in the country.

Walking trail

The Alpine Walking Track, a beautiful long-distance route, runs from Mount Kosciusko in New South Wales to the old gold-mining settlement of Walhalla in Baw Baw National Park (see entry).

Wangaratta J 7

Situation and characteristics

230km/145 miles north-east of Melbourne, at the junction of the Ovens and Hume Highways, is the attractive town of Wangaratta (pop. 16,600), situated on the Ovens River in a fertile region producing wool, wheat, tobacco, hops and wine.

Accommodation

Many hotels, motels and caravan/camping parks.

Features

Within the town are large areas of parkland and lakes. Features of interest are the Aviation Museum, the homestead of Bontharambo (1858) and the grave of the bushranger Daniel Morgan.

Surroundings

To the south of the town are beautiful King Valley and the Paradise Falls. The Ovens Highway runs south-east via Bright to Mount Buffalo National Park. 16km/10 miles south is Glenrowan (pop. 220), where the bushranger and folk hero Ned Kelly was captured in 1880 (see Baedeker Special, p. 61). There is an exhibition in the visitor information centre on the story of the Kelly gang.

Wodonga

Situation and characteristics

66km/41 miles north-east of Wangaratta, on the borders of New South Wales, is Wodonga (pop. 27,500), which has almost joined up with Albury in the neighbouring state. Thanks to its situation on the Murray, close to Lake Hume, it is a popular holiday centre.

The region was explored in the 1820s by Hume and Hovell. Later in the century, before the formation of the Commonwealth of Australia, Wodonga had the largest cattle market on the continent, but after duties were imposed on cattle from New South Wales the market closed down.

Wodonga has numerous fine 19th-century buildings.

Accommodation

Many hotels, motels and caravan/camping parks.

Surroundings

Within easy reach are Beechworth, Rutherglen (see entries) and the mountain valleys of northern Victoria.

★ Warrnambool H 7

Situation and characteristics

Warrnambool (pop. 25,500) is a beautiful coastal town situated at the junction of the Great Ocean Road (see entry) and the Princes Highway,

◀ *In Wilsons Promontory National Park (see page 468)*

264km/164 miles south-west of Melbourne. It has numerous parks and gardens and excellent sport and entertainment facilities.

Accommodation: Many hotels, motels and caravan/camping parks.

Features: Warrnambool's principal tourist attraction is Flagstaff Hill Maritime Village, a 19th-century museum village with old harbour buildings and restored sailing ships. Here too can be seen relics of the clipper "Loch Ard", wrecked off the coast in 1878. By the lighthouse are cannon set up here in 1880, when there were fears of a Russian attack.

Surroundings: 14km/8½ miles west is Tower Hill, an extinct volcano with a crater lake. 54km/34 miles south-east is Port Campbell National Park (see entry).

★Port Fairy

Situation and characteristics: 29km/18 miles west of Warrnambool on the Princes Highway is the fishing town of Port Fairy (pop. 2500). One of the oldest towns in Victoria, it was founded in 1835, under the name of Belfast, on a site where there had been temporary whaling and sealing settlements, and thereafter developed into one of the largest ports in Australia. It has preserved over 50 historic old buildings, including the oldest pub in Australia, first licensed in 1844.

Accommodation: Several motels and caravan/camping parks.

Features: Features of particular interest are the Historical Centre in Bank Street; Battery Hill, an old fort at the mouth of the river; Captain Mills' House, which belonged to a whaling skipper; the Old Caledonian Inn; and the ANZ Bank.

With good beaches, good fishing and large caravan/camping parks, Port Fairy is a popular summer holiday resort. During the school holidays many families come here: at these times, therefore, it is advisable to book accommodation well in advance.

Griffiths Island, with a lighthouse and a colony of muttonbirds, is linked with the town by a causeway.

Welshpool · Port Welshpool J 7

Situation and characteristics: Welshpool (pop. 760), 190km/120 miles from Melbourne, is a small dairying town. 8km/5 miles from the town is Port Welshpool, with a deep-water harbour which is the home of a fishing fleet and a supply base for the oil and gas fields in the Bass Strait. Here too the large drilling rigs are assembled. There is now a catamaran ferry from Port Welshpool to Tasmania.

Accommodation: Motel, caravan/camping parks.

Features: The Maritime Museum in Port Welshpool has an interesting collection of material on the history of seafaring. There are also excellent facilities for water sports.

Surroundings: At Toora, just off the South Gippsland Highway, are the Agnes Falls. 60km/37 miles north of Welshpool is Tarra Bulga National Park (see Morwell).

★★Wilsons Promontory National Park J 7

Location; area: 160km/100 miles south of Melbourne and 30km/19 miles south of Foster; 49,000 hectares/121,000 acres.

Access: On South Gippsland Highway to Foster.

Facilities: The large caravan/camping park at Tidal River (no electricity connections, otherwise excellent facilities) is sometimes full during the main summer season; advance booking advisable. Water sports; walking trails.

Features: With its wild, rugged scenery and good beaches, Wilsons Promontory National Park is one of the best known National Parks in Australia. Occupying the whole of the peninsula which forms the most southerly point on the Australian continent, it consists of an ancient granite promontory with an extraordinary landscape of forest-covered hills, valleys with patches of woodland, swamps, salt marshes and long sand-dunes. There are bathing beaches with calm water and others more suitable for surfing. Parts of the peninsula (with sea-caves, curious rock formations and inlets) are accessible only from the sea. The rich fauna can already be seen from the excellent access road to Tidal River (grazing emus and kangaroos, friendly wombats). Innumerable brightly coloured lorikeets and seagulls congregate on the camping ground. The road ends at the Mount Oberon car park, beyond the township of Tidal River. On the southern tip of the promontory is a lighthouse of 1859.

Walking trails

In the Prom, as the park is familiarly known, there are more than 80km/50 miles of walking trails. The National Park office in Tidal River provides information about the various routes and detailed maps of the park.

Wonthaggi J 7

Situation and characteristics

The old mining town of Wonthaggi (pop. 6710), 140km/87 miles south-east of Melbourne on the Bass Highway, was formerly the main supplier of coal to the Victorian Railways. It began life as a tented town in 1909, when the government opened up the coal-mines. Coal continued to be worked here until 1968. Since then Wonthaggi has become the centre of a pastoral and dairy farming area.

Accommodation

Hotels, motel, caravan/camping park.

Features

The town's main feature of interest is the State Coal Mine Historic Reserve, with a mining museum (conducted tours).

Surroundings

Within easy reach, on a beautiful road, are good beaches at Inverloch, Walkerville and Tarwin Lower. Good surfing, swimming and fishing on Cape Paterson (Bunurong Marine Park).

Yackandandah, 27km/17 miles south, was formerly a supply centre for the goldfields in north-eastern Victoria which were discovered in 1852. It is now famed for its plantations of strawberries and has preserved a number of fine old buildings.

Inverloch

Situation and characteristics

Inverloch (pop. 2100) lies at the south end of the Bass Highway 13km/8 miles east of Wonthaggi on Anderson Inlet (South Gippsland). In summer it is a popular holiday resort with beautiful long beaches (surfing). Anderson Inlet has the most southerly mangrove swamps in Australia. It is named after Samuel Anderson, who settled here in 1835, soon after John Batman, founder of Melbourne, and his companions had established themselves in Port Phillip Bay. Thereafter Inverloch developed into an important coal-shipping port.

Accommodation

Hotel, motel, caravan/camping parks.

Features

Bird-watching at Townsend Bluff and Maher's Landing. There is a beautiful road from Inverloch to Cape Paterson.

Wyperfeld National Park H 7

Location; area

520km/325 miles north-west of Melbourne; 100,000 hectares/250,000 acres.

Best time to visit

Winter and spring; it is very hot in summer.

Access

Via Hopetoun or from Dimboola via Jeparit and Rainbow.

Facilities

Camping and bush camping (permit required); large picnic area with basic facilities, but limited supplies of water.

Features

Bush and heathland provide shelter for the wildlife of this arid region of mallee scrub vegetation. The lakes are usually dry but are sometimes filled by flood water from the Murray. Tall river red gums are relics of earlier wet periods.

Western Australia

General

Golden West
Area: 2,500,000sq.km./965,000sq. miles
Population: 1.662 million
Capital: Perth

Flag

Coat of Arms

Western Australia

Commonwealth of Australia

ACT = Australian Capital Territory

Symbolic animal: numbat, black swan, kangaroo

Symbolic plant: kangaroo paw

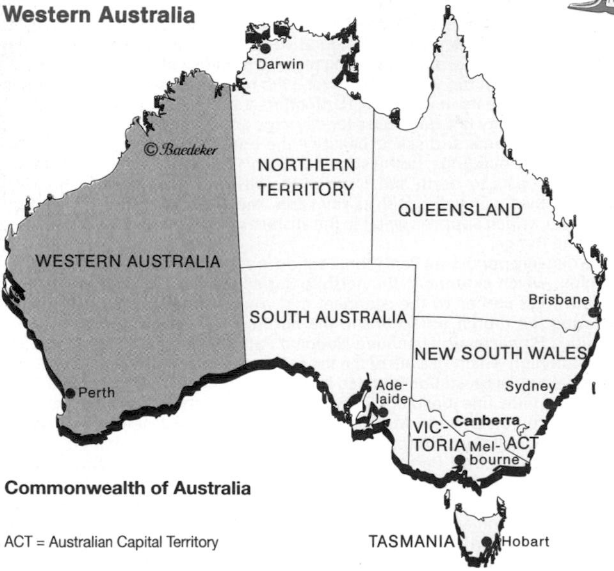

A land of extremes

Western Australia is a land of superlatives and extremes. With an area of 2.5 million sq.km/965,000sq.miles, it is the largest of the Australian states, occupying a third of the area of the continent, with a coastline of over 12,500km/7765 miles.

This immense area has a population of only 1.66 million (1989), or 9.5% of the total population of Australia, and great expanses of the state are almost uninhabited. Two-thirds of the population are concentrated in and around the state capital, Perth.

Western Australia owes its name as the Golden West to the prosperity created by the rich finds of gold in the "golden mile" between Kalgoorlie and Coolgardie in 1892.

Topography

The topography of Western Australia is full of contrasts, and it is famed for its very distinctive flora and fauna – the result of its isolation from the rest of the continent by a belt of desert. Visitors are attracted to Western Australia

◀ *Point Quobba on Australia's west coast*

not only by the fascinating scenery and the adventurous world of the outback but also by the profusion of wild flowers in thousands of different species which carpet the land in the south-west of the state in spring (August–November).

Most of Western Australia is on the western plateau or tableland, at an average altitude of 200–800m (650–2600ft), which rises gradually from the central Australian depression. On the west this plateau is bounded by the Darling Range round Perth, the Hamersley Range in the Pilbara and the Kimberley in the north. To the west of the geologically very ancient granite shield of the Western Australian tableland with its characteristic rounded hills and crags and its mostly infertile soil, are belts of dunes and narrow coastal plains, in which lie Perth and other towns. On the coasts facing the Indian Ocean and the cold and stormy Southern Ocean, with an alternation of rugged cliffs and sheltered beaches, are scattered fishing villages and holiday settlements.

Tourist areas

Perth

Perth, capital of Western Australia, has developed rapidly in recent years. It has, in the literal as well as the figurative sense, a higher profile, with old buildings of pioneering days giving place to high-rise office blocks. Beautifully situated on the wide Swan River, with resplendent modern buildings to demonstrate its new wealth, Perth offers a wide range of attractions for visitors. The city is a good base for day trips and excursions to many other places of interest and scenic beauty – the port of Fremantle with its well restored old buildings, Rottnest Island, 20km/12½ miles offshore, the dune-fringed coasts to north and south of the city with their popular holiday resorts, the Swan valley with its vineyards, the green Avon valley, Mundaring Weir, which supplies water to the eastern goldfields, and the hills of the Darling Range.

South West

The densely populated Perth conurbation is surrounded by the South West region, which extends in the north to Jurien Bay and in the south to the south-west corner of the continent and round it to just east of Albany. Among the tourist attractions in the northern part of the region are the curious Pinnacles in Nambung National Park – limestone columns up to 4m/13ft high which rise out of the flat sandy desert near the sea – and New Norcia, a mission station founded by Spanish Benedictines in the mid 19th century, with fine buildings in Spanish colonial style. To the south the coastal region beyond Mandurah (with Bunbury, Busselton, Margaret River and Augusta as the principal towns) and the hinterland, with the huge karri forests round Pemberton, offer great attractions to nature-lovers, water sports enthusiasts and walkers.

To the east of the South West region, along the south coast, is the Great Southern region centred on Albany on the Southern Ocean, with magnificent coastal scenery and the fascinating hills of the Stirling Range.

Wheat belt and goldfields

Farther north and east are the endless plains of the wheat belt. Where sufficient water is available (supplied by pipelines) wheat alternates with clover grazing for sheep. In the outer regions of the wheat belt, where rainfall is much lower and more irregular, the land must be left fallow after the harvest for one or more years. The chief town in this region of small agricultural townships and large isolated farms, with no particular attractions for tourists, is Merredin, where there is a wheat research institute.

To the east the wheat belt gives place to the goldfields. At Southern Cross, where the first gold was found in 1887, the barren desert-like plain with its saltpans, shimmering pink in the sun, begins. The old gold-mining towns (Kalgoorlie–Boulder, Leonora, Coolgardie) are among Western Australia's main tourist attractions.

To the south of Norseman, from which the Eyre Highway cuts straight across the Nullarbor desert for 1000km/620 miles into South Australia, is recently developed wheat country. Esperance, on the Southern Ocean, offers the attractions of its rocky coasts, beaches of white sand, offshore islands and coastal National Parks.

Mid West

The coastal area round Geraldton, north of Perth, attracts many visitors. Geraldton, the "Sun City", is a favourite holiday centre, particularly during

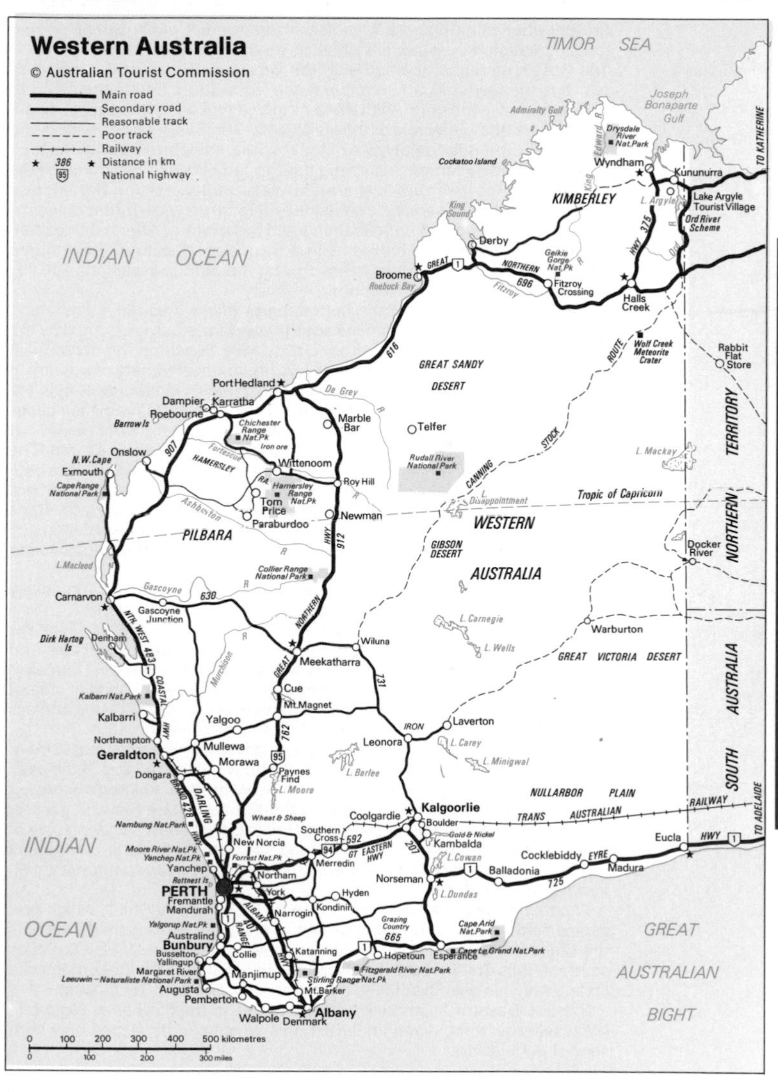

the cool, rainy winter of the south, and large new resort complexes have been developed in recent years. Off the coasts of the central Mid West region is a chain of islands and reefs. To the south of Geraldton is the old pioneer settlement of Greenough, which was soon abandoned because agriculture in this area proved unproductive but has now been well restored. To the north of Geraldton is Kalbarri National Park, with impressive cliffs and rock formations on the coast, scenic gorges on the Murchison River flanked by walls of multi-coloured sandstone and a sea of wild flowers after rain. Inland are endless monotonous expanses of grazing land, punctuated by windmills drawing up the necessary water supply.

North West

The Gascoyne region (named after the Gascoyne River, at the mouth of which is the town of Carnarvon) extends from Shark Bay in the south to Exmouth Gulf in the north, with a beautiful and much indented coast. Shark Bay, and indeed the whole of the continental shelf, is a paradise for game fishers. The friendly dolphins of Monkey Mia, which eat out of visitors' hands, are widely famed. Inland the flat-topped hills and red dunes of the Kennedy Range rise out of the featureless mulga scrub. The endless expanses of reddish sandy plains in the arid interior, with distant ranges of hills on the horizon, are both daunting and fascinating. After the uncertain winter rains, the steppe blossoms in a profusion of colour. This rugged country, traversed a hundred years ago by the gold prospectors, still lies beyond the bounds of civilisation.

Pilbara

The Pilbara region, one of the hottest parts of the Australian continent, extends from Exmouth Gulf in the south-west to the barrier formed by the Great Sandy Desert, reaching from Eighty Mile Beach on the north coast into the Northern Territory. This area has the greatest variety of scenery in Western Australia, with gently undulating plains covered with spinifex grass and much eroded rump mountains. The deep gorges with their oases of green in the valley bottoms, rock ponds and waterfalls were carved out over millions of years by rivers which have long since disappeared. The contrasts between the living green of the vegetation, the water and the bare tabular hills, their colours varying according to the minerals in the rock (iron oxides, copper, asbestos), in the hot, arid climate form the attractions of the two magnificent National Parks in the Pilbara region (Hamersley Range National Park, reached from Wittenoom, and Millstream-Chichester National Park, reached from Roebourne).

The region enjoyed an explosive boom in the 1960s when the immensely rich reserves of iron ore in the Pilbara region began to be worked.

Kimberley

The tropical north of Western Australia was long regarded as a land for tough characters and adventurers, determined gold prospectors and explorers. In this region there are only two seasons, not the usual four as in the south. The hot and sultry summer months (the "wet") with their violent showers of rain and abundantly flowing rivers are followed by the rainless winter (the "dry"), which is the best time to visit the north.

The landscape is patterned by ranges of ancient hills and depressions in the mighty river systems of the Fitzroy in the west and the Ord in the east. Characteristic features are the boab trees with their ability to store up water. The great tourist attractions of the Kimberley are the wild gorges. The rock walls of the 10km/6 mile long Geikie Gorge show a varying play of colour, depending on the position of the sun. Tunnel Creek and Windjana Gorge (a sacred place to the Aborigines) are now under statutory protection as National Parks.

Western Australia's gold rush began in 1885 in Halls Creek, which preserves some remains from that period. A few kilometres from the town is the China Wall, a quartz formation exposed by erosion. 130km/80 miles south of Halls Creek – best seen from the air – is the Wolfe Creek meteorite crater, which is over 850m/930yds in diameter and 50m/165ft deep.

Most of Western Australia's Aborigines live in the Kimberley region, in large self-governing Aboriginal Reserves which can be visited only with special permission.

Places of Interest from A to Z in Western Australia

★Albany C 6/7

Situation and characteristics

Albany (pop. 16,320), 400km/250 miles south-east of Perth on King George Sound, is the oldest European settlement in Western Australia, founded in 1826 as a penal colony. It is the chief town in the Great Southern region (see p. 472) and an important holiday and tourist centre the buildings erected by the early settlers give a remarkably English atmosphere.

Accommodation

Many hotels, motels and caravan/camping parks.

Features

The Albany Residency Museum (open: Mon.–Sat. 10am–5pm, Sun. 2–5pm; admission charge), housed in a mid-19th-century building, has an interesting collection of material on the history of seafaring. Among the exhibits is a replica of the brig "Amity", in which Major Lockyer brought the first convicts to Albany in 1826. The Old Gaol (1851) is also a museum (open: daily 10am–4.30pm; admission charge). The Patrick Taylor Cottage (*c.* 1832) in Duke Street, Albany's oldest building, contains a museum on the history of the town (open: daily 2–4.30pm; admission charge). The Old Farm on Strawberry Hill (open: daily 10am–noon; admission charge) was built in 1836.

Surroundings

Albany lies in a beautiful setting, with good bathing and fishing on beaches near the town. There are impressive views from Mount Clarence (on which is the restored Princess Royal Fortress of 1878) and Mount Melville. To the north of the town are the bizarrely shaped hills of Stirling Range National Park (see entry) and the granite crags of Porongurup National Park (see Mount Barker).

Warning

On the wild south coast there may be danger from sudden high waves.

★★Torndirrup National Park

Location; area

10km/6 miles south of Albany; 3900 hectares/9600 acres.

Best time to visit

Spring (wild flowers) and summer.

Access

From Albany on Frenchman Bay Road.

Facilities

No overnight accommodation; otherwise excellent facilities (information point, ranger station).

Features

The particular interest of Torndirrup National Park lies in the impressive rock formations on the coast. Being so easily accessible, it is one of the most popular National Parks in Australia, drawing a quarter of a million visitors every year.

Along the coast on the south side of King George Sound is a range of cliffs, gullies, blowholes, beaches and promontories. Tarred roads lead to certain particular features. There are magnificent views from the viewing terrace at the Gap, a 30m/100ft deep cleft in the rock. Among other highlights of the park are the Natural Bridge and the Blowholes. There is a good six-hour walk by way of Isthmus Hill to the Flinders Peninsula, Limestone Head and Bald Head.

Also within the park, in Frenchman Bay, is Albany Whaleworld, an interesting whaling museum (open: daily 9am–5pm; admission charge) housed in a former whaling station which closed down in 1978.

West Cape Howe National Park

Location; area

30km/19 miles west of Albany; 3500 hectares/8600 acres.

Best time to visit

Spring and summer.

Access

From South Coast Highway via Lower Denmark Road and Horton South Road.

Facilities	No camping grounds; bush camping permitted.
Features	West Cape Howe National Park takes in the coastal area round West Cape Howe between Forsyth Bluff, in Torbay, and Lowlands Beach. Inland from the impressive coastal scenery are areas of heath and marshland with many species of plants and birds. At the main entrance to the park, on Torbay Hill, are patches of karri forest. The granite and limestone cliffs at Shelley Beach attract many rock-climbing and hang-gliding enthusiasts. There is good fishing off Torbay Head, West Cape Howe and Bornholm Salmon Holes.
Roads	An easily negotiable unsurfaced road leads from the main entrance at Torbay Hill to Shelley Beach. The other tracks in the park are suitable only for four-wheel-drive vehicles.

Augusta C 6

Situation and characteristics	The fishing village of Augusta (pop. 460) lies 330km/205 miles south of Perth on Hardy Inlet, near Cape Leeuwin, the most south-westerly point in Australia. Founded in 1830, it is the third oldest settlement in Western Australia.
Accommodation	Hotel/motel, several caravan/camping parks.
Features	There is an interesting Historical Museum (Blackwood Avenue; open: Sat.–Thu.). In Turner Park are 150-year-old fig-trees.
Surroundings	The Jewel Cave, 8km/5 miles north of Augusta, has some of the largest stalactites and stalagmites in the world. From Cape Leeuwin, with a lighthouse of 1895 (open: Tue.–Sun. 9.30am–3.30pm), there are beautiful views of the coast.

Australind C 6

Situation and characteristics	180km/110 miles south of Perth and 11km/7 miles north of Bunbury (see entry) is Australind (pop. 3670), a popular holiday resort (water sports, fishing) on the Leschenault Estuary. It was the scene of a large-scale but eventually unsuccessful settlement scheme in 1841, when land on the south side of the estuary was allotted to 500 British settlers, but the scheme failed because of the poor quality of the soil.
Accommodation	Caravan/camping parks.
Features	St Nicholas's Church in Paris Road is the smallest church in the country; it was originally built in 1840 as a worker's cottage. Opposite the church is Henton Cottage (*c.* 1841).

Avon Valley National Park C 6

Location; area	80km/50 miles north-east of Perth; 4500 hectares/11,100 acres.
Best time to visit	Spring and autumn.
Access	From Midland on Morangup Road, Quarry Road and road to Toodyay (19km/12 miles gravel road).
Facilities	Bush camping; the park has excellent facilities (camping sites accessible by car, toilets, picnic areas).
Features	An easily accessible National Park with impressive scenery. From Bald Hill there is a good view of the winding Avon River. After the winter rains the Emu Spring Brook, a tributary of the Avon, tumbles over a 30m/100ft high waterfall. The country is very hilly, with dry eucalyptus forest and many grass-trees. The Avon and Brockman Rivers join here to form the Swan River, which flows through the neighbouring Walyunga National Park (see Perth). The river can easily be crossed in summer and autumn, but the ground is steep and rocky.
Walking trails	There are a number of attractive trails along the river.

Badgingarra National Park C 6

Location; area
295km/125 miles north of Perth; 13,100 hectares/32,400 acres.

Best time to visit
August and September (for the wild flowers).

Access
From Brand Highway; car parks on outskirts of park.

Facilities
Bush camping (permit required); no visitor facilities in park.

Features
The park is an area of gently undulating areas of sand covered with heath vegetation which flowers in spring. In the park is found the rare kangaroo paw plant along with relics of a wetter flora of the past.

Walking trails
There is good walking along the fire-breaks round and through the park; otherwise there are no tracks. There is a 2km/1¼ mile long wild flower trail.

Broome D 3

Situation and characteristics
Broome (pop. 5780) is a coastal town in the south of the Kimberley region, some 2400km/1500 miles north of Perth. Its wide sandy beaches, warm and sunny climate and turquoise-coloured sea have brought this old pearl-fishing town, founded in 1883, a tourist boom and a considerable increase in population. It now claims to be "top tourism town".

The site of the settlement was chosen by John Forrest, surveyor-general and first prime minister of Western Australia, and named after the then governor of the state, Frederick Broome. Around 1910 Broome, with some 400 pearl-fishing boats, was the pearl capital of the world, but the development of cultured and artificial pearls led to the decline of the industry. Now there are only very few people who earn their living by pearl-fishing.

Accommodation
Several motels and caravan/camping parks.

Features
The Historical Museum in the old Customs House in Saville Street (open: daily) tells the story of pearl-fishing. In the Japanese cemetery in Anne Street a tall column commemorates the Japanese pearl-fishers who lost their lives in a cyclone in 1908.

Other features of interest are the Broome Crocodile Park and the Pearl Coast Zoological Gardens, in which most species of Australian parrots are represented. 3km/2 miles from the town centre is Cable Beach, starting-point of the cable to Java which provided telegraphic communication with Europe.

Surroundings
At Gantheaume Point, 7km/4½ miles south of Broome, fossilised dinosaur footprints can be seen at low tide.

Broome is a good base for day trips and longer excursions in the Kimberley region.

Bunbury C 6

Situation and characteristics
The port town of Bunbury (pop. 23,000), 190km/120 miles south of Perth, has developed in recent years into a popular tourist centre. From here are shipped the agricultural produce of the fertile hinterland and the mineral sands which are worked in the surrounding area.

Accommodation
Several hotels, motels and caravan/camping parks.

Features
Among the town's fine old buildings are King Cottage (1867–80), a brick-built house at 77 Forrest Avenue which is now a museum (historical collections, Victorian furniture); the Leschenault Homestead on the Old Coast Road, an early settler's house built of clay bricks and timber, with a beautiful garden; the Rose Hotel (1865) at the corner of Victoria and Wellington Streets; and the Eagle Towers Restaurant at 192 Spencer Street, in a former farmhouse (1877) in the style of an Indian bungalow.

Surroundings

From Boulter's Lookout and Marlston Hill Lookout there are good views of the town and surrounding area. 11km/7 miles north of Bunbury is Australind (see entry), another popular holiday centre.

★★Bungle Bungle National Park E 3

Location; area

300km/185 miles south of Kununurra and 160km/100 miles north of Halls Creek; 210,000 hectares/520,000 acres, plus 110,000 hectares/270,000 acres in Conservation Reserve.

Best time to visit

Winter; summer best avoided because of high temperatures and heavy rain.

Access

From Great Northern Highway take Spring Creek Track via Mabel Downs Station (30km/19 miles) to Three Ways intersection in park (a difficult track for 4WD vehicles only; 55km/34 miles, taking 3–4 hours).

There are sightseeing flights from Halls Creek and Kununurra, usually including a visit to the Argyle diamond mine, 70km/43 miles north (day trip). Longer tours in four-wheel-drive vehicles are also on offer.

Facilities

Camping grounds at Bellburn Creek and Kurrajong; bush toilets, picnic areas. There is no refuse disposal service: visitors must take away their own rubbish. Open fires are prohibited, but camping stoves may be used. Visitors must take their own water and provisions.

Features

The National Park was established in 1987 to protect the curious rock formations looking like striped beehives, the flora and fauna, and remains of Aboriginal culture, some of them very old.

The beehive-like rock domes of the Bungle Bungle hills consist of soft sandstone with a coating of silicates and lichens which produces the stripes, orange or greyish-black in colour. The deep gorges and chasms have been carved out by the violent summer monsoon rains of the Kimberley region. Since the sandstone is very friable and liable to break away

Camel-riding, a popular tourist attraction

Weathered hills in Bungle Bungle National Park

when touched access to the rock formations is restricted to the dry riverbeds and climbing on them is prohibited.

The Bungle Bungle hills and surrounding area were for thousands of years the home of Aboriginal tribes, to whom the region was known as Purnululu. The remains of their culture (ceremonial sites, rock paintings, a burial-ground) are strictly protected. The Aborigines who still live in the area take part in the management of the National Park.

Walking trails

From the car park there is an easy walking trail to Cathedral Gorge 2.5km/1½ miles, 1 hour); the difficult trail continuing to Piccaninny Gorge is 18km/11 miles long and takes 8–10 hours.

Roads

Vehicles may drive only on the marked tracks; the trails into the gorges are for pedestrians only.

From the Three Ways intersection at the entrance to the park there are the following tracks. North to the Kurrajong camping ground (5km/3 miles, 15 minutes' drive) and on to the car park at the Echidna Chasm (15km/9 miles; altogether 1 hour); from car park to chasm 1.5km/1 mile on foot (45 minutes). South to the Bellburn Creek camping ground and ranger station (15km/9 miles, 30–45 minutes) and on to Piccaninny car park (15km/9 miles, 45 minutes), then on foot to Cathedral Gorge and Piccaninny Gorge.

Busselton C 6

Situation and characteristics

Busselton (pop. 7780), one of the oldest settlements in Western Australia, lies 240km/150 miles south of Perth on Geographe Bay. It was founded by the Bussell family at the mouth of the Vasse River in the 1830s. It is now the commercial centre of the surrounding agricultural area (dairy farming, beef cattle, wine-growing), a timber town (jarrah forests) and a popular holiday resort with a good surfing beach to the west of the town and sheltered inlets for swimmers.

Accommodation — Numerous hotels, motels and caravan/camping parks; farmhouse holidays.

Features — Two handsome old 19th century buildings are St Mary's Church in Peel Terrace (1844; fine timber roof) and Prospect Villa in Albert Street, a mid-century brick building, now a government office. Opposite, in Victoria Park, is "Ballarat", the oldest steam engine in Western Australia. On the banks of the river is an old butter factory with its original equipment. There is also a Film Museum.

Surroundings — Excursions in the surrounding area are best done in four-wheel-drive vehicles. There are many wineries in the Busselton/Margaret River area which can be visited (tasting and sale of wine).

★Leeuwin-Naturaliste National Park

Location; area — 37km/23 miles west of Busselton; 16,100 hectares/39,800 acres.

Best time to visit — Spring to autumn.

Access — Many side roads off Bussell Highway and Caves Road.

Accommodation — In Busselton, Margaret River and Augusta.

Facilities — Bush camping (permit required); walking trails, picnic areas, toilets, drinking water; fishing, water sports.

Features — This 120km/75 mile long coastal park on the south-west coast extends from Bunker Bay in the north to Augusta in the south. The landscape is very varied, with wide beaches, dunes, rocky coasts, tall cliffs, small islands and reefs. The edges of the cliffs are crumbling: care required. Inland, water has carved out interesting caves in the limestone.

★Cape Arid National Park D 6

Location; area — 125km/78 miles east of Esperance; 280,000 hectares/692,000 acres.

Best time to visit — Spring for wild flowers, summer for water sports and walking.

Access — From Esperance east on Fisheries Road. The last 19km/12 miles to the visitor centre at the west end of the park (Thomas River) are suitable for all vehicles. Some sections of road within the park are for four-wheel-drive vehicles only.

Facilities — Several camping grounds; no drinking water. Visitors must take their own water and camping stove (no wood for fires). The nearest place for supplies is Condingup (55km/34 miles west).

Features — Cape Arid National Park has a varied landscape of sandy plains and heathland, beautiful beaches and rocky promontories. Inland from the coast there are low granite hills, and in the northern part of the park is the Russell Range, with Mount Ragged (594m/1949ft) as its highest peak.

At the east end of the park is Nuytsland Nature Reserve, bordering the Nullarbor Plain. Within the park there are beaches extending for 20km/12½ miles from the mouth of the Thomas River in the west to Cape Arid, above which rises Mount Arid (356m/1168ft). From the hill there are good views of the varied coastal scenery and the innumerable little islands at the east end of the Recherche Archipelago. Granite promontories shelter the sandy beaches (good fishing and water sports in summer). Occasionally whales and seals can be observed.

Walking trails — There are a number of walking trails in the park, and there is also pleasant walking round the inlets and on the beaches.

Roads — The Thomas River at the west end of the park, Seal Creek and Jorndee Creek can be reached on a gravel road. Mount Ragged can be reached only in a four-wheel-drive vehicle.

★Cape Range National Park B 4

Location; area — 1260km/785 miles north of Perth; 50,000 hectares/125,000 acres.

Best time to visit — Winter (May–September), because of the more agreeable temperatures.

Access

From Learmonth–Exmouth road or via Bundegi, 30km/19 miles south of Exmouth. By air from Perth to Learmonth.

Facilities

Camping grounds; picnic and barbecue areas, boat slip. The only water point is north of Milyering. Visitor centre at Milyering, with an exhibition, video films and conducted visits.

Features

An extensive area of grazing land round Cape Range was declared a National Park in 1964. The park extends for 50km/30 miles along the coast between Coral Bay and Exmouth (see entries). An even larger area on the Coral Coast is included in Ningaloo Marine Park (see Coral Bay).

Inland from the rugged limestone cliffs of Cape Range are arid coastal plains and travelling dunes. Rainfall over the year is low, but occasional cyclones bring heavy rain and the depressions in the riverbeds fill up. Mandu Creek and Yardie Creek are good places for bird-watching. The main attractions of the park are the anglers' camps which have been set up on the track which runs the whole length of the park along the coast.

Walking trails

Long cross-country walks are not to be recommended, but there are safe short trails up to the crest of the hills, from which there are good views of the canyons to the east and Exmouth Gulf.

Roads

From the road which runs along the gulf from Coral Bay to Learmonth and Exmouth two tracks (Charles Knife Road and Shothole Canyon Road) run through the National Park to the Thomas Carter Lookout and the Lightfoot Trail, a circuit through the park.

★Carnarvon B 4

Situation and characteristics

Carnarvon (pop. 5850), the chief place in the North West, lies 900km/560 miles north of Perth at the mouth of the Gascoyne River (water sports, fishing), in an irrigated and intensively cultivated agricultural area.

Accommodation

Many hotels/motels and caravan/camping parks.

Church, Carnarvon

Features

The main street of the town, laid out over 100 years ago, is unusually wide so as to leave room for the camel trains then used for the transport of goods to turn. Features of interest are a modest church, the museum in the Civic Centre, the Jubilee Hall (1897) and the museum by the lighthouse.

Christmas Island National Park C 3

Location; area

In the Indian Ocean 800km/500 miles north-west of Port Hedland; 1600 hectares/4000 acres.

Best time to visit

Autumn, winter and spring.

Access

Weekly flights from Perth.

Features

Christmas Island National Park occupies roughly an eighth of the area of the island, which lies to the south of Java in the same latitude as Darwin. It was established to protect the seabirds and the rain forest and offers a fascinating opportunity to explore an unspoiled natural landscape.

There are walking trails and a track for four-wheel-drive vehicles.

★Coolgardie D 6

Situation and characteristis

After Arthur Bayley and William Ford found great quantities of gold nuggets here in 1892 Coolgardie grew from nothing into a town which by 1900 had a population of 15,000, with 23 hotels, six banks and several daily papers. But the superficial deposits of gold were quickly exhausted, the prospectors moved on and many of the town's buildings fell into ruin. Tourism has given a fresh lease of life to what had become an almost dead town. Coolgardie now has a population of just under 1000.

Coolgardie lies 560km/250 miles east of Perth in a semi-arid plain. In the early days of the settlement life in this hot, dry region was inconceivably hard, and many died of disease.

Accommodation

Hotel, several motels, caravan/camping park.

Features

There is an exhibition on the history of the goldfields in the largest building in the town, an imposing stone structure in Bayley Street erected by the government in 1898, with shady arcades, balconies and stucco decoration (open daily; tourist office).

Warden Finnerty's House (Lot 2048, off Hunt Street), built in 1895 as the residence of the mine inspector, with a wide overhanging roof and a verandah running round the house, has been restored by the National Trust. The handsome railway station (1896) is now a museum.

Coral Bay B 4

Situation and characteristics

The little fishing port of Coral Bay lies 150km/95 miles south of Exmouth and 220km/135 miles north of Carnarvon on the Ningaloo coral reef, a miniature edition of Queensland's Great Barrier Reef. Its long white beaches offer ideal conditions for swimming, snorkelling, fishing and boating.

Accommodation

Motel, caravan/camping parks.

Features

Off the coast are ample opportunities for scuba divers, with numerous wrecks round Point Cloates. There are the ruins of a Norwegian whaling station of 1915.

Ningaloo Reef Marine Park

Location

Ningaloo Reef Marine Park extends for some 260km/160 miles from Amherst Point, at the end of the coral reef, in the south to Bundegi on Exmouth Gulf in the north, and also takes in the coastal area of Cape Range National Park (see entry).

Best time to visit: Winter; in summer there is a danger of cyclones.

Access: From North West Coastal Highway, turning off at Minilya Roadhouse, then via Coral Bay or Exmouth. Flights from Perth to Learmonth.

Facilities: Caravan/camping parks in Coral Bay; no visitor facilities in the Marine Park itself. Supply centres are Exmouth and Coral Bay (water, information, boat slipways)

Features: The Marine Park was established in 1987 to protect the Coral Coast and the offshore coral reef. The fantastic coral formations attract divers and snorkellers from far and wide. If you are lucky you may see an Australian *dugong* (sea-cow) grazing on sea-grass. In March and April magnificent whale-sharks frolic in the sea here.

Cossack C 4

Situation and characteristics: Cossack (pop. under 200), the oldest port in the Pilbara region in the hot North West, lies some 1550km/965 miles north of Perth. In the second half of the 19th century it was the supply port for Roebourne (see entry), 12km/7½ miles inland. In those days it was a busy pearl-fishing centre, but its importance declined sharply when the inlet on which it lies silted up.

Accommodation: In Point Samson (see entry).

Features: Old buildings erected between 1869 and 1890 – solidly built of stone to resist cyclones – have been restored and now bear witness to the town's one-time prosperity. The finest is the old Courthouse in Main Street, an imposing two-storey building of 1885-86 which now houses a museum. Other notable buildings are the customs house, the police station and gaol, the post office and the telegraph office.

Cue C 5

Situation and characteristics: 640km/400 miles north-east of Perth, on the Great Northern Highway, is the little township of Cue (pop, 400), which in the 1890s was the commercial centre of the Murchison goldfields. After the end of the gold boom the town declined, and it is only in quite recent years that the population has begun to grow again. Evidence of the town's past prosperity is provided by the solid stone buildings which have survived. Other gold-digging towns in the area (e.g. Daydawn and Big Bell) are gradually being covered by sand.

Accommodation: Hotel, guesthouse, caravan/camping park.

Features: Among notable old buildings are the Masonic Hall in Dowley Street, a two-storey building with a corrugated-iron roof, a tower and handsome window frames, and the government buildings of 1897, with a post office and police station in typical goldfields style.

Dampier C 4

Situation and characteristics: Dampier (pop. 2200) was founded in 1965, the first of the iron ore terminals in the Pilbara region established by the mining companies to ship ore from the Tom Price and Paraburdoo fields. The deep-water harbour loads up to 400 million tons of ore a year. The salt lakes near the port yield 2.5 million tons of salt annually, and mounds of salt are a common feature of the landscape.

Accommodation: Motels, caravan/camping park.

Features: The ore-loading installations of the Hamersley Iron Company can be visited by appointment Mon.–Fri. at 9am and noon.

Surroundings: 10km/6 miles north-east is the North West Shelf Natural Gas Project, with a visitor centre (open: Mon.–Fri. 9am–4.30pm).

Feeding Monkey Mia's dolphins

Denham • Shark Bay B 5

Situation and characteristics

Denham (pop. 1120), 830km/515 miles north-west of Perth, is the most westerly town on the Australian continent and the most important place in Shark Bay. Of the beautiful beaches round the town perhaps the finest is Shell Beach, formed of innumerable tiny shells.

★Monkey Mia

The great tourist attraction in the area is the dolphins of Monkey Mia, which have become accustomed to being fed by visitors. More recently the times for feeding the dolphins have been restricted because the mother dolphins have been concerning themselves less and less with the welfare of their young ones and merely waiting for hours in the shallow water for fish to be thrown by the visitors.

Denmark C 6

Situation and characteristics

Denmark (pop. 1220), a coastal town in the Great Southern/Rainbow Coast region, lies 55km/34 miles west of Albany on the banks of the Denmark River and at the foot of Mount Shadforth (from which there are fine panoramic views). It is a town favoured by artists and craft workers. There are good facilities for water sports and fishing, and on the banks of the river are attractive parks and recreation areas.

Accommodation

Several hotels, motels and caravan/camping parks. Some cattle and sheep farms in the area have accommodation for guests.

Surroundings

Roads of great scenic beauty run through the Valley of Giants with its tall karri trees and to the National Parks along the coast such as the Walpole-Nornalup National Park (see entry) and William Bay National Park (14km/8½ miles west), which has excellent facilities for visitors (information kiosk at park entrance). Wine is grown in the surrounding area.

Derby D 3

Situation and characteristics

Derby (pop. 3260) lies in King Sound in the tropical far North West, 220km/135 miles east of Broome. The area was settled in the 1880s, after the explorer Alexander Forrest had reported favourably on the grazing land round the Fitzroy River. Later Derby became an important supply port for the gold prospectors of Halls Creek (see entry).

The town is a good base for expeditions to the remoter parts of the Kimberley region with their magnificent rivers and gorges. The roads and tracks in the area have been much improved, including the Gibb River Road, which runs north-east for 600km/375 miles from Derby to just short of Wyndham. During the "wet" the roads and tracks are frequently impassable.

Accommodation

Hotels, caravan/camping park.

Features

The museum in the Derby Cultural Centre in Clarendon Street (open daily) has collections of Aboriginal art and old photographs.

Surroundings

Characteristic features of the landscape round Derby are the bottle-shaped boab trees, which can store water in their stout trunks. 7km/4½ miles south of Derby is the Prison Tree, which is said to have served as a gaol in the early days of the settlements.

Esperance D 6

Situation and characteristics

Esperance (pop. 6440) was an important supply port for the Coolgardie and Kalgoorlie goldfields. The town takes its name from a French vessel, the "Espérance", which anchored here in 1792.

Accommodation

Several hotels, motels and caravan/camping parks.

Surroundings

Esperance itself has no outstanding features of interest but it lies in beautiful surroundings. Within easy reach are the Pink Lake (the colour of which is due to its high salt content) and attractive stretches of coast (for example Twilight Bay) with good viewpoints.

The offshore Recherche Archipelago consists of around 100 small islands (bird sanctuaries and nature reserves); the only accommodation for visitors is on Woody Island.

★Cape Le Grand National Park

Location; area

50km/31 miles south-east of Esperance; 31,000 hectares/77,000 acres.

Best time to visit

Spring and summer.

Access

From Esperance on Merivale Road or Fisheries Road.

Facilities

At Wharton, outside the west end of the park, is a privately run caravan park. Within the park there are camping grounds at Le Grand Beach and Lucky Bay. Camping stoves should be brought; there is practically no wood for fires.

Features

From the granite and gneiss hills in the park there are views of the wide sandy plains with banksia vegetation. Narrow inlets with good beaches attract water sports enthusiasts and anglers.

Walking trails

There is a 3km/2 mile long trail from the car park to Frenchman Peak (262m/860ft) on the gentle eastern slopes of the hill.

The Coastal Track (15km/9 miles) runs from Le Grand Beach in the west by way of Hellfire Bay to Rossiter Bay, with spectacular views of the coast. This walk can be split up into five sections: Le Grand Beach to Hellfire Bay (3 hours, strenuous); Hellfire Bay to Thistle Cove (2 hours, strenuous); Thistle Cove to Lucky Bay (¾ hour, easy); Heritage Trail, Thistle Cove (¾ hour, easy); Lucky Cove to Rossiter Bay (2½ hours, not too difficult). There are no roads in the eastern part of the park; there is a track to Dunn Rocks (fishing).

Old telegraph station, Eucla

Eucla H 6

Situation and characteristics

Eucla (pop. under 200), on the Eyre Highway only 12km/7½ miles west of the border with South Australia (1430km/890 miles east of Perth), is a tiny outpost of civilisation in the solitude of the Nullarbor Plain.

From the hill there are views of the ruins of the old telegraph repeater station and settlement, now almost covered by sand, and the Southern Ocean. Eucla lost its function with the opening of the transcontinental telephone line along the Indian–Pacific railway line, 100km/60 miles north. From the Eucla motel and roadhouse there is a rough track to the remains of the telegraph station.

Accommodation

Motel/roadhouse; camping ground.

Eucla National Park

Location; area
Best time to visit

Spring (wild flowers).
Immediately east of Eucla; 3340 hectares/8250 acres.

Access

The Eyre Highway runs along the northern boundary of the park; within the park there are unsurfaced tracks (4WD vehicles only).

Facilities

No accommodation or other facilities for visitors.

Features

Eucla National Park is mainly an area of mallee scrub and heath vegetation. From Wilson Bluff, a striking limestone crag, there are superb views of the rocky cliff-fringed coast of the Great Australian Bight and the Delisser Sandhills (which can also be seen from the Eyre Highway).

Exmouth B 4

Situation and characteristics

Exmouth (pop. 3510), 1275km/790 miles north of Perth on the North West Cape, is one of the youngest towns in Australia, founded in 1967 as a support town for the controversial US naval communications station. The station, now run jointly by the US and Australian Navies, is the principal employer in the area.

The town is well equipped to cater for visitors (water sports facilities, good fishing).

Accommodation

Motels, several caravan/camping parks.

Surroundings

Excursions to Cape Range National Park (see entry) and Ningaloo Marine Park (see Coral Bay).

★Fitzgerald River National Park — C/D 6

Location; area

185km/115 miles north-east of Albany; 243,000 hectares/600,000 acres.

Best time to visit

Spring (wild flowers) and summer (beach activities).

Access

Access is somewhat difficult. Mylies Beach and Barren Beach (picnic area) can be reached from Ravensthorpe (pop. 300), once the centre of a short-lived gold rush, or Hopetoun (pop. 270), a quiet holiday resort on the Southern Ocean. Gordon Inlet is reached on a road which branches off Highway 1 for Bremer Bay. All the roads in the park are suitable only for four-wheel-drive vehicles, and may be closed in winter.

Facilities

Bush camping is permitted; few visitor facilities and no drinking water except at Twin Bays.

Features

Fitzgerald River National Park takes in a highly impressive stretch of coastal landscape. The Fitzgerald River cuts through the Barren Range near Mid Mount Barren (457m/1499ft), which lies directly on the Southern Ocean, with sheer rock faces and steep scree slopes.

In the river valleys there are forests, and the sandy heathland is covered with mallee scrub and under this a dense growth of shrubs which produce a rich show of blossom in spring.

From the Barren Range there are magnificent views of the coast. There are bush trails to the best viewpoints.

Many stretches of coast are suitable for swimming and fishing.

Warning

Swimmers should beware of strong currents and sudden giant waves. The edges of the cliffs are crumbly.

Fitzroy Crossing — E 3

Situation and characteristics

Fitzroy Crossing (pop. 1030) lies 260km/160 miles south-east of Derby at the point where the Great Northern Highway crosses the Fitzroy River. It is a convenient stopover for visitors to Geikie Gorge National Park.

During the season there are boat trips on the river.

Accommodation

On the Great Northern Highway is the Fitzroy River Lodge, a resort complex. There are also a hotel, a motel and caravan/camping parks.

★Geikie Gorge National Park

Location; area

20km/12½ miles north of Fitzroy Crossing; 3100 hectares/7700 acres (mostly a wildlife sanctuary closed to the public).

Best time to visit

Winter and spring.

Access

Great Northern Highway, turn-off for Fitzroy Crossing.

Facilities

Outside the park there is a large new caravan/camping park with excellent facilities, replacing the old one. There are also a rest area, an information desk, toilets and drinking water.

Features

Geikie Gorge National Park is of great geological interest. During the Devonian period, 350 million years ago, a reef 1000km/620 miles long and 20km/12½ miles wide was formed in a huge tropical sea (Geikie Gorge is now more than 300km/185 miles from the sea). In the course of time the Fitzroy, a perennial river flowing throughout the year, cut deep into the

In Geikie Gorge National Park

limestone of the former reef, carving out an impressive gorge and exposing the various fossil-bearing strata and rock formations. Most of the gorge is closed to the public; only a narrow strip on the west bank of the river is accessible.

During the winter the Fitzroy is a quiet river, but in the tropical summer it turns into a raging torrent over 16m/50ft deep and the National Park is flooded to a depth of up to 7m/23ft.

The river is bordered by dense greenery, tropical paperbark trees, river red gums and freshwater mangroves. This area is the home of a rich and varied fauna, including flying foxes and numerous water birds. The freshwater crocodiles, often to be seen on sandbanks in the river, are unlikely to seek human prey. Two unexpected species are the sawfish and the sting ray, saltwater fish which have adapted to life in the Fitzroy River. The marksman fish literally shoots down its insect prey by projecting a stream of water at its target.

The best place for swimming is at the junction of the Margaret River with the Fitzroy, where there is usually a long sandbank. Swimming is not allowed on the east bank.

Flat-bottomed tourist boats sail through the gorge twice daily (9am and 2.30pm; duration 2 hours), offering excellent opportunities for observing wildlife.

Walking trail

There is a walking trail along the west bank of the river to the west rock face before the beginning of the gorge. The variegated strata in the walls of the gorge are reflected in the calm waters of the river; the effect is particularly fine at sunrise and sunset.

★ Fremantle C 6

Situation and characteristics

Fremantle (pop. 24,000), 20km/12½ miles south of Perth, is the port of the Western Australian capital. When James Stirling, landing here in 1829,

St John's Church, Fremantle

selected the site for the port he named it after Captain Charles Fremantle, who had recently taken possession of the west coast of "New Holland" in the name of King George IV. At the end of the 19th century the construction of an artificial harbour made Fremantle an important port shipping agricultural produce and minerals.

Accommodation

Several hotels and motels, caravan/camping park.

Sights in Fremantle

A series of handsome buildings with richly decorated façades, including banks, offices, hotels and the market hall, bear witness to the self-confidence and wealth of turn-of-the-century Fremantle. Although the town is now caught up into the Perth conurbation it has preserved the atmosphere of the 19th century port and many fine buildings.

Round House

The Round House in the High Street (1830–31; open: daily 10am–5pm) was Western Australia's first prison and oldest public building. This fortress-like structure on a limestone hill is not round but twelve-sided, with cells for the prisoners and a house for the governor.

Lionel Samson Warehouse

At 31–35 Cliff Street is the Lionel Samson Warehouse, dating from the turn of the century.

Maritime Museum

The Western Australia Maritime Museum (open: daily) at the south-west end of Cliff Street was built by convict labour in 1851 as a commissariat store and customs house; from 1879 to 1890 it was a post office, and thereafter was restored to serve its present purpose. Its main attraction is the remains of the Dutch East Indiaman "Batavia", which ran aground on the Abrolhos Islands in 1629. During the mutiny which followed the shipwreck 125 men were killed.

Fremantle Markets

At the corner of South Terrace and Henderson Street are the Fremantle Markets (1897), in which markets are still regularly held.

Warders' Quarters

Close by, in Henderson Street, are the Warders' Quarters (1850), a Georgian terrace of prison warders' houses.

Town Hall

The Italian-style Town Hall, at the corner of High Street and Adelaide Street, was designed by the well known Melbourne architects Grainger and D'Ebro and officially inaugurated in 1887, the year of Queen Victoria's Jubilee. The massive and richly decorated tower, with the black swan which is the emblem of Western Australia, has a steep mansard roof. On the ground floor of the Town Hall is the tourist office (open: Mon.-Fri. 9.30am-5pm; shorter hours on Sat. and Sun.).

St John's Church

Adjoining the Town Hall, in Adelaide Street, is the neo-Gothic St John's Church (Anglican), in light-coloured sandstone, built in 1879-82.

Film and Television Institute

Farther along Adelaide Street is the Film and Television Institute, housed in an old boys' school (*c.* 1855), also in light-coloured sandstone.

Fremantle Museum and Arts Centre

An impressive monument of the convict period is the former Lunatic Asylum in Finnerty Street, now occupied by the Fremantle Museum and Arts Centre. Built in the 1860s, it served a variety of purposes before being restored and converted into a museum (the sea and shipping, weapons, ceramics, etc.). In one wing of the buildings are artists' studios and craftsmen's workshops (exhibitions).

Bannister Street Craftshops

An old warehouse in Bannister Street is now occupied by artists and craftsmen (exhibitions of work for sale).

Proclamation Tree

At the corner of Adelaide and Edward Streets is the Proclamation Tree, a handsome Moreton Bay fig-tree planted in 1890 to commemorate the proclamation of Western Australia as an independent state.

Geraldton B 5

Situation and characteristics

Geraldton (pop. 22,000), 425km/265 miles north of Perth in Champion Bay, was founded in 1849 and named Gerald Town after the then governor of Western Australia, Charles Fitzgerald. It developed into the most important port and commercial centre in the Mid West (storage and shipment of wheat and mineral sands).

With its warm and sunny climate, Geraldton is a popular holiday resort well-equipped to cater for visitors. The beautiful coasts and offshore islands offer excellent conditions for water sports and fishing.

Accommodation

Many hotels, motels and caravan/camping parks.

Features

St Francis Xavier Cathedral (corner of Maitland and Cathedral Streets), in pseudo-Byzantine style, was built between 1916 and 1938. The Maritime Museum in Marine Terrace (open: daily) displays equipment from 17th-century Dutch vessels wrecked off the coast, particularly the "Batavia" and the "Zuytdorp". The Geraldton Region Museum is also in Marine Terrace and displays local artefacts. The Lighthouse Keeper's Cottage in Chapman Road houses the Geraldton Historical Society. Other notable buildings are the Cultural Trust Library, in the old railway station of 1897, and the lighthouse on Point Moore (Willcock Drive).

Geraldton is the base of a large lobster-fishing fleet and during the fishing season (mid-November to end of June), the landing and processing of the huge catches can be watched on Fisherman's Wharf.

Surroundings

25km/15½ miles south of Geraldton is Greenough (pop. under 200), founded in the mid-19th century but soon abandoned when wheat-farming in the "front flats" proved unproductive. Some of the old buildings have been restored and opened to the public by the National Trust.

40km/25 miles south of Greenough on the coast road is the fishing port of Dongara (pop. 1500), on a beautiful stretch of coast lined by rocks and reefs, with fine beaches, which draws many visitors.

Halls Creek E 3

Situation and characteristics

Far north in the Kimberley region, on the edge of the Great Sandy Desert, over 2800km/1740 miles from Perth, is Halls Creek (pop. 1180), where the first gold in Western Australia was found in 1885. Within two years 10,000 prospectors came to the diggings, but the numbers fell as the yield of gold declined. Halls Creek is now a cattle-farming centre.

Accommodation
Hotel, motel, caravan/camping parks.

Features
15km/9 miles east of the present town is Old Halls Creek, with only ruins as a reminder of past prosperity. In the cemetery are the graves of many prospectors and of James Darcey, whose death was one of the cases that led to the development of the Flying Doctor Service (see Baedeker Special, p. 275).

Surroundings
Near Halls Creek is the China Wall, a quartz formation which has been exposed by erosion.

Halls Creek is a good base for visits to Wolfe Creek National Park, 130km/80 miles south, and Bungle Bungle National Park, 200km/125 miles north-east on a road suitable for four-wheel-drive vehicles only (see entries).

Hamersley Range G 4

Situation and characteristics
The Hamersley Range, a rump formation of ancient rocks, lies in the rugged and inhospitable terrain of the Pilbara region, whose rich reserves of minerals make such an important contribution to the economy of Western Australia. Mount Meharry (1245m/4085ft), on the eastern edge of Hamersley Range National Park and a few kilometres west of the Great Northern Highway, is the highest peak in Western Australia. The north flank of the range rises steeply up from the arid plain but on the south side the hills fall gently away.

The little settlements of Tom Price, Paraburdoo, Wittenoom (see entry) and Newman (see entry) are good bases for expeditions into this bizarre world of deep gorges, steep rock faces, oasis-like lakes and waterfalls.

The most impressive part of the range, to the east of Tom Price, is now protected by its inclusion in Hamersley Range National Park (see below). Millstream-Chichester National Park (see entry), to the south of Roebourne (see entry), is like a tropical Garden of Eden in its hot and arid surroundings.

★★Hamersley Range National Park

Location; area
80km/50 miles east of Tom Price; 617,600 hectares/1,525,500 acres.

Best time to visit
Late autumn, winter and spring. In summer it is too hot; the winter nights are cold.

Access
South from Wittenboom on Great Northern Highway (new stretch of road). Good unmade tracks in park.

Facilities
There are camping grounds and picnic areas, reached on good gravel roads, near all the main gorges. Camping is permitted only on designated sites. There is a caravan park at Wittenoom.

Features
Hamersley Range National Park (Karijini National Park in the language of the Aborigines) is one of the largest National Parks in Western Australia. Over many millions of years erosion has created deep gorges, the most spectacular of which are in the north of the park. For the most part they run north-south, are up to 100m/330ft deep and have deep rock pools bordered by lush vegetation. In many areas there are tall termite hills and the pebble mounds of the pebblemound mouse.

A track running through the Yampire Gorge leads to most of the scenic highlights of the park. The Fortescue Falls, fed by a groundwater river, do not dry up even in the heat of summer; at the foot of the falls, in a charming setting, is a rock pool. The Kalamina Gorge, to the west of the Yampire Gorge, can be explored on foot. It contains a number of deep water-holes surrounded by dense vegetation. It is possible to drive through the Wittenoom Gorge (to the south of the little township of Wittenoom) for some 30km/20 miles, with beautiful picnic spots beside natural swimming pools under shady trees and steep rock walls. There are magnificent views from the Oxer Lookout at the junction of the Joffre, Hancock and Weano Gorges.

The Wave Rock, over 2000 million years old

To the west of the ranger station is the second highest peak in Western Australia, Mount Bruce (1235m/4052ft). It is possible to drive to the foot of the hill, which can be climbed in 2 hours.

Walking trails

From the Weano and Dales camping grounds there are paths into the Red Gorge. In walking in the gorges it is sometimes necessary to wade through water. Visitors contemplating a long walk in the remoter parts of the park must inform the ranger.

When bathing in the water-holes no soap should be used, since this would upset the biological balance.

Hyden C 6

Situation and characteristics

Hyden (pop. under 200) lies in semi-arid country on the eastern edge of the wheat belt, 350km/215 miles east of Perth. Its main claim to fame is the Wave Rock.

Surroundings

Bates Cave, to the north of Hyden, has Aboriginal rock paintings and handprints.

★★Wave Rock

Situation: 5km/3 miles north-east of Hyden.

Accommodation: Hotel, motel, caravan/camping parks.

Facilities: Visitor facilities in Hyden.

Features: The famous Wave Rock is an extraordinary rock formation of banded granite, 15m/50ft high, in the form of a wave about to break. Rainwater reacting with different chemical substances in the rock has created a series of vertical stripes in shades of grey, red and ochre.

◄ *One of the spectacular gorges in Hamersley Range National Park*

There are other curious granite outcrops in the surrounding area. An 80km/50 miles circuit from Hyden takes in three interesting examples, the Humps, the King Rocks and the Gnama Hole.

Kalbarri B 5

Situation and characteristics

Kalbarri (pop. 2900), 580km/360 miles north of Perth between Geraldton and Carnarvon, is a popular holiday resort which has been growing rapidly in recent years. Situated at the mouth of the winding Murchison River, with constant sunshine, the nearby Kalbarri National Park with its spectacular gorges, good fishing and an extraordinary abundance of wild flowers, the town is attracting increasing numbers of visitors.

Accommodation

Several hotels/motels and caravan/camping parks.

★Kalbarri National Park

Location; area

Just outside Kalbarri, 125km/78 miles north of Geraldton; 186,000 hectares/460,000 acres.

Best time to visit

Winter and spring.

Access

From the south, on Brand Highway; from the north, on North West Coastal Highway; or on road running through the park from Kalbarri. Flights from Perth and Geraldton; coach tours from Perth and Kalbarri.

Accommodation

In Kalbarri.

Facilities

No camping in park. Rest areas, toilets. No drinking water. Open fires prohibited.

Features

Kalbarri National Park takes in an area of magnificent country on both sides of the Murchison River with awe-inspiring gorges and wide sandy plains. The windings of the river have cut deep into the sandstone. There are tracks leading to a number of fine viewpoints with a prospect of sheer sandstone walls and gorges up to 150m/500ft deep (the Loop/Nature's Window, Z Bend, Hawk's Head Lookout, Ross Graham Lookout).

On the coast south of the estuary of the Murchison River (on which canoeing is possible after rain) and the town of Kalbarri are imposing cliffs, which also continue northward, outside the National Park, to Shark Bay. They demonstrate the effects of erosion (Red Bluff, Mushroom Rock, Rainbow Valley, Pot Alley Gorge, Eagle Gorge, Shell House, Island Rock, Natural Bridge). In summer it can be very hot, and long climbing trips should not be undertaken at this time of year. Rain falls mainly in winter (June/July), after which the wild flowers blossom.

Walking trails

From the car parks there are short signposted paths to various viewpoints and longer waymarked trails.

Roads

The roads within the park are unsurfaced tracks, but perfectly negotiable.

Warning

Swimmers should beware of sudden high waves on the cliff-fringed coast, and walkers should keep away from the edges of the cliffs, which tend to be crumbly.

★Kalgoorlie-Boulder D 6

Kalgoorlie

Although Western Australia's gold boom began in the far north, round Halls Creek (see entry), in 1885, the main goldfields lay in the barren regions 500–600km/300–375 miles east of Perth. It was here, round Kalgoorlie and Coolgardie (see entry), that the gold rush reached its peak. In this desolate waste the first nuggets of gold were found in 1893 by an Irishman named Paddy Hannan, and the rich deposits of gold in the famous Golden Mile were a magnet for many thousands of prospectors. In 1896 Kalgoorlie, which had grown from nothing, was declared a town, and in the following year it was linked with Perth by a new railway line. After the

Exchange Hotel, Kalgoorlie

superficial deposits were worked out the extraction of gold continued in deep mines. A further boost was given to Kalgoorlie's economy by the discovery of rich deposits of nickel at Kambalda, to the south of the town. This and the constant influx of visitors have prevented Kalgoorlie from becoming a ghost town: it now has a population of 25,450.

Boulder

Boulder, now amalgamated with Kalgoorlie, grew out of the encampment set up by gold prospectors near the mines. The main problem, the lack of water, was solved by the construction of a pipeline and pumping stations bringing supplies from Mundaring Weir, near Perth, at the beginning of the 20th century. This bold project was initiated and promoted by C. Y. O'Connor, who had previously built Fremantle's artificial harbour – though he committed suicide before the work was completed.

Kalgoorlie-Boulder is easily reached from Perth and also from Norseman, where the Eyre Highway ends after crossing the Nullarbor Plain.

A variety of excursions to the goldfields are on offer. An interesting possibility is a package covering a trip on the "Prospector" tourist train from East Perth Terminal combined with a coach tour to the gold-mines, most of them now abandoned.

From Kalgoorlie-Boulder there are day trips to various (partly abandoned) gold-mining towns within easy reach – Coolgardie (see entry), Broad Arrow, Ora Banda, Kookynie, Leonora (see entry), etc.

Accommodation

Hotels, motels, caravan/camping parks.

Sights in Kalgoorlie

Hannan Street

The handsome buildings, both public and private, in Hannan Street, the town's broad main street, bear witness to its prosperity and self-confidence at the turn of the century, when it had a population of 30,000 and over 90 hotels.

Warning!
The goldfields region is remote, wild, hot, dry and thinly populated. If you intend to leave the main road it is essential to take plenty of water, food and fuel. Before setting out you should check on the condition of the roads and tracks. There are information bureaux in Kalgoorlie and Boulder.

Particular care is required in abandoned mining areas. The workings are mostly unsafe and unfenced.

In Hannan Street, outside the Town Hall, is a bronze statue of Paddy Hannan, who found the first gold in the area. It was erected in 1929, on the 100th anniversary of the settlement of Western Australia.

Statue of Paddy Hannan

The imposing Town Hall of 1908, with its rich interior decoration, reflects the town's immense wealth during the gold boom, as do the Government Buildings of 1899, with the Post Office clock-tower.

Town Hall, Government Buildings

Of the 100 hotels and inns boasted by Kalgoorlie and Boulder in their heyday some fine examples have been preserved in Hannan Street – the York Hotel (1900; 259 Hannan Street), the Exchange Hotel (1900; 135 Hannan Street) and the Palace Hotel (1897; corner of Hannan and Maritana Streets), adjoining which are Palace Chambers (1900; with apartments above the offices on the ground floor). The former British Arms Hotel (1899), a narrow building at 22 Outridge Terrace, now houses the Golden Mile Museum (open daily), with a rich collection of material on gold-mining days and a valuable collection of old photographs of 1894.

Historic hotels and inns

At 272 Hannan Street are the old Market Halls of 1900.

Market Halls

Sights in Boulder

There are many fine Victorian buildings in Burt Street, notably the Town Hall, with a theatre and art gallery, the Courthouse, the Fire Station, the Masonic Temple, the Grand Hotel and the Court Hotel.

Town centre

Boulder's railway station (1897), at the end of the Golden Mile, now houses the Historical Society, which displays memorabilia of early goldfield life (open: daily). A steam train takes visitors round the goldfields.

Railway station

The Eastern Goldfields Heritage Trail covers a 4km/2½ mile walk in Hannan Street in Kalgoorlie and a 3km/2 mile walk around Boulder. The Museum of the Goldfields has an imposing entrance, and from the viewing platform visitors can see the city and mines. The interior exhibits concentrate on gold, and there is also a display of sandal wood items. In the Goldfields War Museum (Burt Street) is a display of machinery and photos pertaining to war.

Surroundings of Kalgoorlie-Boulder

With its spoil-heaps and rusting machinery, the Golden Mile between Kalgoorlie and Boulder does not look particularly inviting, but the Golden Mile Scenic Drive gives a good impression of the wild atmosphere of gold-digging days.

Golden Mile

The Hainault Tourist Mine to the south of Kalgoorlie (Boulder Block Road) was opened up by Harry Sutton in 1893, and until it was closed down in 1968 yielded great quantities of gold. The mine still operates as a tourist attraction. Visitors are taken down in a lift cage to a depth of 60m/200ft and see gold being won from the rock. They are also shown the power station and the original machinery (open: daily).

Hainault Tourist Mine

Karratha C 4

Karratha (pop. 10,000), 1560km/970 miles north of Perth on Nickel Bay, is the new "capital" of the Pilbara region, established in 1968 as part of the Hamersley Iron Project. The discovery of large deposits of natural gas off the coast, on the North West Shelf, gave the town a further boost. Its warm winter climate also attracts visitors, and it is a good base for sightseeing trips and safari tours.

Situation and characteristics

Several motels and caravan/camping parks.

Accommodation

Kojonup C 6

Situation and characteristics

The old mailcoach station of Kojonup (pop. 1100) lies 155km/95 miles north of Albany on the Albany Highway. The stone-built Old Barracks (*c.* 1845) in Sewell Road, in a style very typical of the early years of the colony, with massive walls and chimneys and tiny windows, were originally built to house troops for the protection of the population against Aboriginal attacks. Later they served successively as a church, a school and a dwelling-house; they are now a museum.

Accommodation

Hotels, caravan/camping park.

Kununurra E 3

Situation and characteristics

Kununurra (pop. 3140), the supply centre for the surrounding area (stock farming, irrigated arable farming, mining) and the headquarters of the Ord River Irrigation Project and the Lake Argyle Diamond Mine, lies on Lake Kununurra and the Ord River in the tropical north-east of the Kimberley region, a few kilometres west of the border of the Northern Territory.

Accommodation

Hotel, motels, several caravan/camping parks.

Features

There are fine views of the town and the surrounding irrigated plantations from Kelly's Knob Lookout. The Waringarri Aboriginal Arts Gallery displays Aboriginal arts and crafts.

Surroundings

3km/2 miles east of Kununurra is Hidden Valley National Park, a hilly region traversed by a number of valleys, with occasional boab trees and eucalyptuses growing on the stony slopes. During the dry winter and spring months the river is dry apart from a few pools and water-holes.

There are safari tours and sightseeing flights from Kununurra to Bungle Bungle National Park (see entry) and to the untouched wilderness of the Mitchell Plateau and the lower course of the Ord River. On Lake Argyle (see entry), a huge artificial lake 70km/44 miles south, is a tourist village (water sports, wildlife viewing, walking).

Kwinana C 6

Situation and characteristics

In spite of its nearness to holiday settlements and bathing beaches Kwinana (pop. 11,800), situated on the Cockburn Sound 76km/46 miles south of Perth, has been developing since 1951 into the main centre of Western Australia's heavy industry. The two principal plants are the oil refinery and Alcoa's alumina works; other industries are nickel smelting, chemicals and cement manufacture. Many of the firms can be visited by appointment. In the town's excellent natural harbour are huge loading installations, in particular a grain terminal.

The town is named after the "Kwinana", a ship which was driven ashore in a storm in 1922. The hull has been filled with cement and is used as a diving platform for swimmers.

Surroundings

Excursions to the nearby holiday resort of Rockingham (see entry); boat trips to the offshore islands.

★Lake Argyle E 3

Situation and characteristics

66km/41 miles upstream from Kununurra in the tropical north-east of the Kimberley region the Ord River has been dammed by the 67m/220ft high Top Dam to form Lake Argyle, which has an area of 740sq.km/285sq.miles and stores water for the irrigation of 70,000 hectares/173,000 acres of land during the dry season.

Plans for large-scale irrigation schemes were conceived after the Second World War, when great efforts were being made to develop and populate the empty tropical northern regions of Australia. The Top Dam, completed in 1971, created a reservoir nine times the size of Sydney Harbour, drowning whole valleys and turning the summits of hills into islands. The red slopes on the shores of the lake attract birds, lizards and marsupials.

From the outset the Ord River project had its critics, and the ambitious plans for large-scale irrigation and a resultant increase in prosperity and population were not realised. From the point of view of tourism, however, the project has been a great success.

Features

From Lake Argyle Tourist Village, near the main dam, there are cruises on the lake, angling expeditions and walking trails.

Argyle Downs Homestead, a stone house built by the Durack family in 1886 after a two-year trek driving their cattle from Queensland to the Kimberley region, was taken down before the construction of the dam and re-erected as a museum near the tourist village.

Lake Grace C 6

Situation and characteristics

250km/155 miles north of Albany is Lake Grace (pop. 620), a small agricultural centre in the southern wheat belt. It is named after the two lakes to the west of the town.

Accommodation

Hotel, motels, caravan/camping park.

Surroundings

70km/43 miles north-west is Hyden (see entry), with the famous Wave Rock. To the east of Lake Grace is Holland's Track, an old route to the goldfields to the north-east.

Lancelin C 6

Situation and characteristics

125km/78 miles north of Perth is the little fishing village of Lancelin (pop. 720), in Lancelin Bay, which is now a favourite holiday and recreation area. It lies at the end of the coast road from Perth. From here a track continues north to Nambung National Park (see entry), with the curious Pinnacles (enquire about the state of the road before setting out).

Accommodation

Hotel, several caravan/camping parks.

Features

Thanks to a natural breakwater Lancelin has a safe harbour. Good fishing waters; lobsters are caught on the reef. The waters round Lancelin are popular with sailing enthusiasts and wind-surfers, and the beaches are safe for children.

Laverton D 5

Situation and characteristics

360km/225 miles north-east of Kalgoorlie is Laverton (pop. 1140), an old gold-digging town which has been given a fresh lease of life by the Windarra nickel mine and modern gold-mining operations. From Mount Windarra there is a good view of the opencast nickel mine.

From Laverton there are tracks (part of the Gunbarrel Highway; sometimes in poor condition) through a desert-like landscape and Aboriginal territory (permit required) to Ayers Rock and Alice Springs (see entries) in the Northern Territory. The route is suitable only for four-wheel-drive vehicles, and proper preparation and equipment are essential: all supplies and water must be taken, since they are not available en route. The total distance from Perth via Kalgoorlie, Laverton, Warburton (filling station), Giles, Docker River (filling station) and Ayers Rock to Alice Springs is 2500km/1550 miles.

Accommodation

Hotel, caravan/camping parks.

Leonora D 5

Situation and characteristics

Leonora (pop. 1000), 240km/150 miles north of Kalgoorlie, and the neighbouring settlement of Gwalia flourished as gold-mining towns at the end of the 19th century, and the productive Sons of Gwalia gold-mine closed down only in 1963. The two towns were given a fresh lease of life when nickel and gold mines were opened up at Leinster, to the north, and Laverton to the east.

The country round Leonora is flat and covered with mulga scrub, but when rain falls in spring (August and early September) there is a profusion of wild flowers. Everywhere there are remains of old mining operations.

Accommodation

Several hotels, motel, caravan/camping parks.

Features

Leonora has preserved something of the atmosphere of a gold-mining town of around 1900. Its most notable buildings are the Gwalia State Hotel (1902–03), now the offices of the Western Mining Corporation, and the Gwalia Historical Gallery, in the former offices of the Sons of Gwalia Mine (1898), in which the future US President Hoover worked for a time (at the south end of Gwalia).

In Tower Street are the Grand Hotel, the Post Office and the White House Hotel.

Mandurah C 6

Situation and characteristics

80km/50 miles south of Perth, at the mouth of Peel Inlet, is Mandurah (pop. 18,020), an increasingly popular holiday resort and residential town for commuters to Perth. The sheltered waters of Peel Inlet, into which the rivers Harvey, Serpentine and Murray flow, and the more open waters of the Indian Ocean offer excellent conditions for sailing, boating, swimming and fishing. Early reservation is therefore advisable, particularly during the holiday season.

Accommodation

Many hotels, motels and caravan/camping parks.

Features

There are few remains of the difficult early days of the town. Hall's Cottage, in Leighton Road, was built in 1835 by one of the first settlers. Christ Church in Sholl Street has fine carving in the interior.

Surroundings

Excursions to the numerous artificial lakes in the foothills of the Darling Range, with picnic areas. House boats can be hired in Mandurah.

Manjimup C 6

Situation and characteristics

Manjimup (pop. 3960), 310km/195 miles south of Perth, is surrounded by fertile grazing and arable land (fruit, vegetables, dairy and beef cattle, sheep) and majestic karri and jarrah forests. Some of the trees, up to 70m/230ft high, are over 400 years old.

The first settlers came to the area in the mid 19th century, and since then the basis of the town's economy has been the timber industry. The hard wood of the jarrah tree makes excellent building timber, and the town soon began to export it.

Accommodation

Several hotels, motels and caravan/camping parks.

Features

The Timber Museum in Giblett Street traces the development of the timber industry from its earliest days to the modern wood-chip mills. Many of the mills can be visited.

Shannon National Park

Location; area

53km/33 miles south-east of Manjimup; 60,000 hectares/150,000 acres.

Best time to visit

Spring (for the blossom).

Access

On South Western Highway from Manjimup to the former timber-milling township of Shannon. Coach tours in Westrail buses.

Accommodation: Caravan/camping park.

Facilities: Fishing and swimming in river; canoeing downstream to Broke Inlet. Golf on the old Shannon golf course.

Features: Shannon River takes in the whole river system of the Shannon from its upper course to the north of the South Western Highway to its mouth in Broke Inlet. The hills in the northern and central areas of the park are covered with karri forest or mixed karri, jarrah and marri forest with dense undergrowth which blossoms in spring. On the peaty plains in the south of the park, which are sometimes under water, the vegetation consists mainly of jarrah and banksia.

Warning: In summer, when there is a high risk of bush fires, open fires are prohibited.

Walking trails: Round the old settlement of Shannon there are easy walking trails and a nature trail. There is also good bush walking in the fire breaks, which in some places are even suitable for wheelchairs. The principal walking trails are the Shannon Dam Trail (a 3.5km/2 mile circuit, part of which is suitable for wheelchairs), the Rocks Trail (a 5.5km/3½ mile circuit to the top of the hill, with granite crags) and the Bibbulmun Track (named after a local Aboriginal tribe), which begins near Walpole, in the south of the park, and runs for over 500km/310 miles, with some alternative routes, through the whole length of the great forests in the south-west of Western Australia to end at Kalamunda, south-east of Perth. The Department of Conservation and Land Management (CALM) can supply a description of this long-distance trail and a map showing other long walking trails in the park (information kiosk in centre of park).

Roads: There is a considerable network of tracks (some of them suitable only for 4WD vehicles) throughout the park.

Marble Bar C 4

Situation and characteristics: The old gold-digging town of Marble Bar (pop. 330) lies in the arid interior 200km/125 miles south-east of Port Hedland. Its name comes from the unique bar of red jasper which crosses the (usually dry) Coongan River 6km/4 miles from the little township and gleams when it is wet.

The new line of the Great Northern Highway no longer passes through Marble Bar but between Newman and Port Hedland (see entries) through the Pilbara region farther to the west. The old road, 480km/300 miles long, is now a mere track, leaving Marble Bar isolated.

Marble Bar holds the record as the hottest place in Australia. In 1923–24 the temperature was above 37.8°C/100°F on 160 successive days.

Accommodation: Hotel, motel, caravan/camping park.

Features: Marble Bar, now a typical outback settlement, preserves as a reminder of the gold boom its massive government buildings (1895), built of local stone, which are now occupied by the police station and mining offices.

Surroundings: The barren surrounding country, with its rugged hills and steep-sided gorges, is particularly impressive after rain, when the spinifex grass is covered with blossom.

Margaret River B/C 6

Situation and characteristics: Margaret River (pop. 1280) lies 280km/175 miles south of Perth and a few kilometres from the coast on the river from which it takes its name. It was founded in 1921 by a commune and has prospered as a wine-growing centre.

Accommodation: Hotel, several motels and caravan/camping parks.

Surroundings: The main attractions of the surrounding area are the beautiful coastal scenery and impressive caves (Mammoth Cave, 20km/12½ miles south-west, with fossil remains of prehistoric animals; Lake Cave). Near the mouth of the river is the Wallcliffe Homestead (1865), a two-storey house built by the Bussell family and still in the family. There are many wineries which can be visited (wine tasting and sale).

Meekatharra C 5

Situation and characteristics

Meekatharra (pop. 1000), on the Great Northern Highway half way between Perth and Port Hedland, was formerly of importance as the railhead for cattle which had been driven here from the tropical north; later it prospered from the working of copper, gold and other minerals; and it is now the administrative centre for the surrounding cattle and sheep farming area and a base of the Flying Doctor Service (see Baedeker Special, p. 275).

The airport, with a 2000m/2200yd long runway, is an alternative airport for Perth.

Accommodation

Hotels, motels, caravan/camping park.

Features

The Royal Mail Hotel (1899) recalls the heyday of the gold boom.

★Millstream-Chichester National Park C 4

Location; area

250km/155 miles south-west of Port Hedland; almost 200,000 hectares/500,000 acres.

Best time to visit

Between May and August, when day temperatures are only around 26°C/79°F (though the nights are very cool).

Access

From the Great Northern Highway take the road from Karratha to Wittenoom (180km/112 miles from Karratha, 190km/118 miles from Wittenoom. The tourist facilities at Snake Creek are on this gravel road. The nearest filling stations are some distance away (Roebourne 150km/93 miles, Wittenoom 180km/112 miles, Karratha 190km/118 miles, Tom Price 175km/109 miles).

Crossing Pool, in Millstream-Chichester National Park

Camping grounds (no caravans); bush toilets, campfire sites; water at ranger station. Facilities

The south-western part of the park is particularly beautiful. Perennial rivers and ponds (swimming, rowing) make this area a tropical oasis of lush vegetation. Many plants have adapted to the extreme conditions (e.g. Millstream palms, relics of an earlier, wetter climate). This river oasis is in striking contrast to the hot, arid and dusty country of the Pilbara region. Features

The north-eastern part of the park consists mainly of gentle hills covered with spinifex grass and river valleys which are mostly dry.

In the north-eastern part of the park there is a short trail from Snake Creek (camping ground) to the Snake Pool (rest area; swimming). Walking trails

In the south-western part of the park there are good walks along the river valleys. Before setting out on a long walk visitors should inform the ranger.

Swimmers should check the depth of the water (which may be dangerous for small children). No soap should be used when bathing. Rowing boats and canoes can be hired at Deep Reach and Crossing Pool; motorboats are prohibited.

Moore River National Park C 6

120km/75 miles north of Perth; 17,500 hectares/43,200 acres. Location; area

Spring (wild flowers). Best time to visit

The Brand Highway runs past the park to the north of Gingin. Access

Camping is not permitted. No drinking water. Facilities

This remote National Park, with no facilities for visitors, is typical of the sandy heathland on the northern coastal plains, with dunes and expanses of seasonal or permanent marshland. The fire breaks offer pleasant walking country. Features

Morawa C 5

This little town, the commercial centre of a wheat-growing area in the Mid West, lies 400km/250 miles north of Perth. It is famed for its brilliant show of wild flowers in spring. Situation and characteristics

Hotel, caravan/camping park. Accommodation

The features of most interest are Holy Cross Church, designed and built by the priest and architect John Hawes (along with other churches in and around Geraldton), and the little hermitage behind it, which looks like a miniature church. Features

★Mount Augustus National Park C 4

1000km/620 miles north of Perth, 460km/285 miles east of Carnarvon. Location

Via Carnarvon and Gascoyne Junction or via Meekatharra. Within the park there are good unmade roads. Access

Caravan/camping park at Mount Augustus Station Tourist Resort at the foot of Mount Augustus, via Meekatharra or Cobra Station (50km/31 miles west). Accommodation

None. Facilities

Mount Augustus National Park, established in 1989, lies in the outback of the Gascoyne region. Mount Augustus (1106m/3629ft) rises 717m/2350ft above the surrounding country. The ascent takes 6 hours; it is possible also to drive round it. Features

The rugged outback country is notable for its wildlife, undisturbed by man, and its Aboriginal rock paintings.

Organised tours are run by Westrail, and there are sightseeing flights from Carnarvon (Paggi's Aviation).

Mount Barker C 6

Situation and characteristics
Mount Barker (pop. 1390) lies 360km/225 miles south-east of Perth and 50km/31 miles north of Albany in the Great Southern region. The area was explored at an early stage and the first settlers established themselves here in the 1830s. In recent years the fruit plantations round the town have increasingly given place to vineyards, and the area has rapidly become one of the best known wine-growing regions in Western Australia.

Accommodation
Hotel, motels, caravan/camping parks.

Features
The old police station and gaol (1868) is now a museum. There are fine panoramic views from the summit of Mount Barker (television tower).

Surroundings
Mount Barker is a good base for visits to Porongurup National Park (see below) and Stirling Range National Park (see entry), 80km/50 miles north-east.

Porongurup National Park

Location; area
20km/12½ miles east of Mount Barker; 2572 hectares/6353 acres.

Best time to visit
Late spring and early summer (October–December), when the wild flowers are in brilliant bloom; autumn for walking.

Access
From Mount Barker or from Albany on Chester Pass Road (via Porongurup).

Accommodation
In Karribank and Karri Chalets.

Facilities
Camping is not permitted in the park. Picnic and barbecue areas, ranger station, toilets. At the Tree in the Park car park the road is suitable for wheelchairs.

Features
The Porongurup Range, a 12km/7½ mile long range of hills up to 670m/2200ft high consisting mainly of granite, brings down abundant rainfall, and as a result huge karri trees (formerly common throughout the south-west), flourish at the higher altitudes. Lower down are jarrah and marri forests and expanses of meadowland (wild flowers).

Walking trails
There are walking trails, starting from the picnic areas, to Millinup Pass (2 hours), Castle Rock (2 hours), Wansborough Walk (3 hours), Devil's Slide and Marmabup Rock (3 hours) and Hayward and Nancy Peak (4 hours). There are a number of crags which offer a challenge to climbers.

Warning
In summer there are large numbers of snakes.

Mount Magnet C 5

Situation and characteristics
The old gold-mining town of Mount Magnet (pop. 1000), 560km/350 miles north of Perth, has benefited in recent years from the reopening of some of the old mines (e.g. the Hill 50 Mine, previously worked from 1897 to 1915). Pastoral farming also makes a contribution to the local economy. The town lies at the intersection of the Great Northern Highway with the road running west via Mullewa to Geraldton.

Accommodation
Hotels, motel, caravan/camping park.

Features
To the north of the town, at the Granites (rest area), are Aboriginal rock drawings.

Mundaring C 6

Situation and characteristics
40km/25 miles north-east of Perth in the forest-covered hills of the Darling Range is the little town of Mundaring (pop. 950). Mundaring Weir, an artificial lake created in 1903, supplies water through a 500km/310 mile long pipeline with pumping stations to the eastern goldfields round Kalgoorlie (see entry).

Accommodation: Hotels, caravan/camping park.

Features: Pumping Station No. 1 on Mundaring Road, which closed down in 1955, now houses a museum commemorating C. Y. O'Connor, who devised the pipeline project.

Surroundings: The beautiful artificial lake, a few kilometres south of the town, attracts many visitors. To the west of the town is Forrest National Park (see Perth).

The Bibbulmun Track, a long-distance walking trail, runs for 500km/310 miles from Walpole, on the coast to Kalamunda, near Mundaring Weir.

★★Nambung National Park C 6

Location; area: 200km/125 miles north of Perth; 17,500 hectares/43,200 acres.

Best time to visit: Spring, for the wild flowers which bloom at the end of winter and for the mild climate.

Access: On Brand Highway, turning off at Cervantes. All the roads within the park are unsurfaced tracks. An alternative is the route through the interior by way of Badgingarra National Park (see entry) to Cervantes.

Accommodation: Motel and caravan/camping park in Cervantes.

Facilities: Camping is not permitted in the park; bush camping (with permit) at Hangover Bay. Swimming and bush walking (but it can be very hot in summer). There are picnic areas (with information for visitors) at the Pinnacles car park (reached on a 4WD track), Kangaroo Point and Hangover Bay.

There is no drinking water in the park. Open fires are prohibited. All supplies are available at Cervantes, 2km/1¼ miles north of the park entrance.

Features: The main tourist attraction in Nambung National Park, an expanse of sand and dunes with a 26km/16 mile coastline (good bathing and fishing), is the Pinnacles – thousands of limestone pillars, ranging in height between a few

The Pinnacles, Nambung National Park

centimetres and 4m/13ft, which rise out of a sandy plain almost devoid of vegetation. There has been some controversy over the origin of these bizarre rock pinnacles, but it seems established that a process of chemical change caused by wind and water erosion led to the softer sandstones being washed away, leaving the harder limestone exposed.

Narrogin C 6

Situation and characteristics

Narrogin (pop. 4270), 235km/145 miles south-east of Perth on the Great Southern Highway, grew out of a settlement on an overland route during the construction of the railway line from Albany to Beverley around 1880. It is now the commercial centre of an agricultural area (sheep, pigs, grain).

Accommodation

Hotels, motel, caravan/camping park.

Features

Features of interest are a war memorial of 1922 in the style of classical Greece and the Courthouse (1894), now a museum.

Surroundings

North-west of the town is Dryandra State Forest (area 22,000 hectares/55,000 acres; wandoo woodland, home of the numbat, once found throughout Western Australia; rare plants). Much of the Western Australian wheat belt looked like this before the clearance of the forests.

Newman C 4

Situation and characteristics

Thanks to large-scale irrigation and planting schemes Newman (pop. 5470), 440km/275 miles south-east of Port Hedland in the interior of the Pilbara region, is like a green oasis in the bare and arid surrounding area. Its economy is based on the mining of iron ore. The iron ore extracted on Mount Whaleback, the world's largest opencast iron mine, and on other sites in the area is transported on a private railway line to Port Hedland (422km/262 miles north) for shipment. With the asphalting of the Great Northern Highway and the improvement of its tourist facilities Newman has become a popular stopover on the road to the north. The new line of the road between Newman and Port Hedland (see entry) runs to the west of the old unsurfaced track via Nullagine and Marble Bar (see entry).

Accommodation

Motel, caravan/camping parks.

Features

In addition to the opencast iron mine on Mount Whaleback (conducted tours by appointment) the main attractions of Newman are the Radio Hill Lookout, the Ophthalmia Dam (good for swimming and picnics) and the town's mining and pastoral museum.

★New Norcia C 6

Situation and characteristics

The little town of New Norcia, 130km/80 miles north of Perth, would be of little account but for the foundation of a Benedictine mission in the secluded Moore Valley on the Great Northern Highway in 1846 by two Spanish Benedictines, Rosendo Salvado and José Serra, who named it after Norcia (Nursia) in Italy, birthplace of St Benedict. The purpose of the mission was to convert the Aborigines. The mission now houses a Catholic college for girls.

Accommodation

Hotel (in the former guesthouse of the monastery).

Features

The whole complex has the charm of Spanish colonial architecture. The extensive conventual buildings, with a beautiful inner courtyard, were completed in the early 20th century. The cathedral was built in 1860 and enlarged in 1907. The two richly decorated colleges date from 1908 and 1913.

The New Norcia Museum (formerly Garrido Hall) on the Great Northern Highway (open: daily 10am–4.30pm) has a remarkable collection of art treasures: pictures by Spanish and Italian old masters (including Titian and Raphael), jewellery, antiquities, valuable manuscripts and books.

Among other 19th century relics are a flour mill of 1879, an apiary and a blacksmith's forge.

★Norseman D 6

Situation and characteristics

Norseman (pop. 1900) lies 730km/455 miles east of Perth, half way between Kalgoorlie and Esperance. It is the last place of any size before the journey over the long and featureless Nullarbor Plain to South Australia.

The huge spoil heaps which dominate the townscape recall the great days of the early finds of gold. The gold-bearing quartz reef is still being mined, and there are frequently fossickers at work in the area; permits can be obtained from the Norseman tourist bureau.

Accommodation

Hotels, motels and caravan/camping parks.

Features

The Historical and Geological Museum, housed in the former School of Mines in Battery Road, has an interesting collection of mining equipment and old photographs. The little Post Office dates from 1896. In the main street is a monument to Norseman, a horse which, pawing the ground, brought to light a nugget of gold, thus sparking off the gold boom and giving the town its name. There are conducted tours of the opencast workings by previous appointment.

Surroundings

In the surrounding area are remains of old mine workings and numerous salt lakes.

★Northam C 6

Situation and characteristics

Northam, 100km/62 miles east of Perth on the Great Eastern Highway, is an old settlement in the fertile Avon valley, situated at the junction of the Avon and Mortlock. Founded in 1833, it developed slowly until gold was found to the east of the town and it was linked with the railway system.

Northam is now a regional centre, though the population is tending to decline. On the outskirts of the town is an army training camp.

Accommodation

Hotels, motel, caravan/camping park.

Features

Northam has a number of interesting old buildings: Byfield House (1902–04; 30 Gordon Street), a brick and stucco building with a tower, now occupied by an art gallery and restaurant; the Avon Valley Arts Centre, in an old girls' school (1878); the old Post Office (1892; corner of Hawes and Wellington Streets); the Courthouse (1896); the Italian-style Town Hall (1897–98); the Avon Bridge Hotel (1859); and the Grand Hotel (1904).

The old railway station (*c.* 1886) in Millington Street, now houses a museum. The oldest building in Northam is Morby Cottage (1836) in York Road, a typical colonial-style settler's house.

In Irishtown, a few kilometres north of Northam, is the Buckland Homestead, a two-storey house of 1874 with beautiful gardens.

Nullarbor · Eyre Highway D–F 6

The Eyre Highway, the only east–west road in the south of Australia, runs across the Nullarbor Plain between South and Western Australia. At Ceduna, in the north-west of the Eyre Peninsula (South Australia), it comes close to the Southern Ocean and then runs almost due west for almost 1000km/620 miles. Here begins the Nullarbor (from Latin *nullus arbor,* "no trees"), an endless bare and almost treeless expanse of salt scrub vegetation. Geologically the plain consists of sediment deposited on the bottom of an ancient sea which was later raised, to become a hot and arid desert landscape.

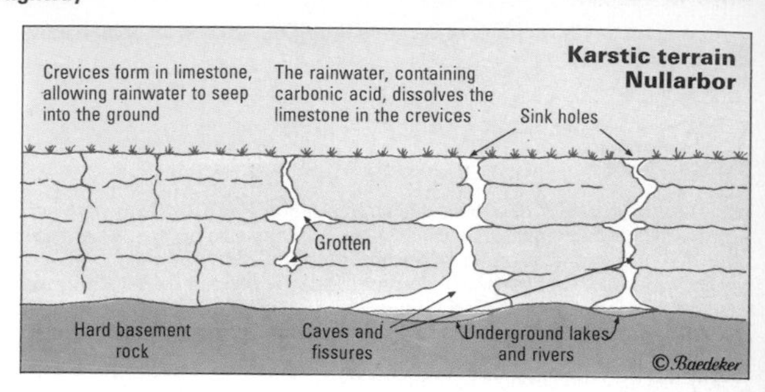

At various points along the course of the Eyre Highway side roads go off to the rocky coast on the stormy Southern Ocean, with its bizarrely shaped limestone cliffs, karstic formations and overhanging rock faces. Here, in addition to the magnificent views of coastal scenery, travellers between June and October may be lucky enough to observe whales passing on their annual migration.

In 1841 John Eyre became the first European to cross the Nullarbor along the Great Australian Bight from Adelaide to Albany. Nowadays, 150 years later, the long, monotonous journey holds no terrors for travellers on the well engineered highway with its filling stations, rest areas and overnight stopovers. The distance from the South Australian border to Norseman (see entry), the end of the Eyre Highway, is 725km/450 miles.

The transcontinental railway runs parallel to the Eyre Highway some 100km/60 miles north, cutting across the empty waste in a dead straight line for 480km/300 miles. A telegraph line was laid along the edge of the Nullarbor Plain in 1877 from Albany to Eucla, linked by way of Port Augusta with the overland telegraph line to Adelaide in the east and Darwin in the north.

Time zones

Travellers from west to east must put the clock forward twice by 45 minutes each time, changing to Western Australian Central Time at Caiguna and to South Australian Standard Time at the state border to the east of Eucla.

Stopovers on Eyre Highway

The first place with a rest area, filling station and overnight accommodation on the journey eastward from Norseman is Balladonia (190km/118 miles), amid the gentle hills of the Fraser Range. The stone fences built by the early settlers can still be seen. 28km/17 miles east of the motel and caravan park, beyond the ruins of the old telegraph station, is the Balladonia Station Homestead (1822). Beyond this is a 145km/90 mile stretch of dead straight road to Caiguna (182km/113 miles from Balladonia). Between Balladonia and Caiguna are rock pools – natural water-holes – at which the camel trains of the 1890s used to halt. At the roadhouse sightseeing flights over the coast are on offer. The next possible stopover is Cocklebiddy, 66km/41 miles from Caiguna. Behind the roadhouse can be seen the ruins of a mission station for the Aborigines. To the north-east are interesting caves; on the coast to the south is a bird-watching station. 91km/57 miles east of Cocklebiddy is Madura, founded in 1876, with the hills of the Hampton Tableland in the background. At Mundrabilla, 114km/71 miles east of Madura, is a bird sanctuary. 68km/42 miles east of Mundrabilla, only 12km/7½ miles short of the South Australian border, is Eucla (see entry), with a police station and a medical post. To the south of the settlement are the ruins of the old telegraph station, now almost completely buried by the sand dunes, which are a favourite subject with photographers. Beyond the state boundary the Eyre Highway continues for another 480km/300 miles over the Nullarbor.

Caiguna

On the South Australian section of the highway are five lookouts with impressive views of grand coastal scenery.

The cliff-fringed coast of the Nullarbor Plain

Onslow C 4

Situation and characteristics

Onslow (pop. 750), formerly an important pearl-fishing port, lies on the north-west coast 1300km/810 miles north of Perth. Gold was found here in 1890. After suffering frequent destruction in cyclones the settlement was moved in 1926 from the mouth of the Ashburton River to a new site 20km/12½ miles east. The ruins of the stone buildings (police station, gaol, hospital, post office) can still be seen on the original site. Onslow has now taken on a new role as supply centre for the offshore oilfields off Barrow Island.

Accommodation

Hotel, motel, caravan/camping park.

Features

Onslow has good fishing waters and a rich native fauna. In spring, after rain, the ground is carpeted with flowers.

Pemberton C 6

Situation and characteristics

Pemberton (pop. 800) lies 335km/210 miles south of Perth at the south-west corner of the continent, surrounded by forests of tall karri trees. The settlement was founded in 1861 by Edward Brockman, who set out to breed horses in this valley. He was soon followed by loggers, and timber-working has since been the mainstay of the town's economy.

Accommodation

Hotels, motels, caravan/camping park.

Features

On the edge of the karri forest is the Pioneer Museum (open: daily), with a display of forestry equipment and specimens of Australian woods; here too is the tourist centre.

In the main street is the Pemberton Sawmill, one of the largest in the world (conducted tours daily).

3km/2 miles south-east is the gigantic Gloucester Tree, a 64m/210ft high eucalyptus which serves as a fire lookout.

Surroundings

30km/19 miles south of Pemberton is Northcliffe (pop. 210). Visitors can travel there on the Timber Tramway, originally built to transport timber but now a tourist train running through magnificent scenery, with forests of majestic karri trees up to 1000 years old.

Pemberton National Park

Location; area

The park lies round Pemberton. It consists of the Beedelup National Park (area 1500 hectares/3700 acres), the Brockman National Park (250 hectares/620 acres) and the Warren National Park (1350 hectares/3330 acres).

Best time to visit

Spring to autumn.

Access

From Pemberton on road to Northcliffe; on foot, access from Bibbulmun Track.

Facilities

Bush camping in Warren National Park. The parks have excellent visitor facilities, particularly Warren N.P. (picnic and barbecue areas, toilets).

Features

The National Parks contain expanses of eucalyptus forest, particularly karri, jarrah and marri trees, with bushy undergrowth with a rich show of blossom. A striking feature is the 100m/330ft high Beedelup Falls. In summer there are good pools for swimming in the Warren River.

Walking trails

There is a wide choice of trails, from short walks to strenuous bush hikes. Information about the various routes can be obtained from CALM (Department of Conservation and Land Management) offices in Manjimup, Pemberton and Northcliffe.

D'Entrecasteaux National Park

Adjoining Pemberton National Park on the south is D'Entrecasteaux National Park, a lonely and magnificent stretch of coastal scenery (access – 4WD vehicles only – from Northcliffe).

★ ★Perth C 6

Capital of Western Australia

Situation and characteristics

Perhaps none of the other Australian capitals has changed so much in recent decades as Perth, capital of Western Australia. With a population of 1.4 million, it is now the third largest city in Australia, coming after Brisbane and just ahead of Adelaide. Bounded on the west by the Indian Ocean and on the east by the foothills of the Darling Range, the Perth conurbation, with an area at present of over 5400sq.km/2085sq.miles, is steadily expanding farther north and south. Its unique situation on the water is no doubt one reason why outdoor activities play such an important part in the city's way of life and why one in four households has either a sailing boat or a motorboat.

History and development

On May 2nd 1829 Captain Charles Fremantle hoisted the Union Jack at the mouth of the Swan River and took possession of the western part of "New Holland" in the name of the British Crown, with the object of anticipating any attempt by the French to settle in the area. The governor of the new colony, James Stirling, landed a few weeks later with the first free settlers. 20km/12½ miles inland they founded a settlement, which was named Perth in honour of the British colonial secretary George Murray, a native of the Scottish town of Perth. The first settlers were faced with considerable problems. The land was much less fertile than had been thought and labour was short. The position improved in 1850, when the first transports of convicts from Britain arrived, and between then and 1868 there were almost 10,000 of these compulsory immigrants, who made a major contribution to the survival of the colony on the Swan River.

With the discovery and extraction of huge deposits of minerals (iron ore,

Perth's Tudor-style London Court ▶

Australia Post
Lotto

bauxite, nickel, diamonds, natural gas) in remote and inhospitable areas Perth became in the 1960s the headquarters of the mining companies.

Heavy industry is concentrated round Kwinana (see entry), on the coast 32km/20 miles south of Perth (deep-water harbour on Cockburn Sound, oil refinery, aluminium and nickel production).

Perth now reflects the country's prosperity, with gleaming façades, new hotels and business centres and a wide range of entertainment and recreation facilities. Both the municipal authorities and private interests are concerned in attracting to the city international events, sporting tournaments and conferences.

The heat of summer is mitigated by the "Fremantle doctor", a wind which blows in from the sea regularly every afternoon. With the constant movement of air, fog and smog are unknown in Perth.

Transport

Perth has excellent communications by air, rail, road and water and is easily reached from any part of Australia.

Air

Perth's international airport lies 20km/12½ miles north-east of the city; the domestic terminal (flights within the state and inter-state flights) is on the west side, 10km/6¼ miles nearer the city. There are direct flights from London to Perth (the nearest destination in Australia for visitors from Europe).

Rail

The transcontinental rail services are very popular, and advance booking is advisable. The Indian Pacific service to Sydney (three times a week) and the Transaustralian to Adelaide (twice a week) depart from the Railway Terminal in East Perth (1.5km/1 mile from the city centre). The popular tourist train to Kalgoorlie, the "Prospector", and the Westrail overland buses also start from there. The City Station in Wellington Street, in the city centre, is the terminus of the suburban lines and of the tourist train to Bunbury, the "Australind".

City transport

Traffic in Perth flows smoothly on multi-lane highways, without the tailbacks and the hassle experienced in other large cities. Parking space is at a premium in the central area, but there is more room in the green belt on the shores of the Perth Water, between the city centre and the Swan River and there is a very large car-park on the south-western edge of the city between the Esplanade and the freeway.

Transperth, the city transport authority, runs a dense network of bus services in the city and suburbs, radiating from the city centre, the jetty on the river and the Central Bus Station in Wellington Street as well as the ferry jetty in Barrack Square.

Within the Free Transit Zone in the city centre travel on the "City Clipper" buses is free, in order to encourage people to use public transport rather than private cars. The buses run at 10 minute intervals on four routes (red, yellow, blue and green). They run from Kings Park in the west to the Causeway in the east and by way of the Bus Terminal and City Station in Wellington Street north to Northbridge and south to the Barrack Square. The City Clippers link the inner districts of East and West Perth and Northbridge with the city centre. Detailed information about routes and timetables can be obtained from Transperth information offices (City Arcade in Hay Street Mall and Central Bus Station, Wellington Street). Day and half-day trips in sightseeing buses usually start near the Central Bus Station.

Ferries

Transperth ferries operate from Barrack Square to South Perth, the Zoological Gardens, Rottnest Island and Fremantle.

Wine cruises

Also starting from Barrack Square are the popular "wine cruises" into the Swan Valley. Lunch or dinner can be taken on board, with the opportunity to taste the region's excellent wines.

Sport

Among the city's principal sports venues are the Ascot and Belmont racecourses on the south bank of the Swan River, to the east of the city centre, the WACA cricket ground near the Causeway and Queens Park and the Australian Football Oval in the Subiaco district. There are golf courses in many parts of the city. The Western Australian Tennis Open is staged

Bird's eye view of Perth

annually in Kings Park. The race for the Perth Cup is run on Ascot racecourse on New Year's Day. There are numerous sailing clubs in inlets on the Swan River and the coast of the Indian Ocean.

Events

The Perth Festival, which lasts three weeks in February/March, has a full programme of music, drama and other events.

Entertainments

Perth offers a wide choice of theatres, concert halls and other places of entertainment, in particular the Perth Concert Hall at the east end of St George's Terrace (1900 seats), the huge Entertainment Centre (8000 seats) to the west of the City Station and Bus Station, His Majesty's Theatre at the corner of King and Hay Streets with its turn-of-the-century splendour and the Playhouse Theatre at the corner of Hay and Pier Streets. The centre of the city's night life is the Northbridge district, in which – in addition to the Art Gallery of Western Australia, the Western Australian Museum and the State Library – there are many restaurants, night spots and discos.

A new night-time attraction is the Burswood Casino in the Rivervale district, east of the Swan River on Great Eastern Highway.

Accommodation

In spite of its isolation from the rest of Australia Perth, thanks to its economic boom, has numerous luxury hotels: indeed it claims to have more top-class hotels than Sydney. In the city centre the leading establishments are the Hyatt Regency and the Sheraton, both in Adelaide Terrace; outside the central area are the Radisson Observation City Hotel in Scarborough and the Burswood Resort Hotel. Among the more reasonably priced hotels in the city centre is Miss Maud, which has the advantage of a central situation (and a generous buffet breakfast).

Information

The best listings of events, entertainments and restaurants are in the Entertainment pages of the "Western Australian", the Perth newspaper with the largest circulation. Also useful is the free brochure "This Week in Perth and Fremantle". For information of all kinds there are the Perth tourist bureaux (Western Australian Tourist Centre on Wellington St., opposite City Railway Station).

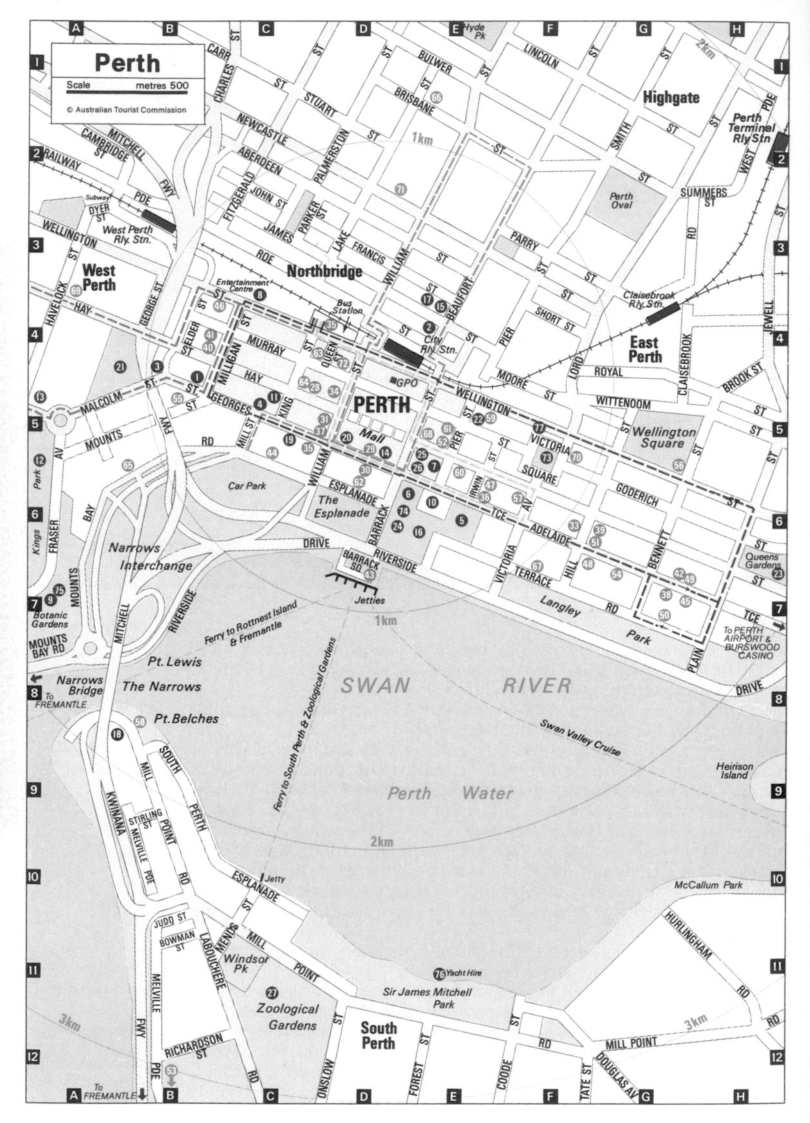

Sights in the City Centre

The central area of Perth is fairly compact, and the main sights can easily be seen on foot using high-level walkways and passages through buildings as

Places of Interest

Aboriginal Art Gallery	1	B5
Art Gallery of W.A.	2	E4
Barracks Archway	3	B4
The Cloisters	4	C5
Concert Hall	5	E6
Council House	6	E6
The Deanery	7	E6
Entertainment Centre	8	C4
Gov'nor Kennedy's Fountain	9	A7
Government House	10	E6
His Majesty's Theatre	11	C5
King's Park	12	A6
Legacy Lookout	13	A5
London Court	14	E5
Museum	15	E4
Old Courthouse	16	E6
Old Gaol	17	E4
Old Mill	18	A9
Old Perth Boy's School	19	C5
Palace Hotel	20	D5
Parliament House	21	A4
Post & Telecom Museum	22	F5
Queen's Gardens	23	H7
Royal Perth Hospital	77	F5
St. Marys RC Cathedral	73	G6
Stirling Gardens	74	E6
Suprome Court	24	E6
Town Hall	25	E5
Treasury Building	26	E6
War Memorial	75	A7
Yacht Hire	76	E12
Zoological Gardens	27	C12

Tourist Information

WA Tourist Centre	28	D5
N.T. Govt. Tourist Bureau	29	D5
Qld. Govt. Travel Centre	30	D6
Tasbureau	31	D5

Motoring Association

Royal Auto. Club of W.A.	33	G6

Post Office

G.P.O. Perth		E5

International Airline

Qantas Airways	34	D5

Metropolitan Transit Information (Buses, Trains & Ferries)

Transport Information Centres	35	D4&C5

Airlines – Domestic

Ansett/Ansett W.A.	36	F6
East-West/Skywest	37	D5
Australian Airlines	38	D6

Coach Terminals

Ansett Pioneer	36	F6
Deluxe Coachlines	38	D5
Greyhound	36	F6
Perth Central Bus Station	35	D5

Rental Cars

Avis	39	G6
Budget	40	B4
Hertz	41	B4
Thrifty	42	H7

Railways

Westrail Travel Centre		E4
City Station		E4
Perth Terminal		H2

Ferries/Cruises

Barrack Street Jetty	43	D7

Accommodation

Deluxe

Hilton International Perth	44	C5
Hyatt Regency Perth	45	H6
Orchard Hotel	46	B4
Perth International	47	E6
Sheraton Perth Hotel	48	F6

Premier

Perth Ambassador	49	G7
Perth Parkroyal Hotel	50	G7
Quality Langley Plaza	51	F6
Transit Inn Hotel	52	E5
Windsor Lodge	53	B12

Moderate

Airways Apartments	54	G7
Aust. Home-a-tel Mount St	55	B5
Bayley's Parkside Motel	56	G5
Chateau Commodore Perth	57	F6
Greetings Town Lodge	58	B8
Inn Town Hotel	59	E5
Kings Ambassador	60	E5
Miss Maud	61	E5
New Esplanade	62	D6
Quality Princes Hotel	63	D4
Town House	64	C5

Budget

Adelphi	65	B5
Backpackers Perth Inn	66	E1
City Waters	67	F7
Criterion	68	E5
CWA House	69	A4
Jewell House	70	F5
Perth City YHA Hostel	71	D2
Wentworth Plaza Hotel	72	D4

Shopping

Clipper Bus Routes:

RED Clipper

YELLOW Clipper

BLUE Clipper

GREEN Clipper

well as pedestrianised precincts. The best starting-point for a tour of the city is St George's Terrace, a wide street some 2km/1¼ miles long on which buildings up to 150 years old have survived in the shadow of skyscrapers reflecting the city's recent prosperity.

Tour of the city

The Perth Tram Company offers City Explorer Tours which take in all the city's major places of interest.

Treasury Building

★St George's Terrace

St George's Terrace runs parallel to the river. Set into the pavement (in 1979, on the 150th anniversary of the establishment of the colony) are 150 bronze tablets commemorating notable figures in 150 years of Western Australian history.

Barracks Archway

The Barracks Archway at the west end of St George's Terrace, a four-storey Tudor-style structure in mellow orange-red brick, is the only relic of the Pensioner Barracks of 1863, demolished to make way for the Mitchell Freeway.

Parliament House

Beyond the Barracks Archway is the modern Parliament House (conducted tours Mon.–Fri. when Parliament is not sitting).

The Cloisters

The Cloisters (200 St George's Terrace, opposite the end of Mill Street), a two-storey building of 1858 in dark-coloured brick, was originally Western Australia's first college of higher education. It is now part of the offices of the Mount Newman Mine Company.

Old Perth Boys' School

Opposite King Street, which runs north off St George's Terrace, is the Old Perth Boys' School (1853), a neo-Gothic building of ecclesiastical aspect which was taken over by the Technical College in 1898, and is now occupied by the National Trust (139 St George's Terrace; open: weekdays 10am–3pm).

Palace Hotel

At the intersection with William Street, on the north side of St George's Terrace, is the former Palace Hotel (1895), a grand hotel of gold boom days which is now, after thorough restoration, part of the Rural and Industries Bank of Western Australia.

Beyond the Palace Hotel is the bank's modern headquarters, Perth's newest high-rise block.

Beyond this, on the north side of St George's Terrace, is the Trinity Church Chapel (1877), an ornate church in Victorian style.

Trinity Church Chapel

One of the most photographed landmarks of Perth is the Tudor-style London Court (1937), a shopping arcade which runs between St George's Terrace and Hay Street Mall (pedestrian zone). The northern entrance is a clock-tower modelled on London's Big Ben; above the clock are four knights who come into action every quarter of an hour. At the southern entrance is a replica of the Gros Horloge, a 16th-century clock-tower in Rouen, with figures of St George and the dragon.

★★London Court

At the corner of St George's Terrace and Barrack Street is the neo-classical Treasury Building (1874) whose reddish sandstone contrasts with the white stucco ornament and projecting, balconies and pillared arcades. The top floor was added in 1905.

★Treasury Building

Round the corner from the Treasury Building, on the east side of Barrack Street, is the Town Hall (1867), with a large clock-tower and small turrets. Showing a remarkable mixture of forms and styles – part neo-Gothic, part French-style – it was the last building in Perth to be erected by convict labour, just before transportation ceased in 1868.

Town Hall

A tablet set into the pavement in Barrack Street marks the spot on which Perth was founded on August 12th 1829.

Opposite the Treasury Building, on the south side of St George's Terrace, are the attractive Stirling Gardens (with a botanic garden established in 1845) and Supreme Court Gardens.

Stirling Gardens, Supreme Court Gardens

In the gardens is the Old Court House (1836), the city's oldest surviving public building. A plain building fronted by a Doric colonnade, it was later used as a theatre, a church and a concert hall. It now belongs to the Law Society of Western Australia and contains a small museum.

Old Court House

Nearby is the Supreme Court of Western Australia. In front of it is Government House, built in 1859-64, which is still the residence of the governor of Western Australia. In ornate neo-Gothic style, it attracted a great deal of criticism because the cost of building far exceeded the original estimates. The gardens of Government House are open to the public on special occasions.

Supreme Court, Government House

Government House is flanked by two ultra-modern buildings, Perth Concert Hall and Council House, the new headquarters of the city authorities. The Concert Hall, a modern functional building with seating for 1900, is used for performances of opera, folk music and rock concerts. In the Music Shell in the Supreme Court gardens, free concerts are given in summer.

Perth Concert Hall, Council House

Opposite Government House is St George's Cathedral, a neo-Gothic brick building erected in 1887 to the design of the Sydney architect Edmund Blacket. Instead of the spire originally planned, the church has a crenellated clock-tower built in 1902 in memory of Queen Victoria, who had died in the previous year. At the corner of Pier Street and St George's Terrace is the Deanery (1859). St George's Terrace ends at the intersection with Victoria Avenue, from which Adelaide Terrace continues east to the Causeway spanning the Swan River by way of Heirisson Island to the Victoria Park district.

St George's Cathedral

Victoria Square

From the east end of St George's Terrace, Victoria Avenue runs north to Victoria Square, in the centre of which stands St Mary's Cathedral, an imposing neo-Gothic church consecrated in 1865. The site for the cathedral was included in the first plan of Perth in 1838.

St Mary's Cathedral

The Royal Perth Hospital is rather overshadowed by the tower block added to it after the Second World War. Within the hospital complex, on Wellington Street, is the original little Colonial Hospital of 1853, with roofed terraces.

Royal Perth Hospital

At the corner of Murray Street and Pier Street, housed in the former Government Printing Office (*c.* 1870), is the Post and Telecom Museum.

Post and Telecom Museum

Perth Mint, where coins are struck and gold bars cast, stands just to the south-east of Victoria Square on the corner of Hyt St. and Hill St. and is open to visitors.

Perth Mint

★Cultural Centre

Beyond the railway line in the Northbridge district, linked by a system of pedestrian bridges with the Forrest Place Complex, is Perth Cultural Centre, with the Art Gallery of Western Australia, the Alexander Library (State Library) and the Western Australian Museum.

Art Gallery of Western Australia

The Art Gallery of Western Australia, in James Street, has a collection of older and modern art, with a special section devoted to Australian art (particularly Hans Heysen and Frederick McCubbin and Aboriginal art) and periodic special exhibitions of international art (open: daily 10am–5pm).

Western Australian Museum

Among exhibits of particular interest in the Western Australian Museum in Francis Street are an 11-ton meteorite from Mundabilla, the skeleton of a blue whale, vintage cars, Aboriginal works of art and material illustrating their way of life and religion. Within the museum complex is the Old Gaol, built by convict labour in 1853, which continued in use as a prison and place of execution until 1888; it is now a museum of Australian culture and history (open: Mon.–Thu. 10.30am–5pm, Fri.–Sun. 1–5pm).

In the Markalinga Centre, near the west end (Barracks Archway) of St George's Terrace, is a gallery of Aboriginal art (exhibition and sale) run by Aboriginal Arts Australia.

General Post Office

In Forrest Place (named after the first prime minister of Western Australia, Sir John Forrest) is the massive General Post Office (1923).

★Kings Park

Like all Australian cities, Perth is well endowed with parks and gardens. The largest of these, immediately west of the city centre, is Kings Park, one of Australia's most beautiful parks. Laid out in 1872 and finely situated on a hill above the broad river and the city, it has an area of 404 hectares/

Art Gallery of Western Australia

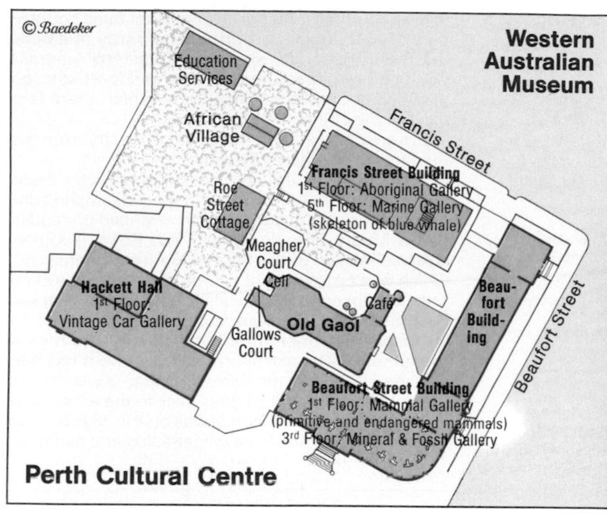
© Baedeker
Western Australian Museum
Education Services
African Village
Francis Street
Francis Street Building
1st Floor: Aboriginal Gallery
5th Floor: Marine Gallery
(skeleton of blue whale)
Roe Street Cottage
Meagher Court
Cell
Hackett Hall
1st Floor:
Vintage Car Gallery
Café
Old Gaol
Gallows Court
Beaufort Building
Beaufort Street
Beaufort Street Building
1st Floor: Mammal Gallery
(primitive and endangered mammals)
3rd Floor: Mineral & Fossil Gallery
Perth Cultural Centre

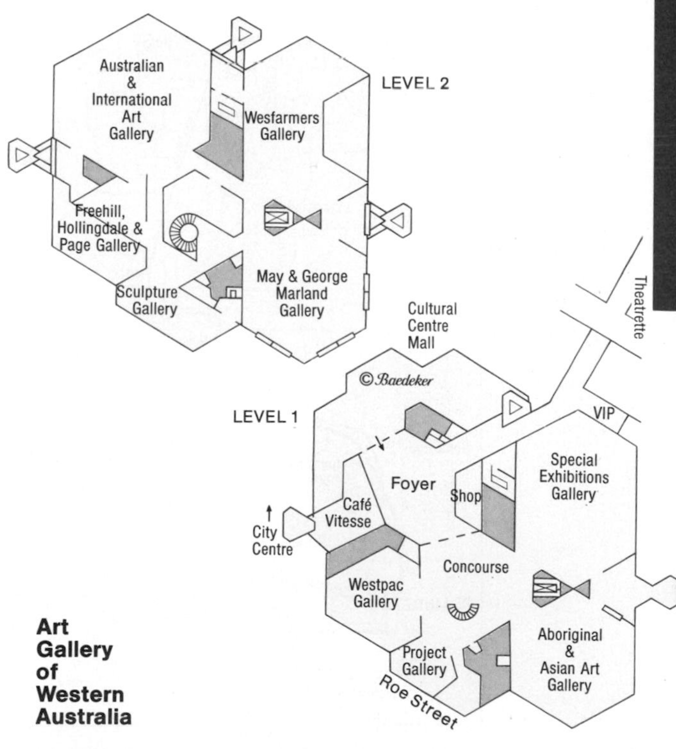
LEVEL 2
Australian & International Art Gallery
Wesfarmers Gallery
Freehill, Hollingdale & Page Gallery
Sculpture Gallery
May & George Marland Gallery
Cultural Centre Mall
Theatrette
© Baedeker
LEVEL 1
VIP
Foyer
Shop
Special Exhibitions Gallery
City Centre
Café Vitesse
Concourse
Westpac Gallery
Aboriginal & Asian Art Gallery
Project Gallery
Roe Street
Art Gallery of Western Australia

998 acres, consisting partly of natural bush country, with a brilliant display of wild flowers in spring, and partly of a botanic garden containing more than 1200 species of Western Australian plants. It is well equipped with roads, cycle tracks and footpaths, ponds, play areas and viewpoints on Mount Eliza, from which there is a superb panoramic view of the city and its environs.

★★Mount Eliza Lookout

War Memorial

There are particularly fine views of the city from the War Memorial and the Pioneer Women's Memorial.

Visitor Centre

On the car park on the city side of Mount Eliza a Visitor Centre will provide detailed information about Kings Park (open: daily 9.30am–3.30pm). Guided tours of the park are also arranged on request.

Kennedy's Fountain

Below Mount Eliza, in Mounts Bay Road, is Kennedy's Fountain, constructed in 1861 in the time of Governor Kennedy. It is fed by a spring which was an important source of water in the early days of the colony.

Old Observatory

The Old Observatory in Havelock Street (which runs north from Kings Park Road), a Victorian building, is now the headquarters of the National Trust, the authority responsible for the protection of national monuments. The astronomical equipment has been removed.

South Perth Mill Point

On the south side of the Narrows Bridge (Kwinana Freeway), on Mill Point, is an old flour mill which goes back to the earliest days of the settlement. This picturesque old windmill was built in 1835 by a miller named Shenton, but it was too far from the wheat-fields and had to close down in 1859. A

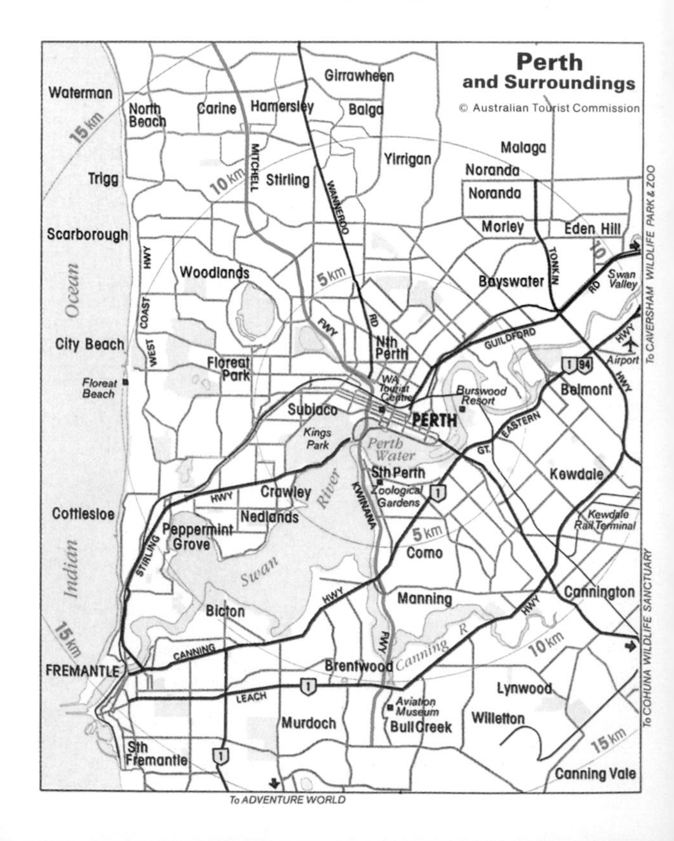

plan to demolish it to make way for road development aroused so much opposition from the people of Perth that this relic of pioneering days was preserved and now houses a museum.

★ Zoological Gardens

On the south bank of Perth Water (Swan River) stretches the interesting and, from an ecological point of view, exemplary Zoological Gardens (open: daily 10am–5pm) which are easily reached from the city by ferry

Of special interest is the Conservation Discovery centre with its nocturnal animal house (open: daily noon–3pm), in which rare nocturnal animals (wombats, kiwis, etc.) can be observed in natural conditions.

Beaches

In Perth water sports, swimming and surfing are not merely holiday activities but part of everyday life. The beaches on the Indian Ocean, in particular Cottesloe, Swanbourne (nude bathing beach), City, Scarborough and Trigg Island beaches, and the sheltered inlets on the winding Swan River (Crawley, Nedlands, Peppermint Grove, Mosman Bay, Como, Canning Bridge, Applecross, Point Walter) are all within easy reach by public transport.

Surroundings of Perth

In addition to the districts of South Perth (see above) and Crawley (bathing beach, University of Western Australia), the suburbs of Nedlands and Dalkeith are worth a visit for the sake of the handsome old houses (7km/4½ miles south-west of the city centre).

Subiaco

Subiaco is a charming suburb, 4km/2½ miles west of the city centre, which has preserved many turn-of-the-century buildings. It has good shops and some comfortable restaurants, a historical museum in City Hall Gardens and a Museum of Childhood (Victorian toys and playthings) in Hamersley Road.

Fremantle
Rottnest Island

See entries.

Hillary's Boat Harbour, ★★ Underwater World

Hillary's Boat Harbour lies 20km/12½ miles to the north-west, on the Indian Ocean. The main attraction is Underwater World (open: daily 9am–5pm). Visitors can walk through a glass underwater tunnel and observe over 200 species of native marine animals, including stingrays, mantas, dolphins and various kinds of shark. Diving with shark in the aquarium and playing with the dolphins are both unique experiences. There are also half-day trips (Sept.–Nov. Tue.–Sun.) to watch the whales when they are diving in the Ocean Ocean off the coast of Fremantle.

Wanneroo

Wanneroo, 40km/25 miles north of the city centre, is now within the Perth conurbation. In the surrounding area are a number of wineries open to visitors (tasting, sales), and some beautiful golf-courses.

★ Neerabup National Park

30–45km/19–28 miles north of Perth and easily reached from Wanneroo, this park covers an area of 1100 hectares/2700 acres. The best time to visit is July–Nov., when the wild flowers are in bloom. There are no visitor facilities, The fire-breaks serve as "walking trails".

Between Lakes Joondalup and Carabooda is a narrow strip of land with the varied vegetation of the sandy coastal plains north of Perth. To the south jarrah woodland predominates, to the south-east limestone from ancient dune systems with dense heath vegetation, while in the north are tall tuart gums.

★ Yanchep National Park

55km/34 miles north of Perth on the road from Wanneroo to Yanchep and covering an area of 2800 hectares/6900 acres, this park is best visited in the spring. There are good tourist facilities (restaurant, guesthouse, shops); a permit is required for bush-camping. Yanchep National Park is one of the favourite recreation areas of the people of Perth. It is a combination of natural vegetation with man-made lawns and gardens. There are also interesting stalactitic caves (conducted tours of Crystal cave, in the east of the park).

Atlantis Marine Park

Near Yanchep National Park (60km/38 miles north of Perth lies Atlantis Marine Park) with its "Two Rocks".

Whiteman Park

Lying 15km/9½ miles north-east of the city centre, Whiteman Park (open: daily 9am–5pm) is a popular recreation spot. Here cattle are herded "cowboy-fashion" and sheep-shearing competitions are held. Round flat bread and "billy tea" are served to the accompaniment of didgeridoo music.

Caversham Wildlife Park/Zoo

Situated outside the city to the south-east, Caversham Wildlife Park and Zoo attracts mainly young visitors.

Guildford

Guildford, situated on the Swan River nearly 20km/12½ miles north-east of the city, was one of the earliest settlements in the interior, founded about 1830. Notable features are St Matthew's Church (1873) in Stirling Square, Guildford Jail, the Courthouse (1866) and the Rose and Crown Inn (1840) in Swan St. The neighbouring Hall Collection is a large private collection of relics of 19th c. Western Australia. Woodbridge Mansion, a well-restored old house just off the Great Eastern Highway, recalls the town's heyday in the late 19th c. (open: Mon.–Sat. except Wed. 1–4pm, Sun. 1–5pm).

★Swan Valley

To the north-east of Perth the Swan River winds through some lovely countryside with many vineyards. This is the oldest wine-producing region in Western Australia and is best visited by ferry from Barrack Square Jetty. Visitors are welcome at no less than 21 wineries.

★Walyunga National Park

40km/25 miles north-east of Perth the early reaches of the Swan River flow through a wildly romantic gorge. The best way to get to this national park is on the Great Northern Highway via Midland. It is ideal for walking, climbing, bathing and white-water rafting.

Within the park was the largest Aboriginal settlement in the Perth area which was still occupied in the late 19th c. Archaeologists have found large numbers of tools and weapons made from stone and bone, and these indicate that the region was occupied by Aborigines for more than 6000 years.

Along the banks of the river runs the Walyunga Aboriginal Heritage Trail, with explanations of the way of life and mythology of the Aborigines. Other trails lead over mountains and through eucalyptus forests and charming valleys.

20km/12½ miles farther north lies Avon Valley National Park (see entry).

John Forrest National Park

25km/15½ miles east of Perth lies John Forrest National Park (1500 hectares/3710 acres) which is particularly attractive in the spring (Aug.–Oct.) Access is from the Great Eastern Highway. Bush camping requires a permit. There are picnic areas and an information centre.

The park, named after John Forrest, the first prime minister of Western Australia, extends along the Great Eastern Highway between Greenmount and Glen Forest. It was established as a nature reserve in 1895, making it the first National Park in Western Australia.

From the crest of the Darling Range there is a good view of Perth. There are short walking trails leading up to waterfalls and pools on Jane Brook. In line with ideas at the turn of the century, the park was laid out in the style of an English park, altering the original landscape and vegetation.

Kalamunda National Park

Kalamunda National Park, 375 hectares/925 acres in area, lies 30km/19 miles east of Perth. It, too, is best visited in late winter and spring (July–Oct.) for the wild flowers. Kalamunda National Park is mainly designed to protect the natural vegetation amid the expanding suburbs of Perth. Piesse Brook follows a winding course through the hilly country on the slopes of the Darling Range, with eucalyptus forest and heathland. There is a network of trails offering scope for long walks.

★Cohuna Koala Park

25km/15½ miles south-east of Perth, near Kelmscott, is Cohuna National Park (open: daily 10am–5pm), which particularly attracts families with children. It is home to Western Australia's largest colony of koalas, together with more than 300 kangaroos. Visitor facilities include a restaurant and picnic sites. Helicopter tours are also available. 10km/6 miles or so south of the city centre, near Bull

Aviation Museum

Creek, the Aviation Museum (open: daily 10.30am–4pm) displays vintage aircraft.

Adventure World

This adventure park is situated some 20km/12½ miles south of Perth.

Pinjarra C 6

Situation and characteristics

Pinjarra (pop. 1590) lies 85km/53 miles south of Perth on the banks of the Murray River, in an area which was settled at a very early stage. It is easily reached on the South Western Highway or on the scenic Old Coast Road from Fremantle. The large Alcoa alumina refinery is the mainstay of the town's economy and has brought an increase in population.

Accommodation

Hotel.

Features

Among buildings preserved from the early days of the settlement are two old settlers' houses (open: weekdays; occupied by a library and an art society) on the South Western Highway, Edenvale (*c.* 1888) and Liveringa (*c.* 1848), and St John's Church (Anglican; *c.* 1845), a plain brick building at the corner of the South Western Highway and Henry Street.

Surroundings

Within easy reach of Pinjarra are the hills of the Darling Range, a number of artificial lakes and the coast, only 20km/12½ miles away, with Mandurah (see entry), Peel Inlet and Yalgorup National Park (see entry).

An old-time steam train runs on the Hotham Valley Railway between Pinjarra and Dwellingup, a quiet little township 25km/15½ miles south-east of Pinjarra. The extensive jarrah forests in the area are popular with walkers.

5km/3 miles north of Pinjarra is Fairbridge Farm, established in 1912 as a home for orphan children from Britain. The farmer's son, Whitmore Fairbridge, born here in 1914, became a leading geologist, concerned particularly with the effects on the climate of glacial melt-water and variations in global sea level.

Point Samson C 4

Situation and characteristics

Point Samson (pop. under 200), 1580km/980 miles north of Perth, is a small fishing village on the north-west coast of the Pilbara region. It was established in 1910 as a port for Roebourne (see entry) and a replacement for the earlier port of Cossack (see entry), which silted up after a cyclone. The village is named after Michael Samson, who accompanied the first settler in the area, Walter Padbury, on a journey of exploration in 1863.

Point Samson is now a quiet little fishing port and, thanks to the beautiful coastal scenery, a favourite holiday place.

Accommodation Motel, caravan/camping park.
Features The sandy beaches are sheltered by a coral reef, which can be explored on foot at low tide. Good water sports and fishing.

Port Hedland C 4

Situation and characteristics

Port Hedland (pop. 11,200), on the north-west coast of the Pilbara region, is 1780km/1105 miles from Perth on the North West Coastal Highway, or 1700km/1055 miles by the inland route on the Great Northern Highway. The town lies on an island which is linked with the mainland by three causeways. In the 19th century, like most ports in the tropical North West, it was a pearl-fishing centre. Its great days began with the iron ore boom of the 1960s, and it is now the Australian port handling the greatest annual tonnage. Here iron ore from enormous opencast mines up to 420km/260 miles in the interior is loaded into huge ore carriers. Visitors are welcome to watch the loading of the ore in the harbour, and the buses of the Mount Newman Mining Company take them on a conducted tour (booking through tourist bureau).

The town's second most important industry is the production of salt by the evaporation of seawater in shallow salt-pans – an activity which has left its mark on the landscape.

Accommodation Several hotels, motels and caravan/camping parks.

Features Facing the harbour control tower is an exhibition illustrating the development of the port. In a limestone ridge opposite the main entrance to the Mount Newman Mining Company are Aboriginal rock drawings.

There is good fishing round the harbour. Boats can be hired. There is a remarkably rich bird life in the area.

Rockingham C 6

Situation and characteristics

Rockingham (pop. 30,640) lies at the south end of the Cockburn Sound 45km/28 miles south of Perth, immediately adjoining the industrial town of Kwinana (see entry). The town is named after a ship which ran aground here in the early days of the settlement.

Once an important port, Rockingham was sidelined by the development of Fremantle in 1897. Thanks to its beautiful sheltered beaches and its convenient proximity to Perth, Rockingham has enjoyed a rapid development as a holiday and commuter town in spite of the neighbouring industrial installations.

Accommodation Several hotels, motel, caravan/camping parks.

Surroundings There are rewarding boat trips to the offshore islands (particularly Penguin Island with its colony of penguins). From Point Peron there are magnificent panoramic views of the ocean, the islands, the coast and the town. Shoalwater Bay Islands National Park extends south from Garden Island to Warnbro Beach (Becher Point).

50km/31 miles east in the direction of the Darling Range are Serpentine Dam and the Serpentine Falls (see Serpentine National Park).

★Roebourne C 4

Situation and characteristics

Roebourne (pop. 1690), the oldest settlement on the north-west coast, was founded in 1864 as the administrative centre of the whole territory north of the Murchison River and was named after John S. Roe, first surveyor-general of Western Australia. It developed into the centre for the mining and pastoral farming industries of the Pilbara region and was linked in 1887 by a horse-drawn tramway with the port of Cossack (see entry), 12km/7½ miles away, and later with Point Samson (see entry).

Accommodation

Hotel, caravan/camping parks.

Features

The iron ore boom in the Pilbara region brought great changes to Roebourne, but the town has preserved a number of old 19th century stone buildings, including the post office (1887), the courthouse (1886) and the police station and gaol (1886), at the corner of Carnarvon Terrace and Queen Street (the gaol can be visited). The Union Bank (1889) in Roe Street now houses the district library and local government offices. Of the town's old hotels only the Victoria Hotel survives. Holy Trinity Church, at the corner of Fisher Drive and Withnell Street, dates from 1894.

Surroundings

The Emma Withnell Heritage Trail runs from the local government offices in Rose Street to Cossack, Wickham and Point Samson (see entries).

40km/25 miles east on the Port Hedland road are the Mount Fisher Rocks, with Aboriginal rock drawings.

Rottnest Island C 6

Situation and characteristics

Rottnest Island, a low-lying island 19km/12 miles off the coast opposite Perth, is a nature reserve (no cars permitted) which attracts many visitors and holidaymakers. It is 11km/7 miles long from east to west and up to 5km/3 miles across. It has a varied coastline with numerous inlets and bathing beaches and many inland lakes.

History

The Dutch navigator Willem de Vlamingh landed on the island in 1696 and pronounced it an earthly paradise. Taking the little rock wallabies or quokkas for rats, he named the island Rottnest ("rats' nest"). From 1838 to 1903 it was used as a place of banishment for rebellious Aborigines.

Access

Boats from Perth (Barrack Street jetty) via Fremantle; flights in light aircraft from Perth.

Features

The Quad, an octagonal limestone building with a large inner courtyard, was built in 1864 as a prison. The cells, after renovation, are now holiday apartments. The nearby Rottnest Hotel, also built in 1864, was originally the summer residence of the governor of Western Australia; the hotel is popularly known as the Quokka Arms.

The Rottnest Museum, housed in a barn and threshing mill of 1857, has collections of historical material and relics of shipwrecks (open: daily; admission charge).

Most of the little limestone houses round the harbour at the east end of the island were built by convict labour. They are among the oldest buildings in Western Australia.

The island has good surfaced roads and walking trails and a range of sports facilities (tennis, golf, bowling, bicycle and boat hire). Safe swimming and fishing in the shelter of the offshore reefs. Bus tours of the island are available.

Scott National Park C 6

Location; area

330–360km/205–225 miles south of Perth; 3200 hectares/7900 acres.

Best time to visit

Spring to autumn.

Access

Difficult access (4WD vehicles only) from Brockman Highway east of Alexandra Bridge; access is easier by boat from Augusta or Alexandra Bridge.

Facilities

Bush camping; no visitor facilities. Water sports, fishing.

Features

Scott National Park lies on the east bank of the Blackwood River and on the Scott River, which flows into the Blackwood. Expanses of marsh and wetland; wooded slopes with jarrah, karri and marri trees and dense shrub undergrowth which blossoms in spring. In the wetlands there are many nesting-places of water birds.

Serpentine National Park C 6

Location; area
60km/37 miles south of Perth; 635 hectares/1568 acres.

Best time to visit
Spring to autumn.

Access
From South Western Highway east on Falls Road (admission charge).

Facilities
Camping (access by car; pre-booking necessary); picnic areas.

Features
Serpentine National Park was established to protect the dry eucalyptus forest, particularly jarrah and marri. It has long been a favourite excursion, particularly when the wild flowers are in bloom.

The main attraction used to be the Serpentine Falls and and a large rock pool at the foot of the falls. Since the construction of a dam farther upstream in the 1960s to supply water for Perth the falls are now worth seeing only in the wet winter season; the rock pool is still there for swimmers.

Walking trails
There are beautiful walks along the river above the falls.

Southern Cross C 6

Situation and characteristics
370km/230 miles east of Perth on the Great Eastern Highway, on the edge of the wheat belt, is the little township of Southern Cross (pop. 900). The first gold was found here in 1887 by two prospectors, Tom Risely and Mick Toomey, who were guided by the Southern Cross constellation. Thereafter the settlement became the centre of the Yilgam goldfield, the first of the eastern goldfields of Western Australia. Close to the town are the opencast workings of Fraser's Mine, the most productive gold-mine in the area and the one which remained in operation longest. Gold is still worked round Southern Cross, for example at Marble Loch to the south and Bullfinch to the north.

Among those who worked in the gold-mine was the notorious Baron Swanston, as he called himself. In reality his name was Frederick Bailey Deeming and he was a multiple murderer, who had killed his family in England and his wife in Melbourne. He was duly executed, and his crimes earned him a place in the Chamber of Horrors in London's Madame Tussaud's.

Accommodation
Hotels, motel, caravan/camping park.

Features
The Old Courthouse (1893) is now a museum (open: daily).

★★ Stirling Range National Park C 6

Location; area
80km/50 miles north of Albany and 450km/280 miles south-east of Perth; 115,600 hectares/285,500 acres.

Best time to visit
Late spring and early summer (October to December) for the wild flowers.

Access
From Albany on the Chester Pass Road, which runs through the park. The roads from Cranbrook, Kendenup and Mount Barker are unsurfaced but perfectly negotiable.

Accommodation
Camping is allowed only at Moingup Springs (with a permit from the ranger). Outside the north entrance to the park is a well equipped caravan/camping park.

Facilities
Ranger, information point, camping ground, rest area.

Features
Conical hills, jagged peaks, rock chimneys and saddles extend from east to west for a distance of 65km/40 miles at heights of up to 1000m/3300ft, while the cultivated plain to the south lies at only 200m/650ft. There are twelve peaks above 750m/2460ft; the highest is Bluff Knoll (1073m/3521ft).

On the slopes of the Stirling Range are eucalyptus forests, but the park is best known for the variety and colour of its flowering shrubs and heath vegetation.There are over 1000 species of plants in the Stirling Range, 60 of them endemic; particularly notable is the darwinia (mountain bells). The fauna also covers a wide range, from giant kangaroos to honey opossums.

The winter is cold and rainy; the hills of the Stirling Range are the only ones in Western Australia that sometimes have snow.

Walking trails

The Stirling Range National Park is a walker's paradise. Some of the hills have paths leading up from the car park to the summit; the ascents are steep, but rewarded by magnificent views. On long and cross-country walks you must be prepared for sudden falls in temperature; and before setting out you should enter details in logbooks held at the Bluff Knoll picnic area and the Moingup Springs camping ground.

The finest walking trails are Bluff Knoll (3 hours), Toolbrunup Peak (3 hours), Mount Trio (2 hours), Mount Hassell (2 hours) and Mondurup Peak (2 hours).

Roads

The Chester Pass Road, which runs from north to south through the park, and the road from the park entrance to the foot of Bluff Knoll are asphalted. Numerous tracks and walking trails branch off the Chester Pass Road. The Stirling Range Drive (an unsurfaced track) runs through the park from Red Gum Pass in the west to the Chester Pass Road.

Stokes National Park

Location; area

80km/50 miles west of Esperance; 10,700 hectares/26,400 acres.

Best time to visit

Spring and summer.

Access

From the South Coast Highway on the Stokes Inlet Road (a good unmade road).

Facilities

Two camping grounds on the shores of the inlet. Much of the park is without roads or tracks. No water.

Features

Stokes National Park takes in Stokes Inlet, long stretches of beach and rocky promontories with dunes and low hills in the hinterland. The quiet waters of Stokes Inlet, into which the Young and Lort Rivers flow, are good for water sports and fishing, boating and canoeing (but not for sailing because of shallows and underwater rocks), and there are pleasant walks along the ocean beaches. On the shores of the inlet and in the neighbouring heath and wetlands there are many species of plants and a rich fauna (particularly water birds).

Warning

Beware of snakes!

Tathra National Park

Location; area

300km/185 miles north of Perth; 4300 hectares/10,600 acres.

Best time to visit

Spring (for wild flowers).

Access

On Brand Highway, turning off at Eneabba into the road to Carnamah (unsurfaced track for part of the way), which runs through the park.

Facilities

No accommodation and no visitor facilities; suitable only for day trips.

Features

Tathra National Park, which is surrounded by arable land, was established to protect the natural heath vegetation and woodlands on the sandy plains; it has a profusion of wild flowers, including rare species.

Tom Price

Situation and characteristics

Tom Price (pop. 3540), 1600km/1000 miles north of Perth, is an iron-mining town in the interior of the Pilbara region. It is the highest town in Australia, situated at an altitude of 747m/2451ft.

The huge deposit of iron ore here was discovered in 1962 and named after the managing director of the American steel corporation who had arranged for prospecting to be carried out in this area. This was the beginning of the Hamersley Iron Project, and within a very short time the multinational mining company had established the town of Tom Price and the port of Dampier (see entry) and built a railway between the two. The town itself has no features of particular interest, consisting mainly of rows of uniform prefabricated houses, a few supermarkets and one or two parks.

Accommodation
Hotel, motel, caravan/camping park.

Surroundings
Tom Price is of interest to visitors only for its proximity to Hamersley Range National Park (see entry) and for the sight of the huge opencast mine workings. There is a good general view from Mount Nameless.

★ Toodyay C 6

Situation and characteristics
Toodyay (pop. 560), 85km/53 miles north-east of Perth in the Avon valley, is a very old foundation dating from the early days of settlement in this area. It has been classed by the National Trust as a Historic Town.

Accommodation
Hotels, motel, caravan/camping parks.

Features
In Stirling Terrace, the town's main street, are many handsome old buildings, including the Freemasons Hotel, which was enlarged and given an extra storey during the gold rush, the Mechanics' Institute (now a public library), the Victoria Hotel and the Post Office. Connor's Mill, a three-storey steam flour mill dating from the 1870s, now houses an information centre and museum. The Old Gaol Museum (*c.* 1865) in Clinton Street was originally a work camp for convicts and later, until the turn of the century, a prison; it is now a museum of pioneering and convict days.

Surroundings
4km/2½ miles south-west of the town on the road to Perth is the Coorinja Winery, established in 1870. To the south-west is Avon Valley National Park (see entry), a beautiful expanse of country with natural bush vegetation.

Tunnel Creek National Park E 3

Location; area
180km/112 miles east of Derby; 90 hectares/225 acres.

Best time to visit
Winter. It is impossible to visit the park in summer, when Tunnel Creek carries a considerable flow of water after heavy rain.

Access
On the Gibb River Road, 125km/78 miles east of Derby. Alternatively from the Great Northern Highway on a track which goes off 42km/26 miles west of Fitzroy Crossing and runs 75km/47 miles north-west.

Facilities
No camping in park; camping ground in Windjana Gorge National Park (see entry), 38km/24 miles north-west. Picnic area.

Features
Here Tunnel Creek has carved out a passage through the Devonian limestone, forming a tunnel 750m/820yd long, between 3m/10ft and 12m/40ft high and 15m/50ft wide. A section of the overlying rock has collapsed, admitting daylight and allowing colonies of flying foxes to reach their sleeping quarters in the tunnel. Visitors passing through the tunnel get a close-up view of the strata of fossil limestone. The cool, humid darkness is rather eerie: an electric torch is essential. There are stalactities at various points, and also Aboriginal rock paintings. There are a number of permanent water-holes fed by springs.

Wagin C 6

Situation and characteristics
Wagin (pop. 1370) lies 180km/112 miles south-east of Perth on the Great Southern Highway, at the junction of two railway lines. The population of the surrounding agricultural area (wheat, sheep) is in steady decline.

In Tunnel Creek National Park ▶

Accommodation — Hotels, motels, caravan/camping parks.

Features — Wagin has preserved a number of Victorian houses. In Ballagin Road is Wagin Historical Village, with old buildings and relics of pioneering times.

★Walpole-Nornalup National Park C 6/7

Location; area — 120km/75 miles west of Albany; 18,000 hectares/44,500 acres.

Best time to visit — Spring and summer.

Access — From South Western Highway north-west of Walpole, or from South Coast Highway east of Walpole (turning off at Bow Bridge into road to Peaceful Bay).

Facilities — Camping grounds at Crystal Springs (South Western Highway) and Coalmine Beach (on Nornalup Inlet) can be reached by car. Numerous rest areas within park. Fishing and water sports.

Features — This National Park in the rainy South West was established in 1910 to protect its majestic karri trees and other giant eucalypts. The park also takes in a 40km/25 mile long stretch of coast on the Southern Ocean, with granite promontories, wide beaches, dunes, heath-covered slopes and sheltered inlets. The central feature of the park is the long Nornalup Inlet, into which the Frankland and Deep Rivers flow. Beyond the Nornalup Inlet is the smaller Walpole Inlet at the mouth of the Walpole River, with the holiday settlement of Walpole. There are tracks and walking trails running along the beaches.

Between the Deep River and the sea is the trackless expanse of Nuyts Wilderness, ideal for bush walkers. The ruggedest part of the National Park with its rock-covered hills, coastal dunes, deep wooded gorge and rocky coast has a rich flora (orchids) and fauna; it is reached on a footbridge over the Deep River at Tinglewood Lodge.

In spring (between September and November) the wild flowers in the wooded areas put on their finest show. In summer (December to February) it is warm and dry (danger of forest fires), but even in summer the nights can be cold.

Walking trail — The Bibbulmun Track, which runs north for over 500km/310 miles to near Perth, starts from Walpole.

Roads — Cars are not allowed in the Wilderness Area. From the South Western Highway and South Coast Highway side roads run through beautiful scenery to waterfalls, karri forests, huge tingle trees (Valley of Giants) and the coastal lagoons on the inlets.

Warning — Beware of sudden giant waves and slippery rocks!

Mount Frankland National Park

Location; area — 25km/15½ miles north-east of Walpole; 30,800 hectares/76,100 acres.

Best time to visit — Spring and summer.

Access — The Beardmore Road, a scenic (unmade) road, branches off Highway 1 90km/56 miles south of Manjimup and runs east by way of Fernhook Falls to Mount Frankland. Mount Frankland can also be reached from Walpole on the North Walpole Road; most of the road is asphalted but the last section is gravel, though in normal weather conditions negotiable by an ordinary car.

Facilities — Bush camping; picnic areas.

Features — There is a spectacular view of this National Park – the great forests (karri, jarrah and tingle tree, with a profusion of wild flowers in late spring) and the catchment area of the Frankland River – from Mount Frankland (422m/1385ft).

An easy walking trail through karri forest runs round the foot of this granite hill, with steep paths leading up to the summit.

Watheroo National Park C 6

Location; area
239km/145 miles north of Perth; 44,500 hectares/110,000 acres.

Best time to visit
Spring (for wild flowers).

Access
From Watheroo (Midlands Road) an unasphalted road runs through the park of Badgingarra.

Facilities
Bush camping (with permit); few visitor facilities. No drinking water.

Features
This National Park is notable for the heath vegetation in a basin with quartz sand and small areas of eucalyptus woodland and tall bushes of banksia. The park contains rare species of flowers and plants more commonly found in the wetter South West.

Windjana Gorge National Park D/E 3

Location; area
150km/95 miles east of Derby; 2100 hectares/5200 acres.

Best time to visit
Winter and spring.

Access
On Great Northern Highway to 42km/26 miles before Fitzroy Crossing, then unsurfaced track to north, 75km/47 miles to Tunnel Creek, 38km/24 miles to Windjana Gorge. Alternatively from Derby on Gibb River Road (150km/95 miles).

Facilities
Caravan/camping ground at entrance to gorge (open: during dry season, April to November); toilets, showers, water, picnic areas, information point.

Features
High jagged limestone walls line the gorge cut by the Lennard River through the Napier Range. The hills – remnants of a reef of the Devonian period, when much of the North West was covered by a tropical sea – rise to 90m/295ft above the surrounding plain. During the wet season in the tropical summer the river becomes a raging torrent and floods the National Park. The park can therefore be visited only during the dry winter, though even during the dry season the river leaves pools of cool water on the bottom of the gorge. Along the banks of the river are trees, mainly river red gums and fig-trees. In the walls of the gorge are caves with Aboriginal rock paintings. In the Classic Face, the north wall of the eastern section of the gorge, the succession of strata in the Devonian limestone is clearly seen.

Freshwater crocodiles may be observed in the gorge, which also has a rich and varied bird life. Swimming is usually possible in the pools in the gorge.

Walking trail
Unlike the impassable Geikie Gorge (see Fitzroy Crossing), the Windjana Gorge can be walked through during the dry season. A 3.5km/2 mile long walking trail runs along the bottom of the gorge from the camping ground, with ample opportunity for observing birds and flying foxes, and with luck also crocodiles.

Wittenoom C 4

Situation and characteristics
Wittenoom lies 290km/180 miles south-east of Roebourne and 320km/200 miles south of Port Hedland at the north end of Hamersley Range National Park, at the mouth of the Wittenoom Gorge. It was originally established to house workers in the asbestos mines, but a decline in demand and health considerations (asbestos as a cause of cancer) led to the closure of the mines in 1966. There was also concern about the danger from minute fibres of asbestos in the spoil heaps. As a result the population of Wittenoom has fallen sharply, and it is now almost a ghost town.

Accommodation
Hotel, caravan/camping park.

Meteorite crater in Wolf Creek National Park

Surroundings

The main tourist attraction in the Wittenoom area is the Hamersley Range (see entry), with its impressive mountain scenery and gorges. Wittenoom Gorge is only 13km/8 miles away, with a road running through it for part of the way. From Oxer's Lookout, at the junction of the Red, Weano and Hancock Gorges, there are spectacular views. Within easy reach, too, is the Yampire Gorge, with the Fortescue Falls.

*Wolfe Creek National Park E 3

Location; area
150km/95 miles south of Halls Creek; 1500 hectares/3700 acres.

Best time to visit
Winter; at other times of year it is too hot.

Access
On Great Northern Highway, turning off into an unsurfaced track 16km/10 miles south of Halls Creek.

Accommodation
In Halls Creek.

Facilities
No water, no visitor facilities.

Features
The central feature of Wolfe Creek National Park is a gigantic meteorite crater 850m/930yd in diameter. In this flat and arid desert region there has been little erosion, and the rim of the crater, 50m/165ft high, is therefore well preserved. Wind-blown sand has partly filled up the interior of the crater.

The crater is named after Wolfe Creek, a winding (usually dry) river to the east.

Wyndham E 3

Situation and characteristics

Wyndham (pop. 1330), the most northerly town in Western Australia, lies 3300km/2050 miles north of Perth in the eastern Kimberley region.

During the gold boom at Halls Creek (see entry) Wyndham flourished as the port of arrival for great numbers of prospectors. After the gold was worked out the export of beef became the mainstay of the town's economy, but in 1985 the meat works closed down. The population is now declining.

The original settlement was round the harbour on Cambridge Gulf; the new town (Wyndham East or Three Mile), mainly a residential and shopping centre, grew up on the Great Northern Highway.

Wyndham is now a service centre for the huge cattle farms in the Kimberley region, the local mine workings, Aboriginal settlements in the area and tourists. The climate is very hot, with heavy rain in summer.

Accommodation

Motel, caravan/camping park.

Features

In the main street are a number of fine old buildings – the post office, Durack's store, the courthouse.

Surroundings

Features of interest in the surrounding area are the Afghan cemetery (graves of the old Afghan camel-men) and Aboriginal rock paintings. The coastal lagoons are home to many species of birds. At the Three Mile caravan park is a gigantic boab tree.

35km/22 miles south is the Telegraph Springs Grotto, a rock pool in a beautiful setting, surrounded on three sides by sheer rock walls.

The road to Kununurra (see entry; 93km/58 miles) runs through impressive gorges.

From the Five Rivers Lookout in the Bastion Range there are magnificent views of the coast, the gulf, the harbour and a number of rivers.

Yalgoo C 5

Situation and characteristics

640km/400 miles north of Perth and 215km/135 miles east of Geraldton, on the road from Geraldton to Mount Magnet, is the little township of Yalgoo (pop. 430), which after the finding of gold here in the late 19th century became an important centre in the Murchison goldfields. Occasional nuggets of gold are still found in the area, and the old Emerald Mine has been reopened, leading to an increase in population.

Accommodation

Motel, caravan/camping park.

Features

Features of interest are the old courthouse and a Dominican chapel (restored).

★Yalgorup National Park C 6

Location; area

130km/80 miles south of Perth; 11,800 hectares/29,100 acres.

Best time to visit

Spring for wild flowers, summer for bird-watching and the beaches.

Access

On Old Coast Road via Mandurah (see entry).

Facilities

Bush camping (with permit); picnic areas, toilets.

Features

Yalgorup National Park takes in a string of coastal lagoons and swamps between lines of dunes and limestone ridges which provide nesting-places for countless numbers of water birds. It is a region of eucalyptus woodland with dense undergrowth; on some hill slopes there are expanses of coastal heath vegetation. There are short walking trails round some of the lagoons, and it is also possible to walk along the fire breaks. On the coast are excellent beaches (water sports).

★York C 6

Situation and characteristics

York (pop. 1120), the oldest settlement in the interior of Western Australia, lies just under 100km/62 miles east of Perth.

In order to secure grazing land for the new colony on the Swan River its first governor, Captain James Stirling, caused the Avon valley to be surveyed and settled at a very early stage. York was declared a town in 1836, but at first, as a result of a shortage of labour, it failed to make headway. It was only in the 1850s, when convict labour was brought in, that roads were built and agricultural produce could be brought to York for sale. The town also developed as a gold-mining centre after the discovery of gold in the Yilgarn district. When the railway was built through Northam, to the north of York, further development passed the town by and it remained a quiet little 19th-century town preserved almost intact down to the present.

Accommodation

Hotels, motels and caravan/camping parks.

Sights in York

The rural setting of the Avon valley and the old houses of the pioneering period and the town's Victorian heyday make York a kind of open-air museum. The National Trust has classed it as a Historic Town, and local people have been at pains to preserve the old buildings.

Balladong Farm

Balladong Farm (Parker Road), the oldest farm in inland Western Australia, is now a "working museum" with demonstrations of old farming practices such as sheep-shearing with a knife and ploughing with horses (open: daily).

Avon Terrace

There are many interesting old buildings in Avon Terrace. At No. 79 is the Town Hall (1911), a brick building with rich stucco ornament and a handsome doorway. The Castle Hotel (1842) at No. 95, one of the oldest hotels in Western Australia, was for many years a coaching inn and was several times enlarged. Between the Castle Hotel and the Settlers' House, at No. 105, is the tourist information bureau. In Settlers' House, built in the mid-19th century and enlarged in 1877, the first newspaper in Western Australia, the "York Chronicle", was printed; it is now a hotel and an elegant restaurant.

York Motor Museum

Opposite, housed in a late 19th-century building, is York Motor Museum with over 200 vintage cars as well as horse-drawn vehicles and motorcycles. Next to it, forming a harmonious group, are the Port Office, the Old Police Station and the Courthouse. The gaol was begun about 1850, the other buildings completed between 1892 and 1895, bearing witness to the town's prosperity at the end of the century. The Police Station and Courthouse, with the gaol, are open daily.

Faversham House

Faversham House in Grey Street, one of the town's oldest dwelling-houses and a handsome example of colonial architecture, was built about 1831 as a two-storey house; a third storey was added around 1850. It now belongs to the Uniting Church.

St Patrick's Church

St Patrick's Church in South Street, with a square tower, was built of local sandstone between 1875 and 1886.

Railway station

The two-storey railway station of 1886, in neo-Gothic style, saw many prospectors passing through on their way east to the newly discovered goldfields. In 1894 the railway line was moved farther north, bypassing York. The building now houses railway items (open: weekends).

Flour mill

At 7–13 Broome Street is a four-storey flour mill of 1891.

Residency Museum

On the opposite (east) side of the Avon, in Brook Street, is the Residency Museum, an early colonial building (1843) with an overhanging roof. Once the residence of the local judge, it now houses a museum, with colonial furniture and a collection of old photographs.

Old York Hospital

Adjoining the Residency Museum is the Old York Hospital, a two-storey brick building of 1896.

Holy Trinity Church

Holy Trinity Church (corner of Newcastle and Pool Streets), one of the earliest churches in the country, was consecrated in 1848 and later enlarged. Its square tower was rebuilt, reduced in height, after suffering earthquake damage in 1968.

Kairey Cottage (1859), with a steep shingle roof and an old-world garden, is now occupied by a group of craft workers and a theatre group (16 Newcastle Street).

Kairey Cottage

Marwick's Barn at 19–21 Newcastle Street, with a shingle roof and roughly built stone walls, is a reminder of York's rural origins. It was formerly a coaching station.

Marwick's Barn

ROTARY CLUB OF BRISBANE
SURF RESCUE
FORCE FIELD

SURF
ESCUE

Practical Information from A to Z

In the Antipodes everything stands on its head!

It is, of course, just a joke when people say that the antipodeans (Greek for "on the other foot") actually stand on their heads! However, Europeans travelling to Australia, on the other side of the world, have to get used to the different conditions in the southern hemisphere and amend their natural way of thinking. The way we are so used to thinking in Europe, namely, instinctively associating north with colder conditions and south with warmer, is completely reversed in Australia – the further north one goes the warmer it gets, and the further south the colder it becomes. When planning a journey travellers must also bear in mind the "topsy-turvy world" of the seasons of the year; in Australia spring lasts from September to November, summer from December to February, autumn from March to May and winter from June to August.

N.B. New telephone numbers

At present all Australian telephone numbers are gradually being altered, and this process is expected to be completed during 1998. The same applies to local dialling codes. The new numbers are quoted in this guide where they are known.

Aborigines

The Aborigines is the name given to the original native inhabitants of the Fifth Continent (see p. 29). Many European and North American tourists are obviously very interested in their culture, as shown by the large numbers who join in tours of the Outback. However, the areas in which they live – most lie in the Northern Territory – can be visited only with a special permit. Some Aboriginal communities are strongly opposed to tourists. Some small Aboriginal tour operators, on the other hand, are now offering bush trips into the Outback, guided tours of places where herbs and plants with special healing properties grow, ornithological excursions and so on.
Central Lands Council, 33 Stuart Highway, PO Box 3321, Alice Springs, NT 5750; tel. (089) 516 211, fax (089) 534 343
Northern Land Council, 9 Rowling St., PO Box 42921, Casuarina, NT 0811; tel.(089) 205 100, fax (089) 452 633
From the "Aussie Helpline" (see Information) visitors can obtain informative material about Aboriginal culture and details of travel agents who operate in this field. The following is a small selection of Australian travel firms who provide contact with the Aborigines:

Aboriginal Tribal Tours, PO Box 271, Babinda, QLD 4861
Tel. (070) 671 637
An-Gnarra Aboriginal Corporation, PO Box, Laura, QLD 4871
Tel. (070) 603 214
Desert Tracks, PO Box 360, Yulara (Ayers Rock Resort), NT 0871
Tel (089) 562 144
Ipolera Cultural Tours, PO Box 176, Ipolera (near Hermannsburg), NT 0872
Tel. (089) 567 466
Jankangyina Tours, 6 Katherine Terrace, Katherine, NT 0850
Tel. (089) 711 381
Seven Sisters Dreaming, 25 O'Shannessy St., Nunawading, VIC 3131
Tel. (059) 662 436

◀ *Who wouldn't mind being rescued here?*

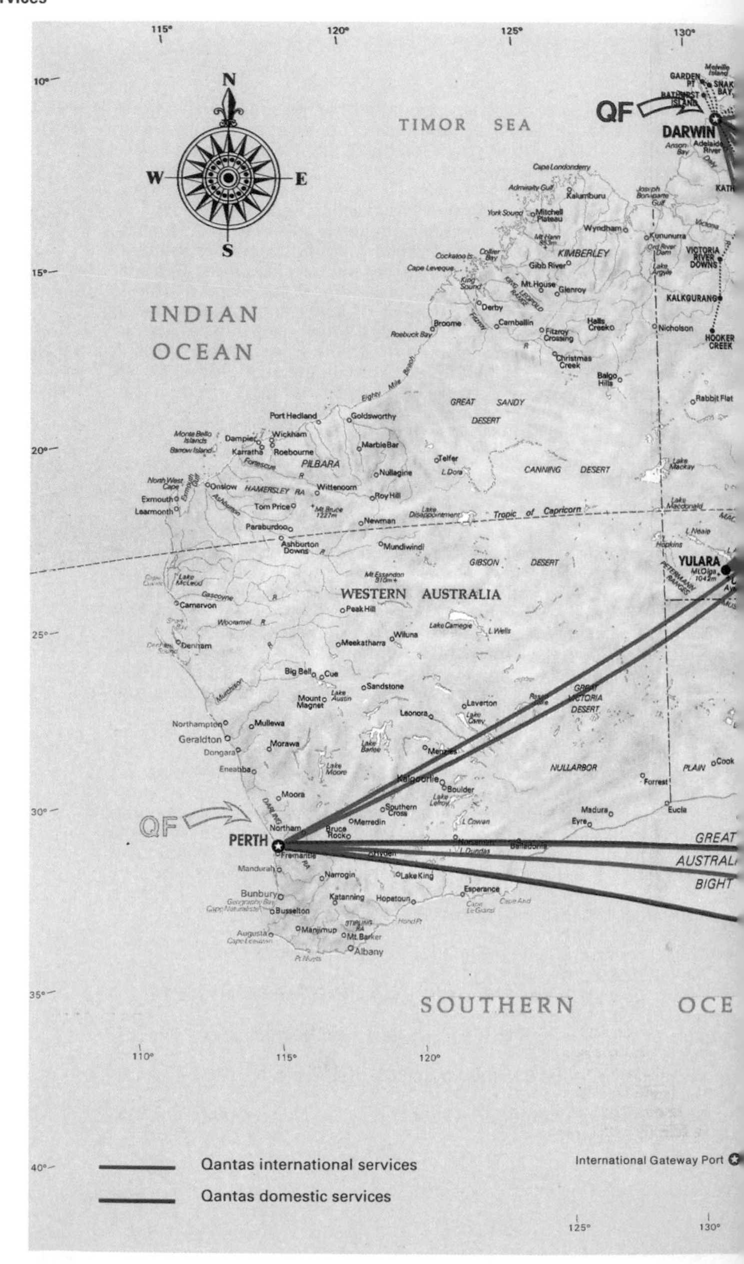
115°
120°
125°
130°
10°
15°
20°
25°
30°
35°
40°
N
W
E
S
TIMOR SEA
QF
DARWIN
INDIAN
OCEAN
Kalumburu
Wyndham
Kununurra
KIMBERLEY
Gibb River
Mt.House
Glenroy
Derby
Broome
Camballin
Fitzroy Crossing
Halls Creek
VICTORIA RIVER DOWNS
KALKGURANG
Nicholson
HOOKER CREEK
Christmas Creek
Balgo Hills
Rabbit Flat
GREAT SANDY
DESERT
Port Hedland
Goldsworthy
Dampier
Wickham
Karratha
Roebourne
Marble Bar
PILBARA
Nullagine
Telfer
CANNING DESERT
Onslow
HAMERSLEY RA
Wittenoom
Roy Hill
Exmouth
Learmonth
Tom Price
Newman
Tropic of Capricorn
Paraburdoo
Ashburton Downs
Mundiwindi
GIBSON
DESERT
YULARA
Carnarvon
WESTERN AUSTRALIA
Peak Hill
Wiluna
Meekatharra
Denham
Big Bell
Cue
Sandstone
Mount Magnet
Laverton
GREAT VICTORIA DESERT
Leonora
Northampton
Mullewa
Geraldton
Dongara
Morawa
Menzies
Eneabba
NULLARBOR
PLAIN
Cook
Kalgoorlie
Boulder
Forrest
Moora
Southern Cross
Merredin
Madura
Eucla
Eyre
QF
PERTH
Northam
Bruce Rock
Fremantle
Mandurah
Narrogin
Lake King
Bunbury
Katanning
Hopetoun
Esperance
Busselton
Augusta
Manjimup
Mt.Barker
Albany
GREAT
AUSTRAL
BIGHT
SOUTHERN
OCE
110°
115°
120°
Qantas international services
Qantas domestic services
International Gateway Port
125°
130°

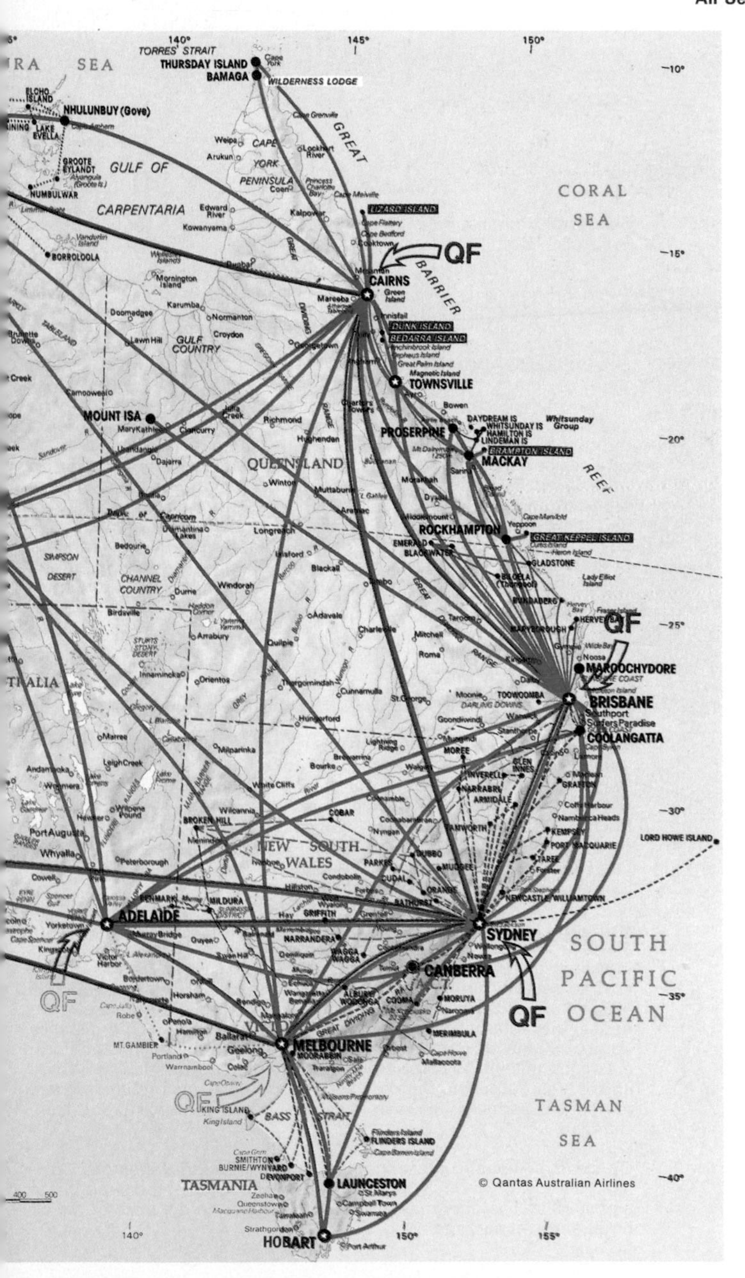
TORRES' STRAIT
THURSDAY ISLAND
BAMAGA
WILDERNESS LODGE
NHULUNBUY (Gove)
GROOTE EYLANDT
NUMBULWAR
GULF OF
CARPENTARIA
BORROLOOLA
CAPE
YORK
PENINSULA
GREAT
BARRIER
REEF
CORAL
SEA
LIZARD ISLAND
QF
CAIRNS
DUNK ISLAND
BEDARRA ISLAND
TOWNSVILLE
MOUNT ISA
GULF
COUNTRY
QUEENSLAND
PROSERPINE
DAYDREAM IS
WHITSUNDAY IS
HAMILTON IS
LINDEMAN IS
Whitsunday Group
BRAMPTON ISLAND
MACKAY
ROCKHAMPTON
GREAT KEPPEL ISLAND
EMERALD
BLACKWATER
GLADSTONE
SIMPSON
DESERT
CHANNEL
COUNTRY
MAROOCHYDORE
BRISBANE
COOLANGATTA
TOOWOOMBA
MOREE
INVERELL
ARMIDALE
TAMWORTH
NARRABRI
KEMPSEY
PORT MACQUARIE
TAREE
LORD HOWE ISLAND
BROKEN HILL
COBAR
NEW SOUTH WALES
PARKES
DUBBO
MUDGEE
ORANGE
BATHURST
NEWCASTLE WILLIAMTOWN
ADELAIDE
RENMARK
MILDURA
GRIFFITH
NARRANDERA
WAGGA WAGGA
SYDNEY
CANBERRA
ALBURY
MORUYA
MERIMBULA
SOUTH
PACIFIC
OCEAN
MT. GAMBIER
MELBOURNE
MOORABBIN
KING ISLAND
BASS
STRAIT
FLINDERS ISLAND
SMITHTON
BURNIE/WYNYARD
DEVONPORT
LAUNCESTON
TASMANIA
HOBART
TASMAN
SEA
© Qantas Australian Airlines

Accidents

See Emergency Services, Safety and Security.

Accommodation

See Hotels. Motels. Resorts. Lodges, Holidays on the Farm; Bed and Breakfast, Youth Hostels.

Air Services

Domestic services

See Getting to Australia

In view of the great distances between the Australian capitals and the need to link small and scattered communities in the empty interior of the continent with the outside world a dense network of domestic air services developed in Australia at an early stage. As a result it is now possible to visit a number of destinations many miles apart within a relatively short period. In addition to the large airports of the state capitals there are numerous smaller airfields in the outback, on the holiday islands off Darwin (NT) and on the Great Barrier Reef (QLD).
In addition to the large national airlines there are many local and regional airlines available to take visitors to destinations in the bush and the desert as well as to more easily accessible places.

Airports

International airports

Adelaide (SA): Adelaide (7km/41⁄2 miles from city centre; transfer time 15 minutes)
Brisbane (QLD): Brisbane (17km/10.5 miles; 25 minutes)
Cairns (QLD): Cairns (6km/4 miles; 15 minutes)
Darwin (NT): Darwin (15km/9 miles; 30 minutes)
Hobart (TAS): Llanherne (18km/12 miles; 35 minutes)
Melbourne (VIC): Tullamarine (25km/15 miles; 35 minutes)
Perth (WA): Perth (20km/12.4 miles; 30–40 minutes)
Port Hedland (WA): Port Hedland (13km/8 miles; 35 minutes)
Sydney (NSW): Kingsford Smith (8km/5 miles; 35 minutes)

Qantas terminals

At most of the larger Australian airports there are two terminals or separate airports for domestic and international flights. Flight numbers indicate which terminal is the right one: Qantas flights QF 1 to QF 399 are international flights handled by the international terminal, while QF 400 and upwards are domestic flights departing from the domestic terminal. The international and domestic terminals are some distance apart at Sydney (2km/1¼ miles), Brisbane (4km/21/2 miles) and Perth (14km/8½ miles); they are side by side at Adelaide, Cairns and Hobart; and at Melbourne and Darwin the two terminals are combined. There are shuttle services between separate terminals (information from Qantas).

Departure tax

On leaving Australia passengers must pay a departure tax of 27 dollars. Stamps for payment of the duty can be bought at the airport or in a post office.The duty may already be included in the price of the air ticket or travel package.

Airlines

Qantas (QF)

Qantas (originally Queensland and Northern Territory Air Services), the Australian international airline, recently amalgamated with the domestic airline company, Australian Airlines. There are over 40 Qantas flights a week from London to Australia, including daily flights to Sydney, Melbourne and Brisbane. Associated with Qantas are a number of smaller airlines flying services within Australia.

United Kingdom

182 Strand, London WC2 1ET, tel. 0171 497 2571
395 King Street, London W6 9NJ, tel. 0181 846 0466
  Reservations from UK, tel. 0345 747 767

United States

Chicago, tel. 800 227 4500
712 Fifth Avenue (11th floor), New York, tel. 800 227 4500
360 Post Street, Suite 905, San Francisco, tel. 800 227 4500
1825 K Street NW, Washington DC, tel. 800 227 4500

Canada

Toronto, tel. 800 227 4500
1111 West Georgia Street, Suite 1705, Vancouver, tel. 800 227 4500

Australia

Sydney (NSW): Hunter and Phillip Streets, tel. 612 691 3636 (information)
  reservations within NSW, tel. (toll-free) 008 112 121
  reservations within Australia, tel. 612 13 13 13
  international reservations, tel. 612 957 0111
  at airport: International Terminal Building, tel. 612 691 3636
Adelaide (SA): tel. 618 237 8541 (international flights), 618 13 13 13 (domestic flights)
Brisbane (QLD): tel. 07 234 3747 (international flights), tel. 07 13 13 13 (domestic flights)
Cairns (QLD): tel. (toll-free) 008 177 767 (international flights), 070 13 13 13 (domestic flights)
Canberra (ACT): tel. 062 275 5518 (international flights), 062 13 13 13 (domestic flights)
Darwin (NT): tel. (toll-free) 008 802 710 (international flights), 089 13 13 13 (domestic flights)
Hobart (TAS): tel. (toll-free) 008 112 121 (international flights), 002 13 13 13 (domestic flights)
Melbourne (VIC): tel. 03 805 0111 (international flights), 03 13 13 13 (domestic flights)
Perth (WA): tel. 09 225 2222 (international flights), 09 13 13 13 (domestic flights)
Townsville (QLD): tel. (toll-free) 008 177 767 (international flights), 077 13 13 13 (domestic flights)

Ansett Australia Airlines (AN)

Ansett Australia flies mainly within Australia and to destinations in Asia and other international destinations.

British Airways

Adelaide (SA)	Level 7, 144 North Terrace, tel. 238 2138
Alice Springs (NT)	Australian Airlines, Todd and Parsons Streets, tel. 505 222
Brisbane (QLD)	243 Edward Street, tel. 223 3123
Broome (WA)	Ansett Western Australia, Baker and Weld Streets, tel. 936 855
Canberra (ACT)	28 Ainslie Avenue, tel. 008 113 722
Darwin (NT)	Australian Airlines, 16 Bennett Street, tel. 801 222
Derby (WA)	Ansett Western Australia, Derby Shopping Centre, tel. 931 488
Hobart (TAS)	86 Murray Street, tel. 347 433
Kalgoorlie (WA)	Ansett Western Australia, 70 Maritana Street, tel. 212 277, 212 764
Melbourne (VIC)	114 William Street, tel. 603 1133
Perth (WA)	1st Floor, 77 St George's Terrace, tel. 483 7711
Port Hedland (WA)	Ansett Western Australia, Shop 16, Boulevard Shopping Centre, tel. 733 122
Sydney (NSW)	64 Castlereagh Street, tel. 258 3300

Singapore Airlines
Sydney (NSW)

Singapore Airlines House
17-19 Bridge Street
tel. 02 236 0144

Alcohol

The purchase, serving and consumption of alcoholic drinks in public places is regulated in varying but very strict ways in the various states of Australia. In addition, alcohol attracts very high rates of duty throughout Australia. Alcoholic drinks can be obtained only in fully licensed bars and restaurants and in special liquor stores and bottle shops. In licensed premises alcohol can be served only between 10am and 10pm, Mondays to Saturdays. There are very strict restrictions applying on Sundays.

BYO

BYO ("bring your own") restaurants have no licence to serve alcohol. Customers may bring in or send for a bottle of wine or beer from a bottle shop and then pay a small corkage charge.

Blood alcohol limit

The blood alcohol limit throughout Australia is 51mg/100ml and there are very frequent police checks.

Bathing Beaches

With a coastline of 47,000km/29,000 miles, including the islands, Australia has innumerable long sandy or rocky beaches and inlets which offer ideal conditions for swimming, surfing and other water sports as well as for beach walks.

It is advisable to bathe only on beaches where there are arrangements for supervision and lifeguards. Bathing near the large cities is not to be recommended, since many beaches are heavily polluted. Protection against the sun is essential – sun-block cream with a high protection factor, protective clothing (including a hat, preferably covering the back of the neck). For walking on the beach (particularly on the coral of the Great Barrier Reef) thick-soled trainers should be worn.

Danger

Flag signals

A red and yellow flag shows that a beach is patrolled and safe; green flags indicate good bathing conditions, yellow flags advise caution, and a red flag means danger.

Currents

In some coastal waters there may be danger from strong currents.

Sharks

There may be sharks in any of the seas round Australia. Never go into the water alone or after dark!

Box jellyfish

In coastal waters in the tropical north of Australia (north of the Tropic of Capricorn) there may be dangerous box jellyfish (sea wasps) between October and May. Their long tentacles contain a very dangerous nerve poison.

Other marine animals

Other dangers on the beach are the stonefish or scorpion fish, cone shells and small blue-ringed octopuses: they are highly poisonous and should not be touched. At the mouths of rivers there may be poisonous sting rays. The spines of sea-urchins can be very painful and difficult to remove from the soles of the feet.

Crocodiles

The saltwater crocodiles (Crocodylus porosus) which live in the coastal waters of northern Australia are a serious hazard for swimmers. Pay heed to warnings about the presence of crocodiles, and never camp within 50m/55yd of the water's edge! The smaller fresh-water crocodiles (C. johnstoni) found in the northern Australian rivers are less dangerous but by no means harmless.

Popular beaches

Ninety Mile Beach at Lakes Entrance, to the east of Melbourne (Vic.), is one of the world's finest sandy beaches. Sydney's Bondi Beach (NSW) is the most popular in Australia, and as a result is often overcrowded; it is a good surfing as well as a bathing beach.

Among other favourite bathing areas in Australia are the beaches on Queensland's Gold Coast (south of Brisbane) and Sunshine Coast (north of Brisbane). While the resorts on the Gold Coast tend to be busy and crowded, with a wide range of entertainment and sports facilities and good surfing beaches, there are still many quiet little holiday villages on the Sunshine Coast. In Queensland, to the north of Maryborough, there are the sheltered beaches in Hervey Bay, very suitable for children with their gradual slope and calm waters. Farther north, off Townsville, is Magnetic Island, which also has beautiful long sandy beaches (particularly Horseshoe Bay, 3km/2 miles long). Another famous beach is Four Mile Beach at Port Douglas, to the north of Cairns (QLD). In the north of Western Australia, at Broome, is the 24km/15 mile long and incredibly broad Cable Beach, with great distances between high and low tide. There are also excellent bathing beaches on the Indian Ocean west and north-west of Perth.

Nude bathing is generally frowned upon, although some beaches and bays exercise a certain degree of tolerance.

Bed and Breakfast

Bed and breakfast (B and B) or "homestay" accommodation is a good way of getting to know the Australians at home, and at very reasonable cost (between 50 and 120 dollars including English breakfast). Credit cards are not usually accepted.

Betting and Gaming

Betting and gambling are the great passion of Australians. Horse-races, dog-races, contests between toads, scorpions or camels – anything and everything may be the occasion for a bet.

Two-up

Since gold-digging times, two-up has been the national (though illegal) game of chance. Two coins are tossed in the air and bets, sometimes for very considerable sums, are made on the chance of two heads or two tails turning up. A mixed result (i.e. a head and a tail) does not count, and there is a re-throw. Although prohibited by law, the game is still widely played and has brought many a player heavy losses.

Casinos

Casinos have been permitted in Australia for a number of years now. Games played include baccarat, blackjack, crap, roulette and even "two-up", which is legal in such establishments. The larger casinos, some of which are open 24 hours a day, insist on clients wearing a jacket and tie; T-shirts, trainers etc. are not allowed.

Casinos (a selection)

Adelaide (SA): Adelaide Casino, North Terrace
Alice Springs (SA): Lasseter's Casino, Barret Drive
Brisbane (QLD): Conrad Treasury Casino, George St.
Cairns (QLD): The Reef Hotel & Casino, Wharf St.
Canberra (ACT): Casino Canberra, Glebe Park
Darwin (NT): MGM Grand Darwin, Mindil Beach
Gold Coast (QLD): Conrad Jupiter's Casino, Gold Coast Highway

Hobart (TAS): Wrest Point Casino, Sandy Bay Road
Launceston (TAS): Country Club Casino, Prospect Vale
Melbourne (VIC): Crown Towers Hotel & Casino, Southbank
Perth (WA): Burswood Casino, Great Eastern Highway
Sydney (NSW): Sydney Harbour Casino
Townsville (QLD): Sheraton Breakwater Casino

Buses

Travelling in the overland buses is the cheapest way to get about in Australia.

Australian Coachlines

The major Australian bus companies are Greyhound Pioneer Australia, McCafferty's Express Coaches and Wayward Bus Touring Company, which run services to all the major commercial and tourist centres. The buses are air-conditioned and have sanitary facilities, and smoking is prohibited in all buses. There are also some smaller regional bus companies, e.g. Tasmanian Redline Coaches.

Bus passes

The large bus companies also offer cheap passes with which one can travel a set number of kilometres within a certain period of time. The Greyhound Pioneer Aussi Pass, for example, is valid for a year, but a minimum of 2000 kilometres must be "bought".

Information

Greyhound Pioneer Australia; tel 13 20 30 (local rate)
McCafferty's Express Coaches; tel. 07 6909 888
Oz Experience; tel. (02) 9907 0522
Tasmanian Redline Coaches; tel. 1-800-030 033 (local rate)
Wayward Bus Touring Company; tel. (08) 8232 6646

Coach tours

Many Australian travel operators have an extensive programme of coach tours, ranging from two-day trips to places of interest within reach of the state capitals to tours lasting several weeks covering particular regions or the whole continent. Some tours provide accommodation in good hotels; others offer cheaper accommodation in tents, with everyone lending a hand; while others again are regular outback safaris. Leading coach tour operators include AAT King Tours, Australian Pacific Tours, Australian Scenic Tours, Contiki Holidays, Evergreen Tours, Greyhound Pioneer, Northern Gateway, Oz Tours, Pinnacle Tours, Sunbeam Tours and Trekabout Australia.
Information about bus tours can be obtained from the Australian Tourist Commission (see Information); bookings can be made through travel agencies.

Bush Fires

During the dry season in particular there is always the danger of bush fires, which threaten vegetation, wildlife and sometimes people's homes. When there is a high risk of fire, therefore, the government imposes a total fire ban prohibiting open fires, with heavy penalties for any contravention of the ban. Warnings are posted up throughout the affected areas and announced in the media. Motorists in danger of being caught in a bush fire should try to park in a clearing and should then switch off the engine, close all windows and lie on the floor of the car with whatever covering is available to protect them from radiant heat. They should on no account leave the car.

Business Hours

Banks See Currency

Chemists See entry

Post offices See Post and Telecommunications

Shops Shop opening hours vary from state to state, but as a rule they are Mon.–Fri. 9am–5pm, Sat. 9am–1pm. In towns there is usually a late night shopping day on Thursday and/or Friday on which shops stay open until 8 or 9pm. Many shops in tourist centres and in pedestrian zones in cities are also open on Sunday.

Supermarkets Department stores Many of these open at 8am and do not close until 10pm.

Small food shops Many small food shops and milk bars are open from early morning to late in the evening.

Local government offices Normally open to the public Mon–Fri. 9am–5pm.

Buying a Car

If you are making a longer stay in Australia and want to buy a second-hand car you should check that it has its annual roadworthiness certificate (RWC, the equivalent of the British MOT). It is also advisable when selling back the car at the end of your stay to sell it in the state in which you bought it.

Camping and Caravanning

Many camping and caravanning parks are well equipped with power points, hot and cold water, waste disposal facilities, showers, toilets and coin-operated washing machines, tumbler driers and irons. Frequently there are also television and recreation rooms, shops, a swimming pool and public telephones, and at some sites blankets and bed-linen can be hired. Almost all parks cater for both tents and caravans. The trailer caravans which were once so popular with Australians are now being challenged by camper vans and mobile homes. On many sites on-site caravans and cabins can be hired, often with their own sanitary facilities. Since hire charges for a long let are relatively lower, many on-site vans and cabins are occupied by long-term tenants.

Reservation During the school holidays and the main holiday season (from the middle of December to the end of February) it is advisable in the most attractive holiday areas to make a booking well in advance.

Charges Currently, the site fee for two people varies between A$10 and A$20 per day. the daily hire charge for a caravan (two people) lies between A$30 (campervan) and A$80 (mobile home). To hire an on-site caravan or cabin will cost between A$20 and A$70 per day.

Site lists Tourist offices in the various states (see Information) and the automobile clubs can provide lists of current camp sites.

Restrictions in the outback and some National Parks In some regions bush camping is restricted or even prohibited. This applies particularly in the case of Aboriginal sites and some National parks containing Aboriginal religious sites or specially protected flora and fauna. Moreover, in the Outback the camping sites are mostly very simple affairs with no facilities and camp fires are prohibited because of the latent risk of bush fires.

Camper vans See Car Rental

Car Rental

The leading international car rental firms operate in Australia and have offices at airports and many railway stations as well as in towns. In addition, of course, there are many local firms. A complete list of recommended car rental firms can be obtained from tourist information offices (see Information).

Hire conditions

The prospective driver must produce a driving licence (national licences are accepted) and be at least 21 years of age. A premium may be charged for drivers under 25.

It is advisable to make a booking before leaving home, since this is likely to be cheaper than hiring on the spot. Tariffs vary according to season, size of car and length of hire. Usually the hire charge covers unlimited kilometres, but some hirers make an additional charge per kilometre beyond a stated limit. Compulsory third party insurance and collision damage waiver are included in car rentals; comprehensive cover and personal accident insurance (recommended) are available at extra charge. When hiring a car you should enquire about any possible additional costs. Expect to pay about A$85 per day for a small car, about A$100 for a medium-sized car and at least A$150 for a 4WD vehicle. It is cheaper to rent by the week.

Most rental companies will ask for a major international credit card for credit identification. With cash rentals it is customary for the estimated rental charge (including insurance and petrol and a refundable deposit of A$500–1500) to be paid in advance.

Normally the car must be returned to the place where it was hired. Where the hire is of some length it may be possible to arrange a one-way rental, though there is likely to be an additional charge for returning the car to its original depot.

Fly/drive

Some travel operators and airlines offer fly/drive packages covering the flight to Australia, the rent of the vehicle and accommodation in hotels or motels. The choice of route is then left to the hirer.

Vehicles

4WD vehicles

Four-wheel-drive (4WD) vehicles are widely used in Australia, and for outback travel they are essential. Most rental companies hiring out 4WD vehicles require the driver to have previous experience in driving them. Moreover in view of the risk of damage on rough tracks – damage to a car caused by the driver is not covered by insurance – the rental charge is higher than for an ordinary car. An alternative to driving a 4WD vehicle yourself is to join an organised tour in 4WD vehicles.

Camper vans

Camper vans and motor caravans can be hired locally in all states. A camper van - a light van whose interior has been converted into living and sleeping areas (2–3 people) by replacing the fixed roof with a "pop-top" – gives you flexibility and independence in planning your journey. The minimum rental period is usually a week, and there are considerable reductions for longer rentals. Rates are at their highest during the main holiday season in December and January.

Motor homes

A motor home has its living area built on to a truck chassis. It is larger than a camper van (sleeping 4–6 people) and not so easily manoeuvrable.

Motorcycles

Motorcycles can at present be hired only in New South Wales and Western Australia. The cost will be at least A$100 per day, with a refundable deposit of A$1000.

Chemists

There should be no problem in obtaining medicines anywhere in Australia. In the major centres and more densely populated areas the standard of service should equal that enjoyed in Great Britain or the United States. Even in the less populated regions a chemist's shop will be found in all the central towns.

Opening hours

Mon.–Fri. 9am–5.30pm, Sat. 9am–noon. In some cities chemists stay open until 9pm one day a week.

Prescribed medicines

Those wishing to obtain prescribed medicines must be able to provide a prescription provided by a doctor registered in Australia.

Currency

The unit of currency is the Australian dollar (A$), which consists of 100 cents (c). There are notes for 5, 10, 20, 50 and 100 dollars and coins in denominations of 5, 10, 20 and 50 cents and 1 and 2 dollars.

Currency regulations

There are no restrictions on the import or export of either Australian or foreign currency, but amounts over 5000 dollars in Australian or other currencies must be declared on arrival and departure.

Banks

Banks are open Mon.–Thu. 9.30am–4pm; on Fridays they often stay open until 5pm. There are branch offices of banks even in quite small towns. Bank desks in airports are open outside the above hours and on Sundays and public holidays.

Changing money

Money can be changed at all international airports, banks and some large hotels. Changing foreign currency and travellers' cheques in banks is a quick and easy process.

Australian dollars and cents

Credit cards, travellers' cheques	Credit cards are widely used in Australia, and most shops, filling stations, hotels and travel agencies accept the usual international cards. It is only in country areas and in small shops that credit cards may be refused. Travellers' cheques, preferably in Australian currency, are acceptable almost everywhere, particularly in banks and hotels. Banks may sometimes charge a commission on changing a cheque. Eurocheques are not accepted in Australia.
Loss of credit cards and cheques	The loss of credit cards or travellers' cheques should be reported at once to the issuing authority.

Customs Regulations

Items for personal use, including cameras, films, etc., may be taken into Australia without payment of duty. Travellers over 18 may also take in 1 litre of alcohol, 250 cigarettes or 250 grams of tobacco and gifts up to a value of A$400 duty-free; travellers under 18 may take in gifts up to a value of A$200.

Drugs

The entry of drugs and narcotics is strictly prohibited; there are frequent checks of luggage for drugs, and penalties are severe. The bringing in of clearly identifiable medicines for personal use is permitted.
Australia has very strict quarantine laws designed to keep out pests and animal diseases. The taking in of foodstuffs, fruit, vegetables, seeds and animal and plant products is prohibited. There are border controls even between individual states; luggage is thoroughly checked, and any fresh fruit, etc., will be confiscated. On all international flights, except from New Zealand, the cabin of the aircraft is sprayed with a disinfectant shortly before landing (passengers suffering from allergies should take any necessary preventive measures).

Information

Detailed information about customs regulations can be obtained from Australian high commissions, embassies and consulates.

Endangered species

Under the Washington convention on the protection of endangered species the trade in or export of endangered species of animals or plants or articles made from them is prohibited.

Diplomatic and Consular Offices

Australian Diplomatic and Consular Offices Abroad

United Kingdom
High Commission

Australia House, Strand,
London WC2B 4LA, tel. 0171 379 4334

Consulate

Chatsworth House, Lever Street,
Manchester M1 2DL, tel. 0161 228 1344

United States
Embassy

1601 Massachusetts Avenue NW,
Washington DC 20036, tel. 202 797 3000

Consulates

2338 Bryant Avenue,
Evanston IL 60201, tel. 847 492 0116

1000 Bishop Street,
Honolulu HI 96813, tel. 808 524 5050

611 North Larchmont Boulevard,
Los Angeles CA 90004, tel. 213 469 4300

International Building, 630 Fifth Avenue,
New York NY 10111, tel. 212 245 4000

1 Bush Street,
San Francisco CA 94104-4979, tel. 415 362 6160

Suite 800, 3 Post Oak Central, 1990 South Post Oak Boulevard,
Houston TX 77056-99976, tel. 713 629 9131

Canada
High Commission

Suite 710, 50 O'Connor Street,
Ottawa, Ontario K1P 6LT, tel. 613 236 0841

Consulates

Suite 3146, 175 Bloor Street E,
Toronto, Ontario M4W 3R8, tel. 416 323 1155

World Trade Centre Complex, Suite 602–999 Canada Place,
Vancouver BC V6C 3E1, tel. 604 684 1177

Diplomatic and Consular Offices in Australia

United Kingdom
British High Commission

Commonwealth Avenue, Yarralumla
Canberra, ACT 2600, tel. 612 6270 6666

Consulates

Hassell Pty Ltd, 70 Hindmarsh Street
Adelaidc, SA 5000, tel. 618 8212 7280

BP House, 193 North Quay
Brisbane, QLD 4000, tel. 617 3236 2575, 236 2577 and 236 2581

90 Collins Street (17th floor)
Melbourne, VIC 3000, tel. 6133 9650 4155

Level 26, Allendale Square, 77 St George's Terrace
Perth, WA 6000, tel. 618 9221 4422

Level 16, The Gateway, 1 Macquarie Place
Sydney Cove, Sydney, NSW 2000, tel. 612 9247 7521

United States
Embassy

Moonah Place, Yarralumla
Canberra, ACT 2600, tel. 612 270 5000

Consulates

386 Wickham Terrace
Brisbane, QLD 4000, tel. 612 9373 9200

24 Albert Road
South Melbourne, VA 3205, tel. 613 9526 5900

16 St George's Terrace (13th floor)
Perth, WA 6000, tel. 618 9231 9400

T & G Tower, Hyde Park Square
Sydney, NSW 2000, tel. 612 9373 9200

Canada
High Commission

Commonwealth Avenue, Yarralumla
Canberra, ACT 2600, tel. 612 273 3844

Consulates

1 Collins Street (6th floor)
Melbourne, VIC 3000, tel. 613 9811 9999

AMP Centre (8th floor), 50 Bridge Street
Sydney, NSW 2000, tel. 612 9364 3000

Distances

Road distances in kilometres between selected towns in Australia *excluding Melbourne–Devonport ferry	Adelaide (SA)	Albany (WA)	Alice Springs (NT)	Ayers Rock (NT)	Brisbane (QLD)	Broken Hill (NSW)	Cairns (QLD)	Canberra (ACT)	Darwin (NT)	Hobart (TAS)*	Kununurra (WA)	Mackay (QLD)	Melbourne (VC)	Mount Isa (QLD)	Perth (WA)	Port Hedland (WA)	Surfers Paradise (QLD)	Sydney (NSW)
Adelaide (SA)	•	2673	1533	1578	2045	506	3352	1196	3022	1001	3219	2783	731	2742	2781	3783	2125	1412
Albany (WA)	2673	•	3588	3633	4349	2810	5656	3846	4614	3674	3787	5087	3404	5106	409	2057	4429	3970
Alice Springs (NT)	1533	3588	•	443	3038	1670	2457	2706	1489	2534	1686	2505	2264	1209	3696	3416	3118	2830
Ayers Rock (NT)	1578	3633	443	•	3254	1715	2900	2751	1932	2579	2129	2948	2309	1652	3741	3859	3334	2875
Brisbane (QLD)	2045	4349	3038	3254	•	1539	1716	1261	3463	1944	3660	976	1674	1829	4457	5390	80	1001
Broken Hill (NSW)	506	2810	1670	1715	1539	•	2846	1101	3159	1123	3356	2277	853	2406	2918	3920	1619	1160
Cairns (QLD)	3352	5656	2457	2900	1716	2846	•	2568	2882	3251	3079	740	2981	1248	5764	4809	1796	2495
Canberra (ACT)	1196	3846	2706	2751	1261	1101	2568	•	4195	918	4392	1999	648	2561	3954	4956	1341	286
Darwin (NT)	3022	4614	1489	1932	3463	3159	2882	4195	•	4023	827	2930	3753	1634	4205	2557	3543	4034
Hobart (TAS)*	1001	3674	2534	2579	1944	1123	3251	918	4023	•	4220	2682	270	3075	3782	5338	2024	1142
Kununurra (WA)	3219	3787	1686	2129	3660	3356	3079	4392	827	4220	•	3127	3950	1831	3378	1730	3740	4516
Mackay (QLD)	2783	5087	2505	2948	976	2277	740	1999	2930	2682	3127	•	2412	1296	5195	4857	1056	1926
Melbourne (VC)	731	3404	2264	2309	1674	853	2981	648	3753	270	3950	2412	•	2805	3512	4514	1754	872
Mount Isa (QLD)	2742	5106	1209	1652	1829	2406	1248	2561	1634	3075	1831	1296	2805	•	4905	3561	1909	2400
Perth (WA)	2781	409	3696	3741	4457	2918	5764	3954	4205	3782	3378	5195	3512	4905	•	1648	4537	4073
Port Hedland (WA)	3783	2057	3416	3859	5390	3920	4809	4956	2557	5338	1730	4857	4514	3561	1648	•	5470	5080
Surfers Paradise (QLD)	2125	4429	3118	3334	80	1619	1796	1341	3543	2024	3740	1056	1754	1909	4537	5470	•	921
Sydney (NSW)	1412	3970	2830	2875	1001	1160	2495	286	4034	1142	4516	1926	872	2400	4073	5080	921	•

Dress

In summer in southern Australia and throughout the year in the tropical north, light clothing of natural fibres is best. Even on hot days, however, it can be quite cool in the evening and at night, and something warm – a pullover or a track-suit – will be appreciated. During the in-between seasons and in winter, warm clothing is required throughout the day in the south.

Stout, comfortable shoes are essential, and in the bush good walking boots should be worn. As well as taking adequate safeguards against the sun (see below), when visiting the beach it is important to wear beach-shoes as a protection against sharp pieces of coral, spines of sea-urchins and razor-sharp shells.

Protection against the sun

The hole in the ozone layer over the Antarctic (see Baedeker Special, pp. 18-19) has led to high ultraviolet radiation in Australia. You should be sure, therefore, to take a sun-block cream with a high protection factor. The saying "Between eleven and three – under a tree" should be taken to heart and the midday sun avoided. The heat is not felt so much if a wind is blowing, as it usually is on the coast, and you may suffer sunburn without being aware of it. Weather reports on radio and television give information daily about the strength of ultraviolet radiation. It is important to wear a hat, and to cover your arms with a long-sleeved shirt/blouse.

Protection against insects

Protection against insect bites is also essential. A product called "Rid" is much used in Australia.

Electricity

Electrical voltage is 240/250 AC, 50 cycles

Australian electrical appliances have a plug with three flat pins, the upper two being set at an angle to the third. Most visitors will therefore require an adaptor.

Emergency Services

The emergency number throughout Australia for police, fire and ambulance is 000. Calls are toll-free; no coin need be inserted in payphones.

Breakdown assistance

Tel. 13 11 11 to contact the automobile clubs anywhere in Australia (see also Motoring in Australia).

Events

In Australia there are numerous local festivals and other events. In addition to lively popular celebrations and sporting events there are now increasing numbers of art and cultural festivals. Agricultural shows are held mainly in September–November.

The following is merely a selection of events throughout Australia. The exact dates can be obtained from the Australian Tourist Commission (see Information).

January

Albany (WA): Wittenoom Cup on the Albany Golf Club course
Arno Bay (SA): Carnival on New Year's Day
Burnie (TAS): New Year's Day Carnival
Corryong (VIC): Folk Festival
Hahndorf (SA): German Festival (Schuetzenfest)
Kundabung (NSW): Rodeo
Longford (TAS): Folk Festival
Melbourne (VIC): Australian Open (tennis)
Port Lincoln (SA): Tunarama Festival
Seaspray (VIC): Surf Fishing Contest
St Helens (TAS): Athletic Carnival
Stanley (TAS): Aquatic Carnival
Sydney (NSW) Surf Carnival
Sydney (NSW) Arts and Music Festival
Sydney (NSW) Opera in the Park

January 26th

Throughout Australia: Australia Day (in Sydney 6km/4 mile race by harbour ferries to Harbour Bridge)

February

Boyup Brook (WA): Country Music Awards
Buninyong (VIC): Gold King Festival (3rd Sun. in Feb.)
Canberra (ACT): St Valentine's Day Jazz Festival
Colac (VIC): Rowing Regatta

	Stanthorpe (QLD): Apple and Grape Festival Sydney (NSW): Chinese New Year
Feb.–April	Peaceful Bay (WA): Salmon fishing season
March	Throughout Australia: Clean Up Australia Day Adelaide (SA): Adelaide Festival (two weeks) Ballarat (VIC): Begonia Festival Barossa Valley (SA) and Hunter Valley (NSW): Vintage Festivals Canberra (ACT): Autumn Flower Show Colac (VIC): Kana Festival Devonport (TAS): Regatta Koo-wee-rup (VIC): Potato Festival (beginning of March) Korumburra (VIC): Karmai (Giant Worm) Festival Melbourne (VIC): Australian Formula One Grand Prix Melbourne (VIC): Moomba Festival Penola (SA): Grape Zenolian Festival (in odd-numbered years) Poowong (VIC): Karmai Festival Sydney (NSW): St Patrick's Day Parade Sydney (NSW): Mardi Gras (parade of gays and lesbians) Tanunda (SA): Essenfest Wagin (WA): Woolarama Wedderburn (VIC): Annual Gold Dig
March/April	Albany (WA): Albany Art Prize Bellbrae and Torquay (VIC): Bells Beach Surfing Championship Berri (SA): Rodeo on Easter Day Burketown (QLD): World Barramundi Fishing Championships Mollymook and Ulladulla (NSW): Blessing of the Fleet (Easter) Monbulk (VIC): Mountain Festival Nuriootpa (SA): Vintage Festival Oakbank (SA): Great Easter Steeplechase Paddington (NSW): Royal Easter Show Port Macquarie (NSW): Carnival of the Pines (Easter) Port Vincent (SA): Aquatic Carnival (Easter) Roma (QLD): Easter in the Country Festival Waikerie (SA): Easter Horse Show Warwick (QLD): Rock Swap Festival
April	Bright (VIC): Autumn Festival (end of month) Canberra (ACT): Nike Marathon (2nd Sunday) Myrtleford (VIC): Hops and Tobacco Festival Katherine (NT): Outback Festival Perth (WA): National Boomerang Throwing Championship Sydney (NSW): Performances by Australian Ballet in Opera House
April–May	Tumut (NSW): Festival of the Falling Leaf
May	Alice Springs (NT): Camel Cup Boyup Brook (WA): Autumn Art Fair Burketown (QLD): Gregory Canoe Race Carnarvon (WA): Carnarvon Tropical Festival (1st weekend) Charleville (QLD): West Queensland Annual Show Crows Nest (QLD): Crows Nest Show Gympie (QLD): Gympie Show Ingham (QLD): Australian-Italian Festival Mount Isa (QLD): Gregory River Canoe Race Renner Springs (NT): Rodeo Roma (QLD): Roma Annual Show Thursday Island (QLD): Torres Strait Cultural Festival Westbury (TAS): Maypole Festival
May/June	Newman (WA): Horse races

Event	Date
Brisbane (QLD): Queensland Day Celebrations Charters Towers (QLD): Goldfields Festival Cooktown (QLD): Cooktown National Park Discovery Festival Darwin (NT): Bougainvillea Festival Grenfell (NSW): Henry Lawson Festival Mount Isa (QLD): Mount Isa Show Townsville (QLD): Pacific Festival Warwick (QLD): Frostbite Regatta	June
Port Macquarie (NSW): Pioneer Week	June-July
Burketown (QLD): Rodeo and races Caboolture (QLD): Pomona Arts and Crafts Festival Cairns (QLD): Cairns Show Darwin (NT): Beer Can Regatta Kalgoorlie-Boulder (WA): Great Gold Festival Mareeba (QLD): Rodeo Festival McLaren Vale (SA): Almond Blossom Festival Mildura (VIC): Pacific Hot Air Balloon Festival Yamba (NSW): Fishing Festival	July
Barcaldine (QLD): Wild flowers	July-Sept.
Coolgardie (WA): Wild flowers	July-Oct.
Crystal Brook (QLD): Annual Show Gympie (QLD): Gympie Country Music Muster Kununurra (WA): Ord River Festival and Ord Tiki Raft Race Mossman (QLD): Mossman Show Mount Isa (QLD): Rodeo and Mardi Gras Newman (WA): Fortescue Festival Noosa (QLD): Festival of the Waters Traralgon (VIC): Latrobe Valley Festival	August
Wollongong (NSW): Festival of Wollongong	Aug.-Sept
Albany (WA): Albany Classic Race Atherton (QLD): Maize Festival Beaudesert (QLD): Beaudesert Show Bencubbin (WA): Marbles Championship Birdsville (QLD): Birdsville Race Meeting Brisbane (QLD): Warana Festival and Parade (Brisbane's biggest festival of drama, music and dance, culminating in a great parade through the streets) Brisbane (QLD): Paniyiri (Greek festival) Broome (WA): National Aboriginal Music Awards Bundaberg (QLD): Harvest Festival Canberra (ACT): Floriade Clermont (QLD): Clermont Rodeo Cowell (SA): Annual Show Cunnamulla (QLD): World Lizard Racing Championship Dunk Island (QLD): Billfish Classic Eudunda (SA): Show Hobart (TAS): Tulip Festival of Tasmania Kalgoorlie-Boulder (WA): Kalgoorlie Cup Kimba (SA): Show Koorda (WA): Corn Dolly Festival Leongatha (VIC): Daffodil Festival Lightning Ridge (NSW): Opal Festival Melbourne (VIC): VFL Grand Final (Australian football) Nowra (NSW): Shoalhaven City Festival Stanley (TAS): Circular Head Arts Festival	September

	Texas (QLD): Texas Roundup (in even-numbered years) Toodyay (WA): Folk Arts Festival Toowoomba (QLD): Carnival of Flowers Yeppoon (QLD): Pineapple Festival of Cultural Arts
Sept.–Oct.	Devonport (TAS): Mersey Valley Music Festival
October	Alice Springs (NT): Henley-on-Todd Regatta ("boat" race in dry river bed) Avoca (VIC): Wool and Wine Festival Beenleigh (QLD): Gem Festival Blackheath (NSW): Rhododendron Festival Boyup Brook (WA): Blackwood Marathon Relay Cambooya (QLD): Fun Day Canberra (ACT): National Festival of Australian Theatre Canberra (ACT): Oktoberfest Crows Nest (NSW): Crows Nest Day and Worm Races Crystal Brook (SA): Rodeo Curdimurka (SA): Curdimurka Outback Ball Cunolly (VIC): Gold Rush Festival Echuca (VIC): Rich River Festival Euroa (VIC): International Sheep-Shearing Championships Glen Innes (NSW): Australian Bush Music Festival Gold Coast (QLD): Tropicana Festival Gympie (QLD): Gold Rush Festival Home Hill (QLD): Harvest Festival Week Jamestown (SA): Annual Show McLaren Vale (SA): Wine Bushing Festival Melbourne (VIC): Melbourne International Festival of the Arts Melbourne (VIC): Oktoberfest Morgan (SA): South Australian State Motorcycle Championships Mount Isa (QLD): Oktoberfest Murray Bridge (SA): Show Penola (SA): Show Warwick (QLD): Rodeo West Wyalong (QLD): Festival of Youth
Oct.–March	Hobart (TAS): numerous festivals, shows and regattas
November	Albany (WA): Perth-Albany Ocean Yacht Race Albany (WA): International Classic Car Race Broome (WA): Mango Festival Canberra (ACT): Osibi African Cultural Festival Childers (QLD): Harvest Festival Coolgardie (WA): Camel Races Crows Nest (QLD): Crows Nest Campdraft Launceston (TAS): Festivale (multi-cultural festival) Marysville (VIC): Wirreanda Festival Melbourne (VIC): Melbourne Cup (first time in November) Ross (TAS): Rodeo Young (NSW): National Cherry Festival
Nov.–April	Albany (WA): Summer Racing Carnival
December	Brisbane (QLD): Carols by Candlelight Gordonvale (QLD): Lions Club Bin Hauling Festival Murray Bridge (SA): Christmas Festival Nerang (QLD): Festival of Arts Port MacDonnell (SA): Regatta Day (Dec. 28th) Sydney (NSW): Performances by Australian Ballet in Opera House Sydney (NSW): Sydney Festival and Carnival (Dec. 31st) Tanunda (SA): Barossa Music Festival Wagin (WA): Annual Festival

The ever-popular barbecue

Food and Drink

Thanks to the large number of immigrants from Mediterranean and Asian countries Australian cuisine is now rich and varied. Particularly innovative Australian chefs have succeeded in establishing a new form of cooking known as "outback cuisine", based on seeds, fruits, herbs and vegetables as eaten and enjoyed by the Aborigines since time immemorial. These include kurrajong seeds, bunya and madcadamia nuts, bush-tomatoes and kakadu plums.

Meals

The Australian breakfast is like the traditional British breakfast, with ham and eggs, cereals or muesli and frequently also an Australian speciality, Vegemite (a dark-coloured yeast spread for bread or toast). Lunch usually consists merely of a sandwich or some form of fast food. The main meal, in the evening, is dinner.

Barbecue

The barbecue, or "barbie", is a regular feature of the Australian life-style. Almost every public picnic or rest area has places for open fires or grill facilities; the most modern work on gas and are coin-operated.

Specialities

Fish and seafood

Australia has excellent fish (barramundi from northern waters, sea-trout and John Dory fish) and seafood, such as Moreton Bay bugs (small crustaceans), mud crabs (river crabs), yabbies, crayfish, prawns, oysters and shellfish. Tasmanian crabs, which may weigh anything up to 15kg/33lb, are among the world's largest crustaceans.

Meat

There is of course also plenty of meat – beef and mutton in abundance, and kangaroo meat, which is lean and tender and tastes like beef. A speciality of the Barossa Valley (SA) is a rabbit casserole. Another favourite dish is carpetbag steak, a thick slice of beef larded with rock oysters. Other specialities are sausage and chicko rolls.

Fruit

Australia has a magnificent range of fresh fruit, including such tropical fruits as mangoes, pineapples, passion fruit and pawpaws.

Sweets

An Australian speciality is pavlova, a concoction of meringue, fruit and cream. Another favourite sweet is Australian flower honey, particularly leatherwood honey from the unspoiled forests of Tasmania. Various sweets incorporating ginger from Queensland are also popular.

Drinks

Soft drinks

Australia's British roots are reflected in the popularity of tea ("billy tea" = black tea). Tap-water is drinkable everywhere in Australia. Bottled mineral waters are not much drunk, although Australia has mineral springs (e.g. in Tasmania); most bottled water is imported from France (and expensive). Australians drink a lot of milk, often in the form of milk shakes. There are also excellent fruit juices, particularly those made from exotic fruits.

Alcoholic drinks

Alcohol is sold only in special liquor shops or bottle shops. A favourite Australian drink, particularly in the hot, dry north and in the interior, is beer, which is always served ice-cold, almost half-frozen. The best-known brands are Fosters, Victoria Bitter (VB for short) and "XXXX" ("Four X"). Australian wines are also excellent, varying in character according to region (see Wine). Spirits such as brandy or Australian-made Bundaberg rum ("Bundy") are expensive because of high excise duties.

In view of the great heat it is better to abstain from alcohol during the day.

Getting to Australia

By air

The flight from Europe to Australia takes between 20 and 30 hours. The fastest route from North America is the direct flight from Los Angeles to Sydney, which takes 15 hours; other flights, with one or more intermediate stops, take correspondingly longer.

International airlines

Many international airlines fly to Australia. The Australian national airline Qantas has services from London to Australia's seven international airports (Sydney, Melbourne, Brisbane, Darwin, Cairns, Perth and Adelaide) and, in North America, from Los Angeles and San Francisco. From London there are flights by British Airways to the major Australian cities. All major airlines fly to Australia, but not all fly to every Australian airport.

It is well worth while comparing the fares on offer by the various airlines and taking advantage of reduced fares available for advance bookings.

Fares

Fares vary considerably according to season and are at their lowest during the Australian winter, and at their highest around Christmas and 0during the main holiday season.

Routes; stopovers

Most services from Europe fly via South-East Asia (e.g. Bangkok, Denpasar/Bali, Hong Kong, Kuala Lumpur, Singapore). Flights from North America usually go via Hawaii or New Zealand. Most airlines have stopover programmes allowing passengers, without extra charge, to spend one or two days at some intermediate point on either the outward or return journey. They may also offer flights within Australia at no additional charge or at reduced rates.

Special rates within Australia for visitors

Visitors flying to Australia can also buy (before leaving home) various passes (Explorer Pass (with Qantas), G'Day Pass, etc.) entitling them to reduced fares on Australian domestic air services. Information from travel agencies and airlines.

By sea

It is also possible to travel to Australia in luxurious cruise ships (Cunard Lines, CTC Lines, P & O Cruises, Royal Viking Lines). The voyage takes at least three weeks. Another alternative – particularly attractive to older travellers – are Fly and Cruise trips. The first part of the journey is by air – mostly to Singapore – and thence by cruise ship to Australia. Details from all good travel agents.

Package tours

Numerous travel operators offer package tours covering the flight to Australia and accommodation and travel within the country. Lists of operators can be obtained from the Australian Tourist Commission (see Information).

Goldfields

Victoria
Goldfields Tourist Route

In Victoria visitors can follow the history of the goldfields on the Goldfields Tourist Route (500km/310 miles), which runs from Ballarat by way of Stawell to Bendigo and from there back to Ballarat. A brochure, "The Goldfields", and other information can be obtained from Tourism Victoria (see Information).

Western Australia
Historic Goldfields Drive

Coolgardie, 550km/340 miles east of Perth (WA), is the best preserved of the old gold-mining towns, with an exhibition on the history of the goldfields. The neighbouring town of Kalgoorlie-Boulder has an interesting Museum of the Goldfields. From here too there are "gold rush tours" and conducted tours of Hannans North Tourist Mine. Kalgoorlie is the starting-point of the Historic Goldfields Drive (171km/106 miles) to Boulder, Coolgardie and Kambalda.

Further information is contained in a brochure, "Golden Heartlands", obtainable from the Western Australian Tourism Commission (see Information).

Dig it yourself

Under the slogan "Dig it yourself" visitors can try their luck as gold prospectors. For this purpose they must have a mining licence (obtainable for a modest charge from the Department of Minerals and Energy) and the necessary equipment, which can be hired: a gold pan, a pick, a shovel, a mining manual and a mineral map; for covering a large area a metal detector can also be useful. The rock must be dug out and then washed in the pan in the hope of finding "pay dirt". Every now and then the lucky finder of a nugget is featured on television or in the press.

Hazards

Natural catastrophes

Forest and bush fires (see entry), particularly after long dry periods, heavy rain in summer, cyclones and sudden spates and floods in dry river beds as a consequence of cloudbursts are not uncommon occurrences in Australia. Bridges and roads may be washed away and forests and houses destroyed by fire.

Dangerous animals

Among dangerous animals which may be encountered in and near water are the sharks which inhabit all the seas round Australia and the crocodiles (now a protected species) which follow tidal waters far inland up the rivers of northern Australia. Warning about crocodiles should be carefully heeded. In the tropical summer the highly poisonous box jellyfish or sea wasps are a danger to bathers. Other poisonous sea creatures are stonefish, which resemble stones on the the seabed, sting rays, small blue-ringed octopuses and cone-shaped shellfish. Poisonous snakes are found in water as well as on land. Normally they make off when disturbed, and usually bite only when attacked. Most snake venom takes full effect only after a few hours, and all hospitals hold sera against snakebites. The shock after the bite is as dangerous as the bite itself. There are also two dangerous species of poisonous spiders, the funnel-web and the redback spider. In addition there are numerous insects in Australia – wasps, bees, ticks, large ants, scorpions and centipedes – which are harmless except for people with an allergy, though often a nuisance.

Help for the Disabled

The Australians are extremely helpful where disabled visitors are concerned. Airlines, railway companies and other transport organisations, as well as hotels etc. will all be pleased to do their best to accommodate disabled travellers and guests if advised in advance of the nature of the handicap. Restaurants, national parks cinemas, theatres and so on mostly cater for the needs of disabled visitors.

Information

National Information Communication Awareness Network (NICAN)
PO Box 407
Curtin, ACT 2605, tel, 06 6285 3713, fax 06 6285 3714
Australian Council for Rehabilitation of the Disabled (ACROD)
33 Thesiger Crescent, Deakin, Canberra, ACT; tel. 02 6282 4333, fax 02 6281 3488

Hitch Hiking

Hitch-hiking is *very* strongly discouraged in many different publications provided by Australian Tourist Board.
In some Australian states hitch-hiking is prohibited; in the remoter parts of the country opportunities of getting a lift are in any case few and far between; and in general, on safety grounds, hitch-hiking is not to be recommended. Women travelling alone should be particularly on their guard. In any event hte various forms of public transport – in particular the overland buses – have and excellent network of services covering the whole country.
An alternative way of getting a life is through the Green Transport Movement (tel. 08 267 5642, toll free), which can put you in touch with someone travelling the way you want to go in return for a contribution towards the cost of petrol. Opportunities for arrangements of this kind are often posted up in youth hostels.

Holidays on the Farm (Farmstay)

A holiday on a farm is a good way of seeing something of life in upcountry Australia. Visitors can watch the everyday activities of the farm (the herding of cattle, sheep-shearing, etc.) and explore the surrounding country on horseback. Good food and country comfort are normally part of the deal but standards do vary. This is not, however, a particularly cheap kind of holiday; the current cost is between A$130 and A$350 per person per day. Holders of a visitor's visa (see Travel Documents) are not officially permitted to take paid work on a farm.
Lists of farmstay sites can be obtained from tourist information offices and automobile clubs. See Information.

Hotels • Motels • Resorts • Lodges

Accommodation of every category and price level

Originally an Australian hotel was merely an inn, the main function of which was to sell liquor but which was required as a condition of its licence to have a few rooms for guests. Nowadays, however, accommodation of every category and price level and of a generally high standard is available. Although many hotels, motels, resorts and lodges are privately owned, including some beautiful old houses, many are owned by large, international hotel chains (Hilton, Hyatt, Inter-Continental, Ritz Carlton, Ramada, Flag, Best Western, Holiday Inn, etc.), and rooms in these can be booked through their international network.

Hotels

Although located mainly in towns and cities, hotels are also to be found in many rural tourist areas, for example, in the wine-producing regions. The better class establishments provide shuttle services to and from the nearest airports and railway stations, and usually offer such amenities as restaurants, bars, swimming pools and fitness centres, and often a coffee shop and boutique.

Motels

Motels (often known as motor inns or roadhouses) are designed to meet the needs of tourists with cars. They are often to be found on the outskirts of towns or in popular tourist areas, and have large car parks and, in many cases, swimming pools, playgrounds and sports facilities.

Resorts

These are mainly luxurious and expensive holiday resorts offering a wide range of sports and leisure facilities. Such complexes may – depending on their location and standard – have their own beaches and provide sailing boats, catamarans, surfboards, diving instruction, riding stables, golf courses, tennis courts and a varied programme of entertainment.

Lodges

Lodges ranging from the simple to the extremely comfortable have been built in the more remote regions far from infrastructure of any kind – in the tropical rain forests of northern Queensland, for example, or near the once semi-inaccessible tropical beaches to the north. In most cases these are wooden buildings – some converted from former hunting-lodges or lumberjacks' huts – with their own water and energy supplies and successfully complement the environment. Often there is a small aircraft runway nearby or approach roads suitable for four-wheel drive vehicles.

Pubs

Some pubs offer reasonably priced food and plain but clean rooms (from $25 a night). Advance reservation is not usually necessary.

Apartments

An economic form of accommodation for a large family or a stay of some length is a self-catering apartment (one or more bedrooms, a living room, a bathroom and a fully equipped kitchen with a washing machine). The rate per night ranges between $120 and $300.

Other types of accommodation

See Bed and Breakfast, Camping and Caravanning, Holidays on the Farm, Youth Accommodation.

Price levels

A rough indication (without prejudice) of the cost of an overnight stay in a double room is as follows (based on those found in the spring of 1997):
Luxury hotels (L): over $220 (suite over $400)
Hotels with very high standards of comfort and amenities (M/L): over $130
Good middle-range hotels (M): $80 to $160
Simple, reasonably priced hotels and motels (M/S): $50 to $100
Very reasonably priced establishments (S): $20 to $70

Additional charges

In many cases an additional charge is made for an extra bed in the room. In many hotels, children sleep free in their parents' room.
Breakfast in rarely included in the cost of the room. Many urban hotels also charge extra for a garage space.
A number of hotels offer special week-end package deals, when the cost of a room is heavily discounted or an additional night's acommodation may be provided free of charge.

Furnishings

In addition to a comfortable bed, wardrobe, table and chair, rooms in Australian hotels usually have a radio, T.V. and kettle. Most also have their own bathroom (shower, bath, W.C.) An increasing number are now air-conditioned.

Room reservations, Information

It is advisable to reserve hotel rooms in advance. Current accommodation guides and telephone numbers for bookings can be obtained from the Australian Tourist Commission (see Information).
In Australia itself local tourist offices will assist. Hotel rooms can also be booked at special desks at all the larger airports.

Flag International

Rooms in several hundred Australian hotels, motels, resorts, inns and apartments can be booked through the Flag International system (in Australia: tel. 13 24 00 free of charge anywhere in the country).
The following is just a brief list of some recommended hotels, arranged alphabetically by state and town or tourist location.

Australian Capital Territory

Canberra

Forrest Motor Inn (M/S), 30 National Circuit, Forrest, ACT 2603
Tel. (02) 6295 3433, fax (02) 6295 2119
77 rooms and suites
Value-for-money motel acommodation in a prime location behind Parliament House and in the vicinity of the National Gallery.

Garden City Premier Inn (M), Jerrabomberra Ave., Narrabundah, ACT 2604
Tel. (02) 6295 3322, fax (02) 6239 6289
72 rooms and suites, swimming pool
Modern and well-appointed accommodation in a quiet location by the Capital Golf Course.

Olims Canberra Hotel (M), c/o Ainslie and Limestone Ave., Braddon ACT 2601, Tel. (02) 6248 5511, fax (02) 6247 0864
125 rooms, restaurant, bistro, bar
The individual rooms of this comfortable hotel are grouped around an attractive garden with a fountain.

New South Wales

Blue Mountains

Blackheath Motor Inn (M/S), 281 Great Western Hwy, Blackheath, NSW 2785
Tel. (02) 4787 8788, fax (02) 4787 8929
18 studios
Simple but well-appointed motel, very suitable as a setting-out point for excursions into the Blue Mountains.

Hawkesbury Lodge (M), 61 Richmond Road., Windsor, NSW 2756
Tel. (02) 4577 4222, fax (02) 4577 6939
74 rooms and suites. golf, tennis, health club with spa and sauna
This well-kept rural hotel lies at the foot of the Blue Mountains in some charming countryside near the Hawkesbury River. The historic town centre of Windsor is but a few minutes away.

Crystal Creek

Crystal Creek Rainforest Lodge (M), Brookers Rd., Murwillumbah, NSW
Tel. (02) 6679 1591, fax (02) 6679 1596
6 cabins. A very comfortable and pleasant lodge in the sub-tropical rain forest by the wildly romantic upper reaches of Crystal Creek.

Sydney

Cambridge Hotel (M), 212 Riley St., Surrey Hills, Sydney, NSW 2010
Tel. (02) 9212 1111, fax (02) 9281 1981
170 rooms, restaurant, bar, swimming pool, fitness centre with sauna. Just a few minutes' walk from the bustling town centre, the hotel has recently been modernised at considerable expense.

Gazebo (M), 2 Elizabeth Bay Road., Elizabeth Bay, Sydney, NSW 2011
Tel. (02) 9358 1999, fax (02) 9356 2951
400 rooms, 2 restaurants, cocktail bar, swimming pool, sauna.
This modern hotel complex is in two parts, the "Tower" and the "Court". There are fine views from the rooms in the "Tower", while those in the "Court" are more generously proportioned. In the immediate vicinity is the Kings Cross entertainment centre.

Ibis Darling Harbour (M/S), 70 Murray St., Sydney 2009
Tel. (02) 9563 0888, fax (02) 9563 0899
255 rooms, restaurant, bar, terrace.
Located by Darling Harbour which, with its hypermodern shopping centre, new exhibition and congress centre and various other attractions, has become the favoured area of this Olympic city. This purpose-built hotel is popular with businessmen and tourists. There is a fine view from the Panorama Restaurant, and the Skyline Bar is the "in-place".

*Inter-Continental (L), 117 Macquarie St., Sydney, NSW 2000
Tel. (02) 9230 0200, fax (02) 9240 1240
500 rooms, several restaurants and bars, lobby, swimming pool. This top class hotel is centrally located near the Botanic Gardens and only a few minutes on foot from Sydney Cove (ferry mooring).

*Ritz Carlton (L), 93 Macquarie St., Sydney, NSW 2000
Tel. (02) 9252 4600, fax (02) 9252 4286
100 rooms, bar with open fireplace.
This relatively small but very fine luxury hotel near the Botanic Gardens is rightly listed as one of the "Leading Hotels of the World". One is likely to meet any number of well-known jet-set personalities in the cosy bar.

*Sheraton on the Park (L), 161 Elizabeth St., Sydney, NSW 2000
Tel. (02) 9286 6686, fax (02) 9286 6000
560 rooms, several restaurants and bars, generously equipped fitness centre with indoor swimming pool, sauna, steam-bath and solarium.
This top class international hotel is very centrally located. Hyde Park and the harbour are a few minutes' walk away. Tasteful elegance is the keynote of this multi-storey hotel.

Sydney Renaissance (L), 30 Pitt St., Sydney, NSW 2000
Tel. (02) 9259 7000, fax (02) 9252 1999
580 rooms, several restaurants and bars, club lounge, brasserie, swimming pool, fitness centre with sauna. A modern, multi-storey luxury hotel for very discerning businessmen and tourists, located very near to the world-famous Sydney Opera House.

Northern Territory

Alice Springs

Alice Springs Vista Hotel (M/L), Stevens Road, Alice Springs, NT 0870
Tel. (08) 8952 6100, fax (08) 8952 1988
140 rooms, restaurant, cocktail lounge, swimming pool, tennis.
This accommodation borders on the luxurious and lies a few kilometres outside the city at the foot of the picturesque MacDonnell Ranges. The hotel restaurant is renowned worldwide.

Plaza Hotel (M/L), Barrett Drive, Alice Springs, NT 0870
Tel. (08) 8952 8000, fax (08) 8952 3822
235 rooms, 3 restaurants, several bars, swimming pool, 2 tennis courts, an 18-hole golf course. A modern hotel on the outskirts of the city by the Todd River, with a fine view of the MacDonnell Ranges. The guests' rooms are generously proportioned and very well appointed.

Ayers Rock
Uluru National Park

Desert Gardens (M), Ayers Rock Resort, Yulura, NT 0872
Tel. (08) 8956 2100, fax (08) 8956 2156
160 rooms, restaurant, café, bar, swimming pool.
This family hotel lies in the centre of a beautiful garden and has recently been completely renovated.

Outback Pioneer Hotel ((M/S), Ayers Rock Resort, Yulara, NT 0872
Tel. (08) 8956 2170, fax (08) 8956 2320
125 rooms, restaurant, bar, swimming pool, barbecue area.
Friendly establishment, good value for money. The rooms are modern and suitably furnished.

*Sails in the Desert (L), Ayers Rock Resort, Yulara, NT 0872
Tel. (08) 8956 2100, fax (08) 8956 2156
228 rooms, several superb restaurants, imposing foyer, cocktail bar, swimming pool, health club, tennis.
Top class hotel with a view of the famous Australian landmark. Its bold and airy sail-like roof provides relaxing shade.

Daly Waters

Daly Waters Pub (S), a few minutes off the Stuart Highway, Daly Waters, NT 0852; tel. (08) 8975 9927, fax (08) 8975 9982
10 rooms and a camp site. A typical, historically meaningful outback pub, but somewhat lacking in comforts.

Darwin	Darwin Travelodge (M), 122 The Esplanade, Darwin, NT 0800 Tel. (08) 8981 5388, fax (08) 8981 5708 180 rooms, restaurant, cocktail bar, swimming pool. This ultra-modern hotel forms part of an international chain and lies in the middle of a tropical park on Darwin's Esplanade.
	Ivan's (S), 97 Mitchell St., Darwin, NT 0800 Tel. (08) 8981 5385, fax (08) 8981 9096. Simple but quite comfortable accommodation for backpackers.
	Mirambeena Resort (M), 64 Cavenagh St., Darwin, NT Tel. (08) 8946 0111, fax (08) 89 81 51 16 220 rooms, restaurant, 2 swimming pools with pool bar, tropical garden with barbecue area, mini-golf. Not far from the Esplanade and and a few minutes on foot from the city centre, this hotel is very suitable for holidaymakers; families with children can feel at home here.
	Novotel Atrium, The Esplanade & Peel St., Darwin, NT 0800 Tel. (08) 8941 0755, fax (08) 8981 9025 140 rooms and studios, 2 restaurants, cocktail bar, swimming pool, fitness centre, garden. This hotel of several storeys is also centrally located on the Esplanade and only a short walk from the city centre. The prettily laid out inner courtyard with its tropical plants is a popular meeting place.
Devil's Marbles/ Stuart Highway	Wauchope Hotel, ca. 8km/5 miles south of the Devil's Marbles, Stuart Highway, NT; tel./fax (08) 8964 1963. 10 rooms, camp site, bar. A popular stop with truckers, and visitors may well see a genuine Australian "Thunder Downunder" haulage vehicle parked here.
Kakadu National Park	*Gagudju Crocodile Hotel (M/L), Flinders St., Jabiru, NT 0886 Tel. (08) 8979 2800, fax (08) 8979 2707 120 rooms, restaurant, several bars, swimming pool. The architecture of this modern building is highly original; from the air it looks like the giant crocodile Ginga, famous in aboriginal legend. It caters for the most discerning tastes and is a suitable setting-out point for excursions into Kakadu National Park.
Katherine	Frontier Katherine (M), Stuart Highway, Katherine, NT 0850 Tel. (08) 8972 1744, fax (08) 8972 2790 98 rooms, swimming pool. The first hotel on the square in the centre of an attractive lawn. Judged by outback standards, the rooms are very comfortably furnished.
	Pine Tree Motel (S/M), 3rd St., Katherine, NT 0850 Tel. (08) 8972 2533, fax. (08) 8972 2920 48 rooms, restaurant, swimming pool. A new and well-run establishment with a well recommended restaurant.
Kings Canyon/ Watarrka National Park	Kings Canyon Resort (M), Watarka National Park, NT 0872 Tel. (08) 8956 7442, fax (08) 8956 7410 100 rooms, camp site. A modern outback hotel with a camp site. Here visitors can obtain a tour pass for the newly constructed Mereenie Loop to Alice Springs.
Larrimah/ Stuart Highway	Larrimah Wayside Inn (S), Larrimah, NT 0852; tel. (08) 8975 2533 10 rooms and a camp site. Legendary outback roadhouse. Nearby is the Larrimah Railway Museum which is worth a visit.
Nhulunburu/ Arnhem Land	The Walkabout Arnhem Land Resort, Nhulunburu, NT 0881 Tel. (08) 8987 1777, fax 8987 2322 40 rooms, restaurant, bar. A pleasant place to relax by the tropical Arafura Lake. The hotel cuisine enjoys a high reputation.

Tennant Creek/ Stuart Highway

Bluestone Motor Inn (S), Paterson St., Tennant Creek, NT 0860
Tel. (08) 8962 2617, fax (08) 8962 2883
60 rooms. A tidy and reasonably comfortable outback motel.

Renner Springs Desert Roadhouse (S), 160km/100 miles north of Tennant Creek, Stuart Highway, NT 0861; tel. (08) 8964 4505, fax (08) 8964 4525
25 rooms and a camp site. Typical outback roadhouse with an informal atmosphere.

Wycliffe Well Roadhouse (S), 135km/84 miles south of Tennant Creek, Stuart Highway, NT 0862; tel/fax (08) 8964 1966
15 rooms and a camp site. A popular stopover with truckers and tourists, because there are several dozen different sorts of beer to be tried here!

Queensland

Airlie Beach

Bush Village (S), Airlie Beach, Cannonvale, QLD
Tel. (079) 466 177, fax (079) 467 227
17 bungalows, swimming pool, diving, snorkelling and hang-gliding. Ideal for backpackers and very suitable as a setting-out point for excursions to the Whitsunday Islands.

Daintree Wilderness Lodge (M), Cape Tribulation Road, Alexandra Bay, QLD 4873; tel (07) 4098 9105, fax (07) 4098 9021
10 cabins. This little lodge was built a few years ago here in the tropical rain forest north of Cairns on sound ecological lines. Eventful excursions can be undertaken from here.

Bedarra Island/ Townsville

*Bedarra Island Resort (L), Bedarra Island, QLD
Tel. (07) 4068 8168, fax (07) 403 602 453
16 villas, restaurant. An exclusive holiday resort in South Seas style, where the guests are cossetted by a world-famous master chef.

Brisbane

Albert Park (M), 551 Wickham Terrace, Brisbane, QLD
Tel. (07) 3831 3111, fax (07) 3832 1290
90 rooms. This well-appointed hotel lies a little way from the city centre near its best known park.

Yellow Submarine (S), 66 Quay St., Brisbane, QLD; tel. (07) 3211 3424
A small hotel for backpackers with 28 beds in a central location.

Cairns

*Cairns International Hotel (M/L), 17 Abbott St., Cairns, QLD 4870
Tel. (070) 311 300, fax (070) 311 801
320 rooms and suites, restaurant. Something of the atmosphere of the colonial period can still be felt in this excellent and central hotel.

Mercure Harbourside Hotel (M), 209 The Esplanade, Cairns, QLD 4871
Tel. (070) 518 999, fax (070) 510 317
170 rooms, restaurant, cocktail bar, swimming pool.
This middle-class hotel has several storeys and lies in a beautiful park directly adjacent to the seaside promenade. From the upper floors there is a fine view of Trinity Bay and the nearby mountains covered in tropical rain forests.

Rosie's, 155 The Esplanade (S), Cairns, QLD 4871
Tel. (070) 510 235, fax (070) 515 191
60 beds, swimming pool.
Located directly on the promenade, this accommodation for backpackers is one of the best of its kind in the whole of Queensland.

Cape Tribulation

Crocodylus Village (S), Cape Tribulation, QLD
Tel. (07) 4098 9166, fax (07) 4098 9131Accommodation for backpackers (120 beds) in tropical rain forest on the edge of Cape Tribulation National Park.

Fern Tree Resort (M), Cape Tribulation, QLD
Tel. (07) 4098 0000, fax (07) 4098 0011
50 rooms and bungalows, restaurant, bar, 2 swimming pools.
This lodge with its attractive wooden buildings lies a few hundred metres from the beach in dense tropical rain forest.

Daydream Island/ Mackay

Daydream Island Resort (M/L), Mackay, QLD 4741
Tel. (07) 4948 8488, fax (07) 4948 8499
300 rooms and studios, several restaurants, atrium lobby, bar, bistro, coffee shop, 2 swimming pools, beach club with fitness centre, children's club, tennis, 9-hole golf course, parasailing, various water sports (including diving and windsurfing).
This resort covers an area of 10ha/25 acres on a small island forming part of the Whitsunday Islands, and is very popular with sportlovers and families with children. Those wishing to explore part of the Great Barrier Reef could not do better than stay at this resort.

Dunk Island

*Dunk Island Resort (L), via Townsville, Dunk Island, QLD 4810
Tel. (070) 688 199, fax (070) 688 528
150 rooms, studios, cabanas and villas, 2 restaurants, coffee shop, 3 bars, children's club, boutique, cricket, golf, tennis, squash, riding, clay-pigeon shooting and archery, bathing beach, various water sports (including diving, catamarans, windsurfing, sea-fishing).

Fraser Island

*Kingfisher Bay Hotel (L); tel. (07) 3221 1811, fax (07) 3221 3270
235 rooms, suites and bungalows, 3 restaurants, several swimming pools, bathing beach, all kinds of water sports.
Kingfisher Bay Hotel is without doubt an architectural jewel as well as fitting into the landscape in an environmentally friendly manner.

Great Keppel Island

*Great Keppel Island Resort (L), via Rockhampton, QLD 4701
Tel. (079) 395 044, fax (079) 391 775
190 rooms and suites, 3 restaurants, fitness centre with sauna, golf, tennis, several bathing beaches, all kinds of water sports (especially sailing, surfing, snorkelling and diving).
Superbly appointed holiday accommodation for those who demand the best, located on Queensland's best-known island for bathers with easy access to the natural beauty of the Great Barrier Reef. The resort attracts mainly younger guests for whom evening entertainment is also provided.

Hamilton Island

Holiday Inn (M/L), Hamilton Island, QLD 4803
Tel. (07) 4946 9999, fax. (07) 4946 8888
750 rooms, suites and bungalows, 9 restaurants, 8 bars, golf, tennis, squash, 8 swimming pools, beach, all water sports (especially sailing, diving and snorkelling), shopping centre, children's club.
Holiday Inn on Hamilton Island is one of Australia's largest holiday resorts, so it will come as no surprise to learn that things are quite lively here all the year round.

Hayman Island

*Hayman Island Resort (L); tel. (079) 469 333
200 rooms and suites, 6 restaurants, several bars, an 18-hole golf course, tennis, swimming pool, sailing, windsurfing, diving and snorkelling.
Hayman Island is almost 400ha/1000 acres in area and lies near the Great Barrier Reef in the region of Whitsunday Passage. This resort is one of the "Leading Hotels of the World". It was recently renovated and is now one of the most luxurious hotels in the southern hemisphere.

Heron Island

Heron Island Resort (M/L), via Gladstone, Heron Island, QLD
Tel. (02) 9364 8350, fax (02) 9369 8937
120 rooms and suites, restaurant, cocktail bar, tennis, swimming pool, sandy beach, diving, snorkelling. Exceedingly friendly and comfortable, this hotel lies on a small island at the southern end of the Great Barrier Reef. Visitors looking for peace and quiet, and nature-lovers will find what they seek here.

Observing nature is the main leisure pursuit (including ornithological walks, watching turtles and whales and snorkelling expeditions to the coral reefs).

Kuranda

Kuranda Rainforest Resort (M), Greenhills Road, Kuranda, QLD 4872
Tel. (07) 4093 7555, fax 4093 7567
40 rooms and 30 cabins. Good accommodation for holidaymakers seeking adventure in the tropical mountain rain forest of Kuranda.

Lindeman Island

Club Mediterranée (M/L); tel. (079) 469 100
220 rooms and suites, restaurant, cocktail bar, golf course, several bathing beaches, all kinds of water sports (especially sailing and diving).
The architecturally pleasing and airy wooden buildings of this well-run holiday hotel were built only a few years ago. It is ideal for those seeking less noise and bustle and who appreciate the beauties of nature on water and on land.

Lizard Island

*Lizard Island Lodge (L),; tel. (070) 603 999, fax (070) 603 991
40 rooms, suites and villas, restaurant, tennis, several bathing beaches, diving, snorkelling, sailing, deep-sea fishing.
This extremely exclusive and expensive establishment is located on the almost unspoiled northernmost island of the Great Barrier Reef. Lizard Island is surrounded by incredibly beautiful coral gardens.

Magnetic Island/ Townsville

Magnetic International Resort (M), Nelly Bay, QLD 4819
Tel. (07) 4778 5200, fax (07) 4778 5806
96 rooms and suites, restaurant, swimming pool, several bathing beaches, water sports (especially diving and snorkelling).
This is one of the newest holiday hotels in the Great Barrier Reef region, and is particularly suitable for families and children.

Mission Beach

Backpackers Lodge, 28 Wongaling Beach Road, Mission Beach, QLD
Tel. (070) 688 317, fax (070) 688 616
74 beds, swimming pool.
Very quietly located and surprisingly comfortable acommodation for backpackers. From here some very worthwhile wild-water trips and excursions to the Great Barrier Reef can be undertaken.

Mossman

*Silky Oaks Lodge (L), Mossman Gorge, QLD 4873
Tel. (07) 4098 1666, fax (07) 4098 1983
60 cabins. Boasting every comfort, this lodge is one of the finest of its kind in Australia. It lies in the tropical rain forest north of Cairns, close to the wildly romantic Mossman Gorge. Injured wallabies are cared for in a compound belonging to the lodge.

Noosa Heads

Backpackers of the Beach (S), 26 Stevens St., Noosa Heads, QLD 4567
Tel. (07) 5447 4739
Fairly new and with modern furnishings, this accommodation for backpackers is quiet and located near the beach.

Sheraton Noosa Resort (M/L), Hastings St., Noosa Heads, QLD 4567
Tel. (07) 5449 4888, fax (07) 5449 2230
110 rooms and studios, 4 restaurants, 4 bars, lobby, shop, swimming pool, fitness centre with sauna and squash courts.
This elegant hotel in the upper price range lies on the "Sunshine Coast" of Queensland, on a promontory between the Noosa River and the sea. It is popular with both gourmets and sports-loving guests. In the vicinity of the hotel are golf courses, tennis courts and water sports. Musical entertainment is provided in the evenings.

Palm Cove

Allamanda (L/M), Palm Cove, Northern Queensland, QLD 4871
Tel. (070) 590 022, fax (070) 590 166
70 rooms, restaurant, bar, terrace, 3 swimming pools, beach.
An attractive establishment in the upper price range in the middle of a tropical park. Suited to those seeking an active holiday, as there is a sports centre nearby with golf, tennis, riding and diving tuition.

Ramada Resort Great Barrier Reef (M/L), Palm Cove, Northern Queensland, QLD 4871; tel. (070) 553 999, fax (070) 553 902
190 rooms, several restaurants, bar, swimming pool, 2 tennis courts, bathing beach. A modern but attractive holiday hotel in a tropical park. Nearby is a diving school, sports centre with golf and riding.

Paradise Village Resort (M), Palm Cove, Northern Queensland, QLD 4871. Tel. (070) 553 300, fax (070) 591 295
30 rooms and apartments. restaurant, cocktail bar, coffee shop, swimming pool. An attractive little hotel in the middle price range located on Palm Cove promenade. A few minutes away there is a diving school and sports centre with golf course, tennis courts and a riding stable.

Port Douglas

Port Douglas Beaches (M/L), 19 The Esplanade, Port Douglas, QLD 4871 Tel. (070) 994 150, fax (070) 995 206
26 apartments, swimming pool.
This comfortable apartment-hotel is aimed mainly at those wishing to self-cater. All apartments have sea views.

*Sheraton Mirage (L), Port Douglas Road, Port Douglas, QLD 4871
Tel. (070) 995 888, fax (070) 995 898
300 rooms and studios, 5 restaurants, lounge, several bars, shopping centre, swimming pool.
This ultra-modern and extremely luxuriously appointed holiday hotel lies near the seashore. Guests can bathe in complete safety in the artificial salt-water lagoon. Also forming part of the hotel is a country club with an 18-hole golf course, sports and fitness centre and sauna.

Smithfield

Kewarra Beach Resort (M/L), Smithfield, QLD 4878
Tel. (070) 576 666, fax (070) 577 525
70 rooms and bungalows, restaurant, cocktail bar, bathing beach, water sports. Aimed at the more discerning guest, this resort lies on a beautiful bay within tropical parkland.

Surfers' Paradise

Parkroyal (M/L), Gold Coast Highway, Surfers' Paradise, QLD
Tel. (07) 5592 9900, fax (07) 5592 1519
380 rooms. From all the rooms in this comfortable hotel visitors can enjoy views of the Pacific and the world-famous surfing beaches.

Townsville

*Sheraton Breakwater Casino Hotel, Sir Leslie Thiess Drive, Townsville, QLD 4810; tel. (077) 222 333, fax (077) 724 741
200 rooms, 2 restaurants, casino, swimming pool.
The "First House on the Square" is busy all the year round.

South Australia

Adelaide

Adelaide Aviators Lodge (M), 782 Tapleys Hill Road, West Beach, SA 5045
Tel. (08) 8356 8388; fax (08) 8353 2868
30 rooms, restaurant, bar, swimming pool. Modern hotel near the beach, about 8km/5 miles outside the city.

Barron Townhouse (M), c/o Hindley St. and Morphett St., Adelaide, SA 5000
Tel. (08) 8211 8255. fax (08)8231 1179
71 rooms, restaurant, bar, swimming pool, sauna. A centrally situated and comfortable hotel for business travellers and tourists.

Old Adelaide Inn (M), 160 O'Connell St., North Adelaide, SA 5006
Tel. (08) 8267 5066, fax (08) 8267 2946
64 rooms, restaurant, bar, swimming pool, sauna.
This superbly appointed and architecturally attractive middle-class hotel lies about 2km/1¼ miles outside the city centre.

*St Francis Winery Resort (M), 14 Bridge St., Old Reynella, SA 5161
Tel. (08) 8322 2246, fax (08) 8322 0921

41 rooms and suites, restaurant, bar, swimming pool, sauna.
An award-winning hotel lying among vineyards to the south of the city. It is housed within the old walls of a wine-cellar dating from the 1860s.

The Grosvenor Vista Hotel, 125 North Terrace, Adelaide, SA 5000
Tel. (08) 231 2961, fax (08) 231 0765
290 rooms, 2 restaurants, cocktail bar, fitness centre with sauna. A friendly urban hotel near the theatre and casino. The rooms are very spacious and well furnished.

Barossa Valley

Barossa Junction Resort (S), Taanunda, SA 5352
Tel. (08) 8563 3400, fax (08) 8563 3660
34 rooms, restaurant. Very original in concept: old railway carriages have been converted into guests' rooms.

Barossa Valley Hotel (M/S), Murray St., Tanunda, SA 5352
Tel. (08) 8563 2303, fax (08) 8563 2279
40 rooms and suites, restaurant, bar, swimming pool, tennis.
This family-friendly hotel is also suitable for the disabled and was renovated at considerable expense in 1996. Special attractions include the gourmet buffet and wine-tasting.

Coober Pedy

The Coober Pedy Experience Motel (S), Coober Pedy, SA 5723
Tel. (08) 8672 5777, fax (08) 8672 5877
6 rooms. Small and very well appointed cave-hotel near a cave-church.

Kangaroo Island

Wisteria Lodge (M), 7 Cygnet Road, Kingscote, SA 5223
Tel. (08) 8553 2707, fax (08) 8553 2200
20 rooms and suites, restaurant, bar, swimming pool.
From this family-friendly and comfortable hotel there are fine views.

Nullarbor

Nullarbor Motel (S), near the Eyre Highway, Ceduna, SA 5690
Tel. (08) 8625 6271, fax (08) 8625 6261
26 rooms. A simple motel at the entrance to Nullarbor National Park. Whale-watching trips are organised.

Oodnadatta

Pink Roadhouse, Oodnadatta, SA 5734
Tel. (08) 8670 7822, fax (08) 8670 7816
10 beds. For a long time this ethnic travellers' inn was a well-kept secret in tourist circles, but now almost every visitor to the outback comes here to admire the colourful signs painted by the landlord.

Pimba

Pimba Roadhouse (S), Pimba, SA 5720
Tel. (086) 737 473, fax (086) 737 557
16 rooms, restaurant. A friendly inn with good cooking, located at the junction of Stuart Highway and Roxby Highway.

Port Augusta

Standpipe Golf Motor Inn (M), Port Augusta, SA 5720
Tel. (086) 424 033, fax (086) 410 571
80 rooms, restaurant, golf course. A very comfortable motel on the outskirts of the city with a cosy restaurant housed in a 19th c. building.

Whyalla

Derham's Foreshore Motor Inn (M), Foreshore & Watson Terrace, Whyalla, SA 5600; tel. (08) 8645 8877, fax (08) 8645 2549
40 rooms. A family-friendly motel near the marina, beach and shopping.

Tasmania

Hobart

Hobart Vista Hotel (M), 156 Bathurst St., Hobart, TAS 7000
Tel. (03) 6232 6255, fax (03) 6234 7884
140 rooms and suites, restaurant.
A centrally situated hotel offering extremely good service.

Islington Hotel (M), 321 Davey St., Hobart, TAS 7000
Tel. (03) 6223 3900, fax (03) 6224 3167
8 rooms. Informal bed-and-breakfast accommodation in one of the city's oldest remaining houses.

Launceston
Strahan

Innkeeper's Colonial Motor Inn (S/M), 31 Elizabeth St., Launceston, TAS 7250; tel. (03) 6331 6588, fax (03) 6334 2765
60 rooms, bar. The old mid-19th c. schoolhouse was recently converted to a guesthouse. It has a cosy and friendly atmosphere.

Franklin Manor (M), Strahan, TAS 7468
Tel. (03) 6471 7311, fax 6471 7267
13 rooms, restaurant.
This small hotel on the west coast of Tasmania was built around the turn of the century. It was recently renovated at considerable expense.

Victoria

Apollo Bay

Apollo International Motor Inn (M), 37 Great Ocean Rd., Apollo Bay, VIC 3233; tel. (03) 5237 6100, fax (03) 5237 6066
24 rooms and suites.
A homely hotel with bathing beach and golf course nearby.

Bendigo

Shamrock Hotel (M), Pall Mall & Williamson St., Bendigo, VIC 3552
Tel. (03) 5443 0333, fax (03) 5442 4494
30 rooms and suites.
A traditional hotel built in Victorian style and reminiscent of the time when Bendigo was a rich gold-prospecting town.

Foster

Foster Motel (M), South Gippsland Highway, Foster, VIC 3960
Tel. (03) 5682 2022, fax (03) 5682 2898
29 rooms and suites, restaurant, swimming pool, sauna.
A very family-friendly and well appointed motel in some extremely charming countryside. Walks in the bush and excursions into the national parks nearby are organised.

Geelong

Ambassador Hotel (M/L), Myers St. and Gheringhap St., Geelong, VIC 3220
Tel. (03) 5221 1684, fax (03) 5221 5814
140 rooms and suites, restaurant, bar, swimming pool, sauna.
Comfortable hotel for the discerning visitor, in a central location.

Lakes Entrance

Bellevue Motor Inn, 191 Esplanade, Lakes Entrance, VIC 3909
Tel. (03) 5155 3055, fax (03) 5155 3429
44 rooms and suites, swimming pool, sauna.
A prize-wining motel with rooms suitably equipped for the disabled. It is at the entrance to the popular Gippsland Lakes.

Melbourne

Adelphi (M), 187 Flinders Lane, Melbourne 3000
Tel. (03) 9650 7555, fax (03) 9650 2710
44 rooms and suites, bar, swimming pool, gymnasium.
This small and really fine hotel with its attractive interior is to be found in the centre of the city opposite Flinders Street Station.

Batman's Hill (M/S), 70 Spencer St., Melbourne, VIC 3000
Tel. (03) 9614 6344, fax (03) 9614 1189
80 rooms, restaurant, bar.
This well furnished accommodation is conveniently situated opposite Spencer Street Station.

Ibis (M/S), 15 Therry St., Melbourne, VIC 3000
Tel. (03) 9639 2399, fax (03) 9639 1988
250 rooms and apartments, restaurant, cocktail bar, business centre.
An ultra-modern multi-storey hotel occupying a central location between Victoria Market and Daimaru Shopping Centre and patronised mainly by

business travellers. It is but a few minutes' walk from here to Chinatown and the Bourke Street Mall.

Savoy Park Plaza (M/L), 630 Little Colins St., Melbourne, VIC 3000
Tel. (03) 9622 8888, fax 9622 8877
160 rooms and suites, 2 restaurants, bar, fitness centre.
This attractive Art Deco hotel was opened back in 1926. It lies on the north-eastern edge of the city centre and is a good setting-out point for exploring Melbourne.

*The Como Hotel (L), 630 Chapel St., Melbourne, , VIC 3000
Tel. (03) 9824 0400, fax (03) 9824 1263
100 rooms and suites, 2 restaurants, lounge, bar, fitness centre with swimming pool and sauna.
This select hotel and meeting place of many well-known personalities lies in the South Yarra area of the city. Ambitious young designers were responsible for the new interior.

*The Regent of Melbourne (L), 25 Collins St., Melbourne, VIC 3000
Tel. (03) 9653 0000, fax (03) 9650 4261
360 rooms, restaurant, bar, fitness centre. The "Regent" is one of the city's top addresses. This extremely luxurious hotel is housed in a skyscraper at the end of Collins St. There is a superb view from the restaurant on the 35th floor.

*The Windsor (L), 103 Spring St., Melbourne, VIC 3000
Tel. (03) 9633 6002, fax (03) 9633 6001
170 rooms, top-class restaurant, Cricketers' Club Bar, health club.
Built in Victorian style, this grand hotel is one of Melbourne's major sights. The decorative faflade and public rooms were recently lovingly restored. It is like going back to "the good old days".

Victoria Vista Hotel (M/S), 215 Little Collins St., Melbourne, VIC 3000
Tel. (03) 9653 0441, fax (03) 9650 9678
530 rooms, restaurant, coffee shop, cocktail lounge, large lobby.
A centrally located and busy hotel with a standard of comfort expected from a middle-class establishment. There are a number of good shops and some popular theatres in the immediate vicinity.

Mount Buffalo

Mount Buffalo Chalet (M), Mount Buffalo National Park, VIC 3745
Tel. (03) 5755 1500, fax (03) 5755 1892
96 rooms. Beautifully situated on Mount Buffalo and popular in both summer and winter. Guests can ride, canoe, walk, ski and join in nature excursions. Early reservation is strongly advisable.

Port Campbell

Southern Ocean Motor Inn (M), Great Ocean Road, Port Campbell, VIC 3269
Tel. (03) 5598 6231, fax (03) 5598 5164
28 rooms, restaurant, bar. A well-run motel in the superb coastal landscape of the Great Ocean Road.

Yarra Glen

The Yarra Glen Grand (M), Bell St., Yarra Glen, VIC 3775
Tel. (03) 9730 1230, fax (03) 9730 1124
10 rooms, restaurant, bar. Rich in tradition and situated in the Yarra Valley which is famous for its wines, this hotel was recently renovated.

Western Australia

Broome/Kimberley

*Cable Beach Club Resort (L), Cable Beach Road, Broome, WA 6725
Tel. (091) 920 400, fax (092) 922 249
260 rooms and studios as well as 80 bungalows, several restaurants and bars, 2 swimming pools, a bathing beach, 12 tennis courts and a children's club. Covering an area of 10ha/25 acres, this resort is one of the finest of its kind in the whole of Australia.

Derby/Kimberley

Spinifex Hotel (S), Clarendon St., Derby, WA 6743
Tel. (091) 911 233, fax (091) 911 576
50 rooms, bar, simple outback accommodation for the more robust traveller.

Fremantle

*The Esplanade Hotel (M). Marine Terrace & Essex St., Fremantle, WA
Tel. (08) 9432 4000, Fax (08) 9430 4539
250 rooms, 2 gourmet restaurants, café, bar. Opened in 1897, this traditional hotel with its encircling balcony has recently been lovingly renovated and now once again radiates its original colonial splendour.

Kalgoorlie

Railway Hotel (M), 51 Forrest St., Kalgoorlie, WA 6430
Tel. (08) 9091 8585, fax (08) 9091 8586
71 rooms, with several restaurants in the immediate vicinity. This very well furnished motel welcomes chidren and was built as part of the redevelopment programme for the railway station quarter.

Kununurra

*El Questro Station (M/L), Gibb River Road, Kununurra, WA 6743
Tel. (091) 691 777, fax (091) 691 383
36 rooms, bungalows and tents.
A luxurious establishment in the grounds of a giant cattle ranch. It would be difficult to imagine a better place for a country holiday.

Margaret River

Captain Freycinet Inn (M/E), Bussell Highway & Tunbridge St., Margaret River, WA 6285; tel. (08) 9757 2033, fax (08) 9757 2959
62 rooms, restaurant, bar, swimming pool.
A friendly hotel catering for the disabled and situated in the middle of some beautiful gardens. It is particularly convenient for those wishing to explore the beautiful woods and caves in the immediate vicinity.

Perth

All Seasons Freeway Hotel (M), 55 Mill Point Road, Perth, WA 6151
Tel. (08) 9367 7811, fax (08) 9367 9159
92 rooms, restaurant, bar, swimming pool.
A friendly and relatively inexpensive hotel in the south of the city, with beautiful views of the Swan River.

Duxton (M/L), 1 St George's Terrace, Perth, WA 6000
Tel. (08) 9261 8000, fax (08) 9325 8060
300 rooms. This comfortable hotel was opened a few months ago and is popular with busimess travellers and tourists alike.

Radisson Observation City (M/L), Esplanade, Scarborough Beach, Perth, WA 6019: tel. (09) 245 10000, fax (09) 245 1345
300 rooms, 4 restaurants, 7 bars, night club, disco, swimming pool, sauna, bathing beach, tennis, riding, water sports.
The facilities offered by this superb hotel near Scarborough Beach are aimed principally at holidaymakers who are keen on sport.

Sheraton (L), 207 Adelaide Terrace, Perth, WA 6000
Tel. (09) 325 0501, fax (09) 325 4032
400 rooms, 2 restaurants, coffee shop, 2 bars, swimming pool, fitness centre, health club with sauna.
This large and ultra-modern hotel occupies a very central location. From its luxuriously appointed rooms guests can enjoy a fine view of the Swan River with the many sailing boats and of the city centre. The "River Room Restaurant" is one of the finest in Perth.

Yanchep

Yanchep Holiday Village (M/S), 56 St Andrew's Drive, Yanchep, WA 6035
Tel. (08) 9561 2244, fax (08) 9561 2338
16 apartments, restaurant, bar, swimming pool, fitness centre.
Near the fantastic beaches north of Perth lies this holiday village from where visitors can explore the surrounding national park.

Australia's most visited tourist areas

An alphabetical list with page numbers of the principal starred places of tourist interest can be found on page 603.

Information

Outside Australia

United Kingdom ATC	The Australian Tourist Commission operates on Aussie Helpline in the UK and the USA, which deals with telephone queries and sends out brochures free of charge.
United States ATC	Aussie Helpline office based in Chicago, tel. 708 635 3612

In Australia

Australin Tourist Commission (ATC) Head Office	Australian Tourist Commission 80 William St., Woolloomooloo, Sydney, NSW 2011: tel 02 360 1111
Australin Capital Territory (ACT)	ACT Tourist Commission CBS Tower (8th floor), Akuna and Bunda Streets, Canberra City, ACT 2601 Tel. 02 205 0666 ACT Tourism Commission's Visitor Information Centre, Jollimont Centre, Northbourne Avenue/Alinga St., Canberra City, ACT 2601; tel. 02 6205 0044
New South Wales (NSW)	New South Wales Tourist Centre, 11–31 York St., Sydney, NSSW 2000 Tel. 13 20 77 (no dialling code needed from anywhere in Australia) Tourism New South Wales, 140 George St., The Rocks, Sydney, NSW Tel. 02 9931 1111
Northern Territory (NT)	Northern Territory Tourist Commission, Tourism House, 43 Mitchell St., Darwin, NT; tel. 08 8989 3900 Darwin Region Tourism Association, 33 Smith Street Mall, Darwin, NT Tel. 08 8981 4300 Central Australian Tourism Industry Association, Hartley St./St Gregory Terrace, Alice Springs, NT; tel. 08 8952 5800
Queensland (QLD)	Queensland Tourist and Travel Corporation, Level 36, Riverside Centre, 123 Eagle St., Brisbane, QLD; tel. 07 3406 5400 Far North Queensland Promotion Bureau, Hartley St., Cairns, QLD: tel. 07 4052 3096
South Australia (SA)	South Australian Tourist Commission, 7th and 8th floors, Terrace Towers, 178 North Terrace, Adelaide, SA; tel. 08 8303 2222 South Australian Travel Centre, 1 King William St., Adelaide, SA Tel. 08 8212 1505
Tasmania (TAS)	Tourism Tasmania, Trafalgar Building, 110 Collins St., Hobart, TAS Tel. 03 6233 8011 Tasmanian Travel and Information Centre, 200 Davey St., Hobart, TAS Tel. 03 6230 8233
Victoria (VIC)	Tourism Victoria, 134 Swanston St., Melbourne, VIC 3001: tel. 03 9658 9968, fax 03 9650 1112
Western Australia (WA)	Western Australian Tourism Commission (WATC), 6th floor, St George's Court, 16 St George's Terrace, Perth, WA 6000; tel. 08 9220 1700
Local information offices	In all those places which are connected in any way with tourism there is an information office which can provide brochures and other material about items of interest in the town or its surroundings.

Language

Australian English

The official language of Australia is English. The spoken language ("Strine") has a distinctive accent, a tendency to shorten words (often adding an "o" or an "ie" on the end) and a rich vocabulary of specifically Australian idioms. As a brief guide to Australian slang the Australian Tourist Commission published in 1991 "A Fair Dinkum Aussie Dictionary". The list given below is a selection of Australian slang terms and words referring to features of Australian life.

Aboriginal languages

Those interested in the Aboriginal languages can consult the dictionaries published by the Institute for Aboriginal Affairs – though these cover only fifty of the two hundred or so Aboriginal languages.

Glossary of Australian Terms

Abo: Aboriginal (a derogatory term)
amber fluid: beer
Apple Isle: Tasmania
arvo: afternoon
Aussie salute: waving your hands in front of your face to ward off flies
back o' Bourke: back of beyond
banana bender: resident of Queensland
barbie: barbecue
beaut: great, fantastic
bell (someone): ring, call
billabong: water-hole in a dry river bed
billy: tin used to boil tea in the bush
boomer: large male kangaroo
bull dust: fine dust in the outback
bush: natural countryside
bushranger: runaway convict, outlaw (19th c.)
bush tucker: native foods, particularly in the outback
BYO: bring your own (drink to a restaurant, meat to a barbecue)
chook: chicken
chunder: vomit
corroboree: Aboriginal ceremony
crook: sick, badly made, broken
cut lunch: sandwiches
daks: trousers
dam: an artificial lake or reservoir (not just the dam itself)
damper: soda bread cooked in a pot on embers
didgeridoo: Aboriginal musical instrument made from a hollow stem
digger: Australian soldier
dumper: giant wave
dunny: outside lavatory
esky: insulated box (to keep beer, etc., cool)
fair dinkum: honestly
fair go: give us a break
fossick: search for gold or precious stones in abandoned diggings
Fremantle doctor: fresh breeze from the Indian Ocean during the hot months
furphy: water-cart; rumour, false report
galah: a noisy parrot, a noisy fool
garbo: garbage collector
g'day: good day (the standard Australian greeting)
googie: egg
grasshopper: tourist in a group
grazier: large-scale sheep or cattle farmer

grog: alcohol
gum: eucalyptus
homestead: farmhouse
hooray, hooroo: goodbye
jackaroo: young male trainee on a farm
jillaroo: young female trainee on a farm
joey: baby kangaroo
jumbuck: sheep
jumbuck barber: sheep-shearer
kiwi: New Zealander
Koori: Aborigines in south-eastern Australia
larrikin: rowdy person
lollies: sweets
manchester: household linen
matilda: swag (see below)
milk bar: general store
mozzie: mosquito
mulga mail: bush telegraph; rumour
neck oil: beer
never-never: remote country in the outback
no worries: that's all right, don't mention it
old man: adult male kangaroo
outback: remote part of the bush
Pat Malone: (one's) own (rhyming slang)
pavlova: meringue and cream dessert
pokie: gambling machine, one-armed bandit
pollie: politician
pom, pommie: Britisher
pull your head in: mind your own business
Rafferty's rules: without any rules
ringer: best sheep-shearer or stockman
ripper: good (exclamation of enthusiasm)
roo: kangaroo
sanger, sango: large glass of beer
sheila: woman
snag: sausage
squatter: large landholder in early colonial times
station: large farm
stubby: small bottle of beer
sunbake: sunbathe
sundowner: casual worker who arrives late for work
swag: bed-roll, personal belongings
swagman: rural tramp
Tassie, Taswegian: resident of Tasmania
tinnie: can of beer
togs: swimming costume
too right!: absolutely!
toot: lavatory
Top End: northern part of the Northern Territory
tucker: food
two-up: illegal gambling game
ute: pickup truck
walkabout: travelling (an Aboriginal expression)
go walkabout: go missing
Westralian: Western Australian
witchetty grub: a large white grub much prized by the Aborigines
woomera: Aboriginal spear-thrower
wowser: killjoy, prude
4WD: four-wheel-drive (vehicle)

Maps

Good tourist maps and road atlases can be obtained from Australian automobile clubs and bookshops. These include "Touring Australia" (a motoring atlas with road maps, town plans and maps of surrounding areas), "Readers' Digest Motoring Guide to Australia" (road atlas with numerous regional maps and town plans), the "Motoring Atlas of Australia" (road atlas with several town plans) and "Geographic Map of Australia" (in four parts, scale 1:2,500 000 with road networks). Topographical maps are available in the following scales: 1:1,000 000 (49 pp.), 1:250,000 (544 pp), 1:100,000 (3060 pp, not yet complete, 1:50,000 (7568 pp, not yet complete).

Medical Aid

Medical care

Australian standards of public health and medical care are in line with those of Europe and North America. Even in country areas almost every town has a resident doctor and a pharmacist. Remote farms in the outback have radio telephones and can call on the Flying Doctor Service. Hospitals have emergency and casualty departments. Visitors who regularly have to take certain medicines should carry a prescription with them which an Australian doctor can confirm or renew in an emergency.

Costs

The costs of hospital, medical or dental care in Australia are high and must be paid in cash. It is advisable, therefore, to take out adequate health insurance cover before leaving home.

Inoculations

Inoculations (cholera, yellow fever) are required only when a visitor has been in an infected area within six days before arrival in Australia. However, as regulations can change at short notice, it is advisable to check the current position before departure.

Motoring in Australia

Hiring a car

If you want to hire a car it is safest to go to one of the well-known international car rental firms. You will then have a reasonable assurance that the car is in good condition. You should in any event check that the engine, lights, brakes, tyres, etc., are all right and that the car meets your requirements. You should also make sure that you have full insurance cover.

Roads

Australia has an excellent network of roads. The main highways and roads between towns are in good condition, but roads into the outback are dusty unsurfaced tracks. The great distances to be covered (see table of distances, p. 550) and the long, straight roads through what is often monotonous country are tiring, and this should be allowed for.

Traffic regulations

Traffic goes on the left, as in Britain, with overtaking on the right; but in spite of this traffic coming from the right has priority.

Speed limits

In built-up areas: 60km/37 miles an hour;
on highways and country roads: 100km/62 miles an hour;
on motorways: 110km/68 miles an hour.
There are no speed limits on the overland stretches in the Northern Territory, but exercise caution and watch out for wild animals on the road!

Seat belts

The wearing of seat belts is obligatory.

Alcohol

The blood alcohol limit is 51mg/100ml. It is preferable to avoid alcohol altogether when driving: there are police checks even in the Outback.

Road signs

Road signs are, in general, easily understandable; speeds and distances are given in kilometres. The only unusual signs are those warning about camels, wombats and kangaroos on the road.

Traffic offences

The police keep an active lookout for drivers exceeding the speed limit or driving under the influence of alcohol; and overstaying your parking time can also get you into trouble. Demands for payment of fines can follow you home, since the car rental firms supply the addresses of their customers to the authorities.

Hazards on the road

Fuel

Petrol (leaded or lead-free) and diesel fuel are sold by the litre. Petrol at present costs about 75 cents a litre; it tends to be cheaper on the east coast than elsewhere in Australia. The more densely populated parts of the country are well supplied with petrol stations; in the outback (where fuel is considerably dearer) there are fewer garages, and it is advisable, therefore, to fill up at every opportunity. Petrol stations accept credit cards and travellers' cheques.

Motoring Organisations

The Australian automobile clubs provide services to members of most foreign motoring organisations on the same basis as to their own members. If you intend to drive a car in Australia, therefore, you should carry the membership card of your own organisation.

AAA

Automobile Association of Australia (AAA, "Triple A")
212 Northbourne Avenue
Canberra, ACT 2601, tel. 06 247 7311, fax 06 257 5320

In states and territories

Australian Capital Territory
National Roads and Motorists' Association (NRMA)
92 Northbourne Avenue
Braddon, ACT 2601, 132 132 (helpline), fax 06 6243 8892

New South Wales:
National Roads and Motorists' Association (NRMA)
151 Clarence Street
Sydney, NSW 2000, tel. 132 132 (helpline), fax 02 9260 8472

Northern Territory:
Automobile Association of the Northern Territory (AANT)
79-81 Smith Street
Darwin, NT 0800, tel. 08 8981 3837, fax 08 8941 2965

Queensland:
Royal Automobile Club of Queensland (RACQ)
300 St Paul's Terrace
Fortitude Valley, QLD 4006, tel. 07 3361 2444, fax 07 3252 3587

South Australia:
Royal Automobile Association of South Australia (RAASA)
41 Hindmarsh Square
Adelaide, SA 5000, tel. 08 8202 4594, fax 08 8202 4520

Tasmania:
Royal Automobile Club of Tasmania (RACT)
Cnr Murray and Patrick Streets
Hobart, TAS 7000, tel. 03 6232 6300, fax 03 6234 8784

Victoria:
Royal Automobile Club of Victoria (RACV)
550 Princes Highway
Noble Park, VIC 3174, tel. 03 9790 2211, fax 03 9790 2628

Western Australia:
Royal Automobile Club of Western Australia (RACWA)
228 Adelaide Terrace, Perth, WA 6000, tel. 09 9421 4444, fax 09 9221 2708

Breakdown Assistance

If you have a breakdown you should inform one of the motoring organisations listed by telephoning 131 111 (countrywide); they will arrange for a breakdown service or a garage to come to your assistance. In the case of an accident it is best to call the police on 000 (free charge, countrywide). See also Safety and Security.

National Parks

More than 3587 National Parks, nature reserves, wildlife reserves and sanctuaries protect some 50 million hectares/124 million acres, or 6.5% of Australia's total area, from exploitation and destruction. No less than eleven National Parks have been designated as World Heritage Sites by UNESCO (see below). These great expanses of unspoiled natural landscape, including areas of great scenic beauty, are open to the public, who in return are expected to behave with consideration and responsibility when visiting the parks. The most important of the National Parks are described in the "A to Z" section of this guide, and almost all of them are shown on the large map at the end of the book.

It is sometimes necessary to close parks to the public for a shorter or longer period without previous notice. Visitors must not enter any park which has been closed, and there are heavy fines for unauthorised entry.

Various travel operators run tours to the best known National Parks. An organised tour of this kind is the best way of seeing some of the more remote parks. Information about operators offering such tours can be obtained from the Australian Tourist Commission (see Information).

World Heritage Sites

Central Eastern Rain Forest Reserves

Over 50 rain forest regions on the border between Queensland and New South Wales are protected sites. They include subtropical, temperate and temperate/cool rain forests on the Pacific coast.

Fossil Mammal Sites

World-famous fossil discovery sites in Riversleigh, Queensland and near the South Australian Naracoorte Caves.

Fraser Island

The world's largest sandy island with some of the world's oldest and highest dunes, with more than 36 lakes and a large rain forest region.

Great Barrier Reef

This is the largest barrier reef of coral anywhere in the world and stretches for several hundred kilometres off the north-east coast of Queensland.

Kakadu National Park

Tropical landscape and home to the Gugudju Aborigines, situated by the East Alligator River (near Darwin) in Northern Australia.

Lord Howe Islands

A group of volcanic islands lying 700km/435 miles off the coast of New South Wales and with the most southerly coral reef in the world.

Shark Bay

An isolated area on the coast of Western Australia with an extremely varied fauna (humpbacked whales, seacrows, dolphins, turtles, etc.)

Tasmanian Wilderness	Rock formations from all epochs of the world's history, in the region of the Cradle Mountains and Lake St Clair.
Uluru – Kata Tjuta (Ayers Rock – The Olgas)	The world-famous, rust-red monolith in the "Red Heart" of Australia and a major site in Aboriginal mythology and culture.
Wet Tropics	Tropical rain forest region in the north-east of Queensland.
Willandra Lakes	A semi-desert region in the south-west of New South Wales, site of archaeological finds tracing one of the oldest human cultures on earth.

Information centres

The whole of Australia	Australian Nature Conservancy Agency, PO Box 636, Canberra, ACT 2601 Tel. 06 250 0200, fax 06 250 0399
Australian Capital Territory	Australian Capital Territory Parks and Conservation Service, PO Box 1119, ACT 2901; tel. 06 207 2334, fax 06 207 2335
New South Wales	New South Wales National Parks and Wildlife Service, PO Box 1967, Hurtsville, NSW 2220; tel. 02 9585 6444, fax 02 9585 6555
Northern Territory	Parks and Wildlife Commission of the Northern Territory, PO Box 496, Palmerston, NT 0831; tel. 08 8999 4537, fax 08 8932 3849
Queensland	Queensland Department of Environment, PO Box 155, Brisbane, QLD 4002 Tel. 07 3225 1779, fax 07 3225 1769
South Australia	South Australia Department of Environment and Natural Resources, PO Box 1047, Adelaide, SA 5001; tel. 08 8204 9399, fax 08 8204 9321
Tasmania	Tasmania Department of Environment and Land Management, PO Box 44A, Hobart, TAS 7001; tel. 03 6233 6461, fax 03 6223 8603
Victoria	Victoria Department of Natural Resources and Environment, PO Box 41, East Melbourne, VIC 3002; tel. 03 9412 4011, fax 03 9412 4835
Western Australia	Western Australia Department of Conservation and Land Management, Locked Bag 104, Bentley Delivery Centre, WA 6983; tel. 09 442 0300, fax (09) 386 1578

Newspapers and Periodicals

Australian press

Dailies

Among the leading Australian dailies are "The Age", the "Sydney Morning Herald", the "Brisbane Courier Mail", the "Canberra Times", the "Adelaide Advertiser", the West Australian" (Perth) and the "Australian" (a national newspaper). The Saturday editions, may have anything up to 200 pages.

Weeklies

The weekly "Bulletin" is one of Australia's best news magazines. Other leading periodicals are the "Australian Business Weekly", the "Times (Australia Magazine)" and "Personal Investment" (with a section on the Australian Stock Exchange).

International press

International newspapers and periodicals are sold in larger towns.

Outback Travel

Where civilisation ends the outback (inland Australia) begins: the endless arid and empty wastes of the interior and the tropical north with its monsoon rain and cyclones. Coming from the narrow coastal strip which has been completely altered by man during 200 years of white settlement, the traveller into the outback finds himself in a boundless expanse of almost untouched natural landscape which can be used only for extensive pastoral farming. Many visitors see a trip in the outback as the realisation of their dream of adventure in the Australian wilderness. Nowadays the outback experience holds little danger for those who plan their trip carefully, are properly equipped and avoid unnecessary risks. Before setting out they should seek the advice of one of the Australian automobile clubs (see Motoring in Australia), the Australian Tourist Commission (see Information) and knowledgeable local people.
Advice on the preparation of an outback trip can be obtained from the Royal Flying Doctor Service, which also hires out emergency radio sets. For further information apply to:

Royal Flying Doctor Service of Australia
Level 5, 15–17 Young St., Sydney, NSW
Tel. 02 9241 2411

High points

The high points of a trip in the outback are the natural wonders in the Northern Territory – in the Red Centre round Alice Springs, round Katherine and in the Top End (Kakadu National Park) – in the north and north-west of Western Australia and in the interior of South Australia, New South Wales and Queensland (Cape York Peninsula).

Organised tours

There are many tour operators and travel agencies running a great variety of tours in the outback. For information apply to the Australian Tourist Commission or the state tourist authorities (see Information).

Travel in the outback

Before setting out it is important to consult the police or other local sources about the condition of the unsurfaced tracks, most of which are negotiable only by four-wheel-drive vehicles and by drivers with experience of 4WD driving. The main roads through the interior are now asphalted, and before leaving these roads you should make sure that you have proper equipment, good maps and up-to-date information about local conditions. Cross-country driving is extremely hazardous (rabbit-holes, sharp-edged rocks, drifting sand and dust) and in addition damages the vegetation, which frequently already suffers from over-grazing. Most car rental firms allow camper vans, mobile homes and ordinary cars to be driven only on asphalted roads, and breakdowns and accidents on unsurfaced tracks will not be covered by insurance – restrictions which do not apply to 4WD vehicles.

Before hiring a car you should check that it has air-conditioning.

The best time for travelling in the outback is between April and October, when it is dry and relatively cool. During the rest of the year heavy rain can make the roads and tracks impassable.

It is essential when travelling in the outback, particularly off the main roads, to carry sufficient supplies of water (5 litres per person per day) and food. You should always take more – preferably a week's reserve supply – than you expect to need. Other essential items are a first aid kit, a large spare can of petrol and the most important spare parts for the vehicle.

Petrol stations are few and far between in the outback, and you should fill up at every opportunity.

Hazards

The greatest danger on the long and monotonous roads in the outback is tiredness and the resultant loss of alertness. Kangaroos, emus, cattle and other animals can suddenly cross the road and may not always be seen in time, particularly at dusk and in the dark. Night driving in the outback is best avoided, and you should never find yourself in the situation of having to drive under pressure of time.

A possible hazard is an encounter with one of the huge "road trains" (multi-axle articulated lorries with several trailers), an important means of transport in the outback, which travel at high speed, often shrouded in impenetrable clouds of dust. Caution is required when meeting a road train, and overtaking one is usually an extremely hazardous operation.

Many roads in the outback are the old tracks on which cattle were formerly driven for many hundred kilometres to the nearest railhead (e.g. the Birdsville Track, the Canning Stock Route), and since the transport of cattle has been taken over by the road trains the tracks are no longer maintained; in particular the water-holes may be no longer usable.

In the event of a breakdown which you cannot deal with you should never leave the vicinity of the car, which provides shade and shelter and is easier for rescuers to see than a person wandering about on his own.

Photography

Films are relatively dear in Australia, so it is advisable to take sufficient supplies with you. Because of the strong sun during the day photographs are most effective in the early morning and late afternoon; sunsets are often magically beautiful. Before photographing people, particularly Aborigines, you should always ask their permission.

Post and Telecommunications

Post
Opening times
Post offices are normally open Mon.–Fri. 9am–5pm. Main post-offices in cities and some large towns are also open Sat. 8.30am–noon.

Stamps
Stamps can be bought not only in post offices but also at hotel reception desks, in motels, at kiosks selling postcards and in some shops.

Poste restante
Large post offices have special poste restante counters, but poste restante mail can also be sent to remote outback post offices. When collecting mail you will be asked to produce evidence of identity (passport, driving licence).

Postal rates to Europe (as at 5/97)
Aerogramms:A$0.75 (Economy Air)
Postcards up to 20g: A$1 (Air Mail), A$0.85 (Economy Air)
Standard letters up to 20g: A$1.50 (Air Mail), A$1.30 (Economy Air)
Letters up to 250g: A$5.30 (Air Mail), A$4.50 (Economy Air), A$2.40 (Sea Mail)
Packages up to 2kg: A$41 (Air Mail), A$29 (Economy Air), A$19 (Sea Mail)
Parcels up to 4kg: A$71 (Air Mail), A$47 (Economy Air), A$27 (Sea Mail)

Time taken to reach Europe
Air Mail: ca. 7 days
Economy Air: ca. 10–14 days
Sea Mail: up to 12 weeks

Telegrams, fax
Telegrams and fax messages are also accepted by post offices.

Telephone
Australia has a very modern telephone system extending into the remotest outback. At present all Australian telephone numbers are gradually being altered, and this process is expected to be completed during 1998. The same applies to local dialling codes. Future dialling codes for the individual states are as follows:
Australia Capital Territory(ACT) and New South Wales (NSW): 02
Victoria (VIC) and Tasmania: 03
Queensland (QLD): 07
South Australia (SA), Northern Territory (NT) and Western Australia (WA): 08

There are numerous coin-operated payphones as well as telephones operated by credit cards or phonecards. The minimum cost of a local public payphone call is 40c. Coin-operated payphones can be used both for local calls (only from red telephones, which accept 10 and 20 cent coins) and trunk and international calls (blue, gold and public telephones, accepting 10, 20 and 50 cent and 1 dollar coins). Phonecards (to the value of 5, 10, 20 or 50 dollars) are widely available from shops, etc., displaying the notice "Phonecards sold here".

International dialling codes
From the United Kingdom to Australia: 00 61
From the USA or Canada to Australia: 011 61
From Australia to the United Kingdom: 00 11 44
From Australia to the USA or Canada: 00 11 1

Public Holidays

This section lists only holidays which are celebrated throughout Australia or in several of the Australian states.

Throughout Australia
New Year's Day
Australia Day (January 26th; anniversary of the landing of the First Fleet in 1788)
Good Friday (March/April)
Easter Monday (March/April)
Anzac Day (April 25th; commemorating Australian losses at Gallipoli in 1915 and other war dead)
Christmas Day

In several states on same day
Easter Saturday (March/April)
Bank holidays (beginning of August, etc.)
Boxing Day (December 26th; not in SA)

Labour Day (1st Monday in March in WA, 2nd Monday in March in VIC, 3rd Monday in March in ACT, 1st Monday in May in QLD, 1st Monday in October in NSW, 2nd Monday in October in SA
Queen's Birthday (September in WA, 2nd Monday in June in other states)

In different states on different days

Radio and Television

The national non-commercial network is the Australian Broadcasting Corporation (ABC), which provides radio and television programmes throughout the country. There are also numerous commercial radio and television stations. Most hotel and motel rooms have radio and television.

Railways

Rail Australia (ROA)

See Maps pages 574-75

Rail Australia (ROA) is a combine of five state-owned railway systems: Australian National, Queensland Rail, the State Rail Authority of New South Wales (State Rail), the Public Transport Corporation of Victoria (V/Line and The Met) and Western Australian Government Railways (Westrail).

Special offers
Rail passes

Rail Australia offers a range of rail passes, the best of which, for visitors who want to see the whole country, are the following:
- the Austrailpass (covering the whole network; valid for 14, 21, 30, 60 or 90 days; can be bought only outside Australia);
- the Austrail Flexipass (covering the whole network; valid on any 8, 15, 22 or 29 days within a period of 6 months). The 8-day Pass excludes Perth and Alice Springs.

In addition there are passes for the various state railway systems such as the East Coast Discovery Pass and NSW Discovery Pass.

Information

ROA Rail Australia
1 Richmond Road
Keswick, SA 5035, tel. 08 217 4681, fax 08 217 4682

Famous Express Trains (a selection)

Luxury travel

The long-distance trains described below offer a high degree of comfort. The First Class sections provide spacious sleeping cars with double beds and en suite facilities (shower/W.C.). The single and double Holiday Class cabins have a wash-basin only, showers and W.C. being at the end of the coach. The Economy Class has seats only. All long-distance trains have a restaurant and/or buffet-car. Those express trains designed primarily with young people in mind ("Spirit of...") also have a mobile disco or dancing.

On the following long-distance trains a luxury package including sleeper and meals or travel as an ordinary passenger can be booked.

Indian Pacific

The Indian Pacific is a railway legend. It runs from Sydney on the Pacific Ocean by way of Broken Hill and Adelaide to Perth, the capital of Western Australia, on the Indian Ocean. This luxurious train takes 64 hours to cover the 4325km/2687 miles. It travels across the Nullarbor Plain between Ooldea (SA) and Nurina (WA) in a dead straight line for 478km/297 miles

Ghan

The Ghan – named after the Afghan camel-drovers of the old Outback who followed the same route – is also world-famous. It covers the 1555km/966 mile stretch from Adelaide (SA) to Alice Springs (NT). The journey takes 20 hours and passes through some unforgettable countryside.

Sunlander, Queenslander, Spirit of the Tropics

The luxurious express trains, the Sunlander and the Queenslander, together with the non-stop Spirit of the Tropics (specially equipped for the younger set) link Brisbane on the east coast with Cairns in the tropical north near the Great Barrier Reef. This 1681km/1045 mile stretch passes through the "Australian Paradise" or Sunshine Route. The journey takes 31 hours.

Spirit of the Outback

This train takes 24 hours to travel the 1326km/824 mile inland run from Brisbane on the Pacific Ocean via Rockhampton to Longreach.

Westlander

The Westlander also travels inland from Brisbane. After 22 hours the 1000km/620 mile journey ends in Cunnamulla or Quilpie in the Outback of Queensland.

Inlander	The Inlander runs from Townsville, on the Coral Sea in north-east Queensland, inland to Mount Isa, taking 19 hours to cover 977km/607 miles.
Overland	The Overland plies on the 774km/480 mile stretch from Melbourne (VIC) to Adelaide (SA) and vice versa. The journey lasts 12 hours.
Australind	The line between Perth (WA) and Bunbury (WA; 185km/115 miles, 2½ hours) is covered by the comfortable railcar known as the Australind.
Prospector	The Prospector travels from Perth (WA) to Kalgoorlie in the Outback of Western Australia (655km/407 miles, 6 hours).
XPT, Explorer	Express Passenger Trains (XPT), comparable with British and European InterCity trains, run from Sydney to Brisbane (987km/613 miles, 14½ hours) and Sydney to Melbourne (961km/597 miles, 10½ hours). The Explorer plies between Sydney and Canberra, taking 4½ to complete the 326km/203 mile trip.
Kuranda Scenic Railway	One of the most beautiful rail routes in the whole of Australia is that taken by the Kuranda Scenic Railway, from Cairns and passing through mountainous country and tropical rainforests and close to many wildly romantic waterfalls en route to Kuranda.
Veteran/steam trains	Many stretches of abandoned railway lines and old steam and diesel locomotives have taken on a fresh lease of life as tourist attractions: for example Puffing Billy in the Dandenongs to the east of Melbourne (VIC), the Zig Zag Railway in the Blue Mountains at Lithgow (NSW) – a day trip from Sydney – and some old Ghan railway stations near Alice Springs in the Outback.

Restaurants

Food to suit all tastes

In the more thickly populated areas of Australia, especially in the cities and main tourist centres, there are restaurants catering for all tastes. Pubs, bistros, cafés and small family restaurants also offer good food at moderate prices. As a result of the influx of immigrants in recent decades there are now innumerable speciality eating-places, ranging from simple Chinese restaurants and Japanese sushi bars to luxurious top-of-the-range establishments offering refined French cuisine. Takeaways, fast-food outlets and "food centres" also have a role to play.

Reservations

Those wishing to visit one of the many good restaurants are advised to reserve a table well in advance.

Reception

In Australian restaurants guests are usually received as they enter and shown to a table. In good restaurants certain standards of dress are observed.

Licensed restaurants

Alcoholic drinks are served only in licensed restaurants. In most licensed establishments alcohol is served only Mon.–Sat. 10am–10pm, Licensing hours on Sundays vary from state to state.

BYO

BYO ("Bring your own") restaurants have no licence to serve alcoholic drinks, but customers can take in their own beer or wine. However, a small charge (about one dollar) is usually made for corkage.

Prices

Generally speaking, prices compare with those in Europe, although top restaurants can be more expensive; a three-course meal in such an establishment may cost between A$70 and A$ 150. A one-course meal in a fast-food outlet costs from A$5.

The following list

Clearly, only a small selection of recommended restaurants can be included in this guide. Details of some further establishments can be found under "Hotels • Motels • Resorts • Lodges".

Australian Capital Territory

Canberra

Fringe Benefits Brasserie, 54 Marcus Clarke St.; tel. (02) 6247 4042
This elegant restaurant is known both for its fine cuisine and excellent wine-list.

New South Wales

Hunter Valley

The Casuarina, Hermitage Road; tel. (049) 987 788
Superior restaurant with fine wines from the region.

Sydney

*Bistro Moncur, 116 Queen St.; tel. (02) 9363 2782
Top-quality restaurant in the city centre with perhaps the best cuisine in the whole of Sydney.

*Doyle's on the Beach, Watson's Bay, 11 Marine Parade; tel. (02) 9337 1350
A world-famous fish restaurant, from the terrace of which there is a fantastic view of the Sydney skyline. Reservation absolutely essential.

Frisco, 46 Dowling St.; tel. (02) 9357 1800
Friendly establishment in – by Australian standards – an historical setting above Woolloomooloo Bay. Various European speciality dishes are on the menu, particularly some excellent salads.

Lord Nelson Brewery, Kent and Argyle Streets; tel. (02) 9251 4044
This is probably Australia's oldest pub and attracts people like a magnet. Its own light and sweet ale goes down well with substantial meals.

Mezzaluna, 123 Victoria St.; tel. (02) 9357 1988
A popular restaurant with a view near Potts Point and excellent Italian cuisine.

Northern Territory

Ayers Rock/ Yulara

*Kuniya Room, in the "Sails in the Desert" hotel; tel. (08) 8956 2200
A top-class hotel will naturally boast an excellent restaurant. Both specialities of the Australian outback and international dishes are prepared superbly well here.

Coober Pedy

Old Miners Dug Out Café, Hutchinson St.; tel. (08) 725 541
This cave-restaurant serves finely prepared regional speciality dishes (including fillet of kangaroo).

Darwin

*The Hanuman, Mitchell Plaza; tel. (08) 8941 3500
A superior restaurant with excellent fish dishes and exquisite Thai creations. The wine menu will be hard to equal.

Swiss Café, Harry Chan Arcade; tel. (08) 8981 5079
Rösti (fried grated potatoes) and Swiss cheese are, of course, on the menu, as well as other delicacies.

Katherine

Pine Tree Restaurant, 3rd St.; tel. (08) 8972 2533
A good outback restaurant.

Nhulunburu/ Arnhem Land

The Walkabout Arnhem Land Resort; tel. (08) 8987 1777
A well-run establishment, the cuisine of which enjoys an excellent reputation.

Port Augusta

Standpipe Golf Motor Inn, at the junction of Highways 1 and 87
Tel. (086) 4240 4033
The restaurant of this motel is housed in an old 19th c. building. Good plain Australian dishes are served in this historical setting.

Queensland

Brisbane

Ecco, c/o Boundary St. and Adelaide St.; tel. (07) 383 1834
Bistro-restaurant with a Mediterranean flavour and cuisine to match (e.g. *gnocchi* – small dumplings – served with spinach and gorgonzola cheese).

*Riverside Restaurant, 123 Eagle St.; tel. (07) 3881 5555
Brisbane's number one gourmet restaurant. Excellent fish and sea-food dishes.

Cairns

*Red Ochre Grill, 43 Shields St.; tel. (070) 510 100
Excellently-prepared speciality dishes are served in a post-modern setting. Primarily these consist of typical Australian delicacies such as fillet of kangaroo and smoked opossum, as well as sea-food and refined and spicy new "outback cuisine" creations.

Noosa Heads

Artis, 8 Noosa Drive; tel. (07) 5447 2300
The very creative chef conjures up exotic new delights in which fish, sea-foods and various fresh vegetables are important ingredients.

*La Plage, 5 Hastings St.; tel. (07) 5447 3308
Showing the influence of French cuisine, this gourmet restaurant offers

moules à la St-Jacques as well as many other delicacies. Wonderful soufflés and desserts round off the meal.

Port Douglas

*Nautilus, 17 Murphy St.; tel. (07) 4099 5330
Many connoisseurs regard this fish restaurant as one of the best in the country.

Townsville

Tongala, 11 Fryer St., North Ward; tel. (077) 724 633
Various Greek delicacies are served in historic surroundings.

South Australia

Adelaide

Aldgate Pump Restaurant, 1 Strathalbyn Road; tel. (08) 8339 2015
This attractive restaurant in Adelaide is particularly busy at week-ends.

Chloe's, 36 College Road; tel. (08) 8362 2574
Well-known establishment in the suburb of Kent Town with excellent French cuisine and exquisite wines.

*Nediz Tu, 170 Hutt St.; tel. (08) 8223 2618
Exquisite Thai and international cuisine which has continually impressed many critics.

Universal Wine Bar, 285 Rundle St.; tel. (08) 8232 5000
A selection of lovingly prepared dishes can be enjoyed in this cosy wine-bar.

Barossa Valley

Heidelberg, Tanunda, Murray St; tel. (085) 632 151
As the name suggests, mainly plain German cooking is served here.

Kaesler Wines, Nuriootpa; tel. (085) 622 711
A popular wine-bar with a varied menu.

The Lyndoch Bakery, Lyndoch; tel. (085) 244 422
South German and Austrian cuisine, including Black Forest cherry gateau.

Tasmania

Hobart

Battery Point Brasserie, Hampden Road; tel. (03) 6223 3186
The Battery Point Brasserie will prove just right for those who like game. A particular speciality of the house is emu ham.

Dear Friends, 8 Brooke St.; tel. (03) 6223 2646
This restaurant is known for its excellent meat dishes (especially lamb) and for its fine wines.

*Mures Upper deck, Victoria Dock Wharf; tel. (03) 6231 1999
Exclusive dishes, especially fish, can be enjoyed in a rustic setting by the harbour.

*West Point Revolving Restaurant, 410 Sandy Bay Road; tel. (03) 6225 0112
Some 80m/260ft above sea-level, there is a wonderful view to be enjoyed from this revolving restaurant. Speciality dishes among the excellent cuisine include superbly prepared sea-foods.

Victoria

Melbourne

Café di Stasio, 31 Fitzroy st.; tel. (03) 9525 3999
Fine Italian food in the St Kilda district of the city.

*Le Chinois, 178 Toorak Road; tel. (03) 9826 3388
Expensive but good restaurant in the trendy district of South Yarra.
Hofbräuhaus, 24 Market Lane; tel. (03) 9663 3361
Bavarian friendliness with beer and schnitzel.

*Le Restaurant, 25 Collins St.; tel. (03) 9653 0000
A magnificent view can be enjoyed from this restaurant on the 35th floor of the "Regent of Melbourne" hotel. Its French-inspired cuisine is currently regarded as the best the city has to offer.

Onions, 50 Commercial Road; tel. (03) 9510 6247
Located in the South Yarra district of the city, this establishment can

offer typical national dishes such as kangaroo steaks and also Asiatic and Mediterranean delicacies.

Sweetwater, 121 Flinders Lane; tel. (03) 9650 5044
A very good eating-place near Flinders Street Station.

Western Australia

Esperance

Gray Starling, 126 Dempster St.; tel. (090) 713 187
A friendly BYO restaurant offering tasty food.

Exmouth

Whalers Restaurant, 5 Kennedy St.; tel. (099) 492 416
The fish dishes are to be recommended.

Fremantle

*Atrium Garden Restaurant in "The Esplanade" hotel; tel. (08) 9432 4000
The finest culinary delights are served in most pleasant surroundings.

Kalgoorlie

Palace Hotel Restaurant, Hannan St. and Maritana St.; tel. (092) 212 788
The original turn-of-the-century splendour has now faded somewhat, but nevertheless it is still possible to eat quite well here.

Perth

Fraser's, Fraser Avenue, Kings Park; tel. (09) 481 7100
This restaurant in the city's most popular park is patronised both for its cuisine and for the beautiful view.

Safety and Security

Insurance

Make sure that you have adequate insurance cover (health insurance, insurance against loss or theft of property and, if you are driving a car, comprehensive car insurance).

Organising your Trip

Good organisation, starting before you leave home, is important. If you know that everything is in order at home this will allow you to enjoy a relaxed holiday.

It is helpful to draw up a check list of what requires to be done and thought of, ticking off each item as it is dealt with.

Decide in plenty of time who is going to water your plants, look after your pets and ensure that mail is not left sticking out of your letter-box as an indication that you are away from home. Leave objects of value, photocopies of important papers and your holiday address with some suitable person or in your bank.

Don't forget:
passports;
tickets and confirmation of bookings;
insurance document;
driving licence (if you expect to be driving a car);
photocopies of important documents (in luggage);
travellers' cheques, credit cards, cash;
maps and guides; and
first aid kit, any medicines you take regularly, spare glasses, if worn, and sun-glasses.

Safety on the Road

Seat belts

The driver must ensure that all occupants of the car wear seat belts. The belts should be properly adjusted – taut and not twisted. A loosely fitting belt can cause additional injury in an accident.

Seat belts are most effective when used with properly adjusted head restraints. These should have their upper edge at least as high as the level of the eyes: only then do they give protection to the cervical vertebrae.

RAIL AUSTRALIA

Australian National Railways (ANR) · Gauges: 1067mm/3ft 6in., 1435mm/4ft 8½in. and 1600mm/5ft 3in.
Queensland Railways (QR) · Gauges: 1067mm/3ft 6in. and 1435mm/4ft 8½in.
State Rail Authority of New South Wales (State Rail/Countrylink/Cityrail/SRA)
Gauge: 1435mm/4ft 8½in.
Public Transport Corporation of Victoria (V/Line & The Met/PTC)
Gauge: 1600mm/5ft 3in.
Western Australian Government Railways (West Rail/WR) · Gauge: 1067mm/3ft 6in., 1435mm/4ft 8½in. and 1067/1435mm

N.B.: In addition to these five state systems there are other regional and local systems

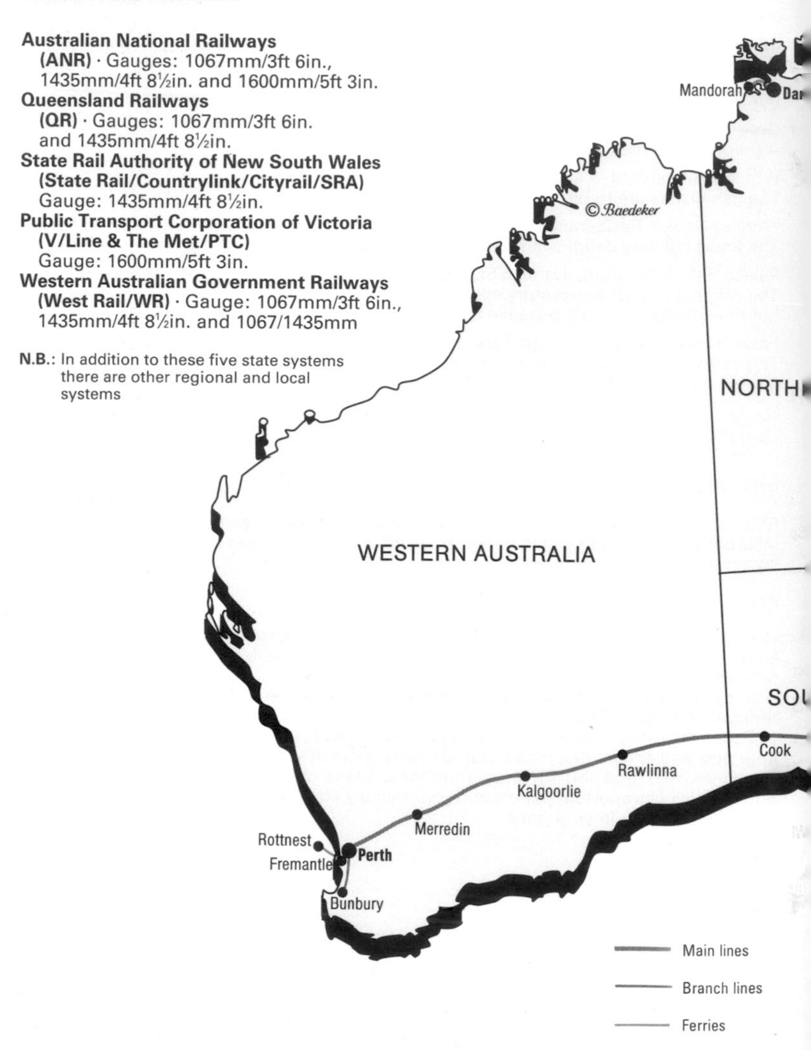

The Australian Railway System
(important main and branch lines)

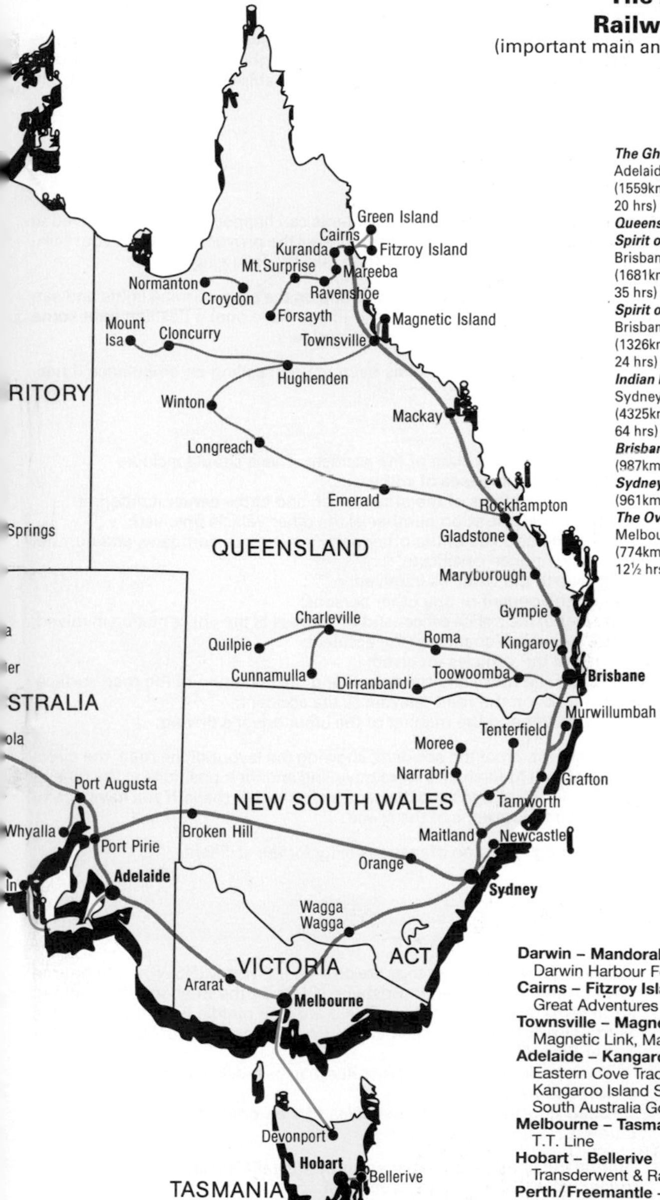

Named trains

The Ghan
Adelaide–Alice Springs
(1559km/969 miles) in 20 hrs)

Queenslander · Sunlander
Spirit of the Tropics
Brisbane–Cairns
(1681km/1045 miles in 35 hrs)

Spirit of the Outback
Brisbane–Longreach
(1326km/824 miles in 24 hrs)

Indian Pacific
Sydney–Adelaide–Perth
(4325km/2687 miles in 64 hrs)

Brisbane–Sydney XPT
(987km/613 miles in 14 hrs)

Sydney–Melbourne XPT
(961km/597 miles in 13 hrs)

The Overland
Melbourne–Adelaide
(774km/481 miles in 12½ hrs)

Ferries

Darwin – Mandorah
Darwin Harbour Ferries

Cairns – Fitzroy Island / Green Island
Great Adventures

Townsville – Magnetic Island
Magnetic Link, Magnetic Marine

Adelaide – Kangaroo Island
Eastern Cove Traders,
Kangaroo Island Sealink,
South Australia Government

Melbourne – Tasmania (Devonport)
T.T. Line

Hobart – Bellerive
Transderwent & Railway Company

Perth / Freemantle – Rottnest Island
Boat Torque Cruises

Spectacle-wearers — Spectacle-wearers drive more safely at night if they have special non-reflective glasses. Tinted glasses should not be worn after dark. Since all glass reflects part of the light reaching it, even a clear windscreen lets through only some 90% of the available light. Tinted windscreens and tinted glasses allow only about half the available light to reach the eye, and safe driving is then no longer possible.

Outback travel — See entry

If you have an accident in Australia

However carefully you drive, accidents can happen. If you are involved in an accident, the first rules are: whatever the provocation, keep your temper; be polite; and keep calm. Then take the following action:

1. Warn oncoming traffic by switching on the car's warning lights and setting out a warning triangle and (if you have one) a flashing light some distance before the scene of the accident.

2. Look after anyone who has been injured, calling an ambulance if necessary.

3. Inform the police.

4. Record full particulars of the accident. These should include:
- names and addresses of witnesses;
- name and address of the other driver, and of the owner if different;
- make and registration number of the other vehicle involved;
- name and address of the other party's insurance company, and number of the insurance certificate;
- damage to the vehicles involved;
- injury to yourself or any other persons;
- number of the police officer and/or address of the police station involved;
- date, time and location of the accident;
- speed of the vehicles involved;
- width of the road, any road signs and the condition of the road surface;
- any marks on the road relevant to the accident;
- the weather and the manner of the other driver's driving.

5. Draw a sketch of the accident, showing the layout of the road, the direction in which the vehicles were travelling and their positions at the time of impact, any road signs and the names of streets or roads. If you have a camera, take photographs of the scene.

6. Make no admission of responsibility for the accident.

Shipping Services

Harbour cruises, river trips, visits to islands — Harbour cruises and river trips are on offer in Sydney (NSW), in Melbourne (VIC) on the Yarra River, in Brisbane (QLD) on the Brisbane River and in Perth (WA) on the Swan River. There are also paddle-boat cruises on the Murray River (SA) from Renmark, Murray Bridge and Goolwa and on the Tamar River (TAS).

The islands in the Great Barrier Reef can be reached in catamarans, hovercraft and water taxis.

Detailed information and timetables can be obtained from local tourist bureaux.

Cruises on east coast — Among the finest travel experiences in Australia are cruises (day trips and longer tours) to the Great Barrier Reef.

Cruise organisers (a selection)

Captain Cook Cruises, Number 6 Jetty, Circular Quay, NSW 2000
Tel. 02 9206 1100, fax 02 9206 1178
Ocean Spirit Cruises, 143 Lake St., Cairns, QLD 4870
Tel. 070 312 920, fax 070 314 344
Proud Australia Holidays, 23 Leigh St., Adelaide, SA 5000
Tel. 08 319 472, fax 08 8212 1520
Quicksilver Connections, PO Box 171, Port Douglas QLD 4871
Tel. 070 995 500, fax 070 995 525
Roylen Cruises, PO Box 169, Mackay, QLD 4740
Tel. 079 553 066, fax 079 553 186
Whitsunday Adventure Sail, Airlie Beach, Whitsunday, QLD 4802
Tel. 079 461 777, fax 079 461 668

Pleasure craft

Boating, sailing and cruising are favourite Australian recreations. House boats, cruisers and sailing craft can be hired, with or without crew, at many places on the coast and on inland waterways and rivers. Among the most popular areas for holidays on the water are Broken Bay and the winding Hawkesbury River (40km/25 miles north of Sydney) and the beautiful Whitsunday Passage off Shute Harbour/Proserpine in Queensland. In Victoria there are the Gippsland Lakes and the Murray River.

Shopping, Souvenirs

Malls and arcades

The enormous strides made in Australia in recent years es exemplified by the shopping malls and excellent shopping arcades which have sprung up in many cities, for example, the arcade in the Queen Victoria Building in Sydney, the Toorak Quarter in Melbourne and Queen Street Mall in Brisbane. Australian fashion designers are now well up to date, and this applies especially to sports garments for ladies and gentlemen. The choice is now comparable with that found in West European and North American cities

Markets

It is well worth looking round the markets in Australian cities, for example Paddy's Market in Sydney (NSW) with its assortment of curios, art and kitsch, the Queen Victoria Market in Melbourne (VIC), the weekly market in Salamanca Place in Hobart (TAS) or the Riverside Centre Market in Brisbane (QLD), where craftsmen offer their products for sale on Sundays.

The Meat Market craft centre in Brisbane offers a wide range of Australian craft products – ceramics, glass, jewellery, wooden articles, leather goods, textiles and furniture. Sullivan Cove, near Hobart (TAS), is the centre for Tasmanian artists and craftsmen (glass-blowers, painters, potters).

Souvenirs

Popular souvenirs from Australia are T-shirts with jokey designs, leather goods, wooden articles (of Huon pine in Tasmania) and fashion accessories such as brooches and earrings in shimmering colours made from coconuts. Bush clothing (e.g. the most popular wind- and weather-proof garment, "Driza-Bone"), Akubra hats (in four versions - Snowy River, Cattleman, Stockman and Down Under) and R. M. Williams' famous moleskin jackaroo jeans in the traditional bone colour and stockman's boots are items of guaranteed quality and durability which will give the wearer the real Australian look. Comical little stuffed animals (koalas, kangaroos, sheep, wombats) will give pleasure to children, and not only to children. When buying examples of allegedly Aboriginal art (particularly boomerangs) it is advisable to examine them carefully to make sure that they are not imports from South-East Asia. Genuine Aboriginal art can be seen, for example, in galleries in Darwin and Alice Springs (NT) and Sydney (NSW) and in the Tiagarra Tasmanian Aboriginal Culture and Art Centre in Devonport (TAS). Other good buys are sheep and kangaroo skins, woollens (especially the popular "Coogi Design"), illustrated books and children's-

Aborignal art

books, modern editions of the Australian classic Banjo Paterson and wall calendars with superb photographs of Australian scenery.

Opals

Opals, available in a wide range of quality and price, are classic souvenirs of a visit to Australia. The main opal-mining areas are Coober Pedy and Andamooka in South Australia, Lightning Ridge in New South Wales and Quilpie in Queensland. A visit to the opal-mines in the outback is a memorable travel experience. Opals can be bought either in the opal fields or in jewellers' shops, usually set in items of jewellery. When buying a "raw" opal you need to know what you are about. If you contemplate buying a valuable and expensive stone you should take into account the duty you may have to pay on returning home. The most popular – and not too expensive – items of opal jewellery are "triplets" (thin layers of opal covered by transparent protective layers).

It should be borne in mind that opals are soft and delicate and should not be exposed to detergents.

Protection of endangered species

It is up to every visitor to act in the spirit of the Washington Conventrion on the Protection of Endangered Species and to help to save threatened flora and fauna by refusing to buy souvenirs the manufacture of which involves the use of such plants and animals or parts thereof. This includes orchids, cacti, some species of insect (mounted butterflies, for example) and birds, living or prepared lizards and their skins, tortoiseshell, corals and shells. The importation of such souvenirs is prohibited in most countries.

Social Conduct

Greetings

Australian manners are relaxed and casual; many of their attitudes stem from the early pioneering days. Australians, particularly in country areas, are talkative and friendly, but their friendliness is without commitment: lasting friendships are the exception rather than the rule.

Australians are not much given to shaking hands, but their greetings are not the less cordial for that. Their standard greeting on meeting anyone is "G'day". They get very readily on to first-name terms, and "mate" is a very common form of address between men.

Dress

In general Australians prefer light casual clothing, but on formal occasions (business meetings, working lunches, a visit to the theatre or a meal in a good restaurant) they attach great importance to appropriately formal dress (jacket, collar and tie, etc.): trainers and jeans are frowned on.

Punctuality

The Australians attach great importance to punctuality.

Smoking

For some time now smoking has been rather frowned upon in Australia. It is forbidden in public buildings, on public transport (aircraft, trains, buses and taxis), in shopping centres and shops as well as in many restaurants. Some pubs and bars have smoking and non-smoking areas. Even in some open-air places – especially in National Parks and the Outback – smoking is prohibited if "Total Fire Ban" signs are up because of the risk of forest and bush fires.

Women travelling alone

In general, women travelling alone should encounter no problems in Australia. They should, however, at all costs avoid hitch-hiking on their own (see Hitch-hiking).

Sport

A sporting country

Australia is one of the world's great sporting nations, In the last forty years or so Australian sportsmen and women have made a name for themselves in athletics, swimming, sailing, tennis, cricket, rugby, hockey and so on. Not for nothing were the 1956 Olympic Games held

in Melbourne, and now Sydney is to be host to the Summer Olympics in the year 2000 (see Baedeker Special p. 00).
Australia offers excellent facilities for all kinds of sporting activities and a varied programme of spectator sports. Even such sports as camel trekking and ballooning, which went out of fashion, are now popular again.

Spectator Sports

Cricket

Cricket, part of Australia's English heritage, is its oldest sport. Still played and watched with the greatest enthusiasm, it has taken on almost the character of a cult. The Mecca of cricket fans is the Melbourne Cricket Ground, and joy is unrestrained when the Australian team defeat their traditional English adversaries there. The cricket season lasts from the beginning of October to the end of March.

Football

Australian football ("Australian rules" or "footy"), a faster variant of American football, is the country's favourite spectator sport; its main stronghold is in Victoria, but is also played in Sydney, Perth and Brisbane. The highlight of the year is the "Grand Final" in Melbourne. In Queensland and New South Wales rugby union and rugby league are more popular. Association football plays a smaller part in Australian life, although the Australian team did reach the final of the World Cup in 1974.

Horse-racing

Racing was one of the first sports organised by the early settlers; the first race was held in 1799. There are now over 400 racecourses in Australia and several hundred meetings every year. The most thrilling are held in Sydney and Melbourne, the highlight of the racing calendar being the Melbourne Cup at Flemington Racecourse on the first Tuesday in November.

Motor sports

One of the great events in motor racing is the Formula 1 World Championship race which is held in Melbourne in March each year. The Sydney-Darwin Safari (7000km/4350 miles) takes place every August. Other major motoring events can be seen in Bathurst (north-west of Sydney, NSW), in Calder (near Melbourne, VIC) and in Longford (TAS).

Tennis

Australia is one of the world's leading tennis nations. The Hopman Cup (mixed doubles) is competed for annually between Christmas and early January. The main event of the tennis season, however, is the Australian Open for men and women, held in Melbourne in the second half of January.

Active Sports

Water sports

Canoeing, kayaking

The sports of canoeing and kayaking are growing in popularity. The world's toughest canoe race is held on the Murray River in December; known as the ICI–Red Cross Murray Marathon, it lasts five days! Kayaking is also attracting more and more enthusiasts.

Diving and snorkelling

There are great opportunities for diving and snorkelling on the Great Barrier Reef, including unforgettably beautiful diving grounds off Lizard Island. The west coast of Australia also offers some beautiful reefs for diving.

Rafting

Raft trips and white-water rafting are possible on many Australian rivers (Tully, Nymboida, Gwydir, Shoalhaven, Mitchell, Franklin, Murray, etc.). Particulary attractive are "Reef 'n Rainforest Tours" which are available in the north of Queensland.

Sailing

Particularly good sailing waters include Whitsunday Passage (Great Barrier Reef), the waters off Fremantle, Sydney Harbour, the Pittwater, the winding Hawkesbury River (40km/25 miles north of Sydney) and Swan River near Perth. The highlight of the sailing year is the Sydney to Hobart Yacht Race, held every year during the Christmas period.

Lawn bowling, a gentle recreation

Surfing

Australia's long coastline offers ideal conditions for surfing. Surfing to the Australians generally means the old-established sport of riding the waves on a surfboard; wind-surfing is less popular. The busiest surfing beaches are supervised by Surf Rescue lifeguards.

Games played on greens

Golf

Australia is a golfer's paradise, with some 1500 courses, most of which welcome visitors. Equipment can be hired at all clubs. There are a number of golf tournaments arranged between mid-November and early March.

Lawn bowling

Lawn bowling is mainly a sport for older people. It is both a recreation and a social occasion, for which the appropriate white uniform must be worn.

Ballooning

Hot-air ballooning has become popular throughout Australia both as an active sport and tourist attraction. It is possible to book at such events for the whole day, with breakfast, lunch and evening meal included. Further details can be obtained from local tourist offices.

Walking

Many of Australia's National Parks and nature reserves have waymarked walking trails. The 5000km/3100 mile long Bicentennial National Trail runs from Cooktown (QLD) to Melbourne (VIC). The 1000km/620 mile long Heyson Trail in South Australia ranks as one of the longest and most beautiful trails in the world. A new trail, Myalls Heritage Trail, opened in 1993 to the north of Newcastle (NSW), passes through varied landscape (rainforest, heathland, dunes, palm forests) from Barrington Tops (1585m/5200ft) to the Myall Lakes on the Pacific Ocean.

Bush-walking

The essential requirements for bush walkers are fitness, a very good sense of direction and proper equipment, which should include comfortable and durable clothing and stout shoes or boots, a hat for protection from the sun as well as sun-cream and insect repellant and a good map and description of the route. Walkers should on no account walk in the wilderness on their own. It is a good idea to join one of the group walks organised by bush-walking clubs. Those wishing to walk through National Parks or other protected areas must have a permit from the bush ranger concerned. It is important to heed warnings and prohibitions.

Cycling

Information about cycle touring can be obtained from local tourist bureaux.

Camel trekking

Camel treks are on offer in the Outback (Frontier Camel Farm, Ross Highway 8km/5 miles south-east of Alice Springs,NT), as are long treks in the Victorian Alps, along some beaches in Queensland, New South Wales and Western Australia, on Bruny Island off Hobart (TAS) and – for those experienced in desert travel – across the Strzelecki Desert and Sturt Stony Desert, both in South Australia.

Winter sports

The winter sports season lasts from June to September, and in many skiing resorts the opening of the season is celebrated with fireworks and ski-jumping. Many resorts offer holiday packages covering skiing instruction and unlimited use of the ski-lifts.

The best snow areas are on the east coast, in the ranges of mountains between Sydney (NSW) and Melbourne (VIC).

New South Wales

The best known skiing resorts in the Snowy Mountains (highest point Mount Kosciusko, 2230m/7317ft) are Smiggin Holes, Perisher Valley (good for families) and Thredbo Alpine Village. Cooma, 425km/265 miles south-west of Sydney, is the main gateway to this skiing area.

Victoria

Victoria's skiing areas, which lie lower than those of New South Wales, are north-east of Melbourne. The most important skiing villages are Mount Buller (240km/150 miles from Melbourne; the largest skiing centre in Australia), Mount Buffalo (320km/200 miles from Melbourne), Mount Hotham (367km/228 miles from Melbourne) and Falls Creek (380km/235 miles from Melbourne).

Taxis

Taxis can be hailed in the street or ordered by telephone, dialling 132 227 (Taxis Australia) throughout Australia.

Time

Time zones

The Australian continent falls within three different time zones:
Eastern Standard Time (EST) in New South Wales, the Australian Capital Territory, Victoria, Queensland and Tasmania: 10 hours ahead of Greenwich Mean Time;
Central Standard Time (CST) in South Australia and the Northern Territory: 9½ hours ahead of GMT;
and Western Standard Time (WST) in Western Australia: 8 hours ahead of GMT.

Summer Time

All Australian states except Queensland and the Northern Territory put their clocks an hour forward in summer (October to March). The exact times of the change are announced in the media.

Tipping

Tipping was not an Australian practice, but it has been introduced by foreign visitors. In good restaurants a 10% tip is normally given by customers satisfied with the service. Porters at airports and railway stations expect A$1 for each piece of luggage carried. The tip for hotel porters is at the discretion of the guest. for taxi-drivers and hairdressers it is normal to round the amount due up to the nearest dollar.

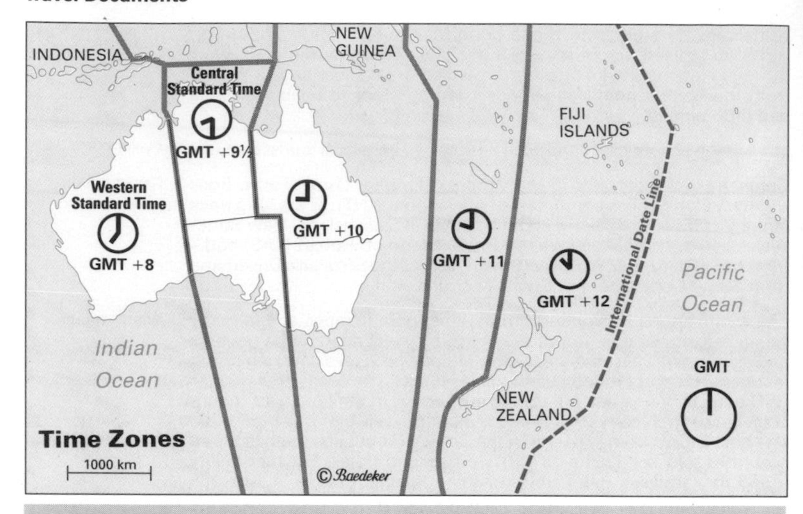

Travel Documents

Personal papers

All visitors to Australia require a passport, and all except New Zealanders must also have a visa. Visas can be obtained from any Australian High Commission, embassy or consulate. Visas for a stay of up to three months are free; for visitors intending to stay more than three months there is a processing fee (£20 in the UK). A working holidaymaker visa, valid for up to a year, allows the visitor to take casual employment (no more than three months with one employer) and attracts a higher processing fee (£75 in the UK).

For visitors travelling to Australia on a package holiday the visa will be obtained by the travel operator; otherwise visitors must make a personal application. Application forms can be obtained from Australian diplomatic and consular offices; a passport photograph must accompany the application. Visitors who apply in person can usually get a visitor or working holiday visa on the spot; by post, allow at least 21 working days.

On entry into Australia visitors may be asked to produce their return flight ticket or evidence that they have enough money to support themselves.

You can have your visa extended while in Australia, but the charges are high: it is better to decide before leaving home how long you want to stay.

Car papers

If you intend to drive a car in Australia you will require to produce your national driving licence accompanied by your passport. An international driving licence by itself is not sufficient.

It is advisable to make photocopies of the operative pages of your passport and other important documents, so that if you lose them they can more easily be replaced. The loss of your passport should be reported at once to the police and to your nearest diplomatic mission or consulate.

Permits for Aboriginal land

A permit is required to enter Aboriginal land (i.e. land administered by the Aborigines themselves). Permits must be obtained in advance from the local Aboriginal Land Council and may take a long time to process. A permit is unlikely to be granted for a purely sightseeing visit. On organised tours the permit will be obtained by the travel operator. No permit is required for transit through Aboriginal territory on public roads.

Watching Wildlife

The Australian Tourist Commission (see Information) can provide a booklet which will explain where in Australia wildlife can be observed.

Kangaroos, wallabies, koalas, wombats

Those who venture into the almost uninhabited Outback may well be fortunate enough, especially at dusk and dawn, to see kangaroos, wallabies and wombats. During the daytime koalas sleep high up in eucalyptus trees.

Whale-watching

During the winter whales travel from the Antarctic into warmer waters, passing close to the Australian coasts. In August and September there are daily whale-watching trips (half day or whole day), particularly in the shallow waters of Hervey Bay on the west coast of Fraser Island (QLD). The Hervey Bay Whale Festival, lasting several weeks, is held annually in August.

Information about operators running whale-watching trips can be obtained from the Australian Tourist Commission (see Information).

Dolphins

In Shark bay, near Monkey Mia on the west coast, live large numbers of dolphins, some of which are so tame that they even venture up to the beach. Dolphins can be seen at a number of other places too.

Bird-watching

The Royal Australian Ornithological Union and various travel operators organise bird-watching trips. Information from Australian Tourist Commission. Particularly rewarding regions for bird-watching include Broome (WA), the Kimberley area of Western Australia, and the tropical rainforests of Northern Queensland (Mossmann region).

Weights • Measures • Temperatures

Australia is now on the metric system; the old imperial measures are rarely encountered.

Equivalents

1 mile = 1.61km
1 foot = 30.48cm
1 inch = 2.54cm

1 pint = 0.568 litre
1 gallon = 4.546 litres

1 ounce = 28.35 grams
1 pound = 0.45 kilogram

Temperatures are given in °C (centigrade/celsius). (°F = 1.8 x °C + 32) The following are a few examples:

+37°C = +98.6°F
+25°C = +77.0°F
+20°C = +68.0°F
+15°C = +59.0°F
+10°C = +50.0°F
+5°C = + 41.0°F
0°C = +32.0°F
-10°C = 14.0°F
-20°C = 4.0°F

When to Go

Seasons

The Australian seasons are the reverse of the seasons of the northern hemisphere. Spring is from September to November, summer from December to February, autumn from March to May, winter from June to August.

The main Australian holiday season is from the middle of December to the beginning of February. There are shorter school holidays in May and August/September, varying from state to state. During these periods it is advisable to make your booking in plenty of time.

A package holiday to Australia will be considerably cheaper if you take it between the end of the Australian summer and the beginning of autumn. It is well worth while to compare the prices offered by different travel operators.

Spring
Western Australia

Spring (September to November) is the best time to see the brilliant show of wild flowers, particularly in Western Australia. After heavy rain great expanses of the arid interior are briefly carpeted with flowers.

Summer
Southern Australia

Southern Australia (particularly Victoria and Tasmania) is at its most beautiful in summer (October to March).

Winter
Southern Australia

During the winter southern Australia has its heaviest rainfall, with a long period of cold, wet weather.

Australian Alps
Tasmania

The best winter sports areas are in the Australian Alps (New South Wales and Victoria) and in Tasmania.

Seasons in the tropical north

In the tropical north of Australia there are only two seasons. The best time to go there is in the dry season between May and October, when the days are warm but the nights cool and sometimes cold (in the Red Centre). From November to April is an oppressively hot rainy season with monsoon rains and frequent cyclones.

Temperature

Temperatures are measured in degrees Celsius (°C).

To convert Fahrenheit to Celsius, deduct 32, multiply by 5 and divide by 9; to convert Celsius to Fahrenheit, multiply by 9, divide by 5 and add 32.

Wine

Vines were brought to Australia by some of the earliest settlers, and later German immigrants planted extensive vineyards in the Barossa Valley. After a long period in the first half of the 20th century when the wine industry declined as a result of economic depression, vine diseases and pests it has made great advances in recent decades. Australian wine now has an international reputation. Australian wineries produce a wide range of wines, from fine wines to cheap table wines sold in large containers. The white wines are usually light and fruity, the red wines dry and full-bodied.

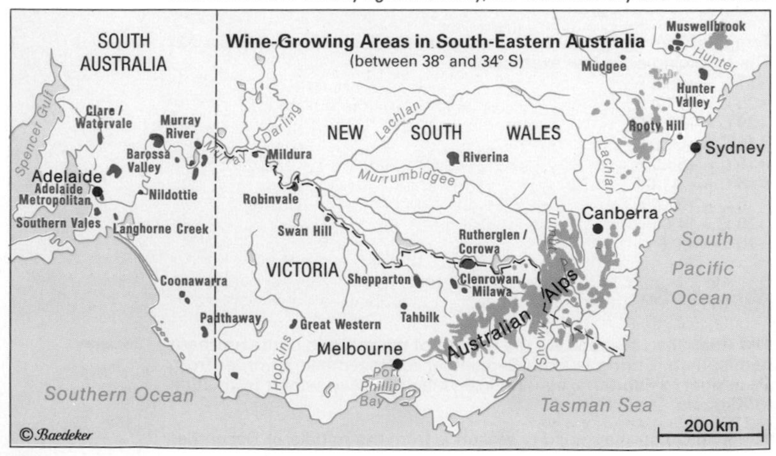

The most favoured grapes are Cabernet Sauvignon, Shiraz (the Australian version of Syrah), Riesling, Chardonnay and Malbeec.

Table wines

The availability of good cheap table wines sold in 4-litre containers has led to a rapid increase in wine consumption. The grapes for these wines come mainly from the climatically favoured irrigated areas on the Murray River (Riverina in New South Wales, Sunraysia in north-western Victoria).

Quality wines

Quality wines, sold in bottles, bear labels indicating the wine-producing area, the type of grape and alcohol content.

The best known areas producing quality wines are in the Yarra Valley, 50km/30 miles north of Melbourne (VIC), the Hunter Valley (NSW), the Barossa Valley and the Clare Valley (SA). Quality wines are also produced on the Margaret River and in the Swan Valley (WA) and in the cooler climate of Tasmania.

Sparkling wine

Australian sparkling wine is also good value, though it tends to be sweet. The best qualities are produced by the *méthode champenoise*.

Visits to wineries

Almost all wineries welcome visitors, offering conducted tours and wine tastings, as well as opportunities for buying wine.

Youth Accommodation

Youth hostels

The Australian Youth Hostels Association, a member of the International Youth Hostel Federation, has more than 140 hostels throughout Australia. Hostellers must present the international youth hostels membership card; there is no age limit. It is also necessary to buy an international guest card valid for a year in all Australian youth hostels.

Information from:
Australian Youth Hostels Association/YHA Australia
Level 3, 10 Mallett Street
Camperdown, NSW 2050, tel. 02 9565 1699, fax 02 9565 1325

VIP Backpacker resorts

The VIP Backpacker Resorts of Australia (BRA) organisation is an association of independently run hostels for backpackers, with the same kind of accommodation and prices as youth hostels. They are found particularly on the east coast. For further information in the UK, tel. 0181 742 8612 or write to:

VIP Backpacker Resorts of Australia
PO Box 600
Cannon Hill, QLD 4170; tel. 07 3890 2767, fax 07 3348 8566

Their quarterly magazine, "For Backpackers by Backpackers", can be picked up in bus stations, airports, hostels and tourist information bureaux. Also useful is "Budget Travel Australia", obtainable from Red Sky Publishing, 70 Brunswick Street, Stockton-on-Tees, Cleveland TS18 1DW, enclosing a large (9x6½in) self-addressed envelope with 45p postage. People living outside UK should send a money order or bank draft for £2 to cover postage and handling costs.

Travellers Accommodation Network (TAN)

Inexpensive accommodation for backpackers is also offered by the Travellers Accommodation Network (TAN). At present this organisation runs more than 100 hotels and holiday complexes all of which are in popular tourist centres. Visitors from Europe can obtain more information from:

Travellers Accommodation Network (TAN),
PO Box 209,
N-1361 Billingstadt (Norway)
Tel./fax 0047 6698 1502

Index

The Principal Sights At A Glance

Most Visited tourist areas in Australia: see map page 571

Note: The places listed above are merely a selection of the principal sights in Australia. There are of course innumerble other sights, to which attention is drawn in the A to Z section of the guide by one or two stars.

181 illustraions, 43 general maps, 35 figures, 27 ground-plans, 13 diagrams, 11 town plans, 6 special maps, 4 special plans, 3 geographical profiles, 1 table
1 large map of Australia

Original German text: Dr Gerlinde Lamping and Prof. Heinrich Lamping, Rosbach v.d. Höhe
Contributions from: Vera Beck, Aichtal (Practical Information from A to Z); Heiner F. Gstaltmayr, Pfullingen (Specials); Prof. Ernst Messerschmid, Reutlingen (Ozone Layer); Werner Voran, Stuttgart (Rock and Pop Music); Reinhard Zakrzewski, Deutsch Evern (Coastal Forms, Beaches, Waves; Climate, in part)

Consultant; Campbell Gome, Australian Tourist Commission, Frankfurt am Main

Preparation of text: Heiner F. Gstaltmayr, Pfullingen
Editorial work: Baedeker-Redaktion

Cartography: Australian Tourist Commission; Christoph Gallus, Hohberg-Niederschopfheim; Gert Oberländer, Munich; Archiv Für Flaggenkunde Ralf Stelter, Hattingen; Mairs Geographischer Verlag, Ostfildern (large map of Australia)

General direction: Dr Peter Baumgarten, Baedeker Stuttgart

Source of illustrations: Baedeker-Archiv (1); Bareth (24); Bildagentur Lade (1); Bildagentur Schapowalow (2); Bildagentur Schuster (9); Deutsche Forschungsanstalt für Luft- und Raumfahrt (1); Grohe (1); Grützner (5); Historia (2); IFA (7); Internationaler Sortenerkennungsdienst (1); Lamping (65); Morgan (3); National Library of Australia (2); Okapia (1); Prax (19); Prokop (2); Rometsch (21); Ullsteinn (4); Warner Brothers (1); Zakrzewski (4); ZEFA (6)

English translation: James Hogarth

Revised text: David Cocking

2nd English edition 1998

Distributed in the United Kingdom by the Publishing Division of the Automobile Association, Fanum House, Basingstoke, Hampshire RG21 2EA

Licensed user: Mairs Geographischer Verlag GmbH & Co., Ostfildern-Kemnat bei Stuttgart

A CIP catalogue record of this book is available from the British Library

Printed in Italy by G. Canale & C.S.p.A – Borgaro T.se – Turin

ISBN 0 7495 1762 x UK

Notes

Notes

Notes

Notes